Data Science and Analytics with Python

Data Science and Analytics with Python

Sandhya Arora
B.E., M.Tech., Ph.D. (Computer Science and Engineering)
Professor, Department of Computer Engineering
MKSSS's Cummins College of Engineering for Women
Pune, Maharashtra

Latesh Malik
B.E., M.Tech., Ph.D. (Computer Science and Engineering)
Associate Professor, Department of Computer Science and Engineering
Government College of Engineering, Nagpur, Maharashtra

DATA SCIENCE AND ANALYTICS WITH PYTHON

UNIVERSITIES PRESS (INDIA) PRIVATE LIMITED

Registered Office
3-6-747/1/A & 3-6-754/1, Himayatnagar, Hyderabad 500 029, Telangana, India
info@universitiespress.com; www.universitiespress.com

Distributed by
Orient Blackswan Private Limited

Registered Office
3-6-752 Himayatnagar, Hyderabad 500 029 Telangana, India

Other Offices
Bengaluru / Chennai / Guwahati / Hyderabad / Kolkata
Mumbai / New Delhi / Noida / Patna / Visakhapatnam

ISBN 978-93-93330-34-5

501925

Typeset in Adobe Garamond Pro 11 points *by*
Cameo Corporate Services Limited, Coimbatore

Printed in India by
B.B. Press, Noida 201 301

Published by
Universities Press (India) Private Limited
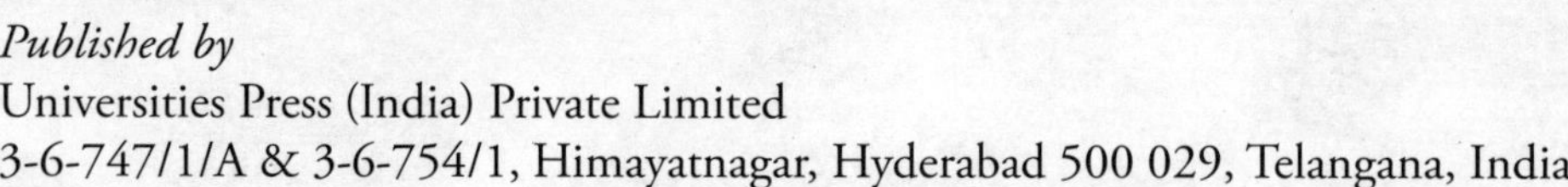
3-6-747/1/A & 3-6-754/1, Himayatnagar, Hyderabad 500 029, Telangana, India

Preface

Data Science and Machine Learning are the leading buzzwords of today. They are very important as they help in solving many business problems. These concepts are underpinned by different statistical techniques, and software programs are used to execute and implement them.

Python is the most popular and fastest growing language in the world. It is very useful in the fields of data science, data analytics and statistical computation because of its versatility. It offers various libraries for clustering, classification, text mining, non-linear/linear modelling and classical statistical testing along with basic programming and very strong built-in functions. Python is a free, open-source, adaptable and extensible language and thus a perfect fit for big data solutions. It also supports many graphical techniques to visualize and present data effectively.

One of the biggest strengths of this book is that we cover the basic concepts of the ecosystem of data science and data analytics, as well as their implementation in Python. If you master both, you will enhance your skills as a data scientist. The book is organized in 18 chapters exploring the basics of data science, data analytics and machine learning. All chapters include relevant case studies and their programming in Python.

Chapter 1 deals with data definition and categorization. It provides an overview of data in the data science context, the different sources of data, data science workflow and ecosystem, main companies involved, the tools used to categorize data and the scales of measurement.

Chapters 2 and 3 will help you understand the basics of Python and set the ground for advanced learning in the data science area. They explain the Python environment, fundamentals of Python programming and libraries such as NumPy and pandas and their related functions with examples.

Chapter 4 details the steps in data visualization in Python. Trends, variations and data insights are more intuitive to humans through visualization techniques and provide a holistic story of the data. Various Python data visualization modules such as Matplotlib, Seaborn and plotly are discussed here, along with visualization software and tools such as Tableau, Looker, Zoho and Microsoft Power BI.

Chapter 5 covers the scikit-learn library. It introduces readers to various algorithms such as support vector machine, classification, regression and K-NN. Modules of this library are used in all subsequent chapters.

Chapter 6 explains the fundamentals of TensorFlow, its architecture and how to leverage the Keras high-level neural network APIs with TensorFlow.

Chapter 7 describes the probability distribution and density functions. Details of discrete and continuous probability distributions are also provided.

Chapter 8 introduces the basic concepts of machine learning, its types and applications. Understanding data is crucial for data science and data-driven machine learning algorithms. Pre-processing of data, removal of noise, handling missing data, data transformation, feature engineering and dimensionality reduction of data are covered in this chapter.

Chapters 9 and 10 deal with descriptive and inferential statistical analysis, such as one-dimensional, two-dimensional and multi-dimensional statistics, correlation and regression analysis, testing of hypothesis, parametric and non-parametric tests and analysis of variance (ANOVA). In these chapters, several mathematical examples and case studies are provided along with the Python code.

Chapter 11 discusses classification techniques such as naive Bayes', decision tree, ensemble techniques, K-NN, support vector machines and their implementation in Python. Classifier evaluation methods, cross-validation, bagging, boosting and stacking ensemble techniques are also explained.

Chapter 12 focuses on the concept of data stream mining and the process of extracting knowledge structures from ordered data records. It explains the classification of streams and implementation techniques with case studies.

Chapter 13 deals with language data processing using Python. Text processing and sentiment analysis are discussed using examples and case studies. CGI/Web programming using Python is also described in this chapter.

Chapter 14 is about clustering. K-means, hierarchical and DBSCAN clustering are covered and application examples and programming in Python are provided.

Chapter 15 discusses association rule mining, specifically the apriori algorithm and its implementation in Python.

Chapter 16 covers time series components, decomposition, autocorrelation and its forecasting.

Chapter 17 discusses deep and convolution neural networks. Activation, loss and regularization functions used in deep learning are explained, along with case studies using Python.

Chapter18 provides a set of case studies that represent well-defined use cases of real-time examples of digital recognition, face and eye detection in images, correlation and feature selection, fake news detection, spam detection and duplicate question detection.

In addition, the book contains more than 300 solved multiple choice questions and programming and concept-based exercises. Also included are the assignment solutions for the AICTE-prescribed data science and analytics syllabus.

Sandhya Arora
Latesh Malik

Acknowledgements

This book is the outcome of queries from students, our lecture notes and laboratory work and material. We have been associated with this subject for more than five years through lectures, workshops and seminars.

Many professionals have helped us write this book. We take this opportunity to thank our mentors, teachers and friends for motivating us throughout this journey. We thank the Principal and colleagues of the Computer Engineering departments at MKSSS's Cummins College of Engineering, Pune, and the Government College of Engineering, Nagpur, for supporting this work.

We also thank all the students who motivated us by asking the right questions at the appropriate time. Without their help in the form of queries and curiosity, the idea of writing this book would never have taken shape.

We acknowledge the support of reviewers with their critical comments and creative suggestions which helped us improve the book. We would also like to thank all the professors who taught us the basics of statistics, data science and machine learning.

Special thanks to Prof. Milind Kolambe, Tanish Rahul Pophale, Mansi Manish Pardeshi, Vivek Deshpande, Jyoti Raghatwan, Deepa Mane, Shreya Malik and Naved Raza Qaisar Ali for their contributions to this book.

We would also like to thank the editorial team of Universities Press for their support in bringing out this book.

Finally, we would like to thank our family for their support, good wishes, encouragement and understanding. Sandhya Arora thanks her husband Aman Arora, daughter Rishika and son Pragnay for being patient and accommodative. Latesh Malik thanks her husband Gagan Malik, daughter Shreya and son Yashmit for their constant support and encouragement.

Sandhya Arora
Latesh Malik

Contents

To

Our Beloved Father,
the Late Sh. B.D. Bhagat
and Our Mother,
Smt. Kaushalya Bhagat

CHAPTER 1

Introduction to Data Science

Learning Objectives

At the end of this chapter, you will be able to:

- Define the main concepts of data science, its work flow and ecosystem
- List the tools used in data science
- Provide an overview of data in a statistical context
- List the different sources of data
- Define big data, list the main companies involved and the tools used
- Categorize data and explain the data sources and scales of measurement

1.0 Introduction

Our world has been transformed by the data science revolution, especially in the post-Internet era. We interact with data science products, knowingly or unknowingly, to manage our daily tasks. If you are looking for information using the Google search engine or asking a question to Siri or Alexa, you are interacting with data science products. Alexa, Siri, Facebook (now Meta), Google, WhatsApp and Instagram are now an integral part of our lives. These platforms store huge amounts of data collected from users – referred to as big data. This is processed further using technologies/methods such as data mining, data analytics, artificial intelligence (AI) algorithms/machine learning (ML), natural language processing (NLP) and neural networks to obtain meaningful reports, assist in useful interactions, make the correct decisions and predict outcomes for users. Alexa, Siri and Google Assistant are some of the popular examples of NLP as virtual assistants that can help users make better decisions, provide easy access to information and provide meaningful insight into hidden data.

Today, data science has become the backbone of nearly every industry. We interact with data products in industries ranging from Travel, Ed Tech, Healthcare, Marketing, Sales, Social Media, Insurance and much more. Data science applications are also heavily used in specialized areas such as personalized healthcare systems, research, Ed Tech and in almost every industry. Contact tracing, based on a mathematical model, has been very effective in limiting the spread of the coronavirus. This mobile phone data-driven technology identifies a person's close contacts after that individual tests positive for the virus and lets the contacts know about the need to self-isolate. Fast forward to, say 2030, to a world with a sophisticated contact tracing mechanism that is used to tackle some other highly contagious disease. What would the impact be? At least it could be limited to the areas where it is identified. In addition, the difficulties associated with a mutating virus, supply chain bottlenecks, hospitals overloaded with patients and even the death rate could be reduced significantly.

Another example of data science in healthcare is the use of data to compare how similar/different a radiotherapy plan is from a trained model. At the centre of the plan would be a search engine that takes a plan as input and finds previous plans from similar patients. The treating physician receives a lot of insight by looking into an optimum plan implemented for similar patients at renowned hospitals and can better predict outcomes for his or her patient. In a nutshell, a patient does not need to travel to the world's best healthcare centres to assess a complex disease when technology can bring the experts to the local hospitals. With the help of data science, it is now possible to estimate accurate diagnostic measures.

The above-mentioned model of radiotherapy has actually been developed and implemented at one of the best cancer centres in the world to bridge the gap between services delivered at smaller hospitals which lack sub-specialities and more sophisticated research-based cancer centres anchored with sub-specialities. These are some of the real-world applications that leverage the methods/technologies used in the data science world related to healthcare.

The Ed Tech area is another fascinating one where a lot of work needs to be done to improve the learning outcome and ultimately to improve career satisfaction. Implementing intelligent solutions such as Student Decision Support systems can help students choose the right set of courses based on their inherent interest, skills and abilities and provide students an option to achieve optimal outcome and ultimately satisfaction. One such system introduced by the faculty of the University of Wisconsin uses Interest-Aligned Planning to extend Holland's theory of personality to college courses for decision support (Fig. 1.1).

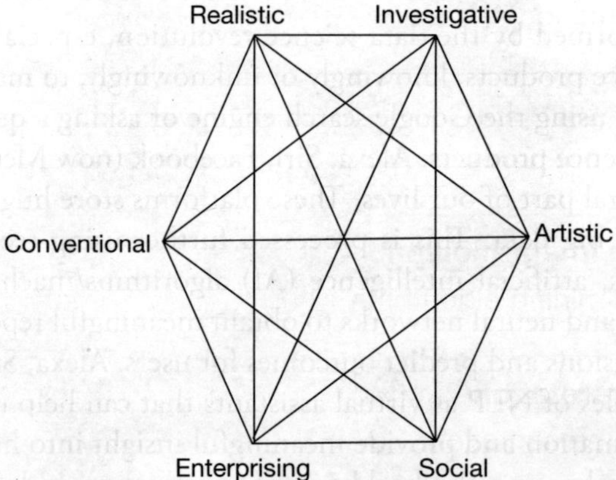

Figure 1.1 Holland's theory of personality

Holland's theory, introduced by John Holland (1959), classifies people and environments using rank ordering of six types: Realistic, Investigative, Artistic, Social, Enterprising and Conventional (RIASEC). The theory uses congruence measures to find the degree of alignment between a profile of an individual's personality types (this profile is usually determined by psychometric tests) and the work (or educational) environment types (the environment profile may be determined by detailed assessments or other mechanisms).

The data generated by such a system can be further applied, using AI/deep learning tools, to find patterns for a successful student, improve the alignment factor based on a student's profile and interest, and thus improve overall satisfaction and productivity.

1.1 Data Science

Data science is a field that involves creating meaning or drawing conclusions from a set of data. Data knowledge is used by machine learning techniques for different applications. A formal and useful definition of data science is that data science is a broad area that encompasses "a set of fundamental principles that support and guide the principled extraction of information and knowledge from data".

Data science is being used because of big data and the advancement of technology with things such as autonomous vehicles and artificial intelligence (AI). Data science extracts meaning from the data we collect using sensors or other methods and allows us to make decisions on new technology based on those conclusions.

1.2 Data Science Stages

- **1. Define the Project Goals**
  a. Meaningful report/result b. Capture the context of data
- **2. Identify Data Sources**
  a. Information extraction b. Structure the data for analysis
- **3. Data Cleaning**
  a. Filter out non-relevant data b. Data transformation
- **4. Data Integration and Quantification**
  a. Data mining algorithms b . Data analysis
- **5. Interpretation**
  a. Data presentation b . Data visualization
- **6. Insight**
  a . Data insight b. Results

Figure 1.2 Data science stages

Figure 1.2 illustrates the important stages of the data science process and also provides a meaningful description of the process at each stage. Data quality is one of the most critical steps of a data science project for a quality outcome. This process will help us understand the various stages of data processing:

1. **Define the Project Goals**: The ultimate business needs or project goals for the given set of data should be contextualized before adopting the data model processing tools. It is important to define the problem clearly, assess the context, and describe the goals with utmost clarity for a better outcome. Before investing in technology and the resources needed for processing a large data set, we need to identify a few high-value outcomes and validate the outcomes to the value to the organization. Once the proof of concept is validated against the intended outcome, the process can be expanded to a full-blown data set.
2. **Identify the Data Sources:** Information extraction from a credible resource is a key element to data quality. The data source should be free from biases and backed up with authenticity. Some of the open data set sources to explore for data sciences projects are:
   - Google Cloud Public Dataset (https://cloud.google.com/datasets)
   - Amazon Web Services Open Data Registry (https://registry.opendata.aws)
   - Kaggle (https://www.kaggle.com/datasets)
3. **Data Pre-processing and Cleaning:** This involves filling in any missing values for the data set and reformatting the data to be used for a machine learning tool. Data cleaning, which also includes eliminating bad data to the extent possible based on the context of the outcome, would be a precursor to a good quality outcome.
4. **Data Integration and Quantification:** Several data analytics techniques are used for data mining and analysis. This area spans multi-disciplinary domains including sociology, computer science, physics and social media, to name a few. Choosing the right tools for the specific domain is an important consideration for optimal outcome. Some of the basic tools used in the industry are:
   - **Descriptive Analysis**: Here, a machine learning tool is used to summarize a portion of the data in a meaningful way.
   - **Predictive Analysis**: Here, a machine learning tool is used to answer a specific question about the data set and predict values based on the data set features.
5. **Interpretation and Insight**: This involves the results of predictive analysis and reflection on the question asked in the predictive analysis section. This aspect of data science aims to uncover the findings, understand complex behaviours, reveal any hidden insight and patterns and draw meaningful conclusions that create business value.

1.3 Data Science Ecosystem

Data science plays a central role in developing a meaningful data product; however, it requires a blend of technologies to work in sync to make this happen. Figure 1.3 illustrates the different technologies used in various proportions to build algorithms and analytic models for a meaningful conclusion. This proportion varies according to the business problem that we are trying to solve and its intended domain.

- **Artificial intelligence (AI)** is a broad concept of mimicking human behaviour demonstrated in machines. These behaviours include identifying patterns, learning from experience and problem solving within the scope defined. The idea is to build intelligence in machines to mimic the behaviour of human beings for solving problems.

- **Machine learning (ML)** is a branch of computer science that deals primarily with data modelling assisted by algorithms to make predictions, determine data patterns and discover insights for solving problems.
- **Neural network (NN)** has its roots in AI and is designed to work like the human brain. It is composed of a series of specific classes of algorithms designed to recognize relationships in a data set, similar to the way in which the human brain interprets relationships or learns from experience. It is a network of nodes, with each node performing a different function and which can act as input to other connected nodes. For example, to identify a picture as that of a dog or some other animal, different nodes would process the specific information and provide an output.
- **Deep learning (DL)** is a subset of NN but with many layers embedded in it. This layered network allows for the processing of vast amounts of data and helps perform complex computations.

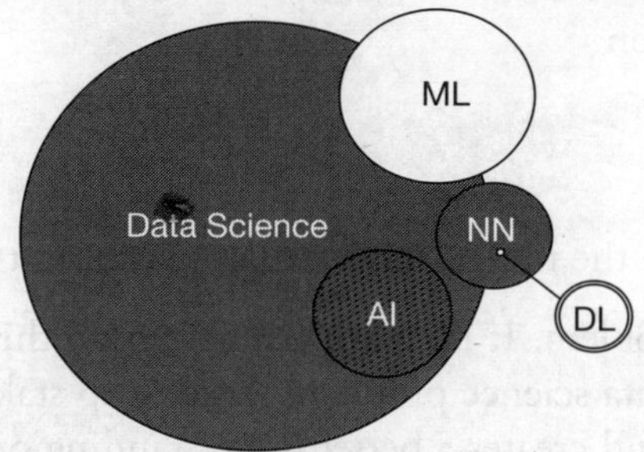

Figure 1.3 Data science ecosystem

1.4 Tools Used in Data Science

Some of the fundamental but powerful methods used in data science are listed below:

- **Linear regression:** This tool is used when there are linear correlations between a set of features and we want to predict the new value of a certain feature based on the linear relationship. This application helps with predictive analysis in AI applications.
- **Clustering:** Clustering uses unsupervised data; this means that the label of each data point is not given and we have to identify the labels based on some method. Clustering analysis can be of many types but the main purpose is to categorize the data points in the set. This application is very helpful for marketing research to identify new groups of customers based on their traits and actions. K-means clustering is the most popular clustering algorithm.
- **Classification:** Classification uses supervised techniques; this means that the label of each data point is given and categorized based on the training data. K-nearest neighbor (K-NN) is a classification data science tool that uses the nearest known clusters to identify the category of unknown data. K-NN uses supervised data where the data set already gives us the labels of each data point. K-NN is useful for pattern recognition. Logistic regression, random forest, decision tree and support vector machines are some other classification algorithms.

- **Principal component analysis (PCA):** This is a machine learning method for reducing a data set's dimension while preserving the parts of the data that identify the data set the most (contain the most variability). This tool is mainly used for processing big data into smaller subsets that would be easier to work with.

1.5 Data Science Workflow

A workflow is a systematic sequence of tasks performed to complete a project. A data science workflow defines the steps in a data science project. It helps us plan, organize and implement the data science project. Generally, data science deals with a six-phase framework iteratively. The six phases are:

1. Ask an interesting question/Define the objective/Give a problem statement
2. Get the data/Data acquisition
3. Explore the data
4. Model the data
5. Reflect or infer
6. Communicate and visualize the results/Dissemination of results

The first step is to define the problem. It may not be easy to do this as it is influenced by the business needs. Correctly defining data science problems helps keep stakeholders' expectations in check, reduces unnecessary iterations, and creates a better understanding of the product for developers, analysts and data scientists. A person who speaks and understands the language of data and business is extremely useful during this process, as they can serve as a link between the business and data science teams.

The second step is to obtain the required quality of data from multiple sources. About 60–70% of the data scientist's time is spent in gathering the right quality of data, as it is necessary to gather all the relevant data, format it so that it can be analyzed, and clean it before analyzing. In the third phase of data exploration, data scientists look for patterns and abnormalities in the data and try to understand it so that hypotheses can be developed that can be tested. After the data is analyzed, an appropriate model can be built for the given data, in the fourth step. Analysis focuses on coding, while reflection focuses on thinking about and sharing analytical results, in the fifth step. The last step is about presenting findings, conclusions and narratives to various stakeholders.

In addition to blogs, several workflow frameworks have become quite well known. Two such frameworks are CRISP-DM (Cross-Industry Standard Process for Data Mining) and OSEMN (Obtain, Scrub, Explore, Model, and iNterpret). Table 1.1 compares different data science workflows.

Table 1.1 Data science workflow comparison

	Harvard	CRISP-DM	OSEMN	Guo's	Tandel's	Joshi's	SciForce	Amazon SageMaker
Understand	Ask an interesting question	Business understanding			Understand the objective		Framing the problem and the goals	
Acquire	Get the data	Data understanding	Obtain	Prepare (acquire)	Import the data	Find, connect and access data	Prepare (acquire)	Fetch
Clean		Data preparation	Scrub	Prepare (clean)	Clean the data	Prepare the data	Prepare (clean)	Clean and prepare
Explore	Explore the data		Explore		Explore the data		Explore	
Model	Model the data	Modelling	Model	Analysis	Model the data	Build models	Analysis	Train the model
Evaluate		Evaluate	Interpret	Reflect			Reflect/ Performance metric	Evaluate the model
Communicate	Communicate / Visualize			Disseminate	Communicate results		Communicate/ Visualize/ Stakeholder meetings	
Deploy		Deployment				Deploy models		Deploy to production
Monitor						Monitor models		Monitor/ Collect Data/ Evaluate

1.6 Automated Methods for Data Collection

Automated methods for data collection means using special tools and software to automate the data capture of paper documents that converts them into digital files. A combination of AI programming and machine learning allows software to quickly read and translate paper files and images and convert them into easily accessible e-files.

The advantages of automated data collection are:

- Faster turnaround time
- Fewer manual processes
- Error reduction
- Cost saving
- Increase in efficiency

Automated data collection (ADC) uses different methods that can change based on the requirements and business needs. Optical character recognition (OCR), optical mark recognition (OMR) and intelligent character recognition (ICR) are a few ADC methods. Various tools and software to automatically collect data include barcode scanners, position scanners, RFID readers, QR codes, and other data collection devices. These tools help in easy and quick readability of documents and, using computer systems, labels and barcodes can be placed on those documents very quickly. Voice data and structured and unstructured data can be collected from different Internet sources using different tools. The algorithm, You Only Look Once (YOLO), has become a favorite among researchers and industry engineers in recent years to identify individuals in videos.

1.7 Overview of Data

All data-based systems involve the collection and interpretation of data, conversion of data into useful information and numerical and statistical analysis. In business and industry, statistical information is required for decision making. In our daily life too, we require information to make informed decisions. For example, before making a purchase, you may want to compare the same product from different manufacturers based on parameters such as customer reviews, cost, size, and so on. Thus, relevant information should be made available to the decision makers.

1.7.1 Data vs Information

Data can be collected from various input sources and devices, but sometimes this data cannot be used directly. It must be processed, interpreted, organized and structured so as to make it meaningful. Processed data is called information. Given below are examples of data and information:

- Temperature readings taken over the past 10 years is data. If this data is analyzed to find global warming patterns, then it is information.
- Traffic to a website is data. If the traffic is analyzed for certain types of virus attacks, it is information.

1.7.2 Growth of Data

Data is growing in many dimensions. Terabytes of data is the average size today and it is expected to increase to petabytes, exabytes and zettabytes. International Data Corporation (IDC) projects that by 2025, the amount of digital data generated globally will reach 163 zettabytes due to the proliferation of devices and sensors. According to projections, the global big data market will increase from $42 billion in 2018 to $103 billion in 2027.

Enterprise executives report that companies have sought big data projects to provide themselves a competitive edge in 83% of cases. By 2025, enterprise firms will create and handle 60% of the 163 zettabytes of current data. About 8% of companies claim that data and analytics have significantly altered the nature of industry rivalry. Among vertical businesses, the education sector has the lowest adoption of big data, but educators are the most inclined to anticipate using it in the future. By 2023, the big data sector is predicted to be worth $77 billion.

1.8 Sources of Data

The amount of data generated and collected is growing exponentially. About 90% of data is generated from the sources discussed below:

- **Internet**: The internet is the main source of data. Online search, internet banking and e-commerce all generate large volumes of data. Today, the number of people with access to the internet is increasing and automation of systems has also contributed to the growth in data.
- **Social media**: The use of social media such as Facebook, Snapchat, Twitter, WhatsApp, Instagram, LinkedIn, and so on, has fuelled data creation. This data includes text, photos, audio and video, which require the storage of huge amounts of data with fast retrieval. For more information about data collected from social media, please see the Data Never Sleeps 5.0 report.
- **Communication**: Digital data for communication between machines, from machines to humans and between humans is increasing daily. We send data through various means such as email, voice SMS, Messenger, Skype and WhatsApp calls. The data can be in the form of text, pictures or videos. Thus, communication systems are a big source of data.
- **Digital photos**: Today, most mobile phones are equipped with high-resolution cameras. Anyone can upload photo albums over the internet. Trillions of photos are stored on servers and retrieved at speed. These photos are also shared on multiple social media networks, generating even more data.
- **Services**: Most people and businesses use services such as Google Maps, internet banking, online trading, and so on. Repositories of information like Wikipedia also allow people to update its pages. Increased use of such services generates a tremendous amount of data.
- **Internet of things (IoT):** Smart devices that interact with each other generate a lot of data. Home automation, e-farming and robotics require devices to interact with each other through the internet. This information, when stored on a cloud or streamed online, becomes a big source of data over time.

Every source of data requires certain related tools and needs to be processed in different ways.

1.9 Big Data

Big data refers to large and complex data sets that can be structured, semi-structured or unstructured and which will typically not fit into the memory available to be processed. Such data may need to be processed in-place, which means that computation must be performed wherever the data resides. It is not possible for such systems to process a vast amount of data within the time frame mandated by the business. Big data comprises the five Vs:

- **Volume**: This refers to the size of the data set. It may be in KB, MB, GB, TB or PB, based on the type of the application that generates or receives the data.
- **Variety**: This refers to the types of data that can exist, such as text, audio, video and photos. It refers to heterogeneous sources of data, both structured and unstructured. Data presented in the form of emails, photos, videos, monitoring devices, PDFs, audio, and so on, are also heterogeneous data that needs to be handled by a single application.
- **Velocity**: This refers to the speed at which data flows into business processes, application logs, networks and social media sites, sensors, devices, and so on. The speed of retrieval of data should remain the same irrespective of the size of the data. Thus, velocity refers to the low-latency, real-time speed at which the analytics need to be applied. A typical example of this would be to perform analytics on a continuous stream of data originating from a social networking site or aggregation of disparate sources of data.
- **Value:** This refers to insight from data. Every data extracted might not be meaningful. As a cost is involved in collecting and analyzing data, the value of data is important.
- **Veracity**: It refers to the trustworthiness of the data. An example of this is GPS data. The reliability and accuracy of this data is very important. Satellite signals are lost sometimes in urban areas because of buildings and other structures. So, in this case, data has been fused with other data sources like road data or data from accelerometers.

1.9.1 Big Data vs Small Data

Big data and small data can be differentiated based on the data source, volume, velocity, variety and value (Table 1.2).

Table 1.2 Big data vs small data

Property	Big data	Small data
Data source	Non-structured data generated from sources such as social media, IoT, Twitter, blogs, devices, video, images, etc. as well as logs generated from systems	Structured data generated from sources such as relational data in tabular form and transaction data
Volume	In TB, PB, EB or ZB	In GB or TB
Velocity	High velocity and real-time data	Low velocity or batch data; can wait for response
Variety	Structured, unstructured or multi-structured data	Structured data

1.9.2 Major Players in Big Data

- Google
- Apache Hadoop
- MapReduce
- Apache Mahout
- Apache HBase
- Apache Cassandra

These are the major players in big data and they provide the data handling tools to store and compute big data. Google provides cloud and big data processing tools. Apache Hadoop can handle multiple computers to solve a problem. MapReduce enables you to process and generate big data sets with a parallel, distributed algorithm on a cluster. Apache HBase handles storage of big data at multiple locations.

1.9.3 Big Data Tools

Table 1.3 lists of the main big data tools in use.

Table 1.3 Types of big data tools and examples

Type of tool	Example
NoSQL databases	CouchDB, MongoDB, Redis, Cassandra, HBase, Hypertable, Voldemort, ZooKeeper, BigTable, Riak
MapReduce	Acunu, Hive, Hadoop, Pig, Cascading, Caffeine, S4, MapR, Flume, Kafka, Oozie, Greenplum, Cascalog
Storage	S3, HDFS, GDFS
Servers	AWS Elastic Beanstalk, Amazon EC2, Elastic, Heroku, Google App Engine
Processing	BigSheets, R language, Mechanical Turk, Solr/Lucene, Datameer, Tinkerpop

1.10 Data Categorization

Data can be categorized according to the scale of measurement. Data has its own property and can be continuous or discrete. Qualitative and quantitative data may be required to represent the system based on the properties of the data.

1.10.1 Entity and Attributes

- **Entity:** An entity can be a single thing, person, place or object. Data can be stored about such entities.
- **Attribute:** An attribute is a measurable or observable property of an entity.
- **Data:** A measure of an attribute of an entity is called data.

1.10.2 Scales of Measurement

The scale of measurement describes the nature of the information assigned to a variable. It defines the way in which variables can be defined or categorized.

The four scales of measurement are nominal, ordinal, interval and ratio. The nominal and ordinal scales are considered as qualitative data, while the interval and ratio scales come under quantitative data. Qualitative data are measures of values and expressed as numbers or categories. They are descriptive and conceptual. Quantitative data is measured using numbers and values. It is concise and close ended. Quantitative data can further be classified as continuous or discrete.

For example, an employee identification number such as 10011 is discrete data. Continuous data can be fitted into a range and includes decimal points. For example, height and age are continuous data as height can be 120.3 cm and age can be 12.5 years. Table 1.4 describes the differences between qualitative and quantitative data.

Table 1.4 Differences between qualitative and quantitative data

Qualitative data	Quantitative data
Countable or measurable	Subjective or descriptive or relating to language
Tells us how much, how often, how many	Describes certain attributes and helps to understand the 'how' and 'why' behind certain behaviours
Analyzed using statistical analysis	Analyzed by grouping the data into meaningful categories or themes

Qualitative Data

- **Nominal scale**: Here, data categories are given names so as to provide a label. There is no hierarchical relationship (order) between the categories. One category is not the parent of or superior to another. Examples: Gender (Male / Female), blood groups (A / B / O / AB), religion (Hindu / Muslim / Christian / Buddhist).
- **Ordinal scale**: Here, the categories can be placed logically in a meaningful order but the difference between the categories is not known. Examples: (a) Rank (First / Second / Third): The ranks can be placed logically in ascending or descending order but the difference in marks between the ranks is not known, nor can it be predicted from the ranks. (b) Rating (Excellent / Very Good / Good): A rating of Excellent or Good is meaningful but the difference between the ratings is not known.

Quantitative Data

- **Interval scale**: Here, the values can be ordered, they are meaningful and the difference between the values can be quantified. Values appear in the form of numbers or numerical values and are meaningful but cannot be multiplied, divided, added or subtracted. Doubling the value has no meaning due to the absence of absolute zero. Examples: (a) Trend analysis: In market analysis, it is useful to know the trends over various time intervals. Trend analysis on interval data can be performed by taking surveys in multiple iterations, using the same question. (b) SWOC analysis: This is performed to analyze the strength, weakness, opportunity and challenge for an organization from interval data. (c) Temperature measurement: Measuring temperature over an interval in Fahrenheit and Celsius.

- **Ratio scale**: This is similar to interval scale data but, in addition, it allows users to compare the intervals or differences. The values can be ordered and are meaningful. Difference and addition is possible, as is doubling, due to the presence of absolute zero. Examples: (a) Temperature measurement: Measurement of temperature on the Kelvin scale is ratio scale data because 100 K is twice as hot as 50 K. The difference in temperature values is also meaningful and can be ordered. (b) Measurement of height in inches. (c) Measurement of weight in kilograms.

Quantitative data may be classified as discrete or continuous, as described below. Fractions are not meaningful here.

- **Discrete**: Values that can be specified as whole numbers, can be counted and which cannot be further divided. For example, the number of classes, number of children, number of votes, PAN number.
- **Continuous:** Any numerical value (including fractions) that is meaningful and which can be measured and broken down further. For example, weight: 1 kg, 1.1 kg, 1.5 kg can be measured in fractions and is meaningful; height: 5 feet, 5.1 feet, and so on; capacity of a tank: 1 litre, 1.5 litres, and so on. These numerical values are continuous.

EXERCISES

Multiple Choice Questions

1. Point out the correct statement:
(a) Raw data is an original source of data
(b) Pre-processed data is an original source of data
(c) Raw data is the data obtained after processing
(d) None of the above

2. Which of the following is performed by a data scientist?
(a) Defining the question
(b) Creating reproducible code
(c) Challenging the results
(d) All of the above

3. Which of the following is the most important language for data science?
(a) Java
(b) Ruby
(c) Python
(d) None of the above

4. Which of the following terms is appropriate for the figure?

(a) Large data
(b) Big data
(c) Dark data
(d) None of the above

5. Which of the following characteristics of big data is relatively more concerned with data science?
(a) Velocity
(b) Variety

(c) Volume
(d) None of the above

6. Data that can be modelled as dimension attributes and measure attributes is called ________ data.
(a) Multi-dimensional
(b) Single-dimensional
(c) Measured
(d) Dimensional

7. The process of viewing the cross-tab (single dimensional) with a fixed value of one attribute is:
(a) Slicing
(b) Dicing
(c) Pivoting
(d) Both slicing and dicing

8. The operation of moving from finer granularity to coarser granularity (by means of aggregation) is called ________.
(a) Roll-up
(b) Drill-down
(c) Dicing
(d) Pivoting

Answers

1. (a) **2.** (d) **3.** (c) **4.** (b) **5.** (b) **6.** (a) **7.** (a) **8.** (a)

Programming/Concept-based Questions

1. What is the smallest and largest unit used to measure the size of data?
Answer: Smallest unit: Bit; Largest unit: Zettabyte

2. How big is a quintillion measure?
Answer: 1 with 18 zeros

3. Give examples of the smallest and largest entities of data.
Answer: A single row of a table, being a single occurrence of that entity. We can also call it an entity instance; this is the smallest entity. The entire database is the largest entity.

4. Give five parameters with which data can be categorized as (i) Simple, (ii) Moderately Complex and (iii) Complex.
Answer: Velocity, Volume, Value, Variety and Veracity

5. What types of data are involved in the following applications?
a. Weather forecasting
b. Mobile usage of all customers of a service provider
c. Anomaly (fraud) detection in a bank
d. Person categorization, that is, identifying a human
e. Air traffic control in an airport
f. Streaming data from all flying aircrafts of Boeing

Answer:
a. Interval scale b. Ratio scale
c. Interval scale d. Ordinal scale
e. Ordinal scale f. Interval scale

6. Consider an image as an entity.

a. What are the attributes necessary to represent an image?
b. Categorize each attribute according to data categorization.
c. Suppose two images are given. Give an idea to check if two images are identical or not.

Answer: Attributes are Pixel colour: Ordinal (While/Grey/Black), Image size: Ratio scale
To check if two images are identical: Their size and pixel colour value at the same positions in the two images should be the same (template-based matching).

7. How you can convert data of interval type to ordinal type? Give an example. What are the problems with such a transformation? Is the reverse possible? Justify your answer.
Answer: For example, "On how many days of the last 30 did a person smoke cigarettes?" typically gets mostly zeros, a smaller number of 1s, 2s and 3s, and then very sparse responses until a second mode at 30. So sometimes we can cut it as 0, 1–2, 3–29, 30, depending on the actual distribution and sample size, reflecting qualitative differences between non-smokers, occasional smokers and daily smokers. The reverse is also possible. Given a category/label data, values can be assigned and converted to intervals. For example, non-smokers can be given an interval 1 or less.

8. What are the different properties used to categorize data according to NOIR data categorization?
Answer: Qualitative or Quantitative

9. Given an entity 'STUDENT' with the following attributes, identify the NOIR category to which each of them belongs.

Scholarship amount	Name	Roll No.	Date of birth	Aadhar No.	Gender	Mobile No.	Email ID

Answer:

Scholarship amount	Name	Roll No.	Date of birth	Aadhar No.	Gender	Mobile No.	Email ID
Ratio	Nominal	Ordinal	Interval	Ratio	Nominal	Nominal	Nominal

BIBLIOGRAPHY

1. Phillips-Wren, G, Esposito, A and Jain, LC. 2021. *Advances in Data Science: Methodologies and Applications*. Springer Nature.
2. Mathews, K. 2020. How Data Science is Being Used to Understand COVID-19. *KD Nuggets*. https://www.kdnuggets.com/2020/04/data-science-understand-covid-19.html
3. Yegulalp, S. 2022. What is TensorFlow? The Machine Learning Library Explained. *InfoWorld*. https://www.infoworld.com/article/3278008/what-is-tensorflow-the-machine-learning-library-explained.html
4. "About Keras". Keras. https://keras.io/about/
5. "What is a Data Science Workflow". Data Science Process Alliance. chttps://www.datascience-pm.com/data-science-workflow/

CHAPTER **2**

Environment Set-up and Basics of Python

Learning Objectives

At the end of this chapter, you will be able to:

- Explain the installation of Python and how to start using it
- Write a simple program and execute it
- Use basic operations on data, control statements, loops, and so on
- Explain the basic concepts of tuples, dictionaries, sets and frozen sets
- Work with files

2.0 Introduction to Python

Python is a simple and powerful language. It enables you to provide solutions to the given problems without worrying about the technical details of the programming language, namely, structure and syntax. It supports high-level programming languages with procedure and object-oriented properties. It is more suitable for scripting and application development.

The Python programming language was introduced by Guido van Rossum. Various popular programming languages such as C, C++ and Java can be coupled with Python. It contains built-in libraries for data structures and GUI (graphical user interface). In Python, a control routine program is an additional feature that allows Python to connect different programs. With the built-in garbage collector, memory management is handled efficiently. In Python, it is not necessary to include various libraries; use of code blocks is also made easy with indentation (whitespace).

In Python, declaration of a variable does not require specification of the data type. Hence, it is called a dynamic typed language. This is applicable for derived types as well. Python is a platform-independent programming language. It contains an interpreter that reads the source code line by line and converts it into machine code. Like Java, Python supports platform independence with the use of byte code. The Python interpreter generates byte code as output. This byte code file can be used and executed by any platform. As Python uses an interpreter rather than a compiler, it takes more time. The advantage of using an interpreter is that syntax errors can be identified immediately after reading each line. Python is very popular for program prototyping. With this, programs can be developed in less time and further modifications can be made quickly with the support of GUIs.

Python supports both procedure-oriented and object-oriented programming languages. In a single Python program, both these programming language features can be used. So, Python programming supports a top-down approach, which allows for the use of functions, as well as a bottom-up approach, which allows for the use of classes and objects.

2.1 Features of Python

- **Unsophisticated**: Python is an unsophisticated language. It allows the user to write programs without following strict rules such as declaring the variable data type, use of curly brackets, etc. It allows the programmer to focus on providing the solution rather than on the structure and syntax of the language.
- **Easy to learn**: Learning Python is easy, even for beginners. Python is a Free/Libre and Open Source Software (FLOSS) provided to share knowledge.
- **High-level**: The programmer need not worry about the low-level details required for the program.
- **Portable**: Python is a platform-independent programming language. With byte code, Python programs can be executed by any platform, and hence, they are portable.
- **Interpreted**: Python programs can be directly executed from byte code, which is an interpreted code. It translates the original source code into platform-independent code.
- **Object-oriented**: Python supports all the principles of object-oriented programming. Python programs can be designed around objects that focus on data. Implementing OOPs principles in Python is simpler than in C++ or Java.
- **Extensible**: Python code can also be written in other languages such as C++, making it a highly extensible language.
- **Embeddable**: The scripting feature can be provided by embedding Python code in C or C++ programs.
- **Extensive libraries**: Python has huge standard libraries for handling regular expressions, threading, GUI, etc.

2.2 Installation of Python

Python can be installed on any operating system. Here, the installation steps for Windows and Linux are discussed.

2.2.1 Windows Operating System

Step 1: Download the Python software from the following URL:
https://www.python.org/downloads/windows/

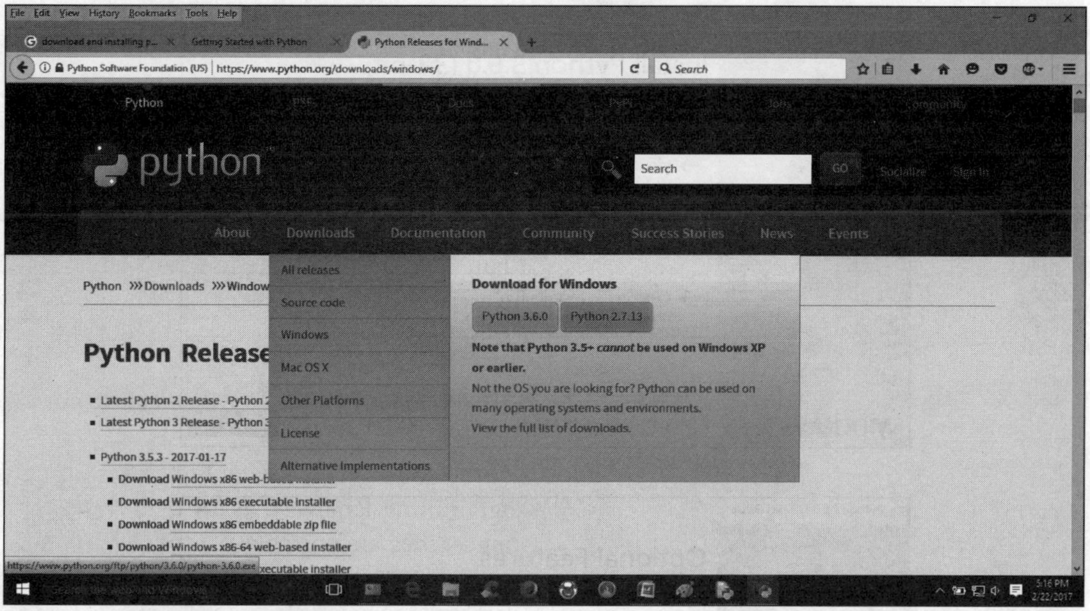

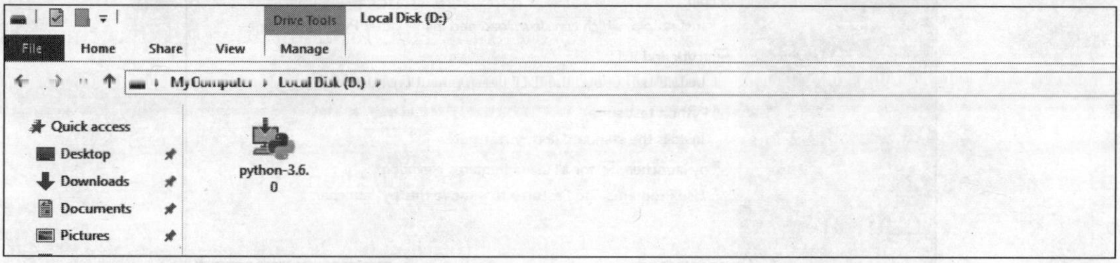

Step 2: Install the downloaded Python software.

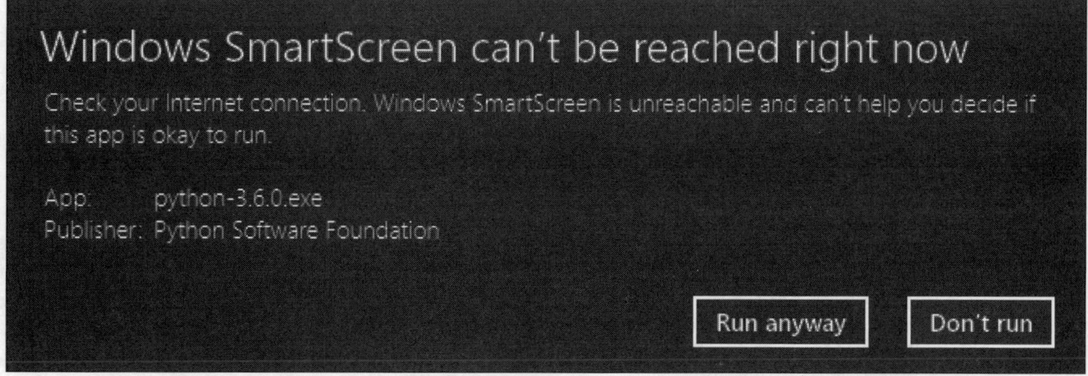

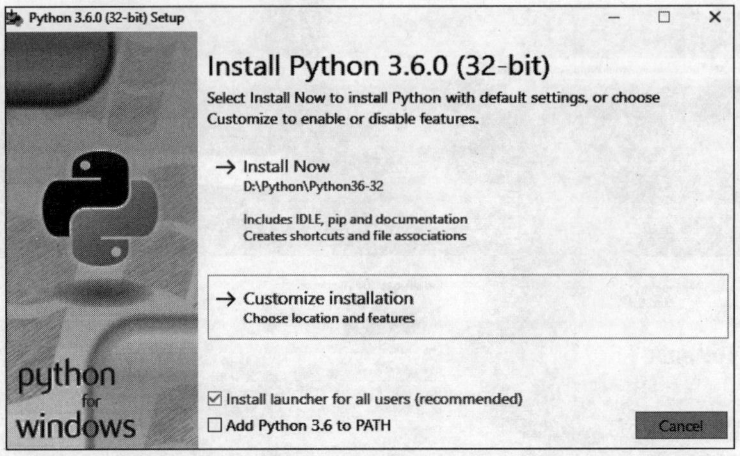
Python 3.6.0 (32-bit) Setup
Install Python 3.6.0 (32-bit)
Select Install Now to install Python with default settings, or choose Customize to enable or disable features.
→ Install Now
D:\Python\Python36-32
Includes IDLE, pip and documentation
Creates shortcuts and file associations
→ Customize installation
Choose location and features
Install launcher for all users (recommended)
Add Python 3.6 to PATH
Cancel
python for windows

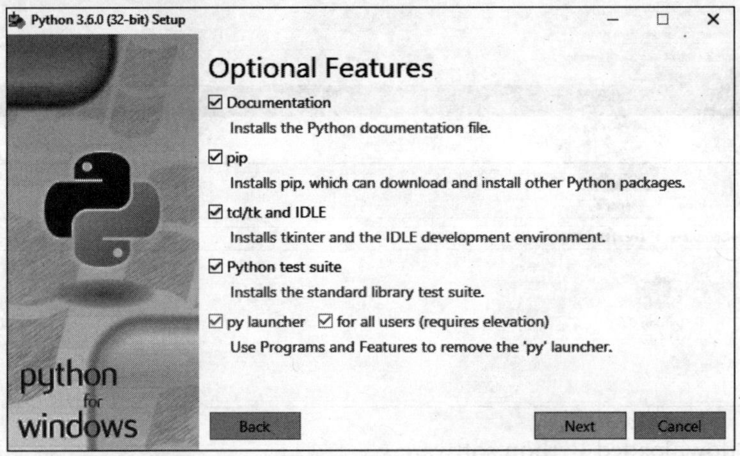
Python 3.6.0 (32-bit) Setup
Optional Features
Documentation
Installs the Python documentation file.
pip
Installs pip, which can download and install other Python packages.
tcl/tk and IDLE
Installs tkinter and the IDLE development environment.
Python test suite
Installs the standard library test suite.
py launcher
for all users (requires elevation)
Use Programs and Features to remove the 'py' launcher.
Back
Next
Cancel
python for windows

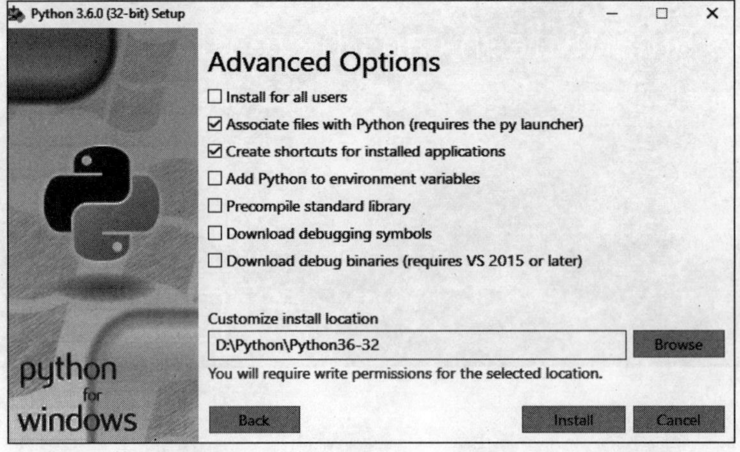
Python 3.6.0 (32-bit) Setup
Advanced Options
Install for all users
Associate files with Python (requires the py launcher)
Create shortcuts for installed applications
Add Python to environment variables
Precompile standard library
Download debugging symbols
Download debug binaries (requires VS 2015 or later)
Customize install location
D:\Python\Python36-32
Browse
You will require write permissions for the selected location.
Back
Install
Cancel
python for windows

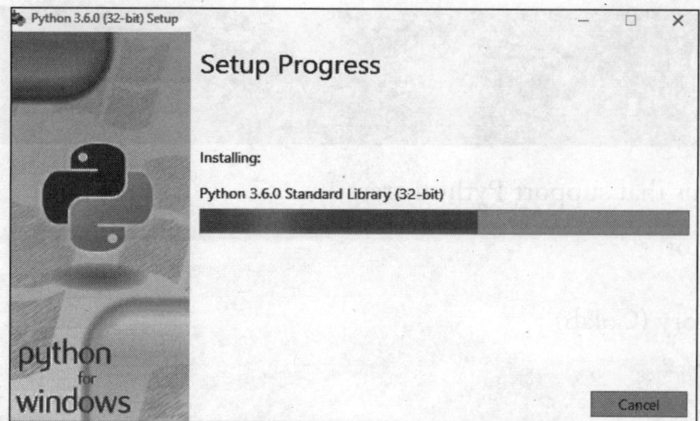

Step 3: Add Python to the system variable. You can specify the settings of the system variable by following these steps:

1. Click *Start* → *My Computer* → *Properties* → *Advanced System Settings* → *Environment Variables* → *System Variables* → *Path* → *Edit.*
2. In the textbox, at the end, paste the path to Python: `D:\Python\Python36-32;`
3. Click *OK.*

2.2.2 Linux Operating System

To install Python on the Linux operating system, follow the steps given below:
Step 1: Install Python from the package manager.

```
>Sudo apt-get install python -pip
```

Step 2: Check for successful installation.

```
>python
```

```
hadoop-04@hadoop-04:~$ python
Python 2.7.6 (default, Jun 22 2015, 17:58:13)
[GCC 4.8.2] on linux2
Type "help", "copyright", "credits" or "license" for more information.
>>>
```

The other platforms that support Python are:

- Anaconda Navigator
- Spyder
- Google Colaboratory (Colab)
- Jupyter Notebook
- PyDev
- IDLE
- Visual Studio Code (VS Code)
- Sublime Text
- Wing
- GNU/Emacs
- Thonny

Sample Program

Write a Python program to print "Hello World!".

Step 1: Open Notepad and type the line shown below:

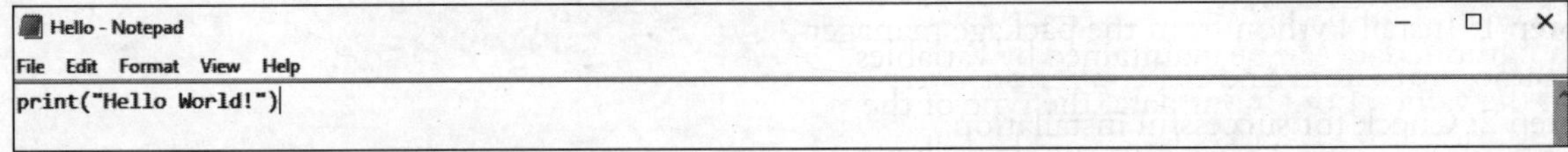

Step 2: Save the file as Hello.py.

Step 3: Click *Start* → *Run*. Type `cmd`. Change to the PythonPrograms directory. Type `python Hello.py`

Output: Hello World!

2.3 Python Identifiers

An identifier represents a name used in a Python program. The length of the identifier can vary. The rules for validating identifiers are listed below:

- The identifier can be a combination of various elements such as uppercase letters, lowercase letters, digits and underscore.
- Keywords cannot be used as identifiers.
- The first letter of the identifier should not be a digit.
- Special characters such as !, @ and # are not permitted to be a part of the identifier.

2.4 Python Indentation

In Python, groups of code or statements are arranged in individual blocks. Each block can be separated by indentation, as shown in Fig. 2.1.

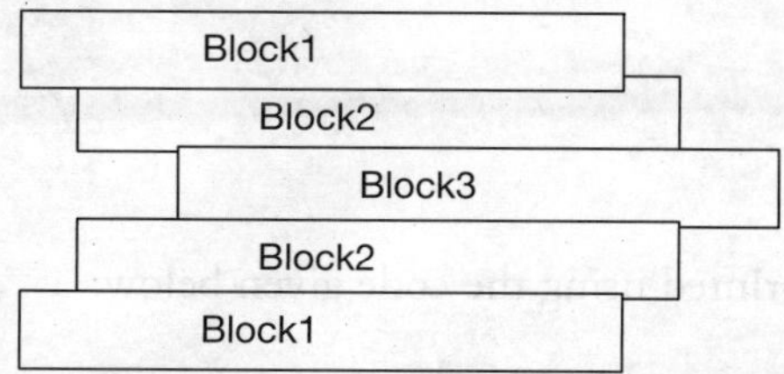

Figure 2.1 Structure blocks in Python with indentation

2.5 Comments in Python

In Python, comments can be specified as follows:

- '#' is used to represent a single-line comment.
- Multiple-line comments begin and end with the "" delimiter.

2.6 Basic Data

In Python, data can be maintained by variables. Variables can be initialized without declaration. Based on the value of the input data, the type of the variable will be automatically considered. The variable name should start with a letter and be followed by a sequence of letters, numbers or underscore (_).

Integer, floating point and string are considered as primitive data types. Character is considered as string data with length 1.

The type of the variable represents the value stored within the variable. Type inferencing is allowed in Python. Therefore, general keywords such as 'int' and 'float' are not required for the variable.

For example, the `var` variable is assigned the value 10 without specifying the data type as `int`.

```
var=10
    var
```

Output: 10

Even though the data type was not specified, we can find it out using the following code:

```
type (var)
```

Output: int

Different variables can be directly assigned values without specifying the data type.

```
var1=10.38
var2="this is a string"
var3="A"
var5=True
var5=False
type (var5)
```

Output: bool

The values of variables can be printed using the code given below:

```
print(var2)
```

Output: this is a string

Even if the `print()` statement is not used, the value can be displayed using only the variable name at the command prompt:

```
var3=2000
var3
```

Output: 2000

The type of the variable can be revealed by:

```
type (var5)
```

Output: bool

Complex numbers can be represented using `j` with an imaginary number, as shown below:

```
var6=27+67j
var6
```

Output: (27+67j)

Two integers can be added using the '+' operator:

```
var7=var+var3
var7
```

Output: 2010

2.7 Operators and Expressions

Python supports a number of operators, explained below.

2.7.1 Arithmetic Operators

For numbers, the usual mathematical rules are applicable.

>>> 1/2 # *returns integer value*
0
>>> 1/2.0 # *returns decimal value*
0.5

Take note of the following operations on strings:

>>> '1' + '2' # *concatenation instead of addition*
12
>>> '1' * 5 # *This is valid in Python*
11111

Table 2.1 Summary of mathematical operators

Symbol	Operation	Example	Output
+	Addition	a = 1+2	3
-	Subtraction	a = 2-1	1
*	Multiplication	a = 2*2	4
/	Division	a = 5.0/2	2.5
//	Truncating division	a = 5.0//2	2.0
%	Modulo	a = 5%2	1
**	Power	a = 5**2	25

2.7.2 Relational Operators

Relational operators are used for comparing values. It returns True or False according to the condition. These operators are also known as comparison operators.

Table 2.2 Summary of relational operators

Operator	Name	Description
==	Equal to	Checks whether two operands are equal
!=	Not equal to	Checks whether two operands are not equal
>	Greater than	Checks whether the left operand is greater than the right operand
<	Less than	Checks whether the left operand is less than the right operand
>=	Greater than or equal to	Checks whether the left operand is greater or equal to the right operand
<=	Less than or equal to	Checks whether the left operand is less than or equal to the right operand

2.7.3 Bitwise Operators

In Python, bitwise operators are used to perform bitwise calculations on integers. The integers are first converted into binary form and operations are then performed on each bit or corresponding pair of bits – hence the name. The result is returned in decimal format.

Table 2.3 Summary of bitwise operators

Operator	Name	Description	Syntax
&	Bitwise AND	Results in bit 1, if both operand bits are 1; otherwise results in bit 0.	x & y
|	Bitwise OR	Results in bit 1, if any of the operand bits is 1; otherwise results in bit 0.	x | y
~	Bitwise NOT	Inverts the individual bits.	~x
^	Bitwise XOR	Results in bit 1, if any of the operand bits is 1 but not both; otherwise results in bit 0.	x ^ y
>>	Bitwise right shift	The left operand's value is moved towards the right by the number of bits specified by the right operand.	x>>
<<	Bitwise left shift	The left operand's value is moved towards the left by the number of bits specified by the right operand.	x<<

2.7.4 Membership Operators

Membership operators are used to test if a sequence is present in an object.

Table 2.4 Summary of membership operators

Operator	Description	Example
in	Returns True if a sequence with the specified value is present in the object	x in y
not in	Returns True if a sequence with the specified value is not present in the object	x not in y

2.7.5 Identity Operators

Identity operators are used to compare objects, not to check if they are equal, but to check if they are actually the same object, with the same memory location.

Table 2.5 Summary of identity operators

Operator	Description	Example
is	Returns True if both variables are the same object	x is y
is not	Returns True if both variables are not the same object	x is not y

2.7.6 Logical Operators

Logical operators are used to combine conditional statements.

Table 2.6 Summary of logical operators

Operator	Description	Example
and	Returns True if both statements are true	x < 5 and x < 10
or	Returns True if one of the statements is true	x < 5 or x < 4
not	Reverses the result and returns False if the result is true	not(x < 5 and x < 10)

2.7.7 Assignment Operators

Assignment operators are used to assign values to variables.

Table 2.7 Summary of assignment operators

Operator	Example	Same As
=	x = 5	x = 5
+=	x += 3	x = x + 3
-=	x -= 3	x = x - 3
*=	x *= 3	x = x * 3

2.8 Data Types

Python supports different types of data such as text, numeric, sequence, mapping, set, Boolean and binary. Some of these are explained in this section.

2.8.1 List

Python supports various built-in data types for data structures. These are sequence or mapping objects. There are two types of sequences: list and tuple. A list consists of homogeneous elements and is created by providing values separated by ','. It does not have a fixed number of elements. It uses square brackets for specification of data. Changes are permitted to the values of a list variable.

The sequencer accesses the elements in a list using an index value. The values are maintained in sequential order. Mapping objects are mainly used to access elements without index values while dictionary objects comprise unordered sets of elements.

To create an empty list:

```
list1=[]
list1
```

Output: []

List is a heterogeneous data type and different types of data such as string, integer, float and Boolean can be assigned to a list:

```
#list is heterogenous datatype
list1=["this is a list",20,3.4,True,False,5+7j]
list1
```

Output: ['this is a list', 20, 3.4, True, False, (5+7j)]

The components of two lists can be combined using the '+' operator:

```
# Create another list
list2=["this is another list",30,40,40.89,4+8j]
list3=list1+list2
list3
```

Output: ['this is a list', 20, 3.4, True, False, (5+7j), 'this is another list', 30, 40, 40.89, (4+8j)]

To print all the elements of a list:

```
print (list3)
```

Output: ['this is a list', 20, 3.4, True, False, (5+7j), 'this is another list', 30, 40, 40.89, (4+8j)]

You can append an element to a list by using the `append()` function along with the element to be added:

```
list3.append("this is an append") #dot+tab
print(list3)
```

Output:

['this is a list', 20, 3.4, True, False, (5+7j), 'this is another list', 30, 40, 40.89, (4+8j), 'this is an append']

List slicing is used to copy selected elements from one list to another. By using [:], all the elements of one list can be assigned to another list.

```
list3[:]
```

Output:

['this is a list', 20, 3.4, True, False, (5+7j), 'this is another list', 30, 40, 40.89, (4+8j), 'this is an append']

The start and end positions can be specified for the slicing operator.

To display the first five elements from index 0 to 4:

```
list3[:5]
```

Output: ['this is a list', 20, 3.4, True, False]

To display elements from index 5 to the last element:

```
list3[5:]
```

Output: [(5+7j), 'this is another list', 30, 40, 40.89, (4+8j), 'this is an append']

To display elements from position 0 to the end of the list:

```
list3[0:]
```

Output:

['this is a list', 20, 3.4, True, False, (5+7j), 'this is another list', 30, 40, 40.89, (4+8j), 'this is an append']

To display elements from position 0 to the sixth element:

```
list3[0:7]
```

Output: ['this is a list', 20, 3.4, True, False, (5+7j), 'this is another list']

To display elements from beginning to end but not the last one:

```
list3[:-1]
```

Output: ['this is a list', 20, 3.4, True, False, (5+7j), 'this is another list', 30, 40, 40.89, (4+8j)]

To display the last element:

```
list3[-1]
```

Output: 'this is an append'

To display elements from beginning to end but not last the three entries:

```
list3[:-3]
```

Output: ['this is a list', 20, 3.4, True, False, (5+7j), 'this is another list', 30, 40]

To display the last three entries:

```
list3[-3:]
```

Output: [40.89, (4+8j), 'this is an append']

To count the number of specific elements using the `count()` function:

```
list3.count(True)
```

Output: 1

To return a copy of a list:

```
list3.copy()
```

Output:

['this is a list', 20, 3.4, True, False, (5+7j), 'this is another list', 30, 40, 40.89, (4+8j), 'this is an append']

To display the index of a specific element:

```
list3.index(40.89) #if it is multiple times then first index will be
given
```

Output: 9

To insert an element at a given index position:

```
list3.insert(2,'mango')
list3
```

Output:

['this is a list', 20, 'mango', 3.4, True, False, (5+7j), 'this is another list', 30, 40, 40.89, (4+8j), 'this is an append']

To calculate the length of a list using `len()`:

```
len (list3)
```

Output: 13

To remove a specific element from a list using `pop()`:

```
list3.pop(1) #takes argument in the form of index
```

Output: 20

To check if the element has been removed from `index 1`:

```
    list3
```

Output:

['this is a list', 'mango', 3.4, True, False, (5+7j), 'this is another list', 30, 40, 40.89, (4+8j), 'this is an append']

To reverse the contents of a list:

```
list3.reverse()
list3
```

Output:

['this is an append', (4+8j), 40.89, 40, 30, 'this is another list', (5+7j), False, True, 3.4, 'mango', 'this is a list']

To update an element in a list at specific index position:

```
list3[2]=89.40
list3
```

Output:

['this is an append', (4+8j), 89.4, 40, 30, 'this is another list', (5+7j), False, True, 3.4, 'mango', 'this is list']

2.8.2 Tuple

A tuple is a list with a fixed number of elements. It uses parentheses for specification of data. Tuple is similar to list, except that it is immutable. No changes are allowed. So, in a tuple, once the data is defined, changes cannot be made. The advantages of immutability are listed below:

- A copy operation with immutable objects is more efficient than with mutable objects.
- A comparison operation with immutable objects is more efficient than with mutable objects.
- For any immutable object, only one copy can be stored.
- In concurrent code, development of synchronized access to immutable objects is not required.
- Lists are used to maintain dynamic data whereas tuples are used to maintain data of fixed size.
- For tuples, new elements cannot be added.
- For tuples, existing elements cannot be removed.

Tuples can be created using small parenthesis, as shown below:

```
tuple1=()
tuple1=('this is an append',(4+8j),89.4,40,30,'this is a
tuple',(5+7j),False,True,3.4,'mango',20)
tuple2=("this is another tuple",2343)
type (tuple2)
```

Output: Tuple

The contents of two tuples can be combined using the '+' operator:

```
tuple3=tuple1+tuple2
tuple3
```

Output:

('this is an append', (4+8j), 89.4, 40, 30, 'this is a tuple', (5+7j), False, True, 3.4, 'mango', 20, 'this is another tuple', 2343)

You can count the frequency of an element in a tuple using the `count()` method:

```
tuple3.count(40)
```

Output: 1

To display elements from beginning to end but not the last three:

```
tuple3[:-3]
```

`Out[98]:`

('this is an append', (4+8j), 89.4, 40, 30, 'this is a tuple', (5+7j), False, True, 3.4, 'mango')

If you try to update a tuple, it will give you an error:

```
tuple3[2]=45.9 #tuple does not update values. they are immutable
---------------------------------------------------------------------------
------ TypeError Traceback (most recent call last) <ipython-input-99-
bfaa9b437295> in <module> ----> 1 tuple3[2]=45.9 TypeError: 'tuple'
object does not support item assignment
```

To display the index of a specific element in a tuple:

```
tuple3.index(40)
```

Output: 3

2.8.3 Dictionary

Python supports the dictionary data type. This is a mapping object. So heterogeneous values can be maintained. Each value should be mapped with a key. The dictionary contains a set of key-value pairs. Within a dictionary, a value can be accessed only with the help of the corresponding key.

A dictionary is a variable used to maintain multiple typed elements. It uses curly brackets for specification of data. It maintains data by using the `{key:value,...}` format. Multiple entries are separated by a comma operator. Change of values is allowed.

A list is a mutable object whereas a dictionary is an implementation of the hash table and key-value pair. A list is an ordered object whereas a dictionary is an unordered object. List elements can be of any type and be accessed with the help of index values. A dictionary can also have multi-typed values. The elements can be accessed with the help of their key.

A dictionary is a mutable object. So all the elements of the dictionary can be changed, updated and removed. A dictionary takes O(1) loop-up speed. This means that the entry will be retrieved in one hit. So, they are efficient for memory operations and for improving look-up speed.

A dictionary can be created empty or using key-value pairs and the keys and values can be known individually too.

```
dict1={}
dict11={'apple':'fruit','almond':'dryfruit','phone':'redmi','pc':'acer'}
#key:value
dict11.keys()
```

Output: dict_keys(['apple', 'almond', 'phone', 'pc'])

To display items from a dictionary:

```
dict11.items()
```

Output: dict_items([('apple', 'fruit'), ('almond', 'dryfruit'), ('phone', 'redmi'), ('pc', 'acer')])

To display values using the `values()` function:

```
dict11.values()
```

Output: dict_values(['fruit', 'dryfruit', 'redmi', 'acer'])

To assign a value to a key:

```
dict11["phone1"]:'vivo'
dict11
```

Output: {'apple': 'fruit', 'almond': 'dryfruit', 'phone': 'vivo', 'pc': 'acer'}

2.9 Sets and Frozen Sets

A set is an unordered collection of unique items. The basic operations on sets are membership testing and duplicate entry elimination. Other mathematical operations such as sum, product, difference and symmetric difference can also be performed on sets.

You can create a new set using curly brackets or the `set()` function. To create an empty set, use `set()` instead of `{}`, because the latter creates an empty dictionary.

Here is a brief demonstration:

```
>>> basket = {'apple', 'orange', 'apple', 'pear', 'orange', 'banana'}
>>> print(basket)            #  duplicates have been removed
{'orange', 'banana', 'pear', 'apple'}
>>> 'orange' in basket       # membership testing True
>>> 'crabgrass' in basket    #Not member False
>>> #  Set operations on two sets
>>> a = set('abracadabraabra')
>>> b = set('alacazamala')
>>> a                                    # print unique letters in a
{'a', 'r', 'b', 'c', 'd'}
>>> a - b                                #print letters in a but not in b
{'r', 'd', 'b'}
>>> a | b                               # print letters in either a or b
{'a', 'c', 'r', 'd', 'b', 'm', 'z', 'l'}
>>> a & b                              # print letters in both a and b
{'a', 'c'}
>>> a ^ b                    # print letters in a or b but not both
{'r', 'd', 'b', 'm', 'z', 'l'}
```

The Python `frozenset()` method creates an immutable set object from an iterable. It is a built-in Python function. As it is a set object, we cannot have duplicate values in the frozen set.

Syntax: `frozenset(iterable_object_name)`

Parameter: `iterable_object_name`

This function accepts an iterable object as input parameter.

Return: Returns an equivalent frozen set object.

The `frozenset()` method can be applied to tuple, list or dictionary. They are mainly used as key in dictionaries or elements of other sets. The example below explains it clearly.

```
# creating a dictionary
Student = {"name": "Ankit", "age": 21, "sex": "Male",
           "college": "MNNIT Allahabad", "address": "Allahabad"}
# making keys of dictionary as frozen set
key = frozenset(Student)
# printing dict keys as frozen set
print('The frozen set is:', key)
```

Output: The frozen set is: frozenset({'address', 'name', 'age', 'sex', 'college'})

2.10 Loops and Conditions

Loops and conditions define control flow and branching using keywords such as `if`, `for` and `while`.

2.10.1 The `if` Statement

In Python, the decision-making statements are used to identify the set of code to be executed according to conditions. The condition will be evaluated and the result can be True or False. Any non-null and non-zero value will be considered as True and any zero or null value will be considered as False.

The three types of decision-making statements are `if`, `if...else` and nested `if`.

The following code accepts a character as input and checks if it is a vowel:

```
a=input("Enter the character:")
if((a=='a') or (a=='e') or (a=='i') or (a=='o') or (a=='u')):
    print("The given character is a vowel")
```

Output:
Enter the character: e
The given character is a vowel

The `if..else` Statement

In a conditional `if` statement, an additional block of code is given as an `else` statement which is performed when the condition is false.

```
if (condition):
    # Executes this block if
    # condition is true
else:
    # Executes this block if
    # condition is false
```

```
# if..else statement example
x = 3
if x == 4:
   print("Yes")
else:
   print("No")
```

Output: No

The Nested `if` Statement

The `if` statement can also be checked inside another `if` statement. This is called a nested `if` statement. It means that the inner `if` condition will be checked only if the outer `if` condition is true and by this, we can check if multiple conditions are satisfied.

```
if (condition1):
   # Executes when condition1 is true
   if (condition2):
      # Executes when condition2 is true
   # if Block is end here
# if Block is end here
```

```
# Nested if statement example
num = 10
 if num > 5:
   print("Bigger than 5")
     if num <= 15:
       print("Between 5 and 15")
```

Output:
Bigger than 5
Between 5 and 15

2.10.2 Loops

Other than decision-making statements, Python programming also supports looping statements. There are two loops in Python: `while` and `for`.

The `while` loop will check for a condition initially and then repeat execution of the block of statements until the evaluated condition becomes false. The syntax for the `while` loop is as follows:

```
while(condition):
   #block of statements
```

Initially, the condition is evaluated. If the condition is true, it will execute the block of statements. After this, the condition is evaluated again and the process is repeated until the condition becomes false.

The code below will accept a number from the keyboard and a `while` loop will be executed for as long as the input number is greater than 0. This code will print numbers from 0 to the input number.

```
a=int(input("Enter the number: "))
i=0
print("Numbers from 0 to ",a)
while(i<a):
  print(i)
  i=i+1
```

Output:
Enter the number: 5
Numbers from 0 to 5
0
1
2
3
4

The `for` loop is used to repeat execution of a block of code a fixed number of times. In Python, the `for` loop will be repeated for all the members of a sequence in order, executing the block each time, whereas in the `while` loop, the condition is evaluated for each iteration. The syntax of the `for` loop is as follows:

```
for variable in range(val1,val2,inr):
#block of statements
```

In the above syntax, `val1` and `val2` represent the minimum and maximum number of the specified range while `inr` specifies the increment value.

The default start value is zero and the `inr` value is one.

```
for i in range(100):
    print(i/25)
```

Output: 0.0 0.04 0.08 0.12 0.16 0.2 0.24 and so on

Nested loops can also be used, but indent must be maintained.

```
for i in range(100):
    for j in range(i):
        print(j);
```

Output: 0 0 1 0 1 and so on

A program to append an incremental value to a list from 0 to 99 using the `for` loop is given below:

```
list1=[]
for i in range(100):
    list1.append(i)
print(list1)
```

Output:
[0, 1, 2, 3, 4, 5, 6, 7, 8, 9, 10, 11, 12, 13, 14, 15, 16, 17, 18, 19, 20, 21, 22, 23, 24, 25, 26, 27, 28, 29, 30, 31, 32, 33, 34, 35, 36, 37, 38, 39, 40, 41, 42, 43, 44, 45, 46, 47, 48, 49, 50, 51, 52, 53, 54, 55, 56, 57, 58, 59, 60, 61, 62, 63, 64, 65, 66, 67, 68, 69, 70, 71, 72, 73, 74, 75, 76, 77, 78, 79, 80, 81, 82, 83, 84, 85, 86, 87, 88, 89, 90, 91, 92, 93, 94, 95, 96, 97, 98, 99]

To print characters in a string:

```
var= "ruchika"
for i in var:
    print(i)
```

Output: r u c h i k a

To append only even numbers to a list, you need to accept a number from the keyboard and append this number if it is even:

```
even=[]
i=int(input("enter the value"))
if i%2==0:
    even.append(i)
print(even)
```

Output: enter the value5 []

To print only the vowels in a string:

```
v="ruchika"
list1=['a','e','i','o','u']
for i in v:
    if i in list1:
        print(i)
```

Output: u i a

2.10.3 The Break Statement

In Python, loops are used to execute blocks of statements repeatedly. The body of the loop will be executed when the condition of the loop evaluates as True. During execution of the loop, if an emergency exit from the loop is required, the 'break' statement is used. It is used to quit the running loop statements. The syntax of the `break` statement is as follows:

```
loop(condition):
    #block of statements
    break
else:
    #block of statements
```

The code below demonstrates the use of the `break` statement. A number is to be input from the keyboard. The `while` loop will execute for as long as the input number is greater than `i`, and the value of `i` will be incremented. If `i=2`, control will come out of the loop.

```
a=int(input("Enter the number: "))
i=0
while(i<a):
  print("Entered into while loop with value of i=",i)
  if(i==2):
    break
  i=i+1
else:
  print("break is not executed")
```

Output:
Enter the number:6

Entered into while loop with value of i= 0 Entered into while loop with value of i= 1 Entered into while loop with value of i= 2

2.10.4 The Continue Statement

The `continue` statement is used to skip the current iteration of the loop. If the condition of the loop evaluates as True, the body of the loop will be executed. During execution, the `continue` statement will stop the current execution of the body and continue to the next iteration. The syntax is as follows:

```
loop(condition):
   #block of statements
   continue
```

2.11 Classes and Functions

In Python, a user can define a function using the 'def' keyword. Such function definition is allowed within a class, module or another user-defined function. The syntax of user-defined functions is as follows:

```
def user_defined_function_name(list_of_arguments):
      body of the user defined function
```

In a Python program, user-defined functions will reduce duplication of data. Whenever execution of the user-defined function is required, the function should be called. The syntax for calling the user-defined function is as follows:

```
user_defined_function_name(list_of_arguments)
```

Data encapsulation is supported with classes. A class consists of both data and functions. The data in the class is called its members and the functions are called methods.

The code below shows how to create a class consisting of two methods: `fun()` and `greeting()`.

```
class classname:
   def fun(self,name):
      self.name=name
   def greeting(self):
      print("Hello %s"%self.name)
```

An object can be created using `classname()`:

```
obj=classname()
```

Functions can be called along with object names:

```
obj.fun("simba")
obj.greeting()
```

Output: Hello simba

2.12 Working with Files

A file contains data stored in memory. All programming languages provide file handling features. Python also supports various file handling operations using streams. A stream represents a continuous flow of data. There are two types of streams: I/O and file.

The I/O stream is used to handle various operations related to input and output devices. The keyword 'input' is used to represent the input stream, while 'print' is used to represent the output stream.

By default, the `input()` command accepts input from the keyboard and prints it.

```
a=input("Enter the input for raw_input: ")
  print("Entered String: ",a)
```

Output:
D:\PythonPrograms>python a1.py
Enter the input for raw_input: 1+2
Entered String: 1+2

Files can be created, deleted and modified using the file stream. To use the file stream, there is no need to import any module. The file object has various attributes, as given below:

- 'closed'represents whether the input file object is closed or not
- 'mode' represents the mode of the file
- 'name' represents the name of the file

2.12.1 Opening, Reading and Writing a File

In Python, the `open()` function is used to open a file. This function takes two arguments. The first argument represents the name of the file and the second argument the mode of the file to be opened. The mode can be read, write or append.

The read mode enables you to perform read operations on the input file. The types of read mode are:

- 'r' is used to open a file for reading only. This is the default mode for opening any file. In this case, the file pointer is placed at the beginning of the file.
- 'r+' is used to open a file for read and write operations. In this case, the file pointer is placed at the beginning of the file.
- 'rb' is used to open a file for reading in binary format. In this case, the file pointer is placed at the beginning of the file.

- 'rb+' is used to open a file for read and write operations in binary format. In this case, the file pointer is placed at the beginning of the file.

To accept input from a file, create the abc.txt file in Notepad. Write the following line and save it. You can open the file in read mode and read it line by line:

Content of "abc.text"

This is the first line in abc.txt.

```
f=open("abc.txt","r")
for line in f:
    print(line)
```

Output:
D:\PythonPrograms>python a1.py
This is the first line in abc.txt

The read operation is performed with the `read()` method. This method should be used with a file stream object.

The `read()` method reads all the contents of the file if no parameter is used:

```
f=open("abc.txt")
s=f.read()
    print(s)
```

Output:
D:\PythonPrograms>python a1.py
This is the second line in abc.txt
This is the third line in abc.txt

The `read()` method reads data from the beginning of a file and returns it as string object. For the `read()` method, we can also specify the size limit of the data to be read.

The `read()` method can take parameters to restrict the number of lines to be read. The file `abc.txt` has two lines and the code below tries to read 6 lines; so this will throw an error:

```
f=open("abc.txt")
s=f.read(6)
    print(s)
```

Output:
D:\PythonPrograms>python a1.py
Output: File exception:: Trying to access contents beyond…….

The write mode of the `open()` function is used to perform write operations on a file. The types of write mode are:

- 'w' is used to create a new file to perform only writing. If the file already exists, it is overwritten. In this case, the file pointer is placed at the beginning of the file.
- 'w+' is used to create a new file to perform reading and writing operations. If the file already exists, it is overwritten. In this case, the file pointer is placed at the beginning of the file.
- 'wb' is used create a new file to perform writing operations in binary format. If the file already exists, it is overwritten. In this case, the file pointer is placed at the beginning of the file.
- 'wb+' is used to create a new file to perform reading and writing operations in binary format. If the file already exists, it is overwritten. In this case, the file pointer is placed at the beginning of the file.

Now if a new line is to be written, open the file in `w+` mode, create a file abc.txt, add a line to it and save it.

The `write()` method can be used to write in a line a file but the old contents will be replaced.

This is the first line in abc.txt.

```
f=open("abc.txt","w+")
   f.write("This is the second line in abc.txt")
```

Output:
This is the second line in abc.txt

In this example, the file abc.txt is already available. So, the `w+` mode overwrites the existing file with the given content. If the file is not available, it creates a new file.

The append mode is used to append data at the end of a file. If the file is already available, the data is appended at the end of the file; otherwise a new file is created and the content is appended to the new file. The types of append mode are:

- 'a' is used to open a file for appending only. In this case, the file pointer is placed at the end of the file.
- 'a+' is used to open a file for read and append operations. In this case, the file pointer is placed at the end of the file.
- 'ab' is used to open a file for appending in binary format. In this case, the file pointer is placed at the end of the file.
- 'ab+' is used to open a file for read and append operations in binary format. In this case, the file pointer is placed at the end of the file.

To append a line, open the file in the 'a' mode; this will ensure that the old contents remain the same and a new line is appended.

This is the second line in abc.txt

```
f=open("abc.txt","a")
   f.write("\nThis is the third line in abc.txt")
```

Output:
This is the second line in abc.txt
This is the third line in abc.txt

2.12.2 Closing a File

Other than read and write, the `close()` method is used to close the file object that is already created.

The code below shows how to read all the contents of a file and print it. At the end, the file is closed using the `close()` function:

```
f1=open("abc.txt")
s2=f1.read()
print("The data from file:")
print(s2)
    f1.close()
```

EXERCISES

Multiple Choice Questions

1. What will be the output of the following code snippet?
```
print(type(5 / 2))
print(type(5 // 2))
```
(a) float and int
(b) int and float
(c) float and float
(d) int and int

2. What will be the output of the following code snippet?
```
def solve(a):
    a = [1, 3, 5]
a = [2, 4, 6]
print(a)
solve(a)
print(a)
```
(a) [2, 4, 6]. [2, 4, 6]
(b) [2, 4, 6], [1, 3, 5]
(c) [1. 3. 5], [1, 3, 5]
(d) None of these

3. What will be the output of the following code snippet?
```
s1 = {1, 2, 3, 4, 5}
s2 = {2, 4, 6}
print(s1 ^ s2)
```
(a) {1, 2, 3, 4, 5}
(b) {1, 3, 5, 6}
(c) {2, 4}
(d) None of the above

4. What will be the output of the following code snippet?
```
square = lambda x: x ** 2
a = []
for i in range(5):
    a.append(square(i))
print(a)
```
(a) [0, 1, 4, 9, 16]
(b) [1, 4, 9, 16, 25]
(c) [0, 1, 2, 3, 4]
(d) [1, 2, 3, 4, 5]

5. What will be the output of the following Python expression if x = 56.236?
```
print("%.2f"%x)
```
(a) 56.236
(b) 56.23
(c) 56.0000
(d) 56.24

6. Which one of the following is the correct way to call a function?
(a) `call function_name()`
(b) `function function_name()`

(c) `function_name()`
(d) None of these

7. Suppose a user wants to print the second value of an array, which has 5 elements. What will be the syntax of the second value of the array?
(a) `array[2]`
(b) `array[1]`
(c) `array[-1]`
(d) `array[-2]`

8. To add a new element to a list, we use which Python command?
(a) `list1.addEnd(5)`
(b) `list1.addLast(5)`
(c) `list1.append(5)`
(d) `list1.add(5)`

9. What will be the output of the following Python code?

```
x = 'abcd'
for i in x:
    print(i.upper())
```

(a) a B C D
(b) a b c d
(c) error
(d) A B C D

10. What will be the output of the following Python code?

```
>>>list1 = [1, 3]
>>>list2 = list1
>>>list1[0] = 4
>>>print(list2)
```

(a) [1, 4]
(b) [1, 3, 4]
(c) [4, 3]
(d) [1, 3]

11. How many types of streams are available in Python?
(a) 1
(b) 2
(c) 3
(d) 4

12. Which of the following streams is used for input devices?
(a) input
(b) read
(c) print
(d) output

13. Which of the following is used for output devices?
(a) input
(b) read
(c) print
(d) output

14. How many types of modes are available for `open()`?
(a) 1
(b) 2
(c) 3
(d) 4

15. What are various modes of `open()`?
(a) read
(b) write
(c) append
(d) all of the above

Answers

1. (a)	2. (a)	3. (b)	4. (c)	5. (d)	6. (c)	7. (b)	8. (c)
9. (d)	10. (c)	11. (b)	12. (a)	13. (c)	14. (c)	15. (c)	

Programming/Concept-based Questions

1. Write a Python program to find the factors of a number.

   Answer:

```
# Python program to find the factors of a number
# This function computes the factor of the argument passed
def print_factors(x):
    print("The factors of",x,"are:")
    for i in range(1, x + 1):
        if x % i == 0:
            print(i)
num = 320
print_factors(num)
```

2. Write a program in Python which counts the frequency of words in a given sentence.

   Answer:

```
#String as input to program
wordstring = 'it was the best of times it was the worst of times '
wordstring += 'it was the age of wisdom it was the age of foolishness'
#Extract words from string
wordlist = wordstring.split()
wordfreq = []
# Calculate word frequencies
for w in wordlist:
    wordfreq.append(wordlist.count(w))
print("String\n" + wordstring +"\n")
print("List\n" + str(wordlist) + "\n")
print("Frequencies\n" + str(wordfreq) + "\n")
print("Pairs\n" + str(zip(wordlist, wordfreq)))
```

   Output:

   String

   it was the best of times it was the worst of times it was the age of wisdom it was the age of foolishness

   List

   ['it', 'was', 'the', 'best', 'of', 'times', 'it', 'was', 'the', 'worst', 'of', 'times', 'it', 'was', 'the', 'age', 'of', 'wisdom', 'it', 'was', 'the', 'age', 'of', 'foolishness']

   Frequencies

   [4, 4, 4, 1, 4, 2, 4, 4, 4, 1, 4, 2, 4, 4, 4, 2, 4, 1, 4, 4, 4, 2, 4, 1]

   Pairs

   <zip object at 0x034AA0A8>

3. Write a program to perform operations on sets.

   Answer:

```
# Program to perform different set operations like in mathematics
# define three sets
```

```
E = {0, 2, 4, 6, 8};
N = {1, 2, 3, 4, 5};
# set union
print("Union of E and N is",E | N)
# set intersection
print("Intersection of E and N is",E & N)
# set difference
print("Difference of E and N is",E - N)
# set symmetric difference
print("Symmetric difference of E and N is",E ^ N)
```

4. Write a program to concatenate two lists.

Answer:

```
list_1 = [1, 'a']
list_2 = [3, 4, 5]
list_joined = list_1 + list_2
print(list_joined)
```

5. What is PYTHONPATH?

Answer: It is an environment variable used when a module is imported. Whenever a module is imported, PYTHONPATH is also looked up to check for the presence of the imported modules in various directories. The interpreter uses it to determine which module to load.

6. What is `__init__`?

Answer: `__init__` is a method or constructor in Python. This method is automatically called to allocate memory when a new object/instance of a class is created. All classes have the `__init__` method.

7. What does `[::-1}` do?

Answer: `[::-1]` is used to reverse the order of an array or a sequence.

For example:

1
2
3

```
import array as arr
My_Array=arr.array('i',[1,2,3,4,5])
My_Array[::-1]
```

Output: array('i', [5, 4, 3, 2, 1])

8. What is the difference between a list and a tuple? When should you use each?

Answer: A list is a mutable data structure while a tuple is an immutable one. A mutable object in Python has the ability to change its values.

Lists are dynamic: you can add items to them or override and remove existing ones. Tuples are fixed-size: they do not have an append or an extend method. You cannot remove items from them.

Both tuples and lists support indexing and allow use of the IN operator to check for existing elements.

BIBLIOGRAPHY

1. "Python Getting Started". W3Schools. https://www.w3schools.com/python/python_getstarted.asp
2. "Python for Beginners". https://www.python.org/about/gettingstarted/
3. "Python Tutorials". Tutorials Point. https://www.tutorialspoint.com/python/index.htm

CHAPTER 3

NumPy and pandas

Learning Objectives

At the end of this chapter, you will be able to:

- Use NumPy to perform scientific computations
- Use NumPy to perform linear algebra, random numbers and Fourier transforms
- Handle multi-dimensional data
- Integrate a variety of data
- Perform statistical operations such as finding minimum, percentile, standard deviation, maximum and variance using the elements in an array
- Use the pandas package for data manipulation and analysis
- Carry out data analysis and manipulation of table data in a DataFrame
- Import data from various file formats
- Perform data manipulation operations, including merging, reshaping, selection, data cleaning and data wrangling

3.0 Arrays

Python does not have built-in support for the array data structure but instead it has the list data structure, which is more generalized and can be used as a multi-dimensional array.

A list is an ordered collection of items of different types. Lists are more flexible than arrays but are difficult to handle when working with regular structures. An array is an ordered collection of items of a single type and works well with a regular structure. A list is a dynamic mutable type and this means you can add and delete elements from the list at any time, in contrast to arrays which are static.

To define a list, you need to write comma-separated items enclosed in square brackets:

```
myItems=[1,2,3,4,5,6]
```

To pick an element from a list, the slicing notation is used. For example, in a list index starting from 0, index 3 would be the fourth element in the list.

```
print myItems[3]
```

Output: 4

Similarly, to change the fourth element, a value can be assigned directly.

```
myItems[3]=100
```

The slicing notation extracts a sublist from the start location to the end location specified in the index, as given below:

```
myItems[2:5]
```

Output: [3,4,5]

Elements will be extracted from `myItems[2]` to `myItems[4]`; the final element specified which is [5] is not included in the slice. Either the start or the end index can be left out; depending on whichever index is left out, the start or end index will change.

For example, `myItem[4:]` refers to the elements from index 4 to the end of the list, `myItem[:4]` returns the elements from the beginning up to `myItem[4]` while `myItem[:]` returns the entire list.

List slicing can be modified by assignment. For example:

```
myItem[0:2]=[1,2]
```

This line of code has the same effect as the following:

```
myItem[0]=1
myItem[1]=2
```

To assign it to a slice, the list does not need to be the same size as the slice; it simply replaces it even if it is of a different size.

To carry out list operations, the list must be scanned:

```
m=0
for ele in myItem:
 if m<ele:
  m=ele
#This uses the for..in construct to scan through each item in the list.
```

Alternatively, the list can be scanned through indexing.

```
Item=0
for i in range(len(myItem)):
 if Item<myItem[i]:
     Item=myItem[i]
```

Range is used to generate the sequence 0, 1, ... end index and all the items in the list are sequentially scanned. For example, if you want to return the index position of the maximum element in the list, you can use:

```
m=0
mi=0
for i in range(len(myItem)):
 if m<myItem[i]:
  m=myItem[i]
  mi=i
```

Or you could use a non-indexed loop and the `index()` method:

```
m=0
for e in myItem:
 if m<e:
  m=e
mi=myItem.index(m)
print mi
```

3.1 NumPy

NumPy is a numerical computation engine used to perform scientific computations. It is the fundamental package for scientific computing. It is an N-dimensional array object containing tools capable of integrating with C/C++/Fortran. It can be used to perform linear algebra, random numbers and Fourier transforms.

NumPy is an efficient multi-dimensional container of generic data. In big data, NumPy allows for seamless and speedy integration with a variety of data. It consists of a table of elements, usually numbers. NumPy dimensions are called axes. The rank of NumPy is the number of axes.

3.1.1 Applications of NumPy

- **Alternative to lists and arrays**: NumPy arrays are similar to Python lists. However, unlike Python lists, NumPy arrays are homogeneous sets of elements. This enables uniformity of mathematical operations, which is not possible with heterogeneous elements. Another advantage of using NumPy arrays is that many functions can be applied to these arrays. These functions do not work when applied to Python lists because of their heterogeneous nature.
- **Minimal memory**: NumPy arrays are objects. Python continually deletes and creates these objects as needed. So it allocates less memory compared to Python lists. NumPy has features to help avoid wasting memory in data buffers. It consists of functions such as copying, viewing and indexing that help save a lot of disk space. Indexing helps return a view of the original array that implements data reuse. It also specifies the data type of the elements, which leads to code optimization.
- **Multi-dimensional arrays**: You can create multi-dimensional arrays with NumPy. These arrays have multiple rows and columns. Multi-dimensional arrays enable creation of matrices. Using matrices also makes code memory efficient.

- **Mathematical operations:** NumPy includes easy-to-use functions for mathematical computations on array data sets, such as linear algebra, bitwise operations, Fourier transforms, arithmetic operations, string operations, etc.

3.1.2 Installing NumPy

The standard Python package manager is called pip. This is used to install additional packages that are not a part of standard Python.

In Windows, you need to navigate to the command prompt and change the current directory to the one where Python is. Then type the following:

```
C:/program files/python35/scripts/pip> pip install numpy
```

To check that NumPy is installed properly, in Python script, check as follows:

```
File  Edit  Shell  Debug  Options  Window  Help
Python 3.6.0 (v3.6.0:41df79263a11, Dec 23 2016, 07:18:10) [MSC v.1900 32 bit (Intel)]
Type "copyright", "credits" or "license()" for more information.
>>> import numpy
>>>
>>> |
```

Type `import  numpy` and press *Enter*. If Python returns with another prompt, everything is working correctly.

In Linux, type the following:

```
sudo pip install numpy
sudo apt-get install libatlas-base-dev gfortran
sudo pip install scipy
sudo pip install matplotlib
```

3.1.3 Two-dimensional NumPy Arrays

A one-dimensional array [1, 2, 2] has one axis and one rank. The axis has a length of 3. Axis represents the dimension and length of axis represents the number of columns.

The array given below has two axes. The first axis has length 2 (two rows) and the second axis has length 3 (three columns)

[[1., 0., 1.],
[0., 2., 2.]]

The Python standard library supports arrays that handle only one-dimensional arrays with less functionality. `Ndarray` is a class of NumPy. Its attributes are given below:

`ndim`	Dimension of the array
`shape`	Size of an array (n, m)
`size`	Total number of elements n*m
`dtype`	Type of elements in the array
`itemsize`	Memory space used by each element

Here is a sample code that creates a NumPy array and performs various operations on it:

```
import numpy as np
x = np.arrange(10).reshape(2, 5)
x
```

Output:
array([[0, 1, 2, 3, 4],
[5, 6, 7, 8, 9]])

```
x.shape
```

Output: (2, 5)

```
x.ndim
```

Output: 2

```
x.dtype.name
```

Output: 'int64'

```
x.itemsize
```

Output: 8

```
x.size
```

Output: 10

3.1.4 Array Creation

An array can be created by using the `array()` function. The data type of an array is deduced from the type of the elements.

```
x = np.array([10,20,30,40])
x
```

Output: array([10,20, 30, 40])

```
x.dtype
```

Output: dtype('int64')

```
y = np.array([0.5,10.2, 30.5, 50.1])
y.dtype
```

Output: dtype('float64')

Two-dimensional arrays can be defined as an array list enclosed in square brackets:

```
x = np.array([(10,20,30), (40,50,60)])
x
```

Output:
array([[10, 20, 30],
[40, 50, 60]])

To create an array of complex numbers:

```
x = np.array( [ [60,70], [80,90] ], dtype=complex)
x
```

Output:
array([[60.+0.j, 70.+0.j],
[80.+0.j, 90.+0.j]])

To create an array filled with zeros:

```
np.zeros(n,m) where n: number of rows, m: number of columns
```

To create an array filled with ones:

```
np.ones()
```

To generate array values from beginning to end increased by a given interval:

```
np.arrange(start value,end value, interval)
x=np.arrange( 1, 10, 2 )
x
```

Output: array([1, 3, 5, 7, 9])

When `arrange()` is used with floating point arguments, the number of elements cannot be predicted due to finite floating point precision. To overcome this problem, the function `linspace()` can be used. It receives as an argument the number of elements that need to be generated.

To generate 9 values from 0 to 9:

```
np.linspace( 0, 3, 9)
```

Output: array([0. , 0.375, 0.75, 1.125, 1.5 , 1.875, 2.25, 2.625, 3.])

3.1.5 Printing Arrays

Arrays can be printed by passing the name of the array to the `print()` function. Before printing, arrays can be rearranged using the `reshape()` function; else it will be displayed in the default layout.

To display a one-dimensional array:

```
x = np.arrange(10)
 print(x)
```

Output: [0 1 2 3 4 5 6 7 8 9]

To reshape the array in 2 rows and 5 columns:

```
x = np.arrange(10).reshape(2,5)
 print(x)
```

Output:
[[0 1 2 3 4]
[5 6 7 8 9]]

If an array is too large, NumPy prints only the corners and skips the other parts:

```
>>> print(np.arrange(1000))
```

Output:[0 1 2..., 999]

3.1.6 NumPy Basic Array Operations

Arithmetic operators are applied element-wise and they result in a new array.

```
x= np.array( [22,33,44,55])
 y = np.array([2,2,2,2])
 z = x+y
z
```

Output: array([24, 35, 46, 57])

The multiply operator (*) in NumPy also operates element-wise, unlike in other languages. It can be performed using the dot function or method:

```
x= np.array( [[1,1],[1,1]])
y= np.array( [[2,2], [2,2]])
z=x*y
x
```

Output:
array([[2, 2],
[2, 2]])

```
z=x.dot(y)
z
```

Output:
array([[4, 4],
[4, 4]])

Aggregate functions can be used on arrays:

```
x=np.array([1,2,3,4,5,6,7,8,9])
x.sum()
```

Output: array([1, 2, 3, 4, 5, 6, 7, 8, 9])

```
x.min()
```

Output: 1

```
x.max()
```

Output: 9

You can perform aggregate functions in multi-dimensional arrays by passing the axis of aggregation.

If you have a two-dimensional array and wish to find the sum of the columns, `axis=0` must be passed in the `sum()` function.

```
b = np.arrange(10).reshape(2,5)
 b
```

Output: array([[0, 1, 2, 3, 4],
[5, 6, 7, 8, 9]])

```
b.sum(axis=0)
```

Output: array([5, 7, 9, 11, 13])

To find the cumulative sum along each row:

```
b.cumsum(axis=1)
```

Output:
array([[0, 1, 3, 6, 10],
[5, 11, 18, 26, 35]])

3.1.7 Universal Functions

NumPy provides familiar mathematical functions such as sin, cos, sqrt and exp. Within NumPy, these functions operate element-wise on an array, producing an array as output.

```
>>> B = np.arrange(4)
>>> B
```

Output: array([0, 1, 2, 3])

```
>>> np.exp(B)
```

Output: array([1. , 2.71828183, 7.3890561, 20.08553692])

```
>>> np.sqrt(B)
```

Output: array([0. , 1. , 1.41421356, 1.73205081])

```
>>> C = np.array([2., -1., 4.])
```

Output: array([2., -1., 4.])

3.1.8 Indexing, Slicing and Iterating

One-dimensional arrays can be indexed, sliced and iterated to read, access and retrieve elements or a subset.

To generate an array of squares:

```
a = np.arrange(5)**2
 a
```

Output: array([0, 1, 4, 9, 16])

To display a particular element from an array, say `a[2]`:

```
a[2]
```

Output: 4

To display the range of elements from index 2 to 4:

```
a[2:4]
```

Output: array([4, 9])

You can iterate in an array. To set every alternate element as 999:

```
a[:4:2]=999
a
```

Output: array([999, 1, 999, 9, 16])

To reverse an array:

```
a[::-1]
a
```

Output: array([16, 9, 999, 1, 999])

Multi-dimensional arrays can have one index per axis. These indices are given in a tuple separated by commas:

```
b = np.arrange(10).reshape(2,5)
b
```

Output:
array([[0, 1, 2, 3, 4],
[5, 6, 7, 8, 9]])

To display an element from two-dimensional array row=1 col=3:

```
b[0,2]
```

Output: 2

To display row 1:

```
b[:1]
b
```

Output: array([[0, 1, 2, 3, 4]])

To display index 2 to 4 from all rows, start from row 0 column 2 and continue up to row 1 column 4:

```
b[0:2,1:4]
```

Output:
array([[1, 2, 3],
[6, 7, 8]])

3.1.9 Splitting an Array

You can split an array horizontally or vertically. The `hsplit()` function will split the array on its horizontal axis. Let us suppose that you want to extract elements from columns 0 to 3. A vertical split will extract data row-wise.

The code given below will generate an array of 2 rows and 9 columns using a random number generator ranging from 1 to 20:

```
a=np.floor(20*np.random.random((2,9)))
a
```

Output:
array([[4., 4., 0., 10.; 7., 0., 14., 3., 10.],
[16., 7., 9., 11., 5., 17., 15., 9., 17.]])

To split an array in three parts:

```
np.hsplit(a,3)
```

Output:
[array([[4., 4., 0.],
[16., 7., 9.]]), array([[10., 7., 0.],
[11., 5., 17.]]), array([[14., 3., 10.],
[15., 9., 17.]])]

To split an array after column 2 and column 5:

```
np.hsplit(a,(2,5))
```

Output:
[array([[4., 4.],
[16., 7.]]), array([[0., 10., 7.],
[9., 11., 5.]]), array([[0., 14., 3., 10.],
[17., 15., 9., 17.]])]

3.1.10 Statistical Functions

NumPy has useful functions to perform statistical operations such as to find the minimum, maximum, standard deviation and variance from the given elements in an array. These functions return the value after applying the said function for a set of values.

```
import numpy as np
a = np.array([[10,20,30],[40,50,60],[70,80,90]])
print (a)
```

Output:
[[10 20 30]
 [40 50 60]
 [70 80 90]]

To print minimum on axis 1:

```
A= np.amin(a,1)
print(A)
```

Output: array([10, 40, 70])

To print minimum on axis 0:

```
A= np.amin(a,0)
print(A)
```

Output: array([10, 20, 30])

To find the maximum of all values:

```
A=np.amax(a)
print(A)
```

Output: 90

To find the maximum on axis 0:

```
A=np.amax(a,0)
print(A)
```

Output: array([70, 80, 90])

Median is the value separating the lower half and upper half of a set of data. Values are sorted and we can obtain the middle value from the sequence.

To calculate median on all values:

```
import numpy as np
a = np.array([[3,4,5],[6,7,8],[9,10,11]])
C= np.median(a)
print(C)
```

Output: 7.0

To calculate median on axis 0:

```
C= np.median(a,0)
  print(C)
```

Output: [6. 7. 8.]

To calculate median on axis 1:

```
C= np.median(a,1)
  print(C)
```

Output: [4. 7. 10.]

Arithmetic mean is calculated by summing the elements along an axis divided by the number of elements. The `numpy.mean()` function calculates the average over an axis and returns a single mean value. It works in a similar way to other statistical functions, if axis is given as the parameter in the function.

Weighted average is the average of values along the specified axis. The `numpy.average()` function works in the same way as `mean()`, but it calculates the weighted average of elements over an axis. A weight matrix should be given along with the array.

Standard deviation is the square root of the average of squared deviations from the mean. The formula for standard deviation is as follows:

```
std = sqrt (mean(abs(x - x.mean())**2))
```

```
import numpy as np
>>> print (np.std([2,2,4,3]))
```

Output: 0.82915619758885

Variance is the average of squared deviations, that is, `mean(abs(y - y.mean())**2)`. The standard deviation is the square root of variance. Variance depicts the variability in values.

```
import numpy as np
>>> print (np.var([2,2,4,3]))
```

Output: 0.6875

3.2 The Pandas Package

In Python, pandas is a package that provides data structures which work with relational or labelled data in a fast, flexible and expressive way. It provides fundamental high-level, building-block, real-world data analysis. Additionally, it has powerful and flexible open source data analysis/manipulation tools. The pandas package is well suited for tabular data with heterogeneously typed columns, ordered and unordered (not necessarily fixed-frequency) time series data and observational/statistical data sets.

Windows: The pandas package can be installed using pip from PyPI. It is executed at the command prompt:

```
pip install pandas
```

Linux: To install pandas for Python 3, you may need to use the package python-pandas:

```
sudo apt-get install python-pandas
```

3.2.1 Object Creation, Selection and Indexing

There are two primary data structures in pandas: Series (one-dimensional) and DataFrame (two-dimensional)

For example, let us create a Series by passing a list of values and allow pandas to create a default integer index:

```
import pandas as pd
import numpy as np
import matplotlib.pyplot as plt
s = pd.Series([1,np.nan,5,np.nan,6,8])
 s
```

Output:
0 1.0
1 NaN
2 5.0
3 NaN
4 6.0
5 8.0
dtype: float64

To create a DataFrame with a start date and periods:

```
>>> dates = pd.date_range('20170101', periods=4)
>>> dates
DatetimeIndex(['2017-01-01', '2017-01-02', '2017-01-03', '2017-01-04'],
dtype='datetime64[ns]', freq='D')
```

To create a DataFrame by passing a NumPy array, index and column label:

```
>>> df = pd.DataFrame(np.random.randn(4,4), index=dates,
columns=list('XYZW'))
>>> df
```

Output:

	X	Y	Z	W
2017-01-01	-1.587228	-0.385051	-0.264195	2.376143
2017-01-02	0.769625	-1.937781	-1.524778	0.936422
2017-01-03	0.550432	0.191810	0.569834	-1.618321
2017-01-04	1.142272	-1.207664	-1.486163	-0.417135

To create a DataFrame that is collection of Series by generating column-wise values:

```
df2 = pd.DataFrame({ 'A': 10.,
  ....:                     'B': pd.Timestamp('20170101'),
  ....:                     'C':
pd.Series(1,index=list(range(4)),dtype='float32'),
  ....:                     'D': np.array([4] * 4,dtype='int32'),
  ....:                     'E': pd.Categorical(["A1","B1","A1","B1"]),
  ....:                     'F': 'test' })
df2
```

Output:

	A	B	C	D	E	F
0	10.0	2017-01-01	1.0	4	A1	test
1	10.0	2017-01-01	1.0	4	B1	test
2	10.0	2017-01-01	1.0	4	A1	test
3	10.0	2017-01-01	1.0	4	B1	test

The Series object has a method `cov()` to compute the covariance between Series (excluding NA/null values):

```
In [5]: s1 = pd.Series(np.random.randn(1000))
In [6]: s2 = pd.Series(np.random.randn(1000))
In [7]: s1.cov(s2)
Out[7]: 0.000680108817431108 71
```

Analogously, DataFrame has a method `cov()` to compute pairwise covariances among the Series in a DataFrame, also excluding NA/null values.

To view data/lookups in DataFrames:

```
df.head()
```

Output:

	X	Y	Z	W
2017-01-01	-1.587228	-0.385051	-0.264195	2.376143
2017-01-02	0.769625	-1.937781	-1.524778	0.936422
2017-01-03	0.550432	0.191810	0.569834	-1.618321
2017-01-04	1.142272	-1.207664	-1.486163	-0.417135

```
df.tail(2)    #display  last two rows
```

Output:

	X	Y	Z	W
2017-01-03	0.550432	0.191810	0.569834	-1.618321
2017-01-04	1.142272	-1.207664	-1.486163	-0.417135

To sort by an axis:

```
>>> df.sort_index(axis=0)
```

Output:

	X	Y	Z	W
2017-01-01	-1.587228	-0.385051	-0.264195	2.376143
2017-01-02	0.769625	-1.937781	-1.524778	0.936422
2017-01-03	0.550432	0.191810	0.569834	-1.618321
2017-01-04	1.142272	-1.207664	-1.486163	-0.417135

```
>>> df.sort_index(axis=1)
```

Output:

	W	X	Y	Z
2017-01-01	2.376143	-1.587228	-0.385051	-0.264195
2017-01-02	0.936422	0.769625	-1.937781	-1.524778
2017-01-03	-1.618321	0.550432	0.191810	0.569834
2017-01-04	-0.417135	1.142272	-1.207664	-1.486163

To select by label:

```
>>> df.loc[dates[0]]
```

Output:

X -1.587228
Y -0.385051
Z -0.264195
W 2.376143
Name: 2017-01-01 00:00:00, dtype: float64

To select a multi-axis by label:

```
>>> df.loc[:,['X','Z']]
```

Output:

	X	Z
2017-01-01	-1.587228	-0.264195
2017-01-02	0.769625	-1.524778
2017-01-03	0.550432	0.569834
2017-01-04	1.142272	-1.486163

To show label slicing, both endpoints are included:

```
>>> df.loc['20170102':'20170104',['X','Z']]
```

Output:

	X	Z
2017-01-02	0.769625	-1.524778
2017-01-03	0.550432	0.569834
2017-01-04	1.142272	-1.486163

For reduction in the dimensions of the returned object:

```
>>> df.loc['20170102',['X','Z']]
```

Output:
X 0.769625
Z -1.524778
Name: 2017-01-02 00:00:00, dtype: float64

To obtain a scalar value and to display the 0th row X value:

```
>>> df.loc[dates[0],'X']
```

Output:
-1.5872280521014948

To select by position:

```
>>> df.iloc[3]
```

Output:
X 1.142272
Y -1.207664
Z -1.486163
W -0.417135
Name: 2017-01-04 00:00:00, dtype: float64

For slicing rows explicitly and to display the 1st to 4th row and all columns:

```
>>> df.iloc[1:4,:]
```

Output:

	X	Y	Z	W
2017-01-02	0.769625	-1.937781	-1.524778	0.936422
2017-01-03	0.550432	0.191810	0.569834	-1.618321
2017-01-04	1.142272	-1.207664	-1.486163	-0.417135

For slicing columns explicitly:

```
>>> df.iloc[:,1:2]
```

Output:	Y
2017-01-01	-0.385051
2017-01-02	-1.937781
2017-01-03	0.191810
2017-01-04	-1.207664

To obtain a particular [row,col] value:

```
>>> df.iloc[1,1]
```

Output: -1.9377809698716892

3.2.2 Handling NaN Values

NaN values are missing or null values. Many values in data sets are missing, either because they exist but are not collected or because they never existed. 'Missing' means null or 'data is not present'. For example, in a data stream, data is continuously generated and stored but due to some fault in the system for a duration, a null value will be stored.

In pandas, missing data can be introduced into a data set by re-indexing. For example:

```
>>> df=pd.DataFrame(np.random.randn(3, 3), index=['a', 'c',
'e'],columns=['one', 'two', 'three'])
   >>> df
```

Output:

	one	two	three
a	0.017773	2.439185	1.742292
c	-0.241506	-0.337997	-0.085486
e	0.243921	-1.319479	0.412318

```
>>> df2 = df.reindex(['a', 'b', 'c', 'd', 'e'])
>>> df2
```

Output:

	one	two	three
a	0.017773	2.439185	1.742292
b	NaN NaN	NaN	
c	-0.241506	-0.337997	-0.085486
d	NaN NaN	NaN	
e	0.243921	-1.319479	0.412318

To detect missing values across different data types, pandas provides the `isnull()` and `notnull()` functions, which are applicable on Series and DataFrame objects:

```
>>> df2['one']
```

Output:
a 0.017773
b NaN
c -0.241506
d NaN
e 0.243921
Name: one, dtype: float64

```
>>> pd.isnull(df2['one'])
```

Output:
a False

b True
c False
d True
e False
Name: one, dtype: bool

```
>>> df2['one'].notnull()
```

Output:
a True
b False
c True
d False
e True
Name: one, dtype: bool

```
>>> df2.isnull()
```

Output:

	one	two	three
a	False	False	False
b	True	True	True
c	False	False	False
d	True	True	True
e	False	False	False

3.2.3 Mapping

The `map()` function maps the values of a Series from a source, which can be a dictionary, Series or function, and returns the Series with the same index as the source.

```
y=Series.map(arg, na_action=None)[source]
arg: function, dictionary, or Series
na_action: {None, 'ignore'}
```

For example, to use `map()` to input a Series to output:

```
>>> s = pd.Series([1,2,3], index=['one', 'two', 'three'])
>>> s
```

Output:
one 1
two 2
three 3
dtype: int64

```
>>> t = pd.Series(['map1', 'map2', 'map3'], index=[1,2,3])
>>> t
```

Output:
1 map1
2 map2
3 map3
dtype: object

```
>>> s.map(t)
```

Output:
one map1
two map2
three map3
dtype: object

The `na_action` parameter is used to control when NaN values occur. 'None' will do nothing and 'ignore' will stop the display of the argument value.

```
>>> s = pd.Series([1, 2, 3, np.nan])
>>> t1 = s.map('this is a test string {}'.format, na_action=None)
```

Output:
0 this is a test string 1.0
1 this is a test string 2.0
2 this is a test string 3.0
3 this is a test string nan
dtype: object

```
>>> t2 = s.map('this is a string {}'.format, na_action='ignore')
```

Output:
0 this is a test string 1.0
1 this is a test string 2.0
2 this is a test string 3.0
3 NaN
dtype: object

3.2.4 Reading Files

Create a file in Python in a directory, say C:\Users\HP\Desktop\python\

test.txt

I am a test file.
How long will you take to read me.

First enter and execute the following line of code at the command prompt:
`Import os`

To read a file from a specific location, set the path and read the file:

```
>>> path = os.path.expanduser('~/Desktop/python/test.txt')
>>> path
'C:\\Users\\HP/Desktop/python/test.txt'
f = open(path, "r") #opens file with name of "test.txt"
```

The 'r' mode tells Python that we want to read. The `file.read(n)` method reads `n` number of characters from the file; if `n` is blank, it reads the entire file. The `file.readline(n)` method reads a line from the text file till EOL.

```
>>> print(f.read(1))
```

Output: I

```
>>>print(f.read())
```

Output: am a test file.
How long will you take to read me.

First, we open the file using `f.open()`. Then `read(1)` will read one character from the file. Python prints out "I". Next, `read()` does not provide any arguments. However, it does not include the "I" that we just read because reading is a sequential process. The next `read()` will start from the current pointer.

```
f = open(path,"r") #opens file with name of "test.txt"
print(f.readline())
print(f.readline())
```

Output:
I am a test file.
How long will you take to read me.

The `readline()` method is used twice, so we know that we will get the first two lines.

```
f = open(path,"r") #opens file with name of "test.txt"
myLine = []
for line in f:
    myLine.append(line)
print(myLine)
```

Output: ['I am a test file.\n', '\n', 'How long will you take to read me.\n']

We open the file as usual, and we create a list. Then, we break the file into lines in the `for` loop using the `IN` keyword. As we loop through each line of the file, we use `myLine.append(line)` to add each line to our `myLine` list.

The `print()` function breaks each line of the file into a string, which we can manipulate. At the end, you should close the file using `f.close()`.

3.2.5 Plots

Python can draw plots using the Matplotlib library. Data can be generated using the Series function of pandas.

```
import pandas as pd
import numpy as np
import matplotlib.pyplot as plt
import matplotlib
matplotlib.style.use('ggplot')
t = pd.Series(np.random.randn(100), index=pd.date_range('1/1/2017',
periods=100))    #generated data on 15 May 2017.
t = t.cumsum()
t.plot()
plt.show()
```

Output:

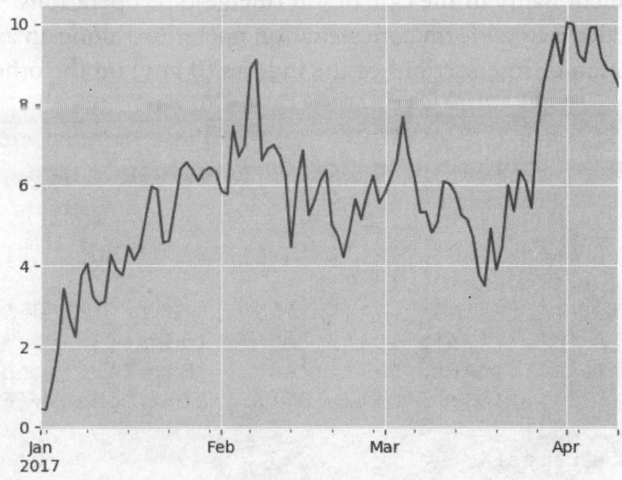

In DataFrame, to plot all the columns with labels:

```
import pandas as pd
import numpy as np
import matplotlib.pyplot as plt
import matplotlib
matplotlib.style.use('ggplot')
t = pd.Series(np.random.randn(100), index=pd.date_range('1/1/2017',
periods=100))
d = pd.DataFrame(np.random.randn(100, 4), index=t.index,
columns=list('XYZW'))
d = d.cumsum()
plt.figure(); d.plot(); plt.show()
```

Output:

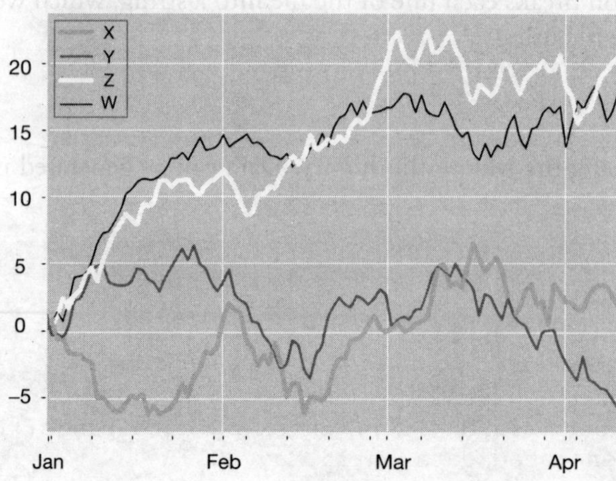

3.2.6 Joins

The pandas package can combine Series, DataFrame and Panel objects with various kinds of set logic and relational algebra functionality in the case of join/merge-type operations.

The `concat()` function can perform concatenation operations along an axis while also performing optional set logic (union or intersection) of the indexes (if any) on the other axes.

```
import pandas as pd
import numpy as np
import matplotlib.pyplot as plt
import matplotlib
df1 = pd.DataFrame({'A': ['A0', 'A1', 'A2'],'B': ['B0', 'B1', 'B2'], 'C':
['C0', 'C1', 'C2'] }, index=[0, 1, 2])
 df2 = pd.DataFrame({'A': ['A3', 'A4', 'A5'], 'B': ['B3', 'B4', 'B5'],'C':
['C3', 'C4', 'C5'], 'D': ['D3', 'D4', 'D5']},index=[3, 4, 5])
df3 = pd.DataFrame({'A': ['A6', 'A7', 'A8'], 'B': ['B6', 'B7', 'B8'],
'C': ['C6', 'C7', 'C8'], 'D': ['D6', 'D7', 'D8']}, index=[6, 7, 8])
frames = [df1, df2, df3]
result = pd.concat(frames)
print(result)
```

Output:

	A	B	C	D
0	A0	B0	C0	NaN
1	A1	B1	C1	NaN
2	A2	B2	C2	NaN
3	A3	B3	C3	D3
4	A4	B4	C4	D4
5	A5	B5	C5	D5
6	A6	B6	C6	D6
7	A7	B7	C7	D7
8	A8	B8	C8	D8

3.2.7 Histograms

Histograms can be drawn by using the functions `DataFrame.plot.hist()` and `Series.plot.hist()`.

```
import pandas as pd
import numpy as np
import matplotlib.pyplot as plt
import matplotlib
df4 = pd.DataFrame({'a': np.random.randn(100)+1, 'b': np.random.
randn(100), 'c': np.random.randn(100)-1, 'd': np.random.randn(100)-2},
columns=['a', 'b', 'c', 'd'])
plt.figure();
df4.plot.hist(alpha=0.5)
plt.show()
```

Output:

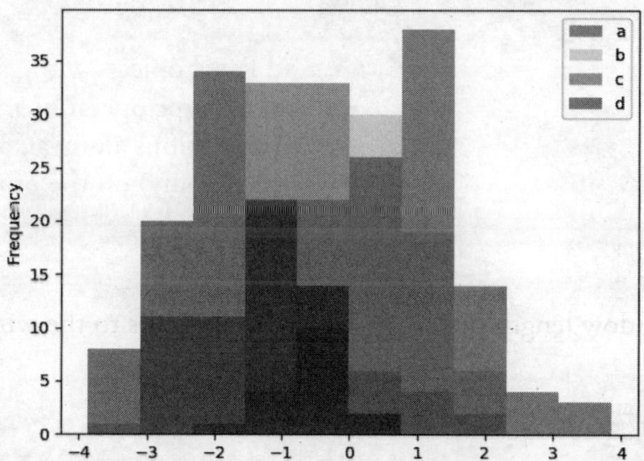


```
df4.plot.hist(stacked=True, bins=20)
df4.plot.hist(stacked=True, bins=20)
```

Output:

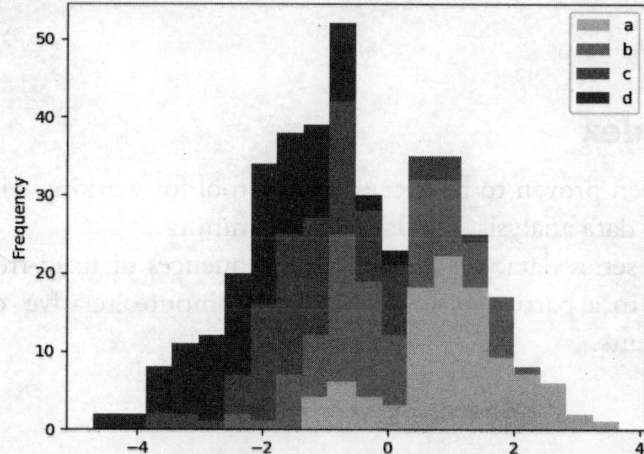

We can perform rolling calculations.

```
>>> df = pd.DataFrame({'B': [0, 1, 2, np.nan, 4]})
>>> df
```

Output:

```
  B
0 0.0
1 1.0
2 2.0
3 NaN
4 4.0
```

For rolling sum with a window length of 2, using the 'triang' window type:

```
>>> df.rolling(2, win_type='triang').sum()
     B
```

Output:

```
0 NaN
1 1.0
2 2.5
3 NaN
4 NaN
```

For rolling sum with a window length of 2, `min_periods` defaults to the window length:

```
>>> df.rolling(2).sum()
```

Output:

```
  B
0 NaN
1 1.0
2 3.0
3 NaN
4 NaN
```

3.2.8 Date Time Index

The pandas package has been proven to be successful as a tool for working with date and time series data, especially in financial data analysis, big data or data mining.

In working with time series data, we can generate sequences of fixed-frequency date and time spans, convert time series to a particular frequency and compute 'relative' dates based on various non-standard time increments.

To create a range of dates:

```
# 24 hours starting from Jan 1, 2017
 rng = pd.date_range('1/1/2017', periods=72, freq='H')
 rng[:5]
print(rng)
```

Output:
DatetimeIndex(['2017-01-01 00:00:00', '2017-01-01 01:00:00',
'2017-01-01 02:00:00', '2017-01-01 03:00:00',
'2017-01-01 04:00:00', '2017-01-01 05:00:00',
'2017-01-01 06:00:00', '2017-01-01 07:00:00',
'2017-01-01 08:00:00', '2017-01-01 09:00:00',
'2017-01-01 10:00:00', '2017-01-01 11:00:00',
'2017-01-01 12:00:00', '2017-01-01 13:00:00',
'2017-01-01 14:00:00', '2017-01-01 15:00:00',
'2017-01-01 16:00:00', '2017-01-01 17:00:00',
'2017-01-01 18:00:00', '2017-01-01 19:00:00',
'2017-01-01 20:00:00', '2017-01-01 21:00:00',
'2017-01-01 22:00:00', '2017-01-01 23:00:00'],
dtype='datetime64[ns]', freq='H')

Indexes can be generated along with dates by specifying the 'index' parameter in the `pandas.Series()` function.

```
ts = pd.Series(np.random.randn(len(rng)), index=rng)
ts.head()
print(ts)
```

Output:
2017-01-01 00:00:00 -0.328165
2017-01-01 01:00:00 -0.043818
2017-01-01 02:00:00 0.874095
2017-01-01 03:00:00 -0.222245
.
.
.
Freq: H, dtype: float64

To change frequency and fill gaps:

```
# Change frequency to 45 minute and fill data
 converted = ts.asfreq('45Min', method='pad')
 converted.head()
print(converted)
```

Output:
2011-01-01 00:00:00 0.469112
2011-01-01 00:45:00 0.469112
2011-01-01 01:30:00 -0.282863
2011-01-01 02:15:00 -1.509059
2011-01-01 03:00:00 -1.135632
.
.
Freq: 45T, dtype: float64

To resample, calculate the daily mean:

```
ts.resample('D').mean()
```

Output:
2017-01-01 0.286062
Freq: D, dtype: float6

3.2.9 Group By

- **Aggregation:** It computes aggregate summary statistics for a group. Examples:
  - Compute group average or sum
  - Compute group counts
- **Transformation:** It performs some group-specific transformations and computing over a specific group. Examples:
  - Standardizing data (z-score) within a group
  - Filling NaN within groups with a value
- **Filtration:** It selects some groups according to group-wise computation. Examples:
  - Discarding some groups based on certain criteria
  - Filtering out groups based on the group aggregate sum or average

You can display aggregate information or columns on which groups are formed using the `SELECT` clause.

```
SELECT Column1, Column2, sum(Column3), count(Column4)
FROM Table1
GROUP BY Column1, Column2
```

The pandas objects can be split on any of their axes. The abstract definition of grouping is to provide a mapping of labels to group names. To create a `GroupBy` object, you need to perform the following:

```
>>> grouped = obj.groupby(key)
>>> grouped = obj.groupby(key, axis=1)
>>> grouped = obj.groupby([key1, key2])
```

The following DataFrame for student data consists of:

```
df = pd.DataFrame({'A': ['std1', 'std2', 'std3', 'std1', 'std2', 'std1'],
'B': ['A1', 'B1', 'C1', 'A2', 'B2', 'A3'], 'C': [6,7,8,6,7,6]})
print(df)
```

Output:

	A	B	C
0	std1	A1	6
1	std2	B1	7
2	std3	C1	8
3	std1	A2	6
4	std2	B2	7
5	std1	A3	6

To group the above data on column A:

```
grouped_df = df.groupby('A')
for key, item in grouped_df:
    print (grouped_df.get_group(key), "\n\n")
```

Output:

	A	B	C
0	std1	A1	6
3	std1	A2	6
5	std1	A3	6

	A	B	C
1	std2	B1	7
4	std2	B2	7

	A	B	C
2	std3	C1	8

To print groupwise sum:

```
print (grouped_df.sum())
```

Output:

A	C
std1	18
std2	14
std3	8

Once groups are created, we can perform aggregate functions:

```
print(grouped_df.aggregate(np.sum))
```

Output:
A
std1 18
std2 14
std3 8

To define multiple indexes for grouping:

```
grouped_df = df.groupby(['A', 'B'])
grouped_df.aggregate(np.sum)
```

Output:

A	B	C
std1	A1	6
	A2	6
	A3	6
std2	B1	7
	B2	7
std3	C1	8

To describe the statistics of a group:

```
print(grouped_df.describe())
```

Output:

A	C	
std1	count	3.0
mean	6.0	
std	0.0	
min	6.0	
25%	6.0	
50%	6.0	
75%	6.0	
max	6.0	
std2	count	2.0
mean	7.0	
std	0.0	
min	7.0	
25%	7.0	
50%	7.0	
75%	7.0	
max	7.0	
std3	count	1.0
mean	8.0	
std	NaN	

```
min     8.0
25%     8.0
50%     8.0
75%     8.0
max     8.0
```

Transformation methods return a DataFrame with the same shape and indices as the original, but with different values. With both aggregation and filter, the resulting DataFrame will usually be smaller in size than the input DataFrame. This is not true of a transformation, which transforms individual values themselves but retains the shape of the original DataFrame.

Filter methods return a subset of the original DataFrame. This means using `filter()` to drop entire groups based on some comparative statistic about that group and its sub-table. Under this definition, we also need to include a number of methods that exclude specific rows from each group.

3.2.10 pandas.io.data

Functions from pandas.io.data and pandas.io.ga extract data from various Internet sources into a DataFrame. Currently the following sources are supported:

- Yahoo! Finance
- Google Finance
- Federal Reserve Bank of St. Louis (FRED)
- Kenneth French's data library
- World Bank
- Google Analytics

It should be noted that various sources support different kinds of data. So not all sources implement the same methods and the data elements returned might also differ.

For example, in Yahoo! Finance:

```
In [1]: import pandas.io.data as web
In [2]: import datetime
In [3]: start = datetime.datetime(2010, 1, 1)
In [4]: end = datetime.datetime(2013, 1, 27)
In [5]: f = web.DataReader("F", 'yahoo', start, end)
In [6]: f.ix['2010-01-04']
Out[6]:
```

Output:

```
Open        1.017000e+01
High        1.028000e+01
Low         1.005000e+01
Close       1.028000e+01
Volume      6.085580e+07
Adj Close   8.755953e+00
Name: 2010-01-04 00:00:00, dtype: float64
```

3.3 Panels

A Panel is a three-dimensional container of data. The term Panel is derived from econometrics and is partially responsible for the name pandas – pan(el)-da(ta)-s.

The names for the three axes are intended to give semantic meaning to describing operations involving Panel data:

- `items` – axis 0, each item corresponds to a DataFrame contained inside.
- `major_axis` – axis 1, it is the index (rows) of each of the DataFrames.
- `minor_axis` – axis 2, it is the columns of each of the DataFrames.

A Panel can be created using the following constructor:

`pandas.Panel(data, items, major_axis, minor_axis, dtype, copy)`

The parameters of the constructor are as follows:

`Data`	Takes various forms like ndarray, Series, map, list, dict, constants and another DataFrame
`items`	axis=0
`major_axis`	axis=1
`minor_axis`	axis=2
`dtype`	Data type of each column
`copy`	Copy data. Default is 'false'

A Panel can be created in multiple ways:

```
From ndarrays
From dict of DataFrames
From 3D ndarray
# creating an empty panel
import pandas as pd
import numpy as np
data = np.random.rand(2,4,5)
p = pd.Panel(data)
print p
```

Output:

<class 'pandas.core.panel.Panel'>
Dimensions: 2 (items) x 4 (major_axis) x 5 (minor_axis)
Items axis: 0 to 1
Major_axis axis: 0 to 3
Minor_axis axis: 0 to 4

EXERCISES

Multiple Choice Questions

1. What will be the output of the following code?

```
import numpy as np
a = np.array([1, 2, 3], dtype =
```

```
complex)
print a
```
(a) [[1.+0.j, 2.+0.j, 3.+0.j]]
(b) [1.+0.j]
(c) Error
(d) [1.+0.j, 2.+0.j, 3.+0.j]

2. Which of the following statements is false?
(a) Ndarray is also known as axis array.
(b) `ndarray.dataitemSize` is the buffer containing the actual elements of the array.
(c) NumPy main object is a homogeneous multi-dimensional array.
(d) In NumPy, dimensions are called axes.

3. What will be the output of the following code?
```
import numpy as np
a = np.array( [7, 10, 2, 4, 13,
16])
med = np.percentile(a, 50)
print(med)
```
(a) 8.5
(b) 11.5
(c) 10
(d) 7

4. What will be the output of the following code?
```
import numpy as np
a = np.arrange(10)
f = np.vectorize(lambda x: x+1)
f(a)
```
(a) [2, 3, 4, 5, 6, 7, 8, 9, 10, 11]
(b) [2, 3, 4, 5, 6, 7, 8, 9, 10]
(c) [1, 2, 3, 4, 5, 6, 7, 8, 9, 10, 11]
(d) [1, 2, 3, 4, 5, 6, 7, 8, 9, 10]

5. Consider an (11 12) shape array. What is the index (x y) of the 100th element?
(a) (8, 3)
(b) (9, 4)
(c) (9, 3)
(d) (8, 4)

Answers

1. (d) **2.** (a) **3.** (a) **4.** (d) **5.** (a)

Programming/Concept-based Questions

1. Define the following vectors and matrices:
```
vec1 = np.array([ -1., 4., -9.])
mat1 = np.array([[ 1., 3., 5.], [7., -9., 2.], [4., 6., 8. ]]
```
(a) Compute `vec2 = (np.pi/4) * vec1`
(b) Compute `vec2 = np.cos( vec2)`
(c) Compute `vec3 = vec1 + 2 * vec2`
(d) The Euclidean norm of a matrix or a vector is available using `la.norm`. Compute `la.norm(vec3)`
(e) Compute the product of `mat1` and `vec3` and set `vec4` equal to the result.
(f) Compute the transpose, determinant and trace of `mat1`.

Answer:
```
import numpy as np
importscipy.linalgasla
vec1 = np.array([ -1., 4., -9.])
mat1 = np.array([[ 1., 3., 5.], [7., -9., 2.], [4., 6., 8. ]])
vec2 = (np.pi/4) * vec1
```

```
vec3 = np.cos( vec2)
print(vec2, vec3)
vec3 = vec1 + 2 * vec2
la.norm(vec3)
print(mat1 @ vec3)
vec4 = mat1 @ vec3
np.transpose(mat1)
```

2. Make a pandas DataFrame with a two-dimensional list.
Answer:

```
# import pandas as pd
import pandas as pd
# List1
lst = [['Geek', 25], ['is', 30],
   ['for', 26], ['Geeksforgeeks', 22]]
# creating df object with columns specified
df = pd.DataFrame(lst, columns =['Tag', 'number'])
print(df)
```

3. Explain re-indexing in pandas.
Answer: Re-indexing is used to conform a DataFrame to a new index with optional filling logic. It places NA/NaN in that location where the values are not present in the previous index. It returns a new object unless the new index is produced as equivalent to the current one, and the value of copy becomes False. It is used to change the index of the rows and columns of the DataFrame.

4. Explain categorical data in pandas.
Answer: Categorical data is defined as a pandas data type that corresponds to a categorical variable in statistics. A categorical variable is generally used to take a limited and usually fixed number of possible values. Examples: gender, country affiliation, blood type, social class, observation time, or rating by the Likert scales. All values of categorical data are either in categories or `np.nan`.

5. How can we create a copy of a Series in pandas?
Answer: We can create a copy of a Series by using the following syntax:

```
pandas.Series.copy
Series.copy(deep=True)
```

The above statements make a deep copy that includes a copy of the data and the indices. If we set the value of `deep` to False, it will neither copy the indices nor the data.

6. How can we delete indices, rows or columns from a pandas DataFrame?
Answer:
To remove an index from a DataFrame:
   1. Reset the index of DataFrame.
   2. Execute `del df.index.name` to remove the index name.
   3. Remove duplicate index values by resetting the index and drop the duplicate values from the index column.

To delete a column from a DataFrame

1. Use the `drop()` method to delete a column from the DataFrame. The axis argument that is passed to the `drop()` method is 0 if it indicates the rows or 1 if it drops the columns.
2. Pass the argument in place and set it to True to delete the column without reassigning the DataFrame.
3. Delete the duplicate values from the column using the `drop_duplicates()` method.

To remove a row from a DataFrame:

1. Use `df.drop_duplicates()` to remove duplicate rows from the DataFrame.
2. Use the `drop()` method to specify the index of the rows that we want to remove from the DataFrame.

7. How do you obtain the number of rows and columns of a pandas DataFrame?
   Answer: Use the `shape` attribute which gives you the shape of the DataFrame:
   ```
   df.shape
   ```
   Thus, there are 6 rows and 3 columns in the DataFrame `df`.

8. How do you convert a pandas Series to a DataFrame?
   Answer: You can use the `Series.to_frame()` method to convert the series object to a DataFrame:
   ```
   series = pd.Series(['butter', 'dynamite','daydream', 'friends'])
   col = 'bts'
   series.to_frame(name=col)
   ```

9. How do you add multiple rows to an existing DataFrame?
   Answer: #Creating a new DataFrame that we want to append
   ```
   df2 = pd.DataFrame({
     'id': [1221, 1200, 1230],
     'age': [36,53,26],
     'gender': ['M','F','M'],
     })

   #Appending multiple rows with DataFrame
   df.append(df2)
   ```

10. What are the `loc[ ]` and `iloc[ ]` methods in pandas?
    Answer: The `loc[ ]` method is a label-based method that is used for selecting data and updating it. Here, you can pass the row or column label you want to select.
    Syntax: `loc[row_label, column_label]`
    The `iloc[ ]` method is an index-based method that is used for data selection. Here, you can pass the row or column positions that you want to select (0-based integer index).
    Syntax: `iloc[row_position, column_position]`

BIBLIOGRAPHY

1. "NumPy quickstart". NumPy. https://numpy.org/doc/stable/user/quickstart.html

CHAPTER 4

Data Visualization

Learning Objectives

At the end of this chapter, you will be able to:

- Describe how visualization tools such as Tableau, Looker and Zoho Analytics can be used
- Use interactive visual analysis techniques on user interaction and the human visual system at the intersection of visual analytics and big data
- Describe the Matplotlib library used to process data sets
- Use Matplotlib to generate plots, scatterplots, histograms, power spectra, bar charts and error charts
- Create interactive, web-based visualizations using the plotly library
- Visualize data at exploratory data analytics and further stages of data analysis
- Visualize maps using Cartopy

4.0 Introduction

Data visualization is the graphical representation of information and data. By using visual elements like charts, graphs and maps, data visualization tools provide an accessible way to view and understand trends, outliers and patterns in data. Additionally, it provides an excellent way for employees or business owners to present data to non-technical audiences.

It helps people see, interact with and better understand data. Whether simple or complex, the right visualization can help everyone have the same understanding, regardless of their level of expertise.

4.1 Visualization Software and Tools

Data visualization tools are software applications that render information in visual formats such as graphs, charts and heat maps for the purpose of data analysis. Such tools make it easier to understand and manipulate vast amounts of data. The data visualization tools can vary greatly. They range from software that emphasizes simplicity and ease of use to more complex platforms that require more advanced technical and data science skills. The end goal is essentially the same for different tools: making data easier to understand and work with. The tools can also process multiple data sets in one visualization and output various types of charts, graphs and maps. Most tools can output both images and interactive graphics. The various output criteria have exceptions.

Visualization tools makes it easy for analysts and statisticians to create visual data models according to their specifications by conveniently providing an interface, database connectivity and machine learning tools in one place.

Some data visualization software tools are described below.

- **Tableau** is a data visualization tool that data analysts, scientists, statisticians and others use to visualize data and draw clear conclusions. Tableau can ingest data and generate the data visualization output in a short amount of time. It also allows us to do this while providing the highest level of security, ensuring that security issues are addressed as soon as they occur or are discovered by users. Tableau also allows users to prepare, cleanse and format data and then create visualizations for actionable insights that can be shared with others. Tableau is available for individual data analysts or at scale for business teams and organizations.
- **Looker** is a data visualization tool that lets you dig deep into data and discover valuable insights. It provides real-time dashboards of data for deeper analysis, allowing businesses to make instant decisions based on visualizations of data received. Looker also provides connections to Redshift, Snowflake, BigQuery and over 50 SQL-compatible dialects, making it easy to connect to multiple databases. Looker data visualizations can be shared with anyone using specific tools.
- **Zoho Analytics** is a business intelligence and data analytics software that allows you to create attractive data visualizations in minutes. By retrieving data from multiple sources and linking them together, you can create multi-dimensional data visualizations that can display business data across multiple departments. Zoho Analytics allows you to share or publish reports. The files can be exported to any format such as Spreadsheet, MS Word, Excel, PPT and PDF.
- **Microsoft Power BI** is a data visualization platform focused on building a data-driven business intelligence culture in every organization. Its analytics tools are used to analyze, aggregate and share data in meaningful ways. It offers hundreds of data visualizations with built-in artificial intelligence and Excel integration capabilities.

4.2 Interactive Visual Analysis

Interactive visual analysis (IVA) is a set of techniques that combines computer processing power with human perceptual and cognitive abilities to extract knowledge from large and complex data sets. These techniques rely heavily on user interaction and the human visual system and are at the intersection of visual analytics and big data. IVA is a suitable technique for analyzing high-dimensional data containing a large number of data points. Simple graphical representations and non-interactive techniques are insufficient for information comprehension.

These techniques involve looking at a data set through various correlated views and iteratively selecting and examining features of interest to the user. The goal of IVA is to gain insights that are not readily apparent from data sets (usually tabular). This may involve generating, testing and validating hypotheses, or simply searching data sets for correlations between different variables.

Here, the goal is to move from the data itself to the information it contains, ultimately revealing knowledge that is not apparent from just looking at the raw numbers.

The most basic form of IVA is the use of multiple coordinated views showing different columns of a data set. IVA requires at least two views. Views usually belong to common information visualization tools such as histograms, scatterplots and parallel coordinates, but can also use volume rendering views if they are appropriate for the data. One view typically shows the independent variables of the data set (such as time or spatial location), while the other shows the dependent variables (such as temperature, air pressure or population density). When the views are linked, when the user selects a data point in one of the views, the corresponding data point is automatically highlighted in the other view. This technique, which allows intuitive exploration of higher-dimensional properties of data, is known as linking and brushing.

The selection made in one of the views need not be binary. IVA's software package allows for progressive levels of interest-of-choice, allowing progressive emphasis on data points as one moves from low to high interest. This enables the 'focus + context' aspect inherent in information retrieval. For example, when examining a tumour in an MRI data set, one may also be interested in the tissue surrounding the tumour.

4.3 Text Visualization

Text visualization is the technique of visually representing written data using graphs, charts or word clouds. It provides an at-a-glance view of the most relevant keywords in the text, summarizes the content, and reveals trends and patterns within the document.

Text visualization is used to summarize large amounts of text, save reading time by automatically highlighting key phrases in a run of text and categorizing text by subject, mood, and more.

- It makes text data easier to understand. Humans can process images much faster than text. Text visualization is an effective way to simplify complex data and convey ideas and concepts.
- Gain insight from qualitative data. Customer feedback contains a wealth of insight. Text visualizations help you identify the most important features, products and topics at a glance.
- Discover hidden trends and patterns. Analyze and visualize insights over time to identify fluctuations and quickly find root causes.

4.4 Creating Graphs with Matplotlib

Matplotlib in Python is a two-dimensional plotting library that generates quality figures for publication and interactive environments across platforms.

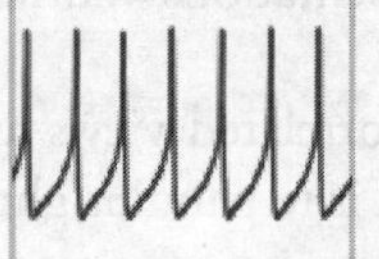

Figure 4.1 Graphs created using Matplotlib

Matplotlib can generate plots, scatterplots, histograms, power spectra, bar charts, error charts, and more (Fig. 4.1).

For simple plotting, Pyplot provides an interface to Matplotlib. It gives full control of the graph area, data representations, font properties, axes properties and line styles to the programmer.

Let us look at the steps involved in installing Matplotlib on Windows and Linux.

4.4.1 Installing Matplotlib on Windows

1. First download Matplotlib from https://pypi.python.org/pypi/matplotlib/ and look for a wheel file (a file ending in .WHL) that matches the version of Python you are using. For example, if you are using a 32-bit version of Python 3.5, you will need to download MATPLOTLIB-1.4.3-CP35-NONE-WIN32.WHL.
2. Use the `pip` command at the command prompt in the related Python directory to install Matplotlib:
   ```
   pip install matplotlib
   ```

4.4.2 Installing Matplotlib on Linux

1. To install Python 3 on Linux, use the following command:
   ```
   $ sudo apt-get install python3-matplotlib
   ```
2. If you want to install a newer version of Python, you need to install several other libraries that Matplotlib depends on:
   ```
   $ sudo apt-get install python3.5-dev python3.5-tk tk-dev
   $ sudo apt-get install libfreetype6-dev g++
   ```
3. Use the `pip` command to install matplotlib:
   ```
   $ pip install --user matplotlib
   ```

4.4.3 A Simple Plot

To use functions defined in Pyplot, you need to import the Pyplot module of Matplotlib instead of all the modules of Matplotlib. This saves memory space. Matplotlib's modules come with some default settings. Programmers can control the default values of almost every property such as colour and style, figure size and dpi, line width, axes, axis and grid properties, text and font properties.

For example, let us generate values and calculate `sin()` and `cos()` and plot the same.

The program given below generates 256 values from –3.14 to +3.14.

```
import numpy as np
import matplotlib.pyplot as pl
Y = np.linspace(-np.pi, np.pi, 256, endpoint=True)
print(Y)
CP = np.cos(Y)
SP= np.sin(Y)
pl.plot(Y,CP)
pl.plot(Y,SP)
pl.show()
```

Output:

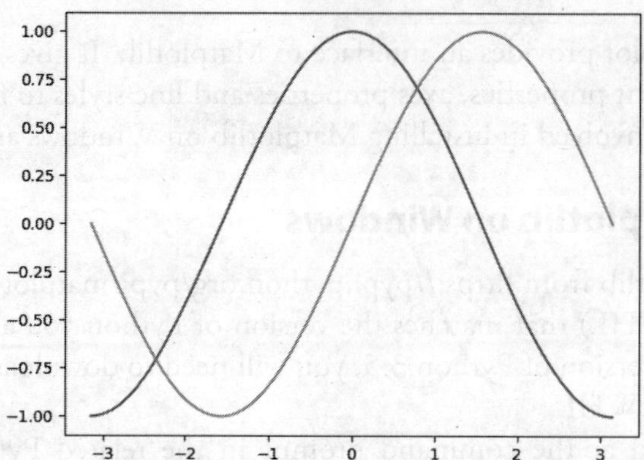

Now, the default values defined by Matplotlib in the above program can be changed. For example, to have the cosine and sine curves in blue and the line width for cosine as 2.5 and sine as 3.5, the following code can be used

```
pl.figure(figsize=(8,6), dpi=200)
pl.plot(Y, CP, color="blue", linewidth=2.5, linestyle="-")
pl.plot(Y, SP, color="blue",  linewidth=3.5, linestyle="-")
```

Output:

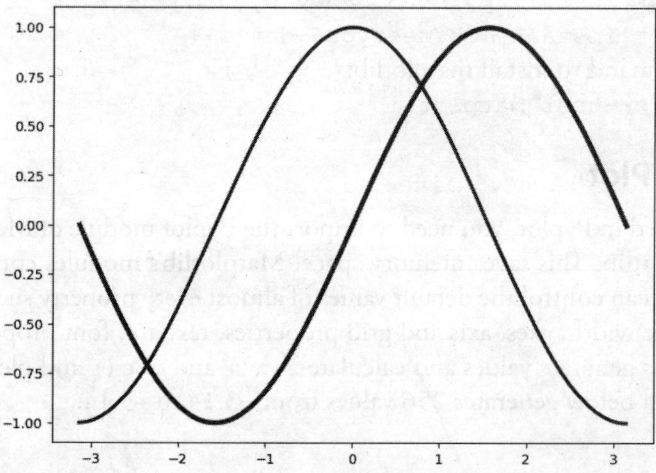

If you want to increase or reduce the current axis limit, it can be multiplied by that factor. Increase in limit can give you more free space and decrease in limit can allow you to analyse the graph minutely.

```
pl.figure(figsize=(8,6), dpi=100)
pl.xlim(Y.min()*2, Y.max()*2)
pl.ylim(CP.min()*2, CP.max()*2)
pl.plot(Y, CP, color="blue", linewidth=2.5, linestyle="-")
pl.plot(Y, SP, color="blue",  linewidth=3.5, linestyle="-")
```

Output:

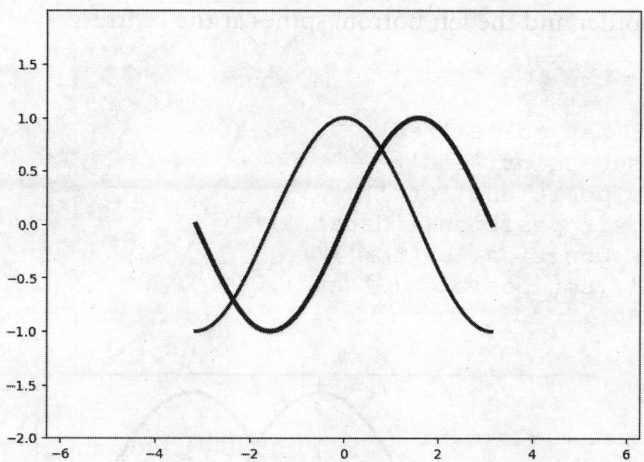

In the above graph, ticks are integer or decimal values. However, if graphs of sine or cosine are drawn, these values are less meaningful. Ticks should be drawn in π or π/2. To do this, the first tick values should be set to not accept default values. After this, commands to display labels accordingly should be given.

To get current ticks, the values (+/-π,+/-π/2) are used for sine and cosine. The code given below restricts *x*-axis ticks to π values and *y*-axis ticks to decimal values ranging from −1 to +1. The first parameter of `xticks` will set the tick colour and the second parameter will label it accordingly.

```
pl.figure(figsize=(8,6), dpi=100)
pl.xticks([-np.pi, -np.pi/2, 0, np.pi/2, np.pi], [r'$-\pi$', r'$-\pi/2$',
r'$0$', r'$+\pi/2$', r'$+\pi$'])
pl.yticks([-1, 0, +1], [r'$-1$', r'$0$', r'$+1$'])
pl.plot(Y, CP, color="blue", linewidth=2.5, linestyle="-")
pl.plot(Y, SP, color="blue",  linewidth=3.5, linestyle="-")
```

Output:

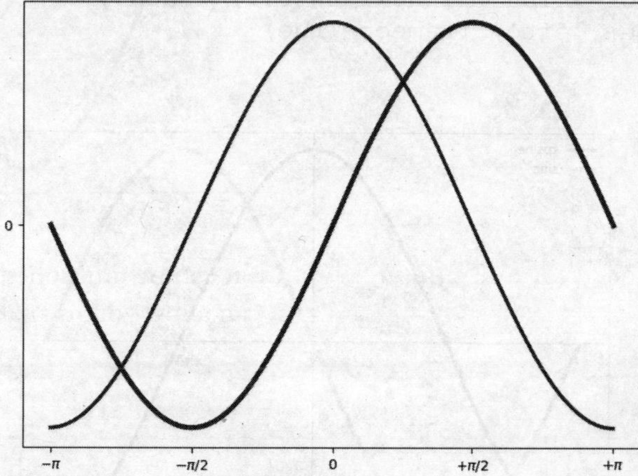

Spines can be placed at left, right, top or bottom. They can be placed at the border or at the centre. If spines are placed at the centre, they can work as reference points and show the symmetry of the graph. To place them in the centre, set the position data as 0. The code given below will place the right top spines at the border and the left bottom spines at the centre.

```
ax = pl.gca()
ax.spines['right'].set_color('red')
ax.spines['top'].set_color('red')
ax.yaxis.set_ticks_position('left')
ax.spines['left'].set_position(('data',0))
ax.xaxis.set_ticks_position('bottom')
ax.spines['bottom'].set_position(('data',0))
```

Output:

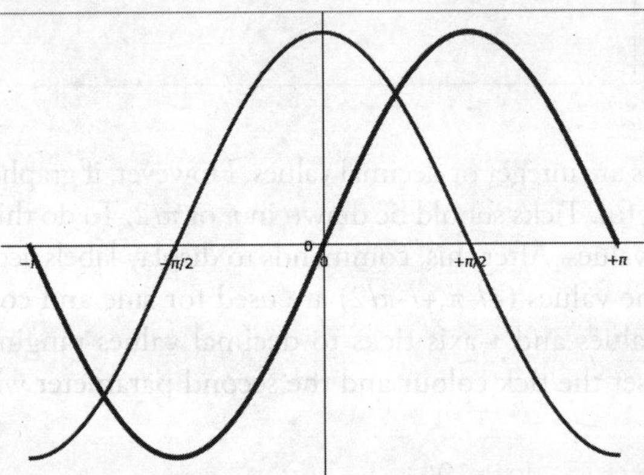

Legend values are used for labelling the graph representation. If more than one data is represented, a label is required to show which curve is representing which data. While giving plot commands, additional parameter labels should be provided. Legends can be added in the upper-left or upper-right corner.

```
pl.plot(Y, CP, color="blue", linewidth=2.5, linestyle="-", label="cosine")
pl.plot(Y, SP, color="blue", linewidth=3.5, linestyle="-", label="sine")
pl.legend(loc='upper left', frameon=True)
```

Output:

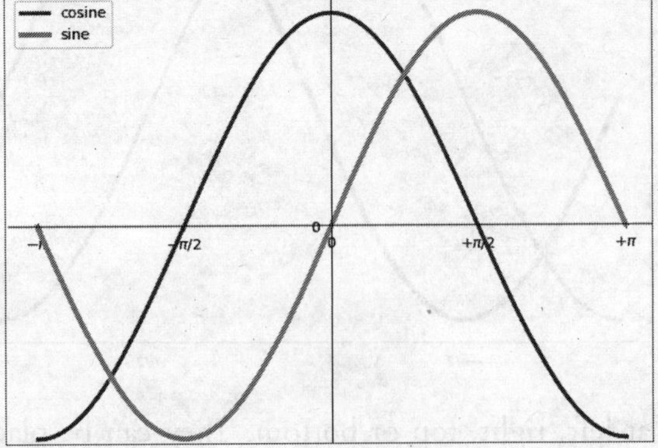

4.4.4 Figures, Subplots, Axes and Ticks

Python uses implicit figures and axis creation but it can be user defined too. The whole window where the graph is displayed is a figure. In a figure, the user can display many subplots and control this area through programming.

Within this figure, there can be one or more subplots. The default is subplot (111). This means only one subplot in the figure can be drawn. The figure can consist of multiple subplots displayed in a regular grid. Division of figures in grids and placement of subplots can be controlled by the programmer.

```
Gca(): get current axes
Gcf: get current figure
```

A figure is the interface where a user can display subplots and axes. The display area for plots is a figure. The user can specify various parameters like figure number, DPI, figure size and edge colour. The user can control the whole area by setting its parameter values.

Figures can be closed by clicking on the X in the upper-right corner or by using the command `close()`. Depending on the argument, it can close the current figure or a specific figure. Figure properties can be set using the set_something methods.

Subplots can be places using axes. The scale values on the axes can be displayed using ticks. Subplots enable you to arrange plots in a regular grid. In the `subplot()` function, you need to pass the number of rows, columns and the number of the plot.

The program given below will draw four subplots in a figure (2,2) and write the heading in the centre of the plot.

```
from pylab import *
subplot(2,2,1)
xticks([]), yticks([])
text(1.5,1.5, 'subplot(2,2,1)',ha='center',va='center',size=14,alpha=.5)
subplot(2,2,2)
xticks([]), yticks([])
text(1.5,1.5, 'subplot(2,2,2)',ha='center',va='center',size=15,alpha=.5)
subplot(2,2,3)
xticks([]), yticks([])
text(1.5,1.5, 'subplot(2,2,3)',ha='center',va='center',size=14,alpha=.5)
subplot(2,2,4)
xticks([]), yticks([])
text(1.5,1.5, 'subplot(2,2,4)',ha='center',va='center',size=14,alpha=.5)
show()
```

Output:

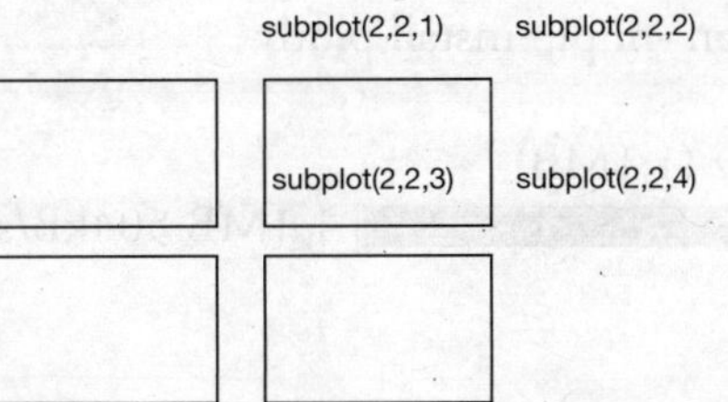

Axes are similar to subplots but permit placement of plots in any region. If a smaller plot is to be placed inside a large one, that can be done with axes. The `axes()` function is provided with the top-left and bottom-right corners of the plot and one axis can be embedded in another. To label the axes, the `text()` function is provided with the location (x,y) where text is to be displayed.

```
from pylab import *
axes([0,0,.8,.8])
xticks([]), yticks([])
text(0.8,0.8,
'axes([0.1,0.1,.8,.8])',ha='center',va='center',size=14,alpha=.6)
axes([0.2,0.2,.4,.4])
xticks([]), yticks([])
text(0.5,0.5,
'axes([0.2,0.2,.3,.3])',ha='center',va='center',size=14,alpha=.6)
show()
```

Output:

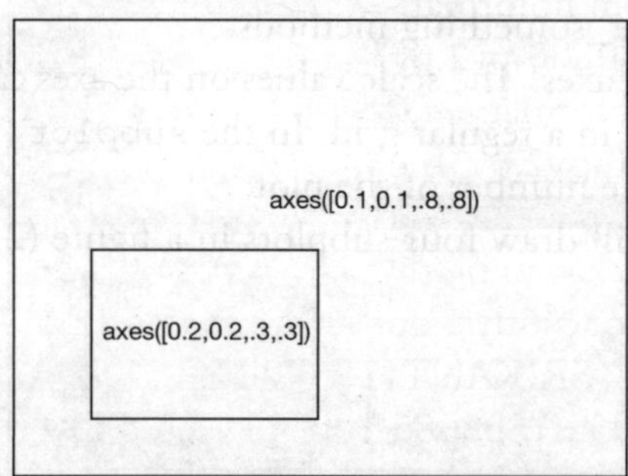

Ticks are labels used to expose the scale on an axis. They make plots easier to understand. Matplotlib provides a completely configurable gadget for ticks. Tick locators are used to specify where ticks need to appear and tick formatters personalize the appearance of ticks. Predominant and minor ticks can be located and formatted independently.

4.5 Creating Graphs with the plotly Package

To install the plotly package, use the following command. For this, pip should be installed and the `PATH` environment variable should contain the address of the scripts folder.

```
python -m pip install plotly
```

Output:

C:\Users\T SRIKANTH>python -m pip install plotly
Collecting plotly
Downloading plotly-2.1.0.tar.gz (1.1MB)
100% |████████████████████████████████| 1.1MB 504kB/s

Collecting decorator>=4.0.6 (from plotly)
Downloading decorator-4.1.2-py2.py3-none-any.whl
Collecting nbformat>=4.2 (from plotly)
Downloading nbformat-4.4.0-py2.py3-none-any.whl (155kB)
100% |████████████████████████████████| 163kB 936kB/s
Collecting pytz (from plotly)
Downloading pytz-2017.2-py2.py3-none-any.whl (484kB)
100% |████████████████████████████████| 491kB 819kB/s
Requirement already satisfied: requests in d:\python\python36-32\lib\site-packages (from plotly)
Requirement already satisfied: six in d:\python\python36-32\lib\site-packages (from plotly)
Collecting traitlets>=4.1 (from nbformat>=4.2->plotly)
Downloading traitlets-4.3.2-py2.py3-none-any.whl (74kB)
100% |████████████████████████████████| 81kB 1.0MB/s
Collecting jsonschema!=2.5.0,>=2.4 (from nbformat>=4.2->plotly)
Downloading jsonschema-2.6.0-py2.py3-none-any.whl
Collecting ipython-genutils (from nbformat>=4.2->plotly)
Downloading ipython_genutils-0.2.0-py2.py3-none-any.whl
Collecting jupyter-core (from nbformat>=4.2->plotly)
Downloading jupyter_core-4.3.0-py2.py3-none-any.whl (76kB)
100% |████████████████████████████████| 81kB 1.0MB/s
Building wheels for collected packages: plotly
Running setup.py bdist_wheel for plotly... done
Stored in directory: C:\Users\T SRIKANTH\AppData\Local\pip\Cache\wheels\33\4b\2f\b3651c-c3166303da7676f5724865089d32f18b8685cc04cffd
Successfully built plotly
Installing collected packages: decorator, ipython-genutils, traitlets, jsonschema, jupyter-core, nbformat, pytz, plotly
Successfully installed decorator-4.1.2 ipython-genutils-0.2.0 jsonschema-2.6.0 jupyter-core-4.3.0 nbformat-4.4.0 plotly-2.1.0 pytz-2017.2 traitlets-4.3.2

4.5.1 Working with plotly in Offline Mode

```
from plotly import __version__
from plotly.offline import download_plotlyjs, init_notebook_mode, plot,
iplot
print(__version__)
```

Output:
D:\PythonPrograms>python s1.py
2.1.0

In the offline mode, graphs can be plotted and saved in the local system. There are two types of plotting in offline mode: `plotly.offline.plot()` and `plotly.offline.iplot()`.

The `plot()` function is used to plot a graph and save it in a local standalone HTML file. The `iplot()` function is used to plot a graph in a Jupyter notebook file. The HTML file will be opened in the local web browser and the Jupyter file will be opened in the Jupyter Notebook.

```
import plotly
from plotly.graph_objs import Scatter, Layout
plotly.offline.plot({
"data": [Scatter(x=[10, 20, 30, 40], y=[40, 30, 20, 10])],
"layout": Layout(title="with plot()")
})
```

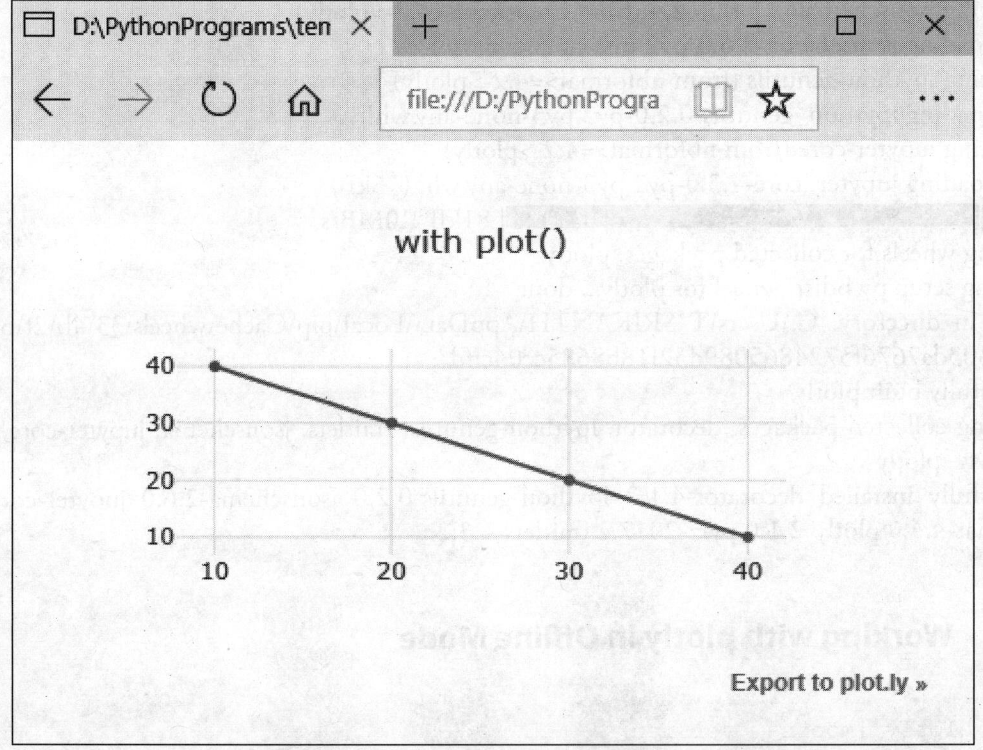

When using `plotly.offline.iplot()`, we need to install ipython using the following command:

```
pip install "ipython[all]"
```

Then install the Jupyter Notebook app using the following command:

```
jupyter notebook
```

With this command, the Jupyter Notebook is opened, as shown below.

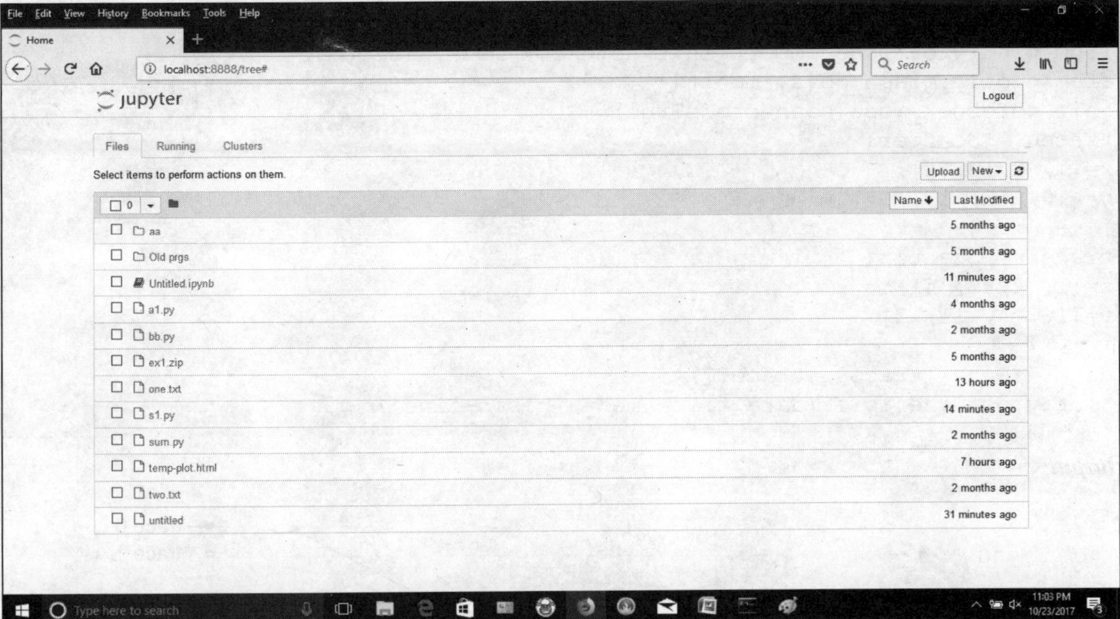

To create a new notebook, click on *New* → *Python3*.

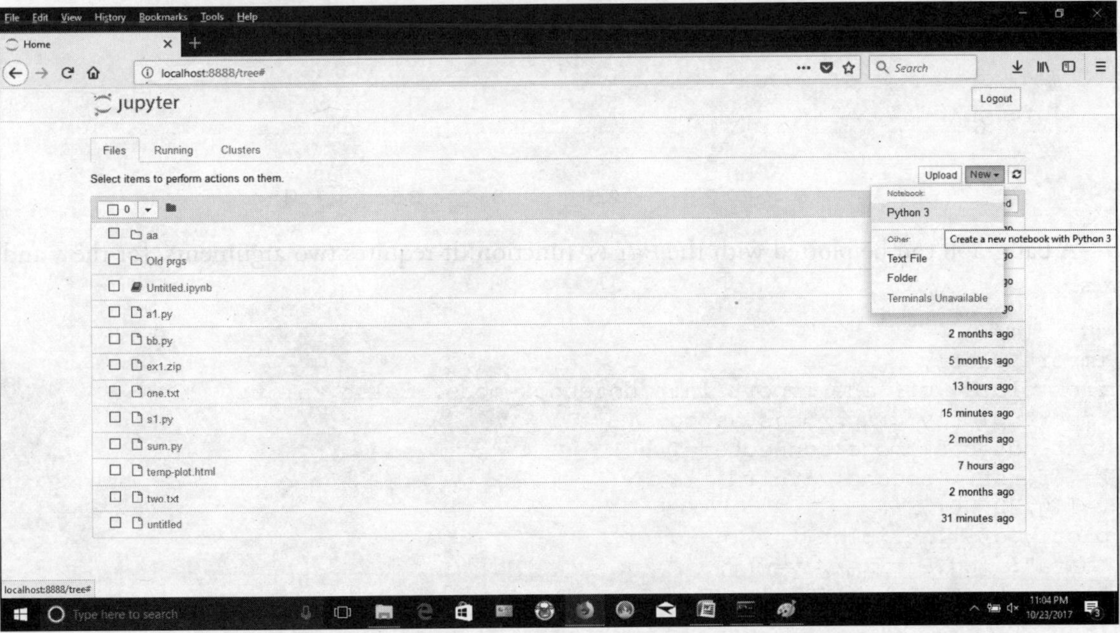

Type the code and click *Run.*

```
import plotly
from plotly.offline import init_notebook_mode, iplot
from plotly.graph_objs import *
init_notebook_mode(connected=True)
trace0 = Scatter(
x=[1, 2, 3, 4],
y=[10, 15, 13, 17]
)
trace1 = Scatter(
x=[1, 2, 3, 4],
y=[16, 5, 11, 9]
)
data = Data([trace0, trace1])
plotly.offline.iplot(data,filename = 'basic-line')
```

Output:

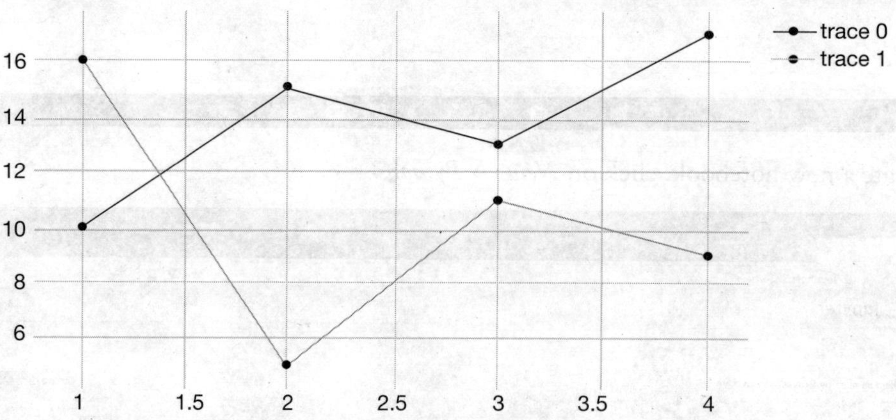

A bar graph can be plotted with the `Bar()` function. It requires two arguments, for the *x* and *y* axes.

```
import plotly
from plotly.offline import init_notebook_mode, iplot, plot
import plotly.graph_objs as pg
init_notebook_mode(connected=True)
k=['first','second','third']
v=[10,20,30]
plotly.offline.iplot({
"data": [pg.Bar(x=k, y=v)],
"layout": pg.Layout(title="Bar Graph")
})
```

Output:

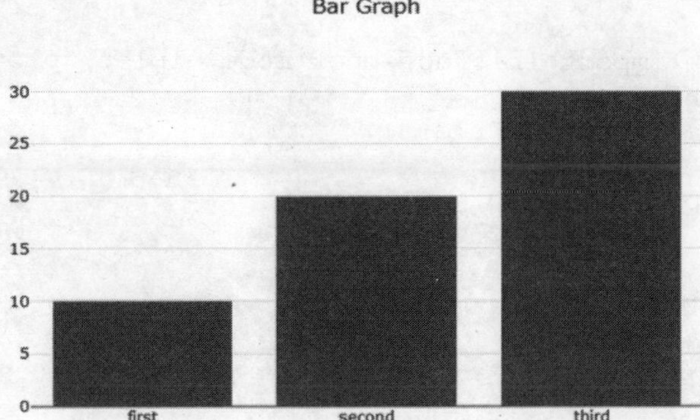

A box graph can be plotted with the `Box()` function. It requires two arguments, for the *x* and *y* axes.

```
import plotly
from plotly.offline import init_notebook_mode, iplot, plot
import plotly.graph_objs as pg
init_notebook_mode(connected=True)
k=['first','second','third']
v=[10,20,30]
plotly.offline.iplot({
"data": [pg.Box(x=k, y=v)],
"layout": pg.Layout(title="Box Graph")
})
```

Output:

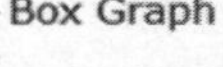

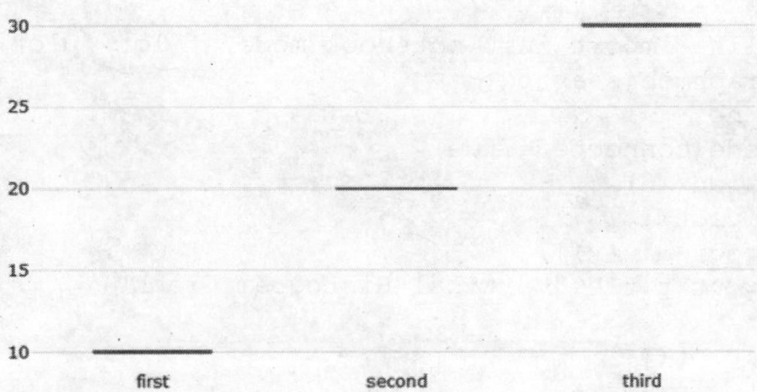

A heat map graph can be plotted using the `Heatmap()` function. It requires a matrix argument.

```
import plotly
from plotly.offline import init_notebook_mode, iplot, plot
import plotly.graph_objs as pg
init_notebook_mode(connected=True)
plotly.offline.iplot({
"data": [pg.Heatmap(z=[[10, 20, 30],
[40, 50, 60],
[70, 80, 90]])],
"layout": pg.Layout(title="Heatmap Graph")
})
```

Output:

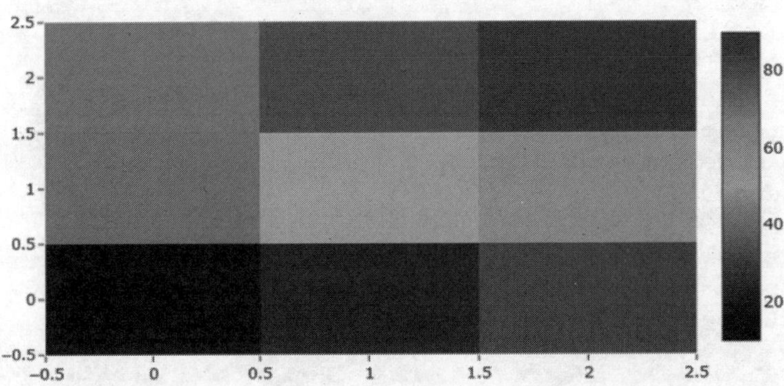

A histogram graph can be plotted using the `Histogram()` function. It requires array values as argument.

```
import plotly
from plotly.offline import init_notebook_mode, iplot, plot
import plotly.graph_objs as pg
import numpy as np
init_notebook_mode(connected=True)
x = np.random.randn(20)
plotly.offline.iplot({
"data": [pg.Histogram(x=x)],
"layout": pg.Layout(title="Vertical Histogram Graph")
})
plotly.offline.iplot({
"data": [pg.Histogram(y=x)],
"layout": pg.Layout(title="Horizontal Histogram Graph")
})
```

Output:

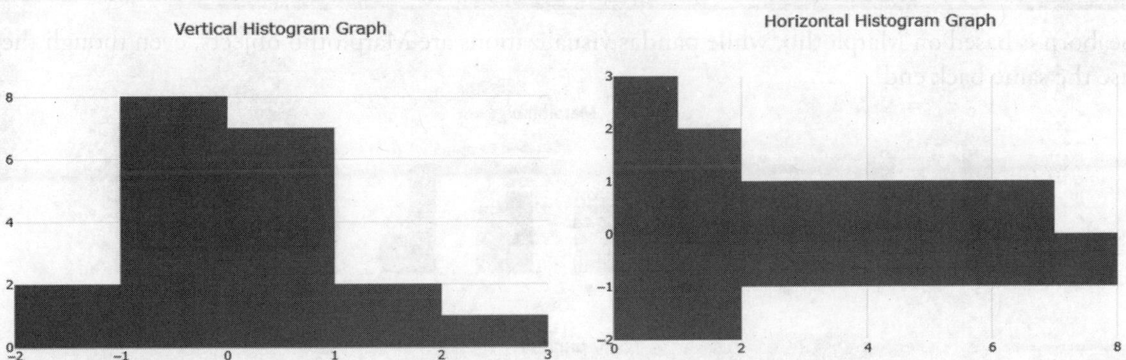

A pie graph can be plotted using the `Pie()` function. It requires array label and value as arguments.

```
import plotly
from plotly.offline import init_notebook_mode, iplot, plot
import plotly.graph_objs as pg
import numpy as np
init_notebook_mode(connected=True)
x = [10,30,20,15,25]
y=['a','b','c','d','e']
plotly.offline.iplot({
"data": [pg.Pie(labels=y, values=x)],
"layout": pg.Layout(title="Pie Graph")
})
```

Output:

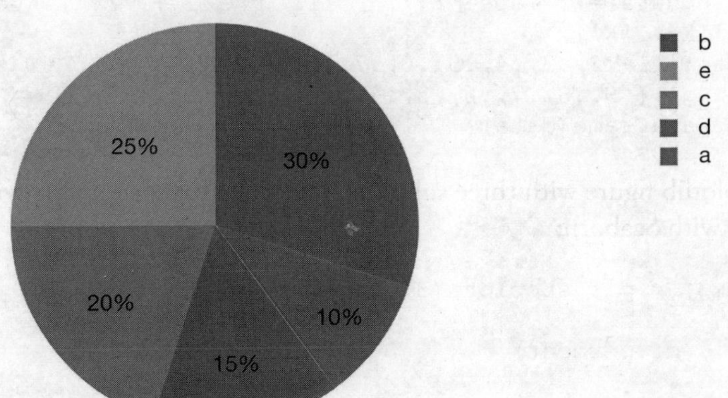

4.6 Data Visualization with Matplotlib, Seaborn and pandas

Seaborn is based on Matplotlib, while pandas visualizations are Matplotlib objects, even though they use the same back end.

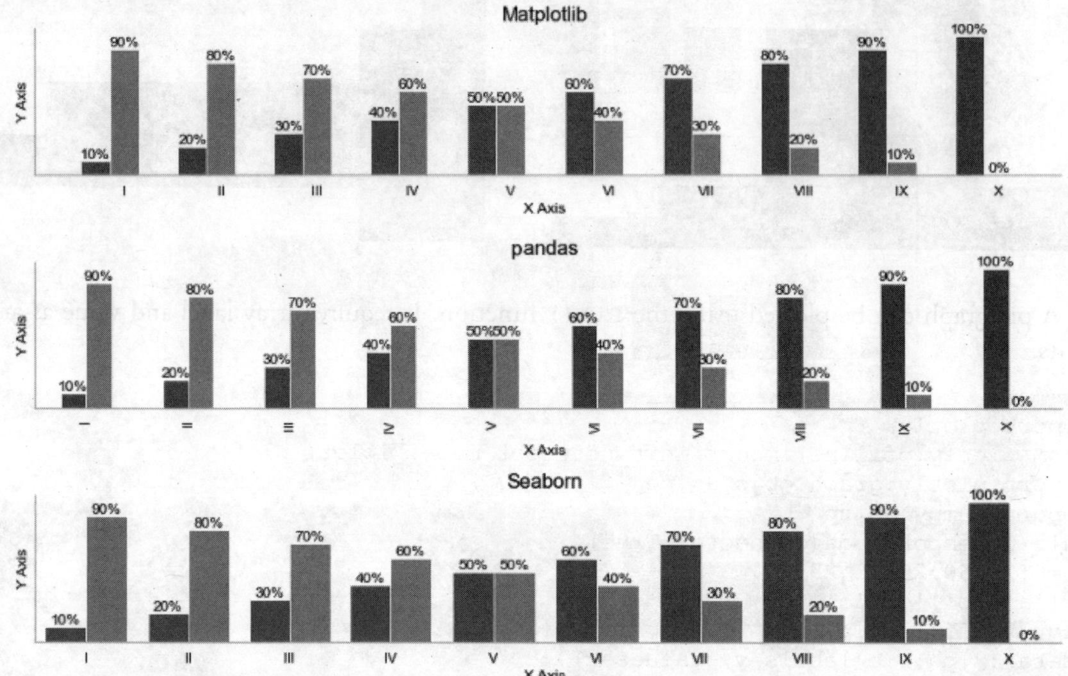

To create dummy data:

```
import pandas as pd
import matplotlib.pyplot as plt
import seaborn as sb
import numpy as npdata = {'label':['I', 'II', 'III', 'IV', 'V', 'VI',
'VII', 'VIII', 'IX', 'X'],
        'percent':[.1,.2,.3,.4,.5,.6,.7,.8,.9, 1],
        'remaining':[.9,.8,.7,.6,.5,.4,.3,.2,.1, 0],
       }df = pd.DataFrame(data)
```

To create a Matplotlib figure with three subplots, plot three bar charts, one with Matplotlib, one with pandas and one with Seaborn:

```
f, (ax1, ax2, ax3) = plt.subplots(3, figsize=(12,8))
# matplotlib
ax1.bar(df.label, df.percent)
# pandas
df.plot(x='label', y='percent', kind='bar', ax=ax2)
# seaborn
sb.barplot(x=df.label, y=df.percent, ax=ax3)
plt.show()
```

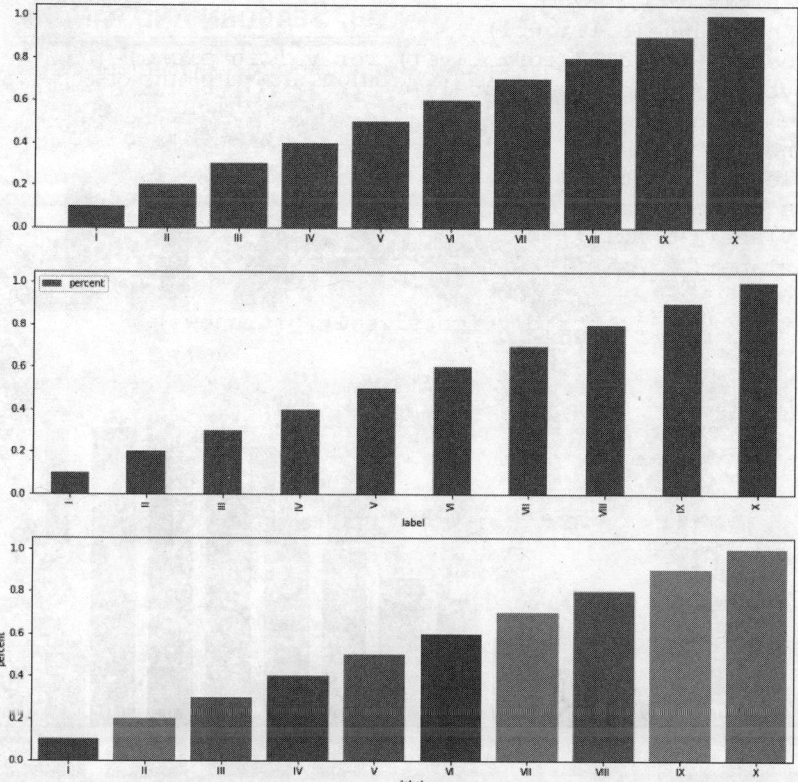

To customize charts, use Seaborn's functions or navigate the Matplotlib objects and make the adjustments. pandas can facilitate plotting, but it does not have methods to edit Matplotlib objects, only to create them.

To set a theme, remove the spines with Seaborn, add labels and edit the ticks, titles and legend with Matplotlib.

```
# seaborn theme
sb.set_theme(style="whitegrid")f, (ax1, ax2, ax3) = plt.subplots(3,
figsize=(10,16))# matplotlib + pandas
ax1.bar(df.label, df.percent)
# pandas + matplotlib
df.plot(x='label', y='percent', kind='bar', ax=ax2)
# seaborn + pandas
sb.barplot(x=df.label, y=df.percent, ax=ax3)# remove espine
sb.despine(f)for ax in [ax1, ax2, ax3]:
   # add labels
    container = ax.containers[0]
    labels = ["{:g}%".format(val*100) for val in container.datavalues]
   ax.bar_label(container, labels=labels)
    # horizontal grid only
    ax.grid(False)
    ax.grid(axis='y')
```

```
# set y ticks
ticks = np.arange(0,1.1,0.1)
tick_labels = ["{:g}%".format(val) for val in ticks]
ax.set_yticks(ticks, tick_labels)
# remove legend
ax.legend([])
ax.get_legend().remove()
# define xy labels
ax.set_ylabel('Y Axis')
ax.set_xlabel('X Axis')
# title
ax.set_title('Hello World', fontsize=16)plt.show()
```

Output:

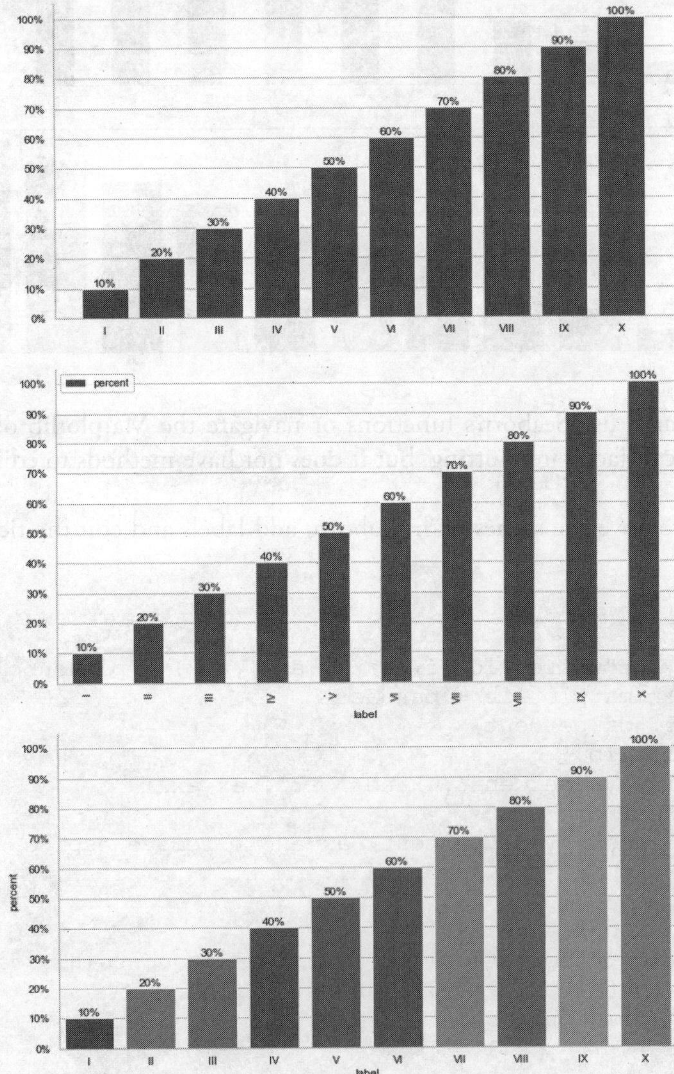

4.7 Exploratory Data Analysis

Exploratory data analysis (EDA) refers to the process of conducting an initial investigation of data to discover patterns, detect anomalies, test hypotheses and validate assumptions using summary statistics and graphs. The main purpose is to help us examine the data before making assumptions. It helps us identify obvious errors, better understand patterns in the data, spot outliers and unusual events, and discover interesting relationships between variables.

Data scientists can use exploratory analysis to ensure that the results they generate are valid and applicable to the desired business outcomes and goals. EDA also assists stakeholders by ensuring they are asking the right questions. EDA helps answer questions about standard deviations, categorical variables and confidence intervals. Once EDA is complete and insight is gained, its capabilities can be used for more advanced data analysis and modelling, including machine learning.

4.7.1 EDA Tools

- Clustering and dimensionality reduction techniques that help create graphical representations of high-dimensional and highly variable data.
- Univariate visualization and summary statistics for each field in the raw data set.
- Bivariate visualization and summary statistics that allow you to assess the relationship between each variable in a data set and the target variable under study.
- Multivariate visualization for mapping and understanding interactions between different fields in the data.
- K-means clustering is a clustering technique in unsupervised learning that assigns data points to K groups. The number of clusters is based on the distance from the centroid of each group. Data points closest to a particular centroid are grouped in the same category. K-means clustering is commonly used in market segmentation, pattern recognition and image compression.
- Predictive models, such as linear regression, use statistics and data to predict outcomes.

4.7.2 Types of Exploratory Data Analysis

- **Univariate non-graphical**: This is the simplest form of data analysis, where the data being analysed consists of only one variable. Since it is a single variable, it has no relation to cause or relationship. The main purpose of univariate analysis is to explain the data and find patterns in it.
- **Univariate graphical**: Non-graphical methods do not give the full picture of the data. So we need a graphical method. Common types of univariate graphs are:
  - o A stem and leaf plot showing all the data values and the shape of the distribution.
  - o A histogram or bar chart where each bar represents the frequency (count) or proportion (count/sum) of cases in a range of values.
  - o A box plot that graphically represents a 5-digit summary of the minimum, first quartile, median, third quartile and maximum values.
- **Multivariate non-graphical**: Multivariate data arises from more than one variable. Multivariate non-graphical EDA techniques generally show the relationship between two or more variables of the data through cross-tabulation or statistics.

- **Multivariate graphical**: Multivariate data uses graphs to show relationships between two or more data sets. The most commonly used charts are cluster bar charts or bar charts, where each group represents one level of a variable and each bar within a group represents the level of another variable.

4.8 Mapping and Cartopy

Cartopy is a Python package that consolidates infrastructure assets and the relationships between them into an intuitive diagram view powered by the Neo4j database. Cartopy is intended to enable a wide range of exploration and automation scenarios. It is particularly suited for uncovering hidden dependencies between assets in a service, allowing you to validate assumptions about security risks.

Service owners can create asset reports, red teams can discover attack paths, and blue teams can identify areas for security improvement. Everyone can benefit from using graphs to explore manually using a web front-end interface or in an automated way by calling APIs.

Cartopy is not the only security graph tool, but it differentiates itself by being fully-featured yet generic and extensible enough to help make anyone better understand their risk exposure, regardless of what platforms they use. Rather than being focused on one core scenario or attack vector like the other linked tools, Cartopy focuses on flexibility and exploration.

```
# Default imports
import numpy as np
%matplotlib nbagg
import matplotlib.pyplot as plt
import cartopy.crs as ccrs
```

Let us start with a simple plot of points:

```
np.random.seed(1)
x = 360 * np.random.rand(100)
y = 180 * np.random.rand(100) - 90
fig = plt.figure()
ax = fig.add_subplot(1, 1, 1)
ax.scatter(x, y)
```

Output:

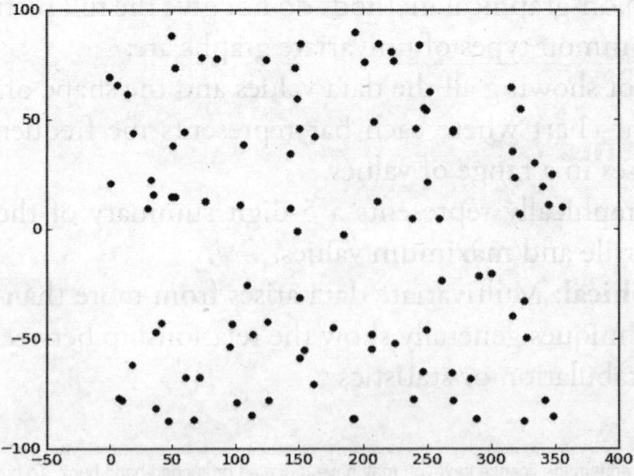

Why have we used x values between 0 and 360 and y values between −90 and 90? This is because it corresponds to the ranges for longitudes and latitudes. Let us rename them.

```
lon = x
lat = y
```

4.8.1 Projections

The first problem with mapping is deciding in which projection to create the map. Some interesting properties of maps are:

- Conformal: Preserve local angles. This means that local shapes are not distorted.
- Equal area: Area is preserved.
- Trade-off: Neither conformal nor equal area, but offset to reduce overall distortion.
- Equidistant: All distances from a point (or two points) are correct. Other equidistant properties are listed in the notes.
- Gnomonic: All great circles are straight lines.

Cartopy has several options. We can start with a basic `PlateCarree()` function (also called equirectangular or equidistant cylindrical). Specify the projection for which the resulting map is created by passing an instance of the projection class to the 'projection' keyword argument of `fig.add_subplot()`.

```
fig = plt.figure()
ax = fig.add_subplot(1, 1, 1,
                     projection=ccrs.PlateCarree())
ax.scatter(lon, lat)
```

Output:

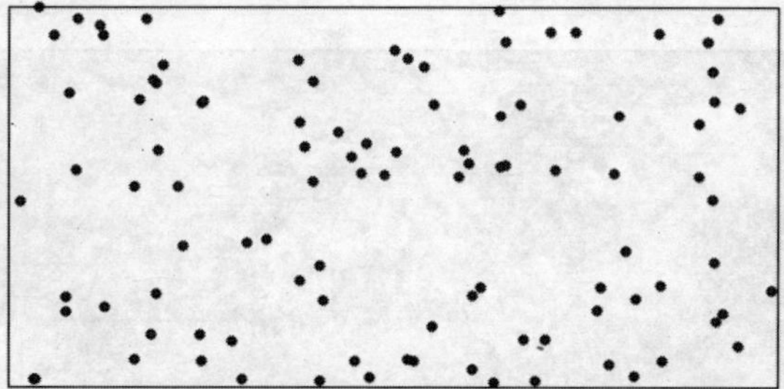

4.8.2 Adding Elements

Let us now add some coastlines:

```
fig = plt.figure()
ax = fig.add_subplot(1, 1, 1,
                     projection=ccrs.PlateCarree())
ax.scatter(lon, lat)
ax.coastlines()
```

Output:

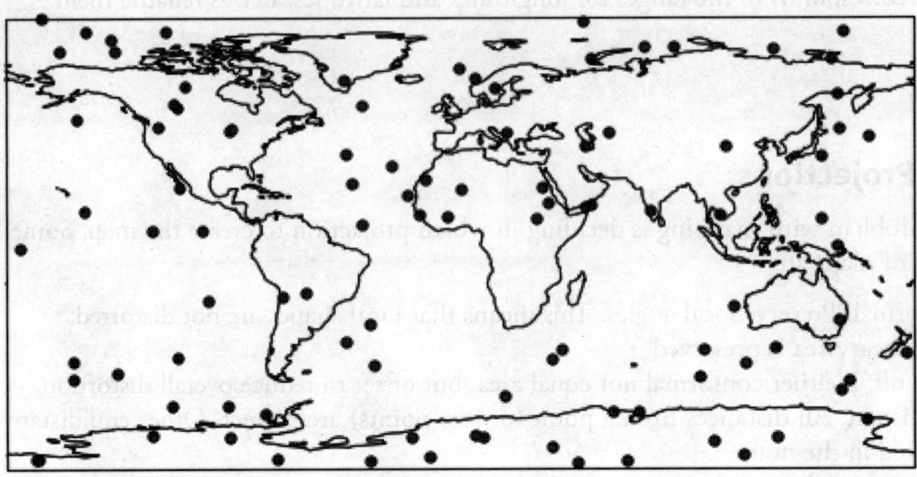

Let us add the oceans and some grid lines:

```
fig = plt.figure()
ax = fig.add_subplot(1, 1, 1,
                    projection=ccrs.PlateCarree())
ax.scatter(lon, lat)
ax.stock_img()
ax.coastlines()
ax.gridlines()
```

Output:

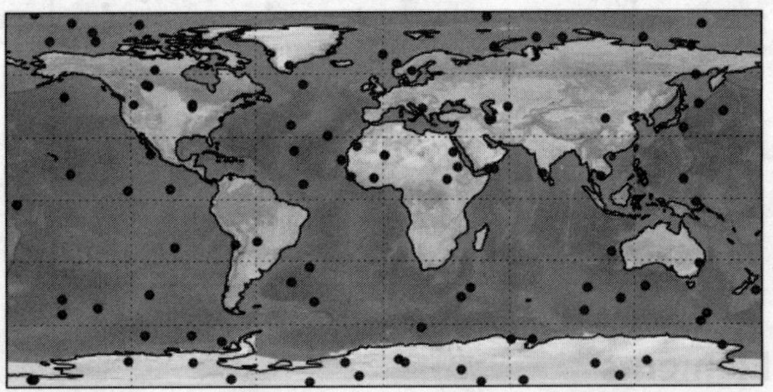

EXERCISES

Multiple Choice Questions

1. Which of the following is false?
   (a) Data visualization includes the ability to absorb information quickly
   (b) Data visualization is another form of visual art
   (c) Data visualization decreases insights and makes you take slower decisions
   (d) None of the above

2. Data can be visualized using?
   (a) Graphs
   (b) Charts
   (c) Maps
   (d) All of the above

3. To create a chart, Pyplot provides:
   (a) `figure()`
   (b) `chart()`
   (c) `plot()`
   (d) `print()`

4. Which of the following options describes a pie chart?
   (a) Comparison in different categories of data
   (b) Relationship between two sets of numeric data
   (c) Contribution of individual values to a total value
   (d) Data trend over a period of time

5. Identify the correct type of chart using the following hints:
   Hint 1: This chart is often used to visualize a trend in data over intervals of time.
   Hint 2: The line in this type of chart is often drawn chronologically.
   (a) Bar chart
   (b) Pie chart
   (c) Line chart
   (d) Scatter plot

6. The plot method on Series and DataFrame is just a simple wrapper around ___:
   (a) `Gplt.plot()`
   (b) `Plt.plot()`
   (c) `Plt.plotgraph()`
   (d) None of the above

7. Plots may also be adorned with error bars or tables:
   (a) True
   (b) False

8. The symbol that represent a single data value (point) is:
   (a) Tick
   (b) Marker
   (c) Title
   (d) Data label

9. Which of the following arguments cannot be used with `hist()`?
   (a) `Bin`
   (b) `Width`
   (c) `Histtype`
   (d) `Cumulative`

10. Which of the following data summary is not included in box plot?
    (a) Median
    (b) Quartile
    (c) Count
    (d) Maximum

Answers

1. (c) **2.** (d) **3.** (c) **4.** (c) **5.** (c) **6.** (b) **7.** (a) **8.** (b)
9. (a) **10.** (c)

Programming/Concept-based Questions

1. Create a figure of size 15 x 8 with two subplots: top and bottom. Draw two lines in the top axes, one green and one orange. Add a legend to the top plot, *Green* and *Orange*. Place this legend at the top-middle of the graph.

Answer:

```
fig, ax = plt.subplots(2, 1, figsize=(15,8))
ax[0].plot(df.index.values, df['a'], c='green')
ax[0].plot(df.index.values, df['b'], c='orange')
ax[0].legend(loc=9) # "9": upper center
ax[1].plot(df.index.values, df['c'], marker='o', lw=0) # set line width
= 0, means no visuable line
```

2. Create a figure with three subplots, aligned vertically. Create a bar graph for *a* and *b* on the first two, but in the last one, draw both *a* and *b*, but place *b* on top of *a*. (Hint: Use the bottom argument in the `Bar()` function). Make sure the colours for *a* and *b* are consistent in all the subplots.

Answer:

```
fig, ax = plt.subplots(3, 1, figsize=(15,18))
ax[0].bar(df.index.values, df['a'])
for i in range(df.shape[0]):
ax[0].text(i, df['a'][i]+1, df['a'][i], horizontalalignment='center')
ax[0].legend('a')
ax[1].bar(df.index.values, df['b'])
for i in range(df.shape[0]):
ax[1].text(i, df['b'][i]+1, df['b'][i], horizontalalignment='center')
ax[1].legend('b')
ax[2].bar(df.index.values, df['a'])
ax[2].bar(df.index.values, df['b'], bottom=df['a'])
for i in range(df.shape[0]):
ax[2].text(i, df['a'][i]+df['b'][i]+1, df['a'][i]+df['b'][i],
horizontalalignment='center')
ax[2].legend(['a','b'])
```

3. Create bars to represent the turnover for each market. Use labels to make sure your audience understands the graph.

Answer:

```
np.random.seed(0)
turnover_data = pd.DataFrame({'boardid': ['DAY', 'DAY_X', 'DAY_U', 'TSE'],
'turnover': np.random.randint(1e6, 1e9, 4)})
# sort by turnover value
turnover_data = turnover_data.sort_values(by='turnover').reset_
index().drop('index', axis=1)
# convert value to Million unit for easy-reading
turnover_data['turnover_simplified'] = turnover_data['turnover'] //
1000000
```

```
# market share
turnover_data['market_share'] = round((turnover_data['turnover'] /
sum(turnover_data['turnover'])*100), 1)
turnover_data
```

4. Read bathing soap and face wash of all the months and display it using subplots.

month_number	facecream	facewash	toothpaste	bathingsoap	shampoo	moisturizer	total_units	total_profit
1	2500	1500	5200	9200	1200	1500	21100	211000
2	2630	1200	5100	6100	2100	1200	18330	183300
3	2140	1340	4550	9550	3550	1340	22470	224700
4	3400	1130	5870	8870	1870	1130	22270	222700
5	3600	1740	4560	7760	1560	1740	20960	209600
6	2760	1555	4890	7490	1890	1555	20140	201400
7	2980	1120	4780	8980	1780	1120	29550	295500
8	3700	1400	5860	9960	2860	1400	36140	361400
9	3540	1780	6100	8100	2100	1780	23400	234000
10	1990	1890	8300	10300	2300	1890	26670	266700
11	2340	2100	7300	13300	2400	2100	41280	412800
12	2900	1760	7400	14400	1800	1760	30020	300200

Answer:

```
import pandas as pd
import matplotlib.pyplot as plt
df = pd.read_csv("D:\\Python\\Articles\\matplotlib\\sales_data.csv")
profitList = df ['total_profit'].tolist()
monthList = df ['month_number'].tolist()
plt.plot(monthList, profitList, label = 'Month-wise Profit data of last year')
plt.xlabel('Month number')
plt.ylabel('Profit in dollar')
plt.xticks(monthList)
plt.title('Company profit per month')
plt.yticks([100000, 200000, 300000, 400000, 500000])
plt.show()
```

Output:

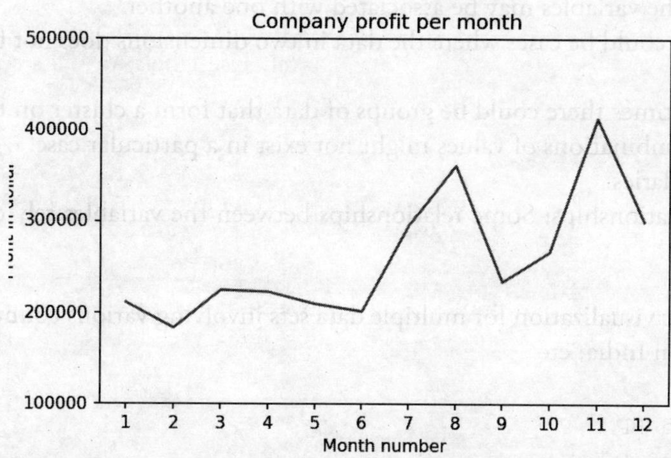

5. How can we visualize more than three dimensions of data in a single chart?
Answer: To visualize data beyond three dimensions, we need to use visual cues such as colour, size and shape.
Colour is used to depict both continuous and categorical data.
Marker size is used to represent continuous data. It can be used for categorical data as well. However, since size differences are difficult to detect, it is not considered the most appropriate choice for categorical data.
Shapes are used to represent different classes.

6. Why is data cleansing important for data visualization?
Answer: Data cleansing is used for identifying and removing errors and inconsistencies from data in order to enhance the quality of data. This process is crucial and emphasized because incorrect data can lead to poor analysis. This step ensures the quality of the data is met to prepare data for visualization.

7. What are some important features of a good data visualization?
Answer: The data visualisation should be light and must highlight essential aspects of the data; looking at important variables, what is relatively important, what are the trends and changes. Besides, data visualisation must be visually appealing but should not have unnecessary information in it.
Key aspects are:
   - Data positioning
   - Bars over circle and squares
   - Use of colour theory
   - Reducing chart junk by avoiding 3D charts and eliminating the use of pie charts to show proportions

8. What features might be visible in scatterplots?
Answer:
   - Correlation: The two variables might have a relationship; for example, one might depend on another. But this is not the same as causation.
   - Associations: The variables may be associated with one another.
   - Outliers: There could be cases where the data in two dimensions does not follow the general pattern.
   - Clusters: Sometimes there could be groups of data that form a cluster on the plot.
   - Gaps: Some combinations of values might not exist in a particular case.
   - Barriers: Boundaries.
   - Conditional relationships: Some relationships between the variables rely on a condition to be met.

9. Build a cartographic visualization for multiple data sets involving various countries of the world, states and districts in India, etc.
Answer:

```
import numpy as np
import pandas as pd
```

```
import matplotlib.pyplot as plt
import seaborn as sns
import geopandas as gpd
import shapefile as shp
from shapely.geometry import Point
sns.set_style('whitegrid')
fp = r'Maps_with_python\india-polygon.shp'
map_df = gpd.read_file(fp)
map_df_copy = gpd.read_file(fp)
map_df.head()
df = pd.read_csv('globallandslides.csv')
pd.set_option('display.max_columns', None)
df = df[df.country_name=="India"]
df["Year"] = pd.to_datetime(df["event_date"]).dt.year
df = df[df.landslide_category=="landslide"]
ls_df["admin_division_name"].replace("Nāgāland", "Nagaland",inplace = True)
ls_df["admin_division_name"].replace("Meghālaya",  "Meghalaya",inplace  =
True)
ls_df["admin_division_name"].replace("Tamil Nādu", "Tamil Nadu",inplace =
True)
ls_df["admin_division_name"].replace("Karnātaka",  "Karnataka",inplace  =
True)
ls_df["admin_division_name"].replace("Gujarāt", "Gujarat",inplace = True)
ls_df["admin_division_name"].replace("Arunāchal  Pradesh",  "Arunachal
Pradesh",inplace = True)
state_df = ls_df["admin_division_name"].value_counts()
state_df = state_df.to_frame()
state_df.reset_index(level=0, inplace=True)
state_df.columns = ['State', 'Count']
state_df.at[15,"Count"] = 69
state_df.at[0,"State"] = "Jammu and Kashmir"
state_df.at[20,"State"] = "Delhi"
state_df.drop(7)
merged = map_df.set_index('st_nm').join(state_df.set_index('State'))
merged['Count'] = merged['Count'].replace(np.nan, 0)
merged.head()
fig, ax = plt.subplots(1, figsize=(10, 10))
ax.axis('off')
ax.set_title('Number of landslides in India state-wise', fontdict={'fon-
tsize': '20', 'fontweight' : '10'})
merged.plot(column='Count',cmap='YlOrRd', linewidth=0.8, ax=ax, edge-
color='0',legend=True,markersize=[39.739192,  -104.990337],  legend_
kwds={'label': "Number of landslides"})
```

BIBLIOGRAPHY

1. "Matplotlib: Visualisation with Python". https://matplotlib.org
2. "Mujizi/Matplotlib tutorial". https://github.com/mujizi/matplotlib-tutorial
3. Interactive Dynamics for Visual Analysis, *ACM Queue*, February 20, 2012, Volume 10, issue 2.
4. Wikipedia on Interactive Visual Analysis. https://en.wikipedia.org/wiki/Interactive_visual_analysis

CHAPTER 5

Python scikit-learn

Learning Objectives

At the end of this chapter, you will be able to:

- Describe the groups of models provided by scikit-learn
- Identify the types of learning and salient frameworks, algorithms and their utility
- Explain case studies using the NumPy, pandas, SciPy and Matplotlib libraries
- Explain how to train and evaluate models using the scikit-learn framework

5.0 Introduction

The scikit-learn (sklearn) library is associated with Python. It is a free, open-source, useful and robust library for machine learning (ML) in Python. It has its own set of functions and syntaxes. It is an easy-to-use library that gives an immense amount of power and flexibility. It covers most ML tasks and scales to most data problems.

The scikit-learn library supports both supervised and unsupervised ML, and creates a range of efficient tools for ML and statistical modelling including classification, regression, clustering and dimensionality reduction through an identical interface in Python. It also provides various tools for model fitting, data pre-processing, model selection, model evaluation and many other utilities. The sklearn library is built on top of NumPy, SciPy and Matplotlib.

5.1 Features of scikit-learn

- It is a simple and efficient tool for processing data and for data analysis.
- It is built using NumPy, SciPy and Matplotlib.
- It is easily accessible to everyone and can be reused in many contexts.
- The scikit-learn library focuses more on data modelling instead of loading, manipulating and summarising data.
- It supports different classification, regression and clustering algorithms including support vector machines, random forests, decision trees, gradient boosting and k-means.

Some of the popular groups of models provided by sklearn are:

- **Supervised learning algorithms**: Linear regression, support vector machine (SVM), decision tree, etc.
- **Unsupervised learning algorithms:** Clustering, factor analysis, principal component analysis, unsupervised neural networks, etc.
- **Clustering**: To group unlabelled data such as k-means.
- **Cross-validation:** To check how accurate a supervised model is with different data subsets.
- **Data sets**: To test and generate data sets with specific properties for analysing model behaviour.
- **Feature extraction**: To select a subset of features out of the original features in order to reduce model complexity, enhance the computational efficiency of the models and reduce generalisation error introduced due to noise by irrelevant features.
- **Feature selection:** To reduce input labels or select significant attributes from which supervised models are created.
- **Parameter tuning:** To increase model accuracy, decrease the time the model runs, and decrease the costs associated with a model.
- **Multi-dimensional learning**: To summarise and represent complex multi-dimensional data.
- **Ensemble methods:** To capture and combine predictions from different supervised models.

5.2 INSTALLATION

The scikit-learn library can be installed using the pip package manager or the Conda package manager. The prerequisites for installing the sklearn library on Windows are:

- 64-bit version of Python 3
- Conda or pip (depending on user preference)

For pip users: These users can type the command given below to install the scikit-learn library on Windows:

```
pip install sklearn
```

To verify successful installation, run the following command:

```
python -m pip show scikit-learn
```

The package manager handles installation of the required dependencies for the scikit-learn library, which is not already installed.

```
import sklearn
```

For Conda users: Open the PowerShell prompt in Anaconda and use the following command:

```
conda install -c conda-forge scikit-learn
```

or

```
conda install sklearn
```

Type *y* for yes when prompted.

To use an environment for installation other than the base environment, use the following command:

```
conda create -n my-envconda activate my env
```

If the preferred method of installation is conda-forge, use the following command:

```
conda config --env --add channels conda-forge
```

5.3 Regression and Classifiers in scikit-learn

5.3.1 Linear Regression

One of the simplest and most widely used ML techniques is linear regression. This is a statistical technique that is used for performing predictive analysis. For continuous/real/numeric variables such as sales, salary, age and product price, among others, linear regression makes predictions. Linear regression is an ML algorithm based on supervised learning. It executes a regression operation. Regression uses independent variables to model a goal-prediction value. It is mostly used to determine how variables and forecasting relate to one another.

The linear regression algorithm, often known as linear regression, demonstrates a linear relationship:

- Between a dependent (*y*) and one or more independent (*x*) variables.
- That determines how the dependent variable's value changes in response to the independent variable
- That represents a sloped straight line giving the relationship between the variables

Hypothesis function for linear regression algorithm: At the time of training, the following is to be given:

- *x*: input training data (also called (parameter))
- *y*: labels/output to data (supervised learning)

In predicting the value of y for a given value of x, the model is trained to fit the best line as the output.

Forms of Linear Regression

Linear regression algorithms can be further categorised as follows:

- **Simple linear regression:** This type of linear regression technique is used when a single independent variable is utilised to determine the value of a numerical dependent variable.
- **Multiple linear regression:** Here, multiple independent variables are used to determine the value of a single output variable.

$Y = M_1X_1 + M_2X_2 + M_3X_3 + \ldots$

Implementation

```
from sklearn.linear_modelimport LinearRegression
regression_model = LinearRegression()
regression_model.fit(X_train, y_train)
```

Predicting the outcomes of the test set

```
y_predict = regression_model.predict(X_test)
```

Applications

- Used in calculating the impact of an independent variable on a dependent variable.
- Used to identify data patterns.
- Used to determine how much change in a dependent variable can be attributed to change in an independent variable.

5.3.2 Polynomial Regression

Polynomial regression is a non-linear regression. The relation between the dependent variable is fitted to the *n*th degree of the independent variable.

Two cases during model fitting that would cause the model to perform poorly are (Fig. 5.1):

- **Underfitting**: When the model cannot sufficiently fit the data, it is said to be underfitted. Low accuracy in the model is caused by underfitting. As a result, the relationship, trend or pattern in the training data cannot be captured by the model. More data needs to be used or the model's parameters should be optimised to prevent underfitting.
- **Overfitting**: This is the opposite of underfitting, and it occurs when a model performs exceptionally well on training data but poorly on test or validation data. The primary cause of overfitting may be due to the model memorising the training data and failing to generalise it on test data sets or unknown data sets. Overfitting can be decreased by performing feature selection or by using regularisation approaches.

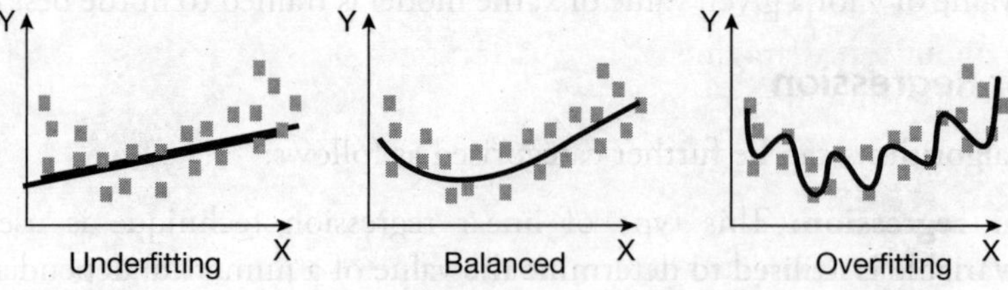

Figure 5.1 Underfitting, balanced fitting and overfitting

5.3.3 Logistic Regression

Like linear regression, logistic regression also represents data using an equation. To predict an output value, input values (*x*) are mixed linearly with weights or coefficient values (*y*). The output value being modelled is a binary value (0 or 1) rather than a numeric value, which is a significant distinction from linear regression.

Here is an illustration of a logistic regression formula:

$$y = e^\wedge(b0 + b1*x) / (1+ e^\wedge(b0 + b1*x))$$

The term *b*0 is the bias or intercept term, *b*1 is the coefficient for the single input value, and *y* is the predicted output.

Implementation: To implement logistic regression, the required library needs to be imported and data for training is to be passed and the best fit line is to be added to the model.

```
from sklearn.linear_model import LogisticRegression
lr = LogisticRegression(random_state = 0)
lr.fit(X_train, y_train)
```

Predicting the outcomes of the test set

```
y_pred_lr = lr.predict(X_test)
```

Applications

Recognizing spam emails: If an email is spam, assign it a class of 1, and if it is not, assign it a class of 0. The mail body's many properties are examined in order to determine this. These properties consist of:

- The sender
- Spelling mistakes
- Keywords such as 'bank details', 'lucky', 'winner' and 'congratulations'
- Contact information or a URL in the email

Text editing: Text is first pre-processed, the features are extracted and logistic regression is used to make an assertion about a text fragment. Logistic regression produces good results in toxic speech detection, topic classification for questions to support and email sorting.

5.3.4 Decision Trees

A decision tree is a form of supervised learning that can be applied to both classification and regression problems. Rules that can be represented by a tree structure are generated by the algorithm using training data.

A decision tree has leaf nodes, internal nodes and a root node, like any other tree representation. A condition on attributes is represented by an internal node. The results of the condition are represented by branches and the class label is represented by a leaf node.

By following the if-else style principles, classification can begin at the root node at the top and work its way down to the leaf node. The class label of the classification problem is the leaf node.

Both categorical and numerical data can be used with decision trees. In contrast, other ML techniques need encoding to numeric values and are unable to handle categorical data.

Implementation

```
from sklearn.tree import DecisionTreeClassifier
dt = DecisionTreeClassifier(criterion = 'entropy', random_state = 0)
dt.fit(X_train, y_train)
```

Predicting the outcomes of the test set

```
y_pred = dt.predict(X_test)
```

Decision tree classifiers for categorical data: For categorical data, conversion from non-numeric data into numeric data is required. One-hot encoding is a method for achieving this. It creates separate columns for each unique value in a categorical column. If the column matches the original value, the column is given the value of 1; otherwise the value is 0.

5.4 Support Vector Machine (SVM)

SVM is a supervised ML technique that can be applied to classification or regression problems. However, classification issues are where it is most frequently used. Each data point in the SVM method is represented as a data point in *n*-dimensional space, with the value of each feature being the value of a certain coordinate. The classification is carried out by selecting the hyper-plane that separates the two classes.

The scikit-learn library includes SVM, and the same methodology is used for it (import library, object creation, fitting model and prediction).

The kernel functions in SVC can be accessed at:

https://scikit-learn.org/stable/modules/svm.html#kernel-functions

When the data points cannot be separated linearly, the polynomial, RBF and sigmoid kernels are very helpful. Here, the RBF kernel is used in this portion.

```
from sklearn.svm import SVC
 svc_rbf = SVC(kernel = 'rbf', random_state = 0)
svc_rbf.fit(X_train, y_train)
```

Predicting the outcomes of the test set

```
y_pred_svc_rbf = svc_rbf.predict(X_test)
```

5.5 K-Nearest Neighbor (K-NN)

The unique feature of the k-nearest neighbor approach is that this formula is determined at the time of prediction rather than fitting. The K-NN algorithm begins by locating the closest neighbours of a new data point when it is introduced. The values of those neighbours are then used to predict the value of the new data point.

Implementation

```
from sklearn.neighbors
import KNeighborsClassifier
knn=KNeighborsClassifier(n_neighbors= 5,metric='minkowski', p = 2)
knn.fit(X_train, y_train)
```

Predicting the outcomes of the test set

```
y_pred_knn = knn.predict(X_test)
```

Minkowski has been used as the fast distance metric function in this case.

5.6 Case Studies

1. **Importing libraries**

```
import numpyas np import pandas aspd
import matplotlib.pyplotas plt
importseabornas snsfrom IPython
import get_ipython
import warnings
warnings.filterwarnings("ignore")
```

2. **Importing a data set**

```
data = pd.read_csv('/content/online_education.csv')
```

The entire data set can be found at:

https://github.com/tanishpophale53/Analysis-and-Classification-of-Online-learning-of-students-according-to-Flexibility-Level/blob/main/online_education.csv

3. **Printing the first five rows of the data set**

```
data.head()
```

	Education Level	Institution Type	Gender	Age	Device	IT Student	Location	Financial Condition	Internet Type	Network Type	Flexibility Level
0	University	Private	Male	23	Tab	No	Town	Mid	Wifi	4G	Moderate
1	University	Private	Female	23	Mobile	No	Town	Mid	Mobile Data	4G	Moderate
2	College	Public	Female	18	Mobile	No	Town	Mid	Wifi	4G	Moderate
3	School	Private	Female	11	Mobile	No	Town	Mid	Mobile Data	4G	Moderate
4	School	Private	Female	18	Mobile	No	Town	Poor	Mobile Data	3G	Low

4. Printing the last five rows of the data set

```
data.tail()
```

	Education Level	Institution Type	Gender	Age	Device	IT Student	Location	Financial Condition	Internet Type	Network Type	Flexibility Level
1200	College	Private	Female	18	Mobile	No	Town	Mid	Wifi	4G	Low
1201	College	Private	Female	18	Mobile	No	Rural	Mid	Wifi	4G	Moderate
1202	School	Private	Male	11	Mobile	No	Town	Mid	Mobile Data	3G	Moderate
1203	College	Private	Female	18	Mobile	No	Rural	Mid	Wifi	4G	Low
1204	School	Private	Female	11	Mobile	No	Town	Poor	Mobile Data	3G	Moderate

5. Printing the dimension of the data set

```
data.shape()
```

Output: (1205, 11)

6. Printing all the columns of the data set

```
data.columns()
```

Output:

```
Index(['Education Level', 'Institution Type', 'Gender', 'Age', 'Device',
       'IT Student', 'Location', 'Financial Condition', 'Internet Type',
       'Network Type', 'Flexibility Level'],
      dtype='object')
```

7. Finding all the duplicate values in the data set

```
data.duplicated().sum()
```

Output: 980

8. Printing the null values of a particular column of a data set

```
data.isnull().sum()
```

Output:

```
Education Level        0
Institution Type       0
Gender                 0
Age                    0
Device                 0
IT Student             0
Location               0
Financial Condition    0
Internet Type          0
Network Type           0
Flexibility Level      0
dtype: int64
```

9. Displaying the information of each column in the data set

```
data.info()
```

Output:

```
 #   Column               Non-Null Count  Dtype
---  ------               --------------  -----
 0   Education Level      1205 non-null   object
 1   Institution Type     1205 non-null   object
 2   Gender               1205 non-null   object
 3   Age                  1205 non-null   int64
 4   Device               1205 non-null   object
 5   IT Student           1205 non-null   object
 6   Location             1205 non-null   object
 7   Financial Condition  1205 non-null   object
 8   Internet Type        1205 non-null   object
 9   Network Type         1205 non-null   object
 10  Flexibility Level    1205 non-null   object
dtypes: int64(1), object(10)
memory usage: 103.7+ KB
```

10. Displaying a short description of the data set

```
data.describe()
```

Output:

	Age
count	1205.000000
mean	17.065560
std	5.830369
min	9.000000
25%	11.000000
50%	18.000000
75%	23.000000
max	27.000000

11. Finding unique values (pandas nunique() is used to obtain a count of unique values)

```
data.nunique()
```

Output:

```
Education Level         3
Institution Type        2
Gender                  2
Age                     6
Device                  3
IT Student              2
Location                2
Financial Condition     3
Internet Type           2
Network Type            3
Flexibility Level       3
dtype: int64
```

12. Plotting a histogram for each column of a data set

```
for i in data.columns:
    plt.figure(figsize=(16,5)) sns.histplot( data[i], bins = 10)
    plt.xticks(rotation = 90)
    plt.show()
```

Output: (You can plot the graph for other columns of the data set in a similar manner)

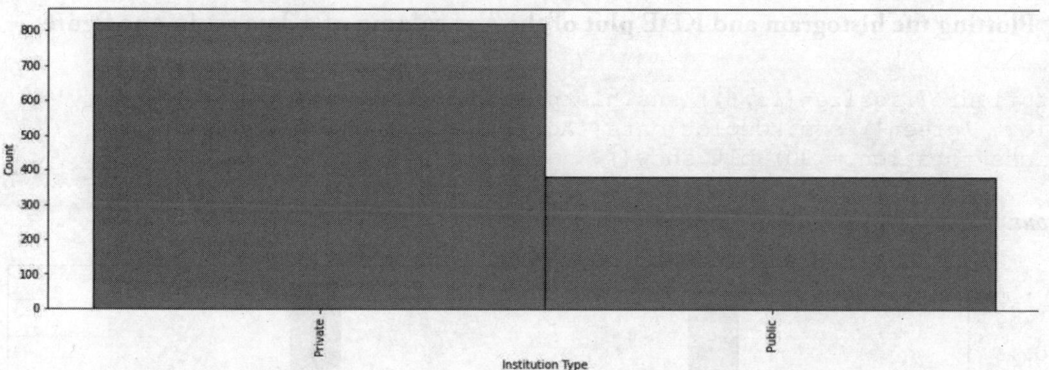

13. Plotting the count plot for each value of a particular column of a data set

```
for i in data.columns:
    plt.figure(figsize=(15,6)) sns.countplot(data[i], data = data, palette
    = 'hls') plt.xticks(rotation = 90)
    plt.show()
```

Output:

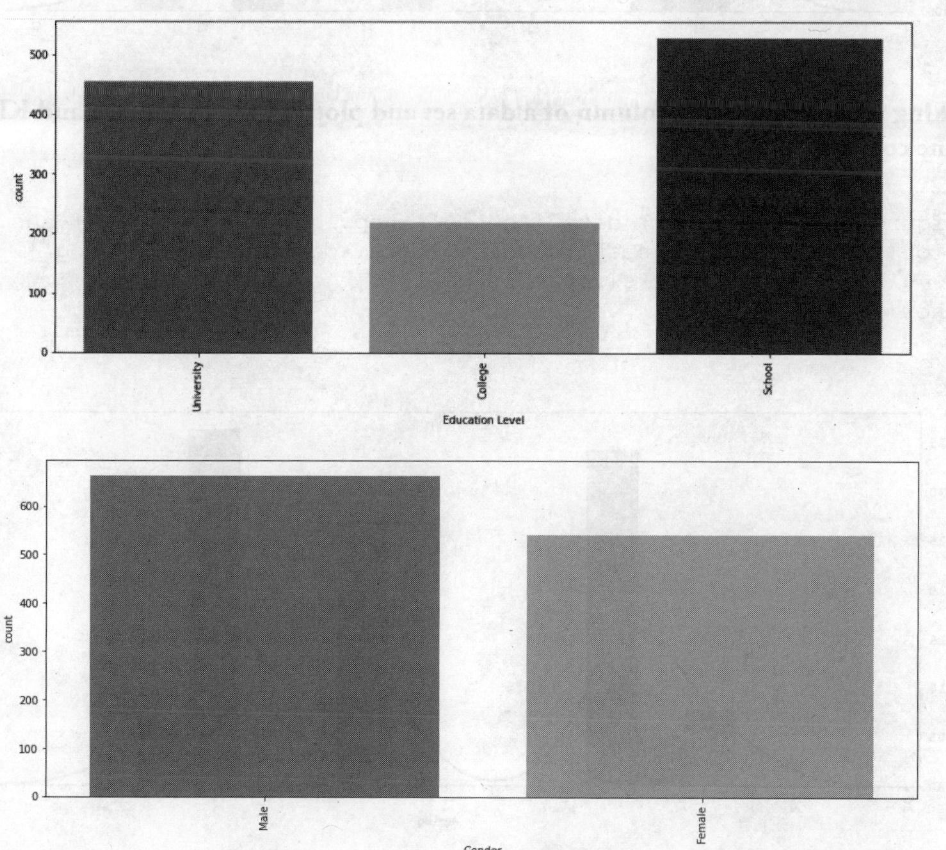

...and so on.

14. Plotting the histogram and KDE plot of the Age column of a data set in one figure

```
plt.figure(figsize=(15,6)) sns.histplot(data['Age'], stat = 'density',
color= 'green') sns.kdeplot(data['Age'], color='black') plt.
xticks(rotation = 90) plt.show()
```

Output:

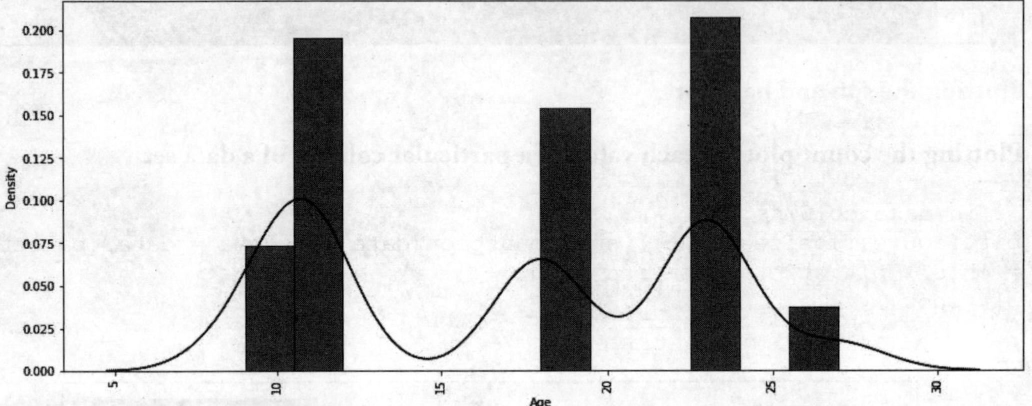

15. Taking the log of the Age column of a data set and plotting the histogram and KDE of the same column

```
plt.figure(figsize=(15,6)) data['AgeLog']= np.log(data['Age']+1) sns.
histplot(data['AgeLog'], stat 'density') sns.kdeplot(data['AgeLog'],
color = 'black') plt.xticks(rotation =90)
plt.show()
```

Output:

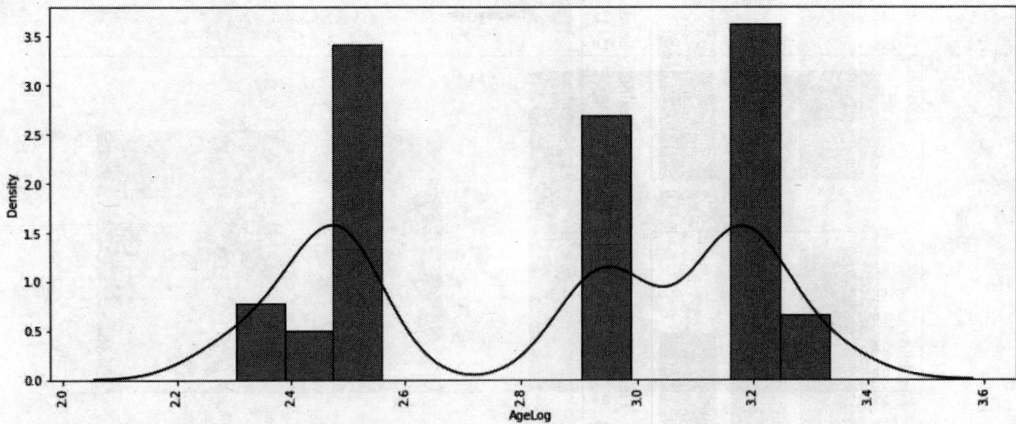

16. Pre-processing the data set using the sklearn library

```
from sklearn.preprocessingimport LabelEncoder
le = LabelEncoder()
FlexibilityLevel = le.fit_transform(data['Flexibility Level'])
data['Flexibility Level'] = FlexibilityLevel
categorical_features = ['Education Level','Gender','Institution
Type','Device','ITStudent','Location','Financial Condition','Internet
Type','Network Type']
```

17. Plotting the sub and bar plot

```
fig, axes = plt.subplots(3, 3, figsize=(10,10))
axes = [ax for axes_row in axes for ax in axes_row]
target =  'Flexibility Level'
for i,c inenumerate(categorical_features):
  sns.barplot(data[c], data[target], ax=axes[i], palette = 'hls')
  axes[i].set_ylabel('Flexibility Level', fontsize=14)
  axes[i].set_xlabel(c, fontsize=14)
plt.tight_layout()
```

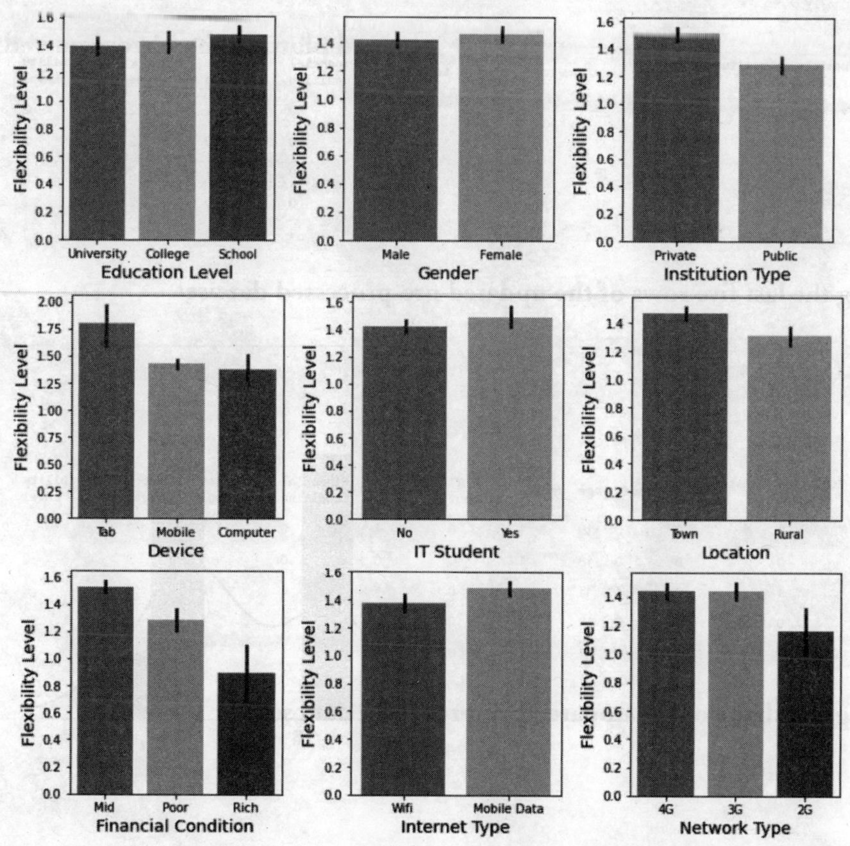

18. Fit transforming

```
EducationLevel= le.fit_transform(data['Education Level'])
Gender = le.fit_transform(data['Gender'])
InstitutionType = le.fit_transform(data['Institution Type'])
Device = le.fit_transform(data['Device'])
ITStudent= le.fit_transform(data['IT Student'])
Location = le.fit_transform(data['Location'])
FinancialCondition =le.fit_transform(data['FinancialCondition'])
InternetType = le.fit_transform(data['Internet Type']) NetworkType =
le.fit_transform(data['Network Type'])
data['Education Level'] = EducationLevel data['Gender'] = Gender
data['Institution Type'] = InstitutionType data['Device'] = Deviceda
data['IT Student'] = ITStudent data['Location'] = Location data['Financial
Condition'] = FinancialCondition data['Internet Type'] = InternetType
data['Network Type'] = NetworkType
```

19. Printing the first five rows of the updated pre-processed data set

```
data.head()
```

Output:

	Education Level	Institution Type	Gender	Age	Device	IT Student	Location	Financial Condition	Internet Type	Network Type	Flexibility Level	AgeLog
0	2	0	1	23	2	0	1	0	1	2	2	3.178054
1	2	0	0	23	1	0	1	0	0	2	2	3.178054
2	0	1	0	18	1	0	1	0	1	2	2	2.944439
3	1	0	0	11	1	0	1	0	0	2	2	2.484907
4	1	0	0	18	1	0	1	1	0	1	1	2.944439

20. Printing the last five rows of the updated pre-processed dat aset

```
data.tail()
```

Output:

	Education Level	Institution Type	Gender	Age	Device	IT Student	Location	Financial Condition	Internet Type	Network Type	Flexibility Level	AgeLog
1200	0	0	0	18	1	0	1	0	1	2	1	2.944439
1201	0	0	0	18	1	0	0	0	1	2	2	2.944439
1202	1	0	1	11	1	0	1	0	0	1	2	2.484907
1203	0	0	0	18	1	0	0	0	1	2	1	2.944439
1204	1	0	0	11	1	0	1	1	0	1	2	2.484907

21. Printing the shape of the updated pre-processed data set

```
X.shape
```

Output: (1205, 11)

```
Y.shape
```

Output: (1205)

22. Splitting the data set into train and test

```
from sklearn.model_selectionimport
train_test_split train_x,test_x,train_y, test_y= train_test_split(x,
y,test_size= 0.2, random_state = 100)
```

23. Fit transforming the data set

```
from sklearn.preprocessingimport StandardScaler
sc = StandardScaler()
train_x sc.fit_transform(train_x)
test_x = sc.fit_transform(test_x)
```

24. Applying various algorithms to obtain the highest accuracy

Applying the XG Boost algorithm

```
import xgboostas xgb
clf = xgb.XGBClassifier()
clf.fit(train_x, train_y)
print(f"Train score={clf.score(train_x, train_y):.3}")
print(f"Test score={clf.score(test_x, test_y):.3}")
y_pred_test = clf.predict(test_x)
```

Output:
Train score=0.759
Test score=0.743

Applying the LGB Classifier algorithm

```
import lightgbmas lgb
clf = lgb.LGBMClassifier()
clf.fit(train_x, train_y)
print(f"Train score={clf.score(train_x, train_y):.7}")
print(f"Test score={clf.score(test_x, test_y):.3}")
clf.score(test_x,test_y)
```

Output:
Train score=0.8350622
Test score=0.846
0.8464730290456431

Applying the Gradient Boosting algorithm

```
from sklearn.ensembleimport GradientBoostingClassifier
gradient_booster =GradientBoostingClassifier(learning_rate=0.1) gradient_
booster.fit(train_x,train_y)
gradient_booster.score(test_x,test_y)
```

Output:
0.7842323651452282

Applying the AdaBoost Classifier algorithm

```
from sklearn.ensembleimport AdaBoost
Classifierabc =AdaBoostClassifier(n_estimators=14,learning_rate=0.1)
model = abc.fit(train_x, train_y)
y_pred = model.predict(test_x) abc.score(test_x, test_y)
```

Output:
0.5809128630705395

Applying the SVM algorithm

```
from sklearnimport svm
from sklearn.svmimport SVC
classifier_svm=SVC(kernel="rbf")
classifier_svm.fit(train_x,train_y)
SVC(C=1.0, cache_size=250, class_weight=None, coef0=0.1, decision_
function_shape='ovr', degree=3, gamma='auto_deprecated', kernel='rbf',
max_iter=-1, probability=False, random_state=None, shrinking=True,
tol=0.005, verbose=False)
classifier_svm.score(test_x, test_y)
```

Output:
0.7717842323651453

Applying the Decision Tree Classifier algorithm

```
from sklearn.treeimport DecisionTreeClassifier
model = DecisionTreeClassifier()
model.fit(train_x, train_y)
y_pred = model.predict(test_x)
print("Training Accuracy:", model.score(train_x, train_y))
print("Testing Accuracy:", model.score(test_x, test_y))
```

Output:
Training Accuracy: 0.8547717842323651
Testing Accuracy: 0.8547717842323651

Generating the classification report

```
from sklearn.metricsimport classification_report
print(classification_report(test_y, y_pred))
```

Output:

```
              precision    recall  f1-score   support

           0       0.81      0.96      0.88        23
           1       0.81      0.88      0.84        92
           2       0.90      0.82      0.86       126

    accuracy                           0.85       241
   macro avg       0.84      0.88      0.86       241
weighted avg       0.86      0.85      0.85       241
```

Representing a tree graphically

```
from sklearnimport tree
plt.figure(figsize=(10,15))
tree.plot_tree(model, filled=True)
 plt.show()
```

Output:

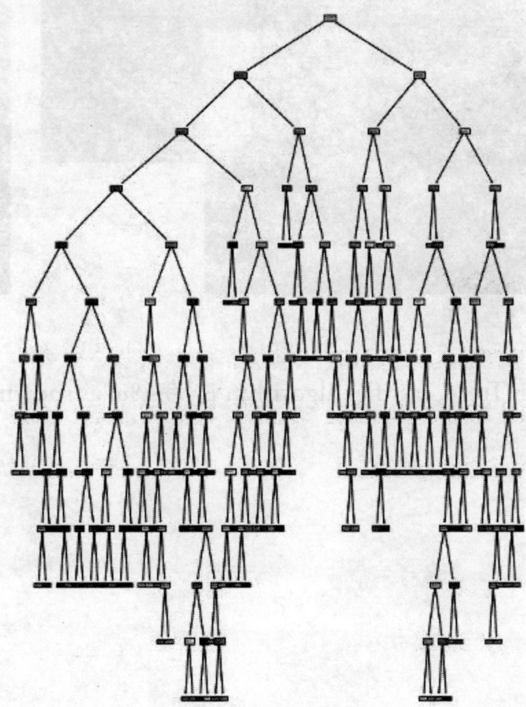

Representing feature importance on output

```
model.feature_importances_
```

Output:
array([0.05918089, 0.09620064, 0.10486635,0.09055473, 0.05481044,0.0610596,0.08365364, 0.17926294,0.09003702, 0.09097999,0.08939375])

Representing the confusion matrix of the Decision Tree Classifier algorithm in terms of heat map

```
from sklearn.metricsimport confusion_matrix
y_pred_clf = clf.predict(test_x)
cf_matrix = confusion_matrix(test_y, y_pred_clf)
sns.heatmap(cf_matrix, annot=True)
plt.title("Confusion Matrix for Decision Tree", fontsize=14,
fontname="DejaVu Sans", y=1.03)
```

Output:

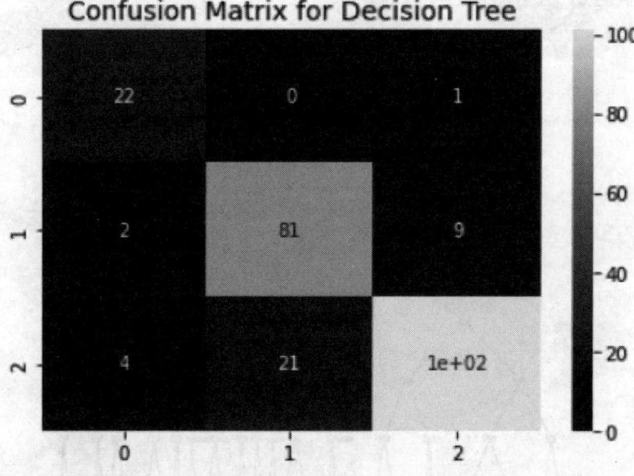

So, accuracy by the Decision Tree Classifier algorithm is 85.4%, as shown in the above diagram.

EXERCISES

Multiple Choice Questions

1. Which of the following is a good test data set characteristic?
   (a) Large enough to yield meaningful results
   (b) Representative of the data set as a whole
   (c) Both (a) and (b)
   (d) None of the above

2. How do you handle missing or corrupted data in a data set?
   (a) Drop missing rows or columns
   (b) Replace missing values with mean/median/mode
   (c) Assign a unique category to missing values
   (d) All of the above

3. Which of the following are features of scikit-learn?
   (a) It is an open-source library and can be commercially used under the BSD licence
   (b) It is used to identify useful attributes to create supervised models
   (c) It is used to extract features from data to define attributes in an image
   (d) All of the above

4. Which of the following statements is false in the case of the K-NN algorithm?
   (a) For a very large value of k, points from other classes may be included in the neighbourhood.
   (b) For a very small value of k, the algorithm is very sensitive to noise.
   (c) K-NN is used only for classification problem statements.
   (d) K-NN is a lazy learner.

5. Which of the following is false about correlation and covariance?
   (a) Zero correlation does not necessarily imply independence between variables.
   (b) Correlation and covariance values are the same.
   (c) Covariance and correlation are always the same sign.
   (d) Correlation is the standardized version of covariance.

6. How do you choose the right node while constructing a decision tree?
   (a) An attribute having high entropy
   (b) An attribute having high entropy and information gain
   (c) An attribute having the lowest information gain
   (d) An attribute having the highest information gain

7. Which of the following is/are true regarding SVM?
   (a) For two-dimensional data points, the separating hyper-plane learnt by a linear SVM will be a straight line.
   (b) In theory, a Gaussian kernel SVM cannot model any complex separating hyper-plane.
   (c) For every kernel function used in a SVM, one can obtain an equivalent closed form basis expansion.
   (d) Overfitting in an SVM is not a function of the number of support vectors.

8. ______ provides some built-in data sets that can be used for testing purposes.
   (a) scikit-learn
   (b) Classification

(c) Regression
(d) None of the above

9. Predicting the amount of rainfall in a region based on various cues is a _______ problem.
(a) Supervised learning
(b) Unsupervised learning
(c) Clustering
(d) None of the above

10. Which of the following can only be used when training data is linearly separable?
(a) Linear hard-margin SVM
(b) Linear logistic regression
(c) Linear soft-margin SVM
(d) The centroid method

11. The k-means algorithm:
(a) Requires the dimensions of the feature space to be no bigger than the number of samples
(b) Has the smallest value of the objective function when k = 1
(c) Minimizes the within-class variance for a given number of clusters
(d) Converges to the global optimum if and only if the initial means are chosen as some of the samples themselves

12. Which of the following is not supervised learning?
(a) PCA
(b) Decision tree
(c) Linear regression
(d) Naive Bayesian

13. For a large k value, the k-nearest neighbor model becomes _______ and _______.
(a) Complex, Overfitted
(b) Complex, Underfitted
(c) Simple, Underfitted
(d) Simple, Overfitted

Answers

1. (c)	**2.** (d)	**3.** (d)	**4.** (c)	**5.** (b)	**6.** (d)	**7.** (a)	**8.** (a)
9. (a)	**10.** (a)	**11.** (c)	**12.** (a)	**13.** (c)			

Programming/Concept-based Questions

1. What is the problem if you call the `fit()` method multiple times with different x and y data? How can you overcome this issue?
Answer: When you use `model.fit(features train, label train)` on an initial model, the model immediately begins to train using the features and labels you have provided. If you call `model.fit(features train2, label train2)` once more, training will restart with the supplied data, and the prior results will be discarded. The following internal model components will be reset: weights, fitted coefficients and bias.
If we want our previously calculated information to be retained and to train further using the subsequent data, we can utilise the `partial_fit()` method to solve this problem.

2. How will you know which ML algorithm to use for your classification problem?
Answer: Although there is no specific rule for selecting an algorithm for a classification problem, you can use the following principles:
   - Test and cross-validate various algorithms if accuracy is a concern.
   - Use low-variance, high-bias models if the training data set is small.
   - Use high-variance, low-bias models if the training data set is large.

3. When will you use classification over regression?
   Answer: When your target variable is categorical, classification is applied; when it is a continuous variable, regression is used. The group of supervised ML algorithms includes both classification and regression techniques.
   Classification issues include the following examples:
   - Making a yes/no judgement
   - Determining gender
   - Species of animal
   - Colour type

   Regression issues include the following:
   - Estimating a product's sales and price
   - Estimating a team's final score
   - Predicting the amount of rainfall

4. What are the assumptions you need to make before starting with linear regression?
   Answer: For a linear regression model, there are essentially five assumptions:
   - Multiple-variate normality
   - No auto-correlation
   - Homoscedasticity
   - The linear relationship
   - No or minimal multicollinearity

5. What is cross-validation?
   Answer: The statistical resampling technique called cross-validation in ML uses various data set subsets to train and evaluate an ML algorithm over a number of rounds. Cross-validation is a technique used to test a model's predictive ability using new data that was not used to train the model. Cross-validation prevents data overfitting.
   K-fold cross-validation is the most common resampling method that divides the entire data set into K sets of equal size.

6. What is semi-supervised ML?
   Answer: Unsupervised learning does not require any training data, whereas supervised learning requires labelled training data. In the case of semi-supervised learning, the training data is made up primarily of unlabelled data and only a small part of it is labelled.

7. How does the support vector machine algorithm handle self-learning?
   Answer: The SVM algorithm has a learning rate and expansion rate which takes care of self-learning. The learning rate neutralizes the hyper-planes for making incorrect moves while the expansion rate provides handling and finding of the maximum separation area between different classes.

8. Which is more important to you – model accuracy or model performance?
   Answer: Model accuracy is an important parameter of model performance. The accuracy of the model and performance of the model are directly proportional; hence, the more accurate the predictions are, the better the performance of the model.

9. You are given a cancer detection data set. Let us suppose when you build a classification model

that you achieved an accuracy of 96%. Why should you not be happy with your model performance? What can you do about it?

Answer: You can do the following:

- Add more data
- Treat missing outlier values
- Perform feature engineering
- Perform feature selection
- Use multiple algorithms
- Carry out algorithm tuning
- Use the ensemble method
- Use cross-validation

BIBLIOGRAPHY

1. skikit-learn. https://scikit-learn.org/stable/
2. skikit-learn 1.2.2. https://pypi.org/project/scikit-learn/
3. Pedregosa et al. scikit-learn: Machine Learning in Python. ACM Digital Library, published November 2011. https://dl.acm.org/doi/10.5555/1953048.2078195
4. scikit-learn-extra documentation. https://scikit-learn-extra.readthedocs.io/en/stable/

CHAPTER 6

Environment Set-up: TensorFlow and Keras

LEARNING OBJECTIVES

At the end of this chapter, you will be able to:

- Explain the TensorFlow basics and its architecture
- Describe how to install and use TensorFlow and Keras
- Write programs using the functions of TensorFlow and Keras

6.0 INTRODUCTION TO TENSORFLOW

TensorFlow (TF) is a library by Google to implement fast computing. It is used to create deep learning models. It was made public in 2015 and the first stable version appeared in 2017. It is an open-source library in which you can implement deep learning models, modify code and redistribute it.

It allows deployment of computation across a variety of platforms such as central processing unit (CPU), graphics processing unit (GPU) and tensor processing unit (TPU) and from desktop to cloud and to servers and mobiles and edge devices. Neural networks work on multi-dimensional data arrays called tensors; hence this library is called TensorFlow. It was earlier called KuberFlow for operation and deployment on Kubernetes.

Its functionality is the same as of a flowchart to perform operations on graphs. The input is fed into one end, then flows through this system of multiple operations and the computed results are provided as output at the other end.

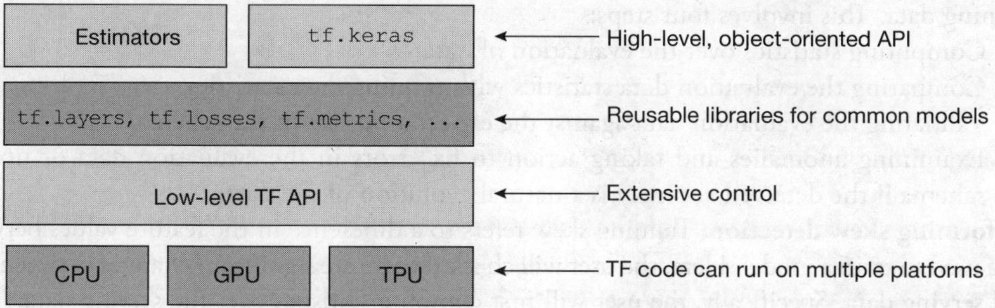

Figure 6.1 Architecture of TensorFlow

TensorFlow has a rich collection of APIs to manage all aspects of machine learning (ML) systems. TensorFlow code can run on multiple platforms and extensive control over it can be given by low-level TF APIs. These APIs are used to create and explore new ML algorithms. TensorFlow provides reusable libraries for common models of deep learning and, on the top layer, high-level object-oriented APIs are available for direct use in programs. The layered architecture of the TensorFlow toolkit is given in Fig. 6.1.

6.1 TensorFlow Features

- **Open-source library:** As it is an open-source library, it is in wide use. Standard reusable models are available to make it easy to solve complex problems.
- **Easy to run:** TensorFlow has its own hardware to train the neural models; this is known as cloud TPU. TensorFlow applications can run on the desktop, cloud, android, servers and on various platforms like CPU, GPU and TPU.
- **Abstraction and flexibility:** TensorFlow is an abstract model and helps reduce code length and development time. It provides reusable code so that the user can focus on logic while using APIs for complex operations.
- **Fast and effective debugging:** TensorFlow uses computational graphing methods that support an easy-to-execute paradigm. It uses multi-dimensional arrays to represent tensors and the connection between them. Representing information in structures makes for fast and effective debugging.
- **Scalable and easy experimentation:** Models built using TensorFlow are scalable and we can use the same model with different data sets. It also allows for synchronous and asynchronous learning techniques.
- **Understanding the training data**: The user can understand the training data using TensorFlow data validation (TFDV). This uses the Facets library to create the visualization that displays the charts showing the distribution of individual features and various statistics. The user can check for potential errors in the data and drill down to understand specific slices of the data.
- **Inferring a schema:** TFDV uses a set of reasonable heuristics to auto-generate the initial schema. In this step, the user will use TFDV to infer an initial schema based on the training data. Then the user will inspect the inferred schema and modify any properties if needed. The schema is represented as a protocol buffer and can be modified through its Python API.
- **Validating the evaluation data:** The user can validate if the evaluation data is even with the training data. This involves four steps:
  - Computing statistics over the evaluation of data
  - Comparing the evaluation data statistics with training data statistics
  - Validating the evaluation data against the expectations set in the schema
  - Examining anomalies and taking action to fix errors in the evaluation data or update the schema if the detected anomaly is a natural evolution of the data
- **Performing skew detection:** Training skew refers to a difference in the feature values between the data used to train a model. Here, the user will check if there are significant changes between training and serving data. Specifically, the user will first compute statistics over the serving data. Then the user will visualize side-by-side the statistics of training and serving data to look for potential errors or drifts and perform skew detection between the training and serving data to identify the features whose distribution over training data is different from that seen over serving data.

6.2 Benefits of TensorFlow

- **Data flow graphs:** TensorFlow combines the data flow of high-level programming models and the low-level efficiency of parameter servers. It is very powerful because it uses TPU which makes computation faster than CPU and GPU.
- **High GPU utilization:** TensorFlow allows concurrent and distributed execution of subgraphs of the overall graph. It is fast and uses a single data flow graph to represent all the computation. GPU utilization is high as it defers execution until the program is complete.
- **Community support:** TensorFlow has huge community support such as Open AI, Google, Twitter and Airbnb. They use TensorFlow back ends for projects.
- **Mobile interfaces:** Nowadays, many applications require mobile interfaces. TensorFlow Lite supports mobile devices. It allow ML programs to run on GPU and TPU while having an interface on mobiles.
- **Large-scale ML:** Large ML models can be created in TensorFlow. Large data sets can be used for training and testing. It provides fault-tolerant, distributed and optimized architecture to support this.

6.3 Installation of TensorFlow

To install TensorFlow, follow the steps given below:

Step 1: Verify the version of Python installed.

Step 2: Use pip to install Anaconda. It will execute and install the Anaconda framework on your system.

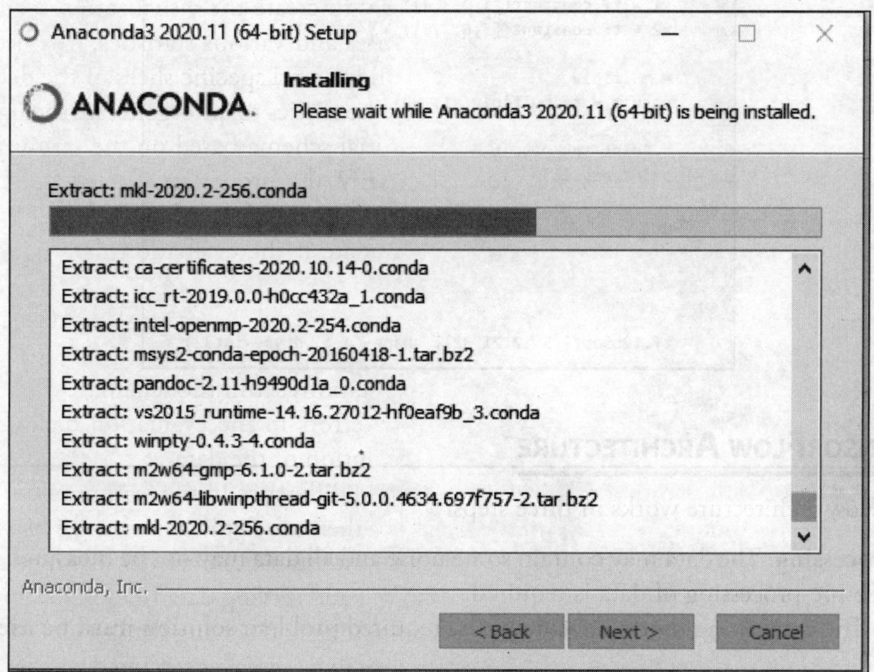

Step 3: After successful installation, at the Anaconda prompt, use the conda command.

Step 4: Initialise installation of TensorFlow, as follows:

```
conda create -n tftensorflow
```

Step 5: The TensorFlow module needs to be activated, as follows:

```
conda activate tf
```

Step 6: Use pip to install Tensorflow in the system.

```
pip install tensorflow
pip install tensorflow-gpu
```

TensorFlow is now ready to be used.

The code for the first program implementation is as follows:

```
>> activate tensorflow
>> python (activating python shell)
>> import tensorflow as tf
>> hello = tf.constant('Hello, Tensorflow!')
>> sess = tf.Session()
>> print(sess.run(hello))
```

```
import tensorflow as tf

# Initialize two constants
x1 = tf.constant([1,2,3,4])
x2 = tf.constant([5,6,7,8])

# Multiply
result = tf.multiply(x1, x2)

# Print the result
print(result)
```

```
tf.Tensor([ 5 12 21 32], shape=(4,), dtype=int32)
```

6.4 TensorFlow Architecture

The TensorFlow architecture works in three steps:

1. **Pre-processing:** The data may contain some noise and all data may not be measured on the same scale. So pre-processing of data is required.
2. **Build**: The computing model specific to the required problem solution must be used. Different

deep learning models such as RNN and CNN can be used to build a model in TensorFlow.

3. **Training and Testing**: Models can be trained with training data and after multiple iterations of training, the system is supposed to estimate the correct output on being given input data.

To use TensorFlow:

```
import tensorflow as tf
import numpy as np
tf.InteractiveSession()
<tensorflow.python.client.session.InteractiveSession at 0x10511300588>
```

A tensor can be created from the input data or as the result of a computation. All the operations are conducted on a graph. Each operation is an op node and they are all connected to each other. The computation result will flow over the edges.

6.4.1 Representation of a Tensor

A tensor is a collection of feature vectors of *n*-dimensions.

To represent 2 x 3 values as a matrix, use the following code:

```
[[1, 2, 3], [4, 5, 6]]
```

To create a three-dimensional matrix with values from 1 to 8 (Fig. 6.2):

```
[ [[1, 2], [[3, 4], [[5, 6], [[7,8] ]
```

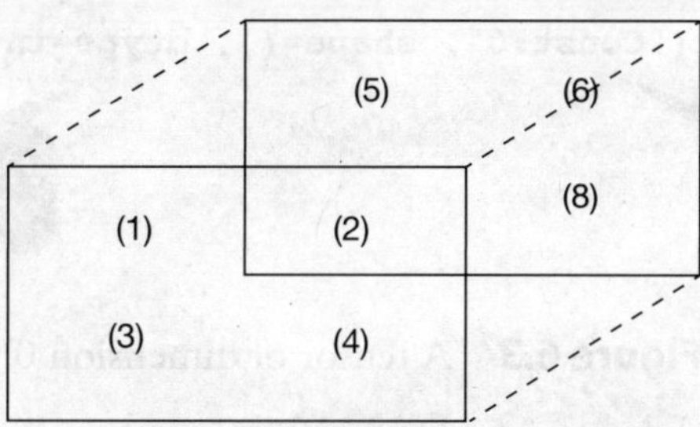

Figure 6.2 A three-dimensional matrix with values from 1 to 8

6.4.2 Types of Tensors

All computations pass through one or more tensors. A tensor is an object defined with three properties:

- A unique label, called its name
- A dimension to define the shape of the tensor
- A data type

The four main types of tensors are:

- `tf.Variable`

- `tf.constant`
- `tf.placeholder`
- `tf.SparseTensor`

6.4.3 Creating a Tensor of *n*-dimensions

To create a tensor of constant type:

`tf.constant(values, dtype, name = "")`

where `name` = name of a variable, `values` = the dimension of the tensor and `dtype.` = data type of tensor.

To create a tensor of dimension 0:

```
tc = tf.constant(1, tf.int16)
print(tc)
```

Output (Fig. 6.3): `Tensor("Const:0", shape=(), dtype=int16)`

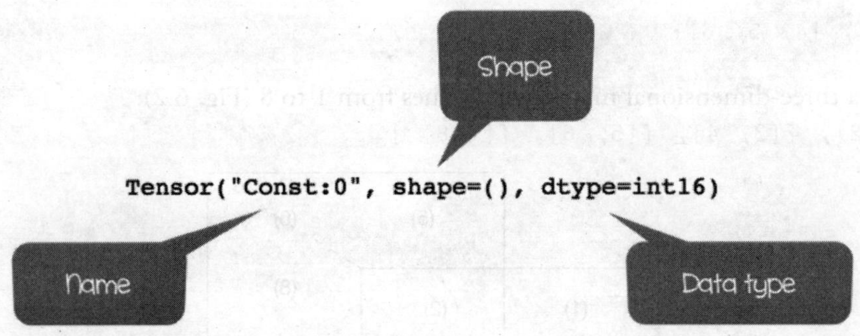

Figure 6.3 A tensor of dimension 0

To create a tensor of three elements in an array of type integer:

```
tc_vector = tf.constant([1,3,5], tf.int16)
print(tc_vector)
```

Output: Tensor("Const_3:0", shape=(3,), dtype=int16)

To create a tensor of type Boolean:

```
tb_boolean = tf.constant([True, True, False], tf.bool)
print(tb_boolean)
```

Output: Tensor("Const_4:0", shape=(3,), dtype=bool)

To create a tensor with multi-dimensional array data:

```
matrix = tf.constant([[1, 2],[2, 1]],tf.int16)
print(matrix)
```

Output: Tensor("Const_5:0", shape=(2, 2), dtype=int16)

To create a 3 x 2 matrix:

```
matrix_33 = tf.constant([[[1, 2][3, 4], [5, 6]],
[[1, 2],[3, 4],  [5, 6]]], tf.int16)
print(matrix_33)
```

Output: Tensor("Const_13:0", shape=(2, 3, 2), dtype=int16)

TensorFlow allows you to create a vector or matrix filled with 0 or 1. For instance, to create a 1-D tensor with a specific shape of 10, filled with 0, you can use the code given below:

```
# zero Matrix
tf.zeros(10)
```

Output: <tf.Tensor 'zeros_1:0' shape=(10,) dtype=float32>

To create a tensor of two rows, one filled with 0s and the other with 1s:

```
a = tf.zeros((2,2))
b = tf.ones((2,2))
a
```

Output: <tf.Tensor 'zeros_2:0' shape=(2, 2) dtype=float32>

```
b
```

Output: `<tf.Tensor 'ones:0' shape=(2, 2) dtype=float32>`

6.4.4 Shape of the Tensor

TensorFlow will guess the shape automatically when a tensor is printed. However, the shape can be displayed using the `shape` property.

A tensor for three rows and three columns of constant data has been created. Its shape can be displayed using the code:

```
m_shape = tf.constant([ [10, 11,20],[12, 13,20], [14, 15,20] ] )
m_shape.shape
```

Output:
TensorShape([Dimension(3), Dimension(3)])
The matrix has 3 rows and 3 columns.

6.4.5 NumPy versus TensorFlow

Both NumPy and TensorFlow are *n*-dimensional array libraries. By default, tensors map multi-linear vector spaces to real numbers. A tensor could be represented as a multi-dimensional array.

TensorFlow provides predefined functions on tensors. TensorFlow computations are defined on a graph. This graph can be seen as having each operation as a node with computations being propagated to the next operation in the graph. The code given below demonstrates the same operations on NumPy and TensorFlow.

To populate NumPy with zeros or ones:

```
import numpy as np
a = np.zeros((2,2))
b = np.ones((2,2))
```

a

Output: array([[0., 0.], [0., 0.]])

b

Output: array([[1., 1.], [1., 1.]])

To populate TensorFlow with zeros or ones:

```
a1 = tf.zeros((2,2))
b1 = tf.ones((2,2))
```

a1

Output: <tf.Tensor 'zeros_4:0' shape=(2, 2) dtype=float32>

b1

Output: <tf.Tensor 'ones_2:0' shape=(2, 2) dtype=float32>

To display the shape of a NumPy array:

```
a.shape
```

Output: (2, 2)

To display the shape of a TensorFlow array:

```
a1.get_shape()
```

Output: TensorShape([Dimension(2), Dimension(2)])

To reshape a NumPy array:

```
np.reshape(a, (1,4))
```

Output: array([[0., 0., 0., 0.]])

To reshape a TensorFlow array:

```
tf.reshape(a1, (1,4))
```

Output: <tf.Tensor 'Reshape:0' shape=(1, 4) dtype=float32>

To multiply two matrices in NumPy:

```
np.dot(a,b)
```

To multiply two matrices in TensorFlow:

```
array([[0., 0.], [0., 0.]])
tf.matmul(a1, b1)
```

Output: <tf.Tensor 'MatMul:0' shape=(2, 2) dtype=float32>

```
# Slicing a tensor
a[0,0], a[:,0], a[0,:]
```

Output: (0.0, array([0., 0.]), array([0., 0.]))

6.4.6 Variable Tensor

A variable tensor allows you to change the data. For this, a variable tensor needs to be created by specifying its name, data type, etc.

```
tf.get_variable(name = "", values, dtype, initializer)
```

where `name` = variable name, `values` = values given to the tensor, `dtype` = data type of the tensor and `initializer` = initializes the tensor with values. If the initializer is specified, there is no need to define values (dimension).

To create a two-dimensional tensor variable initialized with two random values:

```
tv = tf.get_variable("var", [1, 3])
print(tv.shape)
```

Output: (1, 3)

6.4.7 Placeholder

A placeholder is used to feed a tensor. It is used to initialize the data to flow inside the tensor. The `Feed_dict()` method is used supply a placeholder.

```
tf.placeholder(dtype, shape, name)
```

where `dtype` = type of data, `shape` = dimension of the placeholder and `name` = name of the placeholder

The following code will create a placeholder of float type which can be printed using the `print()` command:

```
ph_a= tf.placeholder(tf.float32, name = "ph_a")
print(ph_a)
```

Output: Tensor("ph_a:0", dtype=float32)

6.4.8 Tensor Perceptron

The perceptron model is a generalized model of the McCulloch–Pitts neuron. It takes an input, calculates the weighted sum and returns 1 only if the weighted sum is more than some threshold; otherwise it returns 0. Figure 6.4 shows $x_1,x_2…x_n$ as input and $w_1,w_2,….w_n$ as weights. W_0 is the bias which will become active if the value of x_0 is 1. Output y is the weighted sum of $x_1,x_2…x_n$.

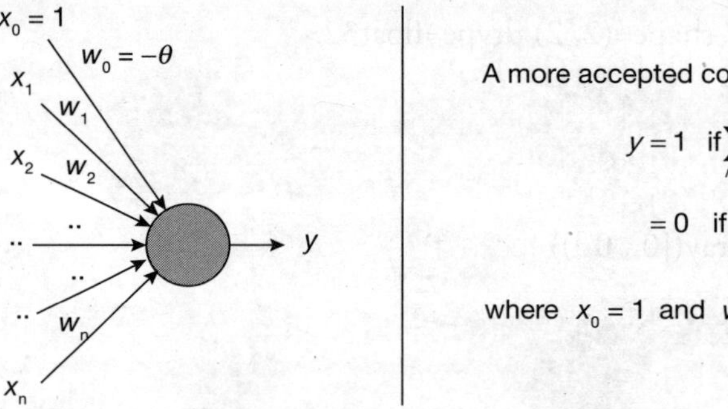

Figure 6.4 Perceptron model

The perceptron model is used to implement linearly separable functions. The code given below accepts data from input file 'data.csv' which consists of input data in columns X and Y trained to classify the data as label 1.

```
import tensorflow as tf
import pandas as pd
import numpy as np
import matplotlib.pyplot as plt
data = pd.read_csv('C:/Users/admin/Desktop/data.csv')
data.head()
```

Output:

	label	x	y
0	1	2.6487	4.5192
1	1	1.5438	2.4443
2	1	1.8990	4.2409
3	1	2.4711	5.8097
4	1	3.3590	6.4423

```
data.info()
```

Output:
<class 'pandas.core.frame.DataFrame'> RangeIndex: 100 entries, 0 to 99 Data columns (total 3 columns): label 100 non-null int64 x 100 non-null float64 y 100 non-null float64 dtypes: float64(2), int64(1) memory usage: 2.4 KB

Data in columns X and Y need to be converted into a matrix using the `as_matrix()` method. This converts the DataFrame to a matrix.

`X=df[['x1','x2','X3']].as_matrix()` where the different `x` are the column names.

```
X= data[['x','y']].as_matrix()
Y = data[['label']].as_matrix()
Y
```

Output:
array([[1], [1], [1], [1], [1], [1], [1], [1], [1], [1], [1], [1], [1], [1], [1], [1], [1], [1], [1], [1], [1], [1], [1], [1], [1], [1], [1], [1], [1], [1], [1], [1], [1], [1], [1], [1], [1], [1], [1], [1], [1], [1], [1], [1], [1], [1], [1], [1], [1], [1], [0], [0], [0], [0], [0], [0], [0], [0], [0], [0], [0], [0], [0], [0], [0], [0], [0], [0], [0], [0], [0], [0], [0], [0], [0], [0], [0], [0], [0], [0], [0], [0], [0], [0], [0], [0], [0], [0], [0], [0], [0], [0], [0], [0], [0], [0], [0], [0], [0], [0]], dtype=int64)

X

array([[2.6487, 4.5192], [1.5438, 2.4443], [1.899, 4.2409], [2.4711, 5.8097], [3.359, 6.4423], [3.2406, 5.8097], [3.8128, 6.3917], [4.4441, 6.8725], [3.6747, 6.7966], [4.7401, 8.163], [3.8917, 7.4038], [4.602, 7.6316], [5.7265, 7.7581], [4.9571, 6.5688], [3.9903, 5.3543], [3.0236, 4.4686], [2.0568, 2.9757], [1.2676, 2.4443], [1.169, 0.9008], [1.7411, 2.1154], [1.386, 3.2794], [1.5636, 4.165], [1.8793, 4.8482], [2.7868, 3.33], [3.5563, 5.1518], [4.0693, 6.2652], [4.3849, 6.2652], [1.5438, 7.2014], [2.412, 7.6569], [1.7806, 6.1387], [1.4057, 4.4939], [2.6093, 4.8735], [3.0828, 5.5314], [3.9311, 6.0121], [4.7598, 7.1508], [5.3122, 7.7075], [5.7068, 8.3148], [5.1149, 8.5172], [5.4109, 8.7449], [3.8128, 7.8593], [3.2406, 6.999], [2.9052, 5.5061], [2.6882, 4.9241], [3.8325, 6.6447], [4.5428, 7.6822], [5.7857, 8.0364], [6.5552, 8.9221], [5.253, 7.8593], [5.2333, 6.5941], [4.7598, 6.0374], [4.5822, 2.7227], [3.6549, 1.9383], [2.9841, 1.6852], [4.4244, 4.3168], [3.7536, 3.4312], [5.2728, 5.4808], [4.8387, 4.1144], [4.4244, 3.2034], [5.3911, 4.1144], [6.0817, 5.1012], [5.5687, 4.8988], [6.4565, 5.9615], [6.0028, 5.7591], [6.7722, 6.6953], [6.6538, 5.7338], [7.1471, 6.6194], [7.5219, 7.2014], [6.8314, 7.2014], [7.6206, 8.5931], [7.1865, 7.7581], [7.7784, 7.7581], [7.6009, 5.1012], [6.496, 4.2156], [5.8055, 3.4818], [5.0163, 2.3684], [4.1876, 1.7864], [3.4379, 0.9008], [5.7857, 0.9008], [6.3382, 1.9636], [4.9571, 1.4069], [6.8511, 2.419], [6.0817, 2.8745], [7.1668, 4.0132], [7.226, 4.6711], [8.1533, 5.1771], [7.4825, 6.2146], [7.0484, 5.4555], [8.5084, 5.9868], [7.5417, 4.0891], [7.2063, 2.3937], [6.5355, 1.331], [5.4503, 1.7358], [5.8449, 2.4443], [4.8979, 3.1781], [5.8055, 4.6711], [7.3641, 5.9868], [6.2592, 4.6711], [8.3703, 7.581], [8.5676, 4.6457], [8.1676, 4.6457]])

The sequence of labels is all ones and then all zeros. To mix all input samples randomly, a random permute of the sequence will be performed and a permuted range will be returned. If `x` is a multi-dimensional array, it is only shuffled along its first index. Now, shuffle the data and labels together.

```
p =np.random.permutation(x.shape[0])
X = X[p]
Y = Y[p]
X
Y
```

Output:
array([[1], [0], [0], [1], [1], [1], [0], [0], [0], [0], [1], [0], [1], [0], [1], [1], [1], [1], [0], [1], [1], [1], [1], [0], [1], [0], [0], [1], [0], [0], [1], [0], [1], [0], [1], [1], [1], [0], [0], [1], [0], [1], [1], [0], [1], [0], [1], [0], [1], [1], [0], [1], [0], [0], [0], [0], [1], [0], [1], [1], [0], [0], [0], [1], [1], [1], [0], [0], [0], [0], [0], [1], [1], [0], [1], [1], [0], [0], [0], [0], [1], [1], [1], [1], [0], [1], [0], [0], [1], [1], [0], [1], [1], [1], [0], [0], [0], [0], [1], [0]], dtype=int64)

The code given below defines a neural network by specifying the number of inputs and outputs. `x` is the matrix for input and `y` is the matrix for output. Weights and bias are initialized with random values with a normal distribution. Then, weighted sum is passed in the activation function `sigmoid()`.

```
num_units = 1
num_inputs = 2
num_outputs = 1
#define place holder for input and output
x = tf.placeholder(tf.float32,[None, num_inputs])
y = tf.placeholder(tf.float32,[None, num_outputs])

weight = tf.Variable(tf.random_normal([num_inputs, num_units]))
bias = tf.Variable(tf.random_normal([num_units]))
bias

# activation_fns(XW +b)
output = tf.add(tf.matmul(x,weight),bias)
output = tf.sigmoid(output)
tf.shape(output)
```

Output: <tf.Tensor 'Shape_5:0' shape=(2,) dtype=int32>

Now, the `loss()` function is to be defined as a cross-entropy method to find the difference between actual output (output) and targeted output (y). Logits means that the function operates on the unscaled output of the earlier layers and that the relative scale to understand the units is linear.

Gradient descent is an optimization algorithm based on a convex function. It is provided with the learning rate and the function `minimize(loss)` to reach local minima.

```
loss = tf.reduce_mean(tf.nn.sigmoid_cross_entropy_with_logits(labels =
y,logits = output))
gdo = tf.train.GradientDescentOptimizer(learning_rate = 0.1).
minimize(loss)
init = tf.global_variables_initializer()
```

The following function will supply batch-wise `batch_size` X and Y values starting from the `idx` index:

```
def get_batch(X,Y,batch_size,idx):
    return(X[batch_size*idx:batch_size*(idx+1)]),Y[batch_size*idx:batch_
size*(idx+1)]
```

Initialize `epochs` and `batch_size`:

```
epochs = 20
batch_size = 20
total_batch = int(X.shape[0]/batch_size)
```

In a session, run the neural network. Training of the perceptron model will iterate for `epochs (20)` times and in every epoch, batch-wise data is inputted. The model can be run using the command `sess.run()`. Once the model is created, it can be tested with the `eval()` function.

```
with tf.Session() as sess:
    sess.run(init)
    for e in range(epochs):
        avg_loss = 0
        for i in range(total_batch):
            x_batch, y_batch = get_batch(X,Y,batch_size,i)
            _,c = sess.run([gdo,loss],feed_dict = {x:x_batch,y:y_batch})
            avg_loss+=c/total_batch
        print("Epoch",e+1,"Loss", avg_loss)
    preds = output.eval({x:X[:4]})
    print(preds)
    sess.close()
```

Output:

Epoch 1 Loss 0.6834026098251342 Epoch 2 Loss 0.6821386337280273 Epoch 3 Loss 0.6804690122604371

Epoch 4 Loss 0.6781767129898072 Epoch 5 Loss 0.6748798489570618 Epoch 6 Loss 0.6698849678039551 Epoch 7 ....Epoch 20 Loss 0.5858666062355041

Predicted output is:

[[0.7922023] [0.14544126] [0.30719584] [0.80818677]]

Check with actual output:

`Y[:4]`

Output: array([[1], [0], [0], [1]], dtype=int64)

Correct output is achieved. Values in the predicted output close to 1 are actually 1 and those close to 0 are actually 0.

6.5 Introduction to Keras

Keras is a built-in library of Python used to create deep learning models. It is built on top of libraries such as TensorFlow and Theano.

Keras is a dynamic framework with faster development of deep learning models and large community support. Keras supports both convolution and recurrent networks. Keras was developed and maintained by François Chollet, a Google engineer, using modularity and extensibility. Keras supports the following features:

- It supports extensible APIs.
- It has minimal structure; it is easy to achieve results in the fewest steps.
- It is compatible with multiple platforms and back ends.
- It runs on both CPU and GPU.
- It is a scalable computing model.

6.6 Installation of Keras

As Keras is a Python-based neural network library, Python must first be installed on the machine. If Python has been properly installed, its version can be checked using a command at the command terminal. The recommended version is the latest version of Python.

To check the version, type the following command at the command prompt:

```
python --version
```

It will display the Python version.

If Python is not installed in the system or only a lower version is installed, download the latest version based on the OS and install it immediately:

1. Go to the download page at python.org.
2. Click and select the latest version of Python for Windows and download it.
3. Run the installer. The system is now equipped with the latest version of Python.
   Before installing Keras, you must install one of its back end engines, that is, TensorFlow. To install TensorFlow using the pip3 package manager, run the following command at the command prompt:
   ```
   pip3 install tensorflow
   ```
   It will extract and install the requires libraries.
4. Now install Keras from PyPI by running the following command at the command prompt:
   ```
   pip3 install keras
   ```
   Now Keras is ready for use.

6.7 Features of Keras

- **Easy and fast**: Keras provides direct APIs to implement deep neural nets. It is easy to use and enables fast prototyping.

- **Multiplatform support**: Programs written in Keras can execute on CPU, GPU and edge devices.
- **Diversified network support**: It provides direct APIs to implement convolutional networks and recurrent networks. It allow you to implement arbitrary network architecture, where multi inputs or multi outputs with layer sharing and model sharing can be specified. Keras allow you to build deep learning models and generative adversarial networks.

6.8 Programming in Keras

To program an ML model in Keras, the following steps need to be performed:

1. Load the data.
2. Select the data.
3. Display the data.
4. Reshape the training and testing data set.
5. Re-scale the training and testing data.
6. Cross-validate the set.
7. Build the model.
8. Evaluate the model.
9. Predict the model.

Let us implement text classification in Keras. This program uses the MNIST data set.

Step 1: Load the data. First load the Keras data set. It returns two tuples of digits and labels, one for the training set and the other for the testing set.

```
from keras.datasets.mnist import load_data
(train_digits, train_labels), (test_digits, test_labels) = load_data()
```

Output:
Using TensorFlow backend.

Downloading data from https://s3.amazonaws.com/img-datasets/mnist.npz 11493376/11490434 [==============================] - 18s 2us/step

Step 2: Select random images of digits from the MNIST data set. Let us display 14 random images from the training set. The seed number (123) you choose is the starting point for the generation of a sequence of random numbers. It will generate the same random numbers for multiple executions.

```
import numpy as np
import matplotlib.pyplot as plt
np.random.seed(123)
rand_14 = np.random.randint(0, train_digits.shape[0],14)
sample_digits = train_digits[rand_14]
sample_labels = train_labels[rand_14]
sample_labels
```

Output: array([4, 9, 0, 4, 6, 3, 8, 5, 3, 6, 8, 7, 7, 9], dtype=uint8)

```
sample_digits
```

Output:
array([[[0, 0, 0,..., 0, 0, 0], [0, 0, 0,..., 0, 0, 0], [0, 0, 0,..., 0, 0, 0],..., [0, 0, 0,..., 0, 0, 0], [0, 0, 0,..., 0, 0, 0], [0, 0, 0,..., 0, 0, 0]], [[0, 0, 0,..., 0, 0, 0], [0, 0, 0,..., 0, 0, 0], [0, 0, 0,..., 0, 0, 0],..., [0, 0, 0,..., 0, 0, 0], [0, 0, 0,..., 0, 0, 0], [0, 0, 0,..., 0, 0, 0]], [[0, 0, 0,..., 0, 0, 0], [0, 0, 0,..., 0, 0, 0], [0, 0, 0,..., 0, 0, 0],..., [0, 0, 0,..., 0, 0, 0], [0, 0, 0,..., 0, 0, 0], [0, 0, 0,..., 0, 0, 0]],..., [[0, 0, 0,..., 0, 0, 0], [0, 0, 0,..., 0, 0, 0], [0, 0, 0,..., 0, 0, 0],..., [0, 0, 0,..., 0, 0, 0], [0, 0, 0,..., 0, 0, 0], [0, 0, 0,..., 0, 0, 0]], [[0, 0, 0,..., 0, 0, 0], [0, 0, 0,..., 0, 0, 0], [0, 0, 0,..., 0, 0, 0],..., [0, 0, 0,..., 0, 0, 0], [0, 0, 0,..., 0, 0, 0], [0, 0, 0,..., 0, 0, 0]], [[0, 0, 0,..., 0, 0, 0], [0, 0, 0,..., 0, 0, 0], [0, 0, 0,..., 0, 0, 0],..., [0, 0, 0,..., 0, 0, 0], [0, 0, 0,..., 0, 0, 0], [0, 0, 0,..., 0, 0, 0]]], dtype=uint8)

Step 3: Display the 14 randomly selected images. Following is the code used to view the images. The 14 images are displayed in a subplot of 2 rows and 7 columns. The random retrieved images and their labels are displayed.

```
num_rows, num_cols = 2, 7
f, ax = plt.subplots(num_rows, num_cols, figsize=(12,5),
                     gridspec_kw={'wspace':0.03, 'hspace':0.01},
                     squeeze=True)
for r in range(num_rows):
    for c in range(num_cols):
        image_index = r * 7 + c
        ax[r,c].axis("off")
        ax[r,c].imshow(sample_digits[image_index], cmap='gray')
        ax[r,c].set_title('No. %d' % sample_labels[image_index])
plt.show()
plt.close()
```

Output:

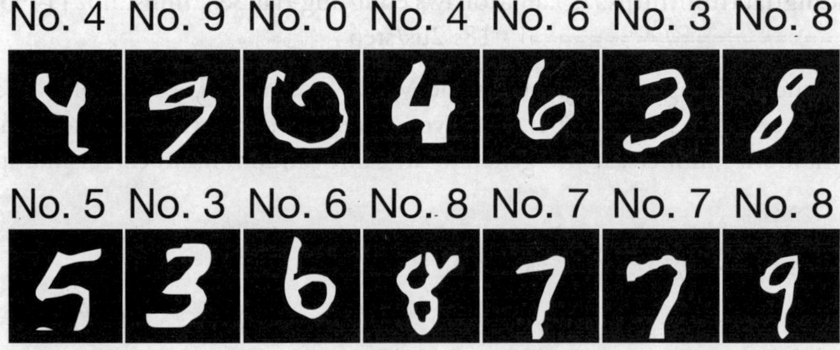

Step 4: Reshape the training and testing data set.

To display a tuple of shape (rows, columns) of the training data set that consists of 6000 images of height 28 and width 28:

```
train_digits.shape
```

Output: (60000, 28, 28)

```
image_height = train_digits.shape[1]
image_width = train_digits.shape[2]
num_channels = 1  # we have grayscale images
# NOTE: image_height == image_width == 28
# re-shape the images data - Preprocessing
train_data = np.reshape(train_digits, (train_digits.shape[0],
                                       image_height, image_width, num_
channels))
test_data = np.reshape(test_digits, (test_digits.shape[0],
                                     image_height, image_width, num_
channels))
```

Step 5: Re-scale the training and testing image data to values between [0.0,1.0] and categorize them in 10 classes.

```
train_data = train_data.astype('float32') / 255.
test_data = test_data.astype('float32') / 255.
# one hot encode the labels - we have 10 output classes
# so 3 -> [0 0 0 1 0 0 0 0 0 0], 5 -> [0 0 0 0 0 1 0 0 0 0] & so on
[3,5,7]
[[0 0 0 1 0 0 0 0 0 0]
 [0 0 0 0 0 1 0 0 0 0]
 [0 0 0 0 0 0 0 1 0 0]]
from keras.utils import to_categorical
num_classes = 10
#Categorise train label and test label data in 10 classes
train_labels_cat = to_categorical(train_labels,num_classes)
test_labels_cat = to_categorical(test_labels,num_classes)
train_labels_cat.shape, test_labels_cat.shape
```

Output: ((60000, 10), (10000, 10))

Step 6: Shuffle the training data set (5 times) and create cross-validation sets.

```
for _ in range(5):
    indexes = np.random.permutation(len(train_data))
train_data = train_data[indexes]
train_labels_cat = train_labels_cat[indexes]
# now set-aside 10% of the train_data/labels as the
# cross-validation sets
val_perc = 0.10
val_count = int(val_perc * len(train_data))
```

```
# first pick validation set from train_data/labels
val_data = train_data[:val_count,:]
val_labels_cat = train_labels_cat[:val_count,:]
# leave rest in training set
train_data2 = train_data[val_count:,:]
train_labels_cat2 = train_labels_cat[val_count:,:]
```

Step 7: Build a model of CNN.

```
from keras.models import Sequential
from keras.layers import Conv2D, MaxPooling2D, Flatten, Dense, Dropout
def build_model():
 model = Sequential()
 # add Convolutional layers
 model.add(Conv2D(filters=32, kernel_size=(3,3), activation=' relu
',padding=' same ', input_shape=(image_height, image_width, num_
channels)))
model.add(MaxPooling2D(pool_size=(2,2)))
model.add(Conv2D(filters=64, kernel_size=(3,3), activation=' relu ',
padding=' same '))
model.add(MaxPooling2D(pool_size=(2,2)))
model.add(Conv2D(filters=64, kernel_size=(3,3), activation=' relu ',
padding=' same '))
model.add(MaxPooling2D(pool_size=(2,2)))
model.add(Flatten())
# Add Dense  layers
model.add(Dense(128, activation=' relu '))
#  Add output layer
model.add(Dense(num_classes, activation=' softmax '))
# compile with adam optimizer & categorical_crossentropy loss function
model.compile(optimizer='adam', loss='categorical_crossentropy',
metrics=['accuracy'])
 return model
model = build_model()
print(model.summary())
```

Output:

WARNING:tensorflow:From C:\ProgramData\Anaconda3\lib\site-packages\tensorflow\python\framework\op_def_library.py:263: colocate_with (from tensorflow.python.framework.ops) is deprecated and will be removed in a future version. Instructions for updating: Colocations handled automatically by placer.

____ Layer (type)

Output Shape Param #

===

conv2d_1 (Conv2D) (None, 28, 28, 32) 320

____

max_pooling2d_1 (MaxPooling2 (None, 14, 14, 32) 0

____

conv2d_2 (Conv2D) (None, 14, 14, 64) 18496

---

max_pooling2d_2 (MaxPooling2 (None, 7, 7, 64) 0

---

conv2d_3 (Conv2D) (None, 7, 7, 64) 36928

---

max_pooling2d_3 (MaxPooling2 (None, 3, 3, 64) 0

---

flatten_1 (Flatten) (None, 576) 0

---

dense_1 (Dense) (None, 128) 73856

---

dense_2 (Dense) (None, 10) 1290

===

Total params: 130,890 Trainable params: 130,890 Non-trainable params: 0

None

```
results = model.fit(train_data2, train_labels_cat2,
                    epochs=15, batch_size=64,
                    validation_data=(val_data, val_labels_cat))
```

Output:

WARNING:tensorflow:From C:\ProgramData\Anaconda3\lib\site-packages\tensorflow\python\ops\math_ops.py:3066: to_int32 (from tensorflow.python.ops.math_ops) is deprecated and will be removed in a future version. Instructions for updating: Use tf.cast instead. Train on 54000 samples, validate on 6000 samples Epoch 1/15 54000/54000 [==============================] - 84s 2ms/step - loss: 0.1761 - acc: 0.9447 - val_loss: 0.0622 - val_acc: 0.9802 Epoch 2/15 54000/54000 [==============================] ……….. val_loss: 0.0295 - val_acc: 0.9927

Step 8: Evaluate the model.

```
import matplotlib
import numpy as np
import matplotlib.pyplot as plt
plt.show(results.history)
test_loss, test_accuracy = model.evaluate(test_data, test_labels_cat,
batch_size=64)
print('Test loss: %.4f accuracy: %.4f' % (test_loss, test_accuracy))
```

Output:

10000/10000 [==============================] - 5s 454us/step Test loss: 0.0240 accuracy: 0.9939

Step 9: Obtain predictions from the model.

```
predictions = model.predict(test_data)
first_preds = np.argmax(predictions, axis=1)[:25]
first_true = np.argmax(test_labels_cat,axis=1)[:25]
print(first_preds)
print(first_true)
```

Output:
[7 2 1 0 4 1 4 9 5 9 0 6 9 0 1 5 9 7 3 4 9 6 6 5 4] [7 2 1 0 4 1 4 9 5 9 0 6 9 0 1 5 9 7 3 4 9 6 6 5 4]

```
# How many mismatches?
(np.argmax(predictions, axis=1) != np.argmax(test_labels_cat,axis=1)).
sum()
```

Output: 61

EXERCISES

Multiple Choice Questions

1. Where in the neural internet architecture does weight sharing occur in TensorFlow?
   (a) Fully related neural community
   (b) Recurrent neural community
   (c) Convolutional neural community
   (d) Both (b) and (c)
2. Y = ax^2 + bx + c (polynomial equation of degree 2)
   Can this equation be represented using a neural network of a single hidden layer with linear threshold?
   (a) Yes
   (b) No
3. Which of following functions should not be used at the output layer to classify an image?
   (a) TanH
   (b) ReLU
   (c) Sigmoid
   (d) None of these
4. The number of nodes in the I/P layer is 10 and that in the hidden layer is 5. What will be the maximum connections from the I/P layer to the hidden layer?
   (a) 20
   (b) 60
   (c) 50
   (d) It is random
5. Identify the type of tensors:
   (a) Variable
   (b) Constant
   (c) Placeholder
   (d) All of the above
6. What is the meaning of `model = sequential()` in Keras?
   (a) No such code in Keras
   (b) Keras should be used only for sequential models like RNNs
   (c) Keras builds sequential models
   (d) Keras creates a computational graph
7. How do you feed external data into placeholders?
   (a) By using the `import` data command
   (b) By using `feed_dict`

(c) By using the `read` data function
(d) Not possible

8. `C=-tf.reduce_sum(Y*tf.log(out)):`
(a) C is a logistic regression line equation
(b) C is a squared error loss function
(c) C is a cross-entropy loss function
(d) C is a linear regression line equation

9. How do calculations work in TensorFlow?
(a) Through vector multiplications
(b) Through RDDs
(c) Through computational graphs
(d) Through map-reduce tasks

10. What is the advantage of TensorFlow?
(a) It has excellent community support.
(b) It is designed to use various back end software (GPUs, ASIC) and is a also highly parallel.
(c) It has a unique approach that allows monitoring of the training progress of the models and tracking of several metrics.
(d) All of the above.

Answers

1. (d)	**2.** (b)	**3.** (b)	**4.** (c)	**5.** (d)	**6.** (c)	**7.** (b)	**8.** (c)
9. (c)	**10.** (d)						

Programming/Concept-based Questions

1. What are types of layers in Keras?
Answer:
- Core
- Convolutional
- Pooling
- Locally connected
- Recurrent
- Embedding
- Merge
- Advanced activation
- Normalization
- Noise

2. What do you understand by dropout and early stopping techniques?
Answer: Dropout means that during the training, randomly selected neurons are turned off or 'dropped' out. It means that they are temporarily obstructed from influencing or activating the downward neuron in a forward pass. Early stopping is a cross-validation strategy where one part of the training set is used as a validation set, and the performance of the model is gauged against this set. So if the performance on this validation set becomes worse, the training on the model is immediately stopped.

3. Explain the following example:

```
for epoch in range(training_epochs):
for (x, y) in zip(train_X, train_Y):
sess.run(optimizer, feed_dict = {X:x, Y:y})
```

Answer: Here, the initializer is run and all the training data is fitted by running a loop for all the epochs.

4. Explain the following code:

```
x = tf.constant(35, name ='x')
y = tf.Variable(x+5, name = 'y')
print(y)
```

Output: `<tf.Variable 'y:0' shape=() dtype=int32_ref>`

Answer: Here, y is effectively an equation that means "when this variable is computed, it takes the value of x (as it is then) and adds 5 to it". But x and y are 'placeholders' which are values that are unassigned and that will be initialized by the session when you run it. In short, the result of the lines of code is an abstract tensor in the computation graph that defines the model but no process is run to calculate the result.

5. Write a code to pass an array of 4 numbers, multiply the two variables and store it as the result.

Answer:

```
import tensorflow as tf
# Initialize two constants
x1 = tf.constant([1,2,3,4])
x2 = tf.constant([5,6,7,8])
result = tf.multiply(x1, x2)
sess = tf.Session()
print(sess.run(result))
sess.close()
```

Output: [5 12 21 32]

6. Define and declare the model structure along with the loss functions.

Answer:

```
Model Structure: y_pred =  tf.add(tf.mul(x_input, weight_matrix), b_
matrix)
Loss functions: loss = tf.reduce_mean(tf.square(y_actual - y_pred))
```

7. Apply the layer to the `tf.data.Dataset` to obtain a data set that yields batches of pre-processed data.

Answer:

```
dataset = dataset.map(lambda x, y: (preprocessing_layer(x), y))
```

With this option, pre-processing will take place in the CPU asynchronously, and it will be buffered before going into the model. In addition, if you prefetch the data set, the pre-processing will take place efficiently in parallel with training.

8. What does this code do?

```
import tensorflow as tf
x = tf.constant([[1, 1, 1], [1, 1, 1]])
tf.reduce_sum(x, 0)
tf.reduce_sum(x, 1)
tf.reduce_sum(x, [0, 1])
```

Answer: x has a shape of (2, 3) (two rows and three columns):

1 1 1

1 1 1

`reduce_sum` computes the sum of elements across the specified dimensions of a tensor and by this, it reduces the input tensor.

By running `tf.reduce_sum(x, 0)`, the tensor is reduced along the first dimension (rows); so the result is [1, 1, 1] + [1, 1, 1] = [2, 2, 2].

By running `tf.reduce_sum(x, 1)`, the tensor is reduced along the second dimension (columns); so the result is [1, 1] + [1, 1] + [1, 1] = [3, 3].

By running `tf.reduce_sum(x, [0, 1])`, the tensor is reduced along both dimensions (rows and columns); so the result is 1 + 1 + 1 + 1 + 1 + 1 = 6 or equivalently [1, 1, 1] + [1, 1, 1] = [2, 2, 2] and then 2 + 2 + 2 = 6.

9. What is a feature cross and how can you create it with TensorFlow?

   Answer: A feature cross is a synthetic feature formed by multiplying (crossing) two or more features. Crossing combinations of features can provide predictive abilities beyond what those features can provide individually.

```
import tensorflow as tf
latitude = tf.feature_column.numeric_column("latitude")
longitude = tf.feature_column.numeric_column("longitude")
bucketized_latitude = tf.feature_column.bucketized_column(latitude,
  boundaries=list(np.linspace(32., 42., 20 - 1)))
bucketized_longitude = tf.feature_column.bucketized_column(longitude,
  boundaries=list(np.linspace(-125., -114., 20 - 1)))
location = tf.feature_column.crossed_column(
  [bucketized_latitude, bucketized_longitude], hash_bucket_size=1000)
```

10. List the limitations of TensorFlow.

    Answer:

    - It does not provide support for OpenCL (Open Computing Language).
    - It requires prior knowledge of advanced calculus and linear algebra along with a good understanding of ML.
    - It has GPU memory conflicts with Theano if imported in the same scope.

BIBLIOGRAPHY

1. "TensorFlow Tutorial". Tutorials Point. https://www.tutorialspoint.com/tensorflow/index.htm
2. Gregor Koehler. "MNIST Handwritten Digit Recognition in Keras". Nextjournal. https://nextjournal.com/gkoehler/digit-recognition-with-keras
3. Srijan. "PyTorch Tensor Method - How to Create Tensors in Python". freeCodeCamp, published December 2020, https://www.freecodecamp.org/news/pytorch-tensor-methods/

CHAPTER 7

Probability

LEARNING OBJECTIVES

At the end of this chapter, you will be able to:

- Define the central limit theorem for a given problem
- Calculate the probability of a random variable using various probability distribution functions
- Apply different types of discrete and continuous probability distribution functions using Python
- Differentiate between discrete and continuous probability distribution functions
- List the applications of probability distribution functions

7.0 INTRODUCTION TO PROBABILITY

Probability is a way to deal with the uncertainty and randomness of processes. It helps us make a judgment about future events based on previous event data. It helps in prediction in an informed manner.

Many statistical methods in data science use probability theory. It can be inferred statistically to predict trends or patterns in data. Hence, probability theory and probability distribution play an important role in computer science.

7.1 PROBABILITY AND STATISTICS

Probability is the chance of an outcome in an experiment (also called an event). It deals with predicting the likelihood of future events. For example, consider an event such as tossing a coin, where the outcome could be head or tail. As another example, let us suppose there are five red balls and six white balls. In a random selection of two balls, what is the probability that both the balls are red (P1) or of selecting two different balls (P2)?

If there is no knowledge about the total number of balls of each colour in the above example, then statistics comes into play. Statistics helps us infer population based on random samples. It analyzes the frequency of past events.

Statistics can answer the following questions:

S1: A random sample of five balls is selected from a bag and two red and three white balls are picked. What is the total population of red and white balls?

S2: An experiment of random sampling of four balls is performed and the number of red balls in each experiment is counted. This experiment is performed 10 times; the average of these trials is 3. What is the true number of red balls in the population?

In probability, a model is given and the question asked is what kind of data is likely to be seen. In statistics, data is given and the question asked is what kind of model is likely to have generated it.

7.2 Random Variables

A random variable stores the output of a random event. The range of values of a random variable can be fixed, but the exact value will be determined only after the occurrence of the event. For example, a random variable can store the side of a flipped coin, as head (0) or tail (1).

If you throw a die and wish to store the outcome, it will be a number in the range 1–6. You need to use a random variable because the outcome of throwing a die is not known. Random variables are used to quantify the outcomes of random occurrences in probability and statistics.

A random variable is different from an algebraic variable. The variable in an algebraic equation is an unknown value that can be calculated. The equation $10 + x = 13$ shows that the specific value of x can be calculated, which is 3. On the other hand, a random variable has a set of values, and any of those values could be the outcome, as seen in the example of the die above.

7.3 Central Limit Theorem

According to this theorem, the average of the sample mean and standard deviation of a sample of large size is equal to the population mean and standard deviation. Distribution of sample mean approximates normal distribution as the sample size becomes larger. The sample size should be greater than 30 for the Central Limit Theorem to hold true. Therefore, if a sample of sufficiently large size is drawn, it can represent the entire population correctly.

The Central Limit Theorem is represented using the formula

$$Z = \frac{\overline{X} - \mu}{\sigma / \sqrt{n}},$$

where $\overline{X}$ = mean of a random sample of size n, μ = mean of the population and σ2 = variance of the population. As $n \to \infty$, the distribution tends to the standard normal distribution.

For example, in an institute, the mean height of male students is 160 cm, with a standard deviation of 20 cm. If a sample of 80 male students is drawn, what is the probability that their mean height will be greater than 155 cm?

Here, $\overline{X} = 155$, $\sigma = 20$, $n = 80$ and $\mu = 160$.

Applying the Central Limit Theorem formula

$$(155 - 160)/(20/\sqrt{80}) = -2.23$$

Looking up the z-score in the z-table of standard normal probabilities
= 98.71%

Thus, 98.71% of students will have a mean height greater than 155 cm.

7.4 Density Functions

Density functions are mathematical functions that describe the probability distribution of a random variable *X*. The following are important density functions:

Probability Mass Function (PMF): This describes the probability of a random variable *X* taking on a particular value *x*. It is only applicable for discrete distributions. PMF is given as:

$$f(x) = P[X = x]$$

It must satisfy two conditions:

(i) $f(x) \geq 0$ for all $x \in S$

(ii) $\sum_{x \in S} f(x) = 1$

Probability Density Function (PDF): This function is for continuous random variables and is equivalent to PMF. A continuous distribution includes infinite numbers of the random variables. So, a range of values is used to infer the likelihood of a random sample. Carrying out integration over the range will fetch the likelihood for the sample.

$$Pr[a \leq X \leq b] = \int_a^b f_X(x)dx$$

Cumulative Density Function (CDF): A cumulative density function at *x* explains the probability of a random variable *X* taking on values less than or equal to *x*. It is applicable to both discrete and continuous distributions. For a constant distribution, all we need to do is integrate the density function from negative infinity to *x*.

$$f_X(x) = \int_{-\infty}^{x} f_X(t)dt$$

The CDF for a random variable *X* sampled from a discrete distribution is given by

$$F_X(x) = P(X \leq x) = \sum_{x_i \leq x} P(X = x_i) = \sum_{x_i \leq x} p(x_i)$$

Finding the CDF of *x* is equal to the probability of a random variable *X* <= *x*, which is, in turn, the summation of the probability of *X* similar to *xi* when *xi* is less than or equal to *x*.

7.5 Probability Distribution

A probability distribution is a list of all of the possible outcomes of a random variable, along with their corresponding probability values.

For example, the probability distribution of a six-sided die roll is shown in Table 7.1.

Table 7.1 Probability distribution of a six-sided die roll

Outcome of die roll	1	2	3	4	5	6
Probability	1/6	1/6	1/6	1/6	1/6	1/6

Probability distributions can be discrete or continuous. Discrete probability distribution is defined using discrete variables, while continuous probability distribution is defined using continuous variables.

Discrete versus continuous variables: If a variable can take any specified value, it is called a discrete variable. For example, you throw a die (the specified values will be 1, 2, 3, 4, 5 or 6) or toss a coin (the specified values will be head or tail).

If a variable can take a specified range of values and all the values in between (continuous), it is a continuous variable. For example, measuring height in centimetres, where the values can be 150 cm, 150.5 cm, 150.6 cm, and so on. Generally, real-time values are stored in continuous variables.

7.5.1 Discrete Probability Distribution

If a random variable is a discrete variable, its probability distribution is called a discrete probability distribution. The probability is distributed amongst all possible discrete outcomes.

For example, if you throw a die, the possible outcomes are 1, 2, 3, 4, 5 and 6. A discrete random variable X can store these values.

The probability distribution for throwing a die may be as is shown in Table 7.2.

Table 7.2 Probability distribution for throwing a die

Outcome	Probability
1	0.16
2	0.16
3	0.16
4	0.16
5	0.16
6	0.16

This relates the output values of a discrete random variable to the probability values.

Binomial probability distribution: A binomial random variable contains a number of successes in n repeated trials of an event. Each event trial has two possible outcomes (success or failure).

Binomial probability distribution is the distribution of the probability of a binomial random variable. It allows you to perform n trials, where the outcome of each trial is success or failure and the probability of success of each trial is P. Every trial is independent, which means that the outcome of one trial is not dependent on another.

The Python code to visualize a binomial distribution is as follows:

```
from numpy import random
import matplotlib.pyplot as plt
import seaborn as sns
sns.distplot(random.binomial(n=10, p=0.5, size=500), hist=True, kde=False)
plt.show()
```

Output:

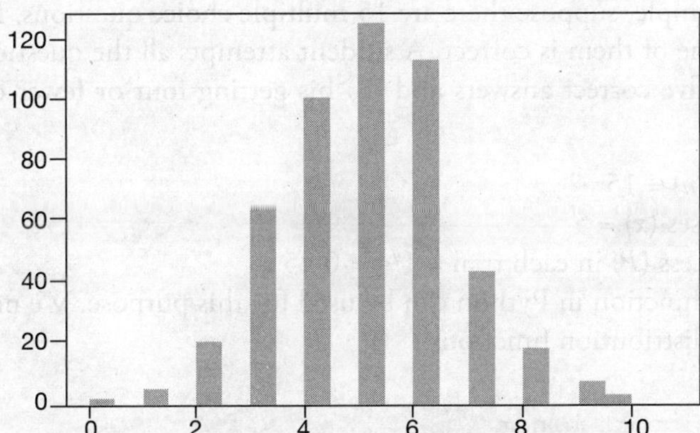

Function `binomial(n,p,size)` can be used for binomial distribution, where `n` is the number of trials, `p` is the probability of occurrence of each trial and `size` is the shape of the returned array. The graph shown above shows 10 trials with the probability of occurrence of each trial as 0.5.

Suppose a coin is tossed in two trials and the number of heads is counted. The binomial probability distribution with the number of heads and their probability is shown in Table 7.3.

Table 7.3 Binomial probability distribution with the number of heads and their probability

Binomial random variable or number of heads	Probability
0	0.25
1	0.50
2	0.25

Mathematical formula: Suppose n trials of an experiment are performed and the number of successes is counted (x). The probability of success in each trial is P. Then, the binomial probability is

$$b(x; n, P) = {}^{n}C_{x} * P^{x} * (1 - P)^{n-x}$$

or

$$bx; n, P) = \{ n! \,/\, [\, x! \,(n - x)! \,] \} * P^{x} * (1 - P)^{n-x}$$

Suppose you toss a coin five times. The probability of getting three heads is shown below:

Number of trials (n) = 5
Number of successes (x) = 3
Probability of success (P) in each trial = ½ = 0.5
Applying the formula for binomial distribution

$$b(3; 5, 0.5) = {}^{5}C_{3} * (0.5)^{3} * (0.5)^{2} = 0.625$$

Taking another example, suppose there are 15 multiple choice questions. Each question has four possible answers and one of them is correct. A student attempts all the questions. The probability of (a) his getting exactly five correct answers and (b) his getting four or fewer correct answers can be computed.

(a) Number of trials (n) = 15
Number of successes (x) = 5
Probability of success (P) in each trial = 1/4 = 0.25
The `pmf(x,n,P)` function in Python can be used for this purpose. We need to import SciPy to use the binomial distribution functions:

```
from scipy.stats import binom
res = binom.pmf(5, 15,.25)
print(res)
```

Output: 0.16514598112553383

(b) To find the probability of four or fewer correct answers, addition of all the binomial probabilities of x = 0, 1, 2, 3, 4 is required.
In Python programming:

```
from scipy.stats import binom
result=binom.pmf(0, 15,.25)+binom.pmf(1, 15,.25)+binom.pmf(2,
15,.25)+binom.pmf(3, 15,.25)+binom.pmf(4, 15,.25)
print(result)
```

Output: 0.6864859415218261

The probability of success of four or fewer correct answers is 68.6%.

Alternatively, the cumulative probability function for binomial distribution `cdf(x,n,p)` can be used.

```
from scipy.stats import binom
prob = binom.cdf(4, 15,.25)
print(prob)
```

Output: 0.6864859415218234

Multinomial distribution: A multinomial distribution is the probability distribution of n repeated trials, where each trial can have a number of possible outcomes (k). The probability of each outcome is $p_1, p_2, \ldots, p_k$. All trials are independent.

Mathematical formula: Suppose a multinomial experiment consists of n trials and k possible outcomes $(E_1, E_2..E_k)$ and the probabilities of k possible outcomes are $p_1, p_2, \ldots, p_k$. The event E_1 occurs n_1 times, E_2 occurs n_2 times,..., and E_k occurs n_k times. The multinomial probability P is calculated as:

$$P = [\, n! \,/\, (\, n_1! * n_2! * \ldots n_k!) \,] * (p_1^{n_1} * p_2^{n_2} * \ldots * p_k^{n_k}),$$

where $n = n_1 + n_2 + \ldots + n_k$.

For example, two chess players play a game and the probability that A would win is 0.30, B would win is 0.50 and that the match would be drawn is 0.20. The players played 10 games. To find out the probability that A would win three games, B would win four games and three games would be drawn, the following computation can be used:

A wins $n_1 = 3$ games with probability p_1 0.30.
B wins $n_2 = 4$ games with probability p_2 0.50.
Match draw $n_3 = 3$ times with probability p_3 0.20.

$$P = [\, n! \,/\, (\, n_1! * n_2! * \ldots n_k!) \,] * (p_1^{n_1} * p_2^{n_2} * \ldots * p_k^{n_k})$$
$$P = [\, 10! \,/\, (\, 3! * 4! * 3! \,) \,] * [\, (0.30)^3 * (0.50)^4 * (0.20)^3 \,]$$
$$P = 0.0567$$

The Python code for this is given below:

```
# multinomial distribtion in python
from scipy.stats import multinomial
#calculate multinomial probability
r=multinomial.pmf(x=[3, 4, 3], n=10, p=[.3,.5,.2])
print(r)
```

Output: 0.05669999999999983

Poisson distribution: A Poisson distribution is the probability distribution that finds the probability of events based on average past probability. Poisson probability is defined as

$$P(x;\, \mu),$$

where x = actual number of successes and μ = mean number of successes.

Mathematical formula: The Poisson probability is defined as

$$P(x;\, \mu) = (e^{-\mu})\, (\mu^x) \,/\, x!,$$

where e = 2.71828

Suppose the average number of cars sold by a company is five per day. The probability that six cars will be sold tomorrow can be calculated as shown below:

μ = 5 (average of 5 cars sold per day)

x = 6 (calculate that 6 cars will be sold tomorrow)

e = 2.71828

Applying the Poisson formula

$$P(x; \mu) = (e^{-\mu})\ (\mu^{x})\ /\ x!$$

$$P(6; 5) = (2.71828^{-5})\ (5^{6})\ /\ 6!$$
$$= 0.762$$

The probability of selling six cars will be 0.76 or 76%.

The Python code to perform this is given below:

```
from scipy.stats import poisson
lmbda = 5
r = poisson.cdf(6, lmbda)
print(r)
```

Output: 0.7621834629729387

The Poisson distribution function `poisson(lam, size)` has two parameters; `lam` is the rate or known number of occurrences and `size` is the shape of the returned array.

```
from numpy import random
import matplotlib.pyplot as plt
import seaborn as sns
sns.distplot(random.poisson(lam=3, size=500), kde=False)
plt.show()
```

Output:

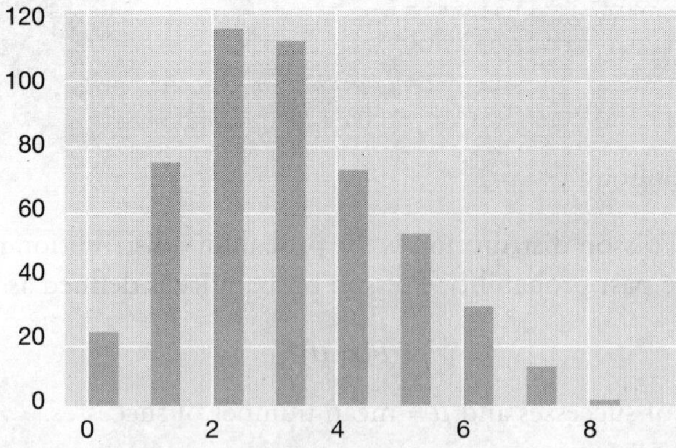

7.5.2 Continuous Probability Distribution

A continuous random variable takes a continuous range of values. Continuous probability distribution is defined over a continuous random variable. It can be represented using an equation or function.

A function that describes a continuous probability distribution is called a probability density function (PDF). Sometimes referred to as density function, PDF has the following properties:

1. $F(b)=Pr\,(X\leq \int_{-\infty}^{x} f(t)\,dt$
2. $f(x) \geq 0$ for any value of x
3. $\int_{-\infty}^{x} f(t)\,d(t)=1$

PDF can be represented using graphs that are continuous over a range. The area under the curve of the density function should be in the given range and the *x* axis should be 1; that is, the sum of all probabilities should be 1.

Continuous uniform distribution: PDF takes continuous uniform values over a range. It can be rectangular or constant (saturated) after some values of *x*, as shown in Fig. 7.1.

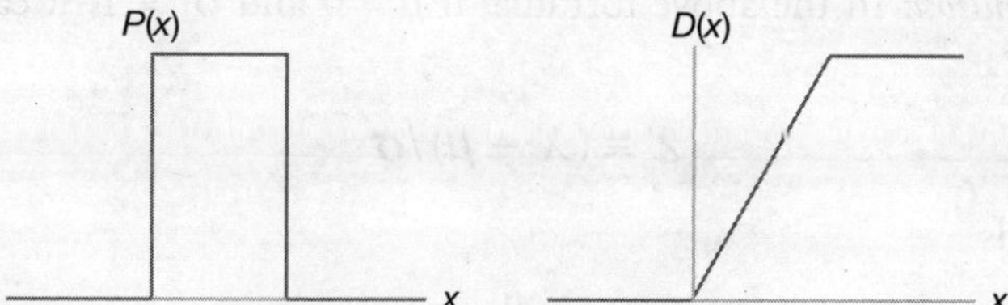

Figure 7.1 Continuous uniform distribution over a range

The PDF and cumulative distribution function over an interval $[a, b]$ is defined as

$$P(x)=\begin{cases} 0 & \text{for } x<a \\ \dfrac{1}{b-a} & \text{for } a\leq x\leq b \\ 0 & \text{for } x>b \end{cases} \tag{1}$$

$$D(x)=\begin{cases} 0 & \text{for } x<a \\ \dfrac{x-a}{b-a} & \text{for } a\leq x\leq b \\ 1 & \text{for } x>b \end{cases}$$

For example, to generate five numbers between 1 and 5 of the uniform distribution, the code in Python is as follows:

```
R = uniform.rvs(1, 5, size = 5)
print(R)
```

Output: [3.8051511 1.09323645 5.00316336 2.16487137 5.03552598]

Normal distribution: This is the continuous probability distribution of a bell-shaped curve, shown in Fig. 7.2. It is also called a Gaussian distribution. The bell-shaped curve is also known as a normal curve. It is used in various instances, such as in the grading of marks in student examinations, rainfall studies, measurement of area and manufacturing parts.

A continuous random variable X having a bell-shaped distribution is called a normal random variable.

Mathematical formula: Normal probability density function is defined as

$$P(x) = \frac{1}{\sigma\sqrt{2\pi}} e^{-(x-\mu)^2/(2\sigma^2)},$$

where X = continuous random variable $x \in (-\infty, \infty)$; μ = mean and σ^2 = variance.

Standard normal distribution: In the above formula, if $\mu = 0$ and $\sigma^2 = 1$, it can be called a standard normal distribution.

$$Z \equiv (X - \mu)/\sigma$$

So $dz = dx / \sigma$ yields

$$P(x)dx = \frac{1}{\sqrt{2\pi}} e^{-z^2/2} dz$$

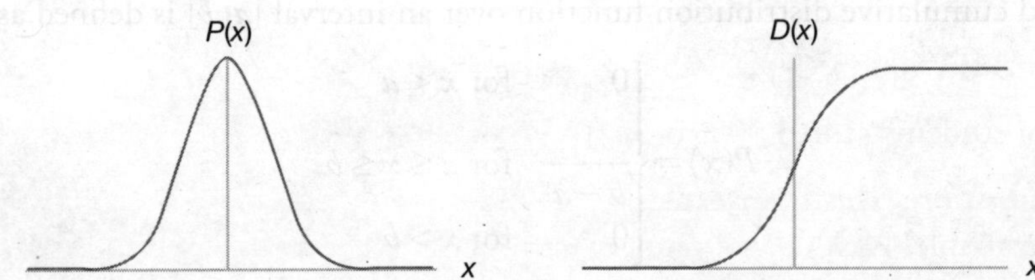

Figure 7.2 Continuous normal distribution

Normal distribution in Python is obtained using the function `random.normal(loc, scale, size)`. It has three parameters `loc`, `scale` and `size`, where `loc` (mean) is where the peak of the bell exists, `scale` (standard deviation) is how flat the graph distribution should be and `size` is the shape of the returned array. The curve of a normal distribution is called the bell curve because of its bell shape.

```
from numpy import random
import matplotlib.pyplot as plt
import seaborn as sns
sns.distplot(random.normal(loc=1, scale=2, size=(2, 3)), hist=False)
plt.show()
```

Output:

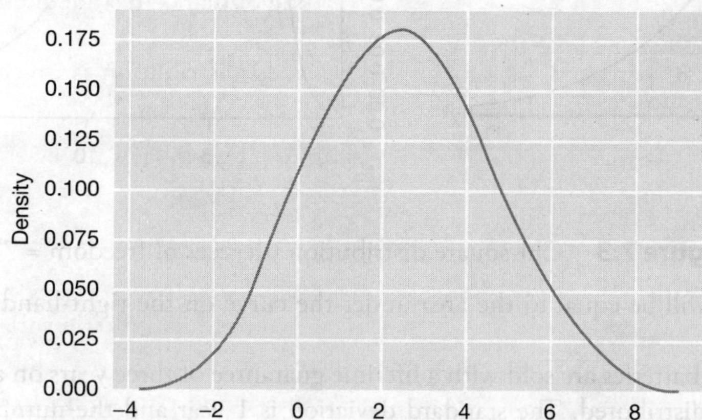

For example, a student examination system follows normal distribution. In a subject, the mean test score is 78 and standard deviation is 20. To find out what percentage of students score 90% or more, the function for normal distribution in Python can be used as follows:

```
import scipy.stats as stats
x=stats.norm(78, 20).cdf(90)
print((1-x))
```

Output: 0.27425311775007355

Therefore, 27% of students scored 90% or more.

Chi-square distribution: This is an extension of the standard normal distribution, where m independent random variables $X_1, X_2, \ldots, X_m$ are involved. Its degree of freedom is m and variance is $2m$.

Mathematical formula:

$$V = X_1^2 + X_2^2 + \cdots X_m^2 \sim X_{(m)}^2$$

The chi-square distribution with $v = n - 1$ degrees of freedom is given by

$$x^2 = \frac{(n-1)S^2}{\sigma^2} = \sum_{i=1}^{n} \frac{(X_i - \overline{X})^2}{\sigma^2}$$

To calculate the probability that a random sample produces a chi-square distribution value greater than χ^2_α, the graph shown in Fig. 7.3 can be used.

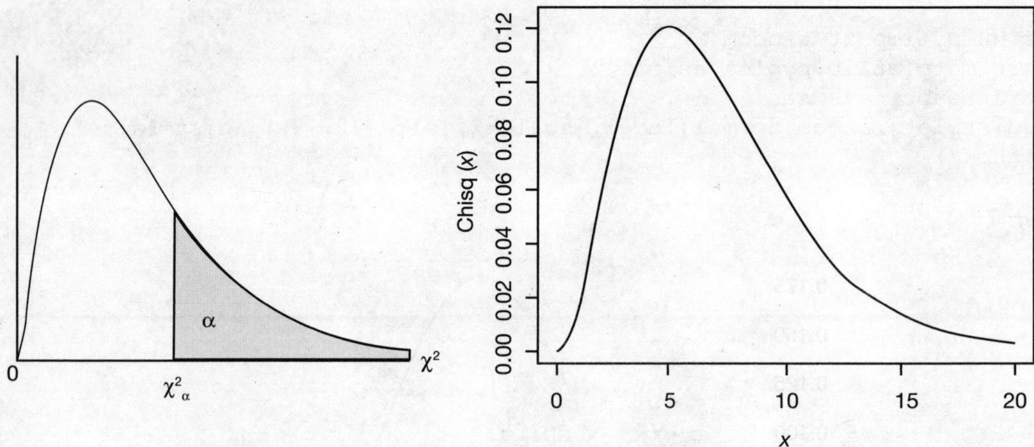

Figure 7.3 Chi-square distribution (degrees of freedom = 7)

The probability will be equal to the area under the curve on the right-hand side of χ^2_α (shaded area).

For example, car batteries are sold with a lifetime guarantee of three years on average. The battery lifetime is normally distributed. The standard deviation is 1 year and the number of batteries is 5. The lifetime of five batteries in years = 1.9, 2.4, 3.0, 3.5, 4.2. Our aim is to find the percentage of confidence that the standard deviation of the battery is 1 year.

$X = 1.9, 2.4, 3.0, 3.5, 4.2$
$n = 5$
$\sigma = 1$ (standard deviation of 1 year)
$\overline{X} = 3.0$

$$s^2 = \frac{\sum (x_i - \overline{x})^2}{n-1} = 0.815$$

$$\chi^2 = \frac{(n-1)s^2}{\sigma^2} = 3.26$$

Checking 3.26 with 4 degrees of freedom in the chi-square table, the value at 95% is obtained. Therefore, the confidence percentage that the standard deviation of the batteries is 1 year is 95%.

As an example, what would be the 86th percentile of the chi-square distribution, if the degree of freedom is 6? The Python function `chi2.ppf()` can be used, with the percentile passed as 0.86.

```
import scipy.stats as stats
x = stats.chi2.ppf(0.86, 6)
print("chi square ", x)
```

Output: chi square 9.653989666546625

Student's t-distribution: This is a form of continuous probability distribution where the sample size is small and standard deviation of the population is unknown. The name is based on the pseudonym "Student" used by William Sealy Gosset, who discovered it.

This distribution is the same as a normal distribution, which is bell shaped, but with heavier tails and lower peaks. It tends to produce values far from the mean. Student's t-distribution is used to estimate the significance of the values. It is used when you want to estimate the mean in a normally distributed population of small size where the standard deviation of the population is not known. It can construct a confidence interval between two mean values of two populations. It is used to study the mean of a population rather that individual members of the population.

Its mathematical formula is

$$T = \frac{\overline{X} - \mu}{S / \sqrt{n}},$$

where $\overline{X}$ = sample mean, μ = population mean, S = sample standard deviation and N = degree of freedom.

As the degree of freedom increases, the t-distribution tends towards standard normal distribution. Some sources state that if $n > 30$, the t-distribution would be the same as standard normal distribution.

Mathematical formula: It can be defined in terms of the Z standard normal random variable as

$$t = \frac{Z}{\sqrt{V / m}} \sim t_{(m)},$$

where Z is the same as in a standard normal distribution, V = chi-square distribution and m = degree of freedom.

Thus, the t-distribution is used to check the means of two samples that are different from each other or to compare means when the standard deviation of the population is not known. A student's t-distribution is shown in Fig. 7.4.

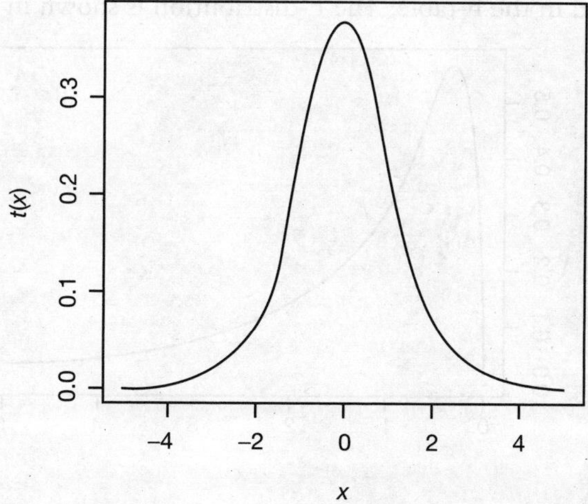

Figure 7.4 Student's t-distribution (degree of freedom = 5)

For example, to find the 12th and 88th percentiles of a student's t-distribution with degree of freedom = 7, the Python function `t.ppf()` can be used as follows:

```
import scipy.stats as stats
  r=stats.t.ppf([.12,.88], df=7)
  print(r)
```

Output: [-1.28401411 1.28401411]

F-distribution: This type of distribution is related to the χ^2 distribution. It is used to test whether two samples have the same variance. A chi-square distribution deals with one variable and one degree of freedom, but F-distribution deals with multiple variables and multiple degrees of freedom. It is a skewed distribution of probabilities similar to a chi-square distribution. The ANOVA model utilizes the F-distribution. It is a method for obtaining the probabilities of a specific set of events.

The F-distribution is defined on two independent random variables having chi-square distribution.

Mathematical formula:

$$F = \frac{V_1 / m_1}{V_2 / m_2} \sim F_{(m_1, m_2)},$$

where V_1 and V_2 are two independent random variables and m_1 and m_2 represent the degrees of freedom.

If the variance of two samples is S_1 and S_2 and the population variance is $\sigma^2{}_1$ and $\sigma^2{}_2$, the F-distribution with n_1 and n_2 degrees of freedom is defined as

$$F = \frac{S_1^2 / \sigma_1^2}{S_2^2 / \sigma_2^2} = \frac{\sigma_2^2 S_1^2}{\sigma_1^2 S_2^2}$$

An F-distribution uses $n_1 - 1$ and $n_2 - 1$ degrees of freedom. The area and percentile of the F-distribution can be found in the F-table. The F-distribution is shown in Fig 7.5.

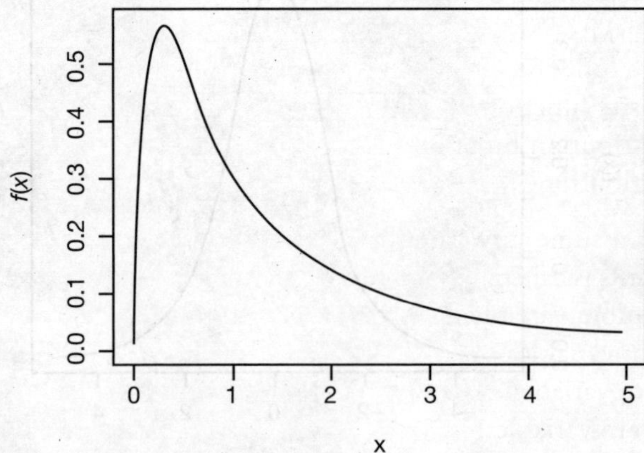

Figure 7.5 F-distribution (degree of freedom = (5,2))

To find out the F-distribution of the 88th percentile, with degree of freedom as 7, 3, the `f.ppf()` function can be used in Python:

```
import scipy.stats as stats
r=stats.f.ppf(q=.88, dfn=7, dfd=3)
print("F distribution ",r)
```

Output: F distribution 4.559048803738592

EXERCISES

Multiple Choice Questions

1. Which of the following standard probability density functions is applicable to discrete random variables?
   (a) Gaussian distribution
   (b) Poisson distribution
   (c) Rayleigh distribution
   (d) Exponential distribution

2. What is the area under a conditional cumulative density function?
   (a) 0
   (b) Infinity
   (c) 1
   (d) Changes with CDF

3. A table with all possible values of a random variable and its corresponding probabilities is called________.
   (a) Probability mass function
   (b) Probability density function
   (c) Cumulative distribution function
   (d) Probability distribution

4. A variable that can assume any value between two given points is called ________.
   (a) Continuous random variable
   (b) Discrete random variable
   (c) Irregular random variable
   (d) Uncertain random variable

5. A variable that can contain certain integer values between two given points is called ________.
   (a) Continuous random variable
   (b) Discrete random variable
   (c) Irregular random variable
   (d) Uncertain random variable

6. The expected value of a discrete random variable 'x' is given by:
   (a) $P(x)$
   (b) $\sum P(x)$
   (c) $\sum x\, P(x)$
   (d) 1

7. Of the following values, which is not possible in probability?
   (a) $P(x) = 1$
   (b) $\sum x\, P(x) = 3$
   (c) $P(x) = 0.5$
   (d) $P(x) = -0.5$

8. In binomial probability distribution, the dependents of standard deviation must include:
   (a) Probability of q
   (b) Probability of p
   (c) Trials
   (d) All of the above

Answers

1. (b) **2.** (c) **3.** (d) **4.** (a) **5.** (b) **6.** (c) **7.** (d) **8.** (d)

Programming/Concept-based Questions

1. Give some examples of random variables. Also, specify the range of values and whether they are continuous or discrete values.

Answer: A discrete variable is a variable whose value is obtained by counting. Examples are number of students present, number of red marbles in a jar, number of heads when flipping three coins, students' grade levels.

A continuous variable is a variable whose value is obtained by measuring. Examples are height of students in a class, weight of students in a class, time it takes to get to school, distance travelled between classes.

2. In the following cases, what are the probability distributions likely to be followed? In each case, you should mention the random variable and the parameter(s) influencing the probability distribution function.

(a) In a retail source, how many counters should be opened at a given time period?

(b) The number of people suffering from cancer in a town

Answer:

(a) Here, the arrival process is Poisson and the service time distribution is deterministic. The system has *n* servers (a ticket booking counter with *n* cashiers). Here, the service time can be assumed to be the same for all customers.

(b) Based on the data, a Gaussian or normal distribution can be used.

3. In the following cases, what are the probability distributions likely to be followed? In each case, you should mention the random variable and the parameter(s) influencing the probability distribution function.

(a) A missile will hit the enemy's aircraft

(b) A student in the class will secure EX grade

(c) Salary of a person in an enterprise

(d) Accident involving cars in a city

(e) People quit education after (i) primary, (ii) secondary and (iii) higher secondary education

Answer:

(a) A good example of this application is the study carried out by Clark (1946) concerning the distribution of flying bomb hits in one part of London during the Second World War. The area was divided into 576 small areas of 0.25 km^2 each. In the data, the number of areas with exactly *k* hits was recorded and compared with the predicted number based on a Poisson distribution, with the number of total hits per number of areas.

(b) Normal distribution, where the cut-off of all grades can be marked on a curve.

(c) The normal probability distribution is very common in the field of statistics. Whenever you measure entities such as people's height, weight, salary, opinions or votes, the graph of the results is very often a normal curve.

(d) It is sensible to use a Poisson random variable representing the number of car accidents in a city.
(e) Normal distribution

4. How can you calculate the mean and standard deviation of a population if the population follows the following probability distribution functions with respect to an event?
(a) Binomial distribution function
(b) Poisson distribution function
(c) Hypergeometric distribution function
(d) Normal distribution function
(e) Standard normal distribution function

Answer:
(a) The mean of the distribution (μ_x) is equal to $n * P$. The variance (s^2_x) is $n * P * (1 - P)$. The standard deviation (s_x) is *sqrt*[$n * P * (1 - P)$].
(b) The mean, or average, number of wins (λ) in n tries will be given by $\lambda = np$.
(c) The mean of the hypergeometric distribution is nk/N, and the variance (square of the standard deviation) is $nk(N - k)(N - n)/N^2(N - 1)$.
(d) To calculate the standard score for an observation, take the raw measurement, subtract the mean, and divide by the standard deviation. Mathematically, the formula for that process is as follows:

$$f(x) = \frac{1}{\sigma\sqrt{2\pi}} e^{-\frac{1}{2}\left(\frac{x-\mu}{\sigma}\right)^2}$$

(e) The standard normal distribution (z distribution) is a normal distribution with a mean of 0 and a standard deviation of 1.

CHAPTER **8**

Machine Learning and Data Pre-processing

LEARNING OBJECTIVES

At the end of this chapter, you will be able to:

- Explore the basics of machine learning
- List the types of machine learning
- Explain the basics of data sets
- Identify the data types
- Describe the data pre-processing tasks
- Implement data reduction, data transformation, data encoding and handling missing values using Python

8.0 INTRODUCTION TO MACHINE LEARNING

Machine learning (ML) is an important sub-branch of Artificial Intelligence (AI). A frequently quoted definition of ML is by Arthur Samuel, one of the pioneers of AI. He stated that, "Machine learning is the field of study that gives the computer the ability to learn without being explicitly programmed."

The key to this definition is that the system should learn by itself without explicit programming. How is this possible? It is widely known that to perform a computation, one needs to write programs that teach the computer how to perform that computation.

In conventional programming, after understanding the problem, a detailed design of the program such as a flowchart or an algorithm is created and converted into programs using a suitable programming language. This approach could be difficult to implement for many real-world problems such as puzzles, games and complex image recognition applications.

AI attempted to understand these problems and develop general purpose rules manually. These rules were formulated into logic and implemented in a program to create intelligent systems. This idea of developing intelligent systems by using logic and reasoning by converting an expert's knowledge into a set of rules and programs is called an **expert system**. An expert system like MYCIN was designed for medical diagnosis after converting the knowledge of many doctors into a system. However, this approach did not progress much as programs lacked real intelligence. The word MYCIN is derived from the fact that most of the antibiotics' names end with 'mycin'.

The above approach was impractical in many domains as programs still depended on human expertise and hence did not truly exhibit intelligence. Then, the momentum shifted to machine learning in the form of data-driven systems. The focus of AI today is to develop intelligent systems by using a data-driven approach, where data is used as input to develop intelligent models. The models can then be used to predict new inputs. Thus, the aim of ML is to learn a model or set of rules from the given data set automatically so that it can predict the unknown data correctly. As humans make decisions based on experience, computers make models based on extracted patterns in the input data and then use these data-filled models for prediction and to make decisions. For computers, the learnt model is equivalent to the human experience.

A **model** is an explicit description of patterns within data in the form of:

- Mathematical equations
- Relational diagrams like trees/graphs
- Logical if/else rules
- Groupings called clusters

In summary, a model can be a formula, procedure or representation that can generate data decisions. The difference between pattern and model is that the former is local and applicable only to certain attributes, but the latter is global and fits the entire data set. For example, a model can be helpful to examine whether a given email is spam or not. The point is that the model is generated automatically from the given data.

Another pioneer of AI was Tom Mitchell. His definition of ML states that, "A computer program is said to learn from experience E, with respect to task T and some performance measure P, if its performance on T measured by P improves with experience E." The important components of this definition are experience E, task T and performance measure P.

For example, the task T could be detecting an object in an image. The machine can gain knowledge of objects using a training data set of thousands of images. This is called experience E. So, the focus is to use this experience E for this task of object detection T. The ability of the system to detect the object is measured by performance measures like precision and recall. Based on the performance measures, course correction can be carried out to improve the performance of the system.

Models of computer systems are equivalent to human experience. Experience is based on data. Humans gain experience by various means. They gain knowledge by rote learning. They observe others and imitate them. Humans gain a lot of knowledge from teachers and books. They also learn many things by trial and error. Once knowledge is gained, when a new problem is encountered, humans search for similar past situations and then formulate the heuristics and use that for prediction. However, in systems, experience is gathered by these steps:

1. Collection of data.
2. Once data is gathered, abstract concepts are formed out of that data. Abstraction is used to generate concepts. This is equivalent to humans' idea of objects; for example, humans have some idea of what an elephant looks like.
3. Generalization converts the abstraction into an actionable form of intelligence. It can be viewed as ordering all possible concepts. So, generalization involves ranking of concepts, inferencing from them and formation of heuristics, an actionable aspect of intelligence. Heuristics are educated guesses for all tasks. For example, if one runs into or encounters danger, it is the result of human

experience or one's heuristics. In machines, it occurs the same way. Heuristics works in most cases, but it may fail too. It is not the fault of heuristics as it is just a 'rule of thumb'. Course correction is carried out by taking evaluation measures. Evaluation checks the thoroughness of the models and carries out course correction, if necessary, to generate better formulations.

8.1 Need for Machine Learning

Machine learning is a promising and flourishing field. It can help the top management of an organization to extract knowledge from the data stored in a structured and unstructured manner in various archives of the organization to facilitate decision-making.

Earlier, the full potential of this data was not utilized. One of the possible reasons was data being scattered across different archive systems and organizations not being able to integrate these sources fully. Secondly, there were very few software tools available that could help to unearth the useful information from data.

Business organizations have now started to use the latest technology, ML, for this purpose. ML has become popular for three reasons:

- **High volume of data to manage:** Companies such as Facebook (now Meta), Twitter and YouTube generate huge amounts of data every year. The rate of data growth is estimated to double every year.
- **Reduced cost of storage:** The hardware cost has dropped. This makes it easy to capture, process, store, distribute and transmit digital information.
- **Availability of complex algorithms:** Especially with the advent of deep learning, many algorithms are available for ML.

With the popularity and ready adoption of ML by business organizations, it has become a dominant technology trend.

8.2 Types of Machine Learning

There are four types of machine learning, as shown in Fig. 8.1.

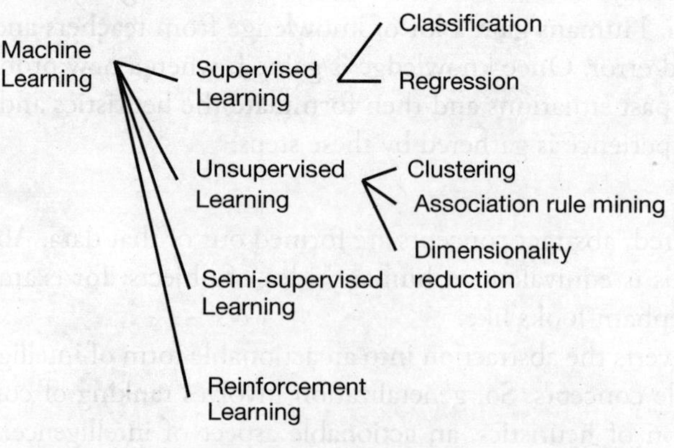

Figure 8.1 Types of ML

Before discussing the types of ML, it is necessary to discuss data. There are two types of data: labelled and unlabelled. Normally, data is represented in the form of a table. It can also be presented as a data point. In tabular form, each row represents a data point. The columns of a table are attributes or features of data. Of all the attributes, the label is the feature that we aim to predict.

To illustrate labelled data, let us take use the Iris flower data set or Fisher's Iris data set. This data set has 50 samples of Iris, with four attributes: length and width of sepals and petals. The target variable is called class. There are three classes: Iris setosa, Iris virginica and Iris versicolor. So data in Table 8.1 is labelled data, where each row has a value for a target variable.

Table 8.1 Iris data set example

Petal length	Petal width	Sepal length	Sepal width	Class
5.5	4.2	1.4	0.2	Setosa
7	5.2	1.7	1.4	Versicolor
7.3	4	1.8	1.8	Virginica

Data may be in the form of images also. Various deep learning models can be used for this data. Unlabelled data comes without a label. Figure 8.2 shows labelled and unlabelled image data.

Figure 8.2 Labelled and unlabelled data example

8.2.1 Supervised Learning

Supervised algorithms use labelled data sets. As the name suggests, there is a supervisor or teacher component in supervised learning. A supervisor provides labelled data so that the model is constructed and generates test data.

In supervised learning algorithms, the supervisor communicates the information that the learner is supposed to know. The learner understands the received information without the supervisor knowing whether the information has been grasped by the learner or not. The supervisor tests the learner by asking a set of questions. Supervised learning typically uses two methods:

- **Classification:** Classification is a supervised learning method. The aim of classification is to predict the 'label' or 'class', that is, in a discrete form. An example is to categorize the given image into cat or dog. A classification algorithm takes a set of labelled data images such as dogs and cats to construct a model that can later be used to classify unknown test image data.

  In classification, learning takes place in two stages. In the first stage, called the training stage, the learning algorithm takes a labelled data set and starts learning. After the training set, samples are processed and the model is generated. In the second stage, the constructed model is tested with a test or unknown sample and assigned a label. This is the classification process.

  For example, in the case of the Iris data set, if the test is given as (6.3, 2.9, 5.6, 1.8, ?), the classification will generate a label for this. Other examples of classification are image recognition, classification of diseases like cancer, classification of plants, email spam detection, sentiment analysis, etc.

  Some of the key algorithms of classification are:

  - Decision tree
  - Random forest
  - Support vector machines
  - Naïve Bayes
  - Artificial neural networks and deep learning networks like CNN
- **Regression:** Regression models, unlike classification algorithms, predict continuous variables such as price. In other words, it is a real number. The regression model takes input x and generates a model in the form of a fitted line of the form $y = f(x)$. Here, x is the independent variable that may be one or more attributes and y is the dependent variable. For example, product sales is dependent on week of sale; linear regression takes the training set and tries to fit it with a line: product sales = 0.66 × Week + 0.54. Here, 0.66 and 0.54 are regression coefficients that are learnt from the data. The advantage of this model is that prediction for product sales (y) can be made for unknown week data (x). For example, the prediction for an unknown eighth week can be made by substituting x with 8 in the regression formula to obtain y.

Both regression and classification models are supervised algorithms. Both have a supervisor and concepts of training and testing are applicable to both. The difference is that regression models predict continuous variables such as product price, while classification concentrates on assigning labels such as class or state.

8.2.2 Unsupervised Learning

This kind of learning takes place by self-instruction. As the name suggests, there are no supervisor or teacher components. In the absence of a supervisor or teacher, self-instruction is the most common kind of learning process. It uses the trial and error method for self-instruction. Here, self-learning takes place with unlabelled data. The algorithm itself observes the examples and data and identifies patterns based on the principles of grouping. Grouping is performed so that similar objects form a group.

Cluster analysis, association rule mining and dimensional reduction algorithms are examples of unsupervised learning algorithms.

- **Cluster analysis:** This aims to group objects into disjoint clusters or groups. Cluster analysis clusters objects based on their attributes. All the data objects of the partitions are similar in some aspects and vary from the data objects in the other partitions significantly.
  Some of the key clustering algorithms are:
  - k-means
  - Hierarchical
  - DBSCAN
- **Dimensionality reduction:** This takes a higher dimension data as input and outputs the data in lower dimension by taking advantage of the variance of the data. It is a task of reducing the data set with few features without losing the generality. Principle component analysis (PCA) is used for dimension reduction.
- **Association rule mining:** Association rule mining finds interesting associations and relationships among large sets of data items. This rule shows how frequently an itemset occurs in a transaction. A typical example is a market-based analysis. These rules help retailers find relationships between items which are frequently purchased together by customers. Apriori algorithm is used to find the association rules.

8.2.3 Semi-supervised Learning

There are circumstances where the data set has a huge collection of unlabelled data and some labelled data. Labelling is a costly process and difficult to perform by humans. Semi-supervised algorithms use unlabelled data by assigning a pseudo-label. Then, the labelled and pseudo-labelled data sets can be combined.

8.2.4 Reinforcement Learning

Reinforcement learning mimics human beings. Instead of data, an environment is given and an agent is supposed to navigate the environment to learn. Like human beings use ears and eyes to perceive the world and take actions, reinforcement learning allows the agent to interact with the environment to get rewards. The agent can be a human, animal, robot or any independent program. The rewards enable the agent to gain experience. The agent aims to maximize the reward, which can be positive or negative (punishment). When the rewards are greater, the behaviour is reinforced and learning becomes possible. Reinforcement learning has various applications in gaming, robotics and in self-driving cars.

8.3 Understanding Data

All facts are data. In computer systems, bits encode facts present in numbers, text, images, audio and video. Data can be directly human-interpretable, such as numbers or text, or be diffused, such as images or videos that can be interpreted only by a computer.

Data by itself is meaningless. It needs to be processed to generate any information. A string of bytes is meaningless. Only when a label is attached such as the height of a person does the data become meaningful. Processed data is called information and it includes patterns, associations and relationships among the data. For example, sales data can be analyzed to extract information such as which product was sold in greater quantities in the last quarter of the year.

Big Data

Data whose volume is less and can be stored and processed by a small computer is called small data. Big data, on the other hand, is data whose volume is much larger. It must satisfy the 6Vs: volume, velocity, variety, veracity, validity and value. Big data is measured in terms of petabytes (PB) and exabytes (EB). One exabyte is 1 million terabytes. The fast arrival speed of data and its increase in volume is noted as velocity of data. Data comes in different forms that range from text, graphs, audio, video and maps to composite data. Data also comes from various resources such as human conversation, transaction records and old archive data. Data sources can be open/public, social media and multimodal. The veracity of data deals with aspects like conformity to facts, truthfulness, believability and confidence in data. Veracity of data is one of the important aspects of data as there may be many sources of error such as technical, typographical and human. Validity is the accuracy of data for taking decisions. Value is the characteristic of big data that indicates the quality of the information that is extracted from the data; it influence the decisions that are taken based on it.

In big data, there are three kinds of data:

- **Structured data:** Here, data is stored in an organized manner such as a database where it is available in the form of a table. The data can be retrieved in an organized manner using tools like SQL.
- **Unstructured data:** This includes video, image and audio. It also includes textual documents, programs and blog data. Nowadays 80% of data is unstructured.
- **Semi-structured data:** This type of data is partially structured and partially unstructured. Examples are XML/JSON data, RSS feeds and hierarchical data.

Once a data set is assembled, it must be stored in a structure that is suitable for analysis. Data can be stored in flat files in plain ASCII or EBCDIC format. Comma-separated values (CSV) and tab-separated values (TSV) are popular spreadsheet formats for storing data.

Data can be stored in database files, which consist of original data and metadata. A relational database consists of sets of tables, having rows and columns. A database management system aims to manage data and improve operator performance by including various tools like database administrator, query processing and transaction manager. Transactional, time-series and spatial are a few types of databases where different types of data are stored.

The World Wide Web (WWW) provides diverse, worldwide online information. Algorithms can be used to mine interesting patterns of information in WWW. eXtensible Markup Language (XML) is a machine-interpretable data format that can be used to present data that needs to be shared across platforms. A data stream is dynamic data, which flows in and out of the observing environment. Typical characteristics of a data stream are huge volume of data, dynamic nature, fixed order movement and real-time constraints. Really Simple Syndication (RSS) is a format for sharing instant feeds across services. JavaScript Object Notation (JSON) is another useful data interchange format that is often used for many ML algorithms.

8.4 DATA SET AND DATA TYPES

A data set can be assumed to be a collection of data objects. The data objects may be records, points, vectors, patterns, events, cases, samples or observations. These records contain many attributes. An attribute can be defined as a characteristic or property of an object. Consider the data set in the sample in Table 8.2.

Table 8.2 Student placement data set

Student ID	CGPA	Interactiveness	Practical knowledge	Communication skills	Job offer
1	>9	Yes	Very good	Good	Yes
2	>8	No	Average	Moderate	No
3	<8	No	Good	Poor	No

Every attribute should be associated with a value. This is called measurement. The type of attribute determines the data types, often referred to as measurement scale types. The data types are shown in Fig. 8.3.

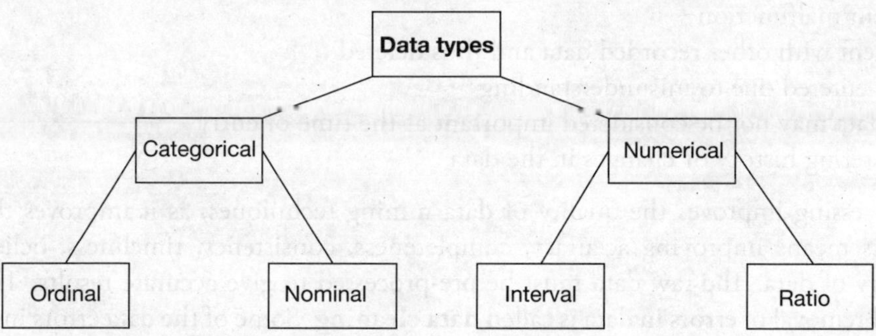

Figure 8.3 Types of data

Broadly, data can be classified into two types:

- **Categorical** or qualitative data can be nominal or ordinal. In Table 8.2, Student ID is nominal data. **Nominal data** are symbols and cannot be processed like numbers. For example, the average of student ID does not make any statistical sense. Likewise, job offer (Yes, No) and interactiveness (Yes, No) are also nominal data. Nominal data types provide only information but have no order. Only operators like (=, ≠) are meaningful for this data.

  Ordinal data provides information and has a natural order. For example, communication skill (Good, Average, Poor) is ordinal data. Poor is certainly less than Average and Average is less than Good, irrespective of value. Any transformation can be applied to this data to obtain a new value.

- **Numerical** or quantitative data can be classified as discrete or continuous. Another classification is interval and ratio. **Discrete data** is recorded as integers. Employee identification number such as 10011 is discrete data. **Continuous data** can be fitted into a range and includes decimal points. For example height, age is continuous data as height, age can be 120.3 cm, 12.5 years, respectively. **Interval data** is numeric data for which the difference between values is meaningful. For example, there is a difference between 30 degrees and 40 degrees. The only permissible operations are + and –. For **ratio data**, both differences and ratio are meaningful. The difference between ratio and interval data is the position of zero in the scale. For example, take Centigrade to Fahrenheit conversion. The zeros of both scales do not match. Hence this is interval data.

8.5 Data Pre-processing

In the real world, the available data is 'dirty'. By this, we refer to:

- Incomplete data
- Outlier data
- Data with inconsistent values
- Inaccurate data
- Data with missing values
- Duplicate data

This 'dirtiness' of data can be caused by the following:

- Equipment malfunction
- Inconsistent with other recorded data and thus deleted
- Data not entered due to misunderstanding
- Certain data may not be considered important at the time of entry
- Not registering history or changes in the data

Data pre-processing improves the quality of data mining techniques, as it improves the quality of the data. This means improving accuracy, completeness, consistency, timeliness, believability and interpretability of data. The raw data must be pre-processed to give accurate results. The process of detection and removal of errors in data is called **data cleaning**. Some of the data errors include human errors such as typographical errors or incorrect measurement and structural errors like improper data formats. Data errors can also arise from omission and duplication of attributes. **Noise** is a random component and involves distortion of a value or introduction of a spurious object. It is often seen when data is a spatial or temporal component. Certain deterministic distortions in the form of a streak are known as artifacts.

Consider Table 8.3. 'Bad' or 'dirty' data can be observed in this table.

Table 8.3 'Dirty' data example

Student ID	Name	Age	Date of birth	Fever	Salary
1	Shreya	136		Low	-1500
2	Tanu	18		High	Yes
3	Rishika	8	10/10/2006	Yes	""
4	Pragnay	17		High	Yes

It can be observed that data such as salary = " " is incomplete. Date of birth for Shreya, Tanu and Pragnay is missing. Rishika's age is recorded as 8 but her date of birth is stated as 10/10/2006. This is called inconsistent data. Shreya's salary is -1500. It cannot be less than 0. It is an instance of noisy data.

Inconsistent data occurs due to problems in conversion, inconsistent formats and differences in units. Outliers are data that exhibit characteristics that are different from other data and have unusual values. Shreya's age is 136. It might be a typographical error. It is often required to distinguish between noise and outlier value. Outlier might be legitimate data and sometimes is of interest to ML algorithms. These errors often occur in the data collection stage. They must be removed so that ML algorithms yield better results as the quality of results is determined by the quality of input data. This removal process is called data cleaning.

8.5.1 Missing Data Analysis

The primary data cleaning process involves missing data analysis. Data cleaning routines attempt to fill in the missing data values and smoothen the noise while identifying the outliers and correcting the inconsistencies in data. This enables machine learning to avoid overfitting of models. Following are a few techniques to solve the problem of missing data:

- A tuple with missing data, especially the class label, is ignored. This method is not effective when the percentage of missing values increases.
- A domain expert can analyze the data tables and carry out analysis and fill in the values manually. However, this is time consuming and may not be feasible for large sets of data.
- A global constant can be used to fill in the missing attributes. The missing value may be 'unknown' or 'infinity'. But some ML algorithms may give spurious results by analyzing these labels.
- Use the attribute mean for all samples belonging to the same class. Here, the average value replaces the missing values of all tuples that fall in this group.
- Use the most probable value to fill in the missing value. The most probable value can be obtained from other methods like classification and decision tree prediction.

8.5.2 Removal of Noise

Noise is a random error or variance in a measured value. It can be removed by using binning, which is a method where the given data values are sorted and distributed into equal frequency bins. The bins are also called buckets. The binning method uses the neighbour values to smooth the noisy data.

Some of the techniques commonly used are 'smoothing by bin mean' where the bin mean removes the values of the bins, 'smoothing by bin median' where the bin median replaces the bin values, and 'smoothing by bin boundary' where the bin value is replaced by the closest bin boundary. The maximum and minimum values are called bin boundaries.

Binning methods may be used as a discretization technique. For example, applying binning technique using bins of size 3 on data {12,14,19,22,24,26,28,31,34}:

Smooth by equal frequency bin method:
Bin1: 12,14,19
Bin2: 22,24,26
Bin3: 28,31,32

Smooth by bin mean method:
Bin1:15,15,15
Bin2:24,24,24
Bin3:30.3,30.3,30.3
Smooth by bin boundary method:
Bin1:12,12,19
Bin2:22,22,26
Bin3:28,32,32

8.5.3 Data Integration and Data Transformation

Data integration involves routines that merge data from multiple sources into a single data source. The main goal of data integration is to detect and remove redundancies that arise from data integration. Data transformation routines perform operations like normalization to improve the performance of ML algorithms. It is necessary to transform data so that it can be processed. In normalization, attribute values are scaled to fit in a range (say, 0–1) to improve the performance of ML algorithms. Some of the normalization techniques used are:

- **Min-Max procedure (MinMax scaler):** It is a normalization technique where each variable V is normalized by its difference with the minimum value divided by the range to a new range, say 0–1. Often, neural networks require this kind of normalization.

$$v' = \frac{v - \min_A}{\max_A - \min_A}(\text{new\_max}_A - \text{new\_min}_A) + \text{new\_min}_A \qquad (1)$$

Consider the marks {88,90,92,94}. To convert these marks to the 0–1 range, normalization can be applied as:

For mark 88

$$v' = \frac{(88-88)}{(94-88)} * (1-0) + 0 = 0$$

For mark 90

$$v' = \frac{(90-88)}{(94-88)} * (1-0) + 0 = 0.33$$

For mark 92

$$v' = \frac{(92-88)}{(94-88)} * (1-0) + 0 = 066$$

For mark 94

$$v' = \frac{(94-88)}{(94-88)} * (1-0) + 0 = 1$$

So the marks {88,90,92,94} are mapped to a new range {0,.33,.66,1}

- **Z-score normalization (Standard scaler):** This procedure takes the difference between the field value and mean value and scales this difference by the standard deviation of the attribute.

$$v' = \frac{v - \mu_A}{\sigma_A} \tag{2}$$

For example, applying z-score normalization on {10,20,30}, mean and standard deviation is required of this data. Mean of 10,20,30 is 20 and standard deviation is 10.

$$\text{Z-score of } 10 = \frac{(10-20)}{(10)} = -1$$

$$\text{Z-score of } 20 = \frac{(20-20)}{(10)} = 0$$

$$\text{Z-score of } 30 = \frac{(30-20)}{(10)} = 1$$

Z-scores are used to detect outliers. Z-score function is extremely sensitive to outliers as it is dependent on the mean.

8.5.4 Data Reduction

Data reduction reduces the data size but produces the same results. There are different ways in which data reduction can be carried out such as wavelet transform, feature selection, sampling and dimensionality reduction.

- **Discrete wavelet transform (DWT)** transforms the given data vector to a numerically different data vector. The transformed vector is of the same size as the original but the wavelet-transformed vector can be truncated. The strongest wavelet coefficients, that is, wavelet coefficients larger than some specified threshold, can be retained and the rest can be set to 0. This helps in data compression. As many data values become 0 after applying this transform, data becomes sparse and computation becomes very fast in wavelet space. Inverse DWT can be applied on a given set of wavelet coefficients, which gives an approximation of the original data.
- **Principal component analysis (PCA)** creates an alternative reduced set of variables from the original data, resulting in dimensionality reduction of data. Original data is projected into smaller spaces. The projection which captures the largest amount of variation in data is found. It works only on numeric data. Data is first normalized to make it more consistent and to make all attributes or variables in the same range. Eigenvectors of the covariance matrix are found. These eigenvectors define the new space, that is, k orthogonal vectors which are k principal components of data, where $k \leq n$. These principal components are considered in decreasing order of 'significance' or strength. Weak components are those with low variance and strong components have high variance. Therefore, strong components give more information to ML models. Since only strong components are stored, the size of data is reduced.

- **Feature subset selection** helps in feature reduction as attributes are redundant and irrelevant sometimes. There are heuristic methods for feature selection:
  - o **Step-wise forward selection:** It works in the forward direction, as it starts with an empty set of features as the reduced set. The best of the original features is determined and added to the reduced set. The best of the remaining original features are added in the set iteratively.
    Initial attribute set= {A1, A2, A3, A4, A5, A6}
    Initial reduced set: {}
    — {A1}
    —{A1,A4}
    —Reduced attribute set {A1,A4, A6}
  - **Step-wise backward elimination:** It works in the backward direction as it starts with a full set of features as the reduced set. The worst of the remaining original features are removed at each step iteratively.
    Initial attribute set= {A1, A2, A3, A4, A5, A6}
    Initial reduced set: {A1, A2, A3, A4, A5, A6}
    — {A1,A4, A5, A6 }
    —Reduced attribute set {A1,A4, A6}
  - **Combination of forward selection and backward elimination:** It combines both techniques discussed above. Here, the best features are added and the worst features are removed from the remaining data.
- In **sampling**, a representative subset of data is selected, which helps to reduce data. Taking out samples randomly can results in poor performance as data may be skewed. So adaptive sampling methods must be used for better performance. Some sampling techniques are as follows:
  - o **Simple random sampling:** Here you choose any item with equal probability.
  - o **Sampling without replacement:** Here, an item is removed from a population after selection.
  - o **Sampling with replacement:** Here, an item is not removed from the population after selecting it. It means that the same sample can appear again.
  - o **Cluster sampling:** Data is clustered and a cluster is randomly selected from the population.
  - o **Stratified sampling:** This works well for skewed data. Here, the data set is partitioned and samples are drawn from each partition (proportionally or in approximately the same percentage of the data).

8.5.5 Dimensionality Reduction Using Python

For each data sample that chooses a set of primary features, the number of feature variables is reduced using the unsupervised machine learning technique known as dimensionality reduction. One of the popular dimensionality reduction methods offered in sklearn is PCA.

By examining the features of the original data set, PCA is a statistical technique that linearly projects the data into a new feature space. Picking out the 'principal' qualities of the data and creating features based on them is the primary idea. It will provide us with a new data set that is small in size but which has all of the same information as the original data set. Computations become fast with a reduced data set.

Here, we use the Iris data set for explanation. It has one target variable, flower category, and four independent variables: sepal length, sepal width, petal length, petal width. We reduce the feature space from four independent variables to two, using PCA. So these two PCA components will have all the information contained by the four independent variables.

First import the libraries and load the Iris data set. Separate the *x* and *y* variables; *x* contains sepal length, sepal width, petal length, petal width and *y* contains species. The `pca()` method and `fit_transform()` are used on *x* data. Features are scaled using `standard scalar()`.

```
from sklearn.preprocessing import StandardScaler
import matplotlib.pyplot as plt
import seaborn as sns
import pandas as pd
df = sns.load_dataset('iris')
x = df.drop('species', axis =1)
y = df['species']
x = StandardScaler().fit_transform(x)
x = pd.DataFrame(x)
from sklearn.decomposition import PCA
pcatwofeatures = PCA()
x_pca = pcatwofeatures.fit_transform(x)
x_pca = pd.DataFrame(x_pca, columns=['PCA1','PCA2','PCA3','PCA4'])
print(x_pca.head())
explained_variance = pca.explained_variance_ratio_
print(explained_variance)
plt.figure(figsize=(10, 10))
sns.scatterplot(x_pca['PCA1'], [0] * len(x_pca), hue=y, s=50)
plt.figure(figsize=(10, 10))
sns.scatterplot(x_pca['PCA2'], [0] * len(x_pca), hue=y, s=50)
plt.figure(figsize=(10, 10))
sns.scatterplot(x_pca['PCA3'], [0] * len(x_pca), hue=y, s=50)
plt.figure(figsize=(10, 10))
sns.scatterplot(x_pca['PCA4'], [0] * len(x_pca), hue=y, s=50)
```

Output:

```
PCA1       PCA2      PCA3      PCA4
0 -2.264703  0.480027 -0.127706 -0.024168
1 -2.080961 -0.674134 -0.234609 -0.103007
2 -2.364229 -0.341908  0.044201 -0.028377
3 -2.299384 -0.597395  0.091290  0.065956
4 -2.389842  0.646835  0.015738  0.035923
[0.72962445 0.22850762 0.03668922 0.00517871]
```

PCA1 gives very accurate information, PCA2 gives less information compared to PCA1, while PCA3 gives less information compared to PCA2, as shown in Figs 8.4, 8.5, 8.6 and 8.7.

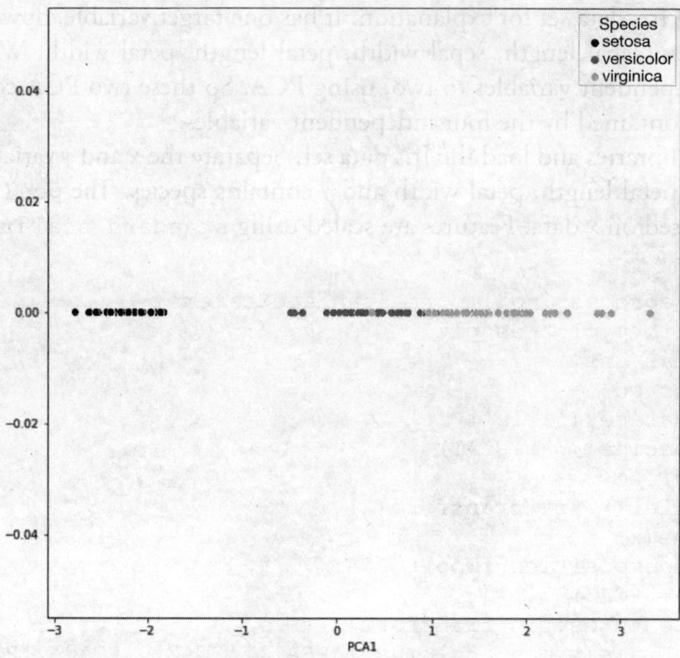

Figure 8.4 Iris flower categorization using the first principal component PCA1

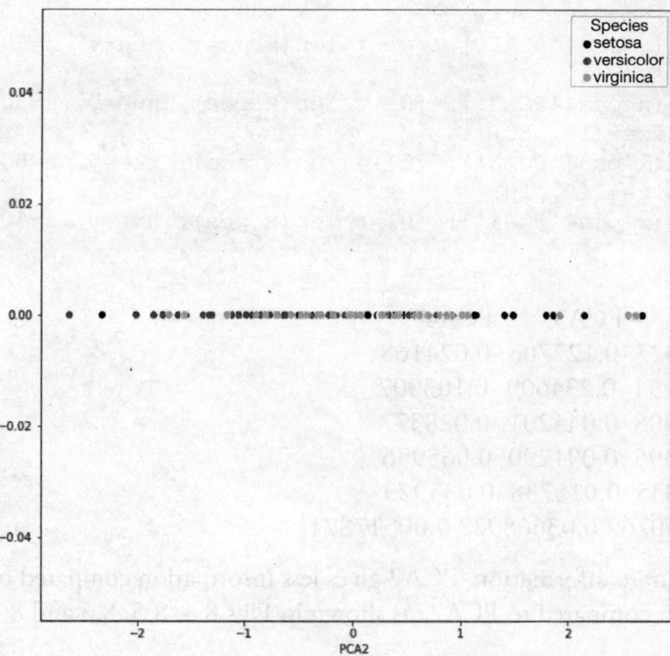

Figure 8.5 Iris flower categorization using the second principal component PCA2

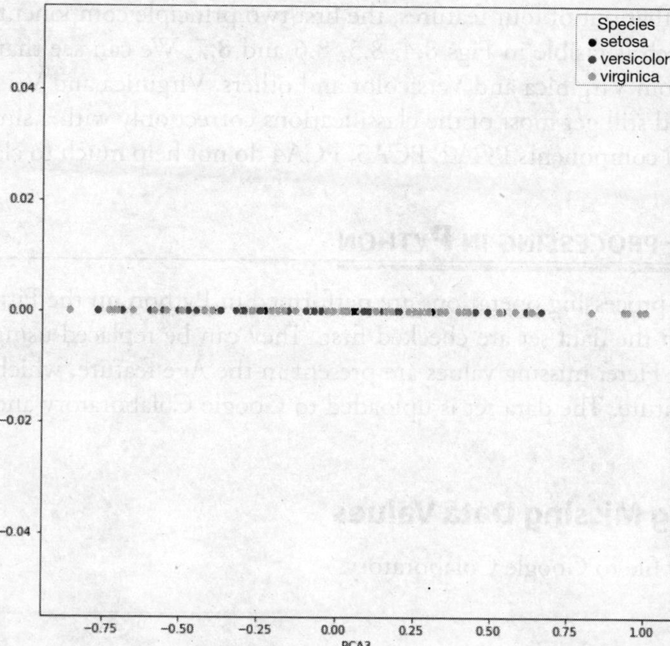

Figure 8.6 Iris flower categorization using the third principal component PCA3

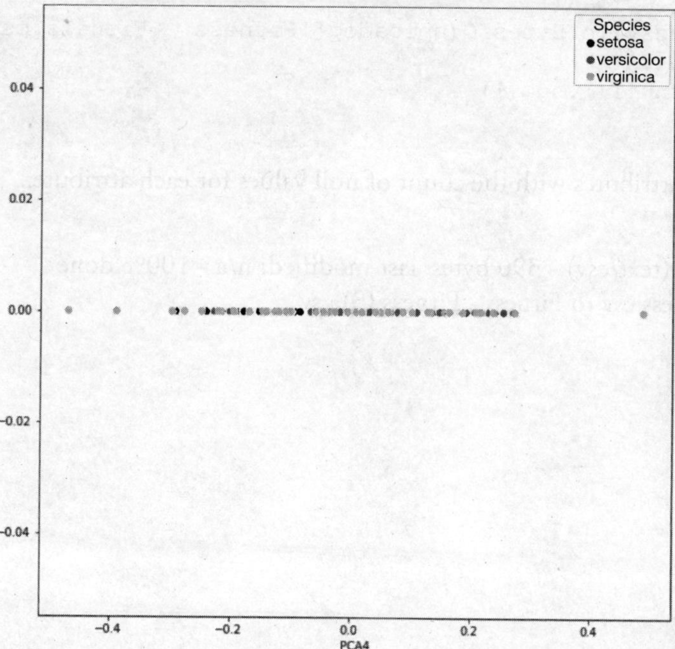

Figure 8.7 Iris flower categorization using the fourth principal component PCA4

Here we can see that out of four features, the first two principle components explain 96% of the variance of data, which is visible in Figs 8.4, 8.5, 8.6 and 8.7. We can see that PCA1 separates the Setosa class clearly from Virginica and Versicolor and others. Virginica and Versicolor are tougher to classify, but we should still get most of the classifications correct only with a single principal component. Other principal components PCA2, PCA3, PCA4 do not help much to classify the data clearly.

8.6 Data Pre-processing in Python

Here, a few data pre-processing operations are performed in Python on the Fitness - Fitness.csv data set. Missing values in the data set are checked first. They can be replaced using the different strategies discussed above. Here, missing values are present in the Age feature, which is replaced with the mean of the same feature. The data set is uploaded to Google Colaboratory and then pre-processing is performed.

8.6.1 Handling Missing Data Values

First, upload the .csv file to Google Colaboratory.

```
import io
from google.colab import files
import pandas as pd
import numpy as np
uploaded= files.upload()
datadf=pd.read_csv(io.BytesIO(uploaded['Fitness - Fitness.csv']))
print("ORIGINAL DATA")
print(datadf.isnull().sum())
print(datadf)
```

This will print data attributes with the count of null values for each attribute.

Output:
Fitness - Fitness.csv(text/csv) - 390 bytes, last modified: n/a - 100% done
Saving Fitness - Fitness.csv to Fitness - Fitness (3).csv
ORIGINAL DATA
ID 0
Age 0
Gender 0
MaritalStatus 0
Fitness 0
Income 0
MilesRun 0
Fit 0
dtype: int64

	ID	Age	Gender	MaritalStatus	Fitness	Income	MilesRun	Fit
0	ST19	32	Female	Single	4	34562	114	yes

1	ST19	33	Male	Single	3	29342	75	no
2	ST19	21	Female	Partnered	3	43214	65	yes
3	ST19	19	Male	Single	3	30987	84	yes
4	ST19	22	Male	Partnered	2	53234	46	yes
5	ST19	22	Female	Partnered	3	28345	64	no
6	ST19	24	Male	Partnered	3	36432	74	no
7	ST19	25	Female	Single	3	30987	86	yes
8	ST19	24	Male	Single	4	31234	142	yes

The .csv file has some missing values in the Age attribute.

```
# The data file with missing values
uploaded= files.upload()
df1=pd.read_csv(io.BytesIO(uploaded['Fitness - Fitness1.csv']))
print("DATA WITH MISSING VALUES IN AGE FEATURE")
print(df1.isnull().sum())
x = df1.iloc[:,:-1].values
print(x)
```

Output:

Fitness - Fitness1.csv(text/csv) - 388 bytes, last modified: n/a - 100% done
Saving Fitness - Fitness1.csv to Fitness - Fitness1 (3).csv
DATA WITH MISSING VALUES IN AGE FEATURE
ID 0
Age 2
Gender 0
MaritalStatus 0
Fitness 0
Income 0
MilesRun 0
Fit 0
dtype: int64
[['ST19' 32 'Female' 'Single' 4 34562 114]
['ST19' 'Male' 'Single' 3 29342 75]
['ST19' 21 'Female' 'Partnered' 3 43214 65]
['ST19' 19 'Male' 'Single' 3 30987 84]
['ST19' 22 'Male' 'Partnered' 2 53234 46]
['ST19' 'Female' 'Partnered' 3 28345 64]
['ST19' 24 'Male' 'Partnered' 3 36432 74]
['ST19' 25 'Female' 'Single' 3 30987 86]
['ST19' 24 'Male' 'Single' 4 31234 142]]

The missing values can be computed by the methods discussed above. Here, `SimpleImputer()` is used for pre-processing this data to handle missing data.

```
from sklearn.impute import SimpleImputer
impute = SimpleImputer(missing_values = np.nan, strategy = 'mean')
''' Using the fit method, we apply the 'imputa' object on the matrix of
our feature x, which is AGE here. The 'fit()' method identifies the missing
values and computes the mean of such feature a missing value is present'''
impute.fit(x[:, 1:2])
x[:, 1:2] = impute.transform(x[:, 1:2])
print("Imputed data (AGE feature missing values replaced with mean of
AGE) ")
print(x)
```

Output:
Imputed data (AGE feature missing values replaced with mean of AGE)
[['ST19' 32.0 'Female' 'Single' 4 34562 114]
['ST19' 23.9 'Male' 'Single' 3 29342 75]
['ST19' 21.0 'Female' 'Partnered' 3 43214 65]
['ST19' 19.0 'Male' 'Single' 3 30987 84]
['ST19' 22.0 'Male' 'Partnered' 2 53234 46]
['ST19' 23.9 'Female' 'Partnered' 3 28345 64]
['ST19' 24.0 'Male' 'Partnered' 3 36432 74]
['ST19' 25.0 'Female' 'Single' 3 30987 86]
['ST19' 24.0 'Male' 'Single' 4 31234 142]]

8.6.2 Categorical Data Encoding

Machine learning algorithms work on numeric data as they are based on forming mathematical equations from the given data; so ML models require categorical data to be converted to numeric data. Encoding techniques help to convert categorical or textual data into numeric data. Encoding techniques such as one-hot encoding and label encoding are available in Python which convert text data into numeric. Here in the Fitness.csv data set, Gender, MaritalStatus and Fit are categorical data. One-hot encoding on the Gender feature and Label encoding on the Fit feature is applied. For our data set, Gender has two values (Male and Female), 0 represents Male and 1 represents Female. Numerical order between Male and Female does not matter. So one-hot encoding helps as it converts the Gender column into three columns and creates a unique binary vector for Male and Female. Male is converted to vector [0.0 1.0] and Female is converted to vector [1.0 0.0]

First, upload the .csv data file and view its contents.

```
# Data Preprocessing -- Encoding of data
import io
from google.colab import files
import pandas as pd
import numpy as np
uploaded= files.upload()
datadf=pd.read_csv(io.BytesIO(uploaded['Fitness - Fitness.csv']))
print("ORIGINAL DATA")
print(datadf)
```

Output:

Fitness - Fitness.csv(text/csv) - 390 bytes, last modified: n/a - 100% done
Saving Fitness - Fitness.csv to Fitness - Fitness (4).csv
ORIGINAL DATA

	ID	Age	Gender	MaritalStatus	Fitness	Income	MilesRun	Fit
0	ST19	32	Female	Single	4	34562	114	yes
1	ST19	33	Male	Single	3	29342	75	no
2	ST19	21	Female	Partnered	3	43214	65	yes
3	ST19	19	Male	Single	3	30987	84	yes
4	ST19	22	Male	Partnered	2	53234	46	yes
5	ST19	22	Female	Partnered	3	28345	64	no
6	ST19	24	Male	Partnered	3	36432	74	no
7	ST19	25	Female	Single	3	30987	86	yes
8	ST19	24	Male	Single	4	31234	142	yes

The Fit feature has 'Yes' or 'No' values. The label encoder (discussed above) is used to encode the Fit feature. Functions `LabelEncoder()` and `fit_transform()` are applied on the Fit attribute.

```
from sklearn.preprocessing import LabelEncoder
ylabel = datadf.iloc[:, -1].values
print(ylabel)
le = LabelEncoder()
ylabel = le.fit_transform(ylabel)
print("Label Encoded Fit Feature values")
print(ylabel)
```

Output:

['yes' 'no' 'yes' 'yes' 'yes' 'no' 'no' 'yes' 'yes']
Label Encoded Fit Feature values
[1 0 1 1 1 0 0 1 1]

A one-hot encoder (discussed above) is used to encode the Fit feature. Functions `OneHotEncoder()` and `fit_transform()` are applied on the Fit attribute.

```
# One-hot encoding on Gender Feature
from sklearn.compose import ColumnTransformer
from sklearn.preprocessing import OneHotEncoder
xinput = datadf.iloc[:,:-1].values
colt = ColumnTransformer(transformers=[('encoder', OneHotEncoder(),
[2])], remainder= 'passthrough')
xinput = np.array(colt.fit_transform(xinput))
print("One-Hot encoding on Gender Feature")
print(xinput)
```

Output:

One-Hot encoding on Gender Feature
[[1.0 0.0 'ST19' 32 'Single' 4 34562 114]

[0.0 1.0 'ST19' 33 'Single' 3 29342 75]
[1.0 0.0 'ST19' 21 'Partnered' 3 43214 65]
[0.0 1.0 'ST19' 19 'Single' 3 30987 84]
[0.0 1.0 'ST19' 22 'Partnered' 2 53234 46]
[1.0 0.0 'ST19' 22 'Partnered' 3 28345 64]
[0.0 1.0 'ST19' 24 'Partnered' 3 36432 74]
[1.0 0.0 'ST19' 25 'Single' 3 30987 86]
[0.0 1.0 'ST19' 24 'Single' 4 31234 142]]

8.6.3 Scaling of Features

In some data sets, features have different values. Some features have very high-range values while others have small-range values. Feature scaling must be performed so that data becomes more relevant and all the features are given the same weight and importance. If the ML model is built on unscaled data, features with high-range values will dominate those with small values and the ML model will treat the small-range value features as though they do not exist. Python has two methods which help to scale data: `StandardScaler()` and `MinMaxScaler()`. `StandardScaler()` is applied on the Miles feature of the Fitness.csv data set.

First, upload the .csv data file and view its contents.

```
# Data Preprocessing-Scaling of Data
import io
from google.colab import files
import pandas as pd
import numpy as np
from sklearn.preprocessing import StandardScaler
from sklearn.preprocessing import MinMaxScaler
uploaded= files.upload()
datadf=pd.read_csv(io.BytesIO(uploaded['Fitness - Fitness.csv']))
print("ORIGINAL DATA")
print(datadf)
```

Output:

Fitness - Fitness.csv(text/csv) - 390 bytes, last modified: n/a - 100% done
Saving Fitness - Fitness.csv to Fitness - Fitness (6).csv
ORIGINAL DATA

	ID	Age	Gender	MaritalStatus	Fitness	Income	MilesRun	Fit
0	ST19	32	Female	Single	4	34562	114	yes
1	ST19	33	Male	Single	3	29342	75	no
2	ST19	21	Female	Partnered	3	43214	65	yes
3	ST19	19	Male	Single	3	30987	84	yes
4	ST19	22	Male	Partnered	2	53234	46	yes
5	ST19	22	Female	Partnered	3	28345	64	no
6	ST19	24	Male	Partnered	3	36432	74	no
7	ST19	25	Female	Single	3	30987	86	yes
8	ST19	24	Male	Single	4	31234	142	yes

Next, print the values of `MilesRun` as we want to apply scaling on this feature.

```
datadf = datadf.iloc[:,[6]]
print("Miles column")
print(datadf)
```

Output:

Miles column
  MilesRun
0 114
1 75
2 65
3 84
4 46
5 64
6 74
7 86
8 142

`StandardScaler()` is applied on the `MilesRun` column.

```
stdc = StandardScaler()
datadf = stdc.fit_transform(datadf)
print("Standard Scaled data of Miles")
print(datadf)
```

Output:

Standard-scaled data of MilesRun
[[1.12817638]
[-0.30656967]
[-0.67445327]
[0.02452557]
[-1.37343212]
[-0.71124163]
[-0.34335803]
[0.09810229]
[2.15825047]]

`MinMaxScaler()` is applied on `MilesRun`. Both scaling techniques use different formulas to scale the data.

```
minmaxdc = MinMaxScaler()
datadf = minmaxdc.fit_transform(datadf)
print("MinMax Scaled data of Miles")
print(datadf)
```

Output:
```
MinMax-scaled data of MilesRun
[[0.70833333]
[0.30208333]
[0.19791667]
[0.39583333]
[0. ]
[0.1875 ]
[0.29166667]
[0.41666667]
[1. ]]
```

EXERCISES

Multiple Choice Questions

1. Unprocessed data or processed data are measurement values that can be expressed as text, numbers or other types of media.
   (a) False (b) True
2. What are the different types of data?
   (a) Ordinal
   (b) Nominal
   (c) Ratio
   (d) All of the above
3. Which of the following is considered the primary source of unstructured data?
   (a) Facebook
   (b) Twitter
   (c) Internet
   (d) All of the above
4. Which of the following are examples of structured data?
   (a) Videos
   (b) Student's name, Student's ID, Student's age
   (c) Audio files
   (d) All of the above
5. Which of the following steps is performed by a data scientist after acquiring data?
   (a) Data transformation
   (b) Data replication
   (c) Data integration
   (d) Data cleansing
6. Which of the following are examples of data quality problems?
   (a) Noise and outliers
   (b) Duplicate data
   (c) Missing values
   (d) All of the above
7. Which method is used for encoding categorical variables?
   (a) `LabelEncoder()`
   (b) `OneHotEncoder()`
   (c) `CategoryEncoder()`
   (d) All of the above
8. Why do we need feature transformation?
   (a) Converting non-numeric features into numeric
   (b) Resizing inputs to a fixed size
   (c) Both (a) and (b)
   (d) None of the above
9. Which one is true about outliers?
   (a) Data points that deviate a lot from normal observations
   (b) Can reduce the accuracy of the model
   (c) Both (a) and (b)
   (d) None of the above

10) Which one of the following is true for imputation methods?
   (a) Imputation with mean/median
   (b) Imputing with random numbers
   (c) Imputing with one
   (d) All of the above

11. Which of the following is a characteristic of a good data set?
   (a) Sufficiently large for getting meaningful predictions
   (b) The bias is lower
   (c) Both (a) and (b)
   (d) None of the above

12. The correct order of pre-processing data is:
   (a) Imputation → Feature scaling → Training
   (b) Feature scaling → Imputation → Training
   (c) Feature scaling → Label encoding → Training
   (d) None of the above

Answers

1. (b) **2.** (d) **3.** (d) **4.** (b) **5.** (d) **6.** (d) **7.** (a) **8.** (c)
9. (c) **10.** (a) **11.** (c) **12.** (a)

Programming/Concept-based Questions

1) Download the crime data set of Boston, that is, crime.csv. Find the count of missing values for the variable SHOOTING and handle the missing values by replacing all the missing values with "N".

Answer:

```
import io
from google.colab import files
import pandas as pd
import numpy as np
uploaded= files.upload()
datadf=pd.read_csv(io.BytesIO(uploaded['crime.csv']))
print(datadf.isnull().sum())
print("DATA MISSING VALUE HANDLING")
datadf.SHOOTING.fillna('N', inplace=True)
datadf.SHOOTING.replace({'Y':True,'N':False}, inplace=True)
print(datadf.isnull().sum())
```

2. Download the crime data set of Boston, that is, crime.csv. Find the count of missing values for the variable DISTRICT. Fill all the DISTRICT missing values with NA.

Answer:

```
import io
from google.colab import files
import pandas as pd
import numpy as np
uploaded= files.upload()
datadf=pd.read_csv(io.BytesIO(uploaded['crime.csv']))
print(datadf.isnull().sum())
print("DATA MISSING VALUE HANDLING")
datadf.DISTRICT.fillna('NA', inplace=True)
print(datadf.isnull().sum())
```

3. Download the crime data set of Boston, that is, crime.csv. Find the duplicate values for the variable INCIDENT_NUMBER and remove them.

Answer:

```
import io
from google.colab import files
import pandas as pd
import numpy as np
uploaded= files.upload()
datadf=pd.read_csv(io.BytesIO(uploaded['crime.csv']))
print(datadf.INCIDENT_NUMBER.unique())
print("DUPLICATE VALUE HANDLING")
datadf.drop_duplicates(subset="INCIDENT_NUMBER",
inplace=True,keep='first')
print(datadf.INCIDENT_NUMBER)
```

4. Download the crime data set of Boston, that is, crime.csv. Find the number of crimes that occurred each YEAR and in each DISTRICT and also find the unique YEAR and DISTRICT in the data set.

Answer:

```
import io
from google.colab import files
import pandas as pd
import numpy as np
uploaded= files.upload()
datadf=pd.read_csv(io.BytesIO(uploaded['crime.csv']))
print(datadf.YEAR.unique())
print(datadf.YEAR.value_counts(dropna=False))
print(datadf.DISTRICT.unique())
print(datadf.DISTRICT.value_counts())
```

5. Download the crime data set of Boston, that is, crime.csv. Find the skew in the numeric data attributes of the data set.

Answer:

```
import io
from google.colab import files
import pandas as pd
import numpy as np
uploaded= files.upload()
datadf=pd.read_csv(io.BytesIO(uploaded['crime.csv']))
print(datadf.skew())
```

Negative number indicates left-skewed distribution and positive number indicates right-skewed distribution.

6. Perform dimensionality reduction on a given data set and create various visualizations like histograms, scatterplots, etc.

Answer:

```
import numpy as np
import matplotlib.pyplot as plt
from sklearn.decomposition import PCA
```

```
# Generate synthetic dataset
np.random.seed(0)
n_samples = 1000
n_features = 4
X = np.random.randn(n_samples, n_features) + 2*np.random.rand(n_features)
y = np.random.randint(0, 2, size=n_samples)
# Perform PCA for dimensionality reduction
pca = PCA(n_components=2)
X_pca = pca.fit_transform(X)
# Create histograms
plt.figure(figsize=(12, 4))
plt.subplot(1, 2, 1)
plt.hist(X_pca[y == 0, 0], color='b', alpha=0.5, label='Class 0')
plt.hist(X_pca[y == 1, 0], color='r', alpha=0.5, label='Class 1')
plt.xlabel('Principal Component 1')
plt.ylabel('Frequency')
plt.legend()
plt.subplot(1, 2, 2)
plt.hist(X_pca[y == 0, 1], color='b', alpha=0.5, label='Class 0')
plt.hist(X_pca[y == 1, 1], color='r', alpha=0.5, label='Class 1')
plt.xlabel('Principal Component 2')
plt.ylabel('Frequency')
plt.legend()
plt.suptitle('Histograms of Principal Components')
plt.show()
# Create scatter plot
plt.figure(figsize=(6, 6))
plt.scatter(X_pca[y == 0, 0], X_pca[y== 0, 1], color='b', alpha=0.5,
label='Class 0')
plt.scatter(X_pca[y == 1, 0], X_pca[y == 1, 1], color='r', alpha=0.5,
label='Class 1')
plt.xlabel('Principal Component 1')
plt.ylabel('Principal Component 2')
plt.legend()
plt.title('Scatter Plot of Principal Components')
plt.show()
```

BIBLIOGRAPHY

1. Harrington, P. 2012. *Machine Learning in Action.* Manning Books. https://www.manning.com/books/machine-learning-in-action

CHAPTER 9

Statistical Analysis: Descriptive Statistics

Learning Objectives

At the end of this chapter, you will be able to:

- Explain and apply descriptive statistical operations on one-dimensional data
- Write code in Python to calculate descriptive statistical operations such as mean, median, mode, standard deviation and variance
- List the Python libraries and methods used for descriptive statistical analysis
- Explain the basics of bivariate and multivariate data analysis
- Describe and implement simple and multiple linear regression and logistic regression for the given data
- Explain the validation methods used for regression
- Describe Simpson's paradox for the given data and write the Python code

9.0 Introduction

Statistics convey different meanings to different people. Some consider statistics as a form of mathematics, whereas others consider it to be the tables, figures and charts found in newspapers, journals, articles, surveys and reports. Statistical analysis is the science of collecting, exploring and presenting different types of data for drawing inferences, making decisions or to uncover underlying trends and patterns. Statistical analysis is applied in all fields of life. It is the backbone of industrial research, basic science research and government planning.

Statistical characteristics are properties that are analysed for each individual in a sample. This is of two types: **qualitative characteristics**, which do not have numerical values associated with it, such as hair colour and nationality, and **quantitative characteristics**, which have numerical values associated with it, such as age and height. Quantitative variables can be further classified as discrete and continuous. **Discrete variable** values are those that can be obtained by counting, whereas **continuous variable** values can be obtained by measuring. Discrete variables can take only certain values whereas continuous variables can take an infinite number of values. Qualitative variables can be classified as nominal and ordinal. **Nominal variables** have no hierarchical relationship (order) between categories whereas **ordinal variables** have categories placed logically in a meaningful order.

In statistics, independent, dependent and controlled are three important types of variables. An **independent variable** is one which you decide to change in an experiment, a **dependent variable** is what you observe or measure and a **controlled variable** is one that does not change. For example, in a study of the growth of plants using different types of fertilizers, we measure how tall a plant grows by adding different brands of fertilizer. Here, the independent variable is the type of fertilizer used for that plant. The dependent variable is the height of the plant. The controlled variables are all the conditions that are kept the same for all plants, such as type of plant, amount of fertilizer given to a plant, amount of water and sunlight given to a plant, temperature of the environment and time given for the plant to grow.

Different types of statistical methods are available for analysis and modelling one-, two- and multi-dimensional data. **One-dimensional data** has a single value corresponding to each individual, such as height, weight, colour, age, length and width. **Two-dimensional data** has two values for each individual, such as length and width of a surface, product model and its sale and age of son and age of father. **Multi-dimensional data** has more than two values. So more than one aspect is studied. Examples are product sale based on product model, demography, salesman and time of sale; a film's IMDB rating based on production house, director, cast and story.

9.1 One-dimensional Statistics

In many situations, only one value is required to represent the data. Measuring mean, median and mode helps us obtain a one value representation of data.

9.1.1 Descriptive Statistics

Descriptive statistics deals with methods which help to describe, summarize and understand data. Calculating central tendency and dispersion of data are some ways of describing data. Central tendency describes the central position for one-dimensional data distribution. Mean, median and mode are the most commonly used measures of central tendency. Measures of variability, spread or dispersion can be described by calculating the standard deviation and variance of the given one-dimensional data.

Mean

Mean is calculated by adding all the items and dividing this total by the number of items. The different mean measurements that can be obtained are simple or arithmetic mean (AM) and weighted mean.

Weighted mean: Mean gives equal weight to all items, but weighted mean given different weights to all items, as the importance of each item varies. Weighted mean is calculated by adding the product of proportion and group mean. It is used when the sample sizes are unequal.

Trimmed mean: If there are extreme values (also called outliers) in a sample, the mean is then greatly influenced by these values. Trimmed mean can be used to offset the effect of these extreme values. Trimmed mean is defined as the mean obtained after discarding the values at the high and low extremes.

Sometimes, data is provided in continuous form; that is, as classes and the frequency for each class. Three methods can be used to calculate the mean of such data:

Direct method: The following formula is used to obtain mean using the direct method:

$$X = \sum fx / N = \sum fx / \sum f$$

where f = frequency, X = value of the variable and N = sum of frequency or $\sum f$.

Assumed mean method: Here, the assumed mean value is taken and the deviations of the variable from it are computed. The following formula is used to calculate the mean X:

$$\bar{X} = A + \frac{\sum fdx}{\sum f} = A + \frac{\sum fdx}{N}$$

where A = assumed mean, $dx = (X - A)$, f = frequency $\sum f$ and N = total number of terms.

Step deviation method: The following formula is used to obtain mean through the step deviation method:

$$X = A + (\sum fdx \;/\; N) * i = A + (\sum fdx \;/\; \sum f) * i$$

where A = assumed mean, $dx = (X - A)$, i = class size or class interval, f = frequency $\sum f$ and N = total number of terms.

Median

Median refers to the middle-most value in a data distribution. Here, one-half of the items in the distribution has a value smaller than the median, while the other half has a value larger than the median. Median is called positional average.

$$\text{Median} = l + \frac{\left(\frac{N}{2} - m\right)}{f} \times c$$

Median class is the class where the $(N/2)^{th}$ item is present. Here, N = number of observations, c = class interval of the median class, l = lower limit of the median class, f = frequency of the median class and m = cumulative frequency of all classes preceding the median.

Mode

Mode is the most common value that occurs in a set of observations. It can be calculated for categorical or character data, whereas mean and median can be calculated only for numeric data.

Measures of Dispersion

The measures of central value discussed above give us only a single value that represents the entire data. Sometimes, it may be necessary to measure the variability of data, as two distributions of data may have the same central values but there can be wide disparity in the data distribution. Measures of dispersion help in measuring the variation among data items. Dispersion measures the extent of spread of observations in a sample.

The main measures of dispersion, such as range, interquartile range, quartile deviation, mean or average deviation, standard deviation, variance and coefficient of variation, can be calculated with standard functions from the native statistical package.

Standard deviation: This measures the variability of a distribution. A small standard deviation means high uniformity of the data series. Standard deviation is defined as the square root of variance, and it is considered as the best measure of variation. Standard deviation is amenable to further algebraic treatment and is less affected by fluctuations of sampling.

Let $X = n\ \{x_1,x_2,x_3,,,x_n\}$ be sample values of n samples. Variance denoted as s^2 is defined as:

$$S^2 = \frac{\sum (X - \bar{X})^2}{N-1},$$

where X = mean of the sample.

The standard deviation s of the samples is the square root of the variance s^2.

Variance: Variance defines how data values are dispersed around the mean value. Variance is the square of standard deviation.

Quartiles: Range is based on two extreme values and does not account for scatter within the data. Quartiles give some indication of the centre and scatter within data and the shape of the distribution. Quartiles along with deciles and percentiles are the measures of position. R has a `quantile()` function that helps in calculating the quartiles.

The first quartile (denoted by Q_1), second quartile (median) and third quartile (denoted by Q_3) are the 25th percentile, 50th percentile and 75th percentile, respectively. The distance between the third and first quartiles is called the interquartile range (IQR) and is defined as

$$\text{IQR} = Q_3 - Q_1$$

9.1.2 Descriptive Statistics in Python

Descriptive statistics in Python can be computed using various methods. Python has a `statistics` module to perform descriptive statistics along with NumPy/pandas; SciPy can also be used to perform descriptive statistics. The functions listed in Table 9.1 can be used to perform descriptive statistics using NumPy and pandas.

Table 9.1 NumPy and pandas functions for descriptive statistics

No	Function name	Description
1	`count()`	Finds the total number of non-null values
2	`sum()`	Finds the sum of the values
3	`mean()`	Finds the mean of the values
4	`median()`	Finds the median of the values

(Continued)

Table 9.1 (Continued)

No	Function name	Description
5	`mode()`	Finds the mode of the values
6	`std()`	Finds the standard deviation of the values
7	`min()`	Finds the minimum of the given values
8	`max()`	Finds the maximum of the given values
9	`abs()`	Finds the absolute value
10	`prod()`	Finds the product of the given values
11	`cumsum()`	Finds the cumulative sum of the given values
12	`cumprod()`	Finds the cumulative product of the given values
13	`describe()`	Gives the summary of statistics including mean, standard deviation and IQR

The Python code using the `statistics` module to calculate descriptive statistics is given below:

```
import statistics as st
numsval=[11,21,32,54,72,96,75,23,72,61]
print('mode is ',st.mode(numsval))
print('mean is ',st.mean(numsval))
print('median is ',st.median(numsval))
print('variance is ',st.variance(numsval))
print('standard deviation is ',st.stdev(numsval))
```

Output:
mode is 72
mean is 51.7
median is 57.5
variance is 803.5666666666666
standard deviation is 28.347251483462493

The Python code using NumPy and pandas to calculate descriptive statistics is given below:

The file Advertising.csv is first uploaded on Google Colab. It has attributes Radio, TV, sales, etc.

```
from google.colab import files
uploaded= files.upload()
import io
import pandas as pd
df=pd.read_csv(io.BytesIO(uploaded['Advertising.csv']))
df.head()
Mean, median and mode of attributes Radio, TV and sales is calculated on
dataframes here.
averageval = df['Radio'].mean()
print('mean of Radio is ',averageval)
```

```
medval = df['TV'].median()
print('median of Tv is ',medval)
modval = df['Sales'].mode()
print('mode of Sales is ',modval)
stdval = df['Radio'].std()
print('standard deviation of Radio is ',stdval)
```

Output:
mean of Radio is 23.264000000000024
median of Tv is 149.75
mode of Sales is 0 9.7
dtype: float64
standard deviation of Radio is 14.846809176168723

The Python code using SciPy to calculate descriptive statistics is given below:

```
from scipy import stats
a=[30,28,32,26,33,25,28,31]
print('mean is ',stats. tmean(a))
print('standard deviation is ',stats.tstd(a))
#print('median is ',stats. median_abs_deviation(a,0))
print('mode is ',stats. mode(a))
```

Output:
mean is 29.125
standard deviation is 2.850438562747845
mode is ModeResult(mode=array([28]), count=array([2]))

9.2 Multi-dimensional Statistics

Statistical processes applied on two- or higher dimensional data is termed multi-dimensional statistics. Correlation, regression analysis, principal component analysis, factor analysis, cluster analysis and discriminant analysis are some of the techniques used for multivariate statistical analysis. These methods are used to analyse the joint behaviour of more than one variable.

We may often come across problems involving the determination of relationships among variables; that is, change or movement in one variable causes movement in another variable. For example, there exists a relationship between the number of hours of study and the marks obtained, rainfall and the production of crops. These require measures of the association between variables. The degree of relationship between the variables is measured through correlation analysis. Regression analysis helps in estimating the value of a variable, given the value of another variable.

9.2.1 Correlation Analysis

The association between variables or correlation can be studied graphically by creating a scatter plot of variables or the correlation coefficient can be calculated. Both these methods of analysis are described below.

Measures of Association (Covariance and Correlation)

In statistics, correlation denotes some form of association between two variables. For example, weight and height are correlated. The measured correlation can be positive, negative or zero (scatter plot in Fig. 9.1).

- **Positive correlation**: If the value of attribute A increases with an increase in the value of attribute B, and vice versa.
- **Negative correlation**: If the value of attribute A decreases with an increase in the value of attribute B, and vice versa.
- **Zero correlation:** When the value of attribute A varies at random with the value of attribute B, and vice versa.

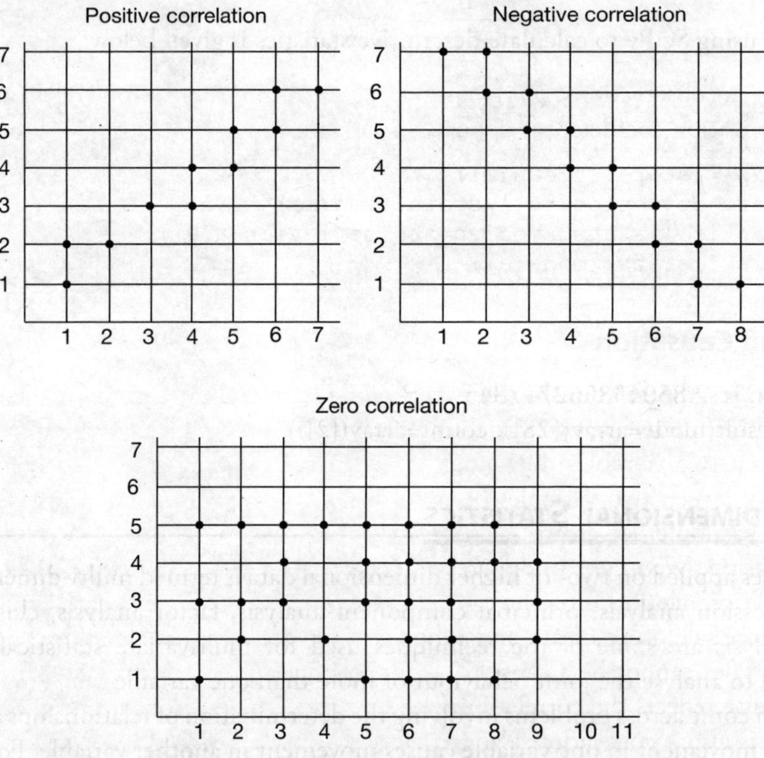

Figure 9.1 Scatter plot of correlation (types of correlation)

Correlation Coefficient

Correlation coefficient is used to describe the linear relationship among quantitative variables. It measures the strength and direction of a relationship. The + and – signs indicate the directions of the relationship, and the magnitude indicates the strength of the relationship (ranging from 0 to 1 for a perfect predictable relationship). If the correlation coefficient is close to 1, it would indicate that the variables are highly positively related; –1 would indicate that the variables are negatively linearly related. A value of 0 would indicate that variables do not move together – there is a weak linear relationship between the variables.

To find the correlation coefficient value between two numerical attributes, Karl Pearson's coefficient of correlation method is used. To find the correlation coefficient between two ordinal attributes, Charles Spearman's coefficient of correlation can be used. A rank can be assigned to the different values of a variable with the ordinal data type.

Correlation and covariance describe the degree of a relationship. Correlation is dimensionless, while covariance is not. Its unit is obtained by multiplying the units of the two variables. Dividing the covariance by the product of *x* and *y*'s standard deviation produces a 'scaleless' quantity, known as the correlation coefficient in general.

Covariance is defined in terms of mean as:

$$s_{xy} = \frac{1}{n-1}\sum_{i=1}^{n}(x_i - \overline{x})(y_i - \overline{y})$$

Here, x_i and y_i are observations, $(\overline{x}, \overline{y})$ = mean of observations and n = total number of observations.

Formally, correlation coefficient is defined by the following formula:

$$r_{xy} = \frac{s_{xy}}{s_x s_y}$$

where s_x and s_y represent the standard deviations, and covariance is represented by s_{xy}.

Correlation and Causation

Correlation identifies the relationship between two variables, but causation identifies the cause-and-effect relationship between two variables or groups. Correlation is different from causation as correlation between two variables does not necessarily mean that one caused the other; there can be a relationship between two variables because of a third variable which causes an effect on both the variables. For example, ice cream sales and temperature are correlated but they do not follow a causation relationship. We might find a correlation between ice cream and sunglasses too, which is clearly not a causation relationship. The cause in both cases is warm weather. It is obvious that warm weather causes more sale of ice cream and sunglasses, but ice cream sales cannot be a cause of warm weather, sunglass sales cannot be a cause of warm weather and ice cream sales cannot be a cause of sunglass sales. Cause reflects the correlation with a reason. The relationship between drinking coffee and productivity is also a correlation. We may feel more productive because of caffeine intake, but it can also be the case that you go to the coffee shop and drink coffee and you are more productive working at a coffee shop than working at home where you have many distractions. So, in this case also the cause–effect relationship is not definite.

The relationship between exercise and muscle growth and overeating and obesity are examples of cause–effect relationships: exercising causes muscle growth and overeating causes weight gain or obesity. It suggests that if *X* happens, then *Y* follows. The cause–effect relationship is very useful in business analysis. It adds real-world context and meaning to correlation. For example, you want to study the factors that actually contributed to a successful channel, you want to find the reasons why customers are buying your product or you want to know the best feature of your product.

9.2.2 Regression Analysis

The purpose of regression analysis is to estimate the value of the dependent variable, given the value/values of the independent variable. It is a statistical modelling method used to formulate the mathematical model of the relationship among variables.

Regression analysis models can be classified as linear and non-linear. Linear models in turn can be categorized as simple and multiple, as shown in Fig. 9.2.

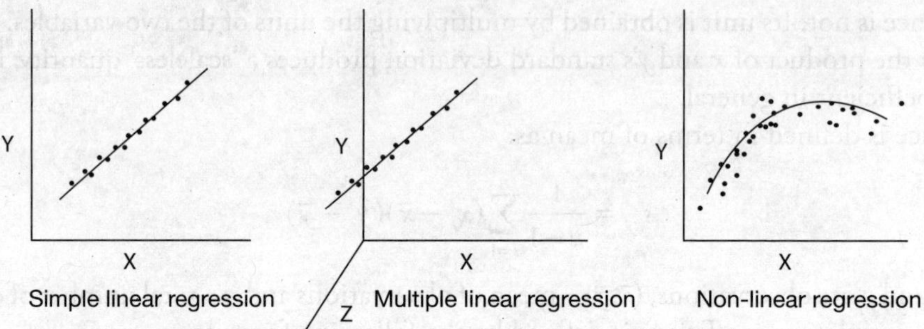

Figure 9.2 Regression analysis models

Simple Linear Regression

In simple linear regression, only two variables are studied: dependent (also called response), usually denoted by *Y*, and independent (alternatively called regressor), usually denoted by *X*. A relationship between *X* and *Y* is a linear relationship of the form shown in Fig. 9.3.

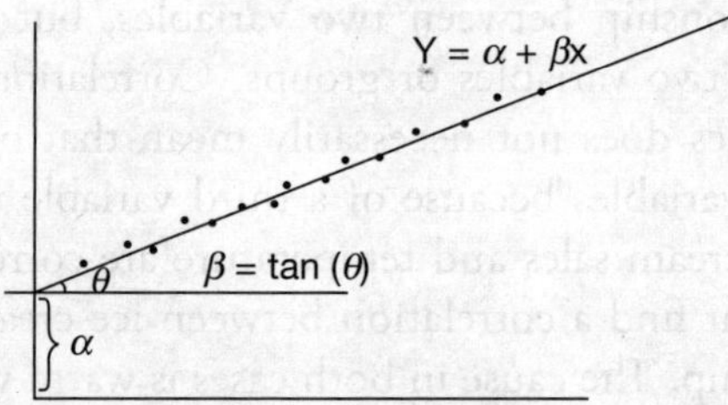

Figure 9.3 Simple linear regression

There are an infinite number of lines but the concept of regression analysis deals with finding the best relationship between *Y* and *X* (and hence, the best fitted values) quantifying the strength of that relationship. The task in regression analysis is to estimate the regression coefficients α and β. It uses the method of least squares to find the optimal values. This method minimizes the sum of the squared vertical distances between the observations and the regression line. Linear regression chooses the estimated parameters or fitted parameters α and β to minimize the sum of squares errors.

$$e = \sum(Y_i - \beta - \alpha X_i)^2 \tag{2}$$

Sum of squares error is preferred for linear regression as it does not cancel out for positive and negative errors and is also differentiable. Minimization of error is achieved by differentiating Eq. 2

with respect to parameters and substituting it with zero. The estimated values for parameters α and β are as follows:

$$\alpha = \frac{\left(\overline{XY}\right) - \left(\overline{X}\right)\left(\overline{Y}\right)}{\left(\overline{X_i^2}\right) - \left(\overline{X}\right)^2} \tag{3}$$

$$\beta = \overline{Y} - \alpha \overline{X} \tag{4}$$

Some assumptions are made for linear regression to draw valid conclusions from it:

- The linear regression parameters β and α are raised to the first power only. Neither β nor α is multiplied or divided by another regression parameter; that is, the relationship between the dependent variable Y and the independent variable X is linear in the parameters β and α.
- The independent variable is not random.
- For all observations, the variance of the error term is the same.
- The error term ε is normally distributed and uncorrelated across observations.

Multiple Linear Regression

When more than one variable is independent (k-independent variables $x_1, x_2 \ldots\ldots x_k$), the regression can be estimated as a multiple regression model. When this model is linear in coefficients like simple linear regression, it is called a multiple linear regression model. The multiple linear regression model is given by

$$y_i = \beta_0 + \beta_1 x_1 + \beta_2 x_2 + \beta_k x_k \tag{5}$$

Non-linear Regression

When the regression equation is expressed in terms of r-degree, $r>1$, it is called a non-linear regression model. When more than one independent variable, $x_1, x_2 \ldots\ldots x_r$, is present, it is called a multiple non-linear regression model (alternatively, polynomial regression model). In general, it takes the form

$$y_i = \beta_0 + \beta_1 x + \beta_2 x^2 + \ldots \beta_r x^r \tag{6}$$

It is useful when the relationship between dependent and independent variables is not linear. Non-linear data can be transformed to linear and can fit a linear regression model on that transformed data, or else polynomial regression as given in Eq. 6 can be used to fit the regression model.

Validation of Regression Methods

For evaluating regression model correctness, the following metrics are used. Each metric has its own advantages and disadvantages.

Mean absolute error: It is defined as the mean of the residuals. The residual is the difference between the predicted value and the actual value.

Mean squared error (MSE): It is defined as the mean of the squares of residuals. MSE value is always positive and closer to zero.

Root mean squared error (RMSE): It is defined as the square root of the mean of the squares of residuals. RMSE value is always positive.

Coefficient of Determination: It is also called the R squared score (R^2 score). It is a measure of how many test samples are likely to be predicted correctly by the regression model. R^2 values nearing 1 represent perfect regression models. R^2 values nearing zero indicate that the model fit is not good. It is a measure of the variations explained by the model.

$$MAE = \frac{1}{N}\sum_{i=1}^{N} | y_i - \hat{y} |$$

$$MSE = \frac{1}{N}\sum_{i=1}^{N} (y_i - \hat{y})^2$$

$$RMSE = \sqrt{MSE} = \sqrt{\frac{1}{N}\sum_{i=1}^{N} (y_i - \hat{y})^2}$$

$$R^2 = 1 - \frac{\sum (y_i - \hat{y})^2}{\sum (y_i - \hat{y})^2}$$

where $\hat{y}$ = predicted value of y and $\bar{y}$ = mean value of y.

Example: A company's sales data (in thousands) for five months is given below. Apply linear regression technique to predict the sales for the 8th and 12th months.

X_i **(Month)**	Y_i **(Sales in thousands)**
1	12
2	18
3	26
4	32
5	38

To fit the linear regression model, the parameters are calculated using the following formulas for $Y = \alpha X + \beta$

$$\alpha = \frac{(\underline{XY}) - (\underline{X})(\underline{Y})}{(\underline{X_i 2}) - (\underline{X})2}$$

$$\beta = \underline{Y} - \alpha \underline{X}$$

X_i	Y_i	$(X_i)^2$	X_i x Y_i
1	12	1	12
2	18	4	36
3	26	9	78
4	32	16	128
5	37	25	185
Sum = 15 Average of X_i = 15/5 = 3	Sum = 125 Average of Y_i = 125/5 = 25	Sum = 55 Average of $(X_i)^2$ = 55/5 = 11	Sum = 439 Average of (X_i x Y_i) = 439/5 = 87.8

$\alpha = ((87.8) - (3)(25)) / (11 - 3^2) = 12.8/2 = 6.4$
$\beta = 25 - 6.4 * 3 = 5.8$
Regression line $Y = 6.4\,X + 5.8$
Sales of the 8th month = 6.4 * 8 + 5.8 = 57
Sales of the 12th month = 6.4 * 12 + 5.8 = 82.6
Given the actual sales of the 8th and 12th months as 60 and 80, errors can be calculated such as MSE, MAE, RMSE and or R^2.
MAE = ½ ((60 – 57)+abs(80 – 82.7)) = 2.85
MSE = ½ ($(60 - 57)^2+(80 - 82.7)^2$) = 8.145
RMSE = sqrt(8.145) = 2.85
$\underline{Y} = 25$
$R^2 = 1 - (((60 - 57)^2+(80 - 82.7)^2) / ((60 - 25)^2 +(80 - 25)^2)) = .9961$
R^2 indicates that the accuracy of the linear regression model is 99.61%.

9.2.3 Python Code for Simple Linear Regression

This code is for simple linear regression using Google Colab.

This code uses the Advertising.csv file, which contains data of TV, Radio, Newspaper and Sales. Here, the strongest linear relationship between data items is found and a linear regression model is fit for those data items. The accuracy of the model is calculated and it also represents the data using different graphical methods

```
# To load.csv file in colab
from google.colab import files
uploaded= files.upload()
```

Output: Advertising.csv(application/vnd.ms-excel) - 5166 bytes, last modified: 4/14/2021 - 100% done
Saving Advertising.csv to Advertising (1).csv

```
#Simple Linear Regression
from matplotlib import pyplot
import io
import matplotlib.pyplot as plt
import pandas as pd
from sklearn.model_selection import train_test_split
from sklearn.linear_model import LinearRegression
from sklearn import metrics
import scipy.stats
dfval=pd.read_csv(io.BytesIO(uploaded['Advertising.csv']))
```

After the .csv file is uploaded, correlation coefficients between TV, Radio, Newspaper and Sales are calculated using Pearson's, Spearman's and Kendall's methods.

```
#Find the correlation between variables
pearsoncorr = dfval.corr(method='pearson')
print(pearsoncorr)
spearmancorr = dfval.corr(method='spearman')
print(spearmancorr)
kendallcorr = dfval.corr(method='kendall')
print(kendallcorr)
```

Output:

```
          TV       Radio    Newspaper Sales
TV        1.000000 0.054809 0.056648 0.782224
Radio     0.054809 1.000000 0.354104 0.576223
Newspaper 0.056648 0.354104 1.000000 0.228299
Sales     0.782224 0.576223 0.228299 1.000000
          TV       Radio    Newspaper Sales
TV        1.000000 0.056123 0.050840 0.800614
Radio     0.056123 1.000000 0.316979 0.554304
Newspaper 0.050840 0.316979 1.000000 0.194922
Sales     0.800614 0.554304 0.194922 1.000000
          TV       Radio    Newspaper Sales
TV        1.000000 0.041202 0.034156 0.621946
Radio     0.041202 1.000000 0.207077 0.419447
Newspaper 0.034156 0.207077 1.000000 0.132271
Sales     0.621946 0.419447 0.132271 1.000000
```

By looking at results shown, it appears that TV and Sales follow a strong linear relationship. A plot is printed for the TV and Sales attributes.

```
dataval1=dfval['TV']
dataval2=dfval['Sales']
# plot
pyplot.scatter(dataval1, dataval2)
pyplot.show()
```

Output:

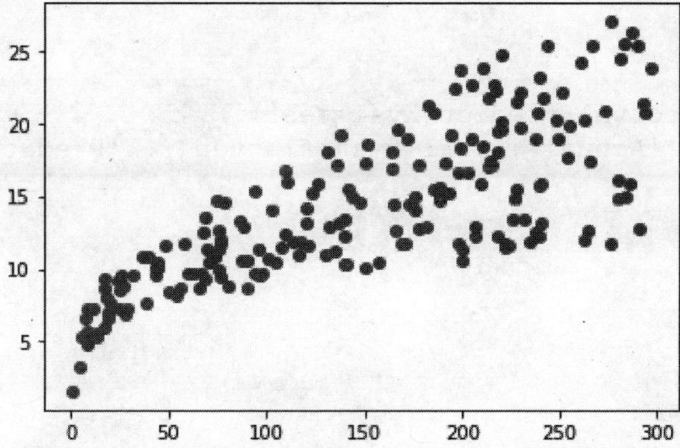

TV and Sales correlation coefficients can be printed using all three methods of correlation.

```
print('Using scipy, coorelation between two variables Tv and Sales')
pearsoncorr=scipy.stats.pearsonr(dataval1,dataval2)[0]
print(pearsoncorr)
spearmancorr = scipy.stats.spearmanr(dataval1,dataval2)[0]
print(spearmancorr)
kendallcorr = scipy.stats.kendalltau(dataval1,dataval2)[0]
print(kendallcorr)
```

Output:
Using scipy, coorelation between two variables TV and Sales
0.7822244248616065
0.8006143768505688
0.6219463551009411

As we see a strong linear relationship between TV and Sales data, the regression model can be built for these parameters, as coded below:

```
Xval = dfval['TV'].values.reshape(-1,1)
yval = dfval['Sales'].values.reshape(-1,1)
Linear Regression model on Tv and Sales data of advertising
Xval_train, Xval_test, yval_train, yval_test = train_test_split(Xval,
yval, test_size=0.3, random_state=0)
regressorval = LinearRegression()
regressorval.fit(Xval_train, yval_train)
#To retrieve the intercept of linear regression model:
print(regressorval.intercept_)
#For retrieving the slope of linear regression model:
print(regressorval.coef_)
```

Output:
[7.31081017]
[[0.04581434]]

```
yval_pred = regressorval.predict(Xval_test)
df = pd.DataFrame({'Actual': yval_test.flatten(), 'Predicted': yval_pred.
flatten()})
print(df)
```

Output:

	Actual	Predicted
0	11.3	10.481163
1	8.4	9.601527
2	8.7	11.452427
3	25.4	20.583225
4	11.7	15.108411
5	8.7	9.885576
6	7.2	7.709395
7	13.2	18.310834
8	9.2	8.401192
9	16.6	16.363724
10	24.2	19.282098
11	10.6	11.305821
12	10.5	14.485336
13	15.6	15.914744
14	11.8	10.811026
15	13.2	12.817694
16	17.4	19.479099
17	1.6	7.342880
18	14.7	10.733142
19	17.0	17.087591
20	26.2	20.487015
21	10.3	13.738562
22	14.9	15.332901
23	12.9	13.344559
24	8.1	9.761877
25	15.2	12.950556
26	12.6	14.897665
27	22.6	16.702750
28	11.6	17.573223
29	8.5	8.460750
30	12.5	10.417023
31	23.7	16.423283
32	16.1	20.170896

33	21.8	18.384137
34	5.6	7.915559
35	6.7	8.167538
36	9.7	10.041345
37	12.9	15.594043
38	13.6	10.444511
39	7.2	8.456169
40	10.8	9.001359
41	9.5	8.753962
42	15.0	13.857680
43	15.9	16.913496
44	17.1	17.179219
45	14.0	12.015943
46	4.8	7.704814
47	8.7	8.085073
48	15.9	13.069673
49	10.4	12.102990
50	12.4	12.341225
51	19.7	17.825202
52	17.6	18.938490
53	15.5	15.781882
54	10.1	9.358711
55	9.7	10.165044
56	21.4	20.729831
57	14.4	15.213784
58	16.6	16.588214
59	5.5	7.645255

To calculate the accuracy of the regression model:

```
print('')
r2_score = regressorval.score(Xval_test, yval_test)
print('accuracy of model is')
print(r2_score*100,'%')
```

Output:
accuracy of model is
72.5606346597073 %

To create a bar graph of the first 15 values to show actual and predicted values:

```
dfval1 = df.head(15)
dfval1.plot(kind='bar',figsize=(16,10))
plt.grid(which='major', linestyle='-', linewidth='0.5', color='green')
plt.grid(which='minor', linestyle=':', linewidth='0.5', color='black')
plt.show()
```

Output:

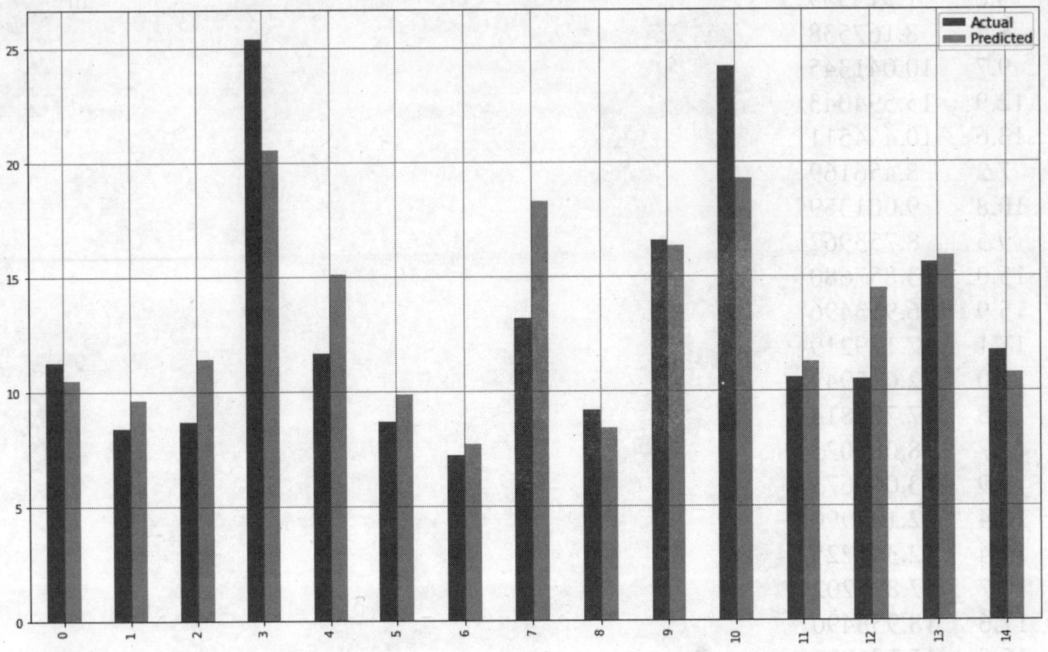

To show the predicted *Y* value in line, with points showing actual *Y* values for test data:

```
plt.scatter(Xval_test, yval_test,  color='gray')
plt.plot(Xval_test, yval_pred, color='red', linewidth=2)
plt.show()
```

Output:

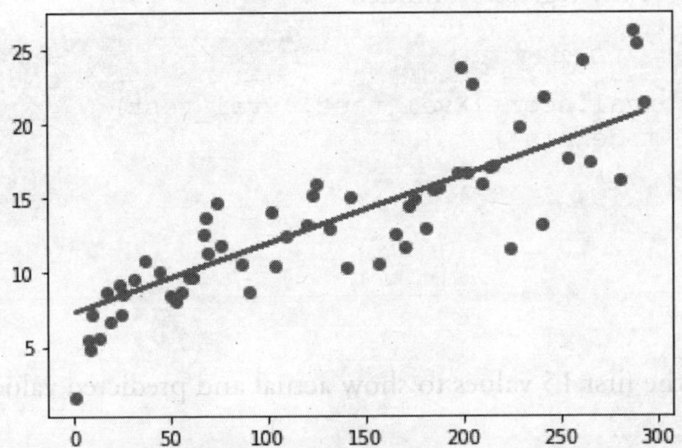

9.2.4 Python Code for Multiple Linear Regression

This code is for multiple linear regression using Google Colab.

This code uses the Advertising.csv file, which contains the data of TV, Radio, Newspaper and Sales. Here, the linear relationship between data items is first determined and a multiple linear regression model is fitted for those data items. Sales data items are considered as dependent variables, whereas TV, Newspaper and Radio are considered as independent variables. Using this model, Sales is predicted based on TV, Newspaper and Radio. The accuracy of the model is also calculated and it also represents the data using different graphical methods. Here, the results show that Sales prediction is better considering TV, Radio and Newspaper together instead of considering only TV data. Accuracy of the multiple linear regression model is 86%, and that of the simple linear regression model is 72%.

```
from google.colab import files
uploaded= files.upload()
#Multiple Linear Regression
from matplotlib import pyplot
import io
import matplotlib.pyplot as plt
import pandas as pd
from sklearn.model_selection import train_test_split
from sklearn.linear_model import LinearRegression
from sklearn import metrics
import scipy.stats
dfval=pd.read_csv(io.BytesIO(uploaded['Advertising.csv']))
#Find the correlation between variables
pearsoncorr = dfval.corr(method='pearson')
print(pearsoncorr)
```

Output:

	TV	Radio	Newspaper	Sales
TV	1.000000	0.054809	0.056648	0.782224
Radio	0.054809	1.000000	0.354104	0.576223
Newspaper	0.056648	0.354104	1.000000	0.228299
Sales	0.782224	0.576223	0.228299	1.000000

Here is a multiple linear regression model which considers TV, Newspaper, Radio in `xval` and Sales data in `yval`.

```
Xval = dfval.iloc[:,0:3]
yval = dfval['Sales'].values.reshape(-1,1)
Xval_train, Xval_test, yval_train, yval_test = train_test_split(Xval,
yval, test_size=0.3, random_state=0)
regressorval = LinearRegression()
regressorval.fit(Xval_train, yval_train)
#To retrieve the intercept:
print('intercept valus is ',regressorval.intercept_)
#For retrieving the slope:
print('coefficient values are ',regressorval.coef_)
```

Output:
intercept value is [2.88025529]

coefficient values are [[0.04391531 0.20027962 0.00184368]]

To predict the sales for test data:

```
yval_pred = regressorval.predict(Xval_test)
df = pd.DataFrame({'Actual': yval_test.flatten(), 'Predicted': yval_pred.
flatten()})
print(df)
```

Output:

	Actual	Predicted
0	11.3	10.058667
1	8.4	7.433188
2	8.7	6.953057
3	25.4	24.168746
4	11.7	11.981720
5	8.7	6.544647
6	7.2	13.194268
7	13.2	14.902403
8	9.2	11.076753
9	16.6	16.250617
10	24.2	23.008116
11	10.6	9.120721
12	10.5	10.293423
13	15.6	15.370966
14	11.8	11.623965
15	13.2	12.105743
16	17.4	18.550308
17	1.6	10.858109
18	14.7	16.138799
19	17.0	17.202814
20	26.2	24.254699
21	10.3	9.438698
22	14.9	15.134194
23	12.9	12.412838
24	8.1	5.669739
25	15.2	15.238767
26	12.6	12.187876
27	22.6	20.951641
28	11.6	13.226718
29	8.5	9.209547
30	12.5	13.398127
31	23.7	21.619445
32	16.1	18.059387
33	21.8	21.147985

```
34   5.6   6.735830
35   6.7   6.167997
36   9.7   7.980426
37  12.9  13.090835
38  13.6  14.862141
39   7.2   6.235971
40  10.8  12.352469
41   9.5   9.194522
42  15.0  15.047177
43  15.9  16.230393
44  17.1  17.172409
45  14.0  13.334122
46   4.8   3.680358
47   8.7  12.539469
48  15.9  15.936748
49  10.4   8.678814
50  12.4  10.624600
51  19.7  19.564653
52  17.6  18.347228
53  15.5  15.246630
54  10.1  10.048464
55   9.7   8.173442
56  21.4  21.490611
57  14.4  14.137309
58  16.6  16.297602
59   5.5   8.905023
```

To calculate the accuracy of the regression model:

```
print('')
r2_score = regressorval.score(Xval_test, yval_test)
print('accuracy of model is')
print(r2_score*100,'%')
```

Output:
accuracy of model is
86.49018906637792 %

To show a bar graph of the first 10 actual and predicted values:

```
dfval1 = df.head(15)
dfval1.plot(kind='bar',figsize=(16,10))
plt.grid(which='major', linestyle='-', linewidth='0.5', color='green')
plt.grid(which='minor', linestyle=':', linewidth='0.5', color='black')
plt.show()
```

Output:

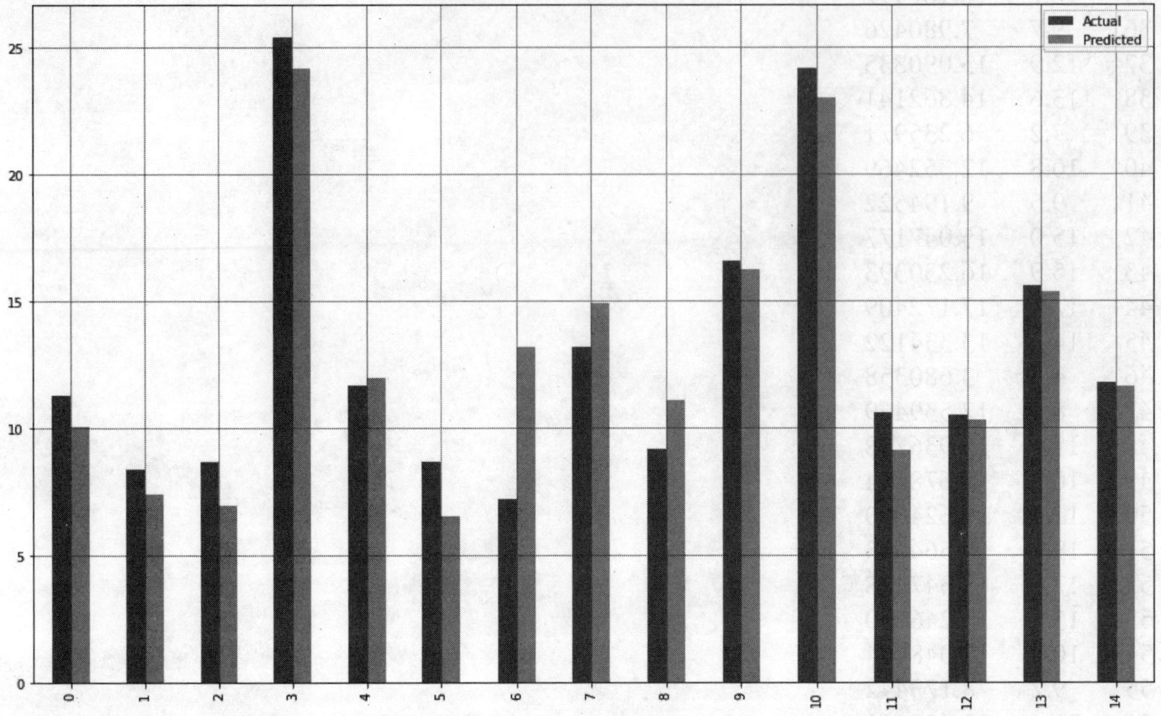

9.2.5 Logistic Regression

Linear regression is used to model data when Y is a continuous variable. However, it cannot be used when the output variable is binary categorical. There are many applications where the output is only 0 or 1. Such problems are called binary classification problems. For example, to identify whether an email is spam or not, review comments about a movie (good or bad), if a credit card transaction is fraudulent or not, whether the given tissue sample is malignant or not, and so on. Logistic regression can be used to model such problems.

Logistic regression takes the log odds of the event $ln(P/1-P)$, where P is the probability of the event. The probability value always lies between 0 and 1. It uses the concept of maximum log likelihood to optimise the results.

$$z_i = \ln\left(\frac{P_i}{1-P_i}\right) = \alpha + \beta_1 x_2 + \cdots + \beta_n x_n$$

Taking the exponent on both sides of the equation gives

$$P_i = E(y=1 \mid x_i) = \frac{e^z}{1+e^z} = \frac{e^{\alpha+\beta_i x_i}}{1+e^{\alpha+\beta_i x_i}}$$

Logistic regression can be built using the `LogisticRegression()` function in python.

9.2.6 Python Code for Logistic Regression

This code uses the marks.csv file, which contains data of marks. The last column value is considered as a dependent variable, which represents the class (0 or 1) for students who were admitted or not based on the marks. Function `LogisticRegression()` from `Sklearn` is used to classify data. Here the confusion matrix is also printed, which reveals the false positive and false negative cases along with the cases that are correctly classified. In this case, out of 25 testing samples, only 2 are misclassified, which indicates that the accuracy of the fitted model is 80%.

```
# Logistics Regression
from google.colab import files
uploaded= files.upload()
from matplotlib import pyplot
import matplotlib.pyplot as plt
import pandas as pd
from sklearn.model_selection import train_test_split
from sklearn import metrics
from sklearn.linear_model import LogisticRegression
from sklearn.metrics import accuracy_score
import io
df=pd. read_csv(io.BytesIO(uploaded['marks.csv']))
#Logistic regression in python
# X = feature values, all the columns except the last column
X = df.iloc[:,:-1]
# y = target values, last column of the data frame
y = df.iloc[:, -1]
# filter out the applicants that got admitted
admitted = df.loc[y == 1]
# filter out the applicants that din't get admission
not_admitted = df.loc[y == 0]
# plots
plt.scatter(admitted.iloc[:, 0], admitted.iloc[:, 1], s=10,
label='Admitted')
plt.scatter(not_admitted.iloc[:, 0], not_admitted.iloc[:, 1], s=10,
label='Not Admitted')
plt.legend()
plt.show()
X_train, X_test, y_train, y_test = train_test_split(X, y, test_size=0.25,
random_state=0)
model = LogisticRegression()
model.fit(X_train, y_train)
predicted_classes = model.predict(X_test)
accuracy = accuracy_score(y_test,predicted_classes)
parameters = model.coef_
print(parameters)
print(accuracy)
dfa = pd.DataFrame({'Actual': y_test, 'Predicted': predicted_classes})
print(dfa)
print(model.predict_proba(X_test))
print(metrics.confusion_matrix(y_test, predicted_classes))
```

Output:

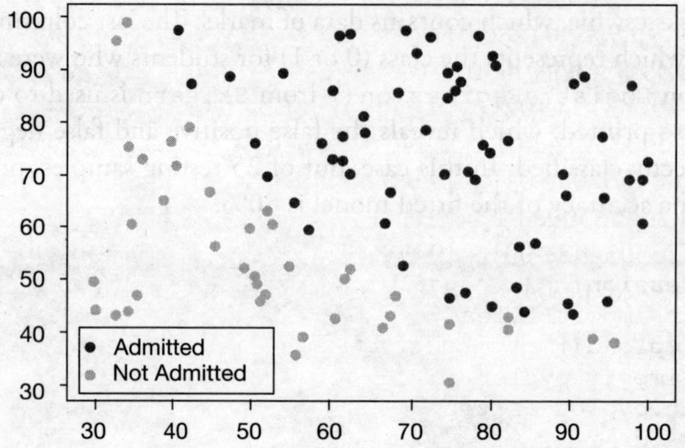


```
[[0.21340326 0.18769604]]
0.92
    Actual  Predicted
26  0       1
86  1       1
2   1       1
55  1       1
75  1       1
92  1       1
16  0       0
73  1       1
54  0       0
94  1       1
53  0       0
91  0       0
78  0       1
13  0       0
7   1       1
30  1       1
22  0       0
24  1       1
33  0       0
8   1       1
43  0       0
62  0       0
3   1       1
71  1       1
45  1       1
```

```
[[6.47880288e-02 9.35211971e-01] [1.84897965e-04 9.99815102e-01] [1.03645803e-02 9.89635420e-01] [9.33606642e-05 9.99906639e-01] [9.89519121e-02 9.01048088e-01] [6.49871656e-04 9.99350128e-01] [7.72508461e-01 2.27491539e-01] [9.02005828e-02 9.09799417e-01] [9.35603474e-01 6.43965258e-02] [8.21374470e-02 9.17862553e-01] [9.87926281e-01 1.20737193e-02] [9.97445751e-01 2.55424881e-03] [2.53166337e-01 7.46833663e-01] [8.55025714e-01 1.44974286e-01] [2.84574779e-04 9.99715425e-01] [1.15432920e-02 9.88456708e-01] [9.99861579e-01 1.38420632e-04] [1.26196191e-01 8.73803809e-01] [9.26858509e-01 7.31414905e-02] [1.53775540e-01 8.46224460e-01] [9.93236966e-01 6.76303442e-03] [9.99843287e-01 1.56712909e-04] [1.46608782e-03 9.98533912e-01] [1.21372870e-04 9.99878627e-01] [5.41056532e-03 9.94589435e-01]]
[[ 9 2]
 [ 0 14]]
```

9.3 Simpson's Paradox

Simpson's paradox is an effect that shows that the trend indicated by a model on a whole data set is different from the trends shown by subsets of data. It occurs when the marginal association between two categorical variables is qualitatively different from the partial association between the same variables after controlling for one or more other variables. For correctly interpreting the data, understanding and identifying this paradox is very important.

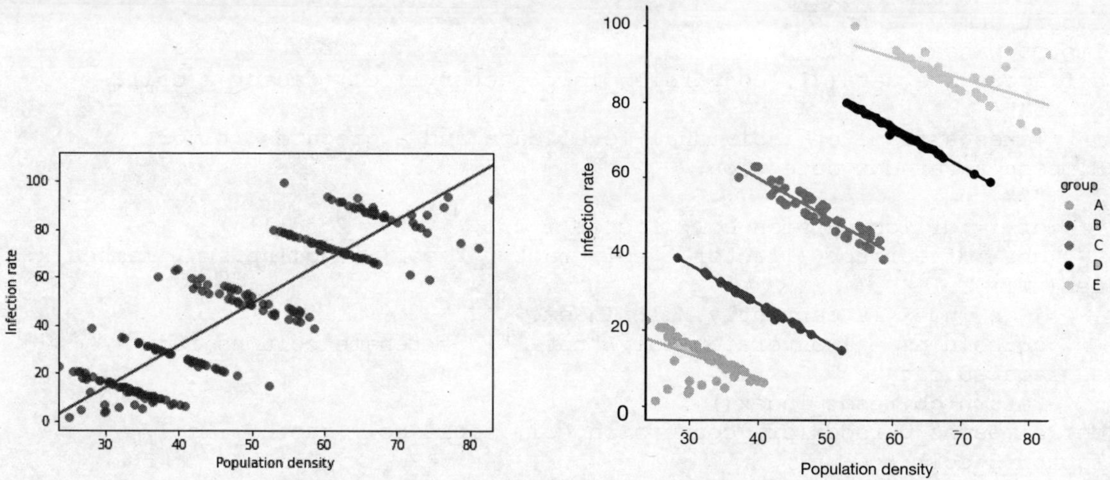

Figure 9.4 Simpson's paradox example

Figure 9.4 shows an infectious disease example; the overall trend in population density and infection rate is positive, but if we look at a small subset of data for cities A, B, C, D, E, each city population density and infection rate is negatively correlated. This may be due to other parameters which have not been included in the build model such as the demography and wealth of residents in that city. This disagreement in the results of the model reveals that more explanatory variables need to be added.

Simpson's paradox is helpful in visualizing data. It gives insight into relationships between variables and models fitted. It is important to identify the question you are trying to answer from the given data set; you also need some contextual information about the data set.

Example: The table given below has Simpson's paradox present in its data. The individual success rates of students enrolled in the statistics and machine learning courses under Prof. Sandhya is higher than under Prof. Arora, but Prof. Arora has a higher overall rate.

	Prof. Sandhya	Prof. Arora
Statistics course	70/90 (77%)	2/10 (20%)
Machine learning course	10/10 (100%)	81/90 (90%)
Total	80/100 (80%)	83/100 (83%)

9.3.1 Python Code for Identifying Simpson's Paradox

This code is used for detecting Simpson's paradox in the given data. Data is grouped by and aggregated using Python functions. Success and failure rates are calculated and Simpson's paradox is detected as global success rate is different from local success rate.

```
# Simpson's paradox example
import numpy as np
import pandas as pd
def aggregate_data(df, conversion_col, factor_1_col, factor_2_col):
    """
    Takes a frame of individual-level data and aggregates it for
Simpson's Paradox detection.
    """
    df_ = df[[conversion_col, factor_1_col, factor_2_col]]
    gb = df_.groupby([factor_1_col, factor_2_col]).agg([np.sum, lambda x:
len(x)])
    # gb index is currently MultiIndex.
    gb.columns = [conversion_col, "total"]  # rename columns for
aggregated data.
    return gb.reset_index()
def simpsons_paradox(df, conversion_col, total_col, factor_1_col,
factor_2_col):
    """
   Determine if simpsons paradox is present.
    """
    # Find the global optimal:
    gbs = df.groupby(factor_1_col).sum()
    print("## Global rates here (%): ")
    print(round((gbs[conversion_col] / gbs[total_col] * 100), 2))
    print()
```

```
    global_optimal = (gbs[conversion_col] / gbs[total_col]).argmax()
    # Check for optimal via segments
    df_ = df.set_index([factor_2_col, factor_1_col])
    rates = (df_[conversion_col] / df_[total_col]).unstack(-1)
    print("## Local rates here (%):")
    print(round(rates * 100, 2))
    print()
    # Find the local optimals
    local_optimals = rates.apply(lambda x: x.argmax(), 1)
    if local_optimals.unique().shape[0] > 1:
        print("## No Simpson's Paradox not detected.")
        print("## Segmented rates do not have a consistent optimal
choice.")
        print("## Local optimals:")
        print(local_optimals)
        print("## Global optimal: ", global_optimal)
        return False
    local_optimal = local_optimals.unique()[0]
    print("## Global optimal: ", global_optimal)
    print("## Local optimal: ", local_optimal)
    if local_optimal != global_optimal:
        print("## Yes Simpson's Paradox detected.")
        return True
    else:
        print("## No Simpson's Paradox not detected.")
        return False
if __name__ == "__main__":
    # Generate data
    d = []
    d += ([('Prof Sandhya', 'Statistics Course', 1)] * 70)        d
+= ([('Prof Sandhya', 'Statistics Course', 0)] * (90 - 70))       d +=
([('Prof Sandhya', 'Machine Learning', 1)] * 10)
    d += ([('Prof Sandhya', 'Machine Learning', 0)] * (10 - 10))
    d += ([('Prof Arora', 'Statistics Course', 1)] * 2)
    d += ([('Prof Arora', 'Statistics Course', 0)] * (10 - 2))
    d += ([('Prof Arora', 'Machine Learning', 1)] * 81)
    d += ([('Prof Arora', 'Machine Learning', 0)] * (90 - 81))
    df = pd.DataFrame(d, columns=['Teacher', 'Course', 'success'])
    gb = aggregate_data(df, 'success', 'Teacher', 'Course')
    simpsons_paradox(gb, 'success', 'total', 'Teacher', 'Course')
```

Output:

```
## Global rates here (%):
Teacher
Prof Arora     83.0
Prof Sandhya   80.0
dtype: float64
```

```
## Local rates here (%):
Teacher          Prof Arora  Prof Sandhya
Course
Machine Learning       90.0       100.00
Statistics Course      20.0        77.78
## Global optimal:  0
## Local optimal:  1
## Yes Simpson's Paradox detected.
```

EXERCISES

Multiple Choice Questions

1. If a single value in data changes, which of the following will always change?
(a) Mean
(b) Median
(c) Mode
(d) All of the above

2. For analysing the central tendency of data, which of these measures are used?
(a) Median and Normal Distribution
(b) Mean, Median and Mode
(c) Mode, Variance and Range
(d) Standard Deviation, Mode and Mean
(e) Mean, Range and Normal Distribution

3. If a distribution has a mean of 23, median of 24 and mode of 25.5, it can be said that the distribution is:
(a) Nothing can be said
(c) Positive skewed
(b) Asymmetrical
(d) Negatively skewed

4. Which of the following is characteristic of the sum of the deviations about the mean?
(a) It is a range
(b) It is equal to zero
(c) It is also called the total standard deviation
(d) It is always positive
(e) It is always negative

5. The middle value of an ordered observation of numbers is the:
(a) Mean (b) Median
(c) Mode (d) Mid-value

6. Which one of these divides a group of data into four sub-groups?
(a) Percentile (b) Deciles
(c) Median (d) Quartile

7. A survey collected the height of students in a school. Height is a/an _____.
(a) Ordinal variable
(b) Continuous variable
(c) Categorical variable
(d) Quantitative variable

8. What would be the sum of deviations of individual data points from their mean for (5, 10, 20, 5, 20)?
(a) 10 (b) 25
(c) 50 (d) 0
(e) None of the above

9. The scores of six persons in an IQ test were 92, 89, 86, 88, 84, 83. The median is:
(a) 87 (b) 86
(c) 88 (d) 92
(e) None of the above

10. Which of the following is a measure of dispersion?
    (a) Median
    (b) Mode
    (c) Interquartile range
    (d) Mean

11. A small sample of Grade 5 students spends the following hours on study per day: 4, 0, 3, 2, 5, 1, 2, 1, 0. The mean number of hours spent on study per day (rounded to the nearest tenth) is:
    (a) 1.7 (b) 2.0
    (c) 2.5 (d) 3.0

12. Logistic regression algorithm is:
    (a) Supervised machine learning
    (b) Unsupervised machine learning

13. Logistic regression is mainly used for:
    (a) Regression (b) Classification

14. Which of the following methods is used to best-fit the data in logistic regression?
    (a) Least Square Error
    (b) Maximum Likelihood
    (c) Entropy
    (d) None of the above

15. Logistic regression algorithm can be used for the three-class classification problem.
    (a) True (b) False

16. Which of the following methods do we use to find the best fit line for data in linear regression?
    (a) Logarithmic Loss
    (b) Entropy
    (c) Least Square Error
    (d) None of the above

17. Suppose the Pearson correlation between V1 and V2 is zero, is it correct to conclude that V1 and V2 do not have any relation between them?
    (a) True (b) False

18. Which of the following statements is true about outliers in linear regression?
    (a) Linear regression is sensitive to outliers
    (b) Linear regression is not sensitive to outliers
    (c) Cannot say
    (d) All of the above are true

19. How many coefficients do you need to estimate in a simple linear regression model?
    (a) 1 (b) 2
    (c) 3 (d) 4

20. If we change the input variable by 1 unit in a simple linear regression model, by how much will the output variable change?
    (a) By 0
    (b) By 1
    (c) Only by intercept
    (d) By its slope

Answers

1. (a)	**2.** (b)	**3.** (d)	**4.** (b)	**5.** (b)	**6.** (d)	**7.** (b)	**8.** (d)
9. (a)	**10.** (c)	**11.** (b)	**12.** (a)	**13.** (b)	**14.** (b)	**15.** (a)	**16.** (c)
17. (b)	**18.** (a)	**19.** (b)	**20.** (d)				

Programming/Concept-based Questions

1. Perform the following statistical operations in Python:
   (a) Create a vector named marks (6.5,5.0,8.4,7.7,10.2,9.8).
   (b) Calculate the mean of the vector.
   (c) Calculate the median of the vector.
   (d) Calculate the standard deviation and variance of the vector.
   (e) Find the maximum and minimum marks in the given vector.

   Answer:

```
import numpy as np
import statistics as st
numsval=[6.5,5.0,8.4,7.7,10.2,9.8]
#print('mode is ',st.mode(numsval))
print('mean is ',st.mean(numsval))
print('median is ',st.median(numsval))
print('variance is ',st.variance(numsval))
print('standard deviation is ',st.stdev(numsval))
print('Maximum is ',max(numsval))
print('minimum is ',min(numsval))
```

2. A manufacturer wants to determine the inner diameter of a piece of chalk. Ideally, the diameter should be 57 mm. The data is as follows: 72, 57, 53, 58, 56, 57, 56, 50. Calculate the measures of central value and dispersion, and comment on the quality of the chalk produced.

   Answer:

```
import numpy as np
import statistics as st
numsval=[72, 57, 53, 58, 56, 57, 56, 50]
#print('mode is ',st.mode(numsval))
print('mean is ',st.mean(numsval))
print('median is ',st.median(numsval))
print('variance is ',st.variance(numsval))
print('standard deviation is ',st.stdev(numsval))
print('Maximum is ',max(numsval))
print('minimum is ',min(numsval))
```

   Output:

   mean is 57.375
   median is 56.5
   variance is 41.69642857142857
   standard deviation is 6.457277179386724 5
   Maximum is 72
   minimum is 50

3. The power of an engine (y) is a function of temperature (x) in °F. Consider the following data:

x	y
4300	1760
4650	1652
3200	1485
3150	1390
4950	1820
4010	1665
3810	1550
4500	1700
3008	1270

Fit a simple linear regression to the data and plot the line through the data.

Answer:

```
import io
import matplotlib.pyplot as plt
import pandas as pd
import numpy as np
from sklearn.model_selection import train_test_split
from sklearn.linear_model import LinearRegression
from sklearn import metrics
import scipy.stats
dfval =
pd.DataFrame({'x':[4300,4650,3200,3150,4950,4010,3810,4500,3008],
              'y':[1760,1652,1485,1390,1820,1665,1550,1700,1270] })
Xval=dfval['x'].values.reshape(-1,1)
yval=dfval['y'].values.reshape(-1,1)
Xval_train, Xval_test, yval_train, yval_test = train_test_split(Xval,
yval, test_size=0.2, random_state=0)
regressorval = LinearRegression()
regressorval.fit(Xval, yval)
#To retrieve the intercept:
print('intercept valus is ',regressorval.intercept_)
#For retrieving the slope:
print('coefficient values are ',regressorval.coef_)
yval_pred = regressorval.predict(Xval)
# calculating Accuracy of Regression model
print('')
r2_score = regressorval.score(Xval, yval)
```

```
print('accuracy of model is')
print(r2_score*100,'%')
# Regression line fitted
plt.scatter(Xval, yval,  color='gray')
plt.plot(Xval, yval_pred, color='red', linewidth=2)
plt.show()
```

Output:

intercept value is [661.79488473]
coefficient values are [[0.23429777]]
accuracy of model is
85.58573089237518 %

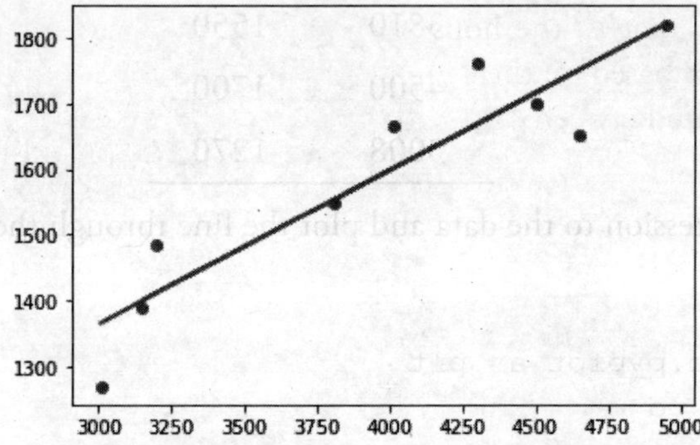

4. Use the Advterising.csv file which contains sales data as a dependent variable. Sales is dependent on TV, Radio and Newspaper. Download the file and study the correlation between Sales and Radio. Also draw a scatter diagram to show the relationship.

Answer:

```
import io
import matplotlib.pyplot as plt
import pandas as pd
import scipy.stats
from google.colab import files
uploaded= files.upload()
dfval=pd.read_csv(io.BytesIO(uploaded['Advertising.csv']))
#Find the correlation between variables
dataval1=dfval['Radio']
dataval2=dfval['Sales']
# plot
pyplot.scatter(dataval1, dataval2)
pearsoncorr=scipy.stats.pearsonr(dataval1,dataval2)[0]
print(pearsoncorr)
```

Output:

0.576222574571055

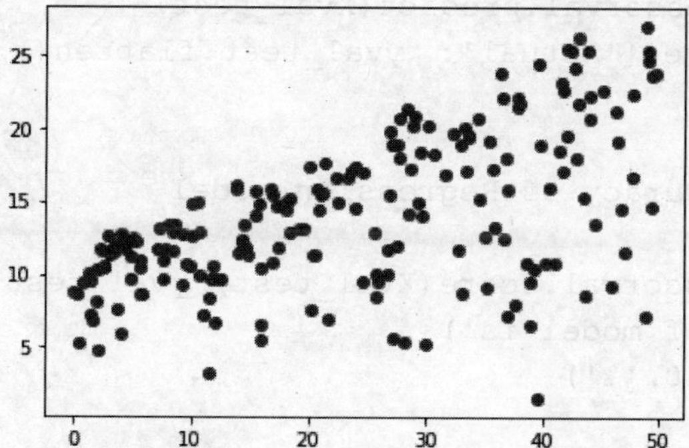

5. Use house price data, that is, the house_prices_train.csv file. Fit a simple linear regression to predict the house price based on the `GrLivArea` feature only. Implement the Python code and view the scatter diagram between `GrLivArea` and `SalePrice` data and calculate the accuracy of the model.

Answer:

```
import io
import matplotlib.pyplot as plt
import pandas as pd
import scipy.stats
from sklearn.model_selection import train_test_split
from sklearn.linear_model import LinearRegression
from sklearn import metrics
from google.colab import files
uploaded= files.upload()
dfval=pd.read_csv(io.BytesIO(uploaded['house_prices_train.csv']))
#Find the correlation between variables
dataval1=dfval['GrLivArea']
dataval2=dfval['SalePrice']
# plot
pyplot.scatter(dataval1, dataval2)
pearsoncorr=scipy.stats.pearsonr(dataval1,dataval2)[0]
print(pearsoncorr)
Xval = dfval['GrLivArea'].values.reshape(-1,1)
yval = dfval['SalePrice'].values.reshape(-1,1)
Xval_train, Xval_test, yval_train, yval_test = train_test_split(Xval,
yval, test_size=0.2, random_state=40)
regressorval = LinearRegression()
regressorval.fit(Xval_train, yval_train)
#To retrieve the intercept:
print('intercept valus is ',regressorval.intercept_)
#For retrieving the slope:
print('coefficient values are ',regressorval.coef_)
```

```
yval_pred = regressorval.predict(Xval_test)
df = pd.DataFrame({'Actual': yval_test.flatten(), 'Predicted': yval_
pred.flatten()})
print(df)
# calculating Accuracy of Regression model
print('')
r2_score = regressorval.score(Xval_test, yval_test)
print('accuracy of model is')
print(r2_score*100,'%')
```

Output:

0.7086244776126522

intercept value is [17161.73473108]

coefficient values are [[108.52724098]]

	Actual	Predicted
0	190000	143704.497715
1	173000	194278.192012
2	392500	196448.736831
3	181000	200572.771988
4	284000	239208.469778
..	...	...
287	102776	145006.824606
288	171750	169642.508309
289	179000	212510.768496
290	309000	283270.529616
291	145000	159766.529380

[292 rows x 2 columns]

accuracy of model is

52.57496998517941 %

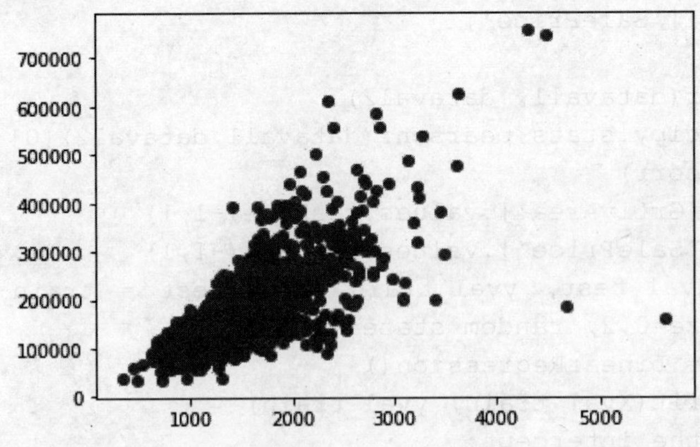

6. Write a program in Python that predicts traffic on a new mode of transport.

Answer:

```
#Importing the libraries
import pandas as pd
from sklearn.preprocessing import LabelEncoder
import matplotlib.pyplot as plt
from sklearn.linear_model import LinearRegression
from sklearn.model_selection import train_test_split
from sklearn.metrics import mean_squared_error
# Load the dataset
df = pd.read_csv('/content/traffic_data.csv')
# Explore dataset
print(df.head())
# Encode the categorical variables
le_weather = LabelEncoder()
df['weather'] = le_weather.fit_transform(df['weather'])
le_traffic = LabelEncoder()
df['traffic'] = le_traffic.fit_transform(df['traffic'])
# Split the data into training and testing sets
X_train,  X_test,  y_train,  y_test  =  train_test_split(df[['time',
'weather']], df['traffic'], test_size=0.2, random_state=42)
# Encode the time column
X_train['time'] = pd.to_datetime(X_train['time'])
X_train['hour'] = X_train['time'].dt.hour
X_train['minute'] = X_train['time'].dt.minute
X_train.drop(columns=['time'], inplace=True)
X_test['time'] = pd.to_datetime(X_test['time'])
X_test['hour'] = X_test['time'].dt.hour
X_test['minute'] = X_test['time'].dt.minute
X_test.drop(columns=['time'], inplace=True)
# Create the model and fit it to the data
model = LinearRegression()
model.fit(X_train, y_train)
# Make predictions on the testing set
y_pred = model.predict(X_test)
# Decode the traffic values
y_pred_decoded      =      le_traffic.inverse_transform(y_pred.round().
astype(int))
y_test_decoded = le_traffic.inverse_transform(y_test)
# Calculate the accuracy of the model
accuracy = sum(y_pred_decoded == y_test_decoded) / len(y_test)
print('Accuracy of the model:', accuracy)
# Calculate the mean squared error
```

```
mse = mean_squared_error(y_test, y_pred)
print('Mean Squared Error:', mse)
# Visualize the predicted vs actual traffic volume
plt.scatter(X_test['hour'], y_test, color='red')
plt.plot(X_test['hour'], y_pred, color='blue')
plt.xlabel('Hour of Day')
plt.ylabel('Traffic Volume')
plt.title('Predicted vs Actual Traffic Volume')
plt.show()
# Preprocess the new data
new_data = pd.DataFrame({'time': ['16:30:00'], 'weather': [0]})
new_data['time'] = pd.to_datetime(new_data['time'])
new_data['hour'] = new_data['time'].dt.hour
new_data['minute'] = new_data['time'].dt.minute
new_data.drop(columns=['time'], inplace=True)
# Predict the traffic volume for the new input
new_pred = model.predict(new_data)
new_pred_decoded = le_traffic.inverse_transform(new_pred.round().
astype(int))
print('Predicted traffic volume:', new_pred_decoded[0])
```

7. Write a program in Python to predict the age of the actors.

Answer:

```
import pandas as pd
fromsklearn.model_selectionimporttrain_test_split
fromsklearn.linear_modelimportLinearRegression
fromsklearn.metricsimportmean_squared_error
# Load the dataset
data =pd.read_csv('actors.csv')# Replace 'actors.csv' with your
dataset file name
# Split the dataset into features (X) and target (y)
X =data[['Name','Gender','Movies']]
y = data['Age']
# Convert categorical features to numerical using label encoding
X['Gender']= X['Gender'].astype('category')
X['Gender']= X['Gender'].cat.codes
# Split the data into training and testing sets
X_train,X_test,y_train,y_test=train_test_split(X, y,test_
size=0.2,random_state=42)
# Initialize and train the linear regression model
model =LinearRegression()
model.fit(X_train,y_train)

# Predict the ages for test data
```

```
y_pred=model.predict(X_test)
# Calculate mean squared error (MSE) as a measure of prediction
accuracy
mse=mean_squared_error(y_test,y_pred)
print(f"Mean Squared Error: {mse}")
# Example prediction for a new actor
new_actor=pd.DataFrame({'Name':['John
Doe'],'Gender':[1],'Movies':[10]})
new_actor['Gender']=new_actor['Gender'].astype('category')
new_actor['Gender']=new_actor['Gender'].cat.codes
age_pred=model.predict(new_actor)
print(f"Predicted Age: {age_pred[0]} years")
```

BIBLIOGRAPHY

1. Avinash Navlani. "Understanding Logistic Regression in Python Tutorial". DataCamp. Published December 2019. https://www.datacamp.com/tutorial/understanding-logistic-regression-python
2. Javier Fernandez. "Introduction to Regression Analysis". Towards Data Science. Published May 9, 2020. https://towardsdatascience.com/introduction-to-regression-analysis-9151d8ac14b3

CHAPTER **10**

Statistical Analysis: Inferential Statistics

LEARNING OBJECTIVES

At the end of this chapter, you will be able to:

- Define a hypothesis for the given problem
- Test the hypothesis using different inferential statistical tests such as t-test, chi-square test and rank-sum test
- Differentiate between one-tailed and two-tailed tests and the types of errors
- Describe the basics of analysis of variance (ANOVA)
- Analyze the given data using one-way and two-way ANOVA
- Explain the mathematics behind inferential statistics
- Apply inferential statistical tests and ANOVA using Python

10.0 INTRODUCTION

To perform statistical analysis, some judgment about the population or sample needs to be made. If the study on a sample is intended to obtain information on the entire population, it is referred to as statistical inference. Inferential statistics deals with the techniques used to help analysts make some judgment about the state of a population or sample. It deals with uncertainty in decision-making and uses the concept of probability.

Two methods are used in inferential statistics: hypothesis testing and estimation. Based on these two methods, two approaches are followed:

- **Approach 1: Hypothesis testing:** Here, tests are conducted based on a hypothesis. In this approach, we make some assumptions about the relationship(s) or value(s) of one or more parameters. Sample statistics is used to make decisions about the assumed parameters. The result of the sample statistics is the probability that indicates whether the decision is correct or incorrect.
- **Approach 2: Measurement of confidence interval:** In this approach, sample statistics is used to estimate one (or more) parameter(s). Estimation is performed in the form of interval measurement and the result takes the form of the level of confidence.

10.1 Hypothesis Testing

A hypothesis is a statement or assumption about the relationship between variables. It can be defined in many ways:

"A hypothesis is an educated prediction that can be tested" (www.study.com)
"A hypothesis is a proposed explanation for a phenomenon" (Wikipedia)
"A hypothesis is used to define the relationship between two variables" (Oxford Dictionary)

Example 1: Avogadro's hypothesis (1811): "The volume of a gas is directly proportional to the number of molecules of the gas."

Statistical hypothesis: This is stated in terms of population parameters, such as variance and mean. The validity of the hypothesis is tested from sample data using some test of the hypothesis. The result of the test of the hypothesis enables us to accept (or reject) the statistical hypothesis.

Example 2: "To determine whether the wages of men and women are equal." "A product in the market is of standard quality." "Whether a particular medicine is effective in curing a disease."

There are two types of hypothesis: null (H_o) and alternative (H_a). The hypothesis to be tested is the null hypothesis; the alternative hypothesis is assumed to be true when the null hypothesis is proved to be false.

Example 3: A null hypothesis might claim that "Men and women are equally intelligent", while the alternative hypothesis might claim that "Women are more intelligent than men."

Example 4: The Government of India's Ministry of Human Resource Development (MHRD) has set up 23 IITs as an initiative to improve the country's human resources. Every year, MHRD conducts the GATE examination carrying 1000 marks to measure the engineering aptitude of graduates. The GATE result data of 300 students for 2018 was collected and the observed mean score was 230. To validate this, statistical hypothesis testing is carried out to determine the mean mark of all the GATE-2018 examinees.

The two hypotheses used here are:

H_0: $\mu = 230$
H_a: $\mu<230$

Note: It is customary to have an equal to sign in the null hypothesis. For the alternative hypothesis, many options are available: H_a: $\mu<230$ or H_a: $\mu>230$ or H_a: $\mu!=230$.

One-tailed Test: In a one-tailed test, the alternative hypothesis states that the population parameter lies entirely above or below (left- and right-tailed test) a specified value.

Two-tailed Test: Here, the alternative hypothesis states that the parameter can lie on both sides of the value specified.

In Fig. 10.1, the dark regions differentiate the one-tailed and two-tailed tests. The alternative hypotheses for one-tailed and two-tailed tests are different, as shown in Fig. 10.2.

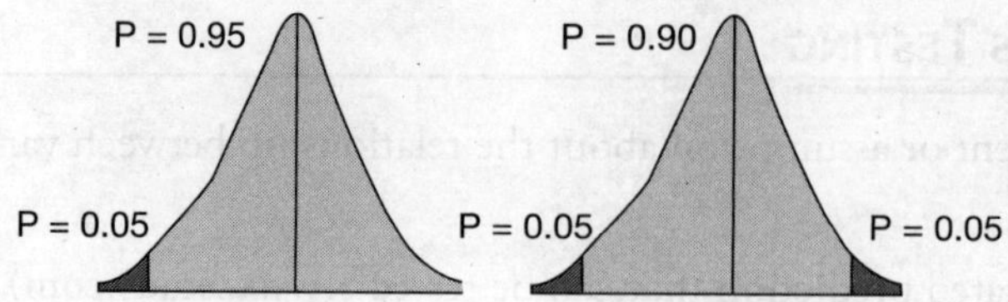

Figure 10.1 One-tailed versus two-tailed test

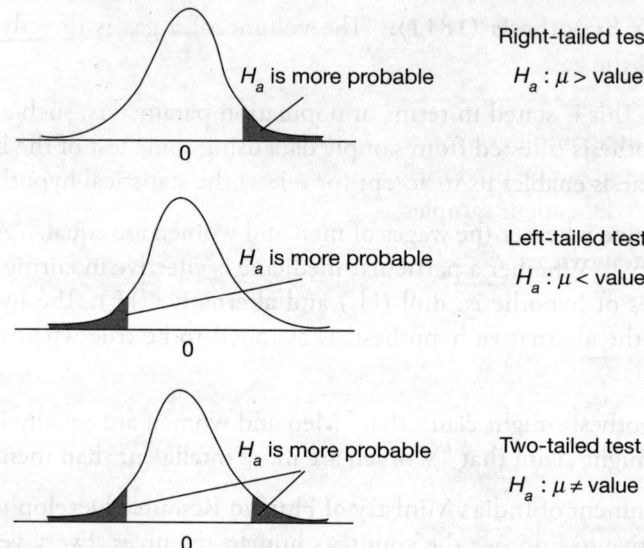

Figure 10.2 Alternative hypotheses for one-tailed and two-tailed tests

For hypothesis testing, the steps given below are performed:

1. Form the null and alternative hypotheses, and the acceptable level of the hypotheses.
2. Determine appropriate test statistics and the rejection region based on samples.
3. Calculate the test statistics from the sample data.
4. Make a decision to accept or reject the null hypothesis.
5. Interpret the result in a language suitable for practitioners.

The standard procedure is to assume that the hypothesis is true. (Just as we presume innocence until guilt is proven). The null hypothesis H_0 is accepted if the test statistics falls within the area of acceptance, and rejected otherwise. The procedure is based on probability theory; that is, there is a chance of making errors.

10.1.2 Types of Errors

Two types of errors can occur in hypothesis testing (Fig. 10.3):

- **Type I:** A type I error occurs when the null hypothesis is incorrectly rejected (the null hypothesis is rejected when it is actually true).

- **Type II:** A type II error occurs when the null hypothesis is incorrectly accepted (the null hypothesis is accepted when it is actually not true).

Decision	Observation: H_0 is true	Observation: H_0 is false
H_0 is accepted	Decision is correct	Type II error
H_0 is rejected	Type I error	Decision is correct

Figure 10.3 Types of errors

10.2 Using the T-Test

A t-test is used for only two samples of inferential statistics. It determines if the means of two populations differ significantly. It can be used for hypothesis testing of the mean of one sample, two independent samples and two dependent samples. The formulae used for t-test statistics are given below:

For one-sample–based t-statistics

$$t = \frac{\bar{X} - \mu}{S_X / \sqrt{n}} \qquad (1)$$

$$df = n - 1$$

where x = mean of the sample, μ = mean of the proposed population, S_x = sample standard deviation, n = number of samples and df = degree of freedom.

For two-independent-samples–based t-statistics

$$t = \frac{m_A - m_B}{\sqrt{\frac{S^2}{n_A} + \frac{S^2}{n_B}}} \qquad (2)$$

where m_A and m_B = means of two different samples, n_A and n_B = sample sizes and S = estimator of the common variance of the two samples, such as:

$$S^2 = \frac{\sum (x - m_A)^2 + \sum (x - m_B)^2}{n_A + n_B - 2} \qquad (3)$$

Here, the degree of freedom is $n_A + n_B - 2$.

For two-dependent (paired)-sample–based t-statistics

This test is treated as the test for two dependent samples. This test is normally applied when sample data with before/after treatment is given, or when the comparison of two variants in A?B testing is required. The mean of the given sample data is computed twice. The paired t-test statistics formula is as follows:

$$t = \frac{m}{s / \sqrt{n}} \qquad (4)$$

where m = mean of the difference in the sample, μ = mean of the population, s = standard deviation of the sample, n = sample size and degree of freedom (df) = $n - 1$.

In t-tests, the same logic is used as in the testing of hypothesis theory in the earlier section. To determine the acceptance or rejection of the null hypothesis, the calculated t-statistics value is compared with the t-critical value given in the table.

10.3 The t-Test in Python

Example 1: A bulb manufacturing company claims that the average life of their bulb is 31 hours. You collect data randomly to test their claim. The data of 8 bulbs from a local vendor was collected and their average life was tested under similar conditions. The following average life of bulbs (in hours) was obtained: 30, 28, 32, 26, 33, 25, 28, 30

Is the actual average life of a bulb 31 hours or does it deviate from this mean life (α = .05 or significance level is 95%)?

Solution: Data indicates testing of the mean against the value 31.00, with a one- or two-tailed t-test of the mean.

$$H_0: \mu = 31.00$$

$$t = \frac{\bar{X} - \mu}{S_X / \sqrt{n}} \quad df = n - 1$$

Compute the test statistics: Computed mean value of the sample is 29 and computed standard deviation of the given sample is 2.775. The t-statistics is calculated as follows:

$$t = \frac{29.00 - 31.00}{2.775 / \sqrt{8}} = -2.04$$

Hypothesis testing: The degree of freedom (*df*) here is 8 – 1 = 7, that is, it is equal to n – 1. A two-tailed test can be performed on this sample data, with α =.05. The absolute value of the calculated t-statistics is 2.04 and the given critical table value of t-statistics is 2.365. Therefore, the null hypothesis is accepted, which indicates that the average life of a bulb does not differ significantly from the population mean. In fact, a conclusion can be made that the average bulb life of the sample did not differ significantly from 31.00.

Python coding of t-test using the SciPy module

```
import numpy as np
from scipy import stats
a=[30,28,32,26,33,25,28,30]
t2, p2 = stats.ttest_1samp(a,31)
print("t = " + str(t2))
print("p = " + str(p2))
alpha = 0.05
if p2 <= alpha:
    print('(reject null hypothesis H0)')
else:
    print('(Null hypothesis H0 holds true)')
```

Output:
t = -2.0367003088692623
p = 0.0811068697473857
(Null hypothesis H0 holds true)

Here, only one sample is given, which is to be tested for the given mean. So the function `stats.ttest_1samp (a,mean)` of the SciPy module is used to test if the population mean of the given data is likely to be a given value. This function takes two parameters: the data sample, specified as `a`, and the `mean` value, against which the population mean is to be checked. This function returns t-statistics and the *p*-value. Here, the function has returned the t-value as −2.0367, which is the same as that achieved through manual calculation. Given that the table value is 2.36 and the calculated value is 2.03, which is less than the given table value, the null hypothesis is accepted.

Example 2: For a random sample of 10 persons trained under training1, the increase in performance in a period was: 9, 15, 14, 8, 12, 13, 17, 16, 6, 10. For another sample of 12 persons trained under training2, the increase in performance in the same period was: 17, 10, 23, 21, 8, 18, 14, 12, 15, 22, 13, 7. Test whether training1 and training2 differ significantly with respect to their effect on increase in performance.

Solution: The null hypothesis taken here in training1 and training2 does not differ significantly as regards their effect on increase in performance. In this example, two independent sample t-tests are applied. The calculated t-value is −1.55 using the formula of two independent samples.

$$t = \frac{m_A - m_B}{\sqrt{\frac{S^2}{n_A} + \frac{S^2}{n_B}}}$$

Mean of the first sample = 12
Mean of the second sample = 15
Standard deviation = 4.66 calculated using the formula:

$$S^2 = \frac{\sum(x - m_A)^2 + \sum(x - m_B)^2}{n_A + n_B - 2}$$

t = ((12 – 15)/4.66)* Sqrt(10*12/(10 + 12)) = 1.51

The table t-value is 2.09. So the null hypothesis is accepted. A conclusion can therefore be made that with respect to the effect of training on increase in performance, training1 and training2 do not differ significantly.

Python code

```
import numpy as np
from scipy import stats
dietA =[10,6,16,17,13,12,8,14,15,9]
dietB =[7,13,22,15,12,14,18,8,21,23,10,17]
```

```
t2, p2 = stats.ttest_ind(dietA,dietB)
print('independent sample statistics')
print("t = " + str(t2))
print("p = " + str(p2))
alpha = 0.05
if p2 <= alpha:
    print('(reject null hypothesis H0)')
else:
    print('(Null hypothesis H0 holds true)')
```

Output:
independent sample statistics
t = -1.5040790787578628
p = 0.1481894350433765
(Null hypothesis H0 holds true)

Here, the SciPy module function `stats.ttest_ind(sample1,sample2)` is used to test two independent samples. Using this function, two independent sample t-tests can be made. It takes two parameters: `sample1` and `sample2`. The result shows that the null hypothesis is accepted as the t-statistic is equal to 1.55, which is less than the given table value of 2.09 at $df = 20$. There is strong evidence that with respect to the training effect on increase in performance, training1 and training2 do not differ significantly.

Example 3: A study was performed to test whether the sales of a company improved after an advertising campaign. Company sales was recorded before and after the campaign. Before the advertisement, the campaign sales was recorded as: 16, 20, 21, 22, 23, 22, 27, 25, 27, 28 and after the campaign, the sales recorded was: 19, 22, 24, 24, 25, 25, 26, 26, 28, 32. A paired t-test can be used to check whether sales improved significantly after the advertising campaign.

Solution: In this example, two dependent sample t-tests are applied. The calculated t-value is 4.47 using the formula of two dependent samples.

$$t = \frac{m}{s / \sqrt{n}}$$

Python code

```
import numpy as np
from scipy import stats
beforesale =[16,20,21,22,23,22,27,25,27,28]
aftersale =[19,22,24,24,25,25,26,26,28,32]
t2, p2 = stats.ttest_rel(beforesale,aftersale)
print('Dependent sample statistics')
print("t = " + str(t2))
print("p = " + str(p2))
alpha = 0.05
if p2 <= alpha:
    print('(reject null hypothesis H0)')
else:
    print('(Null hypothesis H0 holds true)')
```

Output:
Dependent sample statistics
t = -4.47213595499958
p = 0.00154988591170182
(reject null hypothesis H0)

Here, the SciPy module function `stats.ttest_rel(sample1,sample2)` is used to test two dependent samples. Using this function, two dependent sample t-tests can be done. It takes two parameters: `sample1` and `sample2`. The result shows that the null hypothesis is rejected as the calculated t-statistic is equal to 4.47, which is greater than the table value for *df* = 9. There is strong evidence for an increase in sales after the advertising campaign. The table values of t-statistics can be found using predefined tables.

10.4 Chi-Square (χ^2) Test

Chi-square (χ^2) is another important test used in hypothesis testing, mostly for categorical variables. It is a non-parametric test, and the data used is random, mutually exclusive and drawn from a large sample. In the chi-square (χ^2) test, the expectation is measured and compared with the actual observed data. The chi-square test is suitable for unpaired samples. It can compare more than two groups or more than two categories of output variables.

Two main types of chi-square tests are used as a test of independence and as a goodness-of-fit test. The test of independence deals with questions about relationships, such as "Is there a relationship between intelligence and income?", while goodness-of-fit tests if the given sample data is appropriate for the given distribution.

The formula for the chi-square test of independence is given below:

$$\chi_c^2 = \sum \frac{(O_i - E_i)^2}{E_i},$$

where O = observed frequency and E = expected frequency.

Here also the same logic as in testing hypotheses is followed. To accept or reject the null hypothesis, the calculated chi-square value is compared with the chi square-critical value given in the predefined table.

Example 4: In an anti-allergy campaign in a certain locality, a drug was administered to 812 persons out of a total population of 3248. The number of cases of fever after taking the drug is shown below:

Treatment	Fever after taking drug	No fever after taking drug	Total
Drug	20	792	812
No drug	220	2216	2436
Total	240	3008	3248

Is the drug useful in preventing allergies?

Solution:

Treatment	Fever		$(O - E)^2/E$	No fever		$(O - E)^2/E$	Total
	Observed frequency (O)	Expected frequency (E)		Observed frequency (O)	Expected frequency (E)		
Quinine	20	(812*240)/ 3248 = 60	1600/60 = 26.67	792	(812*3008)/ 3248 = 752	1600/752 = 2.128	812
No quinine	220	(2436*240)/ 3248 = 180	1600/180 = 8.89	2216	(2436*3008)/ 3248 = 2256	1600/2256 = .709	2436
Total	240			3008			3248

Chi-square (χ^2) statistics = 26.67 + 8.89 + 2.128 + .709 = 38.39

The calculated chi-square (χ^2) value is greater than the table value of 3.84 at *df* = 1; so the null hypothesis is rejected, which indicates that the drug is useful in preventing allergies.

10.4.1 Chi-square (χ^2) in Python

```
import numpy as np
from scipy import stats
data =[[20,792],[220,2216]]
stat, p, dof, expected = chi2_contingency(data)
print('chi square value is ',stat)
print('expected values are ',expected)
# interpret p-value
alpha = 0.05
print("p value is " + str(p))
if p <= alpha:
print('(reject null hypothesis H0)')
else:
print('(Null hypothesis H0 holds true)')
```

Output:
chi square value is 37.438622931442076
expected values are [[60. 752.]
[180. 2256.]]
p value is 9.43353778612327e-10
(reject null hypothesis H0)

Here, the SciPy module is used to perform a chi-square test on the given data. Function `chi2_contingency(data)` returns the statistical chi-square value, *p*-value, degree of freedom and the expected values. The expected values calculated by the `chi2_contingency(data)` function are the same as those calculated using the mathematical formulas. The value calculated using the chi-square formula is also approximately the same as that calculated by the function `chi2_contingency()`.

10.5 Wilcoxon Rank-Sum Test

The Wilcoxon rank-sum test is a non-parametric test often used for ordinal or continuous data. Two independent data samples are used in this test. Non-parametric tests are useful when the outcome is not normally distributed and the sample size is small (< 30). This test can be used for paired or unpaired data. The Wilcoxon rank-sum test is used to test whether two populations have the same shape or not. In this test, the null hypothesis is taken as equal medians instead of equal means, which is considered as the null hypothesis in the two-sample t-test. If the *p*-value is less than 0.05, the null hypothesis is accepted. In this test, pooling of observations is considered, that is, both samples are combined into one sample and ranking of samples is performed from lowest to highest, from 1 to $n_1 + n_2$, respectively, keeping track of each sample from which the observation comes.

Formulae used for this statistical test are:

$$U_1 = n_1 n_2 + \frac{n_1(n_1+1)}{2} - R_1,$$

$$U_2 = n_1 n_2 + \frac{n_2(n_2+1)}{2} - R_2,$$

where R_1 = group one ranks summation, R_2 = group two ranks summation, n_1 = number of samples in group 1 and n_2 = number of samples in group 2.

Example: For investigating the effectiveness of a new drug for the COVID pandemic, a clinical trial was designed on 10 persons chosen randomly to receive the new drug or a placebo. Shortness of breath over a week after receiving the treatment was recorded. The data values are as follows:

Placebo	12	4	6	5	7
New COVID drug	6	3	1	2	4

Test whether there is significant difference in case of shortness of breath in a week's period in persons receiving the new drug as compared to those receiving the placebo.

Solution: From the data, it appears that there are more cases of shortness of breath in persons receiving the placebo, but this needs to be tested to check if this is statistically significant or not. Here, the ($n_1 = n_2 = 5$) sample size is small, so the non-parametric test or the Wilcoxon rank-sum test is considered.

H_0: The two populations are equal
H_a: The two populations are not equal.

First, ranks are assigned from smallest to largest in combined samples, that is, from 1 to 10, as the total sample size is 10. We should also keep track of the group assignments in the total sample.

		Total sample (Ordered smallest to largest)		Ranks	
Placebo	New drug	Placebo	New drug	Placebo	New drug
12	6		1		1
4	3		2		2
6	1		3		3
5	2	4	4	4.5	4.5
7	4	5		6	
		6	6	7.5	7.5
		7		9	
		12		10	

$$U_1 = 5(5) + \frac{5(6)}{2} - 37 = 3$$

$$U_2 = 5(5) + \frac{5(6)}{2} - 18 = 22$$

Here, U is 3 (smaller value from U_1 and U_2). The null hypothesis is accepted if the U value is large. The critical value of U from the given table is 2. The null hypothesis H_0 is rejected if $U<2$. In our case, the computed U is 3, so this indicates that H_0 is accepted. This means that there is no statistically significant evidence to show that the two populations are not equal.

10.5.1 Wilcoxon Rank-Sum Test in Python

```
import pandas as pd
# Getting our data in to a dictionary
dataval = {'Placebo':[12,4,6,5,7],
      'newTreatment':[6,3,1,2,4]}
# Dictionary to Dataframe
dfval = pd.DataFrame(dataval)
from scipy.stats import mannwhitneyu
# Carrying out the Wilcoxon-Mann-Whitney test
resultsval = mannwhitneyu(dfval['Placebo'], dfval['newTreatment'])
print(resultsval)
```

Output:
MannwhitneyuResult(statistic=3.0, pvalue=0.029276315078413294)

The `mannwhitneyu()` method of the `scipy.stats` module is used. The test statistical value calculated is 3 and the *p*-value is 0.029, which indicates that the null hypothesis must be accepted.

10.6 Introduction to Analysis of Variance

Analysis of variance is used to determine if two or more samples are from the same population. It helps in the design of experiments as well. It is a way of finding out if the experiment results are significant or not.

For example, a study claims that using activities in class enhances concentration and helps children absorb more information. A teacher needs some proof about whether the activities actually work or not. So, the teacher selects random samples of students from three different classes. Five different samples were taken from each class and each class was provided with different environments for the students to study in.

Class 1 children were exposed to activities in every teaching lesson.
Class 2 children were exposed to activities in some teaching lessons.
Class 3 children were exposed to no activity during the lessons.

To check the students' academic performance for all the three groups, the teacher conducted a test after one month and their test scores were collected. It was noticed that activities were useful as the observation data revealed that the mean score of Class 1 students was greater than that of the other two groups.

This may be true, but it may also have occurred because the samples taken from Group A were from the best students and this eventually resulted in good test scores for Group A students (as students were selected at random). So this leads to questions about how to decide if their performance was different because of different situations, and not by chance. Also, we need to know how these three samples were different from each other.

Other examples: Doctors want to determine which therapy is better for psychiatric patients – counselling, feedback or medication. Test the performance of different colleges or a manufacturing process, and so on.

10.6.1 Analysis of Variance

Analysis of Variance (ANOVA) is a statistical technique that is used to check if the means of two or more groups are significantly different from each other or not. It is derived from partitioning of total variability into its component parts. It is used to compare means and the relative variance between data groups. ANOVA has similar applications to techniques such as t-test, z-test and χ^2-test.

The t-test is used to infer the mean of a single population or to compare two populations, but it is not useful for comparing the mean of more than two populations. ANOVA can be used for more than two populations.

For example, two sets of data are shown below:

Set 1			Set 2		
First sample	Second sample	Third sample	First sample	Second sample	Third sample
5.7	9.4	15.2	5.0	4.0	12.0
4.9	9.8	13.4	4.0	8.0	13.0
7.0	9.0	16.0	4.0	11.0	15.0
7.1	11.2	14.6	7.0	12.0	16.0
5.3	10.6	15.8	10.0	15.0	19.0
$\bar{y}$ = 6.0	$\bar{y}$ = 10.0	$\bar{y}$ = 15.0	$\bar{y}$ = 6.0	$\bar{y}$ = 10.0	$\bar{y}$ = 15.0

When the mean for the two sets of three samples is examined, it is noticed that they look similar as their means are the same in both sets. This indicates that there is no significant difference in the two sets. However, the box plots of the data sets indicates that they are quite different. Set 1 observations are more closely bunched compared to Set 2 data. It is also known that the sample mean from a population with small variance will be less variable. This indicates that for Set 1, variance among the observations within the individual samples is small. This is strong evidence to support the view that the two sets are different.

To analyse these types of situations, ANOVA is used. It helps us make inferences about the differences among means. Some terminology with respect to ANOVA is explained below:

Factor: A characteristic under consideration.

Level (also called treatment): A value of the factor.

10.6.2 Variants of ANOVA

Different variants of ANOVA can be defined on the basis of the number of independent and dependent variables. When only one independent variable (factor) is dealt with, it is called one-way ANOVA. When two independent variables or factors are dealt with, it is called two-way ANOVA. Three-way ANOVA deals with three independent variables or factors and when more independent variables are dealt with, it is multivariate ANOVA.

The steps for computing ANOVA are as follows:

1. Create the null hypothesis.
2. Calculate the mean for each of the groups.
3. Calculate the overall combined mean of the groups.
4. Calculate the sum of deviation of each member's score from the group mean, that is, variation within samples.
5. Calculate the deviation of each group mean from the overall mean, that is, variation between samples.

6. Find the F statistic, which is the ratio of the 'between sample' variation to 'within sample' variation, and vice versa.
7. Make the decision using the F-test statistical results.

The null hypothesis is rejected if the calculated value is greater than the given table value. Normality, homogeneity and independence of error are the assumptions made for ANOVA. If these assumptions do not hold, the ANOVA inference results are not valid.

One-way ANOVA

One-way ANOVA studies the effect of the level of a single factor. This type of ANOVA makes certain assumptions. It uses an F distribution and tests the null hypothesis that the two means are equal. This method can be used only for one independent variable and two levels.

The results of a one-way ANOVA test are summarised in Table 10.1. Here, *k* refers to the number of columns and *N* is the total number of samples.

Table 10.1 One-way ANOVA

Source of variation	Sum of squares (*SS*)	Degree of freedom (*df*)	Mean squared	F-ratio
Between samples (*Bts*)	*SS* (*Bts*)	$k - 1$	$\frac{SS\ (Bts)}{k-1}$	$\frac{MS\ (Bts)}{MS\ (Ws)}$
Within samples (*Ws*)	*SS* (*Ws*)	$N - k$	$\frac{SS\ (Ws)}{N-k}$	.
Total	*SS* (*Ws*) + *SS* (*Bts*)	$N - 1$		.

Example: Under controlled conditions, study of the lifespan of electric light bulbs from three different brands. Test the hypothesis that with respect to mean lifespan, there is no difference between the three brands with the assumption that all lifespans are normally distributed with common variance. The significance level is given as 5% and the table value at $k = 3$, $N = 15$ is 3.88; that is, at *df*, v1 = 2, v2 = 12.

Sample 1	Sample 2	Sample 3
8	7	12
10	5	9
7	10	13
14	9	12
11	9	14

Answer: Let us take the null hypothesis as "there is no significant difference in the means of the three samples".

Sample 1 X_1	Sample 2 X_2	Sample 3 X_3
8	7	12
10	5	9
7	10	13
14	9	12
11	9	14
Total = 50	Total = 40	Total = 60
$\bar{x}_1 = 10$	$\bar{x}_2 = 8$	$\bar{x}_3 = 12$

Overall mean $\bar{\bar{x}} = (10 + 8 + 12)/3 = 10$

Variance between samples

$(\bar{x}_1 - \bar{\bar{x}})^2$	$(\bar{x}_2 - \bar{\bar{x}})^2$	$(\bar{x}_3 - \bar{\bar{x}})^2$
0	4	4
0	4	4
0	4	4
0	4	4
0	4	4
Total = 0	Total = 20	Total = 20

Sum of squares between samples = 0 + 20 + 20 = 40

Variance within samples

X_1	$(X_1 - \bar{x}_1)^2$	X_2	$(X_2 - \bar{x}_2)^2$	X_3	$(X_3 - \bar{x}_3)^2$
8	**4**	7	**1**	12	**0**
10	**0**	5	**9**	9	**9**
7	**9**	10	**4**	13	**1**
14	**16**	9	**1**	12	**0**
11	**1**	9	**1**	14	**4**
Sum	**30**		**16**		**14**

Sum of squares within samples is 30 + 16 + 14 = 60

One-way ANOVA table

Source of variation	Sum of squares (*SS*)	Degree of freedom (*df*)	Mean squared
Between	40	2	40/2 = 20
Within	60	12	60/12 = 5
Total	100	14	

$$\text{F-ratio} = 20/5 = 4$$

The given F-table value is 3.88 and the calculated value is 4. So if the calculated value is greater than the given table value, the null hypothesis is rejected. Therefore, there is a significant difference in the sample means.

One-way ANOVA in Python

```
import io
import pandas as pd
from google.colab import files
uploaded= files.upload()
import statsmodels.api as sm
from statsmodels.formula.api import ols
#ANOVA
data=pd.read_csv(io.BytesIO(uploaded['PlantGrowth.csv']))
mod = ols('weight ~ group',data=data).fit()
aov_table = sm.stats.anova_lm(mod, typ=2)
print(aov_table)
```

Output:
sum_sq df F PR(>F)
group 3.76634 2.0 4.846088 0.01591
Residual 10.49209 27.0 NaN NaN

Here, the PlantGrowth.csv file contains two fields: weight and group. The `statsmodels` module is used to fit ANOVA. Function `ols()` with parameters `weight` and `group` is used to fit a one-way ANOVA. First import the API and use `ols()` to set up the model using the formula 'weight ~ group' on the data. The ordinary least squares regression is used with the PlantGrowth data. The object obtained is a fitted model which is used with the `anova_lm()` method to obtain an ANOVA table.

ANOVA can be fitted using SciPy, Pyvttbl, Pingouin and other modules.

Two-way ANOVA

Two-way ANOVA is an extension of one-way ANOVA, where two factors can be taken into account. Two-way ANOVA is used when we need to study the effect of two independent variables, in combination, on a dependent variable. So, you can use two-way ANOVA when you have quantitative dependent variable values at multiple levels of two categorical independent variables.

For example, you may want to study the quality of clothes washed with different types of detergent and quantities of water. You may also want to study if there is a relation between income and gender for anxiety levels in interviews. You may want to find out the effect of fertilizer type and planting density on crop yield.

Table 10.2 summarises the results of a two-way ANOVA test.

Table 10.2 Two-way ANOVA

Source of variation	Sum of squares (*SS*)	Degree of freedom (*df*)	Mean squared	F-ratio
Between samples	SSC	$c-1$	$MSC = \frac{SSC}{c-1}$	$\frac{MSC}{MSE}$
Between rows	SSR	$r-1$	$MSR = \frac{SSR}{r-1}$	$\frac{MSR}{MSE}$
Residual or error	SSE	$(r-1)(c-1)$	$MSE = \frac{SSE}{(r-1)(c-1)}$	
Total	SST	$N-1$	.	.

Example: A tea company has four salesmen and three seasons. Sales values are given salesman-wise and season-wise. Two-way analysis is performed as we need to find out if there is a significant difference between different salesmen and different seasons.

	Salesman			
Season	**A**	**B**	**C**	**D**
Summer	36	36	21	36
Winter	28	29	31	31
Monsoon	26	28	29	29

Solution: The data is classified based on two criteria: salesman and season. The null hypotheses are 'the sales of different salesmen do not differ significantly' and 'there is no significant difference in sales as far as season is concerned'. Variations between rows and columns can be calculated as explained in one-way ANOVA. The calculated values are given below:

Source of variation	Sum of squares (*SS*)	Degree of freedom (*df*)	Mean squared
Between columns (salesman)	42	3	14
Between rows (season)	36.5	2	18.25
Residual	139.5	6	23.25

$$F = 23.25/14 = 1.661$$

The table value of F at v1 = 3 and v2 = 6 is 4.76 at 5% level of significance. The calculated value is 1.661, which is less than 4.76, so the null hypothesis is accepted. Thus, it can be concluded that sales of different salesmen do not differ significantly.

$$F = 23.25/18.25 = 1.274$$

The table value of F at v1 = 2 and v2 = 6 is 5.14 at 5% level of significance. The calculated value is 1.274, which is less than 5.14, so the null hypothesis is accepted. Thus, it can be concluded that there is no significant difference in sales as far as seasons are concerned.

Overall it is concluded that for this data, salesmen and seasons are alike as far as sales is concerned.

Two way ANOVA in Python

The Pingouin library is used to implement two-way ANOVA in Python. You can install it using the following command:

```
!pip install pingouin
```

The code performs analysis of a tea company for four salesmen and three seasons. Sales values are given salesman-wise and season-wise. Two-way analysis is carried out, as we need to find out if there is a significant difference between different salesmen and different seasons. The `pg.anova()` function of the Pingouin library is used to perform two-way ANOVA. The `statsmodels` library can also be used to perform two-way ANOVA. Functions `ols()` and `anova_lm()` of `statsmodels` can also be used.

```
import numpy as np
import pandas as pd
import pingouin as pg
#create data
df = pd.DataFrame({'salesman': np.repeat(['A', 'B', 'C','D'], 3),
                   'season': np.tile(np.repeat(['summer', 'winter',
'monsoon'], 1), 4),
                   'values': [36,28,26,
                              36,29,28,
                              21,31,29,
                              36,31,29]})
```

```
#view data
print(df)
#perform two-way ANOVA
aov = pg.anova(dv='values', between=['salesman', 'season'],
data=df,detailed=True)
print(aov)
```

Output:

	salesman	season	values
0	A	summer	36
1	A	winter	28
2	A	monsoon	26
3	B	summer	36
4	B	winter	29
5	B	monsoon	28
6	C	summer	21
7	C	winter	31
8	C	monsoon	29
9	D	summer	36
10	D	winter	31
11	D	monsoon	29

	Source	SS	DF	MS	np2
0	salesman	42.0	3	14.00	1.0
1	season	36.5	2	18.25	1.0
2	salesman * season	139.5	6	23.25	1.0

The results match exactly with the manual calculations. So it can be concluded that salesmen and seasons are alike as far as sales is concerned.

EXERCISES

Multiple Choice Questions

1. A statement about a population developed for the purpose of testing is called:
   (a) Hypothesis
   (b) Hypothesis testing
   (c) Test statistics
   (d) Level of significance
2. A statement about the value of a population parameter is called an alternative hypothesis.
   (a) False (b) True
3. A quantitative statement about a population is called a statistical hypothesis.
   (a) True (b) False
4. The alternative hypothesis is also called a research hypothesis.
   (a) True (b) False
5. In a criminal trial, a type II error will occur when:
   (a) A guilty person is set free

(b) An innocent person is sent to jail
(c) A guilty person is sent to jail
(d) No decision is made about whether to send a person to jail or to set him free

6. A type I error occurs when we:
(a) Reject a true null hypothesis
(b) Accept a true null hypothesis
(c) Fail to make a decision regarding whether to reject a hypothesis or not
(d) None of the above

7. Analysis of variance is a statistical way of testing a hypothesis about the _________ of several populations.
(a) Standard deviation
(b) Variance
(c) Mean
(d) None of the above

8. Which of the following distributions does the ANOVA test use?
(a) Z
(b) Chi-square
(c) t
(d) F

9. t-test and ANOVA are used for sample mean testing, but ANOVA can be used for more than two populations.
(a) True (b) False

10. In a one-way ANOVA, if the computed F-value is less than the critical F-value, what decision is made regarding the null hypothesis?
(a) Accept H_0 as there is no evidence of a difference in mean
(b) Reject H_0 because there is no evidence of a difference in mean

Answers

1. (a) **2.** (a) **3.** (a) **4.** (a) **5.** (a) **6.** (a) **7.** (c) **8.** (d)
9. (a) **10.** (a)

Programming/Concept-based Questions

1. About 1000 college students are graded according to their IQ level and economic condition. Use the chi-square test to find out whether there is any association between economic condition and the level of IQ.

	High	Medium	Low
Rich	160	300	140
Poor	140	100	160

Answer:

```
import numpy as np
from scipy import stats
data =[[160,140],[300,100],[140,160]]
stat, p, dof, expected = stats.chi2_contingency(data)
print('chi square value is ',stat)
print('expected values are ',expected)
# interpret p-value
```

```
alpha = 0.05

    print("p value is " + str(p))
    if p <= alpha:
        print('(reject null hypothesis H0)')
    else:
        print('(Null hypothesis H0 holds true)')
```

Output:
chi square value is 65.27777777777777
expected values are [[180. 120.]
[240. 160.]
[180. 120.]]
p value is 6.6851423617186904e-15
(reject null hypothesis H0)

2. An IQ test was administered to 5 persons before and after they were trained. IQ before training was 110, 120, 123, 132, 125. After training, IQ became 120, 118, 125, 136, 121. Test whether there is any change in IQ after training. The given t-value at 1% level of significance is 4.6.

Answer: We can use a paired t-test to check whether IQ has changed or not.
H_0: No change in IQ

```
import numpy as np
from scipy import stats
beforesale =[110, 120, 123,132, 125 ]

                        aftersale =[120,118, 125, 136, 121]

t2, p2 = stats.ttest_rel(beforesale,aftersale)
print('Dependent sample statistics, paired t-test')
print("t = " + str(t2))
print("p = " + str(p2))
```

Output:
Dependent sample statistics, paired t-test
t = -0.8164965809277261
p = 0.460050752843961
The calculated value is less than the given t-value. Thus, the hypothesis holds true. Hence, there is no change in IQ after the training programme.

3. Consider a clinical trial designed to investigate the effectiveness of a new psychological treatment. The trial was on 14 persons chosen randomly, that is, they are randomly chosen to receive the treatment or no treatment. They are asked to record the number of times they felt depressed over a week's time after receiving the treatment. The data values are as follows:

Treatment	**7**	**5**	**6**	**4**	**12**	**9**	**8**
No treatment	3	6	4	2	1	5	1

Test whether there is a significant difference in the cases of depression over a week's period in persons receiving the treatment as compared to those receiving no treatment?

Answer:

```
# Wilcoxon Rank Sum Test
import pandas as pd
# Getting our data in to a dictionary
dataval = {'Notrt':[7, 5, 6, 4, 12, 9, 8],
        'Trt':[3, 6, 4, 2, 1, 5, 1]}
# Dictionary to Dataframe
dfval = pd.DataFrame(dataval)
from scipy.stats import mannwhitneyu
# Carrying out the Wilcoxon-Mann-Whitney test
resultsval = mannwhitneyu(dfval['Notrt'], dfval['Trt'])
print(resultsval)
```

The statistical value is 4.5 and the *p*-value is 0.006163481771339872. The null hypothesis is rejected as the given table value is 7. So, the treatment groups differ in the number of depressive cases.

4. Nirma Company wants to study the performance of three detergents and three different water temperatures on the whiteness readings using specially designed equipment. The data values are as follows:

Water temperature	Detergent Surf	Detergent Rin	Detergent Ghadi
Cold	57	55	67
Warm	49	52	68
Hot	54	46	58

Perform a two-way ANOVA using 5% level of significance.

Answer:

```
# Two way ANOVA
import numpy as np
import pandas as pd
import pingouin as pg
#create data
df = pd.DataFrame({'detergent': np.repeat(['A', 'B', 'C'], 3),
'temperature': np.tile(np.repeat(['cold', 'warm', 'hot'], 1), 3),
'values': [57,49,54,
55,52,46,
67,68,58]})
print(df)
#perform two-way ANOVA
```

```
aov = pg.anova(dv='values', between=['detergent', 'temperature'],
data=df,detailed=True)
print(aov)
```

Output:

	detergent	temperature	values
0	A	cold	57
1	A	warm	49
2	A	hot	54
3	B	cold	55
4	B	warm	52
5	B	hot	46
6	C	cold	67
7	C	warm	68
8	C	hot	58

	Source	SS	DF	MS	np2
0	detergent	304.222222	2	152.111111	1.0
1	temperature	73.555556	2	36.777778	1.0
2	detergent * temperature	61.777778	4	15.444444	1.0

Calculated F values are 9.85 and 2.38. So the conclusion is that there is a significant difference between the three varieties of detergent as far as whiteness is concerned, but the water temperature does not make a significant difference.

F1= 152.11/15.45 = 9.85, the given table value is 6.84, so the hypothesis is rejected. There is a significant difference in the varieties of detergent. F2= 36.77/15.45 = 2.38, the given table value is 6.94, so the hypothesis is accepted. Hence, water temperature does not make a significant difference.

5. A group of nine-week-old chickens given a high-protein diet weighed 12, 15, 11, 16, 14, 14 and 16 ounces and a second group of five chickens treated similarly except that they were provided a low-protein diet weighed 8, 10, 14, 10 and 13 ounces. Test whether there is significant evidence that additional protein has increased the weight of the chickens. (The table value for v = 10 at 5% level of significance is 2.33).

Answer: We apply the t-test for independent samples.

```
# t test for independent samples
import numpy as np
from scipy import stats
highprotein =[12,15,11,16,14,14,16]
lowprotein =[8,10,14,10,13]
t2, p2 = stats.ttest_ind(highprotein,lowprotein)
print('independent sample statistics')
print("t = " + str(t2))
print("p = " + str(p2))

alpha = 0.05

if p2 <= alpha:
```

```
    print('(reject null hypothesis H0)')
else:
    print('(Null hypothesis H0 holds true)')
```

Output:
independent sample statistics
t = 2.388832714764773
p = 0.038034359446588985
(reject null hypothesis H0)

BIBLIOGRAPHY

1. t-test Exercise. DataCamp. https://campus.datacamp.com/courses/statistics-with-r/18536?ex=4

CHAPTER 11

Classification

Learning Objectives

At the end of this chapter, you will be able to:

- Explain the basics of classification
- Describe the concept of nearest neighbour learning using the k-nearest neighbor (K-NN) algorithm
- List the fundamentals of entropy, Gini index and information gain
- Describe the structure of decision trees
- Explain the basics of probability and Bayes' theorem
- Explain naive Bayes' algorithm and its types such as Bernoulli, multinomial and Gaussian for continuous and discrete attributes
- Discuss the concepts of support vector machines, hyper-planes, margins and kernel trick
- Explain the basics of ensemble learning, bagging, boosting and stacking
- Explain the random forest algorithm
- Evaluate classifier performance using the confusion matrix
- Explain about exhaustive and non-exhaustive methods of cross-validation

11.0 Introduction

A classification is a statistical machine learning (ML) method that distinguishes different objects based on certain attributes or features. Designating documents as Secret or Confidential is an example of classification. Another example could be assigning documents as Devanagari, Bengali and Gujarati script, classifying a given handwritten character as one of the known characters.

Naive Bayes, k-nearest neighbor (K-NN), logistic regression, decision tree and support vector machine are some of the most commonly used classification algorithms in ML.

Binary classification and multi-class classification are the two main types of classification tasks that you may encounter. **Binary classification** classifies data into two classes, such as email Spam and Not Spam, cancer Detected and Not Detected. **Multi-class classification** has more than two class labels. Face classification, species classification of plants and optical character recognition are examples of multi-class classification. Here the data is classified into one of a range of known classes.

Algorithms designed for binary classification can be used for multi-class classification. The two strategies for this are one-vs-rest and one-vs-one. In the **one-vs-rest strategy**, one binary classification model is fitted for each class versus all the other classes. In the **one-vs-one strategy**, one binary classification model is fitted for each pair of classes. Support vector machine and logistic regression can use these strategies for multi-class classification.

11.1 K-NN Classification

K-NN is the simplest ML algorithm; it is non-parametric. It makes no assumptions about the data. It has no training phase; it immediately classifies new data points as they fall in the proximity of the given data points. Results depend on the value of k.

The set of data points with their class is given. The distance of the new data points (Euclidean or other) is calculated with the other given points and the k-nearest neighbors of the new data points are considered. Among these nearest neighbours, the number of data points of each class is counted and a new point is assigned to the class for which the count was maximum. In Fig. 11.1, the new data point has three neighbour data points of Category 1 and 2 neighbour data points of Category 2. So the new data point is classified under Category 1.

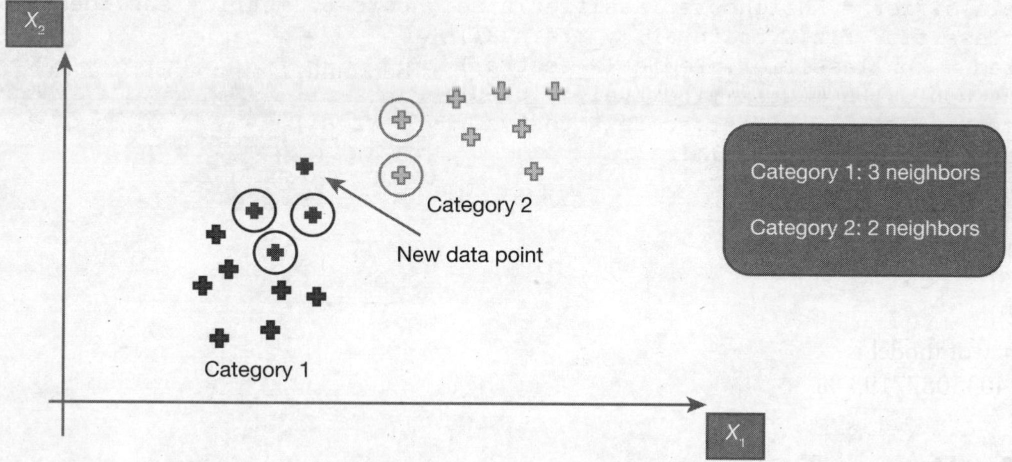

Figure 11.1 K-NN classification

11.1.1 Python Code for K-NN Classification

Breast cancer data is used to classify test data points as 'malignant' or 'benign'. The k value is 5. The distance measure is Euclidean distance. These parameters are specified in the `KNeighborsClassifier()` function of the sklearn library. Data is split into training and test sets. A total of 570 data points are present in the data set. Of these, 114 data points are considered as test data points. The K-NN classifier classifies 109 points correctly. The accuracy of the model is 95.61%.

```
#K-nn Classification
import numpy as np
import pandas as pd
from sklearn import datasets, metrics
from sklearn.preprocessing import StandardScaler
from sklearn.metrics import confusion_matrix
from sklearn.neighbors import KNeighborsClassifier
from sklearn.model_selection import train_test_split
#Upload the dataset and apply a standardscaler to normalize the data.
Data is split in 80% data in training set and 20% data in test set
cancer = datasets.load_breast_cancer()
Xval = cancer.data
yval = cancer.target
scaler = StandardScaler()
X_scaledval = scaler.fit_transform(Xval)
X_trainval, X_testval, y_trainval, y_testval = train_test_split(X_
scaledval, yval, test_size = 0.2, random_state = 1)
#K nearest neighbour classifier is built, which is using euclidean
distance measure to find 5 nearest points. Prediction and accuracy is
also calculated here.
knnclassifier = KNeighborsClassifier(n_neighbors=5, metric='euclidean')
knnclassifier.fit(X_trainval, y_trainval)
y_pred = knnclassifier.predict(X_testval)
print(confusion_matrix(y_testval, y_pred))
r2_score = knnclassifier.score(X_testval, y_testval)
print('accuracy of model is ')
print(r2_score*100,'%')
```

Output:
[[37 5]
[0 72]]
accuracy of model is
95.6140350877193 %

11.2 Decision Trees

A decision tree is a flowchart-like diagram that shows the various outcomes from a series of decisions. It can be used as a decision-making tool, for research analysis or for planning strategy. Tree-based algorithms are the most commonly used type of algorithm in supervised learning scenarios. The decision-tree algorithm works on categorical as well as on numerical data. It is easier to interpret and visualize and has good adaptability.

Generally, the three elements of decision trees are:

- **Root node:** Represents the ultimate objective or big decision you need to make.
- **Branches:** Represent the options that are available when making a decision.
- **Leaf nodes:** Represent possible outcomes for each action.

Advantages
- Requires less effort for data preparation or data cleaning during pre-processing.
- Does not require normalization and scaling of data.
- Missing values do not considerably affect the process of building a decision tree.
- Very intuitive and easy to explain to technical teams as well as stakeholders.

Disadvantages
- Small changes in data can cause large changes in the structure of the decision tree.
- Sometimes, calculations can become more complex compared to other algorithms.
- It often involves more time to train the model.
- Decision tree training is relatively expensive as the complexity and time taken increases with more class labels and tree layers.
- The decision tree algorithm is inadequate for applying regression.

There are two types of decision trees:
- **Regression tree**: A regression tree is used when the dependent variable is continuous. The value obtained by the leaf nodes in the training data is the mean response of observations falling in that region.
- **Classification tree:** A classification tree is used when the dependent variable is categorical. The value obtained by the leaf nodes in the training data is the mode response of observations falling in that region.

Together they are called CART (classification and regression tree).

11.2.1 Working of the Decision Tree Algorithm

Splitting is the process of partitioning the data into subsets. **Pruning or information gain** is the process of shortening branches of the decision tree to limit the tree depth. To keep the decision tree simple, you need to ensure that it is small. To measure the information corresponding to each feature, information gain is calculated using entropy. **Entropy** is a measure to define the degree of disorganization in a system.

Tree selection is the process of finding the smallest tree that fits the data. To keep the decision tree simple, the information present must be pure. Tree selection mainly deals with selecting the best attribute for the root and other internal nodes. Two techniques help in selecting the best attributes: information gain and Gini index.

Information Gain

Information gain tells us how much information a feature or attribute provides about a class. Information gain can be calculated as:

$$\text{Information Gain }(A) = \text{Entropy\_Info }(T) - \text{Entropy\_Info }(T, A)$$

Here, T = training data set, A = set of attributes $\{A_1, A_2, \ldots A_n\}$ and m = number of classes in the training data set. Let P_i be the probability that a data instance d belongs to class C_i. It is calculated as d_{Ci}

$$P_i = \frac{|dCi|}{|T|}$$

P_i = Total no. of data instances that belong to class C_i in T / Total no. of tuples in training set T

Entropy specifies randomness in data. It measures the impurity in a given attribute or feature. It can be calculated as:

$$\text{Entropy\_Info}(T) = -\sum_{i=1}^{m} P_i \log_2 P_i$$

$$\text{Entropy\_Info}(T, A) = \sum_{i=1}^{v} \frac{|A_i|}{|T|} * \text{Entropy\_Info}(A_i)$$

where attribute A has v distinct values $\{a_1, a_2, \ldots. a_v\}$, $|A_i|$ = number of instances for distinct value 'i' in attribute A and Entropy_Info(A_i) = entropy for that set of instances. Entropy and information gain are inversely related, that is, as entropy increases, information gain decreases.

Example: To assess a student's performance during his course of study and predict whether the student will get a job offer or not. The training data set contains 10 instances with attributes CGPA, Interactiveness, Practical Knowledge and Job Offer. The target class is a job offer. Let create a decision tree to solve this problem.

Table 11.1 Student data

SN	CGPA	Interactiveness	Practical Knowledge	Job Offer
1	≥9	Yes	Very Good	Yes
2	≥8	No	Good	Yes
3	≥9	No	Average	No
4	<8	No	Average	No
5	≥8	Yes	Good	Yes
6	≥9	Yes	Good	Yes
7	<8	Yes	Good	No
8	≥9	No	Very Good	Yes
9	≥8	Yes	Good	Yes
10	≥8	Yes	Average	Yes

First, calculate the entropy of target class 'Job Offer'

Entropy_Info(target attribute = job offer) =

$$\text{Entropy\_Info}(7,3) = -\left[\frac{7}{10}\log_2\frac{7}{10} + \frac{3}{10}\log_2\frac{3}{10}\right]$$

$$= -(-.3599 + -.5208) = .8807$$

Now calculate the Entropy_Info and information gain for each attribute. First let us calculate the CGPA attribute, as shown in Table 11.2.

Table 11.2 Entropy information for CGPA

CGPA	Job Offer=Yes	Job Offer=No	Total
≥9	3	1	4
≥8	4	0	4
<8	0	2	2

$$\text{Entropy\_Info(T, CGPA)} = \frac{4}{10}\left[-\frac{3}{4}\log_2\frac{3}{4}-\frac{1}{4}\log_2\frac{1}{4}\right]+\frac{4}{10}\left[-\frac{4}{4}\log_2\frac{4}{4}-\frac{0}{4}\log_2\frac{0}{4}\right]+\frac{2}{10}\left[-\frac{0}{2}\log_2\frac{0}{2}-\frac{2}{2}\log_2\frac{2}{2}\right]$$

$$= .3243$$

$$\text{Gain(CGPA)} = .8807 - .3243 = \mathbf{.5564}$$

Next, calculate the entropy and information gain for attribute Interactiveness.

Table 11.3 Entropy information for Interactiveness

Interactiveness	Job Offer=Yes	Job Offer=No	Total
Yes	5	1	6
No	2	2	4

$$\text{Entropy\_Info(T, Interactiveness)} = \frac{6}{10}\left[-\frac{5}{6}\log_2\frac{5}{6}-\frac{1}{6}\log_2\frac{1}{6}\right]+\frac{4}{10}\left[-\frac{2}{4}\log_2\frac{2}{4}-\frac{2}{4}\log_2\frac{2}{4}\right] = .3898+.3998=.7896$$

$$\text{Gain(Interactiveness)} = .8807 - .7896 = \mathbf{.0911}$$

Likewise, calculate entropy for Practical Knowledge; it will be **0.2246.** So the best split is using CGPA as its information gain is the highest among all the attributes. The CGPA attribute will become the root of the decision tree.

In the next step, the gain of the remaining attributes is calculated and the next level root node is determined from the remaining attributes.

CGPA <8 has Job Offer = 'No', CGPA ≥8 also has Job Offer = 'No'. But CGPA ≥9 has Job Offer = Yes and No for the data shown in Table 11.4.

Table 11.4 Data for CGPA ≥9

Interactiveness	Practical Knowledge	Job Offer
Yes	Very Good	Yes
No	Average	No
Yes	Good	Yes
No	Very Good	Yes

So in this step, the same process of computing Entropy_Info and Gain are repeated with the above subset of data. This subset has only four data items. Of these, three have Job Offer = Yes and only one has Job Offer = No.

Entropy_Info(target attribute = job offer) =

$$\text{Entropy\_Info}(3,1) = -\left[\frac{3}{4}\log_2\frac{3}{4}+\frac{1}{4}\log_2\frac{1}{4}\right]$$

$$= .8108$$

$$\text{Entropy\_Info(T, Interactiveness)} = \frac{2}{4}\left[-\frac{2}{2}\log_2\frac{2}{2}-\frac{0}{2}\log_2\frac{0}{2}\right]+\frac{2}{4}\left[-\frac{1}{2}\log_2\frac{1}{2}-\frac{1}{2}\log_2\frac{1}{2}\right]=0+.4997=.4997$$

$$\text{Gain(Interactiveness)} = .8108 - .4497 = \mathbf{.3111}$$

$$\text{Entropy\_Info(T, Practical knowledge)} = \frac{2}{4}\left[-\frac{2}{2}\log_2\frac{2}{2}-\frac{0}{2}\log_2\frac{0}{2}\right]+\frac{1}{4}\left[-\frac{0}{1}\log_2\frac{0}{1}-\frac{1}{1}\log_2\frac{1}{1}\right]+\frac{1}{4}\left[-\frac{1}{1}\log_2\frac{1}{1}-\frac{0}{1}\log_2\frac{0}{1}\right]=0$$

$$\text{Gain(Interactiveness)} = .8108$$

The gain of Practical Knowledge is high when compared to that of Interactiveness, so it becomes the next level root node. The final decision tree is as shown in Fig. 11.2.

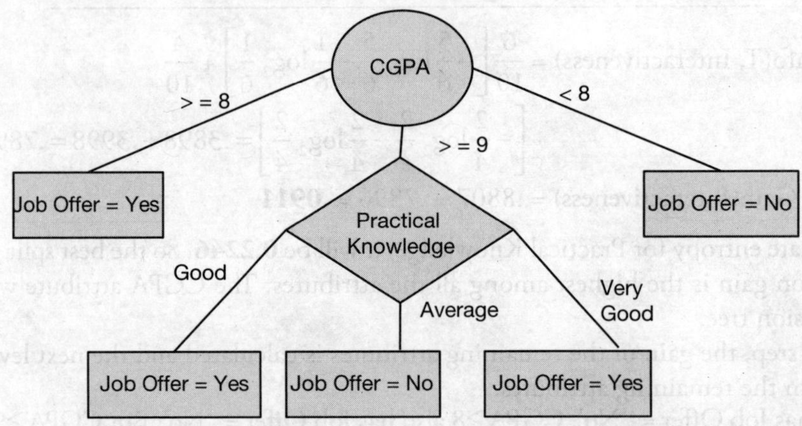

Figure 11.2 Final decision tree for student data set using entropy and information gain

Gini Impurity

This is a measure of misclassification and is used when the data contains multi-class labels. Gini is similar to entropy but is faster to compute. Algorithms such as CART (classification and regression tree) use Gini as an impurity parameter. Python, by default, uses the Gini index for identifying the best attributes for decision making.

Example: You want to find out whether a person is married or not based on the data collected of different persons' age, income and gender, as shown in Table 11.5. An ML algorithm to construct a decision tree which best selects the branches automatically considering each feature (here Age, Salary and Gender) is required to find out how well each feature separates people who are married and who are not.

Table 11.5 Personal data

Married	Age		Income		Gender	
	<30	>30	<50000	>50000	Male	Female
Yes	43	90	59	102	83	96
No	77	30	61	18	37	24

In order to find out which split is better, the information gain is calculated for each feature. The feature with the highest information gain is selected for decision-tree making. Here, there is impurity in each feature as no feature states 100% yes for any case. So the Gini impurity of the left and right leaves are calculated. To do this, subtract the square of the fraction of persons who are married and the square of the fraction of persons who are not married from 1 for that feature. For example, Age Gini impurity can be calculated as

Age
>30 <30
Married Married
No Yes No Yes
30 90 77 43

$$\text{Left impurity} = 1 - \left(\frac{43}{43+77}\right)^2 - \left(\frac{77}{43+77}\right)^2 = .460$$

$$\text{Right impurity} = 1 - \left(\frac{90}{90+30}\right)^2 - \left(\frac{30}{90+30}\right)^2 = .375$$

Impurity at this node is

$$1 - \left(\frac{120}{240}\right)^2 - \left(\frac{120}{240}\right)^2 = .5$$

$$\text{Information gain} = .5 - \left(\frac{120}{240}\right) \times .375 - \left(\frac{120}{240}\right) \times .460$$

$$= .0825$$

Age information gain is calculated as .0825; likewise the information gain of Income and Gender can also be calculated. In this case, information gain of Income is 0.1375 and Gender is 0.1265. So root splitting will be best on Income, rather than the other features. This process continues for subsequent nodes till it goes below the threshold level.

11.2.2 Python Code for Decision Tree

The Iris data set is used here. This data set contains three classes (Setosa, Vercicolor, Virginica) and four features (petal width, petal length, sepal width, sepal length). Python, by default, uses the Gini index for decision trees.

```
import numpy as np
import seaborn as sns
from sklearn.metrics import classification_report, confusion_matrix,acc
uracy_score
from sklearn.preprocessing import LabelEncoder
from sklearn.tree import DecisionTreeClassifier
from sklearn.model_selection import train_test_split
import matplotlib.pyplot as plt
from sklearn.tree import plot_tree
```

Load the Iris data set on Google Colab. Some pre-processing operations such as `isnull()` checking and applying `labelencoder()` on the target variable are performed. After pre-processing, the decision tree ML model is built on the data set. The accuracy of the model is 100%. The decision tree is also printed.

```
df = sns.load_dataset('iris')
df.isnull().any()
target = df['species']
df1 = df.copy()
df1 = df1.shape
X = df1
le = LabelEncoder()
target = le.fit_transform(target)
y = target
dtree=DecisionTreeClassifier()
dtree.fit(X,y)
print('Decision Tree Classifier Created')
ypred=dtree.predict(X)
cm = confusion_matrix(y, ypred)
print(cm)
print("Decision tree model accuracy(in %):", accuracy_score(y, ypred)*100)
#print(y,target)
# Visualising the graph without the use of graphviz
plt.figure(figsize = (20,20))
dec_tree = plot_tree(decision_tree=dtree, feature_names = df1.columns,
 class_names =["setosa", "vercicolor", "virginica"], filled = True,
precision = 4, rounded = True)
plt.savefig("one.png")
```

Output:
Decision Tree Classifier Created
[[50 0 0]
[0 50 0]

[0 0 50]]

Decision tree model accuracy(in %): 100.0

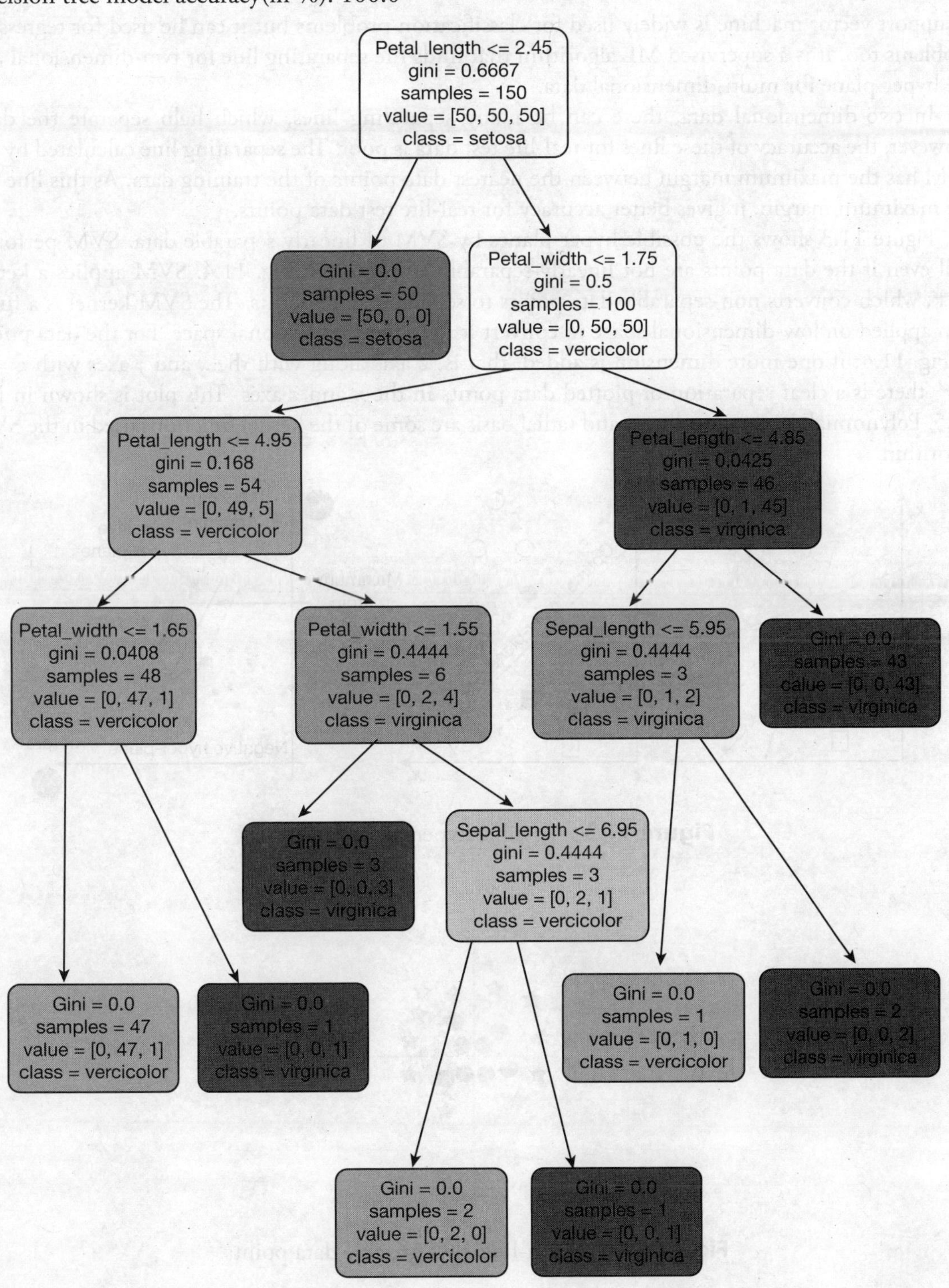

11.3 Support Vector Machine (SVM)

A support vector machine is widely used for classification problems but it can be used for regression problems too. It is a supervised ML algorithm that finds the separating line for two-dimensional and the hyper-plane for multi-dimensional data.

In two-dimensional data, there can be many separating lines, which help separate the data. However, the accuracy of these lines for real-life test data is poor. The separating line calculated by the SVM has the maximum margin between the nearest data points of the training data. As this line has the maximum margin, it gives better accuracy for real-life test data points.

Figure 11.3 shows the possible hyper-planes by SVM of linearly separable data. SVM performs well even if the data points are not linearly separable, as shown in Fig. 11.4. SVM applies a kernel trick, which converts non-separable data points to separable data points. The SVM kernel is a function applied on low-dimensional space to convert it to higher dimensional space. For the data points in Fig. 11.4, if one more dimension is added, that is, z axis along with the x and y axes with $z = x^2 + y^2$, there is a clear separation of plotted data points in the x and z axes. This plot is shown in Fig. 11.5. Polynomial, linear, non-linear and radial basis are some of the kernel functions used in the SVM algorithm.

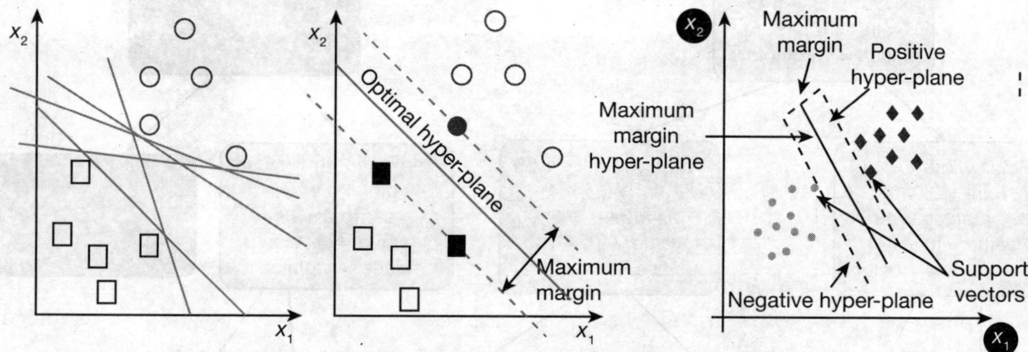

Figure 11.3 Possible hyper-planes and SVM

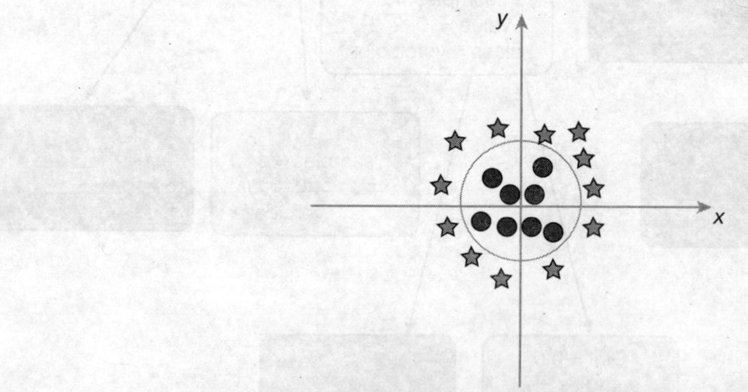

Figure 11.4 Non-linearly separable data points

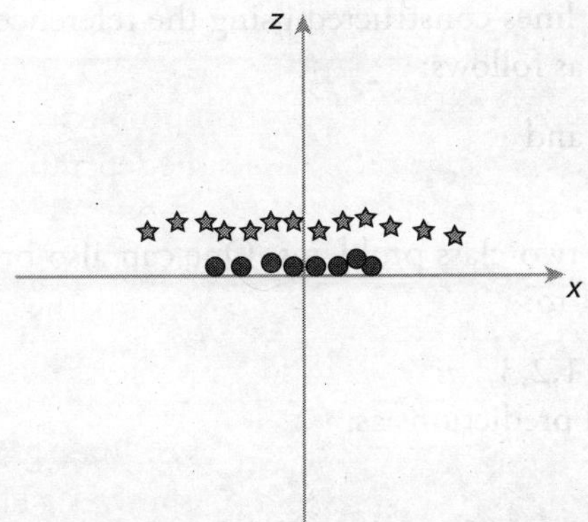

Figure 11.5 Kernel trick applied on Fig. 11.4 data points

The important concepts in SVM are as follows:

- **Support vectors**: These are data points that are closest to the hyper-plane. Line separation will be defined with the help of these data points.
- **Hyper-plane**: As shown in Fig. 11.3, it is a decision plane or space which divides a set of objects into different classes.
- **Margin**: It may be defined as the gap between two lines on the closet data points of different classes. It can be calculated as the perpendicular distance from the line to the support vectors. A large margin is considered as good and a small margin as undesirable.

The main goal of SVM is to divide the data sets into classes to find a maximum marginal hyper-plane (MMH). In contrast to the decision theoretic minimum distance classifier that uses only one decision boundary, SVM uses a reference hyper-plane and two decision boundaries to classify the points. This is shown in Fig. 11.3, where there is a reference hyper-plane with a dark line and two parallel boundaries in dotted lines. The decision boundary should be as far away from the data points as possible, and hence, the distance should be maximized between the line and the nearest data point.

For now, let us consider an SVM that implements a binary classifier. This means that there are only two classes, say +1 and −1. A multi-class SVM can also be implemented. Let us consider a data set:

$$D = \{(x_1,y_1),(x_2,y_2),.....(x_n,y_n)\},\ x \in \Re^n \text{ and } y = \{-1, +1\}$$

The aim of hard margin SVM is to find a hyper-plane that maximally separates the classes. The hyper-plane equation is:

$$h(x) = b + w_1x_1 + w_2x_2 + ... + w_nx_n = 0$$

or $$b + w^Tx = 0$$

where b = intercept, $w_1, w_{2,\ldots}\ w_n$ = coefficients and n = dimension of data points. For two dimensions, the hyper-plane equation can be written as $wx + b = 0$.

The hyper-plane equation separates the data points x into two classes, −1 and + 1. This hyper-plane equation can also be written as $w^T x = 0$. Here, w is the weight vector and b is the bias or offset from the origin.

SVM uses two decision lines constructed using the reference hyper-plane. The two lines act as classifiers. This is written as follows:

H_1: $w.\ x_i + b \geq 0$ for $y = +1$ and
H_2: $w.\ x_i + b < 0$ for $y = -1$

This classifier is suitable for two-class problems. One can also bring the output y into the above equation and that changes it to:

$h(x) = y_i\ (w.x_i + b) \geq 1$ for $i = 1,2,3\ldots n$
or one can alternatively find predictions as:
$h(x_i) = \text{sign}(w.x_i + b)$

The sign of $h(x)$ is always positive if it is correctly classified. Its value is negative if it is incorrectly classified.

- **Kernel trick:** In real-world classification problems, non-linear hyper-planes are required to separate the data as the data can be text, image, video or sequence. One solution to this problem is to map the data into higher dimensional space and define a separating hyper-plane. The mapping process $\phi(x)$ is the vector representation of the feature x. In short, the mapping function transforms the data point in the input space and maps to another point in space called feature space. Normally, the mapping functions are used to map data from a lower dimension to a higher dimension. When the data is mapped from 2D to another feature space, the data points are well segregated in different planes and hence can be separated by a plane. While mapping functions play a major role here, it increases the computation time; also there is no generalized thumb rule describing which transformation should be applied. Kernels are useful in this context as they compute similar values without transforming the data. Kernels are a set of functions used to transform data from low dimension to high dimension and to manipulate data using dot products at higher dimension. Kernels are of different types as given below:
- **Linear:** $k(x,y) = \phi(x).\phi(y) = (x^T.y)^q$ q defines the degree of the polynomial.
- **RBF (Gaussian):** $k(x,y) = \exp\left(\dfrac{(x-y)2}{2\sigma 2}\right)$

Example: Points (4,1), (4,–1) and (6,0) belong to the positive class and points (1,0),(0,1) and (0,–1) belong to the negative class. Let us find an optimal hyper-plane using SVM to classify these points correctly.

Here, the support vectors can be written as

$$s_1 = \begin{pmatrix} 1 \\ 0 \end{pmatrix}$$

$$s_2 = \begin{pmatrix} 4 \\ 1 \end{pmatrix}$$

$$s_3 = \begin{pmatrix} 4 \\ -1 \end{pmatrix}$$

The augmented vector can be obtained by adding the bias, as given below:

$$\overline{s_1} = \begin{pmatrix} 1 \\ 0 \\ 1 \end{pmatrix}$$

$$\overline{s_2} = \begin{pmatrix} 4 \\ 1 \\ 1 \end{pmatrix}$$

$$\overline{s_3} = \begin{pmatrix} 4 \\ -1 \\ 1 \end{pmatrix}$$

From these, a set of three equations can be obtained based on these three support vectors, as follows:

$$\alpha_1 \overline{S_1}\overline{S_1} + \alpha_2 \overline{S_2}\overline{S_1} + \alpha_3 \overline{S_3}\overline{S_1} = -1$$
$$\alpha_1 \overline{S_1}\overline{S_2} + \alpha_2 \overline{S_2}\overline{S_2} + \alpha_3 \overline{S_3}\overline{S_2} = +1$$
$$\alpha_1 \overline{S_1}\overline{S_3} + \alpha_2 \overline{S_2}\overline{S_3} + \alpha_3 \overline{S_3}\overline{S_3} = +1$$

It can be observed that in the first equation, $\overline{s_1}$ is constant, in the second equation, $\overline{s_2}$ is constant and in the third equation, $\overline{s_3}$ is constant. The first equation is for (1,0) that belongs to the negative class −1 and the second and third equations are for the positive class +1.

Substituting the augmented support vectors in the above equations yields:

$$\alpha_1 \begin{pmatrix} 1 \\ 0 \\ 1 \end{pmatrix}\begin{pmatrix} 1 \\ 0 \\ 1 \end{pmatrix} + \alpha_2 \begin{pmatrix} 4 \\ 1 \\ 1 \end{pmatrix}\begin{pmatrix} 1 \\ 0 \\ 1 \end{pmatrix} + \alpha_3 \begin{pmatrix} 4 \\ -1 \\ 1 \end{pmatrix}\begin{pmatrix} 1 \\ 0 \\ 1 \end{pmatrix}$$

$= -1$

$= 2\alpha 1 + 5\alpha 2 + 5\alpha 3 = -1$

$$\alpha_1 \begin{pmatrix} 1 \\ 0 \\ 1 \end{pmatrix}\begin{pmatrix} 4 \\ 1 \\ 1 \end{pmatrix} + \alpha_2 \begin{pmatrix} 4 \\ 1 \\ 1 \end{pmatrix}\begin{pmatrix} 4 \\ 1 \\ 1 \end{pmatrix} + \alpha_3 \begin{pmatrix} 4 \\ -1 \\ 1 \end{pmatrix}\begin{pmatrix} 4 \\ 1 \\ 1 \end{pmatrix}$$

$= +1$

$5\alpha 1 + 18\ \alpha 2 + 16\alpha 3 = +1$

$$\alpha_1 \begin{pmatrix} 1 \\ 0 \\ 1 \end{pmatrix}\begin{pmatrix} 4 \\ 1 \\ 1 \end{pmatrix} + \alpha_2 \begin{pmatrix} 4 \\ 1 \\ 1 \end{pmatrix}\begin{pmatrix} 4 \\ 1 \\ 1 \end{pmatrix} + \alpha_3 \begin{pmatrix} 4 \\ -1 \\ 1 \end{pmatrix}\begin{pmatrix} 4 \\ 1 \\ 1 \end{pmatrix}$$

$= +1$

$5\alpha 1 + 16\alpha 2 + 18\alpha 3 = +1$

Solving these three simultaneous equations will yield the values

$$\alpha 1 = -3$$
$$\alpha 2 = +1$$
$$\alpha 3 = 0$$

The optimal hyper-plane vectors are given as:

$$w = \sum_{i=1}^{3} \alpha i \, X \underline{s_i}$$

$$w = -3 \times \begin{pmatrix} 1 \\ 0 \\ 1 \end{pmatrix} + 1 \times \begin{pmatrix} 4 \\ 1 \\ 1 \end{pmatrix} + 0 \times \begin{pmatrix} 4 \\ -1 \\ 1 \end{pmatrix} = \begin{pmatrix} 1 \\ 1 \\ -2 \end{pmatrix}$$

11.3.1 Python Code for SVM

Implementation here is for the breast cancer data set. It has 31 features. These features are used to classify data into M or B class of diagnosis feature.

First, upload the data set. The last column is used as the target variable, which is stored in `yval`. All the remaining features are in `xval`. Data is pre-processed by applying standard scalar processes and transformed using the `transform()` function.

```
import numpy as np
import pandas as pd
from sklearn.metrics import accuracy_score
from sklearn.model_selection import train_test_split
from sklearn import datasets
from sklearn import svm
from sklearn.preprocessing import StandardScaler
cancerdata = datasets.load_breast_cancer()
df = pd.DataFrame(np.c_[cancerdata['data'], cancerdata['target']],
columns = np.append(cancerdata['feature_names'], ['target']))
df.head()
Xval = df.iloc[:, 0:-1]
yval = df.iloc[:, -1]
x_trainval, x_testval, y_trainval, y_testval= train_test_split(Xval,
yval, test_size= 0.25, random_state=3)
scs = StandardScaler()
x_trainval = scs.fit_transform(x_trainval)
x_testval = scs.transform(x_testval)
#Create a svm Classifier
clfsvm = svm.SVC(kernel='linear') # Linear Kernel
#Train the model using the training sets
clfsvm.fit(x_trainval, y_trainval)
#Predict the response for test dataset
y_predval = clfsvm.predict(x_testval)
from sklearn.metrics import confusion_matrix
cm= confusion_matrix(y_testval, y_predval)
print(cm)
print('Accuracy of SVM is:', accuracy_score(y_testval,
y_predval))
```

Output:
[[51 2]
[1 89]]
Accuracy of SVM is: 0.979020979020979

The `SVC()` function is used to build the SVM for the breast cancer data set. As data is linearly separable, a linear kernel is used here. SVM accuracy is 97.9%.

11.4 Naive Bayes' Classification

This is a supervised learning algorithm used for classification. It is based on Bayes' theorem, which is used to calculate conditional probabilities.

$$P(A|B) = \frac{P(B|A)P(A)}{P(B)}$$

where $P(A/B)$ = probability of event A occurring, given that event B already occurred (also called posterior probability), $P(B/A)$ = probability of event B occurring given that event A already occurred, P(A) = probability of event A occurring and, $P(B)$ = probability of event B occurring.

$$B = (x_1, x_2, x_3, \ldots\ldots x_n)$$

$$P(A/x_1, x_2, x_3, \ldots\ldots x_n) = [P(x_1/A)P(x_2/A)\ldots P(x_n/A) * P(A)] / [P(x_1)\ P(x_2)\ldots P(x_n)]$$

$$= [\ P(A) \prod_{i=1}^{n} P(x_i/A)\ ] / [P(x_1)\ P(x_2)\ldots P(x_n)]$$

where A = argmax $P(A) \prod_{i=1}^{n} P(x_i/A)$, P(A) = class probability and $P(x_i/A)$ = conditional probability.

Given below is an example of naive Bayes'. Here, the data of stolen cars is shown in Table 11.6, which has features such as colour, type of car, origin of car and classified as stolen or not.

Table 11.6 Stolen cars' data

SN	Color	Type	Origin	Stolen
1	Red	Sports	Imported	Yes
2	Red	SUV	Imported	No
3	Yellow	SUV	Domestic	No
4	Yellow	SUV	Domestic	Yes
5	Yellow	SUV	Domestic	No
6	Yellow	Sports	Imported	Yes

(Continued)

Table 11.6 (Continued)

SN	Color	Type	Origin	Stolen
7	Yellow	Sports	Domestic	No
8	Red	Sports	Domestic	Yes
9	Red	Sports	Domestic	No
10	Red	Sports	Domestic	Yes

Probabilities are calculated as given in the above formulae. The new data point which needs to be classified as stolen (Yes or No) will be based on the calculated maximum probability of the class. The new data point given as (Red, Domestic, SUV) can be classified as No for the Stolen class based on the given data.

P(Yes) = Probability of Yes class = 5/10 = .5

P(No) = Probability of No class = 5/10 = .5

Probability of Color, Type and Origin are shown in Tables 11.7, 11.8 and 11.9, respectively.

Table 11.7 Probability of Color feature

Color feature	Yes	No	P(Yes)	P(No)
Red	3	2	3/5	2/5
Yellow	2	3	2/5	3/5
Total	5	5		

Table 11.8 Probability of Type feature

Type feature	Yes	No	P(Yes)	P(No)
Domestic	2	3	2/5	3/5
Imported	3	2	3/5	2/5
Total	5	5		

Table 11.9 Probability of Origin feature

Origin feature	Yes	No	P(Yes)	P(No)
SUV	1	3	1/5	3/5
Sport	4	2	4/5	2/5
Total	5	5		

P(Red/Yes, Domestic/Yes, SUV/Yes) = 3/5 * 2/5 * 1/5 = 6/125
P(Red/No, Domestic/No, SUV/No) = 2/5 * 3/5 * 3/5 = 18/125

So P(Red, Domestic, SUV) will be classified as No, as the probability of (Red, Domestic, SUV) stolen = Yes is lower than the probability of (Red, Domestic, SUV) stolen = No class.

All variations of naive Bayes' classifiers use a common principle, that is, the feature values classified are independent of each other, given the class variable.

Naive Bayes' requires a small volume of training data to estimate the parameters, which are necessary for classification. As the type of data is different such as categorical, binary and numerical, a different approach is required to estimate the parameters of the probability distributions it follows. In the case of numerical data, a Gaussian distribution is used. If the variable is binary, such as 0/1, yes/no, etc., binomial distribution is used and in the case of categorical variables, a multinomial distribution is used.

- **Binary**: Binomial distribution
- **Categorical**: Multinomial distribution
- **Numeric**: Gaussian distribution

These three distributions are so common that the naive Bayes' implementation is often named after these distributions.

11.4.1 Gaussian Naive Bayes'

This works best with continuous data, and the assumption made here is that the data values associated with each class follow normal or Gaussian distribution. The normal distribution curve is bell-shaped and symmetrical about the mean of the feature/attribute value. Feature likelihood value is assumed to be:

$$P(x_i \mid y) = \frac{1}{\sqrt{2\pi\sigma_y^2}} \exp\left(-\frac{(x_i - \mu_y)^2}{2\sigma_y^2} \right)$$

Python Code for Gaussian Naive Bayes'

The Iris data set is used to build the Gaussian naive Bayes' classifier. The `GaussianNB()` function builds the ML model.

```
import pandas as pd
import numpy as np
from sklearn.datasets import load_iris
from sklearn import datasets
from sklearn.model_selection import train_test_split
from sklearn.naive_bayes import GaussianNB
from sklearn.metrics import classification_report, confusion_matrix,
accuracy_score
```

```
iris = load_iris()
Xfeature = iris.data
yresponse = iris.target
X_trainfeature, X_testfeature, y_trainresponse, y_testresponse = train_
test_split(Xfeature, yresponse, test_size=0.4, random_state=1)
gnb_naive = GaussianNB()
gnb_naive.fit(X_trainfeature, y_trainresponse)
ypredresponse = gnb_naive.predict(X_testfeature)
cmt = confusion_matrix(y_testresponse, ypredresponse)
print(cmt)
print("Gaussian Naive Bayes model accuracy(in %):", accuracy_score(y_
testresponse, ypredresponse)*100)
```

Output:

```
sepal length (cm)  sepal width (cm) ...   petal width (cm)  target
0                  5.1              3.5 ...  0.2            0.0
1                  4.9              3.0 ...  0.2            0.0
2                  4.7              3.2 ...  0.2            0.0
3                  4.6              3.1 ...  0.2            0.0
4                  5.0              3.6 ...  0.2            0.0
..                 ...              ... ...  ...            ...
115                6.4              3.2 ...  2.3            2.0
116                6.5              3.0 ...  1.8            2.0
117                7.7              3.8 ...  2.2            2.0
118                7.7              2.6 ...  2.3            2.0
119                6.0              2.2 ...  1.5            2.0
[120 rows x 5 columns]
[[19  0  0]
 [ 0 19  2]
 [ 0  1 19]]
Gaussian Naive Bayes model accuracy(in %): 95.0
```

Here, `GaussianNB()` is used to classify the Iris data set. This data set contains data of three classes (0/1/2), and has 150 rows and 5 columns. The feature vectors used are sepal length, sepal width, petal length, petal width and the target variable is the class of that flower. The data set is split into a training set and a test set, which is 60% and 40%, respectively. After fitting the model on the 60% training data, testing is done on the 40% test data for prediction; the accuracy of Gaussian naive Bayes' on the Iris data set is 95%. Of the 60 test data samples, 57 are correctly classified and only 3 are misclassified.

11.4.2 Multinomial Naive Bayes'

This is used in document classification, in the domain of natural language processing (NLP) and where categorical data values are used for classification. Frequencies of generation of events are represented in the feature vector, which follows a multinomial distribution; that is, it considers the feature vector which represents the number of times it appears in text or data. It calculates the probability of each tag for a given sample and then gives the tag with the highest probability as output.

$$\log p(C_k \mid x) \propto \log\left(p(C_k)\prod_{i=1}^{n} pk_i^{x_i} \right)$$
$$= \log p(C_k) + \sum_{i=1}^{n} x_i \cdot \log pk_i$$
$$= b + w_k^T x$$

An example for multinomial naive Bayes' considers the data shown in Table 11.10, and tries to classify the test data.

Table 11.10 Text data of documents

	Doc No.	Words in document	In I = India?
Training data	1	India Beijing India	yes
	2	India India Shanghai	yes
	3	India Macao	yes
	4	Tokyo Japan India	no
Test data		India India India Tokyo Japan	??

Probabilities cannot be zero, but in the given data, some words do not occur in all documents, so their probabilities will be calculated as zero. To avoid this, Laplace smoothing can be used with values as:

$P = (x_i + \alpha) / (N + \alpha d)$ where $\alpha = 1$ (1)

d = total different words = 6

d = [India, Beijing, Shanghai, Macao, Tokyo, Japan]

$N_{yes} = 8$

N_{yes} = [India Beijing India India India Shanghai India Macao]

$N_{no} = 3$

N_{no} = [Tokyo Japan India]

$P(I) = P(\text{India}) = 3/4$

$P(\underline{I}) = 1/4$

$P(\text{India}/I) = (5 + 1)/ (8 + 6) = 6/14 = 3/7$ as India occurs 5 times in I = India yes category. So applying the formula of Eq. 1 will give this probability,

$P(\text{Tokyo}/I) = (0 + 1)/ (8 + 6) = 1/14$ $P(\text{Japan}/I) = (0 + 1)/ (8 + 6) = 1/14$

$P(\text{India}/\underline{I}) = (1 + 1)/ (3 + 6) = 2/9$ as India occurs once in $\underline{I}$ = India no category. So applying the formula of Eq.1 will give this probability

$P(\text{Tokyo}/\underline{I}) = (1 + 1)/ (3 + 6) = 2/9$ $P(\text{Japan}/\underline{I}) = (1 + 1)/ (3 + 6) = 2/9$

So, the test data (India India India Tokyo Japan) to be categorized in India = yes or no will be determined by the calculated probability as follows:

$P(\text{India India India Tokyo Japan}/ I) = ¾ *(3/7 *3/7 *3/7* 1/14 * 1/14)$
$= .0003$

P(India India India Tokyo Japan/ $\underline{I}$) = ¼ *(2/9 * 2/9 *2/9 * 2/9* 2/9)
= .0001

Probability of test data occurring in I India = yes class is higher than the probability of it occurring in I India = no class. So the test data will be categorized in India = yes.

Python Code for Multinomial Naive Bayes'

Load the diabetes data set for multinomial naive Bayes'.

```
from google.colab import files
uploaded= files.upload()
import io
import pandas as pd
from sklearn.naive_bayes import MultinomialNB
from sklearn.metrics import accuracy_score
datadf=pd.read_csv(io.BytesIO(uploaded['diabetes.csv']))
datadf.head()
Xfeatures = datadf.drop(columns=['Outcome'],axis=1)
Yresponse = datadf['Outcome']
from sklearn.model_selection import train_test_split
X_trainfeatures, X_testfeatures, y_trainresponse, y_testresponse = train_
test_split(Xfeatures, Yresponse, test_size=0.2, random_state=0)
Mclf = MultinomialNB()
model = Mclf.fit(X_trainfeatures, y_trainresponse)
ypred =Mclf.predict(X_testfeatures)
cmt = confusion_matrix(y_testresponse, ypred)
print(cmt)
acc_score = accuracy_score(y_testresponse, ypred)
print('accuracy of multinomial naive bayes is ',acc_score)
```

Output:

```
[[76 31]
 [25 22]]
accuracy of multinomial naive bayes is  0.6363636363636364
```

Here, `MultinomialNB()` is used to classify the diabetes data set. This data set contains 768 rows of pregnancies, glucose, bloodpressure, skinthickness, insulin, BMI, DiabetesPedigreeFunction, age and outcome. Outcome is a dependent variable whose value is 0 or 1, which indicates whether the person is diabetic or not.

The features vector used contains pregnancies, glucose, bloodpressure, skinthickness, insulin, BMI, DiabetesPedigreeFunction and age and the target variable is the outcome. The data set is split into a training set and a test set, which is 80% and 20%, respectively. After fitting the model on the 80% training data, the 20% test data is used for prediction; the accuracy of multinomial naive Bayes' on the diabetes data set is 63.63%. As shown in results, of the 154 test data samples, 98 are correctly classified and 56 are misclassified.

If multinomial naive Bayes' is fitted on the Iris data set, accuracy will be 95%, which is the same as that achieved using Gaussian naive Bayes'.

11.4.3 Bernoulli Naive Bayes'

Bernoulli distribution is used for binary data, where the data values take the form of true/false, yes/no, 0/1, success/failure, presence/absence, etc. It uses the Bernoulli distribution; so feature values are binary and work best on discrete data. This model is also popular for document classification, but binary term occurrences are used as features rather than the frequencies of a word in the document.

The Bernoulli distribution

$$p(x) = P[X = x] = \begin{cases} q = 1 - p & x = 0 \\ p & x = 1 \end{cases}$$

The example demonstrate Bernoulli naive Bayes' for document classification. The data given is related to Sports (S) or Informatics (I). The training set has 11 documents and the aim is to estimate a Bernoulli document model to classify the unlabelled document as S or I. Documents have eight feature words: w_1 = goal, w_2 = tutor, w_3 = variance, w_4 = speed, w_5 = drink, w_6 = defence, w_7 = performance, w_8 = field. We have 6 documents of the Sports (S) category and 5 documents of the Informatics (I) category. B(Sports) has eight feature occurrences (1/0) in 6 documents, so it has a dimension of 6 × 8; and B(Informatics) has eight feature occurrences (1/0) in 5 documents, so it has a dimension of 5 × 8.

B(Sports) =

goal	tutor	variance	speed	drink	defence	performance	field
1	0	0	0	1	1	1	1
0	0	1	0	1	1	0	0
0	1	0	1	0	1	1	0
1	0	0	1	0	1	0	1
1	0	0	0	1	0	1	1
0	0	1	1	0	0	1	1

B(Informatics) =

goal	tutor	variance	speed	drink	defence	performance	field
0	1	1	0	0	0	1	0
1	1	0	1	0	0	1	1
0	1	1	0	0	1	0	0
0	0	0	0	0	0	0	0
0	0	1	0	1	0	1	0

Using the given data, if our aim is to classify b_1 (1 0 0 1 1 1 0 1) and b_2 (0 1 1 0 1 0 1 0) using Bernoulli naive Bayes', calculation of the probabilities are carried out as follows:

N = Total number of documents = 11

N_S = Number of documents in sports = 6 N_I = Number of documents in Informatics = 5 so P(S) = 6/11 P(T) = 5/11

Feature	N_S (feature)	P(feature/S) probability of feature in Sports document	Probability of that feature not occurring	N_I (feature)	P(feature/I) probability of feature in Informatics document	Probability of that feature not occurring
goal	3	3/6	1-3/6 = 3/6	1	1/5	1-1/5 = 4/5
tutor	1	1/6	1- 1/6 = 5/6	3	3/5	1-3/5 = 2/5
variance	2	2/6	1- 2/6 = 4/6	3	3/5	1-3/5 = 2/5
speed	3	3/6	1-3/6 = 3/6	1	1/5	1-1/5 = 4/5
drink	3	3/6	1-3/6 = 3/6	1	1/5	1-1/5 = 4/5
defence	4	4/6	1-4/6 = 2/6	1	1/5	1-1/5 = 4/5
performance	4	4/6	1-4/6 = 2/6	3	3/5	1-3/5 = 2/5
field	4	4/6	1-4/6 = 2/6	1	1/5	1-1/5 = 4/5

$P(S/b_1)$ = Probability of b_1 occurring in S

$b_1 = (1\ 0\ 0\ 1\ 1\ 1\ 0\ 1)$

$P(S/b_1) = 6/11 *(3/6 * 5/6 * 4/6 * 3/6 * 3/6 * 4/6 * 2/6 * 4/6)$

$P(S/b_1) = 5.6 * 10^{-3}$

$P(I/b_1)$ = Probability of b_1 occurring in I

$b_1 = (1\ 0\ 0\ 1\ 1\ 1\ 0\ 1)$

$P(I/b_1) = 5/11 *(1/5 * 2/5 * 2/5 * 1/5 * 1/5 * 1/5 * 2/5 * 1/5)$

$P(I/b_1) = 9.3 * 10^{-6}$

$P(S/b_1)$ is higher, so b_1 will be classified in the Sports category.

$P(S/b_2)$ = Probability of b_2 occurring in S

$b_2 = (0\ 1\ 1\ 0\ 1\ 0\ 1\ 0)$

$P(S/b_2) = 6/11 *(3/6 *1/6 * 2/6 * 3/6 * 3/6 * 2/6 * 4/6 * 2/6)$

$P(S/b_2) = 2.8 * 10^{-4}$

$P(I/b_2)$ = Probability of b_1 occurring in I

$b_2 = (0\ 1\ 1\ 0\ 1\ 0\ 1\ 0)$

$P(I/b_2) = 5/11 *(4/5 * 3/5 * 3/5 * 4/5 * 1/5 * 4/5 * 3/5 * 4/5)$

$P(I/b_2) = 8.0 * 10^{-3}$

$P(I/b_2)$ is higher, so b_2 will be classified in the Informatics category.

Python Code for Bernoulli Naive Bayes'

Load the diabetes data set for Bernoulli naive Bayes'.

```
from google.colab import files
uploaded= files.upload()
import io
import pandas as pd
from sklearn.naive_bayes import BernoulliNB
from sklearn.metrics import accuracy_score
datadf=pd.read_csv(io.BytesIO(uploaded['diabetes.csv']))
datadf.head()
Xfeatures = datadf.drop(columns=['Outcome'],axis=1)
Yresponse = datadf['Outcome']
from sklearn.model_selection import train_test_split
X_trainfeatures, X_testfeatures, y_trainresponse, y_testresponse = train_
test_split(Xfeatures, Yresponse, test_size=0.2, random_state=964)
Bclf = BernoulliNB(binarize=0.0)
model = Bclf.fit(X_trainfeatures, y_trainresponse)
ypred =Bclf.predict(X_testfeatures)
cmt = confusion_matrix(y_testresponse, ypred)
print(cmt)
acc_score = accuracy_score(y_testresponse, ypred)
print('accuracy of bernouli naive bayes is ',acc_score)
```

Output:

```
[[108  0]
 [ 46  0]]
accuracy of bernouli naive bayes is  0.7012987012987013
```

Here, `BernoulliNB()` is used to classify the diabetes data set. This data set contains 768 rows of pregnancies, glucose, bloodpressure, skinthickness, insulin, BMI, DiabetesPedigreeFunction, age and outcome. Outcome is a dependent variable whose value is 0 or 1, which indicates whether that person is diabetic or not. The features vector contains pregnancies, glucose, bloodpressure, skinthickness, insulin, BMI, DiabetesPedigreeFunction and age and the target variable is the outcome variable. The data set is split into a training set and a test set, which is 80% and 20%, respectively. After fitting the model on the 80% training data, the 20% test data is used for prediction; the accuracy of Bernoulli naive Bayes' on the dabetes data set is 70.12%. As shown in results, of the 154 test data samples, 108 are correctly classified and 46 are misclassified.

11.5 Metrics for Evaluating Classifier Performance

Evaluating the performance of classifiers is an excellent way of getting feedback about whether what you are doing is correct or not. It is a tool for comparing the performance of ML models. Ultimately, we need to build a model of high performance accuracy, which can help us make better decisions in real-world scenarios. The most commonly used classification evaluation metric is to calculate its accuracy. However, measuring accuracy is not always the correct measure of evaluating performance as data is not balanced in real-life scenarios such as in spam email detection, financial cases (credit card fraud) and medical diagnosis. So, measuring only accuracy will not give the correct picture of the constructed model. Other measures are required to evaluate the performance of classifiers.

The confusion matrix shown in Fig. 11.6 is a performance measure that gives the details of accuracy, recall and precision. F_1 score and AUC-ROC curve are also used as performance metrics.

		Actual value	
		Positive	Negative
Predicted value	Positive	TP (True positive)	FP (False positive)
	Negative	FN (False negative)	TN (True negative)

- True positive (TP): Observation is positive, and is predicted to be positive.
- False negative (FN): Observation is positive, but is predicted as negative.
- True negative (TN): Observation is negative, and is predicted to be negative.
- False positive (FP): Observation is negative, but is predicted as positive.

Figure 11.6 Confusion matrix

The confusion matrix not only gives a correct picture of the model, such as which classes are incorrectly and correctly predicted or classified, but it also reveals what type of errors are being made by the model. Here TP, FP, FN and TN are calculated for the model, as shown in Figs 11.7 and 11.8, which are useful for measuring precision, recall or sensitivity, specificity, accuracy and the AUC-ROC curve of the model. The relevance of calculating precision, recall, accuracy or specificity depends on the application.

The F_1 score is useful when an optimal blend of precision and recall is required. A good F_1 score (perfect model when F_1 score is 1 and model failure when F_1 score is 0) indicates low false negatives and low false positives, so the model is not disturbed by false alarms.

Classifiers can be characterized based on various performance metrics. When every instance is correctly classified, it is a perfect classifier, that is, its TP = P and TN = N, accuracy will be 1. When every instance is incorrectly classified, it is the worst classifier, that is, its TP = 0 and TN = 0, accuracy will be 0. When the classifier always predicts the positive class correctly, it is an ultra-liberal classifier, that is, its FN = 0 and TN = 0. When the classifier always predicts the negative class correctly, it is an ultra-conservative classifier, that is, its TP = 0 and FP = 0.

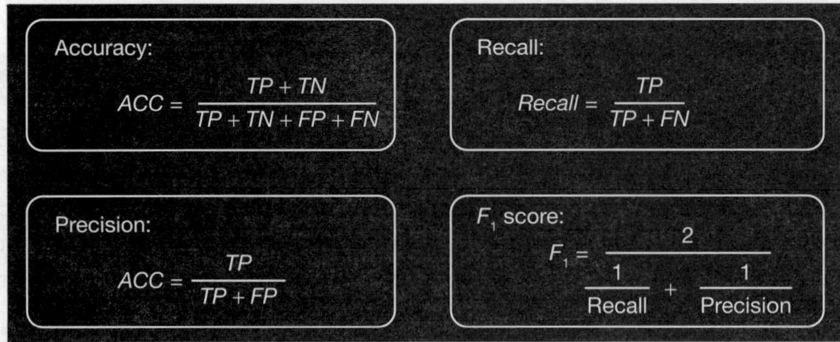

Figure 11.7 Key classification metrics

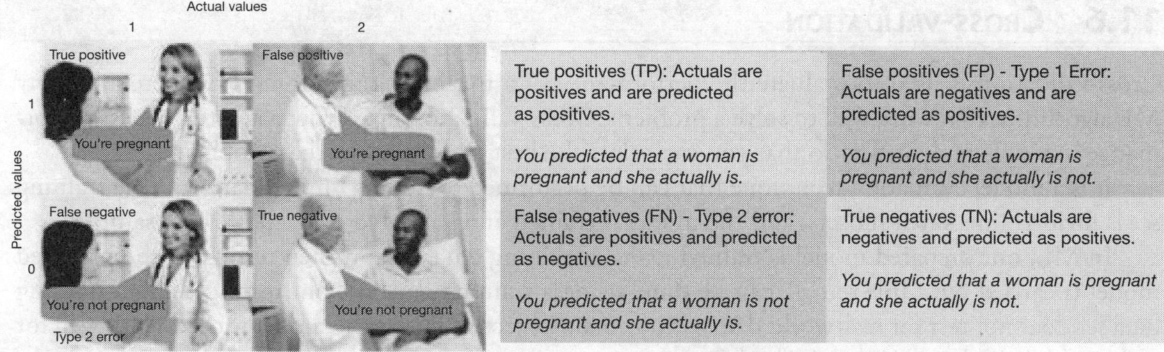

Figure 11.8 TP, FP, FN, TN with examples

Receiver Operating Characteristic (ROC) curve is a visualization method which summarizes the true positive rate (tpr) and false positive rate (fpr) of a model, as shown in Fig. 11.9. It plots tpr versus fpr data, as shown in Fig. 11.10. The performance of the model is assessed by the area under the ROC curve (AUC) shown in Fig. 11.6. If it is less than 0.6, the model is considered a failure, a value between 0.9 and 1 indicates an excellent model, between 0.8 and 0.9 a good model, between 0.7 and 0.8 a fair model and between 0.6 and 0.7 a poor model.

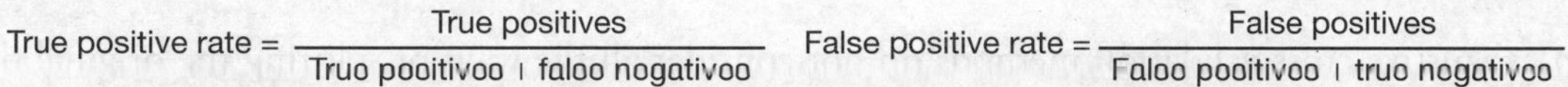

Figure 11.9 True positive rate and False positive rate

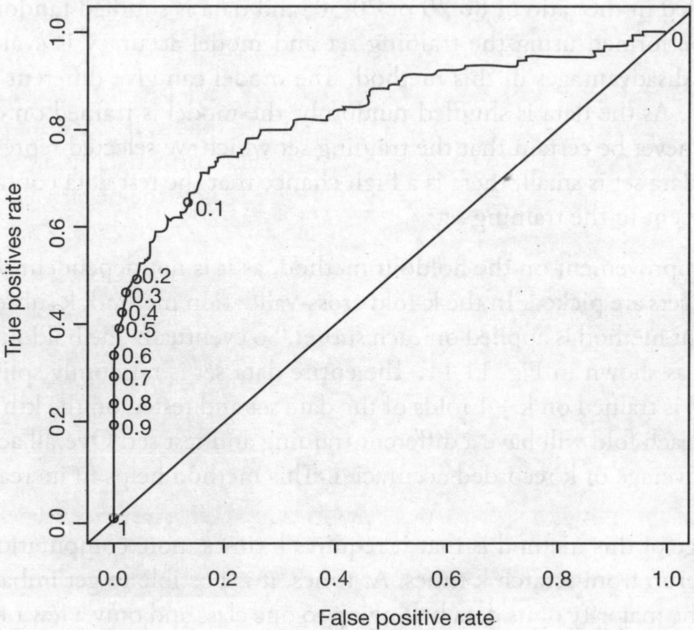

Figure 11.10 ROC curve

11.6 Cross-validation

Cross-validation is used to evaluate the performance of a machine learning model. There are many ML algorithms that work well to solve a problem. Cross-validation helps you evaluate the best performance score of an algorithm so that you can select the best algorithm for that problem.

It is a model evaluation technique that can be performed even on a limited data set. The training set is divided into small subsets, and the model is trained and validated on each of these samples.

In ML, our prepared model is trained using a training data set and then testing of the prepared model is carried out. This testing can be done using a training data set, but testing using a training data set does not test for real-world data. As our main objective is that the model should work well for real-world data, though the training data set may contain real-world data, it is limited; that is, training data represents a small set of possible real-world data points. So to test our trained model, testing is must be carried out on data that the model has not seen earlier. This data set is called the test data set. However, using the training data to train the model and the test data set to test the model, it is possible that some information may be lost that the test data may hold as our model has never been trained for that information.

Cross-validation methods can be categorized as non-exhaustive and exhaustive.

11.6.1 Non-exhaustive Methods

Non-exhaustive cross-validation methods do not consider all the ways of splitting the original data. Holdout and k-fold are non-exhaustive methods.

Holdout method: In this method, the entire data set is divided into a training set and a test set. Usually data is divided in the ratio of 80:20 or 70:30, and data is shuffled randomly before splitting. Model training is performed using the training set and model accuracy is evaluated using the test set. There are some disadvantages in this method. The model can give different results every time it is trained and tested. As the data is shuffled randomly, the model is trained on different data points every time. We can never be certain that the training set which we selected represents the whole data set. Also, when the data set is small, there is a high chance that the test data contains some important information not present in the training set.

K-fold: This is an improvement on the holdout method, as it is not dependent on the way the training and testing data sets are picked. In the k-fold cross-validation method, k subsets of the data set are formed and a holdout method is applied on each subset. So eventually the holdout method is repeated k number of times, as shown in Fig. 11.11. The entire data set is randomly split into k subsets. For each fold, the model is trained on k – 1 folds of the data set and tested on the kth fold. As this process is repeated k times, each fold will have a different training and test set. Overall accuracy of the model is calculated as the average of k recorded accuracies. This method helps in increasing the accuracy of the model.

The disadvantage of this method is that it requires k times more computation as the training algorithm has to be rerun from scratch k times. At times, it is possible to get imbalanced folds, that is, one fold may have the majority of its data belonging to one class and only a few of the other class. This can affect the accuracy of the model and training will also be affected. Stratified k-fold cross-validation helps to avoid this imbalance by using stratification.

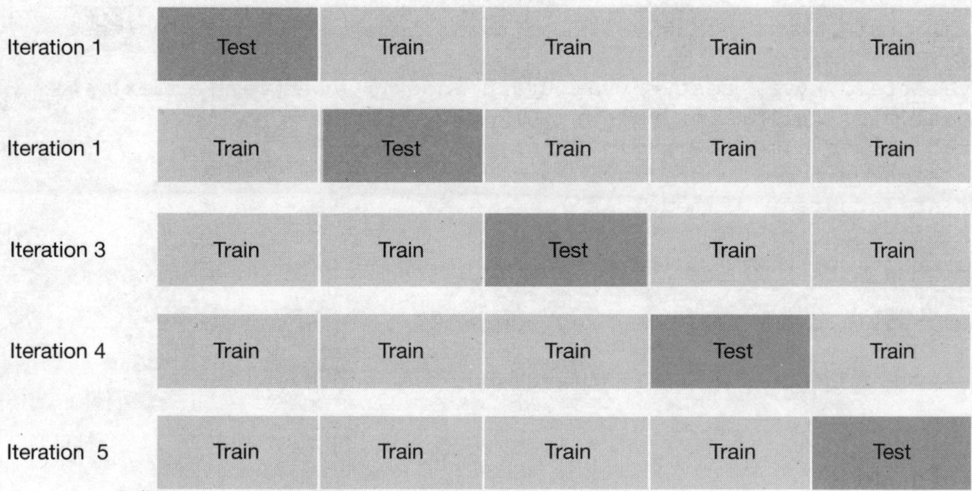

Figure 11.11 K-fold cross validation

Python Code for Non-exhaustive Cross-validation

```
#Importing required libraries
from matplotlib import pyplot
import io
import matplotlib.pyplot as plt
import pandas as pd
from sklearn.model_selection import train_test_split
from sklearn.linear_model import LinearRegression
from sklearn import metrics
import scipy.stats
from sklearn.model_selection import KFold
from sklearn.metrics import accuracy_score
from google.colab import files
uploaded= files.upload()
dfval=pd.read_csv(io.BytesIO(uploaded['Advertising.csv']))
#Loading the dataset
Xval = dfval.iloc[:,0:3]
yval = dfval['Sales'].values.reshape(-1,1)
#Implementing cross validation. 5 fold cross validation is done here. In
each fold ie in each iteration one fold is used as testing set. Overall
accuracy is the average of all classifiers accuracy.
k = 5
kfd = KFold(n_splits=k, random_state=None)
model = LinearRegression()
accuracy_score = []
for train_index, test_index in kfd.split(Xval):
```

```
    Xval_train, Xval_test=Xval.iloc[train_index,:], Xval.iloc[test_
index,:]
    yval_train, yval_test = yval[train_index], yval[test_index]
    model.fit(Xval_train,yval_train)
    pred_values = model.predict(Xval_test)
    r2_score = model.score(Xval_test, yval_test)
    print('accuracy of model is')
    print(r2_score*100,'%')
    accuracy_score.append(r2_score)

avg_accuracy_score = sum(accuracy_score)/k
print('accuracy of each fold - {}'.format(accuracy_score))
print('Avg accuracy: {}'.format(avg_accuracy_score))
```

Output:
accuracy of model is
87.8651980483134 %
accuracy of model is
91.7632116561446 %
accuracy of model is
92.93303235799652 %
accuracy of model is
81.44390391722337 %
accuracy of model is
89.54782879224385 %
accuracy of each fold - [0.878651980483134, 0.917632116561446, 0.9293303235799653, 0.8144390391722337, 0.8954782879224386]
Avg accuracy: 0.8871063495438435

Here, linear regression is performed on the Advertising.csv file, which contains the Sales, TV, Newspaper and Radio fields. Details of this linear regression have been discussed in earlier chapters. K-fold cross-validation with k = 5 is implemented here. The data set is divided into 5 subsets. For each iteration, 4 subsets are used for training and one for testing. Accuracy is calculated for all five iterations and is different for each iteration, that is, 87.86%, 91.76%, 92.93%, 81.44%, 89.54%, respectively. Overall accuracy is the average accuracy of all iterations, which is 88.71%.

11.6.2 Exhaustive Methods

Exhaustive cross-validation methods consider all the ways of splitting the original data into training and testing sets. Leave-one-out and leave-p-out cross-validation methods are exhaustive methods.

Leave-*P*-out: Here, p number of points are taken out from the whole data set consisting of n points. The $(n - p)$ points are used for training the model and the remaining p points are used for testing the model. This process is iterated for all possible combinations of p points. The overall accuracy of the model is the average of all the iteration accuracies. Here, training is performed for every possible combination of data points.

Leave-one-out: If we set the value of p as one, the method is called leave-one-out cross-validation. Taking $p = 1$ makes the method less exhaustive.

Python Code for Exhaustive Cross-validation

```
# importing libraries
import numpy as np
from sklearn.model_selection import LeaveOneOut
# creating the data
X = np.array([[1, 2], [3, 4]])
y = np.array([1, 2])
# Independent variable
print("\nIndependent variable:")
print(X)
# Dependent variable
print("\nDependent variable:")
print(y)
# creating the leave one out function
loo = LeaveOneOut()
loo.get_n_splits(X)
# printing the training and validation data
for train_index, test_index in loo.split(X):
X_train, X_test = X[train_index], X[test_index]
y_train, y_test = y[train_index], y[test_index]
print("\nTraining set:", X_train, y_train)
print("\nValidation set:", X_test, y_test)
```

Output:
Independent variable:
[[1 2]
[3 4]]
Dependent variable:
[1 2]
Training set: [[1 2]] [1]
Validation set: [[3 4]] [2]

First, import libraries into Google Colab. Cross-validation need not be implemented manually. The scikit-learn library in Python provides a simple implementation that will split the data accordingly. An array of a few numbers is taken and printed as an independent variable and dependent variable, x and y, respectively. The function `LeaveOneOut()` is used and data is split using a `for` loop enumerating the splits and iterated through the train index and test index. Finally, the training set and validation set are printed.

11.7 Ensemble Methods: Techniques to Improve Classification Accuracy

Ensemble learning is a popular technique in AI that tries to overcome the risks of single-hypothesis algorithms. The idea behind ensemble learning is to select a collection (ensemble) of hypotheses and combine their individual predictions into a final prediction.

Ensemble methods create one model by combining various ML methods and techniques, to decrease variance and bias and to improve overall accuracy of the model. Bias is an assumption that a model makes to make the target function learn easily. Variance is the estimate of deviation of predictions made by a model as the data set changes. We want every single model to have a high degree of freedom to optimally solve the problem considering the complexity of data we are working with, but we also do not want too much freedom which can increase variance in data. This is called the bias–variance trade-off (Fig. 11.12).

Ensemble learning is applicable in many aspects of real life such as buying a new car, financial policy, shopping, etc. When we buy a car, we do not buy from the first shop based on one advice only. We carry out many comparisons based on car model, price, reviews, opinions of friends and others. Ensemble methods operate on a similar idea. They combine the decisions of more than one model to make better predictions or decisions. Decisions can be combined using very simple methods such as max voting, averaging and weighted averaging.

- **Max** voting, as the name suggests, is used for classification problems. Here, a model's output (prediction) is considered as a vote. The final decision/prediction will be the one which we obtain from the majority of models.
- **Averaging** technique can be used for regression problems or for calculating probabilities in classification problems. As the name suggests, the final decision/prediction will be the average of the predictions of all the models.
- **Weighted averaging** is like the averaging method but here, we assign different weights to each model. Weights define the importance given to that particular model for prediction.

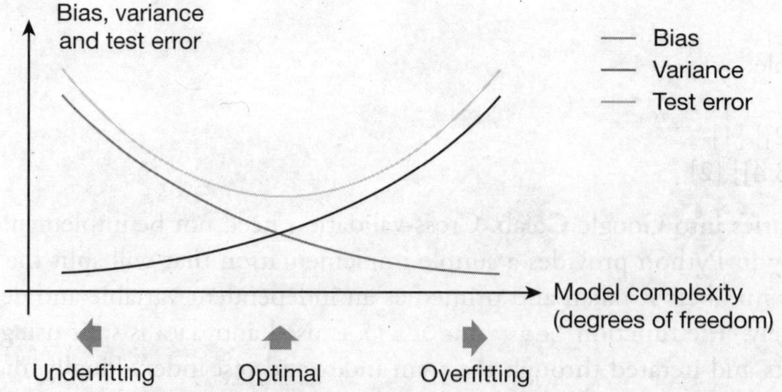

Figure 11.12 Bias–variance trade-off

11.7.1 Bagging

Bagging stands for bootstrap aggregation. In this method, various homogeneous base models are learned independently, in parallel with each other and combined using averaging. For example, we can train M different trees on different subsets of the data and compute the final prediction using voting or averaging. Here, the samples are selected at random from the data set for training, testing and validating. Samples are replaced in the data set.

Bagging uses bootstrap sampling to obtain the data subsets for training the base models. For aggregating the outputs of base models, bagging uses voting for classification and averaging for regression. This method of random picking of samples with replacement improves the accuracy of the overall model. Also, it prevents overfitting and generalises the model for unseen data. For example, we apply bagging when we want to decide what movie we want to watch by asking multiple suggestions from multiple friends; the movie we will watch will be the one which got the highest votes. Some of the methods used in Python for bagging are bagged decision trees, random subspaces, random forest, extra trees and custom bagging.

Python Code for Bagging

We can use the pima-indians-diabetes.data.csv file, which has 8 features such as the number of times pregnant, glucose tolerance test value, blood pressure value, triceps skin fold thickness value, insulin value, BMI value, diabetic pedigree value, age and class value (0/1). Date is to be classified in two classes. Here, the decision tree classifier is used as the base classifier. The aim is to improve accuracy of the model using bagging.

As we can see from the results, single decision tree accuracy is less than the bagging classifier. The bagging method is computationally very intense as we build many base models and then combine them. Here, we build 100 decision trees. The data is chosen with replacement at random, which means that if any data packet is selected again, it is allowed. We create 100 decision trees which are basically trained on different training sets and tested on different test data. We split the data in 10 folds. Each fold's test accuracy is printed and the overall bagging classifier accuracy is also printed. If we apply `GradientBoostingClassifier` (boosting technique) on the same data samples and the same number of trees, accuracy is 77.32%.

```
from sklearn import model_selection
from sklearn.ensemble import BaggingClassifier
from sklearn.tree import DecisionTreeClassifier
from google.colab import files
uploaded= files.upload()
import io
import pandas as pd
from sklearn.metrics import accuracy_score
datadf=pd.read_csv(io.BytesIO(uploaded['pima-indians-diabetes.csv']))
datadf.head()
from sklearn.model_selection import train_test_split
```

```
array = datadf.values
X = array[:,0:8]
Y = array[:,8]
seed = 7
kfoldval = model_selection.KFold(n_splits=10, random_state=seed)
cartclassifier = DecisionTreeClassifier()
# Single model fit and accuracy calculation
X_trainval, X_testval, y_trainval, y_testval = train_test_split(X, Y,
test_size = 0.2, random_state = 4)
cartclassifier.fit(X_trainval,y_trainval)
pred_values = cartclassifier.predict(X_testval)
r2_score = cartclassifier.score(X_testval, y_testval)
print('accuracy of single decision tree model is')
print(r2_score*100,'%')
num_trees = 100
model = BaggingClassifier(base_estimator=cartclassifier, n_estimators=num_
trees, random_state=seed)
results = model_selection.cross_val_score(model, X, Y, cv=kfoldval)
print('Each bagging model accuracy is ', results)
print('Overall Bagging classifier accuracy ',results.mean())
```

Output:

accuracy of single decision tree model is 75.32467532467533 %

Each bagging model accuracy is [0.66233766 0.85714286 0.75324675 0.64935065 0.81818182 0.81818182 0.84415584 0.82894737 0.67105263 0.80263158]

Overall Bagging classifier accuracy 0.770522898154477

If we add the following code of boosting, we obtain an accuracy of 0.7732057416267942 on the same data samples and the same number of trees.

```
#Adaboost on same data
from sklearn.ensemble import GradientBoostingClassifier
model = GradientBoostingClassifier(n_estimators=num_trees, random_
state=seed)
results = model_selection.cross_val_score(model, X, Y, cv=kfold)
print('Gradientboost classifier accuracy is ', results.mean())
```

11.7.2 Boosting

In this method, various homogeneous base models are learned sequentially, in an adaptive way and combined using averaging. For aggregating the outputs of base models, boosting uses majority voting for classification and averaging/weighted sum for regression. Data points that are mispredicted are given more weight so that the next model in sequence can pay more attention to predict it correctly. The basic concept of boosting is to correct the previous model's errors. The previous model's errors are fed into the next model in sequence and are used to correct the mistakes till the last model predicts the most accurate results. Some of the methods used in Python for boosting are AdaBoost, gradient boosting machine, stochastic gradient boosting, XGBoost and LightGBM.

Python Code for Boosting

We use the breast cancer data set for this case study. This data set contains 10 features, to be classified as benign or malignant. The data set contains 699 rows, all as numeric values. Here, the sklearn library methods such as `AdaBoostClassifier` and `GradientBoostingClassifier` are used. The `StandardScalar()` method is used to scale our data set as all the data value ranges are different.

```
import pandas as pd
from sklearn import datasets, metrics
from sklearn.model_selection import train_test_split
from sklearn.preprocessing import StandardScaler
from sklearn.ensemble import RandomForestClassifier, AdaBoostClassifier,
GradientBoostingClassifier
import xgboost as xgb
cancer = datasets.load_breast_cancer()
Xval = cancer.data
yval = cancer.target
scaler = StandardScaler()
X_scaledval = scaler.fit_transform(Xval)
X_trainval, X_testval, y_trainval, y_testval = train_test_split(X_
scaledval, yval, test_size = 0.2, random_state = 1,    stratify = y)
abc = AdaBoostClassifier(n_estimators=200, random_state= 1, learning_
rate=0.01)
gbc = GradientBoostingClassifier(n_estimators=200, random_state=1,
learning_rate=0.01)
xgb_clf = xgb.XGBClassifier(n_estimators=200, learning_rate=0.01, random_
state=1)
abc.fit(X_trainval, y_trainval)
gbc.fit(X_trainval, y_trainval)
xgb_clf.fit(X_trainval, y_trainval)
print('AdaBoost: ', abc.score(X_testval, y_testval))
print('Gradient Boost: ', gbc.score(X_testval, y_testval))
print('XGBoost: ', xgb_clf.score(X_testval, y_testval))
```

Output:
AdaBoost: 0.9473684210526315
Gradient Boost: 0.9736842105263158
XGBoost: 0.956140350877193

We use the parameter 'stratify = y' in the `train_test_split()` method, which means that we want to retain the same proportion of class in the training and test sets. For example, if there are 100 observations in the original data set of which 80 are class 'a' and 20 are class 'b' and we set stratify = True, with a 0.8:0.2 train-test split, we will get a training set with 64 examples of class 'a' and 16 examples of class 'b'. Accuracy of the model changes if we do not specify this parameter, as it changes the data set for different classifiers.

11.7.3 Stacking

Stacking is an ensemble learning technique that combines multiple classification or regression models in parallel through a meta-classifier or meta-regressor. The base level models are trained based on a complete training set and the meta-model is trained on the outputs of the base level model as features.

Overall, bagging focuses on getting an ensemble model which has less variance than its components, however boosting and stacking focus on an ensemble method which has less bias than its components.

11.7.4 Random Forest

A forest is made up of many trees. The random forest algorithm uses the same analogy for classification or regression problems. Random forest, a supervised learning algorithm, is mostly used for classification purposes. It creates multiple decision trees with different data samples and predictions are made by each tree. The final solution is selected by means of voting, and is the best solution. Random forest is thus an ensemble method which uses bagging to improve accuracy and reduces overfitting by averaging the results of all the trees.

In a random forest algorithm, trees are trained not only on different sets of data but also on different features, which allows them to make the best decision. Decision trees consider all the possible features of the given data and pick the feature that is best for the most separation between data in the left node and right node. It selects the feature which gives the best information gain in order. However, in a random forest, each tree picks a random subset of features. So each tree is built on different features. This allows more variations in the tree model and eventually results in better diversification and lower correlation across trees.

For example, you want to decide on where to go for a one-month vacation, so you ask many friends to decide where you should go. Friend-1 asks you about the likes and dislikes of your past travel experiences and some other questions. Based on your answers, he gives you some advice. Then you ask some more friends, they also ask some other questions and advise you accordingly. After seeking all possible advice, you choose the place which is recommended by most of your friends. This is an example of a typical random forest algorithm approach.

Figure 11.13 explains the overall working of the random forest algorithm. It selects 'm' features from a total of 'n' features, where $m < n$. It calculates the best split point among the 'm' features, and splits the nodes to subnodes using this. Splitting continues till the leaf nodes are reached. This process is repeated for the creation of all the trees, that is, 'n' number of trees. After the creation of this random forest, prediction is made on the test data. The outcome of each tree (vote) is stored and the final prediction is the highest voted predicted output.

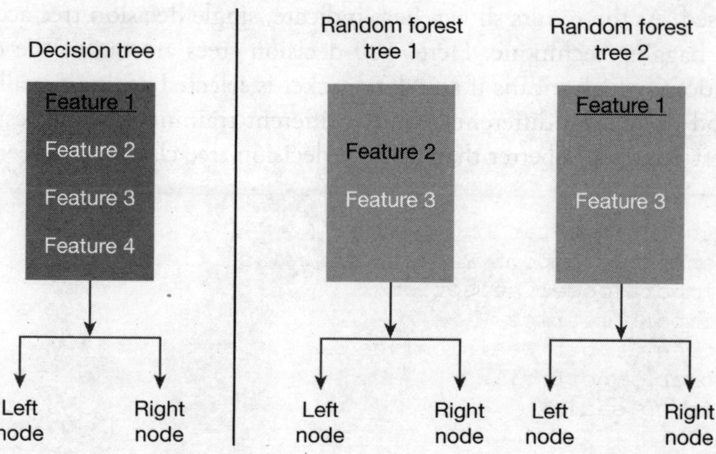

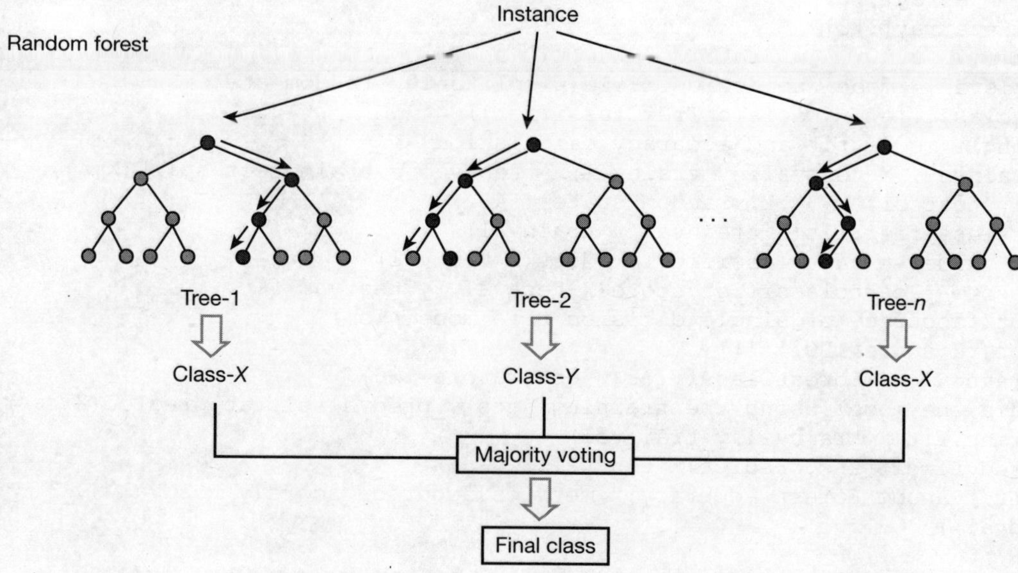

Figure 11.13 Random forest approach

Python Code for Random Forest

The file pima-indians-diabetes.data.csv is used here; it has 8 features such as number of times pregnant, glucose tolerance test value, blood pressure value, triceps skin fold thickness value, insulin value, BMI value, diabetic pedigree value, age and class value (0/1). Date is to be classified in two classes. Here, the decision tree classifier is used as the base classifier. To improve accuracy of the model, a random forest is used. As the results shown here indicate, single decision tree accuracy is lower than the random forest bagging technique. Here, 100 decision trees are built. The data is chosen with replacement at random, which means if any data packet is selected again, it is allowed. 100 decision trees are created and trained on different features, different training sets and tested on different test data. Random forest accuracy is better than a single decision tree classifier, as seen in the results.

```
# Random Forest implementation
from sklearn.ensemble import RandomForestClassifier
from sklearn import model_selection
from sklearn import metrics
from sklearn.tree import DecisionTreeClassifier
from google.colab import files
uploaded= files.upload()
import io
import pandas as pd
from sklearn.metrics import accuracy_score
datadf=pd.read_csv(io.BytesIO(uploaded['pima-indians-diabetes.csv']))
datadf.head()
from sklearn.model_selection import train_test_split
array = datadf.values
Xval = array[:,0:8]
Yval = array[:,8]
seed = 7
#kfoldval = model_selection.KFold(n_splits=10, random_state=seed)
cartclassifier = DecisionTreeClassifier()
# Single model fit and accuracy calculation
X_trainval, X_testval, y_trainval, y_testval = train_test_split(Xval,
Yval, test_size = 0.2, random_state = 4)
cartclassifier.fit(X_trainval,y_trainval)
pred_values = cartclassifier.predict(X_testval)
r2_score = cartclassifier.score(X_testval, y_testval)
print('accuracy of single decision tree model is')
print(r2_score*100,'%')
clfranc=RandomForestClassifier(n_estimators=120)
#Train the model using the training sets y_predval=clfran.predict(X_test)
clfranc.fit(X_trainval,y_trainval)
y_predval=clfranc.predict(X_testval)
print("Random Forest Accuracy:",metrics.accuracy_score(y_testval, y_
predval))
```

Output:
accuracy of single decision tree model is 72.07792207792207 %
Random Forest Accuracy: 0.7662337662337663

The `RandomForestRegressor()` class of the sklearn.ensemble library can also be used to solve the regression problem using random forest.

EXERCISES

Multiple Choice Questions

1. Which machine learning algorithm is based on the idea of bagging?
   (a) Random forest
   (b) Classification
   (c) Regression
   (d) Support vector machine

2. Which of the following is a disadvantage of decision trees?
   (a) Factor analysis
   (b) They are robust for outliers
   (c) They are prone to be overfit
   (d) None of the above

3. Which of the metrics below is used to evaluate the ML classifier?
   (a) F_1 score
   (b) Confusion matrix
   (c) ROC curve
   (d) All of the above

4. Classification technique is:
   (a) Supervised
   (b) Unsupervised
   (c) Both
   (d) None of the above

5. Which of the following is a classification algorithm?
   (a) K-means
   (b) Logistics regression
   (c) Polynomial regression
   (d) None of the above

6. Classification is appropriate:
   (a) When you predict continuous value output
   (b) When you predict discrete value output
   (c) When you predict continuous and discrete value output
   (d) None of the above

7. Which algorithm is considered as a lazy learning algorithm?
   (a) Naive Bayes'
   (b) Decision tree
   (c) SVM
   (d) K-NN

8. Which algorithm is the best for text classification?
   (a) Naive Bayes'
   (b) Decision tree
   (c) SVM
   (d) Random forest

9. What does K refer to in K-NN algorithm?
   (a) Number of classes in output
   (b) Number of neighbours
   (c) Number of feature attributes
   (d) None of the above

10. Hyper-planes can be best described as:
    (a) Mapping functions from input to output
    (b) Decision function
    (c) Decision boundary
    (d) All of the above

11. Why is naive Bayes' called naive?
    (a) Because it is a lazy classifier
    (b) Because its accuracy is low
    (c) Because it is a bad classifier
    (d) Because of its assumptions

12. Which of the following algorithms are similar in nature?
    (a) SVM and K-NN
    (b) K-NN and K-means
    (c) Decision tree and random forest
    (d) Decision tree and naive Bayes'

13. Which of the following is not a kernel used in SVM?
    (a) Polynomial

(b) Gaussian
(c) Sigmoid
(d) All of the above are kernels

14. Which of the following clustering algorithms merges and splits data points to modify non-optimal partitions?
(a) K-means clustering
(b) Agglomerative clustering
(c) Divisive clustering
(d) None of the above

15. Which one of the following is true for logistic regression?
(a) Logistic regression is a linear regression technique and is used to model data having binary outcome
(b) Logistic regression is a linear regression technique and is used to model data having numeric outcome
(c) Logistic regression is a non-linear regression technique and is used to model data having binary outcome
(d) Logistic regression is a non-linear regression technique and is used to model data having numeric outcome

Answers

1. (a)	**2.** (c)	**3.** (d)	**4.** (a)	**5.** (b)	**6.** (b)	**7.** (d)	**8.** (a)
9. (b)	**10.** (c)	**11.** (d)	**12.** (c)	**13.** (c)	**14.** (a)	**15.** (c)	

Programming/Concept-based Questions

1. Implement the decision tree classifier on the breast cancer data set and classify your data. The data set contains features 'id', 'diagnosis', 'radius_mean', 'texture_mean', 'perimeter_mean', 'area_mean', 'smoothness_mean', 'compactness_mean', 'concavity_mean', 'concave points_mean', 'symmetry_mean', 'fractal_dimension_mean', 'radius_se', 'texture_se', 'perimeter_se', 'area_se', 'smoothness_se', 'compactness_se', 'concavity_se', 'concave points_se', 'symmetry_se', 'fractal_dimension_se', 'radius_worst', 'texture_worst', 'perimeter_worst', 'area_worst', 'smoothness_worst', 'compactness_worst', 'concavity_worst', 'concave points_worst', 'symmetry_worst', 'fractal_dimension_worst' which are classified as M or B (malignant or benign).

Answer:

```
#Implementation of Decision Tree Algorithm:on breast cancer data set
import io
import pandas as pd
import numpy as np
import seaborn as sns
from sklearn.metrics import classification_report, confusion_matrix,accuracy_score
from sklearn.preprocessing import LabelEncoder
from sklearn.tree import DecisionTreeClassifier
from sklearn.model_selection import train_test_split
```

```
import matplotlib.pyplot as plt
from sklearn.tree import plot_tree
from sklearn.tree import DecisionTreeClassifier
from google.colab import files
uploaded= files.upload()
datadf=pd.read_csv(io.BytesIO(uploaded['breast-cancer-data.csv']))
Xfeatures = datadf.drop(columns=['diagnosis'],axis=1)
Yresponse = datadf['diagnosis']
from sklearn.model_selection import train_test_split
X_trainfeatures,  X_testfeatures,  y_trainresponse,  y_testresponse  =
train_test_split(Xfeatures, Yresponse, test_size=0.2, random_state=4)
dtree=DecisionTreeClassifier()
dtree.fit(Xfeatures,Yresponse)
print('Decision Tree Classifier Created')
ypred=dtree.predict(Xfeatures)
cm = confusion_matrix(Yresponse, ypred)
print(cm)
print("Decision tree model accuracy(in %):", accuracy_score(Yresponse,
ypred)*100)
```

Output:

Decision Tree Classifier Created
[[357 0]
[0 212]]
Decision tree model accuracy(in %): 100.0

2. Implement the random forest classifier on the breast cancer data set and classify your data. The data set contains features 'id', 'diagnosis', 'radius_mean', 'texture_mean', 'perimeter_mean', 'area_mean', 'smoothness_mean', 'compactness_mean', 'concavity_mean','concave points_mean', 'symmetry_mean', 'fractal_dimension_mean','radius_se', 'texture_se', 'perimeter_se', 'area_se', 'smoothness_se', 'compactness_se', 'concavity_se', 'concave points_se', 'symmetry_se','fractal_dimension_se', 'radius_worst', 'texture_worst','perimeter_worst', 'area_worst', 'smoothness_worst', 'compactness_worst', 'concavity_worst', 'concave points_worst','symmetry_worst', 'fractal_dimension_worst' which are classified as M or B (malignant or benign).

Answer:

```
# random forest on breast cancer data set implementation
import io
import pandas as pd
import numpy as np
import seaborn as sns
from  sklearn.metrics  import  classification_report,  confusion_
matrix,accuracy_score
```

```
from sklearn.preprocessing import LabelEncoder
from sklearn.tree import DecisionTreeClassifier
from sklearn.model_selection import train_test_split
import matplotlib.pyplot as plt
from sklearn.tree import plot_tree
from sklearn.tree import DecisionTreeClassifier

from google.colab import files
uploaded= files.upload()

datadf=pd.read_csv(io.BytesIO(uploaded['breast-cancer-data.csv']))
Xfeatures = datadf.drop(columns=['diagnosis'],axis=1)
Yresponse = datadf['diagnosis']
from sklearn.model_selection import train_test_split
X_trainfeatures, X_testfeatures, y_trainresponse, y_testresponse =
train_test_split(Xfeatures, Yresponse, test_size=0.3, random_state=4)
from sklearn.ensemble import RandomForestClassifier
rfclf = RandomForestClassifier(n_estimators= 100, random_state=3)
rfclf_model = rfclf.fit(X_trainfeatures, y_trainresponse)
rfclf_predictions = rfclf_model.predict(X_testfeatures)
print(confusion_matrix(y_testresponse, rfclf_predictions))
#print(classification_report(y_testval, rfclf_predictions))
print('Random forest accuracy is',accuracy_score(y_testresponse, rfclf_
predictions))
```

Output:

```
[[109  8]
 [  1 53]]
Random forest accuracy is 0.9473684210526315
```

3. Implement the Gaussian naive Bayes' classifier on the breast cancer data set and classify your data. The data set contains features `'id'`, `'diagnosis'`, `'radius_mean'`, `'texture_mean'`, `'perimeter_mean'`, `'area_mean'`, `'smoothness_mean'`, `'compactness_mean'`, `'concavity_mean'`,`'concave points_mean'`, `'symmetry_mean'`, `'fractal_dimension_mean'`,`'radius_se'`, `'texture_se'`, `'perimeter_se'`, `'area_se'`, `'smoothness_se'`, `'compactness_se'`, `'concavity_se'`, `'concave points_se'`, `'symmetry_se'`,`'fractal_dimension_se'`, `'radius_worst'`, `'texture_worst'`,`'perimeter_worst'`, `'area_worst'`, `'smoothness_worst'`, `'compactness_worst'`, `'concavity_worst'`, `'concave points_worst'`,`'symmetry_worst'`, `'fractal_dimension_worst'` which are classified as M or B (malignant or benign).

Answer:

```
# Gaussian naive bayes on breast cancer data set implementation
import io
import pandas as pd
```

```
import numpy as np
import seaborn as sns
from   sklearn.metrics   import   classification_report,   confusion_
matrix,accuracy_score
from sklearn.preprocessing import LabelEncoder
from sklearn.tree import DecisionTreeClassifier
from sklearn.model_selection import train_test_split
import matplotlib.pyplot as plt
from sklearn.tree import plot_tree
from sklearn.tree import DecisionTreeClassifier

from google.colab import files
uploaded= files.upload()

datadf=pd.read_csv(io.BytesIO(uploaded['breast-cancer-data.csv']))
Xfeatures = datadf.drop(columns=['diagnosis'],axis=1)
Yresponse = datadf['diagnosis']
from sklearn.model_selection import train_test_split
X_trainfeatures,  X_testfeatures,  y_trainresponse,  y_testresponse  =
train_test_split(Xfeatures, Yresponse, test_size=0.3, random_state=4)
from sklearn.naive_bayes import GaussianNB
gnb_naive = GaussianNB()
gnb_naive.fit(X_trainfeatures, y_trainresponse)
ypredresponse = gnb_naive.predict(X_testfeatures)
cmt = confusion_matrix(y_testresponse, ypredresponse)
print(cmt)
print("Gaussian Naive Bayes model accuracy(in %):", accuracy_score(y_
testresponse, ypredresponse)*100)
```

Output:

```
[[117  0]
 [ 53  1]]
Gaussian Naive Bayes model accuracy(in %): 69.00584795321637
```

4. Implement the Bernoulli naive Bayes' classifier on the breast cancer data set and classify your data. The data set contains features `'id'`, `'diagnosis'`, `'radius_mean'`, `'texture_mean'`, `'perimeter_mean'`, `'area_mean'`, `'smoothness_mean'`, `'compactness_mean'`, `'concavity_mean'`,`'concave points_mean'`, `'symmetry_mean'`, `'fractal_dimension_mean'`,`'radius_se'`, `'texture_se'`, `'perimeter_se'`, `'area_se'`, `'smoothness_se'`, `'compactness_se'`, `'concavity_se'`, `'concave points_se'`, `'symmetry_se'`,`'fractal_dimension_se'`, `'radius_worst'`, `'texture_worst'`,`'perimeter_worst'`, `'area_worst'`, `'smoothness_worst'`, `'compactness_worst'`, `'concavity_worst'`, `'concave points_worst'`,`'symmetry_worst'`, `'fractal_dimension_worst'` which are classified as M or B (malignant or benign).

Answer:

```
import io
import pandas as pd
import numpy as np
import seaborn as sns
from   sklearn.metrics   import   classification_report,   confusion_
matrix,accuracy_score
from sklearn.preprocessing import LabelEncoder
from sklearn.tree import DecisionTreeClassifier
from sklearn.model_selection import train_test_split
import matplotlib.pyplot as plt
from sklearn.tree import plot_tree
from sklearn.tree import DecisionTreeClassifier

from google.colab import files
uploaded= files.upload()

datadf=pd.read_csv(io.BytesIO(uploaded['breast-cancer-data.csv']))
Xfeatures = datadf.drop(columns=['diagnosis'],axis=1)
Yresponse = datadf['diagnosis']
from sklearn.model_selection import train_test_split
X_trainfeatures,  X_testfeatures,  y_trainresponse,  y_testresponse  =
train_test_split(Xfeatures, Yresponse, test_size=0.3, random_state=4)
from sklearn.naive_bayes import BernoulliNB
gnb_naive = BernoulliNB()
gnb_naive.fit(X_trainfeatures, y_trainresponse)
ypredresponse = gnb_naive.predict(X_testfeatures)
cmt = confusion_matrix(y_testresponse, ypredresponse)
print(cmt)
print("Bernouli Naive Bayes model accuracy(in %):", accuracy_score(y_
testresponse, ypredresponse)*100)
```

Output:

[[117 0]
[54 0]]
Bernouli Naive Bayes model accuracy(in %): 68.42105263157895

5. Implement the decision tree classifier on the diabetes data set, download the pima-indians-diabetes.csv file and classify your data.

Answer:

```
decision tree for diabetic data set
from sklearn import model_selection
from sklearn.tree import DecisionTreeClassifier
from sklearn.metrics import accuracy_score, confusion_matrix
```

```
from google.colab import files
uploaded= files.upload()
import io
import pandas as pd
from sklearn.metrics import accuracy_score
datadf=pd.read_csv(io.BytesIO(uploaded['pima-indians-diabetes.csv']))
datadf.head()
from sklearn.model_selection import train_test_split
array = datadf.values
Xval = array[:,0:8]
yval = array[:,8]
x_trainval, x_testval, y_trainval, y_testval= train_test_split(Xval,
yval, test_size= 0.3, random_state=3)
cartclassifier = DecisionTreeClassifier()
cartclassifier.fit(x_trainval, y_trainval)
ypredresponse = cartclassifier.predict(x_testval)
cmt = confusion_matrix(y_testval, ypredresponse)
print(cmt)
print("Decision Tree model accuracy(in %):", accuracy_score(y_testval,
ypredresponse)*100)
```

Output:

```
[[115 40]
 [ 24 52]]
Decision Tree model accuracy(in %): 72.2943722943723
```

BIBLIOGRAPHY

1. Yesha Shastri. "Getting Started with scikit-learn for Classification in Machine Learning". *KDnuggets*, published December 2022, https://www.kdnuggets.com/getting-started-with-scikit-learn-for-classification-in-machine-learning.html

2. "Classification Algorithm in Machine Learning". JavaTpoint, https://www.javatpoint.com/classification-algorithm-in-machine-learning

3. Arnab Mondal. "A Complete Guide to Understand Classification in Machine Learning". *Analytics Vidhya*, last modified September 2022, https://www.analyticsvidhya.com/blog/2021/09/a-complete-guide-to-understand-classification-in-machine-learning/

4. Badreesh Shetty. "Supervised Machine Learning Classification: An In-depth Guide". Built In, last modified October 2022, https://builtin.com/data-science/supervised-machine-learning-classification

CHAPTER 12

Prescriptive Analytics: Data Stream Mining

LEARNING OBJECTIVES

At the end of this chapter, you will be able to:

- Explain the concepts of data streams and mining
- Describe query processing on streams
- List the steps of data stream filtering
- Explain sampling in data streams and the different types of sampling
- Detect concept drift and explain its various methods
- List the classifier methods
- Explain rare class problems
- List the issues, controversies and problems in data stream mining

12.0 INTRODUCTION TO STREAM CONCEPTS

Data that flows continuously is known as a data stream. Large volumes and high speeds make data stream classification difficult. In the past decades, researchers have given a lot of attention to data stream mining. Data streams cannot be stored and analyzed afterwards as the volume is huge. If we try to do this, it will exhaust the whole memory. Data streams flow at a rapid rate, so the processing should be very fast and classification should take less time. Data distribution plays an important role in the mining process. Usually in data distribution, data is first stored and then analyzed. However, in data stream mining, the data distribution is dynamic. This dynamic nature of the data stream changes over time.

12.1 MINING DATA STREAMS

The necessity of handling a large amount of data gave birth to the field of data mining. Here, the processing time is analyzed and memory is allocated for static data sets. Larger data sets can be handled by the data mining approach, but it fails when dealing with continuous streams of data. Usually, a previously trained model cannot be updated when a new type of data arrives, as at that time, the model cannot handle the new data; instead, the model should be retrained using the new data. However, this is a very tedious process. In response to the continuous supply of data, a stream data mining approach has recently emerged. Data stream algorithms are capable of dealing with huge volumes of data and also with the changing nature of the data, which is not addressed by data mining.

A data stream is an enormous amount of data that is generated in an uncontrolled manner at a quick rate from many applications such as call detail records, log records, sensor applications, emails, blogging, twitter posts, etc. In recent years, data stream mining has gained the attention of many researchers. As the volume of data in a data stream is huge, it is very difficult to store all the data, analyze it and use its characteristics in the future. Massive volume and high speed are the characteristics that make data streams difficult to handle using traditional data mining techniques.

In data mining, the underlying data distribution is static. In a data stream, the underlying data distribution keeps changing as the data may span a long time and the sources that generate it may undergo some changes. Data streams are not stable but dynamic in nature; this means they change with time and these changes are known as concept drift. A rising problem in data streams is the handling of concept drift. Several algorithms have been developed to handle data streams.

Data stream mining fulfills the following characteristics:

- **Continuous stream of data**: A high amount of data in an infinite stream. We do not know the entire data set.
- **Concept drifting**: The data changes or evolves over time.
- **Volatility of data**: The system does not store the data received (limited resources). When data is analyzed, it is discarded or summarized.

Data mining uses a huge range of algorithms (classification, regression, outlier detection and recommender systems). These algorithms need to handle concept drift and huge quantities of data using limited resources (Fig. 12.1). Some algorithms need pre-processing using the previous data-based techniques. For instance, naive Bayes', decision stump, Hoeffding tree or ADWIN.

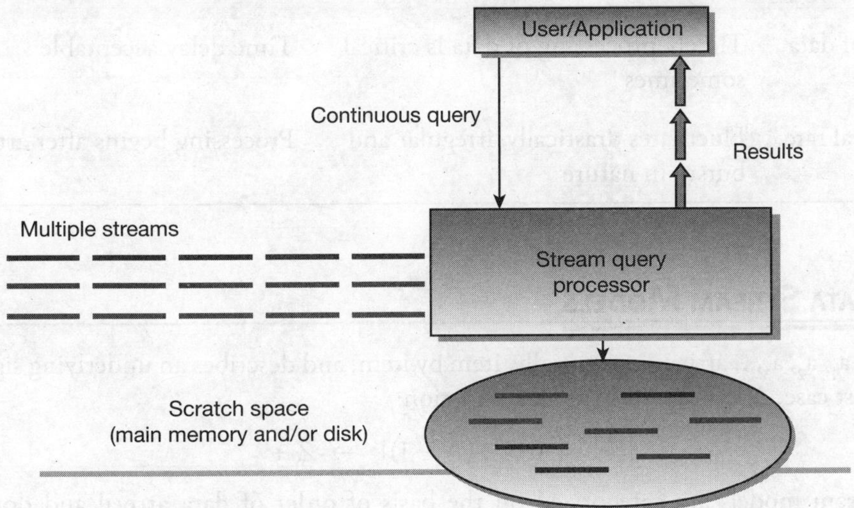

Figure 12.1 Components of data stream mining

12.2 Data Stream Management System (DSMS)

Data stream processing handles a continuous stream of data whereas database management systems (DBMS) manage data after it is stored. Table 12.1 shows a comparison between DSMS and traditional DBMS.

Table 12.1 Comparison of DSMS and traditional DBMS

Data operation	DSMS	DBMS
Newly arriving data	Append only at the end	Unordered data sets that rely on random or repeated access to individual data records
Queries	Issued once and can remain active over a long period of time	Computed once and results are reflected in the state of the database
Volume	Volume, rate and high dimensionality of data make it challenging to store. DSMS computes the result by storing only a small portion of the original stream in the form of data summary structures such as sketches and histograms.	Volume of data is not a challenge
Processing of data	Timely processing of data is critical sometimes	Time delay acceptable
Stream arrival rate	Fluctuates drastically, irregular and bursty in nature	Processing begins after arrival of data

12.3 Data Stream Models

Input stream a_1, a_2, a_3,... arrives sequentially, item by item, and describes an underlying signal A, when in the simplest case, A is a one-dimensional function:

$$0 \ldots (N-1)] \;\rightarrow Z+$$

Data stream models are categorized on the basis of order of data arrival and domain values. Various models and characteristics are given in Table 12.2.

Table 12.2 Data stream models and their characteristics

Data stream model	Characteristic
Unordered cash register model	Individual items are not pre-processed and domain values do not arrive in an ordered way
Ordered cash register model	Individual items are not pre-processed and domain values arrive in an order way
Unordered aggregate model	Individual items are pre-processed and domain values do not arrive in an ordered way
Ordered aggregate model	Individual items are pre-processed and domain values arrive in an ordered way

12.3.1 Window Specification

Queries in data stream models are evaluated on unbounded streams of data and the nature of the data is not known. To perform various operations such as aggregation or join, the entire data would be required to produce results. It is necessary to retain streaming data on fast retrieval storage to achieve accuracy. Most data streaming applications use only past recent data, and not the entire past stream. Due to these constraints, window based models were developed.

These models are used to limit the scope of the input data over which the query is being evaluated. A window specifies a finite set of recent records from the data stream that are processed at a time to evaluate the query. It has the following parameters:

- **Upper bound:** The most recent timestamp of the items to be processed.
- **Lower bound:** The oldest timestamp of the items to be processed.
- **Size:** The number of records or timestamp duration to be processed.
- **Mode of adjustment:** Represents how the window changes state on the arrival of a new item.

Based on the scope of data, windows can be categorized as follows:

- **Physical window**: It is defined based on the number of records. Based on the type of processing, it can be further categorized as:
  - o **Count-based sliding:** The most recent N items of the stream are processed.
  - o **Count-based tumbling**: Streams are divided into non-overlapping partitions and the data in the current partition is considered for processing.
  - o **Partitioned**: Stream records are partitioned based on the value of grouping attributes.
- **Logical window**: It is defined in ascending or descending order of attributes of records. It can also be defined in terms of timestamps, as follows:
  - o **Landmark**: The window starts from an identified landmark (specific timestamp) and the upper bound can be fixed as a future timestamp.
  - o **Fixed-band**: The window is defined by combining both the landmark window variants, fixing the upper and lower bounds according to a band window function, which allows the expression of arbitrary time intervals ('bands').

- o **Time-based sliding**: The window is defined only with the items that arrive before T time units. As the window slides, new items join it and old items expire.
- o **Time-based tumbling**: This is similar to count-based tumbling. Streams are divided into non-overlapping partitions. A new window is created as soon as the old one ceases to exist.
- o **Punctuation-based:** Special annotations are used to represent the end of the processing window.

12.3.2 Persistent Queries

A query on unbounded and continuous data is called a persistent query. Such queries are issued once and they process data continuously and produce results on data streams.

Monotonic persistent queries: If the result of a query does not shrink over time, it is said to be monotonic. If query X is persistent and X (t1) $\subseteq$ X(t2) for $\forall$ t1 $\leq$ t2, then query X is monotonic. For example, in selection predicate, if a new tuple satisfies the query, it is added to the result; if it does not satisfy the query, the tuple will be part of the result for the upper timestamp for consideration again.

Blocking persistent queries: These queries do not produce output until the entire input data is provided. For example, aggregation operations such as SUM, MAX and COUNT cannot produce results until they have all the input data on which these operations are applied. Selections and projections are non-blocking. This is because as and when a tuple satisfies the criteria, it is included in the output.

To make blocking operations feasible on persistent queries, the following techniques can be used:

- **Limiting the scope**: By limiting the scope of data using windows or augmentation, blocking operations can be applied. The data size will become finite and will fit in memory and blocking operations will be applied on the current window rather than the entire stream.
- **Incremental evaluation**: Incremental evaluation updates the result as new data arrives. Values seen thus far are used to compute the result. For example, MAX of values of a stream is the maximum value seen thus far and this updates as and when greater values arrive in a new tuple.

12.4 DATA STREAM FILTERING

This identifies sequence patterns in a data stream. Stream filtering is the process of selection or matching instances of a desired pattern in a continuous stream of data. Assume that a data stream consists of tuples. The steps in filtering are:

1. Accept the tuples that meet a criterion in the stream.
2. Pass the accepted tuples to another process as a stream.
3. Discard the remaining tuples.

Filtering techniques are broadly classified as implicit or explicit.

12.4.1 Implicit Filtering

The DSMS handles the high rate and burstiness of streams in various ways to ensure stability under heavy load. Some of them use various load shedding techniques that lighten the load by only processing some of the elements from the stream and discarding others without processing them. The stream's load shedding mechanism places random sampling operators at various points in the query plan to uniformly sample the stream, dynamically adjusting the sampling rate with respect to operator selectivity and data arrival rate. The goal of this approach is to reduce the load while minimizing the negative impact on query result accuracy.

The strategy of removing tuples early in the query plan makes the query evaluation process for subsequent operators in the plan more efficient. However, when multiple queries share parts of the plan, the question of where to distribute the load becomes more complicated, as the above strategies can affect the results of different queries differently.

12.4.2 Explicit Filtering

Implicit filtering techniques often undermine various data stream analysis problems, such as computing sketches and patterns of various elements to estimate quantiles, heavy beats and other characteristics of the stream. Other issues include IP network flow size estimation and worm signature generation by finding the most common substrings in the network. Therefore, in such cases, it is better to include the filter criteria that best match the returned query as part of the query process itself.

12.5 Sampling Data in a Stream

Stream sampling is a filtering technique. Here, data is represented by a small subset of the stream satisfying certain characteristics of input.

Sampling algorithms are based on set resemblance, approximation of quantiles, count distinction, etc. Sampling uses statistics with variants such as fixed or variable size and biased or not. Sampling in streams widely uses sampling in statistics but with some constraints.

Stream sampling has many challenges. Sampling in one pass over high-speed data cannot be stored at its matching rate. Therefore, even when items repeat, it is difficult to identify them. Thus, even uniform sampling of distinct items in the data stream is tricky. Further, a fixed sample size is required when the size of the stream is unknown. Streams are unpredictable and it is difficult to ensure certain properties.

12.5.1 Reservoir Sampling

Reservoir sampling solves the problem of selecting a random sample of size n from a pool of N records where N is unknown for a stream. Let TP be the tolerance parameter and x denote the number of items processed thus far. The final sample is stored in the array. It is a process of creating a reservoir of candidates.

The basic algorithm can be described as follows:

1. Select n data records for the sample and save them in a reservoir of size $TP * n$.
2. Process the rest of the records within the time window in the following manner:
   - In each iteration, generate an independent random variable $\phi\ (n, x)$.
   - Skip over the next ϕ data records.
   - Make the next data record a candidate by replacing one at random. The index of the record being replaced is (n * random()), where random() is a random number generator that returns a real number in the unit interval.

3. If the current number of candidates exceeds n records, randomly choose n samples from the reservoir of candidates.

12.5.2 Min-Hash Computation

The resemblance of two sets A and B can be calculated as

$$\rho\,(A,B) = |A \cap B| \,/\, |A \cup B|$$

where $|A \cap B|$ = size of the intersection and $|A \cup B|$ = size of the union.

A min-hash signature is an approximate representation of resemblance.

Let $h_i(a)$ be a hash function. The signature of set A, S(A), is:

$$s_i(A) = \min(h_i(a) \mid a \in A)$$
$$S(A) = (s_i(A), \ldots\, s_n(A))$$

If $S(A)$ and $S(B)$ are two min-hash signatures, then

$$\hat{p}(A,B) = \sum_{i=1}^{i=n} I(si(A),\ si(B))$$

where $I(x, y)$ = indicator function, returning 1 if $x = y$ and 0 otherwise.

12.5.3 Subset-Sum Sampling

This algorithm collects a sample S of tuples from R in such a way that we can accurately estimate sums from the sample.

Let us assume that the schema of R is (C, x), where C is an attribute we use for subset selection and x is the measure attribute. Then

$$E[\sum (t \cdot x \mid t \in S \wedge t \cdot C = c)] = \sum (t \cdot x \mid t \in R \wedge t \cdot C = c)$$

In the basic subset-sum sampling algorithm, the user sets a threshold z, which determines the sample size. Each tuple t is sampled with probability $p(x) = \min\{1, t{\cdot}x/z\}$.

The idea behind this algorithm is that tuples with large values of $t{\cdot}x$ contribute the largest amount to a sum. Therefore, all large tuples are sampled; however, small tuples cannot be discarded without biasing some subset-sum. The algorithm samples one small tuple every time the combined weight of the small tuples exceeds z. To estimate the sum, the measure $t{\cdot}x$ of the sampled small tuple is adjusted to z, since it represents a weight of threshold z:

$$t{\cdot}x = \max\{t{\cdot}x,\ z\}$$

The result of the algorithm described above is a sample of arbitrary size, which introduces an element of unpredictability.

The algorithm works in the following manner:

- Collect samples according to the basic subset-sum sampling algorithm, keeping a count of the number of sampled tuples in a sample count.

- If the sample count is count > γ*N (for example, $\lambda = 2$), estimate a new value of z which will result in N tuples. Subsample S using the basic subset-sum sampling and the new value of z, and continue with basic subset-sum sampling.
- When all the tuples from R have been processed, if sample count > N, adjust z and subsample S using basic subset-sum sampling.

12.6 Concept Drift

The process of finding and extracting potential information in a data stream is known as data stream mining. The data stream is a continuous flow of data that is not easy to handle as it arrives at a rapid rate. The data stream is different from traditional static data sets, as it is continuous, unlimited and dynamic in nature. The underlying data distribution changes over the time; this problem is known as concept drift. Concept drift makes data stream classification difficult. Many researchers have classified the data stream changes into main four categories: noise, blip, gradual and sudden.

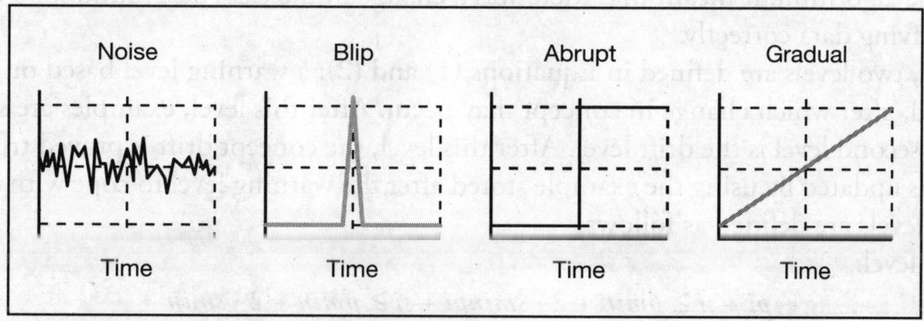

Figure 12.2 Types of concept drift

In Fig. 12.2, noise shows non-significant changes. Blip is a rare event, also referred to as an outlier. Outliers should be detected carefully, as fraud detection and intrusion detection are the few areas where outlier detection plays an important role. In gradual concept drift, the new concept replaces the old one in a gradual manner whereas the replacement of old with new occurs suddenly in sudden (or abrupt) concept drift. Figure 12.3 shows a detailed picture of gradual and sudden concept drift.

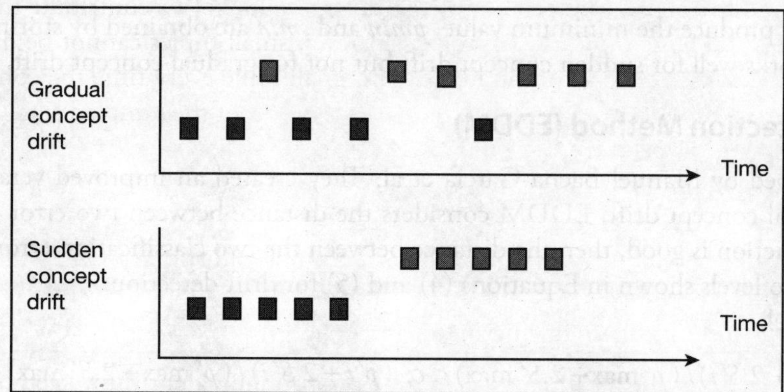

Figure 12.3 Gradual and sudden concept drift

12.6.1 Concept Drift Detection Techniques

Concept drift is an issue in data stream mining and it can be handled in two ways: passive approach and active approach. In the passive approach, the model automatically updates after a certain period of time to adapt to concept drift. This method entails high computation cost as the model frequently updates without knowing the actual existence of concept drift. No explicit drift detection techniques are applied in this approach.

The other approach uses an active strategy which explicitly checks for the existence of concept drift. If concept drift is detected, the model is updated to cope with it. This saves a lot of computation cost, thus allowing for more focus on the active strategy.

A number of drift detection techniques have been mentioned in the literature.

Drift Detection Method (DDM)

Gama et al. observed the error rate of the classifier and assumed that if there was a particular increase in errors in the algorithm, it meant that there was a change in the class distribution. So the algorithm was not classifying data correctly.

In DDM, two levels are defined in Equations (1) and (2): a warning level based on the statistical test is checked, after which change in concept may occur. After this level, examples are stored for further use. The second level is the drift level. After this level, the concept drift is proved true. So, the existing model is updated by using the example stored after the warning level to cope with concept drift.

The two levels are defined as follows:

Warning level:

$$pi + si \geq pmin + 2 \cdot sminpi + si \geq pmin + 2 \cdot smin \tag{1}$$

Drift level:

$$pi + si \geq pmin + 3 \cdot sminpi + si \geq pmin + 3 \cdot smin \tag{2}$$

where binomial distribution is used. Let us assume there are *n* examples in a sample and *i* is the point in the sequence that is considered. The error rate is the probability of misclassifying *pi*. Standard deviation is defined in Eq. (3) as

$$si = \sqrt{pi(1 - pi) / i}\sqrt{pi(1 - pi) / i} \tag{3}$$

When *pi* + *si* produce the minimum value, *pmin* and *smin* are obtained by storing the value of *pi* and *si*. DDM works well for sudden concept drift but not for gradual concept drift.

Early Drift Detection Method (EDDM)

This was developed by Manuel Baena-Garcia et al. They created an improved version of DDM to cope with gradual concept drift. EDDM considers the distance between two error classifications. If the method prediction is good, then the distance between the two classification errors will be greater.

There are two levels shown in Equations (4) and (5) for drift detection:

Warning level:

$$(p'i + 2.S'i) / (p'\max + 2.S'\max) < \alpha \ \ (p'i + 2.S'i) / (p'\max + 2.S'\max) < \alpha \tag{4}$$

Drift level:

$$(p'i + 2.S'i) / (p' \max + 2.S' \max) < \beta \ (p'i + 2.S'i) / (p' \max + 2.S' \max) < \beta \tag{5}$$

Here, $p'i$ is the average distance between two errors and $S'i$ is the standard deviation. When $p'i+2.S'i$ gives the maximum value, the values of $p'i$ and $S'i$ are stored and give the value of $p'max$ and $S'max$. If the warning level is reached, then examples are stored after that level. If the drift level is achieved, it means that after that level, concept drift is true. So, in this case, the model is updated again using the examples stored after the warning level. A minimum of 30 errors have been considered. $\alpha = 0.95$ and $\beta = 0.90$ were calculated through some experimentation.

EDDM is the most popular drift detection method. It detects gradual concept drift at an early stage. EDDM can be used with any classification method. It handles noise very well. EDDM uses the distance between classification errors instead of the number of errors.

Dynamic Concept Drift Detection (DCDD)

This was proposed by Nosrati and Pour et al. The aim was to enhance the performance of DDM and EDDM. Three levels are defined here: control, warning and alarm. It is assumed that no change occurs at the control level. Warning level and alarm level are the same as warning level and drift level, respectively, in DDM and EDDM. The significant levels are defined in Equations (6) and (7) as:

Warning level:

$$r / (n - W) > s / W \text{ and } P < ad \quad r / (n - W) > s / W \text{ and } P < ad \tag{6}$$

Alarm level:

$$r / (n - W) > s / W \text{ and } P < aw \quad r / (n - W) > s / W \text{ and } P < aw \tag{7}$$

where W = size of a window, ad = warning level, aw = drift level, n = number of examples learned by a classifier, s = number of correct classifications among the most recent W examples, r = number of correct classifications among n - W examples and P = P value test. The idea behind this approach is to compare overall accuracy with current accuracy and, if they are found to be different, it means that there is concept drift. If not, then there is no concept drift.

Drift Detection Method based on Hoeffding's Inequality (HDDM)

Here, moving averages and weighted moving averages are used. Moving averages are more helpful to detect sudden changes whereas the weighted moving average is helpful in detecting gradual changes. Three states are defined: stable, warning and drift. As in the previous methods, this method also considers that in a stable state, there is no change in the data. In the warning state, changes may appear but in the drift state, the drift has occurred.

When the warning state is achieved, the examples are stored in a buffer and later used for the learning of the new classifier. This new classifier replaces the old classifier when the drift state is achieved. The error bound $\varepsilon_\delta \varepsilon_\delta$ is defined in Eq. (8):

$$\varepsilon_\delta = \sqrt{\frac{1}{2n} \ln \frac{1}{\delta}} \varepsilon_\delta = \sqrt{\frac{1}{2n} \ln \frac{1}{\delta}} \tag{8}$$

HDDM works well for both gradual and sudden concept drift detection as it requires less time and memory.

Error Distance-based Approach for Drift Detection (EDIST)

This is an advanced approach. The basic concept of EDIST is the same as EDDM. The difference is that EDIST uses two data windows for detection of concept drift whereas EDDM uses the distance between two classification errors. Among the two windows, the first is a global window that keeps recently read examples while the second keeps the current collected examples. EDIST has three levels for the detection of concept drift:

- Control level: No change takes place here.
- Warning level: Change may happen; so the examples are stored for the future when this level is achieved.
- Drift level: The concept drift is true and a global window is used to keep the examples after the warning level; this global window is then used for relearning of the model.

EDIST works well with synthetic and real-world data sets. However, it cannot handle data when a fast drift has occurred.

Detection by Statistical Testing of Equal Proportions (STEPD)

This was proposed by Nishida. STEPD works on the basis of two accuracies: one is recent accuracy, which is gained from recent examples, and the second is overall accuracy, which is gained by considering the whole data set but not the recent examples. It was assumed that if the target concept was stationary, then the accuracy of the recent examples would be the same as overall accuracy. So, if the recent accuracy decreases, it means there is concept drift.

STEPD has two levels: warning and drift. When $\hat{p}\hat{p}$ is less than the warning level, the examples are stored in memory for further use, and when $\hat{p}\hat{p}$ is less than the drift level, the model is relearned with the stored examples. $\hat{p}\hat{p}$ is calculated as follows:

$$\hat{p}\hat{p} = (r_0 + r_r)/(n_0 + n_r) \tag{9}$$

STEPD compares the measure T, which is defined as:

$$T(r_0, r_r, n_0, n_r) = \frac{\left|\frac{r_0}{n_0} - \frac{r_r}{n_r}\right| - 0.5\left(\frac{1}{n_0} + \frac{1}{n_r}\right)}{\sqrt{\hat{p}(1-\hat{p})\left(\frac{1}{n_0} + \frac{1}{n_r}\right)}} \; T(r_0, r_r, n_0, n_r) = \frac{\left|\frac{r_0}{n_0} - \frac{r_r}{n_r}\right| - 0.5\left(\frac{1}{n_0} + \frac{1}{n_r}\right)}{\sqrt{\hat{p}(1-\hat{p})\left(\frac{1}{n_0} + \frac{1}{n_r}\right)}} \tag{10}$$

where $r_0\, r_0$ = number of correct classifications for overall examples $n_0 n_0$ but not including recent examples and $r_r r_r$= number of correct classifications for the recent examples $n_r n_r$.

12.7 Data Stream Classification

Here, the data stream is taken as input for the classifier and a learning model is created on its basis. Once the model is created, it can be used to predict/classify unknown data streams. The classifier should be capable of handling data stream mining issues. It can be of two types: single and ensemble.

12.7.1 Single Classifier

A single classifier can process data quickly and give results in a small amount of time. In the case of data streams, the single classifier's performance is poor as the volume of data is very high. If new data enters the data stream, the single classifier will not be able to handle concept drift properly. So it is not suitable for data stream mining. Examples of single classifiers are Bayesian classifier, decision trees, naïve Bayes', SVM and nearest neighbour.

12.7.2 Ensemble Classifier

The concept of ensemble classifier is an innovation in the field of data mining. In the ensemble classification method, all the classifiers in the ensemble work collaboratively to classify the data stream (Fig. 12.4). A group of classifiers gives a better performance than a single classifier. It can also handle data streams properly as it can adapt to changes and it gives good accuracy. The classifiers in the ensemble can be similar or different.

Ensemble classifiers can be created using:

- A single learning method with different subsets of training data
- Different learning methods

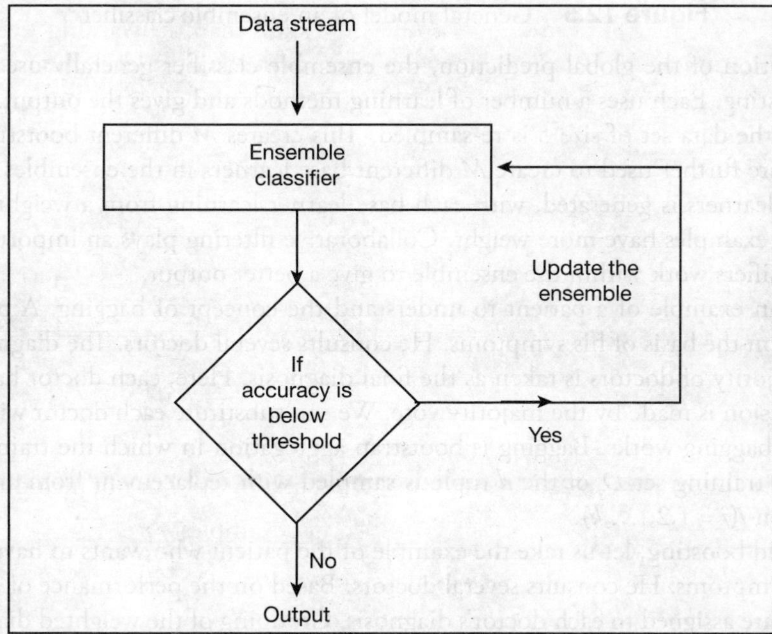

Figure 12.4 Basic structure of ensemble classification and updating

A data stream is provided as input to the ensemble classifier. It tries to classify the given input using the base (or individual) classifier predictions, after training, and combines their predictions to give a global prediction. If the prediction given by any classifier is below the specified threshold, the ensemble is updated (a new classifier is added and a poorly performing one is removed). This will help the ensemble to improve its performance (Fig. 12.5).

Ensemble classifiers cope with concept drift by updating the model frequently. They thus have greater accuracy. However, along with accuracy, there are two more important parameters: time and memory. To obtain a good performance, selection of base learners is very important.

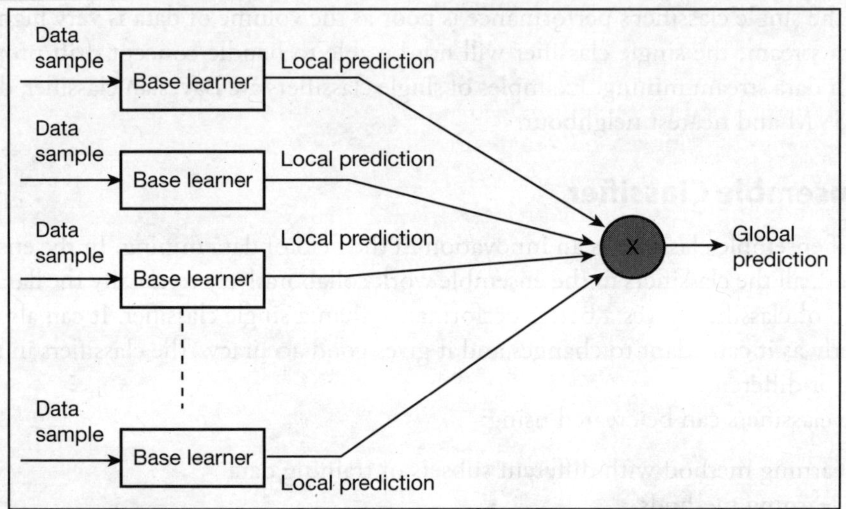

Figure 12.5 General model of an ensemble classifier

For computation of the global prediction, the ensemble classifier generally used two methods: bagging and boosting. Each uses a number of learning methods and gives the output.

In **bagging**, the data set of size *S* is re-sampled. This creates *M* different bootstrap training sets of size *S*, which are further used to create *M* different base learners in the ensembles. In **boosting**, a series of *M* base learners is generated, with each base learner learning from a weighted training set. The misclassified examples have more weight. Collaborative filtering plays an important role in how the different classifiers work within the ensemble to give a better output.

Let us take an example of a patient to understand the concept of bagging. A patient wants to have a diagnosis on the basis of his symptoms. He consults several doctors. The diagnosis that is suggested by the majority of doctors is taken as the final diagnosis. Here, each doctor has an equal vote and the final decision is made by the majority vote. We can substitute each doctor with a classifier to understand how bagging works. Bagging is bootstrap aggregation in which the training set is bootstrap-sampled. A training set D_i of the d tuple is sampled with replacement from an original set of tuples for iteration $i (i = 1,2,\ldots,k)$.

To understand boosting, let us take the example of the patient who wants to have a diagnosis on the basis of his symptoms. He consults several doctors. Based on the performance of the previous diagnoses, weights are assigned to each doctor's diagnosis. Grouping of the weighted diagnoses will give the final diagnosis. We can substitute each doctor with a classifier to understand how boosting works.

Each training tuple is assigned a weight. A group of classifiers is trained. When a classifier M_i is trained, the weights are updated so that the next classifier M_{i+1} will give more attention to the examples that were incorrectly classified by M_i. The final output will be the combination of each classifier's vote where the accuracy of that classifier will determine the weight of its vote.

Suppose there is an ensemble with m base learners from $h_1,\ldots\ldots,h_m$. A weighted training set has been maintained. Each base learner h_m is trained from the weighted training set whose weights are calculated by the classification errors of the preceding model h_{m-1}. In particular, the examples misclassified by h_{m-1} are given more weight in the training set for h_m such that the weights of all the misclassified examples constitute half the total weight of the training set. The same procedure is illustrated in Fig. 12.6.

Here 'a' is the training example that is given to the first model h_1. But h_1 misclassified it, so the weight of the misclassified example should be increased. The height of example 'b' is more than 'a'. Similarly, 'b' is given to the next model that correctly classifies it, so the weight of the example decreases. The height of 'c' is less than 'b'. Similarly, for all the levels of the model, the weight of the example is updated based on the output of the previous model. The corresponding algorithm is shown in Fig. 12.7.

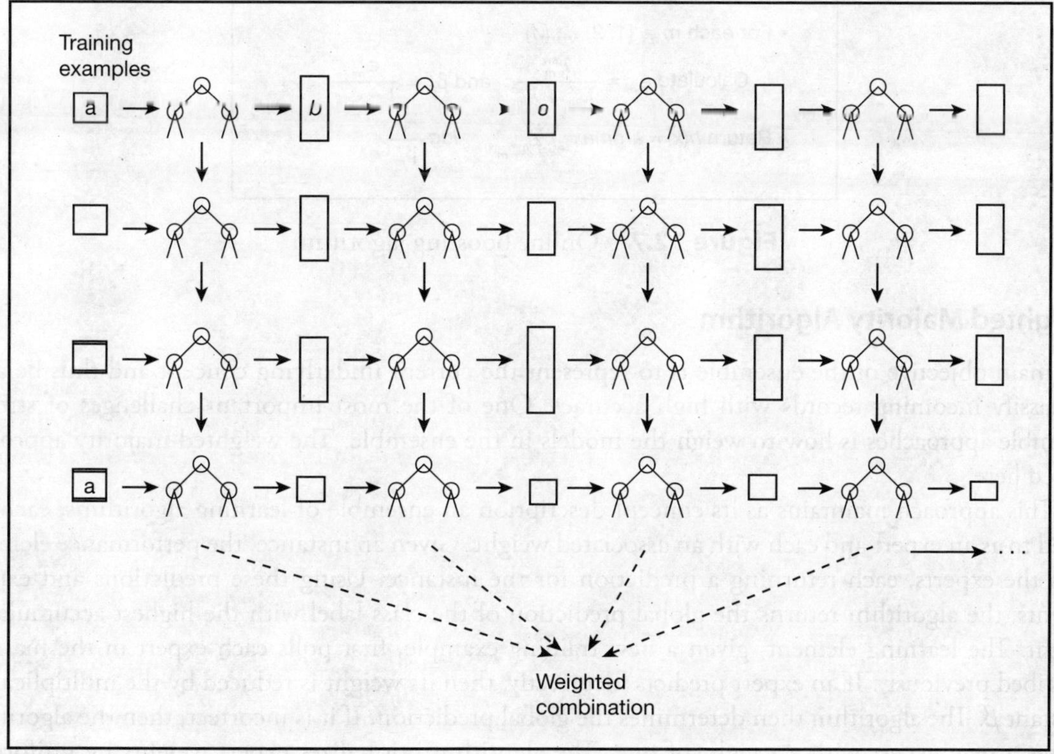

Figure 12.6 General concept of online boosting

Online Boosting (h_M, *OnlineBase, d*)

- Set the example's "weight" $\lambda_d = 1$.
- For each base model h_m, ($m \in \{1, 2, \ldots M\}$) in the ensemble,
  - 1. Set *k* according to *poisson* (λ_d).
  - 2. Do k times
    h_m = *Online Base* (h_m, *d*)
  - 3. If h_m (*d*) is the correct label,
    - * then
      - $\lambda_m^{sc} \longleftarrow \lambda_m^{sc} + \lambda_d$
      - $\lambda_d \longleftarrow \lambda_d \left(\frac{N}{2\lambda_m^{sc}} \right)$
    - * else
      - $\lambda_m^{sw} \longleftarrow \lambda_m^{sw} + \lambda_d$
      - $\lambda_d \longleftarrow \lambda_d \left(\frac{N}{2\lambda_m^{sw}} \right)$

To classify new examples:

- For each $m \in \{1, 2, \ldots, M\}$
  Calculate $\epsilon_m = \frac{\lambda_m^{sw}}{\lambda_m^{sc} + \lambda_m^{sc}}$ and $\beta_m = \frac{\epsilon_m}{1 - \epsilon_m}$
- Return $h(x) = argmax_{c \in C} \sum_{m:h_m(x) = y} log \frac{1}{\beta_m}$.

Figure 12.7 Online boosting algorithm

Weighted Majority Algorithm

The main objective of the ensemble is to represent the current underlying concept and thus be able to classify incoming records with high accuracy. One of the most important challenges of stream ensemble approaches is how to weigh the models in the ensemble. The weighted majority approach is used here.

This approach maintains as its concept description an ensemble of learning algorithms, each referred to as an expert and each with an associated weight. Given an instance, the performance element polls the experts, each returning a prediction for the instance. Using these predictions and expert weights, the algorithm returns the global prediction of the class label with the highest accumulated weight. The learning element, given a new training example, first polls each expert in the manner described previously. If an expert predicts incorrectly, then its weight is reduced by the multiplicative constant β. The algorithm then determines the global prediction. If it is incorrect, then the algorithm creates a new expert with a weight of one. The algorithm normalizes expert weights by uniformly scaling them such that the highest weight will be equal to one. This prevents any newly added experts from dominating the decision making of existing ones. The algorithm also removes experts with weights less than the user-defined threshold θ. Finally, the algorithm passes the training example to each expert's learning element. Note that normalizing weights and incrementally training all experts gives the base learners an opportunity to recover from concept drift. Large and noisy problems require the parameter p, which governs the frequency at which the weighted majority creates experts, removes them and updates their weights.

Base Learner

The base learner is used to learn a model that represents the data stream's underlying concept. Any classification algorithm that can learn incrementally and which treats each feature independently can be used for this task. The base learner can be selected according to the nature of the data to be mined, choosing the algorithm that best suits it (such as high accuracy, noise handling, memory consumed and faster processing time). We use the Hoeffding tree algorithm as the base learner.

Hoeffding Tree

This is an incremental, any-time decision tree induction algorithm that is capable of learning from massive data streams, assuming that the distribution generating examples does not change over time. Hoeffding trees exploit the fact that a small sample can often be enough to choose an optimal splitting attribute. This idea is supported mathematically by the Hoeffding bound, which quantifies the number of observations (or examples) needed to estimate some statistics within a prescribed precision (such as the goodness of an attribute). More precisely, the Hoeffding bound states that with probability $1 - \delta$, the true mean of a random variable of range R will not differ from the estimated mean after n independent observations by more than:

$$\varepsilon = \sqrt{\frac{R^2 \ln\left(\frac{1}{\delta}\right)}{2n}}$$

$$\varepsilon = \sqrt{\frac{R^2 \ln\left(\frac{1}{\delta}\right)}{2n}}$$

The Hoeffding tree induction algorithm induces a decision tree from a data stream incrementally, briefly inspecting each example in the stream only once, without needing to store the examples after they have been used to update the tree. The only information stored in memory is the tree itself, which has sufficient information in its leaves in order to grow, and can be used to form predictions at any point in time between processing training examples.

Partition of Data

As the data stream is massive in volume, partitioning of data for classification is very important. The windowing concept is used for this purpose..

The adaptive sliding window is used in ensemble classification. A window is maintained that keeps the most recent examples. According to some set of rules, the older examples are dropped from the window. This technique does not store the whole window explicitly but instead stores only the statistics required for further computation.

1. Initialize the window W.
2. Initialize the width, variance and total.
3. For each $t > 0$
   set input(X_t, W)
   The window W is partitioned into two sub-windows
4. If change is detected, drop the old window.

5. Update the width, variance and total.
6. Change the alarm level.
7. Use the current data of the new window to update the learning model.
8. End for

12.8 Rare Class Problem

Imbalanced data is one of the main issues in data classification. The skewed nature of data makes its classification difficult. A number of data sets suffer from the problem of class imbalance, such as medical data, where normal data outnumbers the examples of disease but minority samples are more important than the majority data. Misclassification of minority samples carries very high risk in medical science. Intrusion detection, fault detection, anomaly detection and detection of fraudulent telephone calls are other examples of imbalanced datasets.

Thus, we need techniques that can deal with imbalance in data sets. We also need evaluation parameters or techniques that show the clear classification status of minority samples. Most algorithms do not bother about the distribution of classes in the data set. So the same data set will be directly used for classification and result in a bad detection rate for minority classes. Figure 12.8 shows class imbalanced problems. Here, the rectangle shows the minority class samples whereas the circle shows the majority class samples. We have drawn a decision boundary to separate the minority and majority classes but it is not easy to classify the minority class efficiently through the classifier as it is trained with the majority class.

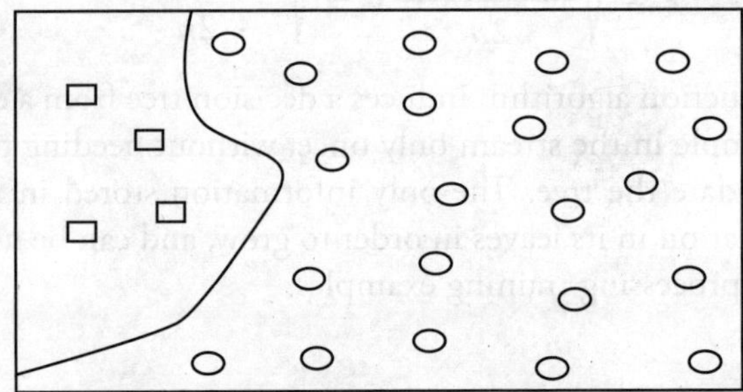

Figure 12.8 Imbalanced data set

A data-level approach tries to balance the data set first and then apply the classification. The second approach is the algorithmic approach, where an algorithm is designed to handle the rare class problems. The third approach is the hybrid approach in which the data-level approach as well as the algorithmic approach are combined to handle the rare class problem.

12.9 Issues, Controversies and Problems

A good algorithm handles the different issues of data stream mining. Data that grows continuously in volume and in speed and which results in changes in the underlying concepts are the challenges of data stream mining.

The two fundamental issues in data stream mining are:

- **Issues related to performance**: As the data stream flows continuously, a lot of memory and time is required to store and process it. To address this issue, the algorithm used for data stream mining should have the following properties:
  - o As the data flows continuously and rapidly, the algorithm should be able to scan the data in one pass.
  - o As the data volume is high, the algorithm should not store all the data in memory; rather only important statistics related to the model should be stored.

  Even if an algorithm takes minimal time and memory, incorrect predictions will be of no use. So accuracy is another important parameter.
- **Issues related to adaptation**: In data mining, the underlying concepts that map the features to class labels are not variable. However, in data streams, the underlying concepts that map features to class labels are variable; this is known as concept drift. Handling concept drift is a big concern in data stream mining. An algorithm which has learned from the data stream but where concept drifts may occur at any time and to which the algorithm cannot adapt would be of no use. A good algorithm needs to adapt to the changes and handle concept drift properly.

Evaluating the accuracy of a classifier: Different techniques are used to assess accuracy:

- **Holdout method**: The given data set is randomly partitioned into training set and testing set. The training set is used to build the model whereas the testing set is used to test the model.
- **Random subsampling**: It is a variation of the holdout method. The holdout method is repeated *n* times in the random subsampling and the average of the accuracy will give the final overall accuracy.
- **Cross validation**: In *n*-fold cross validation, the data is randomly partitioned into *n* partitions. Each partition is a subset of the data set of equal size and mutually exclusive subsets $D_1, D_2 .... D_n$. In the ith iteration, D_i is used as the test set and the remaining $n - 1$ sets are used for training the model.
- **Bootstrap**: Here, the given tuples are sampled uniformly with replacement. The model can select the same tuple more than once.

Limitations of data stream mining: Various issues related to data stream mining have already been discussed in the chapter. The main limitations of data stream mining are:

- As the data volume is huge, we need to sample the data. Sampling of data is closely related to accuracy. If we choose the proper sampling method, the accuracy increases.
- All parameters are not useful for the analysis of data. Some attributes contribute more towards classification while others do not. So the selection of attributes that are important for classification is significant. If we choose the wrong attributes for classification then it will affect the accuracy of the model.
- The time and memory requirements of data stream mining are greater than in traditional data mining. If the ensemble classifier is used for classification of data streams, its accuracy is also affected by other parameters such as how many classifiers are grouped to prepare an ensemble. If the number of classifiers is greater, it will take more time and more memory for classification as each classifier needs to give its own prediction and then all these predictions are combined to give the final prediction. The input parameters also play an important role, such as selection of attribute, weight of each classifier or weight of each tuple if boosting is used. The size of the window is also important if the windowing technique is used.

12.10 Applications of Data Mining

- **Financial Analysis**: Banks and financial institutes provide a number of services like credit cards, loans, insurance and stock investment. Data mining can be applied on financial data to predict the future. Using data mining, classification and clustering of customers for targeted marketing can be performed. Financial crimes and money laundering are big threats to the financial industry, but with the help of data mining techniques, this can be detected and reduced as well. Similarly, credit card fraud can also be avoided by using data mining techniques. Before granting a loan, analysis is carried out for loan payment prediction.
- **Retail Industry**: Today, online shopping is very popular. A wide number of websites offer online shopping. This leads to a huge volume of data. Data mining on this retail data discloses the customer's choices, buying behaviours, shopping patterns and trends. This will help to increase the quality of customer services; goods consumption ratio is increased and customer satisfaction and retention reduce the cost of business.
- **Recommendation Systems**: When a customer shops online, there are a number of products available in the websites. Recommender systems recommend different products to the consumers related to their choice, like online news articles, CDs, books, etc. Recommender systems may use a content-based approach, collaborative approach or a hybrid approach. In the content-based approach, items are recommended to the user on the basis of a query entered by the user in the past. In the collaborative method, the recommendations are given to the user based on other choices of other users who show similar interests. In the hybrid approach, a combination of a content-based approach and a collaborative approach is used.
- **Intrusion Detection**: Security is a primary requirement of all networks. There is a huge volume of data generated by the networks. So data mining techniques come into the picture to deal with it. To preserve data security and prevent attacks, intrusion detection systems (IDS) are used. The classification technique of data mining is frequently used for IDS. Standard data sets are available such as KDD CUP 99. Most researchers make use of this standard data set and apply a number of data mining techniques for practical experimental purposes.
- **Healthcare**: This is another area where data mining techniques play an important role. A number of decision support systems give assistance to doctors to maximize the accuracy levels. Analysis can be performed for different symptoms of diseases and to find the exact diagnosis based on different data mining techniques. It is difficult to analyze continuous data like ECG in an electrical signal which is generated by the heart. Wireless sensors can be used to monitor signals like ECG, EEG and BP. These sensors generate continuous data that is dynamic in nature; data stream mining algorithms are used to handle this type of data.

Rare class problems are widely available in the world. There are a wide variety of applications in which rare class problems exist. We have listed a few of them:

- **Scene classification:** An ensemble SVM can be used for handling rare class problems in scene classification.
- **Remote sensing data classification:** Mine classification is an example of remote sensing classification. Here, the number of targets (mines) are very few than other normal data. Infinitely imbalanced logistic regression (IILR) is used to solve rare class problems in mine classification.

- **Predicting final grades:** Nowadays educational mining is very popular. Applying data mining techniques in the educational domain raises the standard of the education system. Many re-sampling approaches like SMOTE, random over-sampling and random under-sampling are used to balance imbalanced data sets and improve the prediction rate for final grades.
- **Customer behaviour prediction:** Most real-world applications suffer from imbalanced data. Many rare class balancing techniques can be used for customer behaviour prediction.

12.11 Implementation of Data Streams in Python

In Python, data streams can be implemented using generators, iterators and iterables. The iteration pattern simply allows us go over a sequence without materializing all its items explicitly at once.

We can use two approaches to handle data streams. Approach 1 is to create an array of squares, and then use `sum()` to loop over it. Here, there is sequential access for iteration of the list. Approach 2 uses generators. Elements are evaluated in the stream and arrays are not created.

```
numbers = range(100000)
```

Approach 1:

```
sum([n**2 for n in numbers])
333328333350000
```

Approach 2

```
sum(n**2 for n in numbers)
333328333350000
```

An iterator is an object that manages a single pass over a sequence. Iterators are used mostly to iterate or convert other objects to an iterator using the `iter()` function. Generators are mostly used in loops to generate an iterator by returning all the values in the loop without affecting the iteration of the loop. Both iterables and generators produce an iterator, allowing us to carry out *"for record in iterable_or_generator: ..."* without worrying about keeping track of where we are in the stream, how to get to the next item, how to stop iterating, and so on.

To create a generator object and iterate to each word in string and print. Add exclamation marks after each word.

```
generator = (word + '!' for word in 'I love my India'.split())
for val in generator:
  print (val)
I!
love!
my!
India!
If you execute it once more
for val in generator:
  print (val)
```

It will not print any word because there is no more data; the generator stream is exhausted.

On the other hand, an iterable creates a new iterator every time it is looped over. The iterable interface is: return an iterator from `__iter__()`. So implementing `__iter__` as a generator is the easiest way to create streamed iterables. Every generator is an iterator implicitly.

```
class BeyonceIterable(object):
  def __iter__(self):
     for word in 'I love my India'.split():
        yield word + '!'
Iterator is created here:
iterable = BeyonceIterable()
for val in iterable:
  print (val)
I!
love!
my!
India!
Another iterator is created here:
for val in iterable:
  print (val)
```

Output:
I!
love!
my!
India!

So iterables are more universally useful than generators because we can go over the sequence more than once. If the data stream comes from a source that cannot be readily repeated (such as hardware sensors), a single pass through a generator may be the only option.

```
from google.colab import files
uploaded = files.upload()
for fn in uploaded.keys():
  print('User uploaded file "{name}" with length {length} bytes'.format(
      name=fn, length=len(uploaded[fn])))
with open("testassociate.txt", "r") as f:
    mylist = [l for l in f if "am" in l]

for item in mylist:
    print(item)
```

Output:
I am associate professor

Here is the output from file.txt for all the rows that have a "am" substring

If you expand the generator expression from the code above into a full generator function, you will get something like this:

```
def my_generator(step=4):
    with open("testassociate.txt", "r") as f:
        for l in f:
            if "am" in l:
                yield l

myiterator = my_generator()
for item in myiterator:
    print(item)
We have the output from all strings of file.txt where there is a "am"
substring
I am associate professor
from __future__ import print_function

import itertools

def my_generator3():
    # Infinite counter
    counter = itertools.count()
    while True:
        yield next(counter)

myiterator = my_generator3()
myiterator2 = my_generator3()

for item in myiterator:
    print(item, end=" ")
    if item == 3:
        # Let's close the generator in the right way
        myiterator.close()
print()

for item in myiterator2:
    print(item, end=" ")
    if item == 2:
        # Everything's terrible
        myiterator2.throw(Exception("Everything is bad"))
print()
```

Output:
0 1 2 3
0 1 2

Exception Traceback (most recent call last)
<ipython-input-34-bce7250d5b68> in <module>()
23 if item == 2:
24 # Everything's terrible
---> 25 myiterator2.throw(Exception("Everything is bad"))
26 print()

<ipython-input-34-bce7250d5b68> in my_generator3()
7 counter = itertools.count()
8 while True:
----> 9 yield next(counter)
10
11 myiterator = my_generator3()
Exception: Everything is bad

With `close()`, we can make the generator stop when it is called the next time, and with the help of `throw()`, we make it throw an exception. The `send ()` method allows you to send data to the generator before calling the next block of the code.

```
from __future__ import print_function

import itertools

def my_coroutine():
    # Infinite counter
    counter = itertools.count()
    while True:
        y = (yield next(counter))
        if y:
            # Let's change the initial point of the counting
            counter = itertools.count(y)

myiterator = my_coroutine()

for item in myiterator:
    print(item, end=" ")
    if item == 1:
        # Let's send the number to the generator
        myiterator.send(4)
    elif item == 6:
        myiterator.close()
print()
```

Output: 0 1 5 6

EXERCISES

Multiple Choice Questions

1. Which attribute is not an indicator for data streaming?
   (a) Limited amount of memory
   (b) Limited amount of processing time
   (c) Limited amount of input data
   (d) Limited amount of processing power
2. Which of the following statements about data streaming is true?
   (a) Stream data is always unstructured.

(b) Stream data often has high velocity.
(c) Stream elements cannot be stored on a disk.
(d) Stream data is always structured.

3. Which of the following statements about sampling is correct?
(a) Sampling reduces the number of data fed to a subsequent data mining algorithm.
(b) Sampling reduces the diversity of the data stream.
(c) Sampling increases the amount of elements in a data stream.
(d) Sampling increases the amount of data fed to a data mining algorithm.

4. Which of the following is a generator expression?
(a) [*x***2 for *x* in my_list]
(b) (*x***2 for *x* in my_list)
(c) {*x***2 for *x* in my_list}
(d) *x***2 for *x* in my_list

Answers

1. (c) **2.** (b) **3.** (b) **4.** (b)

Programming/Concept-based Questions

1. What are the different ways to apply classification methods in order to improve the accuracy rates of a medical data set?

Answer:

- By excluding anomalous values and contradictions.
- By including the factors that strongly influence the objective function.
- By adding examples.
- By using decision trees or rules to yield valuable insights.

2. Suggest a classification technique for streaming data; that is, a class is defined by a set of patterns.

Answer:

- Decision trees for data streams
- Rule-based methods for data streams
- Nearest neighbour methods for data streams
- SVM methods for data streams
- Neural network classifiers for data streams
- Ensemble methods for data streams

3. Which algorithm is better for classification and clustering among SVM and k-means in data streams?

Answer: SVM and k-means are very different algorithms. SVM is supervised (supervised classification) and k-means is unsupervised (clustering).

For supervised classification, SVM is the best algorithm and very precise; that is, the most efficient kernel (linear, RBF, etc...). For clustering, k-means is one of the simplest ways to aggregate samples. Two parameters need to be taken in account: the number of clusters a priori (classes) and the metric such as Euclidean, Mahalanobis, etc.

4. How can we collect the timeline tweets of specific users using stream API in Python?
   Answer:
   Step 1: In Python, import TweePy and set up the authentication and stream listener with API keys.
   Step 2: Create the StreamListener class. In the same file, create a new class called StreamListener that inherits from TweePy's StreamListener class and overrides the on_status and on_error methods so that we can customize it.
   Step 3: Initialize the stream with filters. Start the stream by specifying the tags we want to use to filter tweets.
   Step 4: Process and store data.
   Step 5: Handling retweets, extended tweets and quote tweets.
   Step 6: Share with collaborators.

5. Which is the best method to detect concept drift (model accuracy or distribution difference)?
   Answer: It depends on the goal for drift detection (to understand the data behaviour over time or to update a classification model), the expected type of change (real/virtual), and whether access to labeled data is allowed. For example, if the change occurs only in *P*(*X*) - virtual drift, it cannot be detected by error monitoring. However, it can be detected by comparing the distributions using labeled or unlabeled data. This kind of change does not impact the accuracy of a classifier, but their identification can help to understand the process of data generation. On the other hand, if the change occurs only in *P*(*Y*|*X*) - real drift, it can be identified by error monitoring and by comparing the distribution using labeled data.

6. How can we detect noise from real streams?
   Answer:
   - The sliding nested window technique
   - Random forest and genetic algorithm to analyze noisy data
   - Reverse indexing and incremental clustering in noisy data streams
   - Classifying data streams using an adaptive random forest (ARF) algorithm

7. What are the concept drift detection methods? How can you choose this method in data streams and is there a preferable method?
   Answer:
   - Drift Detection Method (DDM) (Preferable)
   - Early Drift Detection Method (EDDM)
   - Dynamic Concept Drift Detection (DCDD)
   - Drift Detection Method based on Hoeffding's Inequality (HDDM)
   - Detection Method Using Statistical Testing STEPD

   HDDM considers that in a stable state, there is no change in the data. In the warning state, changes may appear but in the drift state, a drift has occurred.
   STEPD works on the basis of two accuracies: recent, which is gained from recent examples, and overall, which is gained by considering the whole data set but not the recent examples.

8. How can we assess the performance of an ensemble that results from an optimization framework?

Answer: The simplest way is by selecting a set of M models, creating N replications and getting the statistics. This is a highly skewed approach, as it only considers the randomness of ensemble creation, but not the randomness of the optimization technique.
An alternative is creating N replications and, for each of them, running the entire method (from hyper parameter optimization to ensemble creation). Then, take the statistics for the N measures. Create N replications and, for each of them, run the optimization algorithm and create K ensembles. In the end, we could extract statistics from all K*N measures.

9. Which is the most accurate algorithm for ensemble learning with a categorical data set?
Answer: Random forest algorithm.

BIBLIOGRAPHY

1. Dongre, S and Wankhade, K. 2012. Intrusion Detection System Using New Ensemble Boosting Approach. *International Journal of Modeling and Optimization* 2(4): 488–492.
2. Dongre, S, Malik, L and Thomas, A. 2016. Modality of Ensemble Boosting Classifier for concept drift handling in Evolving Data Streams. *International Journal KASMERA*, 44(2): 20–44
3. Wankhade, K and Dongre, S. 2012. A New Adaptive Ensemble Boosting Classifier for Concept Drifting Stream Data. *International Journal of Modeling and Optimization* 2(4): 493–497
4. Gilbert, AC, Kotidis, Y, Muthukrishnan, S and Strauss, M. 2001. Surfing wavelets on streams: One-pass summaries for approximate aggregate queries. *VLDB* 79–88.
5. Rozenbaum, I. *Filtering Techniques For Data Streams*, Dissertation, The Graduate School-New Brunswick Rutgers, The State University of New Jersey
6. Dongre, S and Malik, L. *Analysis and Designing of Classification Methods for Data Stream Mining*, Dissertation, Rastrasant Tukdoji Maharaj Nagpur University, Nagpur
7. “Data Streaming in Python”. Rare Technologies. https://rare-technologies.com/data-streaming-in-python-generators-iterators-iterables/#:~:text=There%20are%20tools%20and%20concepts,neatly%20and%20natively%20in%20Python
8. “Let’s tame data streams in Python”. HackMag. https://hackmag.com/coding/lets-tame-data-streams-with-python/
9. “Big data, streams and samples”. https://chauff.github.io/documents/bdp-quiz/streaming.html

CHAPTER 13

Language Data Processing in Python

Learning Objectives

At the end of this chapter, you will be able to:

- Explain the components of natural language processing
- Perform text processing such as tokenization and lexicon normalization of text data
- Remove stopwords and pre-process text data using regular expressions
- Perform part-of-speech tagging and vectorization on text data
- Demonstrate CGI/web programming in Python
- Apply language data processing in various real-life cases such as review and recommendation systems

13.0 Natural Language Processing

Text and speech are the most common forms of unstructured data. Such data contains rich information. Extracting useful information from text is difficult and time-consuming. Humans have the ability to extract important information from written text. Natural language processing (NLP) is used to perform the task of extracting information and analyzing text data (Fig. 13.1). Tasks such as sentiment analysis, cognitive assistance, fake news identification, real-time language translation and chatbot construction can be performed using NLP.

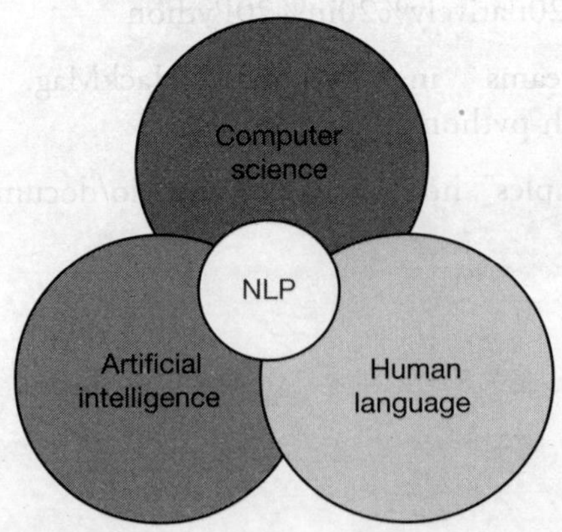

Figure 13.1 Natural language processing

NLP has two components: natural language understanding (NLU) and natural language generation (NLG). NLU extracts metadata such as concepts, entities, keywords, relations, emotions and semantics from text and helps in understanding and analyzing human language. The analyzed data must then be converted into natural language form, which requires text planning, sentence planning and text realization. NLG works as a translator to perform these tasks.

NLP has basic five steps:

- Lexical analysis
- Syntactic analysis
- Semantic analysis
- Discourse integration
- Pragmatic analysis

The first phase of NLP is **lexical analysis**, which divides the text into paragraphs, sentences and words and converts it into meaningful lexemes. In linguistics, a **lexeme** is a basic abstract unit of meaning that approximately corresponds to a collection of forms that one root word can take. The second step, **syntactic analysis or parsing**, is used to check the grammar and word arrangement and show the relationship among the words. Next, **semantic analysis** focuses on the literal meaning of the words, phrases and sentences. This step is concerned with representation of meaning. In NLP, the meaning of the sentence depends on the sentences that precede it and follow it. **Discourse integration** helps to perform this task. The fifth and the last phase of NLP is **pragmatic analysis**. It helps us discover the intended effect by applying a set of rules that characterize cooperative dialogues.

13.1 Text Processing in Python

Python has a toolkit called NLTK to perform text processing and text-related operations. The basic steps of text processing in NLTK are discussed in this section.

13.1.1 Tokenization

Tokenization is the first step in text processing using NLTK. Here, the paragraphs are broken down into smaller components.

To convert paragraphs into sentences or chunks of words, NLTK and its sub-package Punkt are used:

```
import nltk
nltk.download('punkt')
```

To tokenize text into sentences, we use the function `sent_tokenize()`:

```
#sentence tokenization
from nltk.tokenize import sent_tokenize
fulltext="""This is a syntax of paragraph in python programming.
Hello participants we are learning about NLP.
First step is tokenization"""
tokenized_texts=sent_tokenize(fulltext)
print('TOKENIZED TEXT IS:',tokenized_texts)
```

Output:
TOKENIZED TEXT IS: ['This is a syntax of paragraph in python programming.', 'Hello participants we are learning about NLP.', 'First step is tokenization']

Next, to tokenize text into words, we use the function `word_tokenize()`:

```
#word Tokenizing
from nltk.tokenize import word_tokenize
tokenized_wordset=word_tokenize(fulltext)
print('TOKENIZED WORDS ARE:', tokenized_wordset)
```

Output:
TOKENIZED WORDS ARE: ['This', 'is', 'a', 'syntax', 'of', 'paragraph', 'in', 'python', 'programming', '.', 'Hello', 'participants', 'we', 'are', 'learning', 'about', 'NLP', '.', 'First', 'step', 'is', 'tokenization']

13.1.2 Frequency Distribution

To calculate the frequency distribution of words, we use the function `FreqDist()`:

```
from nltk.probability import FreqDist
fdist=FreqDist(tokenized_wordset)#should pass the words list
print(fdist)
```

Output: <FreqDist with 20 samples and 22 outcomes>

To find the most frequent patterns, we use the function `most_common()`:

```
fdist.most_common(5)
```

Output: [('is', 2), ('.', 2), ('This', 1), ('a', 1), ('syntax', 1)]

To draw the frequency distribution plot:

```
#To plot frequency distribution plot, import  matplotlib.pyplot
import matplotlib.pyplot as plts
fdist.plot(30,cumulative=False) # (here max no of words i.e frequency is
30, and as  words are getting repeated cumulative=false is set)
plts.show() #reexecting bcoz 1st time i"ll store in memeory and then
it"ll display plot
```

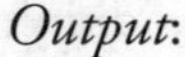

Output:

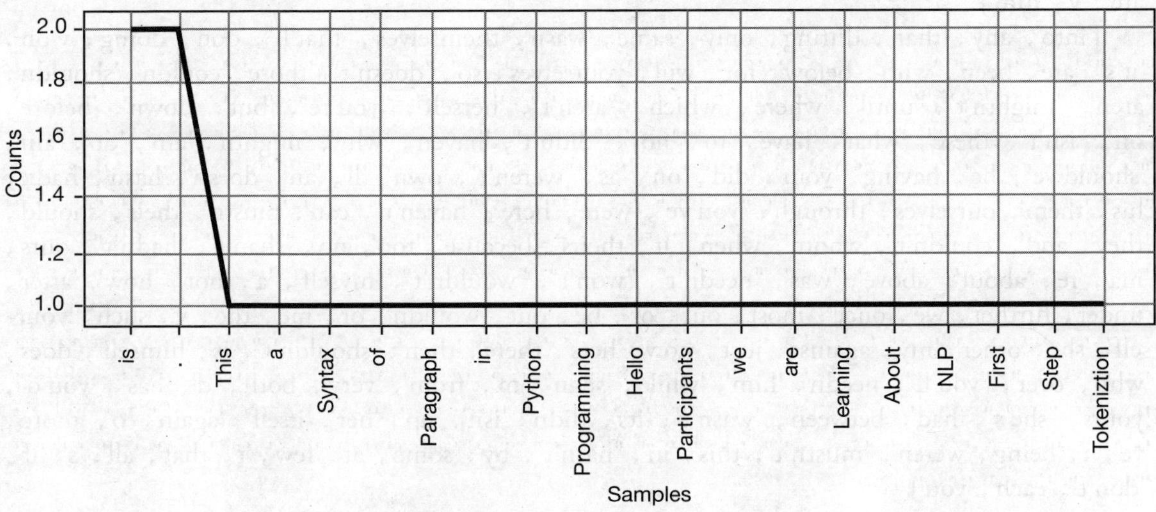

13.1.3 Stopwords

Words such as 'is', 'am', 'are', 'the', 'a', 'an', 'this' and 'that' are called stopwords; they are considered as noise in the text.

```
from nltk.corpus import stopwords
nltk.download('stopwords')
stop_wordset=set(stopwords.words("english"))
print(stop_wordset)
```

The following stopwords will be downloaded from NLTK data after execution of the above code:

{'we', 'will', "won't", 'she', 'here', 'can', 'against', 'while', 're', 'isn', 'when', 'only', 'now', 'do', "you'd", 'having', 'ourselves', 'both', "shouldn't", 'hers', 'those', 'doing', 'won', 'above', "you've", 'i', "haven't", 'as', 'for', 'off', 'some', 'our', 'from', 'weren', 'any', 'so', 'ours', "wasn't", 'to', 'which', "should've", 'where', 'they', 'because', 'too', 'not', 'how', "it's", 'herself', 'shan', 'below', "you're", 'and', 'its', 'through', 'other', 'on', 'yourself', 'should', 'by', 'such', 'been', "hasn't", 'under', 'aren', 'all', 'in', 've', 'hadn', 'hasn', "hadn't", 'during', 'until', 'most', 'o', 'has', 'have', 'is', 'once', 'me', "isn't", 'but', 'yourselves', 'shouldn', 'itself', 't', 'what', "she's", 'again', "wouldn't", 'be', 'their', "needn't", 'did', 'than', 'wasn', "don't", 'll', 'mustn', 'before', 'few', "that'll", 'just', 'does', "weren't", 'up', "mustn't", 'needn', 'if', 'same', "doesn't", 'down', 'them', 'was', 'being', 'wouldn', 'themselves', 'it', 'further', 'the', 'couldn', 'no', 's', 'after', "aren't", 'or', 'doesn', 'why', 'don', 'of', 'this', 'with', 'mightn', 'each', 'at', 'ma', 'who', 'her', 'were', 'these', "didn't", 'yours', 'theirs', 'very', 'that', 'd', 'a', "mightn't", 'then', 'haven', 'he', 'you', 'my', 'myself', "you'll", 'are', 'over', "couldn't", 'more', 'nor', 'your', 'about', 'whom', 'there', 'himself', 'between', 'own', 'am', 'his', 'an', 'out', 'had', 'm', 'into', "shan't", 'didn', 'ain', 'y', 'him'}

{'into', 'any', 'than', 'during', 'only', 'same', 'wasn', 'themselves', "that'll", 'don', 'doing', 'won', "it's", 'are', 'been', 'with', 'below', 'for', 'will', 'yourselves', 'so', "doesn't", 'those', 'couldn', 'shouldn', 'aren', "mightn't", 'until', 'where', 'which', "aren't", 'herself', "you're", 'but', 'down', 'before', 'off', "isn't", 'these', 'what', 'have', 'to', 'nor', "didn't", 'haven', 'why', 'mightn', 'am', 'do', 'ain', "should've", 'he', 'having', 'your', 'did', 'on', 'as', "weren't", 'own', 'll', 'an', 'doesn', 'hasn', 'hadn', 'his', 'them', 'ourselves', 'through', "you've", 'were', 'here', "haven't", 'can', 'mustn', 'their', 'should', 'they', 'and', "couldn't", 'whom', 'when', 'it', 'theirs', 'because', 'too', 'no', "shan't", "hadn't", 'ours', 'ma', 're', 'about', 'above', 'was', "needn't", "won't", "wouldn't", 'myself', 'a', 'not', 'how', 'after', 'under', 'further', 'we', 'once', 'most', 'our', 'of', 'be', 'out', 'wouldn', 'or', 'me', 'the', 'y', 'such', 'yourself', 'she', 'other', 'my', 'against', 'just', 'now', 'hers', 'there', 'then', "shouldn't", 'is', 'himself', 'does', 'who', 'over',"you'll", 'needn', 'him', 'while', 'shan', 'm', 'from', 'very', 'both', 'd', 'has', "you'd", 'yours', "she's", 'had', 'between', "wasn't", 'its', 'didn', 'isn', 'up', 'her', 'itself', 'again', 'o', 'more', 've', 'i', 'being', 'weren', "mustn't", 'this', 'in', "hasn't", 'by', 'some', 'at', 'few', 't', 'that', 'all', 's', 'if', "don't", 'each', 'you'}

To remove all the stopwords from the original text, we need to filter out the stopwords extracted above:

```
filtered_sentset=[]
for wd in tokenized_wordset:
    if wd not in stop_wordset:
        filtered_sentset.append(wd)
print("Tokenized Sentence is as follows: ",tokenized_wordset)
print("Filtered Sentence is: ",filtered_sentset)
```

Output:

Tokenized Sentence is as follows: ['This', 'is', 'a', 'syntax', 'of', 'paragraph', 'in', 'python', 'programming', '.', 'Hello', 'participants', 'we', 'are', 'learning', 'about', 'NLP', '.', 'First', 'step', 'is', 'tokenization']

Filtered Sentence is: ['This', 'syntax', 'paragraph', 'python', 'programming', '.', 'Hello', 'participants', 'learning', 'NLP', '.', 'First', 'step', 'tokenization']

13.1.4 Lexicon Normalization

Text normalization is required to prepare words and text for further processing. Stemming and lemmatization are the techniques used in text normalization. Both techniques remove the common morphological and inflexional endings from words in English, but the actual word may not be produced in **stemming** whereas an actual language word is produced in **lemmatization**.

For example, the stemmed word of 'trying' is 'tri', whereas the lemmatized word is 'try'. Likewise, the stemming word of 'troubled' is 'troubl' whereas the lemmatized word is 'trouble'. Text normalization is necessary because one word in root form can have different forms occurring in the text.

PorterStemmer is a stemming technique which does not follow linguistics. It applies algorithmic rules to generate stems instead of maintaining a look-up table for the actual stems of the word. This is why PorterStemmer does not generate the actual stem words.

For example,

Try
Try---Trying
Try---Tried
Try--Tries

```
#stemming
from nltk.stem import PorterStemmer
from nltk.tokenize import sent_tokenize,word_tokenize
pss=PorterStemmer()
stemmed_wordset=[]
for w in filtered_sentset:
    stemmed_wordset.append(pss.stem(w))

print("Filtered Sentence is as: ",filtered_sentset)
print("Stemmed Sentence is as: ",stemmed_wordset)
```

Output:

Filtered Sentence is as: ['This', 'syntax', 'paragraph', 'python', 'programming', '.', 'Hello', 'participants', 'learning', 'NLP', '.', 'First', 'step', 'tokenization']

Stemmed Sentence is as: ['thi', 'syntax', 'paragraph', 'python', 'program', '.', 'hello', 'particip', 'learn', 'nlp', '.', 'first', 'step', 'token']

The lemmatization process uses the WordNet corpus and a stopwords corpus to produce the lemma. This makes lemmatization slow. You also need to define the parts of speech to obtain the correct lemma. Stemming follows a faster algorithm. Porter's algorithm is the most common algorithm used for stemming.

```
from nltk.stem.wordnet import WordNetLemmatizer
nltk.download('wordnet')
lems=WordNetLemmatizer()
from nltk.stem.porter import PorterStemmer
stems=PorterStemmer()
wordtemp='trying'
print("Lemmatized words: ",lems.lemmatize(wordtemp,pos="v"))#v=part of
speech and by default it is noun
print("stemmed Word:",stems.stem(wordtemp))
```

Output: Lemmatized words: try stemmed Word: tri

```
from nltk.stem.wordnet import WordNetLemmatizer
nltk.download('wordnet')
lems=WordNetLemmatizer()
from nltk.stem.porter import PorterStemmer
stems=PorterStemmer()
wordtemp='goooood'#it will get this word as start op sentence hence we
are getting diff op here
print("Lemmatized words: ",lems.lemmatize(wordtemp,pos="v"))#v=part of
speech and by default it is noun
print("stemmed Word:",stems.stem(wordtemp))
```

Output: Lemmatized words: goooood stemmed Word: goooood

Given below is the code that shows the difference in output between the stemmed and lemmatized words of a given sentence:

```
#Using nltk toolkit work tokenization
import nltk
nltk.download('punkt')
#sentence tokenization
from nltk.tokenize import sent_tokenize
fulltext="""This is a syntax of paragraph in python programming.
Hello participants we are learning about NLP.
First step is tokenization"""
tokenized_textset=sent_tokenize(fulltext)
print('TOKENIZED TEXT IS:',tokenized_textset)
from nltk.tokenize import word_tokenize
tokenized_wordset=word_tokenize(fulltext)
print('TOKENIZED WORDS ARE:', tokenized_wordset)
from nltk.probability import FreqDist
fdists=FreqDist(tokenized_wordset)#should pass the words list
print(fdists)
fdists.most_common(5)

from nltk.corpus import stopwords
nltk.download('stopwords')
stop_wordset=set(stopwords.words("english"))
filtered_sentset=[]
for w in tokenized_wordset:
    if w not in stop_wordset:
        filtered_sentset.append(w)
print("Tokenized Sentence: ",tokenized_wordset)
print("Filtered Sentnce: ",filtered_sentset)
```

```
from nltk.stem import PorterStemmer
from nltk.stem.wordnet import WordNetLemmatizer
nltk.download('wordnet')
lems=WordNetLemmatizer()
stems=PorterStemmer()
pss=PorterStemmer()
stemmedwordset=[]
for w in filtered_sentset:
    stemmedwordset.append(pss.stem(w))
print("Stemmed Sentence: ",stemmedwordset)

lemmazied_wordset=[]
for w in filtered_sents:
    lemmazied_wordset.append(lems.lemmatize(w,pos="v"))
print("lemmazied Sentence: ",lemmazied_wordset)
```

Output:

TOKENIZED TEXT IS: ['This is a syntax of paragraph in python programming.', 'Hello participants we are learning about NLP.', 'First step is tokenization']

TOKENIZED WORDS ARE: ['This', 'is', 'a', 'syntax', 'of', 'paragraph', 'in', 'python', 'programming', '.', 'Hello', 'participants', 'we', 'are', 'learning', 'about', 'NLP', '.', 'First', 'step', 'is', 'tokenization']

Filtered Sentence: ['This', 'syntax', 'paragraph', 'python', 'programming', '.', 'Hello', 'participants', 'learning', 'NLP', '.', 'First', 'step', 'tokenization']

Stemmed Sentence: ['thi', 'syntax', 'paragraph', 'python', 'program', '.', 'hello', 'particip', 'learn', 'nlp', '.', 'first', 'step', 'token']

lemmatized Sentence: ['This', 'syntax', 'paragraph', 'python', 'program', '.', 'Hello', 'participants', 'learn', 'NLP', '.', 'First', 'step', 'tokenization']

Apart from PorterStemmer, Lancaster and Snowball stemming are also used. However, Snowball is more advanced than PorterStemmer.

13.1.5 Regular Expression Removal

The following code can be used to remove patterns in text that are not required. It also helps to find certain patterns like usernames in email IDs.

```
##regular expression in text
from nltk.tokenize import sent_tokenize
fulltext="""This is a syntax of paragraph in python programming.
Hello participants we are learning about NLP.
email is sandhya_arora@gmail.com
site link is https://sandhya/sandhyaarora
First step is 'tokenization'"""
import re
line = re.sub('\S*@\S*\s?'," ",fulltext) #email remove
print(line)
line = re.sub("\'"," ",fulltext) #single quote remove
print(line)
```

```
line = re.sub('_'," ",fulltext) #underscore remove
print(line)
line = re.sub('http\S*\s?'," ",fulltext) #link remove
print(line)
#hasgtag remove
line = ' '.join([i for i in fulltext.split() if i.find('#') < 0])
print(line)
line = ' '.join([i for i in fulltext.split() if i in re.findall(r'\
w+',fulltext)]) #only keep words and numbers
print(line)
```

Output:

This is a syntax of paragraph in python programming.
Hello participants we are learning about NLP.
email is site link is https://sandhya/sandhyaarora
First step is 'tokenization'
This is a syntax of paragraph in python programming.
Hello participants we are learning about NLP.
email is sandhya_arora@gmail.com
site link is https://sandhya/sandhyaarora
First step is tokenization
This is a syntax of paragraph in python programming.
Hello participants we are learning about NLP.
email is sandhya arora@gmail.com
site link is https://sandhya/sandhyaarora
First step is 'tokenization'
This is a syntax of paragraph in python programming.
Hello participants we are learning about NLP.
email is sandhya_arora@gmail.com
site link is First step is 'tokenization'

This is a syntax of paragraph in python programming. Hello participants we are learning about NLP. email is sandhya_arora@gmail.com site link is https://sandhya/sandhyaarora First step is 'tokenization' This is a syntax of paragraph in python Hello participants we are learning about email is site link is First step is

13.1.6 Part-of-Speech (POS) Tagging

This is used to identify the parts of speech in the text.

```
fulltext="""This is a syntax of paragraph in python programming.
Hello participants we are learning about NLP.
email is sandhya_arora@gmail.com
site link is https://sandhya/sandhyaarora
First step is 'tokenization'"""
```

```
import spacy
from spacy.tokenizer import Tokenizer
nlp = spacy.load("en_core_web_sm")
fulltext_tokens_spacy = nlp(fulltext)
for token_in_text in fulltext_tokens_spacy:
 print(token_in_text.text, ': ', token_in_text.pos_, ': ', token_in_text.
is_stop)
```

Output:
This: DET: True
is: AUX: True
a: DET: True
syntax: NOUN: False
of: ADP: True
paragraph: NOUN: False
in: ADP: True
python: PROPN: False
programming: NOUN: False
.: PUNCT: False
: SPACE: False
Hello: INTJ: False
participants: NOUN: False
we: PRON: True
are: AUX: True
learning: VERB: False
about: ADP: True
NLP: PROPN: False
.: PUNCT: False
: SPACE: False
email: NOUN: False
is: AUX: True
sandhya_arora@gmail.com: X: False
: SPACE: False
site: NOUN: False
link: NOUN: False
is: AUX: True
https://sandhya: PROPN: False
/: SYM: False
sandhyaarora: PROPN: False
: SPACE: False
First: ADJ: True
step: NOUN: False

is: AUX: True
': PUNCT: False
tokenization: NOUN: False
': PUNCT: False

13.1.7 Vectorization or Word Embedding

After applying tokenization and cleaning the text, a machine learning model can be built on the text data. For this, you need to extract features from the clean text data because the machine does not understand the text; it only understands data.

Vectorization is a technique that helps you to map words to a vector of numbers. The function `CountVectorizer()` is used to obtain this count.

```
fulltext=['Movie story was nice and movie was good too']
import pandas as pd
from sklearn.feature_extraction.text import CountVectorizer
text_count_vec = CountVectorizer(ngram_range=(1,1))
print(text_count_vec)
text_count_vec.fit(fulltext)
count = text_count_vec.transform(fulltext)
print(count)
```

Output:
CountVectorizer()
(0, 0) 1
(0, 1) 1
(0, 2) 2
(0, 3) 1
(0, 4) 1
(0, 5) 1
(0, 6) 2

Here, the words of the given text "Movie story was nice and movie was good too" are counted. Words are indexed in alphabetical order. You can check the complete vocabulary of the whole document using this.

Text	movie	story	was	nice	and	good	too
Count	2	1	2	1	1	1	1
Index	2	4	6	3	0	1	5

`CountVectorizer()` ignores words with a lower count, that is, it may not give importance to rare words. Sometimes, rare words are more important in applications than the words that occur frequently. So, the most frequent words sometimes need to be penalized.

Term Frequency-Inverse Document Frequency (TF-IDF) of the bag-of-words model provides the overall weight of a word in a document. The function `TfidfVectorizer()` helps us obtain this calculated weighted score.

```
fulltext=['Movie story was nice and movie was good too']
from sklearn.feature_extraction.text import TfidfVectorizer
tfidf_vectext = TfidfVectorizer (analyzer='word', ngram_range=(1, 1),
stop_words = 'english')
tfidf_vectext.fit(fulltext)
tfidftext = tfidf_vectext.transform(fulltext)
print(tfidftext)
```

Output:
(0, 3)   0.3779644730092272
(0, 2)   0.3779644730092272
(0, 1)   0.7559289460184544
(0, 0)   0.3779644730092272

13.2 CGI/Web Programming Using Python

The Common Gateway Interface (CGI) is a standard protocol used to exchange information between a user script file and a web server. With this protocol, web pages can be dynamically generated at the web server. These dynamic web pages are generated using CGI scripts which are executed in the web browser. The browser sends the requested CGI script to the web server, which executes it and the response is transferred to the web browser.

13.2.1 Configuring the Apache Server

To execute Python-based CGI scripts, the following steps are required:

1. Navigate to the Python installation directory:

   D:\Python\Python36-32

2. Install the web server. This chapter uses the Apache Tomcat web server installed using XAMPP. The path of the XAMPP installation directory is:

   c:\xampp

3. In the XAMPP folder, navigate to the Apache folder.
4. In the Apache folder, navigate to the conf directory.
5. To configure the Apache web server to run Python CGI scripts, add the following lines of code at the end of the file httpd.conf:

   ```
   AddHandler cgi-script.py
   ScriptInterpreterSource Registry-Strict
   ```

6. Open the XAMPP Control Panel and restart Apache:

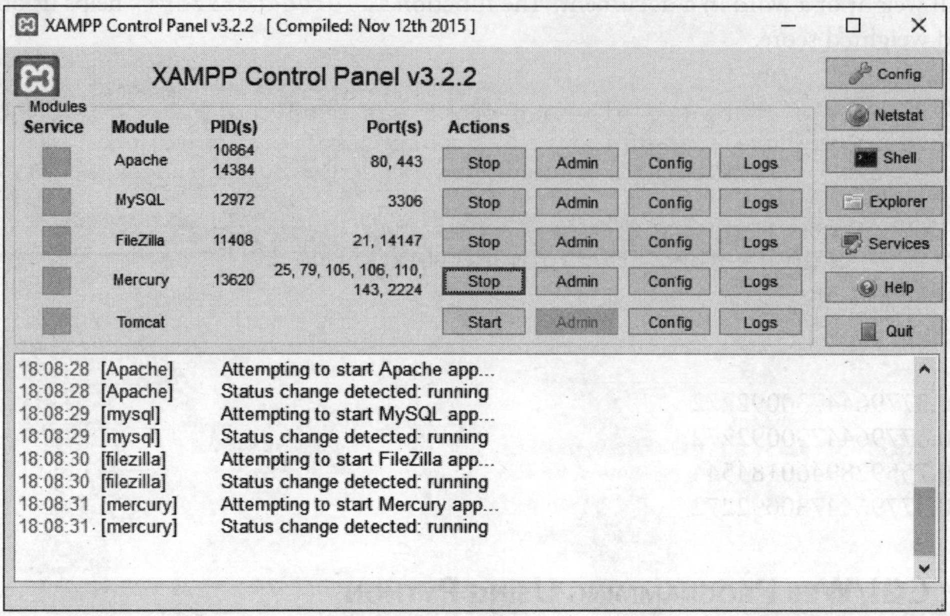

13.2.2 Running the Python CGI Script on the Apache Server

After configuring the Apache web server with the Python CGI script feature, perform the following steps.

1. Create a folder (PP) in the htdocs folder.

   C:\xampp\htdocs\PP

2. In this folder, create a Python CGI script. The first line of the script should be the path of the Python files.

   C:\xampp\htdocs\PP\s1.py

```
#!D:/Python/Python36-32/python.exe
print("Content-Type: text/html\n")
    print ("Hello World!")
```

3. Open the web browser and type the following URL:

   http://localhost/PP/s1.py

Output:

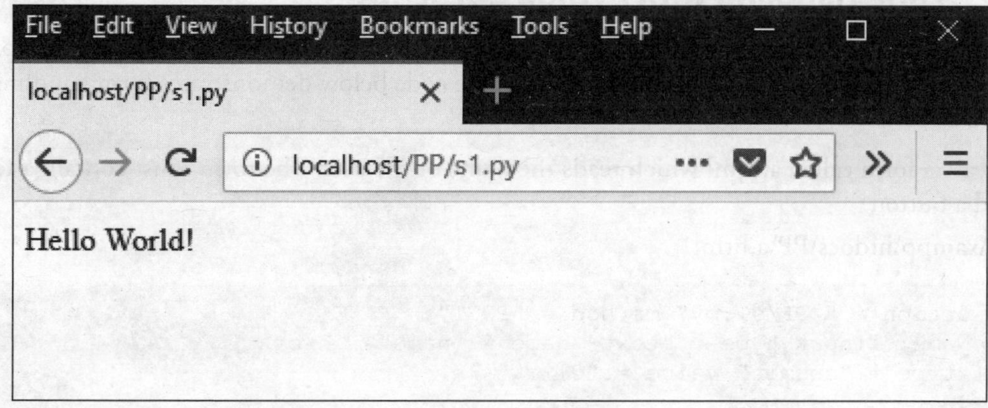

13.2.3 Python CGI Environment Variables

With the Python CGI script, the environment variables of the operating system can be accessed. For this, the os module needs to be used. This module allows the Python script to interact with the operating system.

```
#!D:/Python/Python36-32/python.exe
import os
print("Content-Type: text/html\n")
print("<h1>CGI Environment Variables </h1><br>")
for p in os.environ.keys():
       print(p,":",os.environ[p],"</br>")
```

Output:

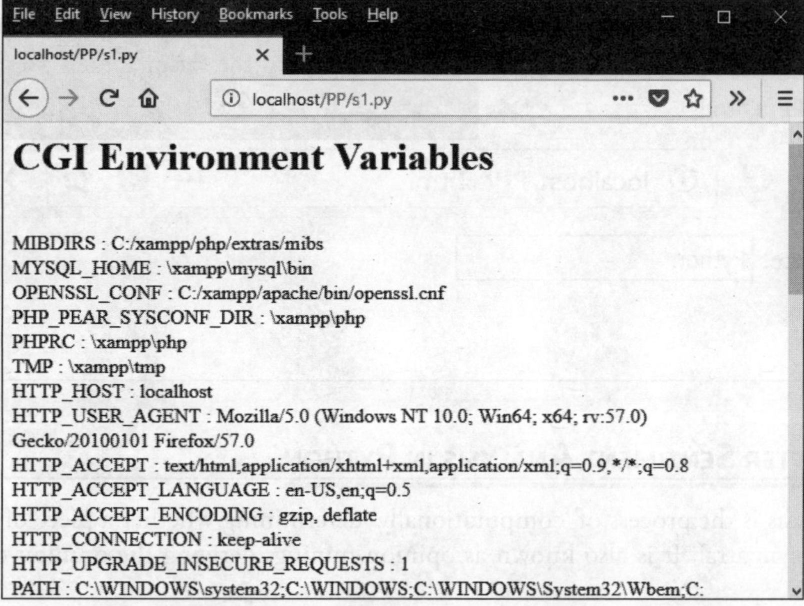

13.2.4 Form Handling with Python CGI Script

Data can be transferred between the web browser and the web server. The form data can be communicated using the POST or GET methods. The sample code below demonstrates form handling with Python CGI script.

1. Create a form called a.html which reads the name of the user. The form must contain a textbox and a button.

   C:\xampp\htdocs\PP\a.html

```
<form action = "/PP/s1.py" method = "POST">
First Name: <input type = "text" name = "name">  </br>
<input type = "submit" value = "Click" />
   </form>
```

2. Write the Python CGI script that receives form data using POST or GET. The current example uses POST. The cgi module in Python is used to handle form data with POST or GET requests. The `FieldStorage()` function in the cgi module receives data from the form.

   C:\xampp\htdocs\PP\s1.py

```
#!D:/Python/Python36-32/python.exe
import cgi
f=cgi.FieldStorage()
name=f.getvalue('name')
print("Content-Type: text/html\n")
   print("Hello",name)
```

Output:

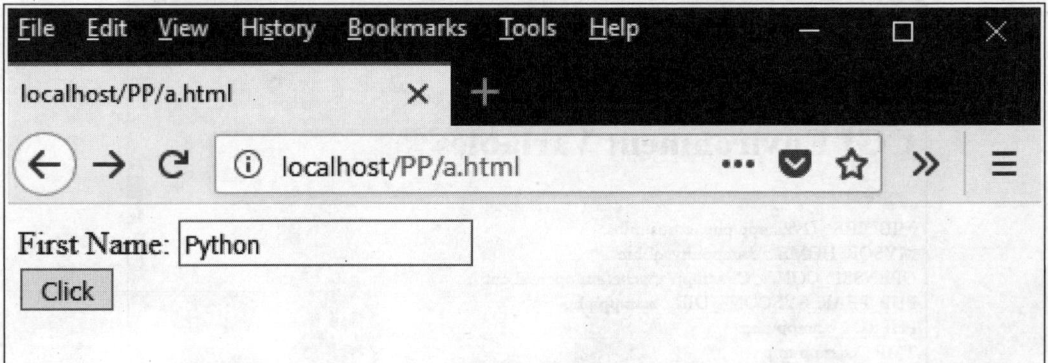

13.3 Twitter Sentiment Analysis in Python

Sentiment analysis is the process of 'computationally' determining whether a piece of writing is positive, negative or neutral. It is also known as opinion mining, deriving the opinion or attitude of a speaker.

- **Business:** Companies use sentiment analysis to develop their marketing strategies, to understand customers' feelings towards products or brands, how they respond to campaigns or product launches and why consumers do not buy some products.
- **Politics:** Here, it is used to keep track of political views and detect consistencies and inconsistencies in statements and actions at the government level. It can be used to predict election results as well.
- **Public actions:** Sentiment analysis is used to monitor and analyze social phenomena, to spot potentially dangerous situations and to determine the general mood of the blogosphere.

Installation:

- **Tweepy:** This is a Python client for the official Twitter API. You can install it using the command given below, found in the scripts directory of Python. This command can be executed at the command prompt:
  ```
  pip install tweepy
  ```
- **TextBlob:** This is a Python library for processing textual data.
  You can install it using the following command:
  ```
  pip install textblob
  ```

Authentication: In order to fetch tweets through the Twitter API, you needs to register an app through the Twitter account:

1. Open https://apps.twitter.com/ and click the Create New App button.
2. Fill in the application details. You can leave the callback URL field empty.
3. Once the app is created, you will be redirected to the app page.
4. Open the Keys and Access Tokens tab.
5. Copy Consumer Key, Consumer Secret, Access Token and Access Token Secret.

Program code:

```
import re
import tweepy
from tweepy import OAuthHandler
from textblob import TextBlob
class TwitterClient(object):
''' Generic Twitter Class for sentiment analysis.'''
def __init__(self):
'''Class constructor or initialization  method.'''
consumer_key = 'XXXXXXXXXXXXXXXXXXXXXXX'
consumer_secret = 'XXXXXXXXXXXXXXXXXXXXXXXXXXXXX'
 access_token = 'XXXXXXXXXXXXXXXXXXXXXXXXXXX'
access_token_secret = 'XXXXXXXXXXXXXXXXXXXXXXXXX'
# attempt authentication
try:
# create OAuthHandler object
self.auth = OAuthHandler(consumer_key, consumer_secret)
# set access token and secret
self.auth.set_access_token(access_token, access_token_secret)
```

```
# create tweepy API object to fetch tweets
self.api = tweepy.API(self.auth) except:
print("Error: Authentication Failed")
def clean_tweet(self, tweet):
'''Utility function to clean tweet text by removing links, special
characters using simple regex statements.'''
return ' '.join(re.sub("(@[A-Za-z0-9]+)|([^0-9A-Za-z \t])|(\w+:\/\/\S+)",
" ", tweet).split())
def get_tweet_sentiment(self, tweet):
'''Utility function to classify sentiment of passed tweet using textblob's
sentiment method'''

# create TextBlob object of passed tweet text
analysis = TextBlob(self.clean_tweet(tweet))
# set sentiment
if analysis.sentiment.polarity > 0:
return 'positive'
elif analysis.sentiment.polarity == 0:
return 'neutral'
else:
return 'negative'
def get_tweets(self, query, count = 10):
''' Main function to fetch tweets and parse them.'''
# empty list to store parsed tweets
tweets = []
try:
# call twitter api to fetch tweets
fetched_tweets = self.api.search(q = query, count = count)
# parsing tweets one by one
for tweet in fetched_tweets:
# empty dictionary to store required params of a tweet
parsed_tweet = {}
# saving text of tweet
parsed_tweet['text'] = tweet.text
# saving sentiment of tweet
parsed_tweet['sentiment'] = self.get_tweet_sentiment(tweet.text)
# appending parsed tweet to tweets list
if tweet.retweet_count > 0:
# if tweet has retweets, ensure that it is appended only once
if parsed_tweet not in tweets:
tweets.append(parsed_tweet)
else:
tweets.append(parsed_tweet)
# return parsed tweets
return tweets
except tweepy.TweepError as e:
# print error (if any)
print("Error: " + str(e))
```

```
def main():
    # creating object of TwitterClient Class
    api = TwitterClient()
    # calling function to get tweets
    tweets = api.get_tweets(query = 'XXXX', count = 20)
    # print(tweets)
    # picking positive tweets from tweets
    ptweets = [tweet for tweet in tweets if tweet['sentiment'] ==
'positive' ]
    # percentage of positive tweets
    print("Positive tweets percentage: {} %".format(100*len(ptweets)/
len(tweets)))
    # picking negative tweets from tweets
    ntweets = [tweet for tweet in tweets if tweet['sentiment'] ==
'negative']
    # percentage of negative tweets
    print("Negative tweets percentage: {} %".format(100*len(ntweets)/
len(tweets)))
    # percentage of neutral tweets
    #print("Neutral tweets percentage: {} %".format(100*len(tweets -
ntweets - ptweets)/len(tweets)))
    # printing first 5 positive tweets
    print("\n\nPositive tweets:")
    for tweet in ptweets[:10]:
    print(tweet['text'])
    # printing first 5 negative tweets
    print("\n\nNegative tweets:")
    for tweet in ntweets[:10]:
    print(tweet['text'])

if __name__ == "__main__":
    # calling main function
    main()
```

Output:
Positive tweets percentage: 36%
Negative tweets percentage: 21%

13.4 Twitter Sentiment Analysis for Film Reviews

Every day, hundreds of reviews about various trending films are posted on Twitter. These are an important source of feedback for corporations. Analysis of such data can be performed using machine learning (ML) as well as non-machine learning approaches. Here, we use multinomial naive Bayes' for Twitter sentiment analysis and comparison with lexicon-based analysis. Thus, the ML approach of multinomial naive Bayes' is used to classify tweet data into positive, negative and neutral reviews. The non-ML approach of lexicon-based analysis uses the `TextBlob()` function in Python to classify the same data and compare it with the results obtained from naive Bayes'.

The data set has been created by fetching 150 tweets about Film1, and manually labelling them as positive, negative and neutral. The final data set contains 102 entries after removal of duplicate tweets, and it has been saved to a .csv file.

The following code shows the data gathering process:

```
keys = pd.read_csv('twitter keys.csv')
consumerKey = keys['keys'][0]
consumerSecret = keys['keys'][1]
accessToken = keys['keys'][2]
accessTokenSecret = keys['keys'][3]
authenticate = tweepy.OAuthHandler(consumerKey,consumerSecret)
authenticate.set_access_token(accessToken, accessTokenSecret)
api = tweepy.API(authenticate, wait_on_rate_limit=True)
The twitter API is accessed after authentication of twitter keys.
```

Code for naive Bayes' ML model for tweet data: While working on model development, data is divided into training set and testing set. The testing data set is different from the training data set. This splitting takes place before training of the model. While splitting the data set, you need to ensure that it occurs in a random manner. Python scikit has a model selection library, with the method `train_test_split()`, which helps us to carry out splitting in a random manner.

Code for defining functions in lexicon-based analysis: The `getPolarity()` function returns a float value associated with each tweet. Based on this polarity, the `analysis()` function classifies the tweets as positive, negative and neutral.

```
import tweepy
from textblob import TextBlob
import pandas as pd
import matplotlib.pyplot as plt
import re
import string
from google.colab import files
uploaded= files.upload()
import io
tweet_data=pd.read_csv(io.BytesIO(uploaded['tweet_data.csv']))
print(tweet_data)
labeled_tweets=tweet_data
labeled_tweets['Tweet'] = labeled_tweets['Tweet'].apply(cleanText)
from sklearn.model_selection import train_test_split
#Splitting into training and testing data
x_train, x_test, y_train, y_test = train_test_split(labeled_
tweets['Tweet'], labeled_tweets['class'], random_state=50)
from sklearn.feature_extraction.text import CountVectorizer
vect = CountVectorizer(ngram_range=(1,1)) #Return a matrix showing the
frequency distribution of words
X_train = vect.fit_transform(x_train)
```

```
X_test = vect.transform(x_test)
print("test data:")
print(x_test)
from sklearn.naive_bayes import MultinomialNB
mnb = MultinomialNB(alpha =0.2)
mnb.fit(X_train,y_train)
result= mnb.predict(X_test)
print(result)
from sklearn.metrics import accuracy_score
from sklearn.metrics import confusion_matrix
#Printing accuracy of the our model
print(accuracy_score(result,y_test))
print(confusion_matrix(y_test,result))
x=["Film1 is a must watch hero has worked his best", "spent 500 rupees on
Film1 ticket at esquare", "Film1 was unexpectedly a good movie","Film1
was a waste of time and money"]
test = vect.transform(x)
pred= mnb.predict(test)
print("prediction is:{}".format(pred))
def getPolarity(text):
  return TextBlob(text).sentiment.polarity
def analysis(score):
  if score<0:
    return 'negative'
  elif score==0:
    return 'neutral'
  return 'positive'
df = pd.DataFrame(x_test, columns=['Tweet'])
df['Polarity'] = df['Tweet'].apply(getPolarity)
df['Analysis'] = df['Polarity'].apply(analysis)
print(accuracy_score(df['Analysis'],y_test))
print(confusion_matrix(y_test,df['Analysis']))
import matplotlib.pyplot as plt
plt.hist(labeled_tweets['class'])
plt.show()
```

Output:

tweet_data.csv(text/csv) - 15731 bytes, last modified: 3/13/2023 - 100% done
Saving tweet_data.csv to tweet_data (6).csv
Tweet class
0 Last night watched Film1 2 what a mass enterta... positive
1 Why are people excited fir Film1 2? negative
2 From the bottom of my heart i respect everyone... positive
3 Wouu this is really awesome Film1 2 now break... positive
4 Hero is getting huge love and response from au... positive
.. ..

```
97 RT @KRKBoxOffice: Actor1 fulfills his m... neutral
98 6 दनि में फलि्म #Film1 ने 80 करोड़ से अधकि की... neutral
99 Film Film1 - the real picture !! https://t.co/... neutral
100 #Film1 box office collection Day 6: #Actor1... positive
101 شويه كلام ورأي عن الفيلم الممتع #Film1..\nMy... neutral
[102 rows x 2 columns]
test data:
55 He should've made Fiml1 2 no
39 Those who watchedFiml1 despite watc...
21 What are they going to replace FIlm...
63 5300 Film1 makes SuperStarHero...
57 the way everyone in the theatre clapped when...
17 Film1 is full of mocking Pandits And Brahmans...
50 5300 FIlm1 makes SuperStarHero1 an...
40 SundayMorning Bollywood has not yet learnt th...
54 i literally loved the movie Film1 Actor1...
52 5300 Film1 makes SuperStarHero an allr...
58 Film1 SuperStarHero Amazing allround...
34 Film1 is a worse movie than the the first one...
89 Film1 had a phenomenal first weekend\n\n...
16 People are not boycotting whole industry the...
98 6 दनि में फलि्म Film1 ने 80 करोड़ से अधकि की क...
15 hero1 The real superstar and genuine human bei...
25 May be my tweet was not comprehended proper...
18 Left in middleits very strange why this movie...
74 Whats the fate of Actor2 film...
3 Wouu this is really awesome Film1 2 now break...
42 I screamed too loudly while watching a scene...
12 10 snaps because you went to see Film1...
8 The box office collection of Film1 2 is provin...
Name: Tweet, dtype: object
['negative' 'negative' 'negative' 'positive' 'neutral' 'negative'
'positive' 'negative' 'positive' 'positive' 'positive' 'positive'
'neutral' 'neutral' 'negative' 'neutral' 'neutral' 'neutral' 'positive'
'negative' 'negative' 'neutral' 'positive' 'negative' 'negative'
'positive']
0.9230769230769231
[[9 0 1]
[1 7 0]
[0 0 8]]
prediction is:['positive' 'neutral' 'positive' 'negative']
```

```
0.38461538461538464
[[1 3 6]
[0 4 4]
[0 3 5]]
```

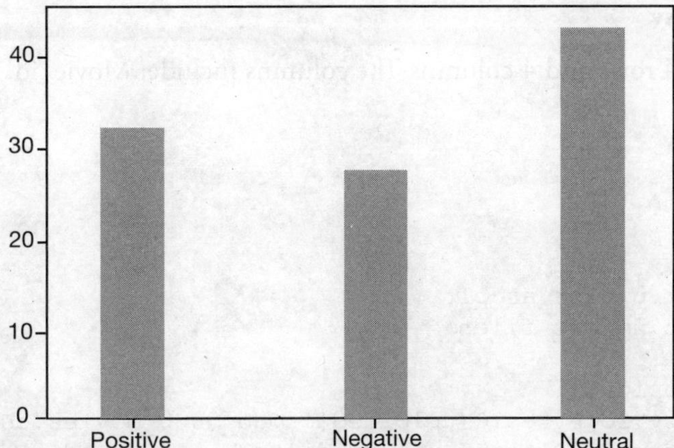

Naive Bayes' classification has an accuracy of 92% whereas lexicon analysis (`TextBlob()`)has an accuracy of only 38%. This is because `TextBlob()` ignores the context in which the reviews may be made. This is often the case with real life data. There is no way to improve the results of `TextBlob()` classification, as its parameters cannot be tuned. However, labelled data is used in the ML approach, so the model can learn to classify textual data correctly.

13.5 Case Study: A Recommendation System for a Film Data Set

This aims to recommend films to users based on the content they watch. A recommender system is a simple algorithm used to provide the most relevant information to a user by searching for some patterns in the data set. Film recommendation systems help to recommend films based on the preferences of the user.

Three types of algorithms are used for recommendations:

- Collaborative filtering system (used by Amazon)
- Content-based filtering system (used by Netflix)
- Hybrid filtering system

Of these, content-based filtering is popular.

The algorithm in this case study uses content-based filtering which filters and predicts film choices based on previous actions or explicit feedback.

The data sets used in this case study can be found at:

https://www.kaggle.com/datasets/tmdb/tmdb-movie-metadata

There are two csv files:

tmdb_5000_movies.csv

In this dataset, we have a total of 4804 rows and 20 columns.

The columns include: Budget, Genres, Homepage, Id, Keywords, Original_language, Original_title, Overview, Popularity, Production_companies, Production_countries, Release_date, Revenue, Runtime, Spoken_languages, Status, Tagline, Title, Vote_average, Vote_count

tmdb_5000_credits.csv

This has a total of 4814 rows and 4 columns The columns include: Movie_id, Title, Cast, Crew

Code:

```
import numpy as np
import pandas as pd
import io
import matplotlib.pyplot as plt
from google.colab import files
# First read the files
uploaded= files.upload()
movies=pd.read_csv(io.BytesIO(uploaded['tmdb_5000_movies.csv']))
credits=pd.read_csv(io.BytesIO(uploaded['tmdb_5000_credits.csv']))
```

In the next step, we merge the relevant fields from both the data sets. This will help us to recommend films based on the user's previous choice. Other fields such as Release_date, Revenue and Runtime, are not helpful for this task and thus we do not consider them.

After merging, we clean the data. Data cleaning is the process of fixing or removing incorrect, corrupted, incorrectly formatted, duplicate or incomplete data within a data set.

The data cleaning steps are:

1. Remove duplicates.
2. Remove irrelevant data.
3. Standardize capitalization.
4. Convert data type.
5. Clear formatting.
6. Fix errors.
7. Language translation.
8. Handle missing values.

As part of the data cleaning process, we first remove all duplicate values and use the `dropna()` method to remove the rows that contain null values. This method has various parameters that help us deal with null values, such as:

`df.dropna()`: All NA records are deleted.
`df.dropna(how=all)`: Only records with all rows as NA will be deleted.
`df.fillna(0)`: Null is replaced with 0.

AST is a tree representation of the source code of a computer program that conveys the structure of the source code. AST is a module in the Python standard library that builds an Abstract Syntax Tree.

```
movies = movies.merge(credits,on='title')
movies = movies[['movie_
id','title','overview','genres','keywords','cast','crew']]
movies.dropna(inplace=True)
movies.isnull().sum()
movies.duplicated().sum()
import ast
def convert(text):
  L=[]
  for i in ast.literal_eval(text):
    L.append(i['name'])
  return L
movies['genres'] = movies['genres'].apply(convert)
movies['keywords'] = movies['keywords'].apply(convert)
def convert_2(text):
  L = []
  counter = 0
  for i in ast.literal_eval(text):
    if counter < 3:
      L.append(i['name'])
    counter+=1
  return L
movies['cast'] = movies['cast'].apply(convert_2)
#movies.head()
def convert_3(text):
  L = []
  for i in ast.literal_eval(text):
    if i['job'] == 'Director':
      L.append(i['name'])
  return L
movies['crew'] = movies['crew'].apply(convert_3)
movies['overview'] = movies['overview'].apply(lambda x:x.split())
def remove_space(L):
  L1 = []
  for i in L:
    L1.append(i.replace(" ",""))
  return L1
```

The `remove_space()` function eliminates empty spaces in all the columns. If the spaces between the words are not removed, the word is considered as two individual words. For example, for 'Sam Washington', 'Sam' and 'Washington' are considered as two different words. Hence, we remove the spaces from the columns.

```
movies['cast'] = movies['cast'].apply(remove_space)
movies['crew'] = movies['crew'].apply(remove_space)
movies['genres'] = movies['genres'].apply(remove_space)
movies['keywords'] = movies['keywords'].apply(remove_space)
movies['Mark'] = movies['overview'] + movies['genres'] +
movies['keywords'] + movies['cast'] + movies['crew']
new_movies=movies[['movie_id','title','Mark']]
new_movies['Mark'] = movies['Mark'].apply(lambda x: " ".join(x))
new_movies['Mark'] = new_movies['Mark'].apply(lambda x:x.lower())
```

We need to import scikit-learn's `CountVectorizer()` which is used to convert a collection of text documents to a vector of term/token counts. A given text is thus transformed into a vector on the basis of the frequency (count) of each word that occurs in the entire text.

Stemming is the process of producing morphological variants of a root/base word. Stemming programs are commonly referred to as stemming algorithms or stemmers. For example, a stemming algorithm reduces the words 'chocolates', 'chocolatey' and 'choco' to the root word 'chocolate' which is exactly what is done here in the above function. When you pass the text data through the `CountVectorizer()` function, it returns a matrix of the number count of each word. We use 'cosine_similarity' to find the similarity. Cosine similarity is a metric used to measure how similar two items are. Mathematically, it measures the cosine of the angle between two vectors projected in a multi-dimensional space. For an output value in the range 0–1, 0 means no similarity, whereas 1 means that both the items are 100% similar.

```
from sklearn.feature_extraction.text import CountVectorizer
cv = CountVectorizer(max_features=5000,stop_words='english')
vec = cv.fit_transform(new_movies['Mark']).toarray()
vec[1]
import nltk
from nltk.stem.porter import PorterStemmer
ps=PorterStemmer()
def stemming(text):
  list2=[]
  for i in text.split():
    list2.append(ps.stem(i))
  return " ".join(list2)
new_movies['Mark']= new_movies['Mark'].apply(stemming)
new_movies['Mark']
vector1 = cv.fit_transform(new_movies['Mark']).toarray()
vector1[1]
cv.get_feature_names()
from sklearn.metrics.pairwise import cosine_similarity
similarity = cosine_similarity(vector1)
similarity
```

```
def recommend(movie):
  fetch_index = new_movies[new_movies['title'] == movie].index[0]
  distance=similarity[fetch_index]
  final_list=sorted(list(enumerate(distance)),reverse=True,key = lambda
x: x[1])[1:6] #list of tuples
  for i in final_list:
    print(new_movies.iloc[i[0]].title)
recommend('Batman Begins')
```

Output:
The Dark Knight
Batman
Batman
The Dark Knight Rises
10th & Wolf

13.6 Case Study: Text Mining and Visualization in Word Clouds

Here, we perform text mining on tweet data and visualize the most important words as a word cloud.

A word cloud depicts word usage in a document by randomly arranging and enlarging individual words according to their frequency. Some issues with word clouds are that they only support the most basic types of textual analysis, they are frequently used in contexts where textual analysis is inappropriate, and they leave viewers to infer the context of the data on their own without giving a narrative. However, in the case of tweets, textual analysis is the most crucial study as it gives a basic understanding of the terms that are frequently used in the corpus.

We used the Python module wordcloud to create a word cloud. The file used here is stock.csv, which contains tweets relating to stocks. The tweets are initially pre-processed and the polarity of tweets is calculated and categorized as negative, positive and neutral sentiments. The word cloud is visualized for all three sentiments.

Code:

```
# Cloud from tweets
import pandas as pd
import io
import matplotlib.pyplot as plt
from google.colab import files
uploaded= files.upload()
dataset=pd.read_csv(io.BytesIO(uploaded['stock.csv']))
dataset
#preprocessing
pat1 = r'@[A-Za-z0-9]+' # this is to remove any text with @....
pat2 = r'https?://[A-Za-z0-9./]+'  # this is to remove the urls
combined_pat = r'|'.join((pat1, pat2))
```

```
pat3 = r'[^a-zA-Z]' # to remove every other character except a-z & A-Z
combined_pat2 = r'|'.join((combined_pat,pat3)) # we combine pat1, pat2
and pat3 to pass it in the cleaning steps
len(dataset['text'])
import nltk
nltk.download('stopwords')
import re
from nltk.corpus import stopwords
from nltk.stem.porter import PorterStemmer
ps = PorterStemmer()
cleaned_tweets = []
for i in range(0, len(dataset['text'])):
    tweets = re.sub(combined_pat2,' ',dataset['text'][i])
    tweets = tweets.lower()
    tweets = tweets.split()
    tweets = [ps.stem(word) for word in tweets if not word in
set(stopwords.words('english'))]
    tweets = ' '.join(tweets)
    cleaned_tweets.append(tweets)
cleaned_tweets[10:20]
dataset['cleaned_tweets'] = cleaned_tweets
!pip install vader
nltk.download('vader_lexicon')
from nltk.sentiment.vader import SentimentIntensityAnalyzer
sia = SentimentIntensityAnalyzer()
for tweet in cleaned_tweets[:10]:
    print(tweet)
    s = sia.polarity_scores(tweet)
    for k in sorted(s):
        print('{0}: {1}, '.format(k, s[k]), end='')
        print()
def findpolarity(data):
  sid = SentimentIntensityAnalyzer()
  polarity = sid.polarity_scores(data)
  if(polarity['compound'] >= 0):
    sentiment = 1
  if(polarity['compound'] < 0):
    sentiment = 0

  return (sentiment)
sentiment = []
for i in range(0, len(cleaned_tweets)):
    s = findpolarity(cleaned_tweets[i])
    sentiment.append(s)
print(len(sentiment))
print(len(cleaned_tweets))
tweet_sentiment = pd.DataFrame()
tweet_sentiment['cleaned_tweets'] = cleaned_tweets
tweet_sentiment['sentiment'] = sentiment
```

```
tweet_sentiment.to_csv('master_tweet_sentiment.csv', index=False)
tweet_sentiment.shape[0]
positive_tweet = []
negative_tweet = []
neutral_tweet = []
for i in range(0, tweet_sentiment.shape[0]):
    if tweet_sentiment['sentiment'][i] == 0:
        neutral_tweet.append(tweet_sentiment['cleaned_tweets'][i])
    elif tweet_sentiment['sentiment'][i] == 1:
        positive_tweet.append(tweet_sentiment['cleaned_tweets'][i])
    elif tweet_sentiment['sentiment'][i] == -1:
        negative_tweet.append(tweet_sentiment['cleaned_tweets'][i])
negative_tweet[:10]
print(len(negative_tweet))
positive_tweet[:10]
print(len(positive_tweet))
neutral_tweet[:10]
print(len(neutral_tweet))
!pip install wordcloud
from wordcloud import WordCloud, STOPWORDS
stopwords = set(STOPWORDS)
import matplotlib.pyplot as plt
def show_wordcloud(data, title = None):
    wordcloud = WordCloud(
        background_color='black',
        stopwords=stopwords,
        max_words=200,
        max_font_size=40,
        scale=3,
        random_state=1 # chosen at random by flipping a coin; it was
heads
    ).generate(str(data))
    fig = plt.figure(1, figsize=(12, 12))
    plt.axis('off')
    if title:
        fig.suptitle(title, fontsize=20)
        fig.subplots_adjust(top=2.3)
    plt.imshow(wordcloud)
    plt.show()
show_wordcloud(positive_tweet)
show_wordcloud(neutral_tweet)
show_wordcloud(negative_tweet)
```

Output:

Positive tweets word cloud

Neutral tweets word cloud

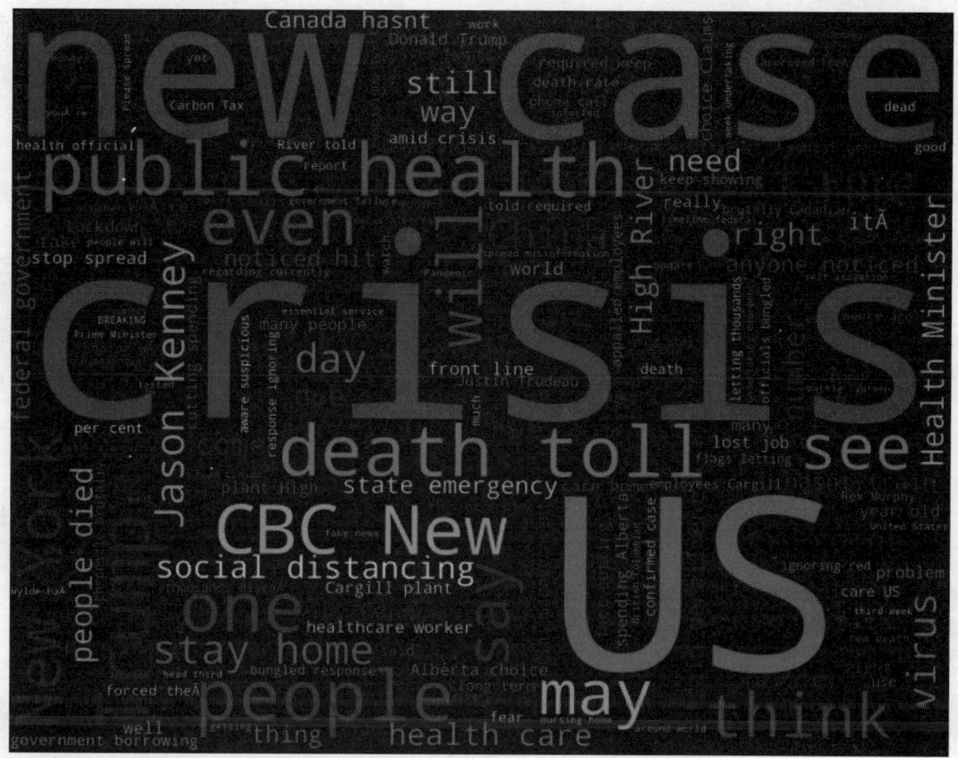

Negative tweets word cloud

EXERCISES

Multiple Choice Questions

1. What is the main challenge of NLP?
   (a) Handling tagging
   (b) Handling tokenization
   (c) Handling ambiguity of sentences
   (d) Handling stemming

2. Choose the correct area where NLP can be applied:
   (a) Text summarization
   (b) Chatbots
   (c) Discourse analysis
   (d) All of the above

3. NLP is a:
   (a) 4th generation language
   (b) 5th generation language
   (c) 6th generation language
   (d) None of the above

4. TFIDF stands for ____________.
   (a) Team Frequency and Inverse Document Frequency
   (b) Term Frequency and Inverse Document Frequency
   (c) Top Frequency and Inverse Document Frequency

(d) Table Frequency and Inverse Document Frequency

5. Which one of the following models cannot be used for text classification?
(a) Naive Bayes' model
(b) Support vector machine
(c) K-means algorithm
(d) OLAP

6. __________ are words that occur very frequently in the corpus but which do not add any value to it.
(a) Tokens
(b) Words
(c) Stopwords
(d) None of the above

7. One of the most common applications of NLP is in chatbots; give some examples of chatbots __________.
(a) Mitsuku bot
(b) Cleverbot
(c) Jabberwacky
(d) All of the above

8. The key tasks of NLP are:
(a) Automatic Summarization
(b) Discourse Analysis
(c) Machine Translation
(d) All of the above
(e) None of the above

9. How many phases does NLP have?
(a) 3
(b) 4
(c) 5
(d) 6

10. "Ram loves his father and Shyam does too" contains which type of ambiguity?
(a) Syntactic
(b) Lexical
(c) Semantic
(d) No ambiguity

Answers

1. (c) **2.** (d) **3.** (b) **4.** (b) **5.** (d) **6.** (c) **7.** (d) **8.** (d)
9. (c) **10.** (c)

Programming/Concept-based Questions

1. Tokenize the given text data and print the tokens;
Input:
textdata = """Last week, the University of Cambridge shared its own research that shows if everyone wears a mask outside home, the dreaded 'second wave' of the pandemic can be avoided."""
Answer:
```
tokensoutput=nltk.word_tokenize(text)
for token in tokensoutput:
   print(token)
```

2. Print the sentences of the given text data using NTLK.
Input: text = """The outbreak of coronavirus disease 2019 (COVID-19) has created a global health crisis that has had a deep impact on the way we perceive our world and our everyday lives. Not only the rate of contagion and patterns of transmission threatens our sense of agency, but the safety measures put in place to contain the spread of the virus also require social distancing

by refraining from doing what is inherently human, which is to find solace in the company of others. Within this context of physical threat, social and physical distancing, as well as public alarm, what has been (and can be) the role of the different mass media channels in our lives on individual, social and societal levels? Mass media have long been recognized as powerful forces shaping how we experience the world and ourselves. This recognition is accompanied by a growing volume of research, that closely follows the footsteps of technological transformations (e.g. radio, movies, television, the internet, mobiles) and the zeitgeist (e.g. cold war, 9/11, climate change) in an attempt to map mass media major impacts on how we perceive ourselves, both as individuals and citizens. Are media (broadcast and digital) still able to convey a sense of unity reaching large audiences, or are messages lost in the noisy crowd of mass self-communication?
"""

Answer:

```
doc=nlp(text)
for sentence in doc.sents:
   print(sentence)
   print(' ')
nltk.sent_tokenize(text)
```

3. Remove all the punctuations in the given text.

Input:

text=""""The match has concluded !!! India has won the match. Will we win the finals too ?"""

Answer:

```
# Removing punctuations in spaCy
import spacy
nlp=spacy.load("en_core_web_sm")
nlp
doc=nlp(text)
newtokens=[]
# Check if a token is a punctuation through is_punct attribute
for token1 in doc:
   if token1.is_punct==False:
      newtokens.append(token1.text)
" ".join(newtokens)
```

4. Tokenize the given input text with stopwords ('is', 'the', 'was') as delimiters.

Input:

text = """Walter was feeling anxious. He was diagnosed today. He probably is the best person I know."""

Answer:

```
# Solution
textdata = "Walter was feeling anxious. He was diagnosed today. He
probably is the best person I know."
stop_words_and_delims = ['was', 'is', 'the', '.', ',', '-', '!', '?']
for sw in stop_words_and_delims:
    textdata = textdata.replace(sw, 'DELIM')
```

```
txt-words = [txt.strip() for txt in textdata.split('DELIM')]
words_filteredtxt = list(filter(lambda aw: aw not in [''], txt-words))
words_filteredtxt
```

5. Remove all the stopwords ('was', 'a', 'the', …) from the given text data.
Input: text="""the outbreak of coronavirus disease 2019 (COVID-19) has created a global health crisis that has had a deep impact on the way we perceive our world and our everyday lives. Not only the rate of contagion and patterns of transmission threatens our sense of agency, but the safety measures put in place to contain the spread of the virus also require social distancing by refraining from doing what is inherently human, which is to find solace in the company of others. Within this context of physical threat, social and physical distancing, as well as public alarm, what has been (and can be) the role of the different mass media channels in our lives on individual, social and societal levels? Mass media have long been recognized as powerful forces shaping how we experience the world and ourselves. This recognition is accompanied by a growing volume of research, that closely follows the footsteps of technological transformations (e.g. radio, movies, television, the internet, mobiles) and the zeitgeist (e.g. cold war, 9/11, climate change) in an attempt to map mass media major impacts on how we perceive ourselves, both as individuals and citizens. Are media (broadcast and digital) still able to convey a sense of unity reaching large audiences, or are messages lost in the noisy crowd of mass self-communication?
"""

Answer:

```
# Method 1# Removing stopwords in nltk
from nltk.corpus import stopwords
mylistofstopwords=set(stopwords.
words('english'))
newtokens=[]
# Tokenization using word_tokenize()

                alltokens=nltk.word_tokenize(text)

for token in all_okens:
  if token not in mylistofstopwords:
    newtokens.append(token)
" ".join(newtokens)
```

6. Apply stemming and convert each token to its root form in the given text data.
Input:
text= """Dancing is an art. Students should be taught dance as a subject in schools. I danced in many of my school function. Some people are always hesitating to dance."""
Answer:

```
# Stemming with nltk's PorterStemmer
from nltk.stem import PorterStemmer
stemmer_obj=PorterStemmer()
stemmedtokens=[]
for token in nltk.word_tokenize(text):   stemmedtokens.append(stemmer_
obj.stem(token))
```

```
" ".join(stemmedtokens)
```

7. Correct the spelling errors in the following text.
Input: textinput= """He is a great person. He believes in God"""
Answer:

```
# Import textblob
from textblob import TextBlob
# Using textblob's correct() function
textinput = TextBlob(textinput)
print(textinput.correct())
#> He is a great person. He believes in god
```

8. Extract the usernames from the email addresses in the text.
Input: textinput = """The new registrations are potter709@gmail.com, elixir101@gmail.com. If you find any disruptions, kindly contact granger111@gamil.com or severus77@gamil.com """
Answer:

```
# Using regular expression to extract usernames
import re
# \S matches any non-whitespace character
# @ for as in the Email
# + for Repeats a character one or more times
extractedusernames= re.findall('(\S+)@', textinput)
print(extractedusernames)
```

9. Find the similarity between any two text documents.
Input:
text1_data="John lives in Canada"
text2_data="James lives in America, though he's not from there"
Answer: `# Finding similarity using spaCy library`

```
document1=nlp(text1_data)
document2=nlp(text2_data)
document1.similarity(document2)
#> 0.792817083631068
```

10. Perform text mining on a set of documents and visualize the most important words in a visualization such as word cloud.
Answer:

```
import nltk
from nltk.corpus import stopwords
from nltk.tokenize import word_tokenize
from wordcloud import WordCloud
import matplotlib.pyplot as plt
doc1 = "Apple unveils new iPhone"
doc2 = "Google announces new search engine"
doc3 = "Microsoft launches new operating system"
doc4 = "Facebook releases new social media platform"
```

```
docs = [doc1, doc2, doc3, doc4]
stop_words = set(stopwords.words('english'))
word_tokens = []
for doc in docs:
  words = word_tokenize(doc)
  words = [word.lower() for word in words if word.isalpha() and word.
lower() not in stop_words]
  word_tokens.extend(words)
freq_dist = nltk.FreqDist(word_tokens)
wordcloud = WordCloud(width=800, height=800, background_color='white').
generate_from_frequencies(freq_dist)
plt.figure(figsize=(8,8), facecolor=None)
plt.imshow(wordcloud)
plt.axis("off")
plt.tight_layout(pad=0)
plt.show()
```

11. Build a recommendation system on a given data set and evaluate its accuracy.
Answer:

```
import pandas as pd
import numpy as np
from sklearn.metrics.pairwise import cosine_similarity
from sklearn.metrics import mean_squared_error
from sklearn.model_selection import train_test_split
# Load the dataset
movies=pd.read_csv('movies.csv')
ratings=pd.read_csv('ratings.csv')
# Merge the two datasets
data=pd.merge(ratings, movies, on='movieId')
# Calculate the average rating for each movie
movie_ratings=pd.DataFrame(data.groupby('title')['rating'].mean())
movie_ratings['num_ratings']        =pd.DataFrame(data.groupby('title')
['rating'].count())
# Create a pivot table for the ratings data
ratings_pivot=data.pivot_table(index='userId',        columns='title',
values='rating')
# Fill missing values with 0
ratings_pivot.fillna(0, inplace=True)
# Calculate the cosine similarity between the movies
movie_similarity=cosine_similarity(ratings_pivot.T)
# Define a function to get similar movies
defget_similar_movies(movie_title, movie_similarity):
    movie_idx=ratings_pivot.columns.get_loc(movie_title)
            returnsorted(list(enumerate(movie_similarity[movie_idx])),
```

```
key=lambdax:x[1], reverse=True)[1:11]
# Define a function to make recommendations
defrecommend_movies(user_ratings, movie_similarity):
        movie_ratings['score']  =movie_similarity.dot(user_ratings)  /
np.array([np.abs(movie_similarity).sum(axis=1)]).T
                 recommended_movies=movie_ratings.sort_values('score',
ascending=False).index.values
    returnrecommended_movies
# Split the data into training and test sets
train_data, test_data=train_test_split(data, test_size=0.2)
# Create a user-item matrix from the training data
train_matrix=train_data.pivot_table(index='userId',   columns='title',
values='rating')
# Fill missing values with 0
train_matrix.fillna(0, inplace=True)
# Calculate the cosine similarity between the users
user_similarity=cosine_similarity(train_matrix)
# Define a function to predict ratings
defpredict_ratings(user_id, movie_title, user_similarity, train_matrix):
    movie_idx=ratings_pivot.columns.get_loc(movie_title)
    sim_scores=user_similarity[user_id-1]
    top_k_users=np.argsort(sim_scores)[-10:]
    ratings=train_matrix.loc[top_k_users, movie_title]
    weights=sim_scores[top_k_users]
    pred_rating= (weights.dot(ratings) /weights.sum())
    returnpred_rating
# Make predictions for the test set
test_data['predicted_rating']  =test_data.apply(lambdarow:   predict_
ratings(row['userId'],  row['title'],  user_similarity,  train_matrix),
axis=1)
# Calculate the MSE and RMSE
mse=mean_squared_error(test_data['rating'],      test_data['predicted_
rating'])
rmse=np.sqrt(mse)
print('MSE:', mse)
print('RMSE:', rmse)
# Recommend movies for a user
user_id=1
user_ratings=train_matrix.loc[user_id].values
recommended_movies=recommend_movies(user_ratings, movie_similarity)
print('Recommended movies:', recommended_movies)
```

12. Write a program in Python to identify the tweets which are hate tweets and those which are not.

Answer:

```
import pandas as pd
import re
import nltk
nltk.download('punkt')
from nltk.corpus import stopwords
from nltk.tokenize import word_tokenize
from sklearn.model_selection import train_test_split
from sklearn.feature_extraction.text import TfidfVectorizer
from sklearn.linear_model import LogisticRegression
from sklearn.metrics import accuracy_score
df  =  pd.read_csv('https://raw.githubusercontent.com/t-davidson/hate-
speech-andoffensive-
language/master/data/labeled_data.csv')
# Pre-process and tokenize the tweet
df['tweet'] = df['tweet'].apply(lambda x: re.sub('[^a-zA-Z0-9\s]', '',
x))
df['tweet'] = df['tweet'].apply(lambda x: x.lower())
stop_words = set(stopwords.words('english'))
df['tweet'] = df['tweet'].apply(lambda x: ' '.join([word for word in
word_tokenize(x) if word not in stop_words]))
# Vectorization
tfidf = TfidfVectorizer(max_features=10000)
X = tfidf.fit_transform(df['tweet'])
y = df['class']
# Train-test split
X_train, X_test, y_train, y_test = train_test_split(X, y, test_size=0.2,
random_state=42)
# Model training
lr = LogisticRegression()
lr.fit(X_train, y_train)
# Model evaluation
y_pred = lr.predict(X_test)
accuracy = accuracy_score(y_test, y_pred)
print("Accuracy:", accuracy)
# Use the model to predict new tweets
new_tweet = "I hate people who are different from me. They don't belong
here."
# Preprocess the sample tweets
new_tweet = re.sub('[^a-zA-Z0-9\s]', '', new_tweet)
new_tweet = new_tweet.lower()
new_tweet = ' '.join([word for word in word_tokenize(new_tweet) if word
```

```
not in
stop_words])
# Vectorize the sample tweets
new_tweet_vec = tfidf.transform([new_tweet])
# Predict the labels of the sample tweets
new_tweet_pred = lr.predict(new_tweet_vec)
# Print the result
if new_tweet_pred[0] == 0:
print("Hate tweet")
else:
print("Good tweet")
```

BIBLIOGRAPHY

1. "Natural Language Toolkit". Javatpoint, https://www.javatpoint.com/natural-language-toolkit
2. Wakeupcoders. "Part 1: Introduction to Natural Language Processing (NLP)". Analytics Vidhya, published June 2020, https://medium.com/analytics-vidhya/part-1-introduction-to-natural-language-processing-nlp-a66ad8773b3
3. Diego Lopez Yse. "Your Guide to Natural Language Processing", Towards Data Science, published January 2019, https://towardsdatascience.com/your-guide-to-natural-language-processing-nlp-48ea2511f6e1/
4. "Tweepy, Getting Started", https://docs.tweepy.org/en/stable/getting_started.html#models

CHAPTER **14**

Clustering

LEARNING OBJECTIVES

At the end of this chapter, you will be able to:

- Explain the concept of clustering
- Highlight the role of distance measures in clustering
- Explain the taxonomy of clustering algorithms
- Explain hierarchical, partitioned clustering and density-based clustering algorithms
- Apply clustering techniques on data
- Implement clustering techniques using Python

14.0 INTRODUCTION

Clustering is an unsupervised machine learning technique used to group similar objects together. It is a form of learning by observation and not by examples. Clustered data will have minimum intra-class distance and maximum inter-class distance. Groups are formed in such a way that data points in the same group have similar properties, whereas data points in another group will have different properties. Data points are unlabelled for unsupervised learning and they help in finding hidden structures within data. The structure of the data determines the best grouping. For example, based on the income of a person, four different groupings can be formed:

- Earning less than \$10,000
- Earning between \$10,000 and \$30,000
- Earning between \$30,000 and \$60,000
- Earning more than \$60,000

Here, income is used for grouping a person. However, income does not indicate the affinity of the persons within each group. This means that there is no inherent reason to believe that a person earning \$80,000 will behave differently from a person earning \$10,000 or \$120,000. Income is chosen for grouping based on easy-to-understand points of delineation. If more variables are added, such as qualification, house size, age, experience and expenditure, the grouping will change altogether. Thus, as more dimensions are added to data, grouping becomes more meaningful and complex.

Clustering techniques help us find natural groupings of persons considering many dimensions. It does not make any prediction but finds the similarities between data points according to data attributes and groups similar data.

Different clustering methods use different distance measures. K-means utilizes Euclidean/Manhattan/city block distance between points, DBSCAN uses distance between the nearest points, affinity propagation and spectral clustering are based on graph distances, Gaussian mixtures are based on Mahalanobis distance. Clustering techniques have numerous applications in marketing, economics, biology, city planning, real estate and various branches of science.

14.1 Distance Measures

Distance measure is the building block of clustering algorithms. It is the measure of similarity and dissimilarity of data. Similarity is a numerical measure that defines how alike the data points are. If similarity is high, data are more alike. Dissimilarity is a numerical measure that defines how different the data points are. If dissimilarity is high, data are more different. Different data types such as numeric, binary, ordinal and categorical have different distance measure metrics.

Numeric data distance measures:

- **Euclidean Distance:** It is one of the most common distance measures used for quantitative data. The Euclidean distance between x and y data points with n features is given below:

$$d(x, y) = \sqrt{\sum_{i=1}^{n}(y_i - x_i)^2}$$

- **Manhattan Distance:** This is also called city block distance, absolute value distance, L1 norm and boxcar. The Manhattan distance between x and y data points with n features is given below:

$$d(x, y) = \sum_{i=1}^{n}| x_i - y_i |$$

- **Minkowski Distance:** In general, all distances formulated above can be generalized as given below. Here p is a parameter. When the value of p is 1, the distance measure is called the Manhattan distance and when the value of p is 2, the distance measure is called the Euclidean distance. The Minkowski distance between x and y points with n features is given as:

$$D(x, y) = \left(\sum_{i=1}^{n}| x_i - y_i |^p\right)^{\frac{1}{p}}$$

- **Chebyshev Distance:** This is also called supremum distance or maximum value distance. The Chebyshev distance between two points x and y with n features is given as:

$$D_{\text{Chebyshev}}(x, y) := \max_i(| x_i - y_i |)$$

Binary data distance measures: Binary data can have only two values. The distance measures discussed above cannot be applied for binary data. To find the distance between binary attributes, a contingency table needs to be created. The entries in the contingency table can be constructed by counting the number of matching transactions: 0-0,0-1,1-0,1-1.

Attributes matching	0	1
0	*a*	*b*
1	*c*	*d*

Here a = number of attributes where x attribute is 0 and y is also 0.
b = number of attributes where x attribute is 0 and y is 1.
c = number of attributes where x attribute is 1 and y is 0.
d = number of attributes where x attribute is 1 and y is also 1.

- **Jaccard Coefficient:** This is calculated for binary attributes as follows:

$$J = d \,/\, (b + c + d)$$

- **Simple Matching Coefficient (SMC):** This is defined as the ratio of the number of matching attributes and the number of attributes.

$$\text{SMC} = (a + d) \,/\, (a + b + c + d)$$

- **Hamming Distance:** This indicates the number of positions at which the characters or binary attributes are different. For example, the Hamming distance between (1 0 1) and (1 1 0) is 2 as both differ in two positions. The distance between "hood" and "wood" is 1 as both differ in just one position.
- **Symmetric Data Distance:** Here, both attribute values are equally valuable and carry the same weight. For example, Gender attribute is symmetric (male, female) as both are equally valuable. The distance for these attributes is calculated as:

$$\text{Distance} = (b + c) \,/\, (a + b + c + d)$$

- **Asymmetric Data Distance:** If both attribute values are not equally valuable and do not carry the same weight. For example, positive and negative outcomes of a disease test or examination. The distance for these attributes is calculated as:

$$\text{Distance} = (b + c) \,/\, (b + c + d)$$

Categorical data distance measures: Categorical data is a symbol or code to represent a value. For example, Gender attribute, where code 0 can represent male and 1 can represent female. To find the distance between categorical attributes, we need to check if they are equal or not. If they are equal, the distance will be 0; otherwise the distance will be 1.

Ordinal data distance measures: Ordinal attributes are similar to categorical attributes but they have an inherent order. For example, qualification and job designation has an order. Job designation can be 1, 2 or 3, where 1 is higher than 2 and 2 is higher than 3. The distance between x and y can be calculated as:

$$\text{Distance(X,Y)} = \left|\text{position}(X) - \text{position}(Y)\right| \,/\, n - 1$$

Here, 'position' refers to the attribute position in the order and n refers to the total number of orders.

14.2 K-MEANS CLUSTERING

K-means is the most widely used clustering algorithm. It is an iterative partitioning algorithm. The goal is to find K groups in the data. Here, K stands for the specified requested non-overlapping clusters that need to be created. The value K = 2 means that there will be two clusters, and value K = 3 means that there will be three clusters, and so on. Data points are clustered based on feature similarity, which is calculated using Euclidean distance. K-means clustering starts with using K different randomly-initiated centroid points; every data point is assigned to the nearest centroid. After every point has been assigned, the centroid is recalculated as the average of all of the points assigned to it. This process is repeated till either the centroids are stabilized or a defined number of iterations has been reached. This process optimizes the position of the centroids.

The K-means algorithm steps are as follows:

1. Choose a K value and select k random points from the data as centroids. (It can be different from the input data set).
2. Assign each data point to its closest centroid by computing the Euclidean distance. Here *x*, *y* are data points of *n* dimension.

$$d(x, y) = \sqrt{\sum_{i=1}^{n}(y_i - x_i)^2}$$

3. Recompute the centroids of newly formed clusters by averaging (arithmetic mean) the points assigned to that cluster.
4. Repeat steps 2 and 3 till the centroids are stabilized or a defined number of iterations has been reached.

14.2.1 Python Code for K-means Clustering

Example 1: The grades_km_input.csv file contains data of the marks of 619 students in Maths, Science and English. This data needs to be grouped into three groups. The results shown here are: group 1 has 207 students, group 2 has 210 students and group 3 has 202 students. The notations used for group 1, group 2 and group 3 are 0, 1 and 2. It takes 300 iterations to reach the three-group formation.

```
from matplotlib import pyplot
import io
import pandas as pd
from sklearn.cluster import KMeans
import numpy as np
from google.colab import files
uploaded= files.upload()
dfval=pd.read_csv(io.BytesIO(uploaded['grades_km_input.csv']))
kmeans = KMeans(n_clusters=3, random_state=0).fit(dfval)
print("Cluster parameterrs are ",kmeans)
print("Cluster centres are ",kmeans.cluster_centers_)
kmeans.predict(dfval)
```

Output:

Cluster parameterrs are KMeans(algorithm='auto', copy_x=True, init='k-means + + ', max_iter=300, n_clusters=3, n_init=10, n_jobs=None, precompute_distances='auto', random_state=0, tol=0.0001, verbose=0)

```
Cluster centres are [[306.5 85.04326923 77.26442308 79.11538462]
[515.42857143 72.8 66.61904762 66.04285714]
[101.5 95.5 90.21287129 93.59405941]]
array([2, 2, 2, 2, 2, 2, 2, 2, 2, 2, 2, 2, 2, 2, 2, 2, 2, 2, 2, 2, 2, 2,
2, 2, 2, 2, 2, 2, 2, 2, 2, 2, 2, 2, 2, 2, 2, 2, 2, 2, 2, 2, 2, 2,
2, 2, 2, 2, 2, 2, 2, 2, 2, 2, 2, 2, 2, 2, 2, 2, 2, 2, 2, 2, 2, 2,
2, 2, 2, 2, 2, 2, 2, 2, 2, 2, 2, 2, 2, 2, 2, 2, 2, 2, 2, 2, 2, 2,
2, 2, 2, 2, 2, 2, 2, 2, 2, 2, 2, 2, 2, 2, 2, 2, 2, 2, 2, 2, 2, 2,
2, 2, 2, 2, 2, 2, 2, 2, 2, 2, 2, 2, 2, 2, 2, 2, 2, 2, 2, 2, 2, 2,
2, 2, 2, 2, 2, 2, 2, 2, 2, 2, 2, 2, 2, 2, 2, 2, 2, 2, 2, 2, 2, 2,
2, 2, 2, 2, 2, 2, 2, 2, 2, 2, 2, 2, 2, 2, 2, 2, 2, 2, 2, 2, 2, 2,
2, 2, 2, 2, 2, 2, 2, 2, 2, 2, 2, 2, 2, 2, 2, 2, 2, 2, 2, 2, 2, 2,
2, 2, 2, 2, 2, 2, 2, 2, 2, 2, 2, 2, 2, 2, 2, 2, 2, 2, 2, 2, 2, 2,
2, 2, 2, 2, 0, 0, 0, 0, 0, 0, 0, 0, 0, 0, 0, 0, 0, 0, 0, 0, 0, 0,
0, 0, 0, 0, 0, 0, 0, 0, 0, 0, 0, 0, 0, 0, 0, 0, 0, 0, 0, 0, 0, 0,
0, 0, 0, 0, 0, 0, 0, 0, 0, 0, 0, 0, 0, 0, 0, 0, 0, 0, 0, 0, 0, 0,
0, 0, 0, 0, 0, 0, 0, 0, 0, 0, 0, 0, 0, 0, 0, 0, 0, 0, 0, 0, 0, 0,
0, 0, 0, 0, 0, 0, 0, 0, 0, 0, 0, 0, 0, 0, 0, 0, 0, 0, 0, 0, 0, 0,
0, 0, 0, 0, 0, 0, 0, 0, 0, 0, 0, 0, 0, 0, 0, 0, 0, 0, 0, 0, 0, 0,
0, 0, 0, 0, 0, 0, 0, 0, 0, 0, 0, 0, 0, 0, 0, 0, 0, 0, 0, 0, 0, 0,
0, 0, 0, 0, 0, 0, 0, 0, 0, 0, 0, 0, 0, 0, 0, 0, 0, 0, 0, 0, 0, 0,
0, 0, 0, 0, 0, 0, 0, 0, 0, 0, 0, 0, 0, 0, 0, 0, 0, 0, 0, 0, 0, 0,
0, 0, 0, 0, 0, 0, 0, 0, 0, 0, 0, 0, 0, 0, 0, 0, 0, 0, 0, 0, 0, 0,
0, 0, 0, 0, 0, 0, 0, 0, 0, 0, 0, 0, 0, 0, 1, 1, 1, 1, 1, 1, 1, 1,
1, 1, 1, 1, 1, 1, 1, 1, 1, 1, 1, 1, 1, 1, 1, 1, 1, 1, 1, 1, 1, 1,
1, 1, 1, 1, 1, 1, 1, 1, 1, 1, 1, 1, 1, 1, 1, 1, 1, 1, 1, 1, 1, 1,
1, 1, 1, 1, 1, 1, 1, 1, 1, 1, 1, 1, 1, 1, 1, 1, 1, 1, 1, 1, 1, 1,
1, 1, 1, 1, 1, 1, 1, 1, 1, 1, 1, 1, 1, 1, 1, 1, 1, 1, 1, 1, 1, 1,
1, 1, 1, 1, 1, 1, 1, 1, 1, 1, 1, 1, 1, 1, 1, 1, 1, 1, 1, 1, 1, 1,
1, 1, 1, 1, 1, 1, 1, 1, 1, 1, 1, 1, 1, 1, 1, 1, 1, 1, 1, 1, 1, 1,
1, 1, 1, 1, 1, 1, 1, 1, 1, 1, 1, 1, 1, 1, 1, 1, 1, 1, 1, 1, 1, 1,
1, 1, 1, 1, 1, 1, 1, 1, 1, 1, 1, 1, 1, 1, 1, 1, 1, 1, 1, 1, 1, 1,
1, 1, 1, 1, 1, 1, 1, 1, 1, 1, 1, 1, 1, 1, 1, 1, 1, 1, 1, 1, 1, 1,
1, 1, 1, 1], dtype=int32)
```

If multi-dimensional data needs to be visualized in 2D, it must be reduced to 2D. If the centroids and groups of data need to be visualized, the code is modified as shown below. Dimension reduction can be performed using PCA.

```
from matplotlib import pyplot
import io
import pandas as pd
from sklearn.cluster import KMeans
import numpy as np
import matplotlib.pyplot as plt
from google.colab import files
uploaded= files.upload()
dfval=pd.read_csv(io.BytesIO(uploaded['grades_km_input.csv']))
#plotting data
from sklearn.decomposition import PCA
pca = PCA(2)
#Transform the data
datadf = pca.fit_transform(dfval)
kmeans = KMeans(n_clusters= 3)
#predict the labels of clusters.
label = kmeans.fit_predict(datadf)
print(label)
#Getting unique labels
u_labels = np.unique(label)
#plotting the results:
#Getting the Centroids
centroids = kmeans.cluster_centers_
u_labels = np.unique(label)
#plotting the results:
for i in u_labels:
    plt.scatter(datadf[label == i, 0], datadf[label == i, 1], label
                = i)
plt.scatter(centroids[:,0], centroids[:,1], s = 80, color = 'k')
plt.legend()
plt.show()
```

Output:

```
[0 0 0 0 0 0 0 0 0 0 0 0 0 0 0 0 0 0 0 0 0 0 0 0 0 0 0 0 0 0 0 0 0 0 0 0 0
 0 0 0 0 0 0 0 0 0 0 0 0 0 0 0 0 0 0 0 0 0 0 0 0 0 0 0 0 0 0 0 0 0 0 0 0 0
 0 0 0 0 0 0 0 0 0 0 0 0 0 0 0 0 0 0 0 0 0 0 0 0 0 0 0 0 0 0 0 0 0 0 0 0 0
 0 0 0 0 0 0 0 0 0 0 0 0 0 0 0 0 0 0 0 0 0 0 0 0 0 0 0 0 0 0 0 0 0 0 0 0 0
 0 0 0 0 0 0 0 0 0 0 0 0 0 0 0 0 0 0 0 0 0 0 0 0 0 0 0 0 0 0 0 0 0 0 0 0 0
 0 0 0 0 0 0 0 0 0 0 0 0 0 0 0 0 0 2 2 2 2 2 2 2 2 2 2 2 2 2 2 2 2 2 2 2 2
 2 2 2 2 2 2 2 2 2 2 2 2 2 2 2 2 2 2 2 2 2 2 2 2 2 2 2 2 2 2 2 2 2 2 2 2 2
 2 2 2 2 2 2 2 2 2 2 2 2 2 2 2 2 2 2 2 2 2 2 2 2 2 2 2 2 2 2 2 2 2 2 2 2 2
 2 2 2 2 2 2 2 2 2 2 2 2 2 2 2 2 2 2 2 2 2 2 2 2 2 2 2 2 2 2 2 2 2 2 2 2 2
 2 2 2 2 2 2 2 2 2 2 2 2 2 2 2 2 2 2 2 2 2 2 2 2 2 2 2 2 2 2 2 2 2 2 2 2 2
 2 2 2 2 2 2 2 2 2 2 2 2 2 2 2 2 2 2 2 2 2 2 2 2 2 2 2 2 2 2 2 2 2 2 2 2 2
 2 2 2 1 1 1 1 1 1 1 1 1 1 1 1 1 1 1 1 1 1 1 1 1 1 1 1 1 1 1 1 1 1 1 1 1 1
 1 1 1 1 1 1 1 1 1 1 1 1 1 1 1 1 1 1 1 1 1 1 1 1 1 1 1 1 1 1 1 1 1 1 1 1 1
 1 1 1 1 1 1 1 1 1 1 1 1 1 1 1 1 1 1 1 1 1 1 1 1 1 1 1 1 1 1 1 1 1 1 1 1 1
 1 1 1 1 1 1 1 1 1 1 1 1 1 1 1 1 1 1 1 1 1 1 1 1 1 1 1 1 1 1 1 1 1 1 1 1 1
```

```
1 1 1 1 1 1 1 1 1 1 1 1 1 1 1 1 1 1 1 1 1 1 1 1 1 1 1 1 1 1 1 1 1 1 1 1 1
1 1 1 1 1 1 1 1 1 1 1 1 1 1 1 1 1 1 1 1 1 1 1 1 1 1 1 1]
```

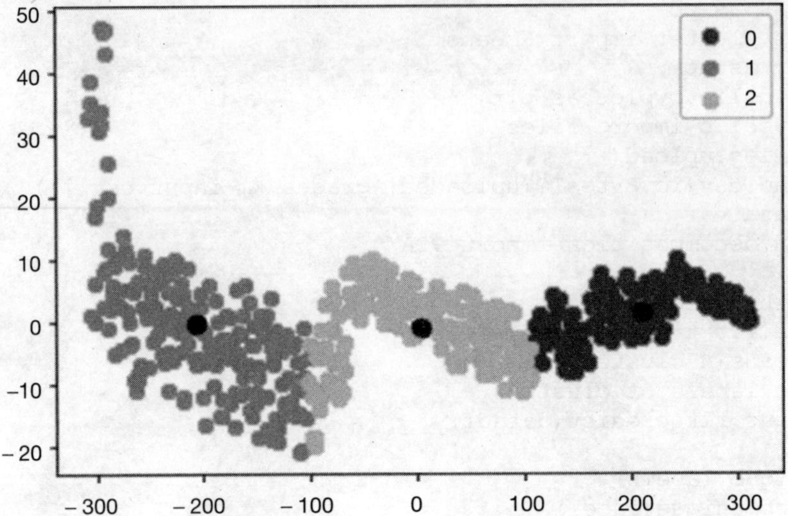

Example 2: A healthcare chain wants to open a series of hospitals within a region. It has data about the location of highly accident-prone areas in the region. The chain needs to decide the number of the hospitals to be opened and the location of these hospitals, so that all the accident-prone areas are covered. The K-means clustering algorithm is the most appropriate to determine the location of these hospitals to cover that region. Here, the km_data.csv file contains the location latitude and number of accidents for that location.

```
import pandas as pd
import numpy as np
import matplotlib.pyplot as plt
from sklearn.preprocessing import MinMaxScaler
from sklearn.cluster import KMeans
from math import sqrt
df = pd.read_csv("km_data.csv",encoding='latin-1')
#read the location data
#add a column for no. of accidents using randomly generated numbers
#dataset is randomly sampled 3 times and each sample is provided with
#randomly generated numbers
df1=df.sample(100, random_state=30)
df2=df.drop(df1.index).sample(80, random_state=30)
df3 = df.drop(df1.index)
df3 = df3.drop(df2.index)
np.random.seed(99999999)
df1['No. of Accidents'] = np.random.randint(0, 40000, df1.shape[0])
df2['No.of Accidents'] = np.random.randint(50000, 100000, df2.shape[0])
df3['No.of Accidents'] = np.random.randint(80000, 150000, df3.shape[0])
data = pd.concat([df1,df2,df3])
```

```
#scale the data
scaler = MinMaxScaler()
data[['latitude','No.ofAccidents']]= scaler.fit_
transform(data[['latitude','No. of Accidents']])
#applying k-means clustering to group data into 4 clusters
k=4
km = KMeans(n_clusters=k)
y_pred = km.fit_predict(data[['latitude', 'No. of Accidents']])
data['cluster']=y_pred #add the predicted cluster values as a column to
the dataset
#plot each cluster as a scatter plot
for i in range(k):
   plt.scatter(data[data.cluster==i]['latitude'],data[data.cluster==i]
['No. of Accidents'])
plt.xlabel("Latitude")
plt.ylabel("No. of Accidents")
print("Centroid values using inbuilt KMeans are: ")
sno=1
for i in km.cluster_centers_:
plt.scatter(i[0],i[1],marker="*",s=100,label="centroid {}".format(sno))
 sno=sno + 1
 print(i)
plt.legend()
plt.show()
```

Output:

Centroid values using inbuilt KMeans are:
[0.39613256 0.30321862]
[0.50697146 0.83881822]
[0.67967907 0.14859177]
[0.71794245 0.5813726]

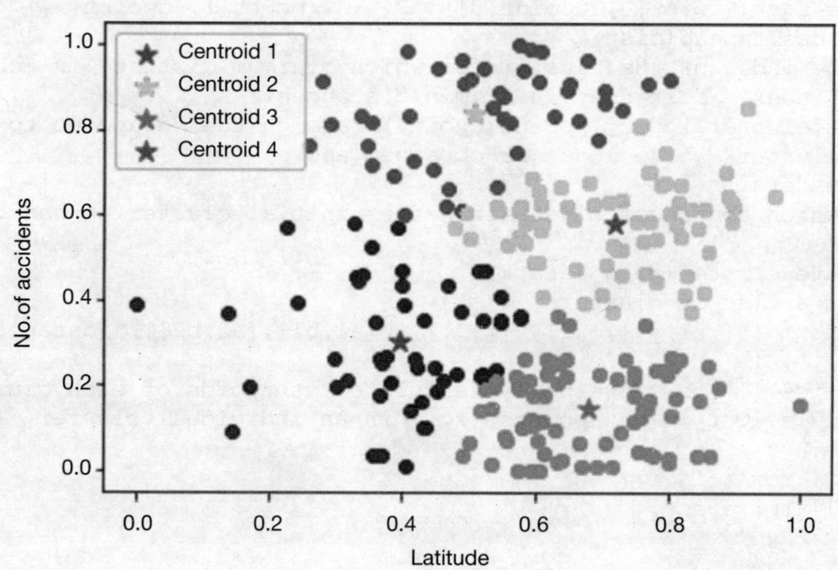

User-defined functions for k-means clustering for the km_data.csv file

```
#creating an array of the datapoints
user_data = []
for x,y in zip(data['latitude'],data['No. of Accidents']):
 user_data.append([x,y])
#function which randomly chooses the centroids (required initially)
def choose_centroids(X,k):
 #X is an array with each element of type [latitude, no. of accidents]
  np.random.seed(90)
 positions = np.random.choice(range(len(X)), size=k, replace=False)
#randomly sample k no. of index values
  centroids=[]
 #choose the datapoints at the indices sampled above, they will be the
#centroids
 for i in positions:
   centroids.append(X[i])
 return centroids
#function which creates the initial clusters using the centroids chosen
by choose_centroids()
def initiate_cluster(X,k):
 #X is an array with each element of type [latitude, no. of accidents]
 centroids = choose_centroids(X,k)
 clusters = [] #will store the clusters as lists, so data points in one
list belong to one cluster
 #create k no. of empty sub-lists for k no. of clusters
 for i in range(k):
   clusters.append([])
 #find distance of each datapoint from each cluster centroid
 for dpoint in X:
   distances=[] #store the distances from each centroid
   for point in centroids:
     dist = sqrt((point[0]-dpoint[0])**2  +  (point[1]-dpoint[1])**2)
     distances.append(dist)
   #find the index of the cluster for which minimum distance is #obtained
   cluster_index = distances.index(min(distances))
   clusters[cluster_index].append(dpoint) #assign the datapoint to that
list(i.e. cluster) whose index is obtained above
 return clusters
#function which continues clustering after initial clustering has been
performed
def calculate_cluster(X,og_data,k):
 #here X is a list of clusters
 #X is of form [ [[x1,y1],[x2,y2],...], [[a1,b1],[a2,b2]], [datapoints of
cluster 3],... ]
 new_centroids=[] #to store newly calculated centroids of each cluster
 #below i is a list of datapoints [x,y] in an individual cluster
 for i in X:
   x = [a[0] for a in i]
   y = [a[1] for a in i]
```

```
    centroid = [np.mean(x),np.mean(y)]
    new_centroids.append(centroid)
  clusters = [] #will store clusters as lists, so datapoints in one list
#belong to one cluster
  #creating k no. of empty sublists to store datapoints of k no. of
#clusters
  for i in range(k):
    clusters.append([])
  #find distance of each datapoint from each cluster centroid and assign
the point to cluster with minimum distance
  for dpoint in og_data:
    distances=[]
    for point in new_centroids:
      dist = sqrt((point[0]-dpoint[0])**2  +  (point[1]-dpoint[1])**2)
      distances.append(dist)
    cluster_index = distances.index(min(distances))
    clusters[cluster_index].append(dpoint)
  return clusters
#function to check if two clustered datasets are equal
def equality(cluster_1, cluster_2):
  for x,y in zip(cluster_1, cluster_2):
    if not (((len(x) == len(y)) and (all(i in x for i in y)))):
      return False
  return True

#function for performing the whole process of kmeans clustering using the
above functions
def fit_kmeans(X,k):
  clusters = initiate_cluster(X,k) #creating initial clusters
  old_clusters = calculate_cluster(clusters,X,k) #perform clustering on
initially created clusters
  new_clusters = calculate_cluster(old_clusters,X,k) #recluster again
  #keep reclustering until the datapoints stop changing clusters
  while not(equality(old_clusters,new_clusters)):
    old_clusters = calculate_cluster(old_clusters,X,k)
    new_clusters = calculate_cluster(old_clusters,X,k)
   #plot each cluster as a scatter plot
  for i in new_clusters:
    plt.scatter([a[0] for a in i],[a[1] for a in i])
  plt.xlabel("Latitude")
  plt.ylabel("No. of Accidents")
  print("cluster centroids are: ")
  global new_centroids
  new_centroids=[]
  for i in new_clusters:
    x = [a[0] for a in i]
    y = [a[1] for a in i]
    centroid = [np.mean(x),np.mean(y)]
    new_centroids.append(centroid)
  sno=1
```

```
 for i in new_centroids:
   plt.scatter(i[0],i[1],marker="*", s=100, label="centroid {}".
format(sno))
   sno = sno + 1
   print(i)
 plt.legend()
 plt.show()
 return
fit_kmeans(user_data,k)
```

Output:

cluster centroids are:
[0.3975908984795953, 0.28642034239739017]
[0.7180242213722119, 0.5822410919925798]
[0.4967087261507008, 0.8242655976854173]
[0.6817238823525831, 0.14801280894564953]

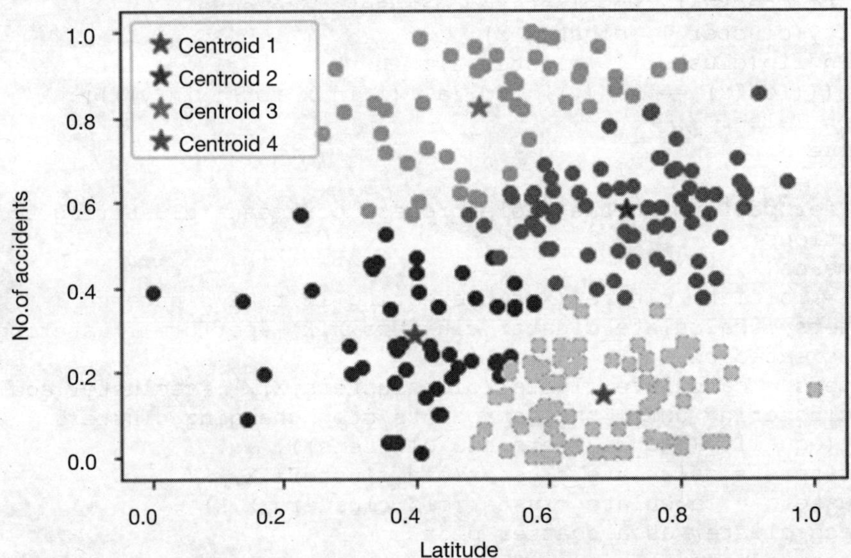

14.3 Hierarchical Clustering

Hierarchical methods produce nested partitions of data with hierarchical relationships among them. Hierarchical relationships are generally shown in the form of dendrograms (Fig. 14.1).

Hierarchical methods include agglomerative methods and divisive methods. Agglomerative clustering uses a bottom-up approach, whereas divisive clustering uses a top-down approach for grouping samples. In agglomerative methods, initially all the individual samples are considered as a separate cluster, that is, a cluster with a single element. They are merged subsequently, and the process continues to obtain a single cluster or desired number of clusters. Divisive methods consider all the samples in a single cluster and then partition it. This partition process is continued until the cluster is split into smaller clusters or the desired number of clusters.

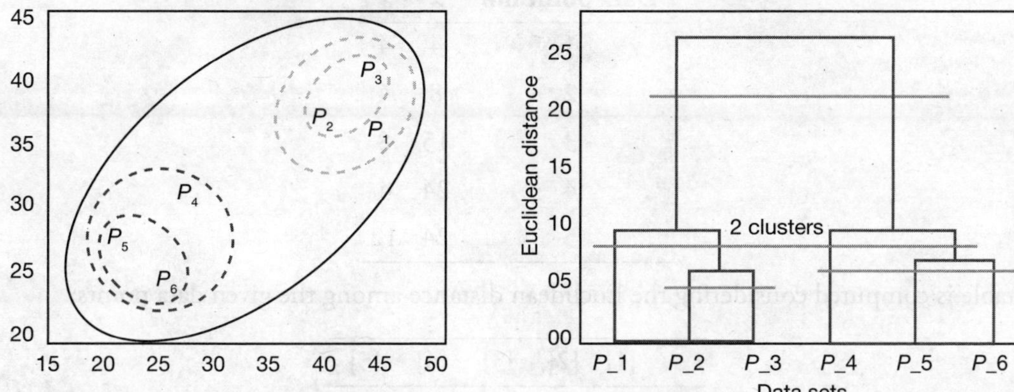

Figure 14.1 Dendrogram

Agglomerative clustering can be performed using following three methods:

- **Single linkage or MIN algorithm:** In this algorithm, the distance (*x, y*), where *x* is from one cluster and *y* is from another cluster, is the smallest distance of two points where the points are in different clusters.

$$D_{SL}(c_i, c_j) = \text{minimum}_{a \in ci,\, b \in cj}\, d(a, b)$$

- **Complete linkage or MAX algorithm:** In this algorithm, the distance (*x, y*), where *x* is from one cluster and *y* is from another cluster, is the largest distance of two points where the points are in different clusters.

$$D_{CL}(c_i, c_j) = \text{maximum}_{a \in ci,\, b \in cj}\, d(a, b)$$

- **Average linkage or MIN algorithm:** In this algorithm, the average distance of all pairs of points across the clusters is used to form a cluster. The average value computed between cluster c_i and c_j is given as follows:

$$D_{AL}(c_i, c_j) = \text{avg}_{a \in ci,\, b \in cj}\, d(a, b)$$

or

$$D_{AL}(c_i, c_j) = \frac{1}{m_i m_j} \sum_{a \in ci, b \in cj} d(a, b)$$

Here m_i and m_j are the sizes of clusters.

Example 1: Five data points of two dimensions are considered. We apply the single linkage algorithm, complete linkage algorithm and average linkage algorithm on the given data to form two clusters.

Data points:

Data point no.	x	y
1	4	4
2	8	4
3	15	8
4	24	4
5	24	12

A table is computed considering the Euclidean distance among the given data points:

	{1}	{2}	{3}	{4}	{5}
{1}	0	4	11.7	20	21.5
{2}		0	8.1	16	17.9
{3}			0	9.8	9.8
{4}				0	8.0
{5}					0

Here, the minimum distance is 4, which is between data points 1 and 2. So data points 1 and 2 form a single cluster {1,2} and the distances are modified based on the algorithm chosen. If single linkage algorithm is applied, distances will be modified as follows:

$$D_{SL}(c_i, c_j) = \text{minimum}_{a \in ci,\, b \in cj}\; d(a, b)$$

The distance between groups {1,2} and {3} is computed using the formula:

Minimum ({1,3},{2,3}) = Minimum { 11.7, 8.1} = 8.1

Thus, the distance between {1,2} and {4} is:

Minimum ({1,4},{2,4}) = Minimum {20, 16} = 16

Thus, the distance between {1,2} and {5} is:

Minimum ({1,5},{2,5}) = Minimum { 21.5, 17.9} = 17.9

	{1,2}	{3}	{4}	{5}
{1,2}	0	8.1	16	17.9
{3}		0	9.8	9.8
{4}			0	8.0
{5}				0

The similarity matrix is modified, and there are still four different clusters. So the minimum distance is found again in the modified similarity matrix and the clusters are formed. {4} and {5} will be combined in a single cluster now as the minimum distance is 8. The distances will be modified according to the formula as:

	{1,2}	{3}	{4,5}
{1,2}	0	8.1	16
{3}		0	9.8
{4,5}			0

The distance of {1,2} with {4,5} will be calculated as:

Minimum (({1,2},{4}), ({1,2},{5})) = Minimum {16, 17.9} = 16

There are still three clusters, so one more iteration of the process can be applied on the data. The next minimum distance in the similarity matrix is 8.1, which is between {3} and {1,2}. So they are combined from a single cluster as {1,2,3}. After applying the single linkage algorithm on the given data points, the two clusters formed are {1,2,3} and {4,5}.

Complete linkage algorithm can also be applied on the same data. Here, initially {1} and {2} clusters are combined as they have minimum distance 4 between them. The distances are modified using the formula:

$$D_{CL}(c_i, c_j) = \text{maximum}_{\;a \in ci,\, b \in cj}\; d(a, b)$$

The distance between groups {1,2} and {3} is computed using the formula:

Maximum ({1,3},{2,3}) = Maximum { 11.7, 8.1} = 11.7

Thus, the distance between {1,2} and {4} is:

Maximum ({1,4},{2,4}) = Maximum {20, 16} = 20

Thus, the distance between {1,2} and {5} is:

Maximum ({1,5},{2,5}) = Maximum { 21.5, 17.9} = 21.5

	{1,2}	{3}	{4}	{5}
{1,2}	0	11.7	20	21.5
{3}		0	9.8	9.8
{4}			0	8.0
{5}				0

The minimum distance is 8, between {4} and {5}. So they form one cluster and distances are modified again considering the formula given above.

	{1,2}	{3}	{4,5}
{1,2}	0	11.7	21.5
{3}		0	9.8
{4,5}			0

The distance of {1,2} with {4,5} will be calculated as:

Maximum (({1,2},{4}), ({1,2},{5})) = Maximum {20, 21.5} = 21.5

There are still three clusters, so one more iteration of the process can be applied on the data. The next minimum distance in the similarity matrix is 9.8, which is between {3} and {4,5}. So they are combined to form a single cluster as {3,4,5}. After applying the complete linkage algorithm on the given data points, the two clusters formed are {1,2} and {3,4,5}

Similarly, the **average linkage algorithm** can be applied on the same data. Here, initially {1} and {2} clusters are combined as they have a minimum distance of 4 between them. The distances are modified using the formula:

$$D_{AL}(c_i, c_j) = \text{avg}_{a \in ci, b \in cj}\, d(a, b)$$

or

$$D_{AL}(c_i, c_j) = \frac{1}{m_i m_j} \sum_{a \in ci, b \in cj} d(a, b)$$

The distance between groups {1,2} and {3} is computed using the formula:

Average ({1,3},{2,3}) = Average { 11.7, 8.1} = 9.9

Thus, the distance between {1,2} and {4} is:

Average ({1,4},{2,4}) = Average {20, 16} = 18

Thus, the distance between {1,2} and {5} is:

Average ({1,5},{2,5}) = Average { 21.5, 17.9} = 19.7

	{1,2}	{3}	{4}	{5}
{1,2}	0	9.9	18	19.7
{3}		0	9.8	9.8
{4}			0	8.0
{5}				0

The minimum distance is 8, between {4} and {5}. So they form one cluster and the distances are modified again considering the formula given above.

	{1,2}	{3}	{4,5}
{1,2}	0	9.9	18.9
{3}		0	9.8
{4,5}			0

The distance of {1,2} with {4,5} will be calculated as:

Average (({1,2},{4}), ({1,2},{5})) = Average {18, 19.7} = 18.9

There are still three clusters, so one more iteration of the process can be applied. The next minimum distance in the similarity matrix is 9.8, which is between {3} and {4,5}. So they are combined to form a single cluster as {3,4,5}. After applying the average linkage algorithm on the given data points, the two clusters formed are {1,2} and {3,4,5}.

14.3.1 Hierarchical Clustering in Python

The agglomerative clustering algorithm is implemented for the data given in the example above. The data needs to be clustered into two groups.

```
# Agglomerative clustering
import numpy as np
import matplotlib.pyplot as plt
import pandas as pd
import scipy.cluster.hierarchy as sch
from sklearn.cluster import AgglomerativeClustering
d = {"x": [4, 8, 15, 24, 24], "y": [4, 4, 8, 4, 12]}
df = pd.DataFrame(d)
print(df)
dendro = sch.dendrogram(sch.linkage(df, method = 'ward'))
plt.title('Dendrogram')
plt.xlabel('data points')
plt.ylabel('Euclidean-distances')
plt.show()
AC = AgglomerativeClustering(n_clusters = 2, affinity = 'euclidean',
linkage = 'ward')
cluster = AC.fit_predict(df)
print (cluster)
```

Output:

```
   x  y
0  4  4
1  8  4
2 15  8
3 24  4
4 24 12
```

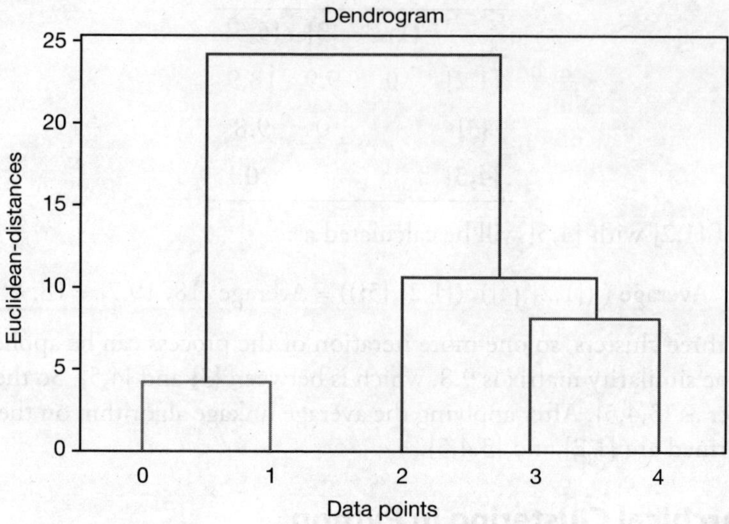

[1 1 0 0 0]

The given data is clustered into two groups, where data points 1 and 2 are in one cluster and data points 3, 4 and 5 are in another cluster.

14.4 DBSCAN Clustering

The K-means clustering algorithm has some challenges to address. Firstly, it may cluster loosely related data together. It clusters every data point, that is, even if the data point is very far in vector space, it will cluster the point. Using a very far point to make clusters may affect the outcome of the whole cluster. DBSCAN clustering algorithm addresses this problem. Another challenge in K-means clustering is that it works on the value of K, that is, the value of K should be known a priori or a number of clusters beforehand. Many times, the K value is not known apriori. In DBSCAN, it is not required that the number of clusters must be specified; that is, the value of K. DBSCAN only needs a function to calculate the distance between data points and some information for defining closeness. The distance that will be considered as close needs to be specified. DBSCAN produces reasonably good results. It produces good results for arbitrary shape clusters also.

DBSCAN is a density-based clustering algorithm. It uses the concept of density and connectivity to define a cluster. The main idea is that a cluster is considered as a region of high density, separated from other clusters by another region of low density. The functioning of this algorithm is based on two parameters: the size of neighbourhood eps (ε) and the minimum number of points MinPts (m) (Fig. 14. 2).

A point is called a core point if it has more than the specified number of points (m) within the ε-neighbourhood. A point is called a border point if it has fewer than m points but is a neighbour of a core point. The noise point is a point which is neither a core point nor a border point. The idea is that every data point should have at least a minimum number of neighbours in a neighbourhood. The neighbourhood of radius ε should have at least m points. The notion of density connectedness determines the quality of the algorithm. A point X is densely reachable to Y if X is the ε-neighbourhood of Y and Y is a core point. The point X is densely reachable from Y if there is a set of core points that leads from Y to X. Points X and Y are densely connected if Z is a core point and thus points X and Y are densely reachable from Z.

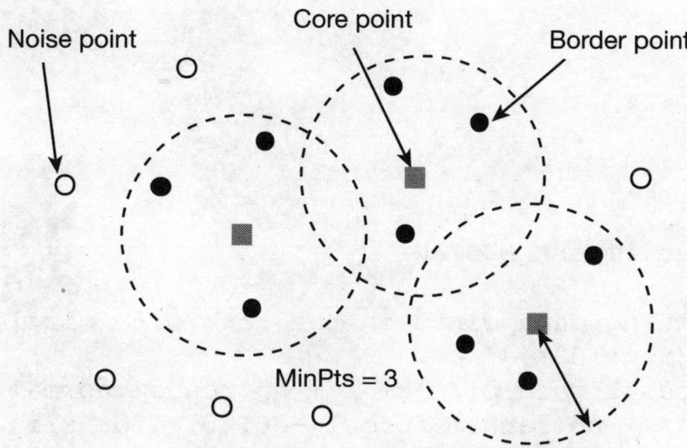

Figure 14.2 DBSCAN points

Steps in DBSCAN clustering:

1. Arbitrarily pick a point *p* in the data set and proceed till all the points are visited. Compute the distance between *p* and all the other data points.
2. Mark it as a core point by finding all the points from *p* with respect to its neighbourhood and check if it has a minimum number of points *m*.
3. A new cluster is formed if it is a core point or an existing cluster is enlarged.
4. Move to the next point if it is a border point.
5. Remove the point if it is a noise point.
6. Merge the mergeable cluster dist $(c_i, c_j) < \varepsilon$.
7. Repeat steps 3 to 6 for all data points.

14.4.1 DBSCAN Code in Python

Let us apply DBSCAN to cluster spherical data. To visualize data easily, let us create a data set with only two features. A function `PointsInCircum()` is created which takes the radius and number of data points as arguments and returns an array of data points which when plotted forms a circle. Three concentric circles of different radii are created here as one circle is not sufficient to see the clustering ability of DBSCAN. Some noise is also added to this data to check how this algorithm deals with noise.

About 2300 spherical training data points are generated with corresponding labels. The plotted data points in the output show that it forms a circle. After that, the features of the training data need to be standardized and DBSCAN is applied from the sklearn library.

The optimum value of epsilon is 30 in this case, and the MinPts value is 6. These optimum values can be found out using the K-distance graph method. The DBSCAN algorithm is trained using these parameters. The results shown here indicate that three clusters are formed with 0, 1 and 2 values as their labels. −1 indicates noise data. About 2300 points are created in total, 1030 points are in cluster 0, 730 points are in cluster 1, 318 points are in cluster 2, and 222 are noise points.

```
#DBSCAN Algorithm
import numpy as np
import pandas as pd
import math
import matplotlib.pyplot as plt
import matplotlib
from sklearn.cluster import DBSCAN
np.random.seed(42)
# Function for creating datapoints in the form of a circle
def PointsInCircle(r,n=100):
    return [(math.cos(2*math.pi/n*x)*r + np.random.normal(-30,30),math.
sin(2*math.pi/n*x)*r + np.random.normal(-30,30)) for x in range(1,n + 1)]
# Creating data points in the form of a circle
df=pd.DataFrame(PointsInCircum(500,1000))
df=df.append(PointsInCircum(300,700))
df=df.append(PointsInCircum(100,300))
# Adding noise to the dataset
df=df.append([(np.random.randint(-600,600),np.random.randint(-600,600))
for i in range(300)])
plt.figure(figsize=(10,10))
plt.scatter(df[0],df[1],s=15,color='red')
plt.title('Whole Dataset',fontsize=22)
plt.xlabel('Feature 1 values',fontsize=16)
plt.ylabel('Feature 2 values',fontsize=16)
plt.show()
#DBSCAN and its plot
dbscan_optclus=DBSCAN(eps=30,min_samples=6)
dbscan_optclus.fit(df[[0,1]])
df['DBSCAN_opt_labels']=dbscan_optclus.labels_
print(df['DBSCAN_opt_labels'].value_counts())
# Plotting the resulting clusters
plt.figure(figsize=(10,10))
plt.scatter(df[0],df[1],c=df['DBSCAN_opt_labels'],cmap=matplotlib.colors.
ListedColormap(colors),s=14)
plt.title('DBSCAN Clustering on whole dataset',fontsize=22)
plt.xlabel('Feature 1 values',fontsize=16)
plt.ylabel('Feature 2 values',fontsize=16)
plt.show()
```

Output:

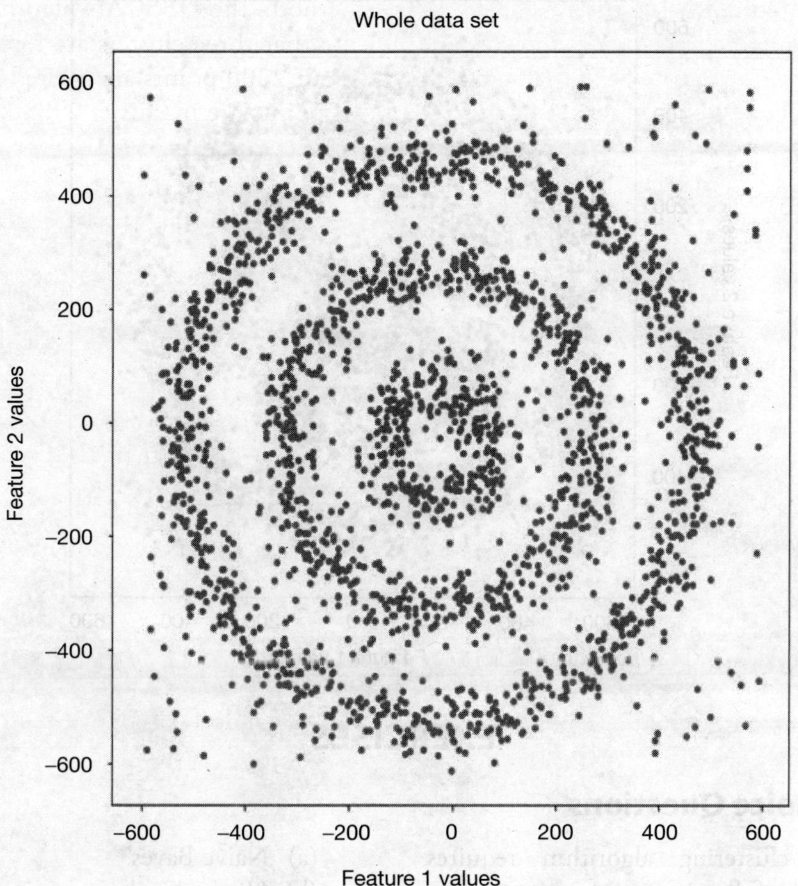


```
0    1030
1     730
2     318
-1    222
Name: DBSCAN_opt_labels, dtype: int64
```

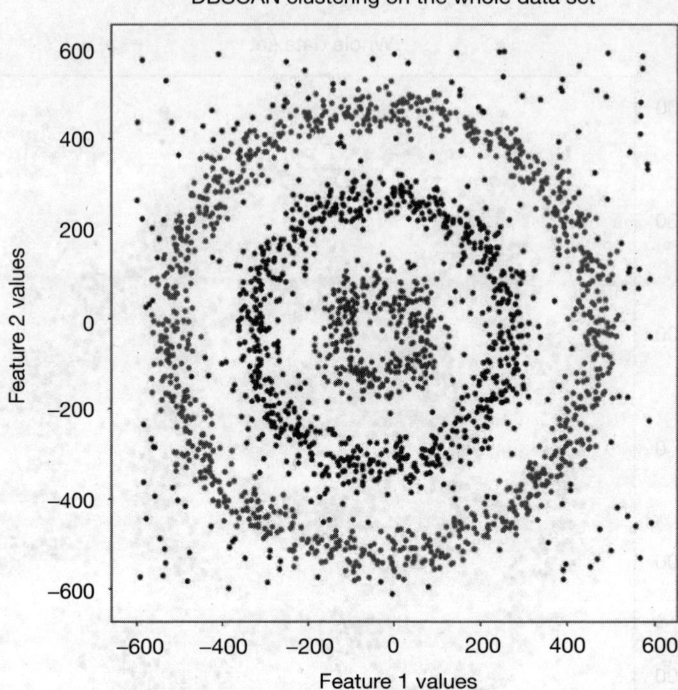

EXERCISES

Multiple Choice Questions

1. K-means clustering algorithm requires which of the following?
   (a) Distance metric
   (b) Value of k or number of clusters
   (c) Initial random guess for cluster centroids
   (d) All of the above

2. Which one of the following statements is incorrect?
   (a) K-means clustering is a method of vector quantization
   (b) The aim of K-means clustering is to partition n data points into k clusters
   (c) K-means is the same as k-nearest neighbour
   (d) All of the above

3. For clustering, which of the following techniques requires merging?
   (a) Naive Bayes'
   (b) Hierarchical
   (c) Partition-based
   (d) All of the above

4. Clustering is ___________ type of learning?
   (a) Supervised
   (b) Unsupervised
   (c) Semi-supervised
   (d) None of the above

5. The task of dividing data into groups is called:
   (a) Clustering
   (b) Classification
   (c) (a) and (b)
   (d) None of the above

6. Which of the following is not a clustering method?

(a) Partition-based
(b) Hierarchical
(c) Density-based
(d) Project-based

7. Which one of the following clustering methods has good accuracy and the ability to merge two clusters?
(a) Density-based
(b) Hierarchical
(c) Grid-based
(d) Partition-based

8. Which of the following clustering methods considers the clusters as a dense region having some similarity and which are different from less dense regions?
(a) Density-based
(b) Partition-based
(c) Grid-based
(d) None of these

9. Hierarchical clustering is a deterministic algorithm.
(a) True
(b) False

10. Time complexity of hierarchical clustering is:
(a) $O(n^3)$
(b) $O(n^2)$
(c) $O(n \log n)$
(d) None of the above

Answers

1. (d) **2.** (c) **3.** (b) **4.** (b) **5.** (a) **6.** (d) **7.** (a) **8.** (a)
9. (a) **10.** (a)

Programming/Concept-based Questions

1. Create a spherical data set of 2300 data points. Add some noise points and apply k-means clustering on that data set.

Answer:

```
#DBSCAN Algorithm
import numpy as np
import pandas as pd
import math
import matplotlib.pyplot as plt
import matplotlib
from sklearn.cluster import DBSCAN
np.random.seed(42)
# Function for creating datapoints in the form of a circle
def PointsInCircle(r,n=100):
    return [(math.cos(2*math.pi/n*x)*r + np.random.normal(-30,30),math.
sin(2*math.pi/n*x)*r + np.random.normal(-30,30)) for x in range(1,n + 1)]
# Creating data points in the form of a circle
df=pd.DataFrame(PointsInCircum(500,1000))
df=df.append(PointsInCircum(300,700))
df=df.append(PointsInCircum(100,300))
# Adding noise to the dataset
df=df.append([(np.random.randint(-600,600),np.random.rand-
int(-600,600)) for i in range(300)])
plt.figure(figsize=(10,10))
```

```
plt.scatter(df[0],df[1],s=15,color='red')
plt.title('Whole Dataset',fontsize=22)
plt.xlabel('Feature 1 values',fontsize=16)
plt.ylabel('Feature 2 values',fontsize=16)
plt.show()
#K-means and its plot
from sklearn.cluster import KMeans
k_meansclus=KMeans(n_clusters=4,random_state=42)
label=k_meansclus.fit(df[[0,1]])
df['KMeans_labels']=k_meansclus.labels_
# Plotting resulting clusters
colors=['purple','red','blue','green']
plt.figure(figsize=(10,10))
plt.scatter(df[0],df[1],c=df['KMeans_labels'],cmap=matplotlib.colors.
ListedColormap(colors),s=14)
plt.title('K-Means Clustering on whole dataset',fontsize=22)
plt.xlabel('Feature 1 values',fontsize=16)
plt.ylabel('Feature 2 values',fontsize=16)
plt.show()
```

Output:

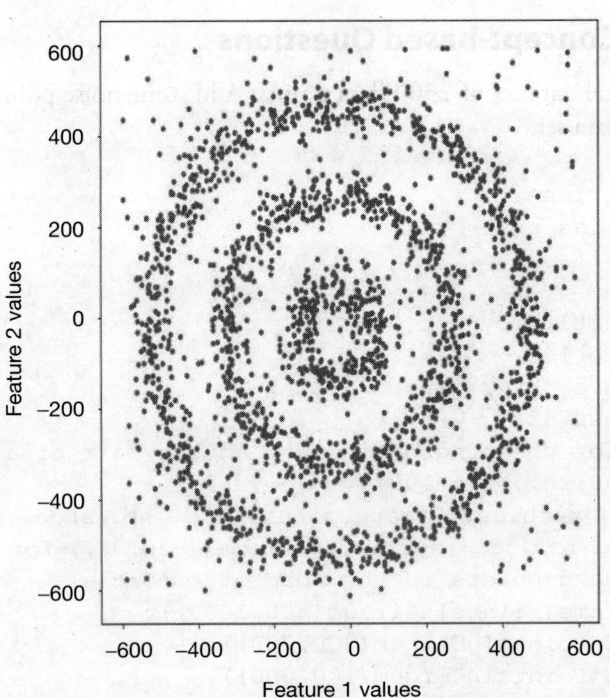

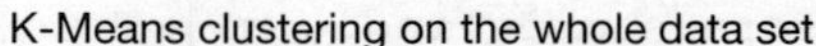

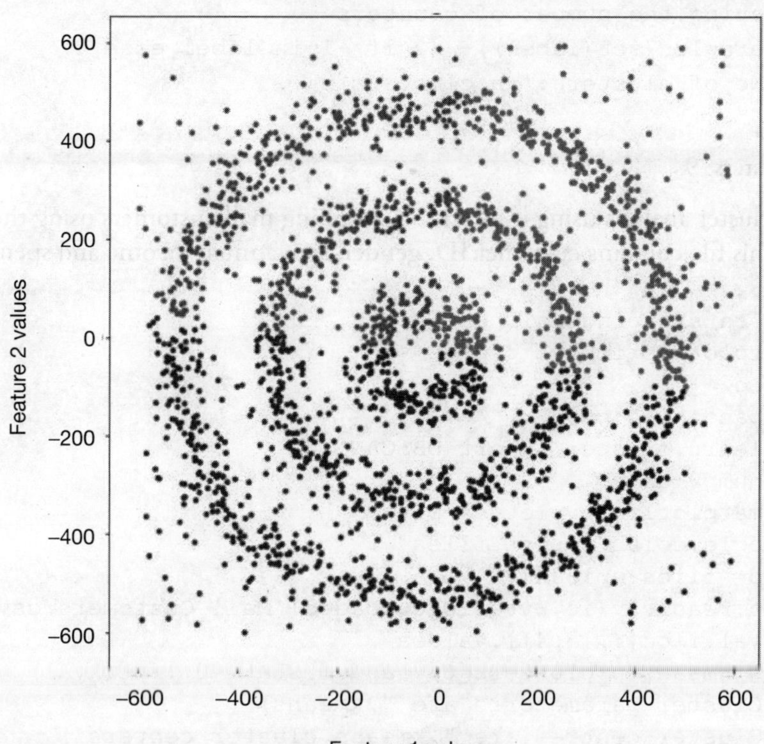

2. Perform cluster analysis using DBSCAN on shopping mall customers using the Mall_Customers.csv file. This file contains customer ID, gender, age, annual income and spending score.

Answer: Annual score and spending score are considered for analysis.

```
#DB SCAN on mall customers
from matplotlib import pyplot
import io
import pandas as pd
from sklearn.cluster import DBSCAN
import numpy as np
import matplotlib.pyplot as plt
from google.colab import files
uploaded= files.upload()
dfval=pd.read_csv(io.BytesIO(uploaded['Mall_Customers.csv']))
xval=dfval.iloc[:,[3,4]].values
dbscan_cluster=DBSCAN(eps=3,min_samples=4,metric='euclidean')
model=dbscan_cluster.fit(xval)
label=model.labels_
from sklearn import metrics
#identifying the points which makes up our core points
sample_cores=np.zeros_like(label,dtype=bool)
```

```
sample_cores[db.core_sample_indices_]=True
#Calculating the number of clusters
n_clusters=len(set(label))- (1 if -1 in label else 0)
print('No of clusters:',n_clusters)
```

Output:
No of clusters: 9

3. Perform cluster analysis using k-means on shopping mall customers using the Mall_Customers.csv file. This file contains customer ID, gender, age, annual income and spending score.

Answer:

```
#Kmeans on shopping mall data
from matplotlib import pyplot
import io
import pandas as pd
from sklearn.cluster import DBSCAN
import numpy as np
import matplotlib.pyplot as plt
from google.colab import files
uploaded= files.upload()
dfval=pd.read_csv(io.BytesIO(uploaded['Mall_Customers.csv']))
xval=dfval.iloc[:,[3,4]].values
kmeans = KMeans(n_clusters=6, random_state=0).fit(xval)
print("Cluster parameterrs are ",kmeans)
print("Cluster centres are ",kmeans.cluster_centers_)
l=kmeans.predict(xval)
print(l)
label = kmeans.fit_predict(xval)
print(label)
#Getting unique labels
u_labels = np.unique(label)
#plotting the results:
#Getting the Centroids
centroids = kmeans.cluster_centers_
u_labels = np.unique(label)
#plotting the results:
for i in u_labels:
    plt.scatter(xval[label == i, 0], xval[label == i, 1], label = i)
plt.scatter(centroids[:,0], centroids[:,1], s = 80, color = 'k')
plt.legend()
plt.show()
```

Output:
Cluster parameterrs are KMeans(algorithm='auto', copy_x=True, init='k-means + + ', max_iter=300,
n_clusters=6, n_init=10, n_jobs=None, precompute_distances='auto',
random_state=0, tol=0.0001, verbose=0)
Cluster centres are [[26.30434783 20.91304348]

```
[78.55172414 82.17241379]
[ 87.75 17.58333333]
[ 55.0875 49.7125 ]
[109.7 82. ]
[ 25.72727273 79.36363636]]
[0 5 0 5 0 5 0 5 0 5 0 5 0 5 0 5 0 5 0 5 0 5 0 5 0 5 0 5 0 5 0 5 0 5 0 5 0
5 0 5 0 5 0 3 0 5 3 3 3 3 3 3 3 3 3 3 3 3 3 3 3 3 3 3 3 3 3 3 3 3 3 3 3 3
3 3 3 3 3 3 3 3 3 3 3 3 3 3 3 3 3 3 3 3 3 3 3 3 3 3 3 3 3 3 3 3 3 3 3 3 3
3 3 3 3 3 3 3 3 3 3 3 3 1 2 1 3 1 2 1 2 1 2 1 2 1 2 1 2 1 2 1 3 1 2 1 2 1
2 1 2 1 2 1 2 1 2 1 2 1 2 1 2 1 2 1 2 1 2 1 2 1 2 1 2 1 2 1 2 1 2 4 2 4 2
4 2 4 2 4 2 4 2 4 2 4 2 4 2 4]
[0 5 0 5 0 5 0 5 0 5 0 5 0 5 0 5 0 5 0 5 0 5 0 5 0 5 0 5 0 5 0 5 0 5 0 5 0
5 0 5 0 5 0 3 0 5 3 3 3 3 3 3 3 3 3 3 3 3 3 3 3 3 3 3 3 3 3 3 3 3 3 3 3 3
3 3 3 3 3 3 3 3 3 3 3 3 3 3 3 3 3 3 3 3 3 3 3 3 3 3 3 3 3 3 3 3 3 3 3 3 3
3 3 3 3 3 3 3 3 3 3 3 3 1 2 1 3 1 2 1 2 1 2 1 2 1 2 1 2 1 2 1 3 1 2 1 2 1
2 1 2 1 2 1 2 1 2 1 2 1 2 1 2 1 2 1 2 1 2 1 2 1 2 1 2 1 2 1 2 1 2 4 2 4 2
4 2 4 2 4 2 4 2 4 2 4 2 4 2 4]
```

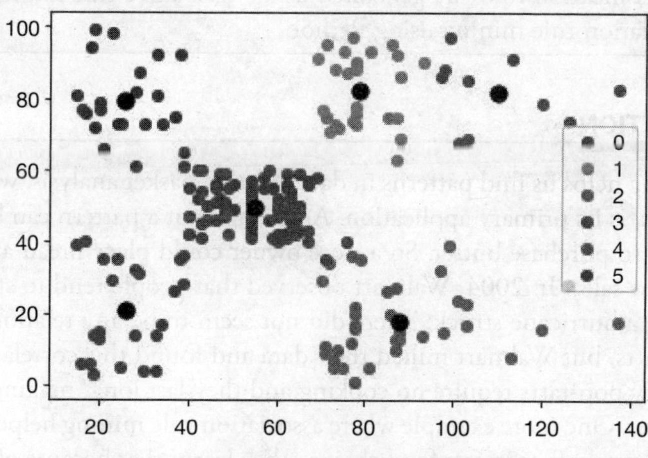

BIBLIOGRAPHY

1. George Seif. "The 5 Clustering Algorithms Data Scientists Need to Know". KD Nuggets, published June 2018, https://www.kdnuggets.com/2018/06/5-clustering-algorithms-data-scientists-need-know.html
2. Sauravkaushik8 Kaushik, "An Introduction to Clustering and Different Methods of Clustering". Analytics Vidhya, last modified February 2023, https://www.analyticsvidhya.com/blog/2016/11/an-introduction-to-clustering-and-different-methods-of-clustering/
3. Alan Fielding. Multivariate Statistics, k-means procedure, https://www.alanfielding.co.uk/multivar/kmeans.htm

CHAPTER **15**

Association Rule Mining

Learning Objectives

At the end of this chapter, you will be able to:

- Explain the basic concept and applications of association rule mining
- Demonstrate support, confidence and lift in the apriori algorithm
- Describe how classification rules are generated using associative rule mining algorithms
- Implement association rule mining using Python

15.0 Introduction

Association rule mining helps us find patterns in data. Market basket analysis, which tries to find patterns in user purchases, is its primary application. An example of a pattern can be that the customers who purchase bread also purchase butter. So a store owner could place bread and butter together in his/her store to increase sales. In 2004, Walmart observed that people tend to stock up or buy strawberry pop-tarts before a hurricane struck. There did not seem to be any relation between hurricanes and strawberry pop-tarts, but Walmart mined their data and found this correlation. Later it was discovered that strawberry pop-tarts require no cooking and they last long, making them the most purchased item in a disaster. One more example where association rule mining helped to find the business strategy was in combo meal offers in fast food chains. They learnt that because of the high salt content of fast food, people feel thirsty. Thus customers bought food and drinks together.

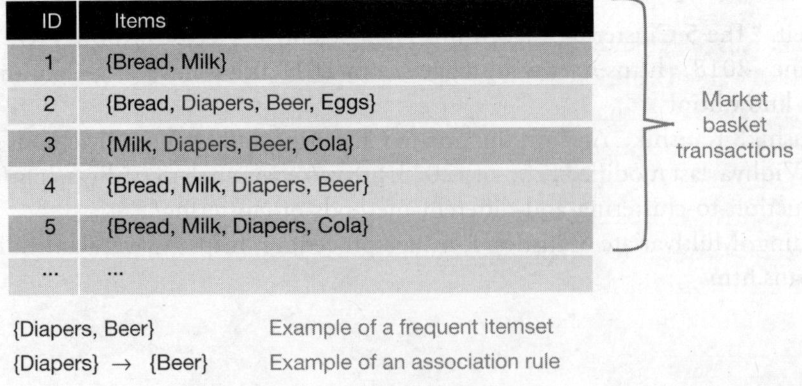

Figure 15.1 Association rule mining

Therefore, finding patterns using data mining is very helpful for companies' decision making. The ultimate aim of association rules is to discover interesting patterns and relationships among items from a given transaction. They help to identify the items that are frequently bought together. Association rules give an idea of user purchasing behaviour as well. Figure 15.1 shows the general idea behind association rules.

15.1 The Apriori Algorithm

The Apriori algorithm is the most basic algorithm of association rule finding. 'Apriori' means 'using previous knowledge'. So, this algorithm finds frequent items using an iterative approach. First, it finds 1-frequent item sets, and using this, it finds 2-frequent item sets and continues to do so until no more frequent item sets can be found. 1-frequent item sets could be {bread}{milk}{butter} and 2-frequent item sets could be {bread, milk} {milk, butter}. The apriori property of the item set helps to reduce the search space. This property states that if {milk, butter} is a frequent item set, then {milk} and {butter} should also be frequent items. This property tells us that all subsets of frequent items must also be frequent.

This algorithm needs values for minimum support and confidence threshold. The formulae are given below:

$$\text{Support (A)} = \frac{\text{Number of transactions in which A appears}}{\text{Total number of transactions}}$$

$$\text{Confidence (A} \rightarrow \text{B)} = \frac{\text{Support (AUB)}}{\text{Support (A)}}$$

$$\text{Lift (A} \Rightarrow \text{B)} = \frac{\text{Confidence (A} \Rightarrow \text{B)}}{\text{P (B)}}$$

$$= \frac{\text{P (A U B)}}{\text{P (A) P (B)}}$$

The support parameter indicates how frequently that item appears in transactions. Specifying minimum support value in apriori helps to prune the transactions. If the data item does not match the minimum support value, that particular data item is not considered further for finding association rules. Support indicates the popularity of the item.

Confidence indicates the likelihood of occurrence of both data items A and B. The apriori algorithm takes an iterative approach to find frequent item sets, using "join" and "prune". The algorithm states that if the P(I) value is less than the minimum support value, that is, threshold value, then the item I is not frequent. All those item sets and supersets can be pruned or ignored when the support value is below the minimum threshold value. The steps in the apriori algorithm (Fig. 15.2) are:

1. **Join:** This deals with the generation of (K+1) item sets using the K-item set by joining items.

2. **Prune:** In this step, reduction of the size of the candidate item set occurs. Scanning of the count of each item set is performed and cross-checked against the minimum support value. Based on count value and the minimum support threshold value, the item is regarded as frequent or infrequent.

- Join step: C_k is generated by joining L_{k-1} with itself
- Prune step: Any (k–1)item set that is not frequent cannot be a subset of a frequent k–item set
- Pseudo-code: C_k: Candidate item set of size k

```
    L_k: Frequent item set of size k
  L_k: (Frequent items);
  for (k = 1; L_k 1 = Ø; k++) do begin
      C_k+1: candidates generated from L_k;
      for each transaction t in database do
          increment the count of all candidates in C_k+1
          that are contained in t
      L_k+1 = candidates in C_k+1 with min_support
      end
      return ∪_k L_k;
```

Figure 15.2 Apriori algorithm (*C*: Candidate item set of size *k*; *L*: Frequent item set of size *k*)

15.2 An Example of an Apriori Algorithm

Here, a table of 6 transactions of purchasing of milk, butter, jam, bread and paneer are shown. Using these transactions, the association rules can be found. Here, the support threshold = 50% and confidence = 60%.

Table 15.1 Transactions

Transaction	List of items
T1	milk, butter, jam
T2	butter, jam, bread
T3	bread, paneer
T4	milk, butter, bread
T5	milk, butter, jam, paneer
T6	milk, butter, jam, bread

Solution: Here, the threshold value for support is 50%, that is, 0.5 x 6 = 3. So, the minimum support is 3.

Step 1: Count each item

Table 15.2 Item count

Item	Count
milk	4
butter	5
jam	4
bread	4
paneer	2

Step 2: Prune

We can see from Table 15.2 that paneer does not meet the minimum support value criterion. So this item will not be considered further. Only milk, butter, jam and bread meet min_sup count as their count values are more than 3.

Table 15.3 Data after pruning

Item	Count
milk	4
butter	5
jam	4
bread	4

Step3: Join

The 2-item set can be formed from Table 15.3. Occurrences of the 2-item set can be found from the transactions given in Table 15.1.

Table 15.4 2-item sets

Item	Count
milk, butter	4
milk, jam	3
milk, bread	2
butter, jam	4
butter, bread	3
jam, bread	2

Step 4: Prune

From Table 15.4, we can see that the item sets {milk, bread} and {jam, bread} do not meet the minimum support value; thus these transactions are deleted or pruned and not considered for further processing.

Table 15.5 Pruning of 2-item sets

Item	Count
milk, butter	4
milk, jam	3
butter, jam	4
butter, bread	3

Step 5: Join and prune

Using Table 15.1, the 3-item set can be formed and their occurrences can be found. For the item set {milk, butter, jam}, subsets {milk, butter}, {milk, jam}, {butter, jam} meet the minimum support criterion and they occur in Table 15.5. So {milk, butter, jam} is considered as frequent.

For item set {milk, butter, bread}, subsets {milk, butter}, {milk, bread}, {butter, bread}, {milk, bread} are not frequent, as they do not meet the minimum support criterion and do not occur in Table 15.5. Hence {milk, butter, bread} is not frequent and it is pruned and not considered for further processing.

Table 15.6 3-item sets

Item
milk, butter, jam
milk, butter, bread
milk, jam, bread
butter, jam, bread

Only {milk, butter, jam} is frequent.

Step 6: Generate association rules

We can form the association rule by using the frequent item set discovered above, as:
{milk, butter} => {jam}
confidence = support {milk, butter, jam} / support {milk, butter} = (3/4)* 100 = 75%
lift = confidence / support {jam} =.75 / (4/6) = 1.12
{milk, jam} => {butter}
confidence = support {milk, butter, jam} / support {milk, jam} = (3/3)* 100 = 100%
lift = confidence / support {butter} = 1 / (5/6) = 1.2
{butter, jam} => {milk}
confidence = support {milk, butter, jam} / support {butter, jam} = (3/4)* 100 = 75%

lift = confidence / support {milk} =.75 / (4/6) = 1.12
{milk} => {butter, jam}
confidence = support {milk, butter, jam} / support {milk} = (3/4)* 100 = 75%
lift = confidence / support {butter, jam} =.75 / (4/6) = 1.12
{butter} => {milk, jam}
confidence = support {milk, butter, jam} / support {butter} = (3/5)* 100 = 60%
lift = confidence / support {milk, jam} =.60 / (3/6) = 1.2
{jam} => {milk, butter}
confidence = support {milk, butter, jam} / support {jam} = (3/4)* 100 = 75%
lift = confidence / support {milk, butter} =.75 / (4/6) = 1.12
All of the above association rules are strong as the minimum confidence threshold here is 60%.

15.3 An Example Using Python: Transactions in a Grocery Store

The example above illustrates an application of the Apriori algorithm in a relatively simple case that generalizes to those used in practice. Companies like Walmart have made extensive use of the Apriori algorithm in correlating products bought by its customers.

Here, the sample data is of 6 transactions of 5 items: milk, butter, jam, bread and paneer. Data is inserted in the file apriorifile1.csv as shown:

Milk	Butter	Jam		
	Butter	Jam		Paneer
			Bread	Paneer
Milk	Butter		Bread	
Milk	Butter	Jam		Paneer
Milk	Butter	Jam	Bread	

The `apriori()` function from the `apyori` package implements the Apriori algorithm to create frequent item sets and association rules. The `apyori` package can be installed using the command:

```
pip install apyori
```

Here, the minimum support value is set as 0.5 and confidence value as 0.6. In output, only {milk, butter, jam} is considered as frequent. All the subsets of {milk, butter, jam} have confidence greater than 60%.

```
import io
import numpy as np
import pandas as pd
from apyori import apriori
from google.colab import files
uploaded= files.upload()
```

```
dfval=pd.read_csv(io.BytesIO(uploaded['apriorifile1.csv']))
dfval.head()
print(dfval.shape)
listrecordset = []
for i in range(0, 6):
    listrecordset.append([str(dfval.values[i,j]) for j in range(0, 5)])
print(listrecordset)
rulesofassociation = apriori(listrecordset, min_support=0.5, min_
confidence=0.6, min_lift=1.2, min_length=2)
resultsofassociation = list(rulesofassociation)
print(resultsofassociation)
```

Output:

(6, 5)

[['nan', 'Butter', 'Jam', 'nan', 'Paneer'], ['nan', 'nan', 'nan', 'Bread', 'Paneer'], ['Milk', 'Butter', 'nan', 'Bread', 'nan'], ['Milk', 'Butter', 'Jam', 'nan', 'Paneer'], ['Milk', 'Butter', 'Jam', 'Bread', 'nan'], ['Milk', 'Butter', 'Jam', 'nan', 'nan']]

[RelationRecord(items=frozenset({'Jam', 'Milk', 'Butter'}), support=0.5, ordered_statistics=[OrderedStatistic(items_base=frozenset({'Butter'}), items_add=frozenset({'Jam', 'Milk'}), confidence=0.6, lift=1.2), OrderedStatistic(items_base=frozenset({'Jam', 'Milk'}), items_add=frozenset({'Butter'}), confidence=1.0, lift=1.2)])........................

It displays all the subsets of {milk, butter, jam} with their support and confidence. All the subsets have confidence values greater than 60.

EXERCISES

Multiple Choice Questions

1. What is the application of association rule mining?
   (a) Spam detection
   (b) Outlier analysis
   (c) Market basket analysis
   (d) Social network analysis

2. What is the meaning of support (item)?
   (a) Total number of transactions containing item
   (b) Total number of transactions not containing item
   (c) Number of transactions containing item / Total number of transactions
   (d) Number of transactions not containing item / Total number of transactions

3. Choose the data mining task that is the most suitable for the following scenario: Given the records of books that a group of people have read, find the relationship of the genre pattern.
   (a) Classification
   (b) Clustering
   (c) Association rule mining
   (d) Prediction

4. What happens if the support threshold value is reduced?
   (a) Frequent item set number remains the same
   (b) Frequent item sets will change as some values will be added to the current set

(c) Frequent item sets will change as some values will become infrequent while others will become frequent
(d) Cannot say

5. A collection of one or more items is called:
(a) Support
(b) Support count
(c) Item set
(d) Lift

6. What is the formula used to calculate confidence (A -> B)?
(a) Support(A ∩ B) / Support (A)
(b) Support(A ∪ B) / Support (A)
(c) Support(A ∩ B) / Support (B)
(d) Support(A ∪ B) / Support (A)

7. When do you consider an association rule fruitful?
(a) When only min_confidence value is satisfied
(b) When only min support value is satisfied
(c) When both min_support and min_confidence values are satisfied
(d) Other measures are required

8. Which of the following is used to measure the interestingness of association rules?
(a) Recall
(b) Accuracy
(c) F1 score
(d) Lift

9. The Apriori algorithm works on which of the following principles?
(a) If a rule is infrequent, its specialized rules are also infrequent
(b) If a rule is infrequent, its generalized rules are also infrequent
(c) Apriori uses both (a) and (b)
(d) None of the above

10. Which association rule would you select?
(a) Having high support and medium confidence
(b) Having high support and low confidence
(c) Having low support and high confidence
(d) Having low support and low confidence

Answers

1. (c) **2.** (c) **3.** (c) **4.** (b) **5.** (c) **6.** (b) **7.** (c) **8.** (d)
9. (a) **10.** (c)

Programming/Concept-based Questions

1. Perform association rule mining for OnlineRetail.xlsx and find out the rules of shopping for different countries like UK, Norway, Germany and Switzerland.

Answer:

```
# Online Retail association rule mining
import io
import numpy as np
import pandas as pd
from mlxtend.frequent_patterns import apriori, association_rules
from google.colab import files
uploaded= files.upload()
dfval=pd.read_excel(io.BytesIO(uploaded['Online Retail.xlsx']))
```

```
dfval.head()
# Exploring the columns of the data
dfval.columns
# Exploring the different regions of transactions
dfval.Country.unique()
# Transactions done in France
basketof_Norway = (dfval[dfval['Country'] =="Norway"]
        .groupby(['InvoiceNo', 'Description'])['Quantity']
        .sum().unstack().reset_index().fillna(0)
        .set_index('InvoiceNo'))
def hot_encode(x):
    if(x<= 0):
        return 0
    if(x>= 1):
        return 1

# Encoding the datasets
basketof_encoded = basketof_Norway.applymap(hot_encode)
basketof_Norway = basketof_encoded
print(basketof_Norway)
# Building the model
frq_itemset = apriori(basketof_Norway, min_support = 0.05, use_colnames
= True)
#Collecting the inferred rules in a dataframe
asso_rules  =  association_rules(frq_itemset,  metric  ="lift", min_
threshold = 1)
asso_rules = asso_rules.sort_values(['confidence', 'lift'], ascending
=[False, False])
print(asso_rules.head())
```

2. Create a .csv file having the following transactions:
1 milk butter jam
2 butter jam bread
3 bread paneer
4 milk butter bread
5 milk butter jam paneer
6 milk butter jam bread
Find out the association rules for this data.
Answer:

```
import pandas as pd
import numpy as np
from apyori import apriori
data=pd.read_csv("/content/ML a6 CSV - Sheet1.csv")
records=[]
```

```
for i in range(1,6):
    records.append([str(data.values[i,j])for j in range (1,4)])
rule=apriori(records, min_support=0.5)
final=list(rule)
print(len(final))
print(final)
```

Output: 2

[RelationRecord(items=frozenset({'bread'}), support=0.6, ordered_statistics=[OrderedStatistic(items_base=frozenset(), items_add=frozenset({'bread'}), confidence=0.6, lift=1.0)]), RelationRecord(items=frozenset({'jam'}), support=0.6, ordered_statistics=[OrderedStatistic(items_base=frozenset(), items_add=frozenset({'jam'}), confidence=0.6, lift=1.0)])]

3. You have a list of shopping items purchased by many people. Find out the frequently purchased combinations of 2 items. Implement Apriori, a frequent pattern analysis algorithm, using Python using the store_data.csv file.

Answer:

```
import io
import pandas as pd
from apyori import apriori
from google.colab import files
# To open csv file
def open_file(name):
uploaded=files.upload()
data = pd.read_csv(io.BytesIO
(uploaded[name]),header=None)
df=[]
for i in range(0, 20):
    df.append([str(data.values[i, j]) for j in range(0,6)])
return df
# For apriori analysis
def apriorialgo(df):
association_rules = apriori(df, min_support=0.45, min_confidence=0.7,
min_lift=1.2, min_le
ngth=2)
association_results = list(association_rules)
# To display
rule=[]
support=[]
confidance=[]
lift=[]
for item in association_results:
    pair = item[0]
```

```
        items = [x for x in pair]
        rule.append(items[0] + " -> " + items[1])
        support.append(str(item[1]))
        confidance.append(str(item[2][0][2]))
        lift.append(str(item[2][0][3]))
    dataframe=pd.DataFrame({" Rules ":rule,"Support":support,
    "Confidance":confidance,"Lift":
    lift})
    print(dataframe)
    Data=open_file("store_data.csv")
    apriorialgo(Data)
```

Output:

	Rules	Support	Confidence	Lift
0	APPLE -> CHIPS	0.45	0.75	1.36
1	BUTTER -> CHIPS	0.45	1.0	1.33
2	BUTTER -> WINE	0.45	0.818	1.25

CHAPTER **16**

Time Series Analysis Using Python

LEARNING OBJECTIVES

At the end of this chapter, you will be able to:

- Explain time series data, its components and modelling
- Perform analysis on time series data such as decomposing and plotting
- Check the stationarity of time series data
- Perform forecasting and autocorrelation for time series data
- Build an ARIMA model for time series forecasting and evaluate it
- Implement time series analysis using Python

16.0 INTRODUCTION

Time series data is a collection of information or observations made at regular or irregular periods of time. A time series is often a collection of data points recorded at regularly spaced intervals. The number of data points captured may be hourly, daily, weekly, monthly, quarterly or yearly.

16.1 COMPONENTS OF A TIME SERIES

- **Trend:** This shows a general direction of the time series data over a long period of time. Trends can be increasing (upward), decreasing (downward) or horizontal (stationary).
- **Seasonality:** This shows a trend that repeats with respect to timing, direction and magnitude. The duration could be a year or shorter. Some examples include an increase in water consumption in summer due to hot weather.
- **Cyclical:** These are the trends with no set repetition over a particular period of time. A cycle refers to a period of ups and downs, booms and slumps, mostly observed in business. Cycles do not exhibit seasonal variation, but generally occur over a time period of 3–12 years depending on the nature of the time series.
- **Irregular variation:** These are fluctuations in the time series data which become evident when trend and cyclical variations are removed. These variations are unpredictable, erratic and may or may not be random.

16.2 Additive and Multiplicative Time Series

Depending on the nature of the trend and seasonality, a time series can be modelled as additive or multiplicative, wherein each observation in the series can be expressed as a sum or a product of the components.

Additive time series: Value = Base Level + Trend + Seasonality + Error

Multiplicative time series: Value = Base Level × Trend × Seasonality × Error

16.3 Time Series Analysis

The statistical techniques for studying time series data are included in time series analysis. We can extract useful statistics, patterns and other aspects of the data using these techniques. Line charts are used to illustrate time series. Therefore, time series analysis entails comprehending the fundamental properties of the time series data in order to produce insightful and precise predictions.

The publicly available gold price time series data is used here. This data set provides the monthly price of gold in 19 countries. We have selected the gold price of United States only (in USD): https://www.kaggle.com/datasets/odins0n/monthly-gold-prices

16.3.1 Reading and Displaying Data

In the data set, Month and Price are the two columns that make up the data for a time series. This is stored in the goldRateUS.csv file.

Let us read the time series data set as a pandas data frame using the `read_csv()` function. This file is stored in the Dataset directory, which in turn is stored in another directory that is the parent directory of the source code directory of Python.

To start, let us import the pandas library and read the gold price data into a data frame:

```
#Reading and Displaying Data
import pandas as pd
df = pd.read_csv("../dataset/goldRatesUS.csv")
print(df.head())
print(df.tail())
```

Output:

```
  Month   Price
0 01-1981 506.5
1 02-1981 489.0
2 03-1981 513.8
3 04-1981 482.8
4 05-1981 479.3

    Month   Price
235 08-2000 277.0
236 09-2000 273.7
```

237 10-2000 264.5
238 11-2000 269.1
239 12-2000 274.5

16.3.2 Converting to Datetime Format

Next, we convert the Month column into a datetime object. This will allow it to programmatically pull time values such as the year or month for each record.

To do this, we use the `to_datetime()` method in pandas:

```
#Converting to Datetime Format
df['Month']=pd.to_datetime(df['Month'])
```

16.3.3 Setting the Index

In this step, the Month column is changed into an index. This will make it easier for us to work with some packages later.

```
#Set Index
df.index = df['Month']
del df['Month']
print(df.head())
```

Output:

```
  Month    Price
1981-01-01 506.5
1981-02-01 489.0
1981-03-01 513.8
1981-04-01 482.8
1981-05-01 479.3
```

16.3.4 Plotting

We will create a time series plot using the Matplotlib and Seaborn libraries. We will then be able to plot the time series data visually. Let us first import Seaborn and Matplotlib. Next, we will overlay our time series with the seven-month rolling mean and seven-month rolling standard deviation.

To make a Matplotlib plot of the time series:

```
#Plotting
import matplotlib.pyplot as plt
import seaborn as sns
sns.lineplot(data=df)
plt.ylabel('Monthly Gold Price Change in United States')
plt.show
```

Output:

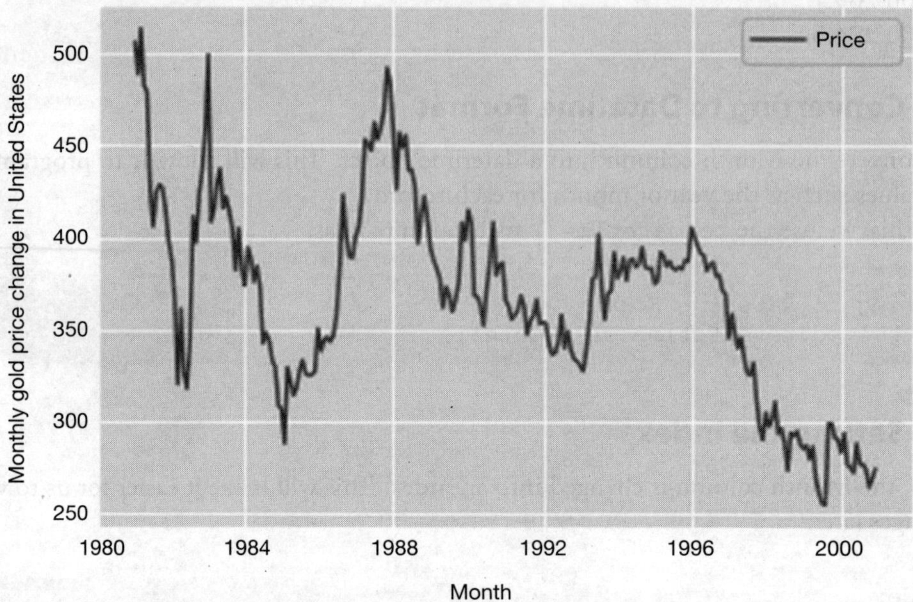

16.3.5 Stationarity

Stationarity is a key part of time series analysis. Simply put, it means that the manner in which time series data changes is constant. A stationary time series will not have any trends or seasonal patterns. You should check for stationarity because not only does it make modelling time series easier, but it is also an underlying assumption in many time series methods. Specifically, stationarity is assumed for a wide variety of time series forecasting methods including autoregressive moving average (ARMA), autoregressive integrated moving average (ARIMA) and seasonal ARIMA (SARIMA).

We will use the Dickey–Fuller test to check for stationarity in our data. This test will generate critical values and a *p*-value, which will allow us to accept or reject the null hypothesis that there is no stationarity. If we reject the null hypothesis, that means we accept the alternative, which is that stationarity is present.

These values allow us to test the degree to which present values change with past values. If there is no stationarity in the data set, a change in present values will not cause a significant change in past values.

Method 1: Time series plot

Many time series are obviously non-stationary. We can understand this by looking at their plots. From the previous step, we can see that the time series has a strong downward trend, so it is non-stationary. When the time series is harder to judge, we can use other methods.

Method 2: ACF plot and PACF plot

These two plots are helpful throughout the process of fitting ARIMA models. ACF (autocorrelation function) is the correlation of a time series with its lags. A lag is the measurement of the temporal difference under consideration. The correlation between values that are separated by one period of time is known as a lag 1 autocorrelation. A lag k autocorrelation, in more general terms, is the correlation between values that are k time periods apart. ACF measures the linear relationship between lagged values of the time series. For example, we can measure the autocorrelation of y_t and y_{t-k} for different values of k.

ACF is straightforward to measure. However, the relationships among lags are more complicated. For example, we can assume that y_t and y_{t-1} are correlated, and y_{t-1} and y_{t-2} are also correlated. Due to their correlations with y_{t-1}, y_t and y_{t-2} must also be correlated. How can we measure if there is new information in y_{t-2} to predict y_t, besides their relationships with y_{t-1}?

For this, we need partial autocorrelations. PACF (partial autocorrelation function) shows the partial correlation of the time series with its lags, after removing the effects of lower-order lags. For example, the partial autocorrelation of y_t and y_{t-k} is the correlation that is not explained by their relationships with the lags $y_{t-1}, y_{t-2}, \ldots, y_{t-k+1}$. It measures the balance amount of variance in y_{t-k} to predict the future value of y_t.

Method 3: ADF test

Apart from plots, we can also check for stationarity with statistical tests such as ADF or augmented Dickey–Fuller. This tests the null hypothesis for a unit root (non-stationary).

H_0: $\beta = 1$ (the time series is non-stationary)

H_a: $\beta < 1$ (the time series is stationary)

If the result shows a large p-value, it means the test failed to reject the null hypothesis. So the ADF test also suggests that our time series is non-stationary. The calculated p-value is 0.112912, which is greater than 0.05; this indicates that we cannot reject the null hypothesis. Hence, the series is not stationary.

Let us test for stationarity in our gold price data.

To start, let us calculate the seven-month rolling mean:

```
#Stationarity Check
rolling_mean = df.rolling(7).mean() # (a seven-month rolling mean)
rolling_std = df.rolling(7).std()
plt.plot(df, color="blue",label="Original Gold Price")
plt.plot(rolling_mean, color="red", label="Rolling Mean #Gold Price")
plt.plot(rolling_std, color="black", label = "Rolling Standard Deviation
in #Gold Price")
plt.title("Gold Price Time Series, Rolling Mean, Standard Deviation")
plt.legend(loc="best")
```

Output:

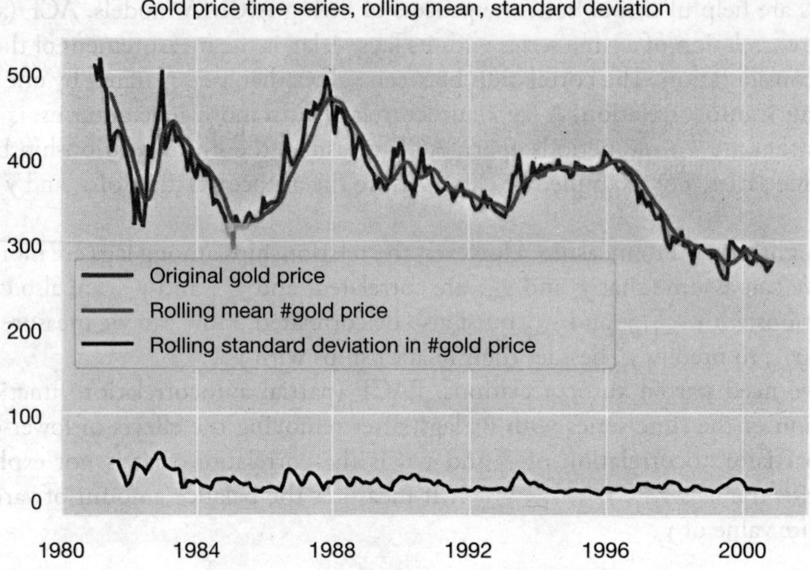


```
#ADF Test
from statsmodels.tsa.stattools import adfuller
dftest = adfuller(df['Price'],autolag="AIC")
dfoutput=pd.Series(dftest[0:4], index=['Test Statistic','p-value','Lags
Used','No. of Obs'])
for key,value in dftest[4].items():
    dfoutput['Critical Value (%s)'%key] = value
print(dfoutput)
```

Output:
Test Statistic -2.510618
p-value 0.112912
Lags Used 1.000000
No. of Obs 238.000000
Critical Value (1%) -3.458128
Critical Value (5%) -2.873762
Critical Value (10%) -2.573283
dtype: float64

16.3.6 Autocorrelation

Checking the time series data for autocorrelation in Python is another important part of the analytic process. It is a measure of how correlated a time series data is at a given point in time with past values.

This has huge implications across many industries. For example, if our gold price data has strong autocorrelation, we can assume that high gold price today suggests a strong likelihood that it will be high tomorrow as well.

The pandas data frame has an autocorrelation method that we can use to calculate the autocorrelation in our gold price data.

Let us compute the one-month lag:

```
#Autocorrelation (Lag1)
autocorrelation_lag1 = df['Price'].autocorr(lag=1)
print("One Month Lag: ", autocorrelation_lag1)
```

Output:
One Month Lag: 0.949978416397146
Code (3,6 and 9 month Lag)

```
#Autocorrelation (Lag 3,6,9)
autocorrelation_lag3 = df['Price'].autocorr(lag=3)
print("Three Month Lag: ", autocorrelation_lag3)
autocorrelation_lag6 = df['Price'].autocorr(lag=6)
print("Six Month Lag: ", autocorrelation_lag6)

autocorrelation_lag9 = df['Price'].autocorr(lag=9)
print("Nine Month Lag: ", autocorrelation_lag9)
```

Output:
Three Month Lag: 0.8721367603675548
Six Month Lag: 0.752823863863704
Nine Month Lag: 0.6451075457397619

16.3.7 Decomposition

Trend decomposition is another useful way to visualize trends in time series data. Let us import `seasonal_decompose()` from the statsmodels package:

```
#Decomposition
from statsmodels.tsa.seasonal import seasonal_decompose
decompose = seasonal_decompose(df['Price'],model='additive',period=7)
decompose.plot()
plt.show()
```

Output:

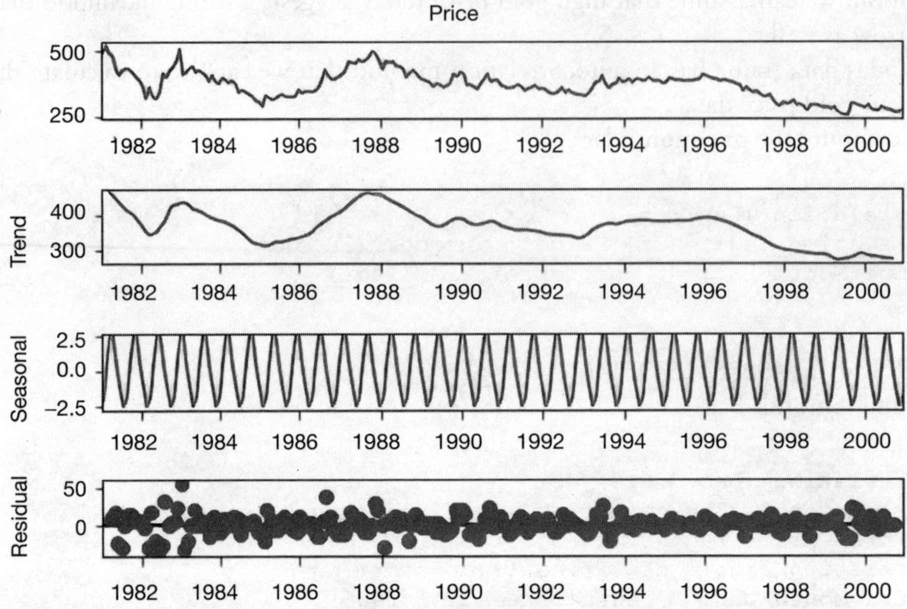

16.3.8 Forecasting

By using historical and current data, time series forecasting enables us to anticipate future values in a time series. Here, we will forecast the gold price using the ARIMA approach, which enables us to estimate future values as a linear mixture of past values. We will use the auto_arima package, which enables us to skip the laborious process of hyperparameter tuning.

Let us first divide our data into training and testing groups and visually represent the split:

```
#Forecasting (Plot train and Test data)
df['Month'] = df.index
train = df[0:230]   #df[ pd.to_datetime(df['Date']) < pd.to_
datetime("07-12-2002") ]
train['train'] = train['Price']
del train['Month']
del train['Price']
test = df[231:]  #df[ pd.to_datetime(df['Date']) > pd.to_
datetime("07-12-2002") ]
del test['Month']
test['test'] = test['Price']
del test['Price']
plt.plot(train, color = "black",label="train")
plt.plot(test, color = "red",label="test")
plt.title("Train/Test split for Gold Price Data")
plt.ylabel("Gold Price")
plt.xlabel('Year-Month')
```

```
plt.legend()
sns.set()
plt.show()
```

Output:

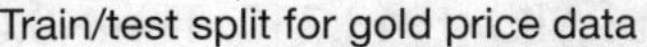

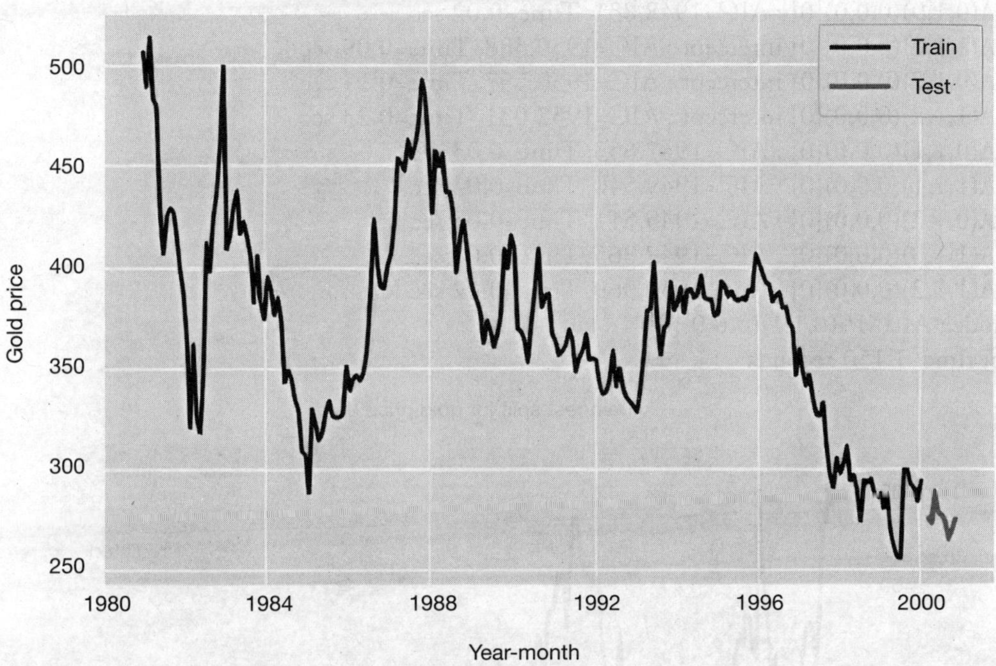


```
#Forecasting (View Prediction)
import pmdarima (# Install this package first (!pip install pmdarima))
from pmdarima import auto_arima
model = auto_arima(train, trace=True, error_action='ignore', suppress_
warnings=True)
model.fit(train)
forecast = model.predict(n_periods=len(test))
#forecast = pd.DataFrame(forecast,index = test.
index,columns=['Prediction'])
plt.plot(train, color = "black",label="Train")
plt.plot(test, color = "red",label="Test")
plt.plot(forecast, color = "green",label="Predicted")
plt.title("Train/Test split for Gold Price Data")
plt.ylabel("Gold Price")
plt.xlabel('Year-Month')
plt.legend()
sns.set()
plt.show()
forecast
```

Output:

Performing stepwise search to minimize aic
ARIMA(2,1,2)(0,0,0)[0] intercept : AIC=1953.059, Time=0.32 sec
ARIMA(0,1,0)(0,0,0)[0] intercept : AIC=1950.144, Time=0.02 sec
ARIMA(1,1,0)(0,0,0)[0] intercept : AIC=1949.004, Time=0.04 sec
ARIMA(0,1,1)(0,0,0)[0] intercept : AIC=1948.750, Time=0.05 sec
ARIMA(0,1,0)(0,0,0)[0] : AIC=1948.831, Time=0.02 sec
ARIMA(1,1,1)(0,0,0)[0] intercept : AIC=1950.588, Time=0.09 sec
ARIMA(0,1,2)(0,0,0)[0] intercept : AIC=1950.557, Time=0.11 sec
ARIMA(1,1,2)(0,0,0)[0] intercept : AIC=1952.031, Time=0.23 sec
ARIMA(0,1,1)(0,0,0)[0] : AIC=1947.653, Time=0.03 sec
ARIMA(1,1,1)(0,0,0)[0] : AIC=1949.540, Time=0.04 sec
ARIMA(0,1,2)(0,0,0)[0] : AIC=1949.511, Time=0.05 sec
ARIMA(1,1,0)(0,0,0)[0] : AIC=1947.865, Time=0.02 sec
ARIMA(1,1,2)(0,0,0)[0] : AIC=1950.969, Time=0.12 sec
Best model: ARIMA(0,1,1)(0,0,0)[0]
Total fit time: 1.150 seconds

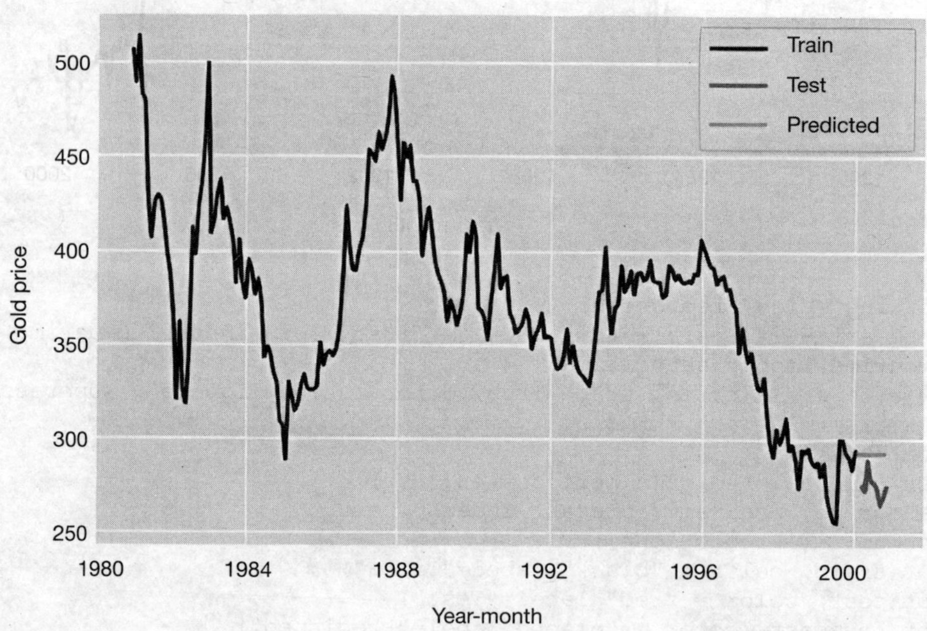

2000-03-01 292.544838
2000-04-01 292.544838
2000-05-01 292.544838
2000-06-01 292.544838
2000-07-01 292.544838
2000-08-01 292.544838
2000-09-01 292.544838

2000-10-01 292.544838
2000-11-01 292.544838
Freq: MS, dtype: float64

16.3.9 Evaluation

Finally, let us calculate the root mean squared error (RMSE):

```
#Measure Error
from math import sqrt
from sklearn.metrics import mean_squared_error
rms = sqrt(mean_squared_error(test,forecast))
print("RMSE: ", rms)
```

Output:
RMSE: 18.972239903975044

16.4 Case Study on Time Series Analysis

The Electric_Production.csv file contains information about date and electricity consumption. We will perform time series analysis on this. Along with some plotting of data, its stationarity, correlation, decomposition and forecasting is carried out and the ARIMA model is evaluated by calculating its RMSE.

```
import numpy as np
import pandas as pd
import io
import matplotlib.pyplot as plt
from google.colab import files
import seaborn as sns
uploaded= files.upload()
df=pd.read_csv(io.BytesIO(uploaded['Electric_Production.csv']),parse_
dates=['DATE'],infer_datetime_format=True)
print(df)
```

Output:

Saving Electric_Production.csv to Electric_Production (1).csv

	DATE	IPG2211A2N
0	1985-01-01	72.5052
1	1985-02-01	70.6720
2	1985-03-01	62.4502
3	1985-04-01	57.4714
4	1985-05-01	55.3151
..	...	...
392	2017-09-01	98.6154
393	2017-10-01	93.6137

394 2017-11-01 97.3359
395 2017-12-01 114.7212
396 2018-01-01 129.4048
[397 rows x 2 columns]

```
ind=df.set_index(['DATE'])
ind.rename(columns={'IPG2211A2N':'value'},inplace=True)
ind.head()
plt.xlabel('Year')
plt.ylabel('Electricity production')
plt.plot(ind)
#Creating a rolling window of a specified size and performing calculations
on the data in this window which, of course, rolls through the data.
Checking stationarity in the data.
rolling_mean = ind.rolling(7).mean()
rolling_std = ind.rolling(7).std()
#Overlaying original data set with seven-month rolling mean and seven-
month rolling standard deviation.
plt.plot(ind, color="blue",label="Original Data")
plt.plot(rolling_mean, color="red", label="Rolling Mean Value")
plt.plot(rolling_std, color="black", label = "Rolling Standard Deviation
in Value")
plt.title("Electricity Time Series, Rolling Mean, Standard Deviation")
plt.legend(loc="best")
```

Output:

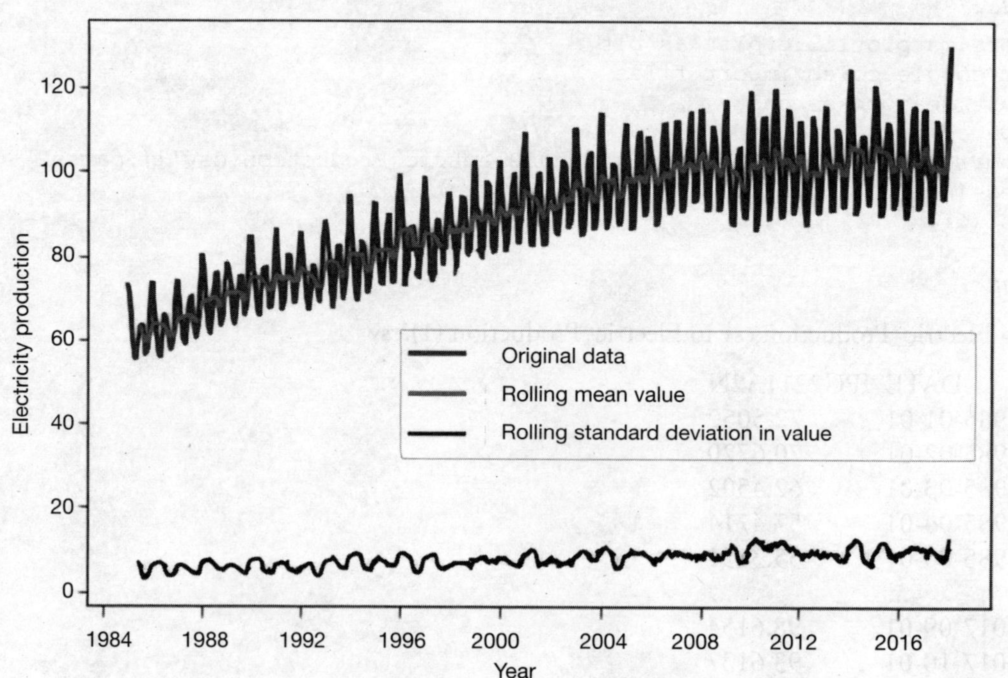

```
from statsmodels.tsa.stattools import adfuller
adft = adfuller(ind,autolag="AIC")
output_df = pd.DataFrame({"Values":[adft[0],adft[1],adft[2],adft[3],
adft[4]['1%'], adft[4]['5%'], adft[4]['10%']] , "Metric":["Test
Statistics","p-value","No. of lags used","Number of observations used",
"critical value (1%)", "critical value (5%)", "critical value (10%)"]})
autocorrelation_lag1 = ind['value'].autocorr(lag=1)
print("One Month Lag: ", autocorrelation_lag1)
autocorrelation_lag3 = ind['value'].autocorr(lag=3)
print("Three Month Lag: ", autocorrelation_lag3)
autocorrelation_lag6 = ind['value'].autocorr(lag=6)
print("Six Month Lag: ", autocorrelation_lag6)
autocorrelation_lag9 = ind['value'].autocorr(lag=9)
print("Nine Month Lag: ", autocorrelation_lag9)
from statsmodels.tsa.seasonal import seasonal_decompose
decompose = seasonal_decompose(ind['value'],model='additive', period=6)
decompose.plot()
plt.show()
```

Output:
One Month Lag: 0.8717308657532121
Three Month Lag: 0.5355867575850725
Six Month Lag: 0.9266842332406335
Nine Month Lag: 0.5180088174990667

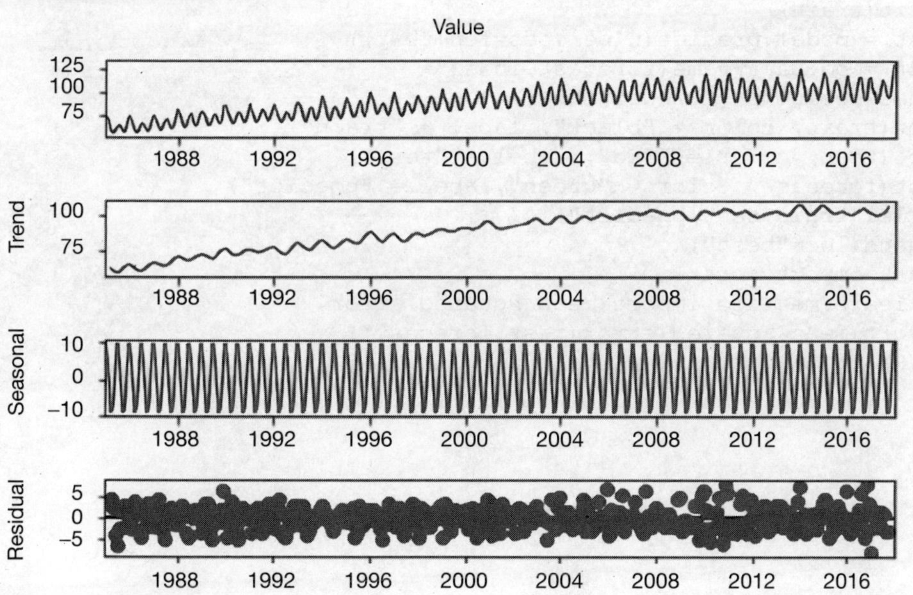

```
#Forecasting using ARIMA enables us to forecast future values in terms of
a linear combination of past values.
ind['Date'] = ind.index
train = ind[ind['Date'] < pd.to_datetime("2015-09-01", format='%Y-%m-
%d')]
train['train'] = train['value']
del train['Date']
del train['value']
test = ind[ind['Date'] >= pd.to_datetime("2015-09-01", format='%Y-%m-
%d')]
del test['Date']
test['test'] = test['value']
del test['value']
plt.plot(train, color = "black",label="training")
plt.plot(test, color = "red",label="testing")
plt.title("Train/Test split for electric production Data")
plt.ylabel("Value")
plt.xlabel('Year-Month-date')
plt.legend(loc="best")
sns.set()
plt.show()
#!pip install pmdarima
from pmdarima.arima import auto_arima
model = auto_arima(train, trace=True,error_action='ignore', suppress_
warnings=True)
model.fit(train)
forecast = model.predict(n_periods=len(test))
forecast = pd.DataFrame(forecast,index =
test.index,columns=['Prediction'])
plt.plot(train, color = "black", label = "train")
plt.plot(test, color = "red", label = "test")
plt.plot(forecast, color = "green",label = "predict")
plt.title("train,test,predict")
plt.legend(loc="best")
from math import sqrt
from sklearn.metrics import mean_squared_error
rms = sqrt(mean_squared_error(test,forecast))
print("RMSE: ", rms)
```

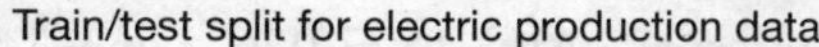

Output:

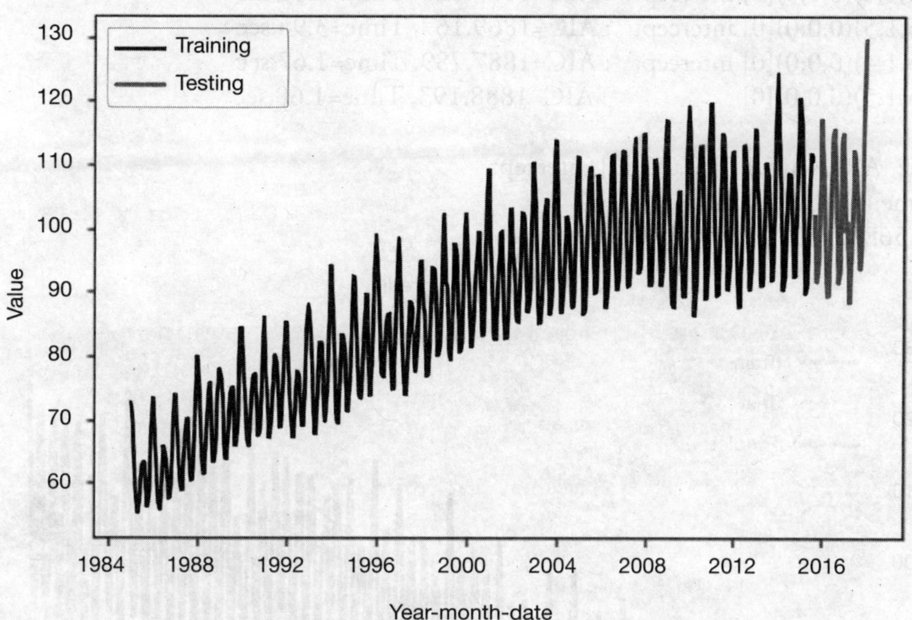

Installing collected packages: pmdarima
Successfully installed pmdarima-2.0.3
Performing stepwise search to minimize aic
ARIMA(2,1,2)(0,0,0)[0] intercept : AIC=inf, Time=0.98 sec
ARIMA(0,1,0)(0,0,0)[0] intercept : AIC=2527.135, Time=0.05 sec
ARIMA(1,1,0)(0,0,0)[0] intercept : AIC=2471.677, Time=0.10 sec
ARIMA(0,1,1)(0,0,0)[0] intercept : AIC=2406.464, Time=0.17 sec
ARIMA(0,1,0)(0,0,0)[0] : AIC=2525.204, Time=0.05 sec
ARIMA(1,1,1)(0,0,0)[0] intercept : AIC=2407.180, Time=0.18 sec
ARIMA(0,1,2)(0,0,0)[0] intercept : AIC=2313.827, Time=0.31 sec
ARIMA(1,1,2)(0,0,0)[0] intercept : AIC=2282.181, Time=0.53 sec
ARIMA(1,1,3)(0,0,0)[0] intercept : AIC=2238.163, Time=0.50 sec
ARIMA(0,1,3)(0,0,0)[0] intercept : AIC=2238.122, Time=0.41 sec
ARIMA(0,1,4)(0,0,0)[0] intercept : AIC=2220.306, Time=0.50 sec
ARIMA(1,1,4)(0,0,0)[0] intercept : AIC=2221.102, Time=0.67 sec
ARIMA(0,1,5)(0,0,0)[0] intercept : AIC=2151.950, Time=0.83 sec
ARIMA(1,1,5)(0,0,0)[0] intercept : AIC=2140.507, Time=0.90 sec
ARIMA(2,1,5)(0,0,0)[0] intercept : AIC=1886.429, Time=2.21 sec
ARIMA(2,1,4)(0,0,0)[0] intercept : AIC=1880.464, Time=2.53 sec
ARIMA(2,1,3)(0,0,0)[0] intercept : AIC=1952.501, Time=1.09 sec
ARIMA(3,1,4)(0,0,0)[0] intercept : AIC=1889.983, Time=1.60 sec
ARIMA(3,1,3)(0,0,0)[0] intercept : AIC=1922.089, Time=1.28 sec
ARIMA(3,1,5)(0,0,0)[0] intercept : AIC=1876.743, Time=1.70 sec

```
ARIMA(4,1,5)(0,0,0)[0] intercept   : AIC=1874.039, Time=1.98 sec
ARIMA(4,1,4)(0,0,0)[0] intercept   : AIC=1877.026, Time=1.58 sec
ARIMA(5,1,5)(0,0,0)[0] intercept   : AIC=1869.167, Time=3.94 sec
ARIMA(5,1,4)(0,0,0)[0] intercept   : AIC=1887.289, Time=1.67 sec
ARIMA(5,1,5)(0,0,0)[0]             : AIC=1888.193, Time=1.68 sec

Best model:  ARIMA(5,1,5)(0,0,0)[0] intercept
Total fit time: 27.493 seconds
RMSE:  6.568623588021505
```

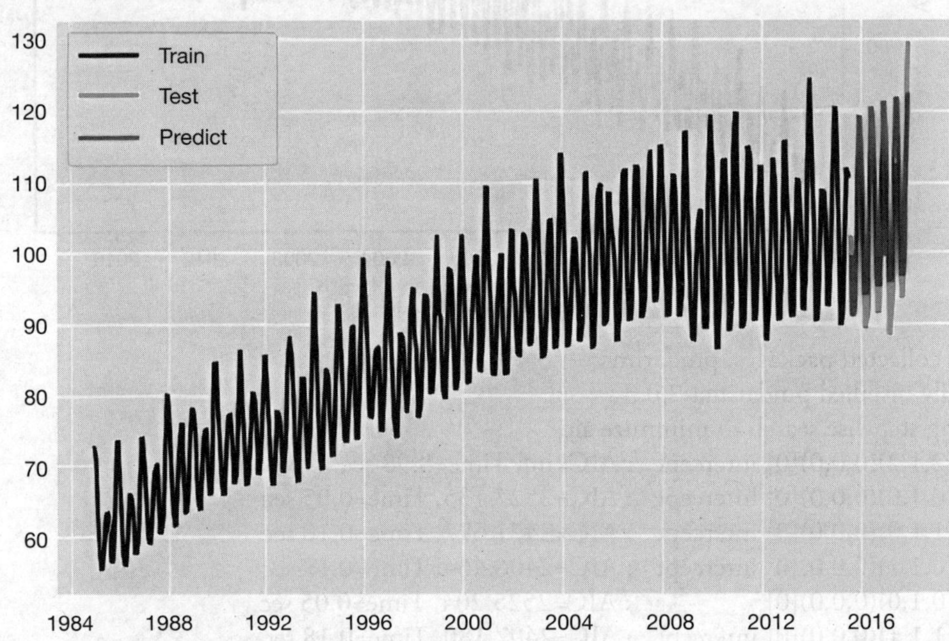

EXERCISES

Multiple Choice Questions

1. A series of observations made over a specific time period is called a:
   (a) Theano
   (b) Scikit
   (c) Time series
   (d) Tensor

2. A time series consists of ______ elements:
   (a) 1
   (b) 2
   (c) 3
   (d) 4

3. Which of the following describes the time series' cyclical behaviour?
   (a) Level
   (b) Trend
   (c) Seasonality
   (d) Noise

4. Rain-related wheat crop damage includes:
   (a) Cyclical movement
   (b) Random movement
   (c) Secular trend
   (d) Seasonal movement

5. The time series' additive model is as follows:
   (a) Y = T + S + C + I
   (b) Y = TSCI
   (c) Y = a + bX
   (d) Y = a + b X, c X 2

6. The rise and fall of a time series over periods longer than one year is called:
   (a) Secular trend
   (b) Seasonal variation
   (c) Cyclical variation
   (d) Irregular variation

7. The graph of a time series is called:
   (a) Line graph
   (b) Trend
   (c) Historigram
   (d) Histogram

8. In the measurement of secular trend, the moving averages:
   (a) Smooth out the time series
   (b) Give the trend in a straight line
   (c) Measure the seasonal variations
   (d) None of these

Answers

1. (c) **2.** (d) **3.** (c) **4.** (b) **5.** (a) **6.** (c) **7.** (c) **8.** (a)

Programming/Concept-based Questions

1. Download the data set of min-max temperature of India from 1901 to 2017 from https://data.gov.in/catalog/all-india-seasonal-and-annual-minmax-temperature-series
   Carry out trend decomposition in the time series data using the additive model for JAN- FEB MIN temperature.

   Answer:

```
import numpy as np
import pandas as pd
import matplotlib.pyplot as plt
from google.colab import files
uploaded= files.upload()
import io
datadf=pd.read_csv(io.BytesIO(uploaded['temperature.csv']))
datadf.head()
```

   #Trend decomposition in time series data ADDITIVE MODEL

```
from statsmodels.tsa.seasonal import seasonal_decompose
decompose=seasonal_decompose(datadf['JAN-FEB -
MIN'],model='additive',period=7)
```

```
decompose.plot()
plt.show()
```

Output:

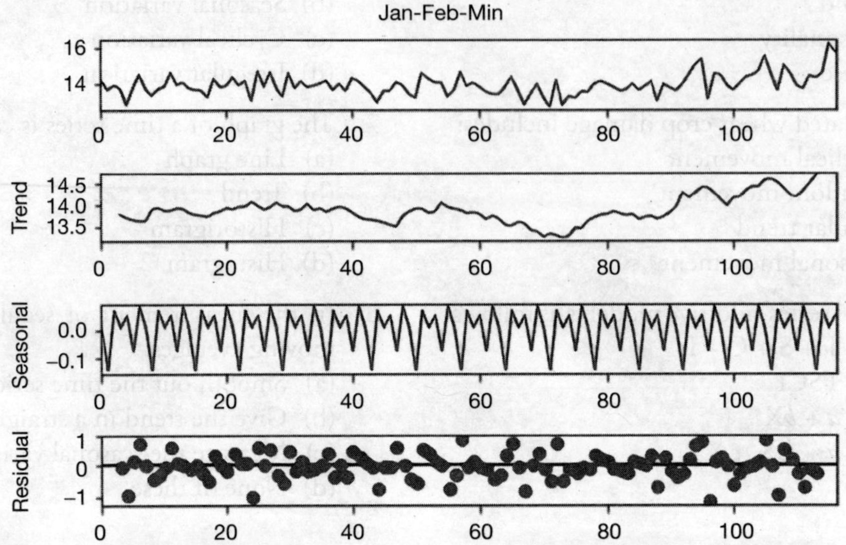

We can see an increasing trend in temperatures after the year 1960 in the month of January.

2. Download the data set of min-max temperature of India from 1901 to 2017 from https://data.gov.in/catalog/all-india-seasonal-and-annual-minmax-temperature-series
Perform trend decomposition in the time series data using the multiplicative model for JAN-FEB MIN and OCT-DEC MAX temperature.
Answer:

```
import numpy as np
import pandas as pd
import matplotlib.pyplot as plt
from google.colab import files
uploaded= files.upload()
import io
datadf=pd.read_csv(io.BytesIO(uploaded['temperature.csv']))
datadf.head()
#Trend decomposition in time series data MUltiplicative model
from statsmodels.tsa.seasonal import seasonal_decompose
decompose=seasonal_decompose(datadf['JAN-FEB -
MIN'],model='multiplicative',period=7)
decompose.plot()
plt.show()
```

```
decompose=seasonal_decompose(datadf['OCT-DEC -
    MAX'],model='multiplicative',period=7)
decompose.plot()
plt.show()
```

Output:

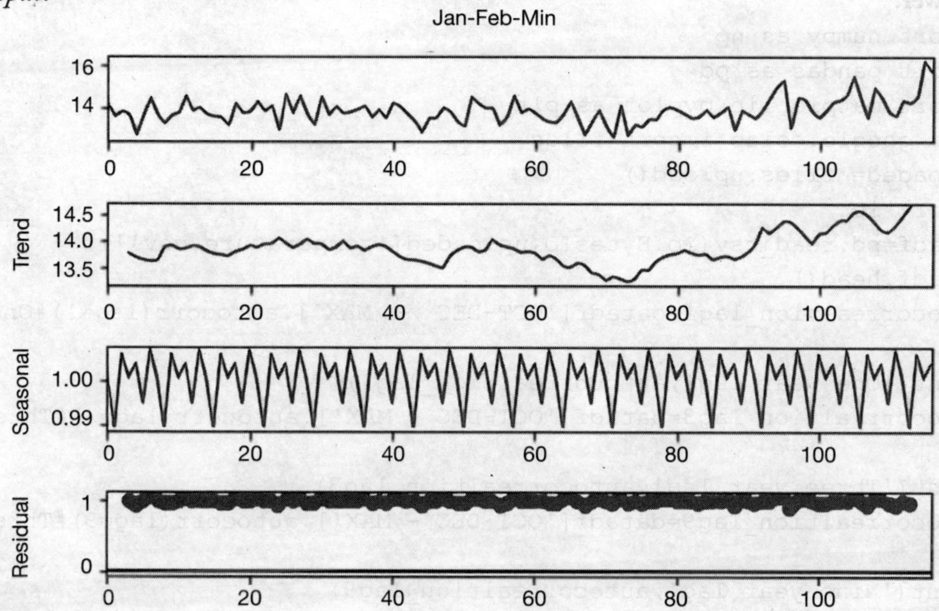

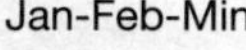

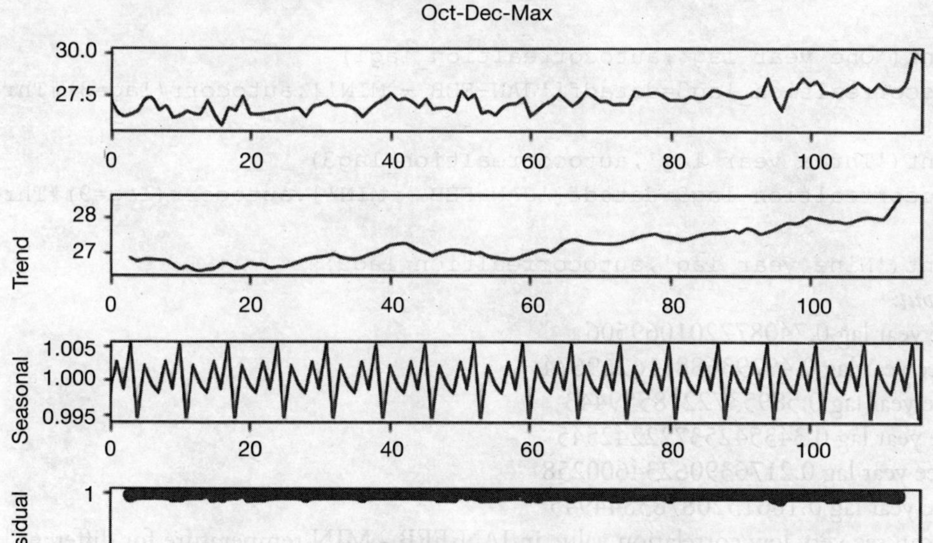

3. Download the data set of min-max temperature of India from 1901 to 2017 from https://data.gov.in/catalog/all-india-seasonal-and-annual-minmax-temperature-series
Perform autocorrelation analysis on the data of JAN- FEB MIN and OCT-DEC MAX temperature.
Answer:

```
import numpy as np
import pandas as pd
import matplotlib.pyplot as plt
from google.colab import files
uploaded= files.upload()
import io
datadf=pd.read_csv(io.BytesIO(uploaded['temperature.csv']))
datadf.head()
autocorrealtion_lag1=datadf['OCT-DEC  - MAX'].autocorr(lag=1)#One  year
lag
print('One year lag',autocorrealtion_lag1)
autocorrealtion_lag3=datadf['OCT-DEC - MAX'].autocorr(lag=3)#Three year
lag
print('Three year lag',autocorrealtion_lag3)
autocorrealtion_lag9=datadf['OCT-DEC - MAX'].autocorr(lag=9)#Three year
lag
print('Nine year lag',autocorrealtion_lag9)
autocorrealtion_lag1=datadf['JAN-FEB  -  MIN'].autocorr(lag=1)#One  year
lag
print('One year lag',autocorrealtion_lag1)
autocorrealtion_lag3=datadf['JAN-FEB - MIN'].autocorr(lag=3)#Three year
lag
print('Three year lag',autocorrealtion_lag3)
autocorrealtion_lag9=datadf['JAN-FEB - MIN'].autocorr(lag=9)#Three year
lag
print('Nine year lag',autocorrealtion_lag9)
```

Output:
One year lag 0.740877201069506
Three year lag 0.49293688116269674
Nine year lag 0.5895372218559443
One year lag 0.34354253722242545
Three year lag 0.21763906234600258
Nine year lag 0.10613208783844945
We can see very low correlation value in JAN-FEB - MIN temperature for different lag values, and very high correlation value in OCT-DEC - MAX temperature.

4. Download the data set with file name sales-of-shampoo-over-a-three-ye.csv from https://www.kaggle.com/datasets/djokester/sales-of-shampoo-over-a-three-year-period
Carry out autocorrelation analysis on the data and give the autocorrelation plot. Also perform stationarity of the given time series using Dickey–Fuller and other statistical tests.
Answer:

```
import numpy as np
import pandas as pd
import matplotlib.pyplot as plt
df=pd.read_csv("sales-of-shampoo-over-a-three-ye.csv")
df.head()
df['Sales of shampoo over a three year period'] = df[
    'Sales of shampoo over a three year period'].astype(float)
plt.plot(df['Month'] , df["Sales of shampoo over a three year period"],
linewidth=3)
plt.title('Sales by Month')
plt.xlabel('Month')
plt.ylabel('Sales')
s = df['Sales of shampoo over a three year period'].squeeze()
s = s.astype(np.float)
x = pd.plotting.autocorrelation_plot(s)

# plotting the Curve
x.plot()

# Display
plt.show()
df_meanrolling = df['Sales of shampoo over a three year period'].
rolling(5).mean()
plt.plot(df_meanrolling)
df_stdrolling = df['Sales of shampoo over a three year period'].
rolling(5).std()
plt.plot(df_stdrolling)
from statsmodels.tsa.stattools import adfuller
from numpy import log
import pandas as pd
res = adfuller(df['Sales of shampoo over a three year period'])
print('Augmented Dickey-Fuller Statistic: %f' % res[0])
print('p-value: %f' % res[1])
```

Output:

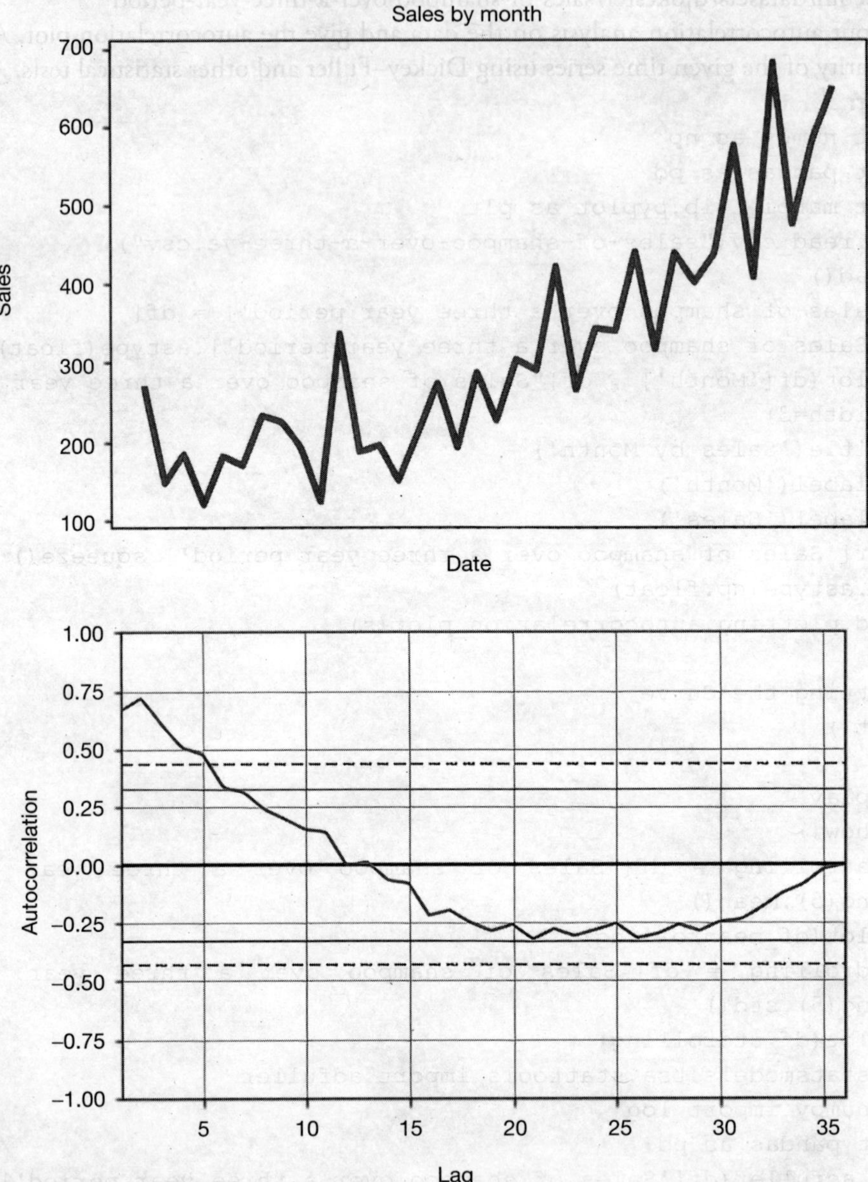

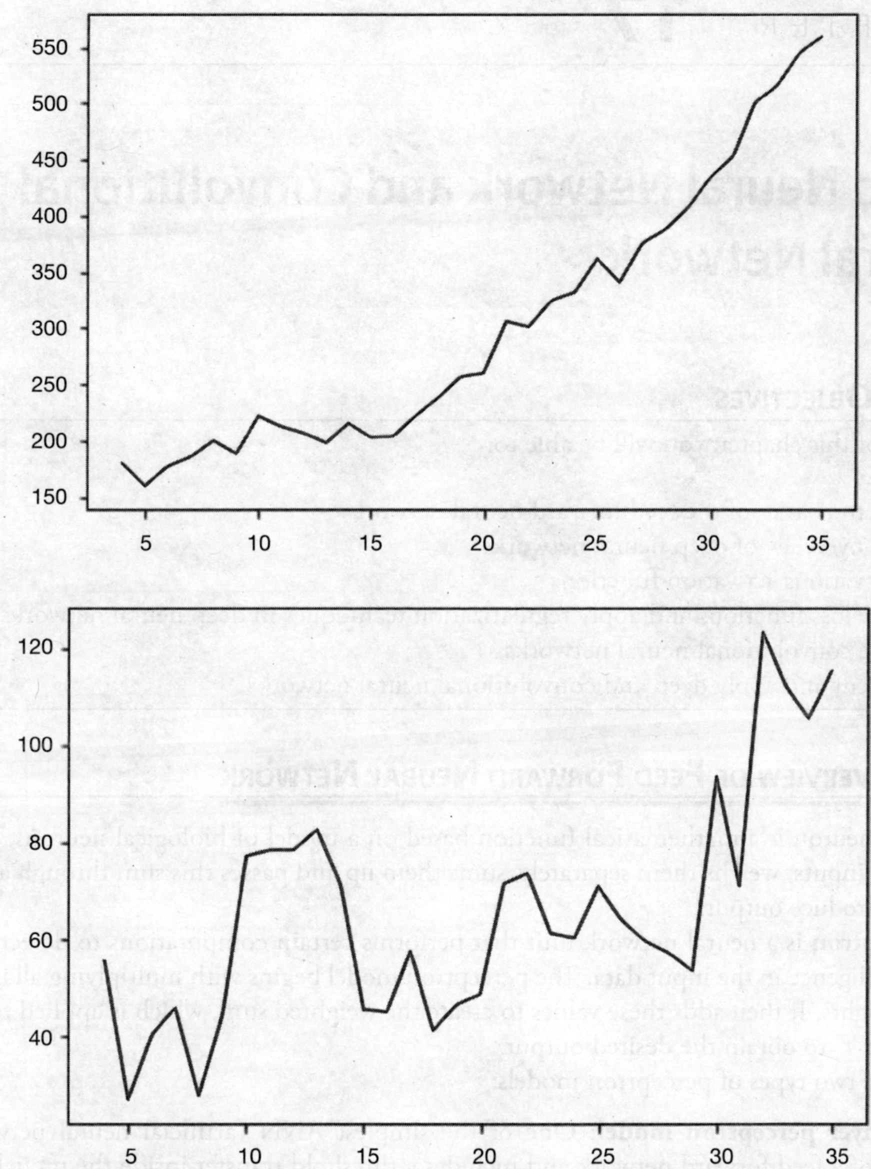

Augmented Dickey-Fuller Statistic: 3.060142
p-value: 1.000000

CHAPTER 17

Deep Neural Network and Convolutional Neural Network

Learning Objectives

At the end of this chapter, you will be able to:

- Explain the basics of the feed forward neural network
- Give an overview of deep neural networks
- Explain various activation functions
- Describe loss functions and apply regularization techniques in deep neural networks
- Describe convolutional neural networks
- Implement and apply deep and convolutional neural networks

17.0 Overview of Feed Forward Neural Network

An artificial neuron is a mathematical function based on a model of biological neurons, where each neuron takes inputs, weighs them separately, sums them up and passes this sum through a non-linear function to produce output.

A **perceptron** is a neural network unit that performs certain computations to detect features or business intelligence in the input data. The perceptron model begins with multiplying all input values and their weights. It then adds these values to create the weighted sum, which is applied to an activation function 'f' to obtain the desired output.

There are two types of perceptron models:

- **Single-layer perceptron model**: One of the simplest ANN (artificial neural network) types consists of a feed forward network and includes a threshold transfer inside the model. The main objective of the single-layer perceptron model is to analyze linearly separable objects with binary outcomes. It can learn only linearly separable patterns.
- **Multi-layer perceptron model**: This is similar to the single-layer perceptron model, but has more hidden layers.

A deep neural network is a neural network with a certain level of complexity, with more than two layers. Deep neural networks use sophisticated mathematical modelling to process data in complex ways. A feed forward neural network is an ANN in which the connections between nodes do not form a cycle. Feed forward is the simplest type of neural network as information is only processed in one direction. While the data may pass through multiple hidden nodes, it always moves in one direction and never backwards.

A deep feed forward neural network is correlated with a coordinated directed acyclic graph (DAG) in portraying the manner in which the neurons are joined with one another (Fig. 17.1).

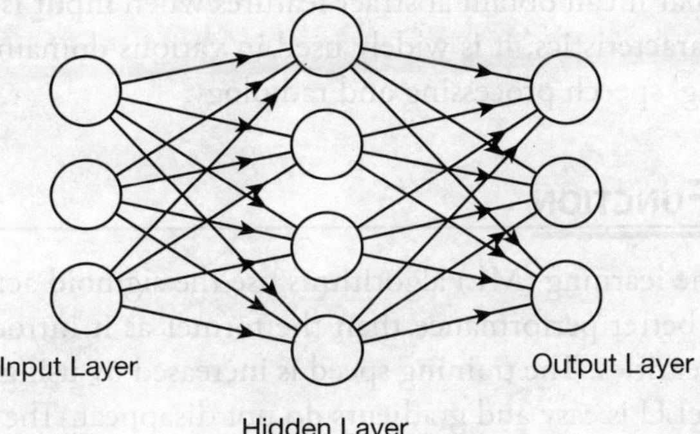

Figure 17.1 Feed forward neural network

The feed forward neural network is commonly seen in its simplest form as a single-layer perceptron. Here, a series of inputs enter the layer and are multiplied by the weights. Each value is then added to obtain the sum of the weighted input values. If the sum of the values is above a specific threshold, usually set at zero, the value produced is often 1, whereas if the sum falls below the threshold, the output value is −1.

The single-layer perceptron is an important model of feed forward neural networks and is often used in classification tasks. Furthermore, they can incorporate aspects of machine learning. Using a property known as the delta rule, the neural network can compare the outputs of its nodes with the intended values, thus enabling the network to adjust its weights through training in order to produce more accurate output values.

17.1 Overview of Deep Neural Network

A deep neural network comprises a series of completely associated layers. The units in each layer compute a weighted amount of the approaching feature and the outcome is sent to an activation function such as TanH or ReLU. The output layer calculates the model output and the loss is determined by how much the computed output varies from the actual result.

There is no particular rule for selecting the hidden layer, through amended ReLUs are the default as they are straightforward and easy to streamline. ReLUs utilize the initiation work $f(x)$ = max0, x. Other grounded hidden units utilize the strategic sigmoid actuation work $f(x) = \sigma(x)$ or the TanH function work $f(x) = \tanh(x)$. In contrast to ReLU, the sigmoidal units soak across the vast majority of their area, making slope-based learning very difficult.

Deep learning is an emerging and interesting area among researchers. Convolutional neural networks (CNN) representative of neural networks show excellent performance and have been used to achieve remarkable results in deep learning. The term convolution was first used by LeCun et al. and the CNN for handwritten pin code recognition was the first version of Lenet-5. Subsequently, many improvements were carried out on different components of the CNN. It is better regarded than the traditional model due to important characteristics such reduced number of training parameters using weight sharing and improved generalization.

Secondly, feature extraction and classification use the learning process. Also, large network implementation is easier in CNN than in any other model of artificial neural networks. Another important characteristic of CNN is that it can obtain abstract features when input is passed through the deeper layers. Due to all these characteristics, it is widely used in various domains such as computer vision, natural language processing, speech processing and radiology.

17.2 Activation Function

Most conventional machine learning (ML) algorithms use the sigmoid activation function. Rectified linear unit (ReLU) shows better performance than the former as it introduces non-linearity. Multi-layer networks use non-linearities. The training speed is increased by using ReLU. In addition, partial derivative calculation of ReLU is easy and gradients do not disappear. The performance of DNN and CNN significantly increases by selecting the proper activation function for the specific task.

17.2.1 ReLU

ReLU is the most commonly used activation function. The ReLU activation is represented as:

$$a_{i,j,k} = \max(z_{i,j,k}, 0),$$

where (i, j) = location and k = channel number.

ReLU is a linear function where it is zero for negative values and it is the same or equal to that value for zero and positive values. It uses a simple max operation and is faster than TanH or sigmoid. Using ReLU, deep networks can be trained efficiently. Graphically it is represented as shown in Fig. 17.2.

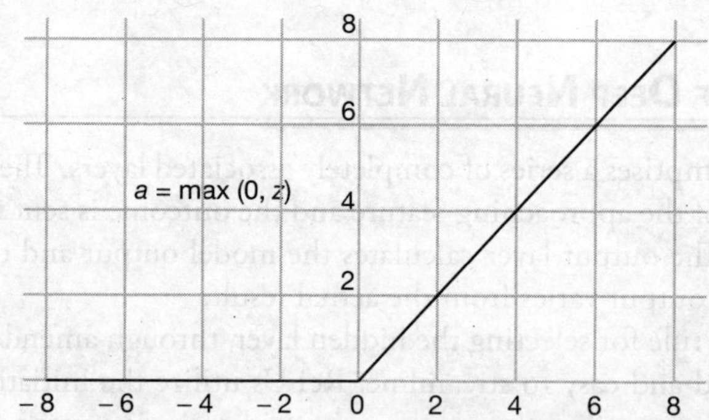

Figure 17.2 ReLU activation function

17.2.2 Leaky ReLU

One of the disadvantages of ReLU is that it has zero gradient and causes the dying ReLU problem. Here, some ReLU neurons die for all inputs and remain inactive no matter what input is supplied.

Network performance is affected if there are a large number of dead neurons. This problem is overcome by leaky ReLU, which is represented below:

$$a_{i,j,k} = \max(z_{i,j,k}, 0) + \lambda \min(z_{i,j,k}, 0),$$

where the value of λ is predefined and in the range of (0, 1). Instead of mapping the negative part to zero, like ReLU, leaky ReLU compresses it. Graphically it is represented as shown in Fig. 17.3.

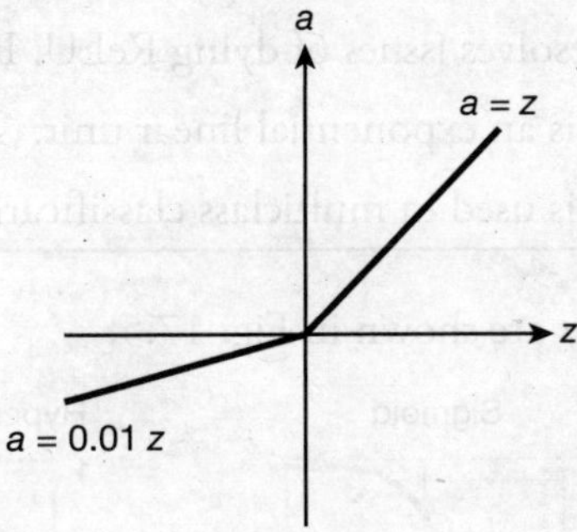

Figure 17.3 Leaky ReLU activation function

17.2.3 Parametric ReLU

To improve accuracy, parametric ReLU or PReLU is used. The performance of PReLU is increased by adaptive learning of parameters. PReLU is represented below:

$$a_{i,j,k} = \max(z_{i,j,k}, 0) + \lambda_k \min(z_{i,j,k}, 0),$$

where λ_k = k^{th} channel's learning parameter. Though it is an extra parameter, there is no risk of overfitting and the computational cost is also negligible. Graphically it is represented as shown in Fig. 17.4.

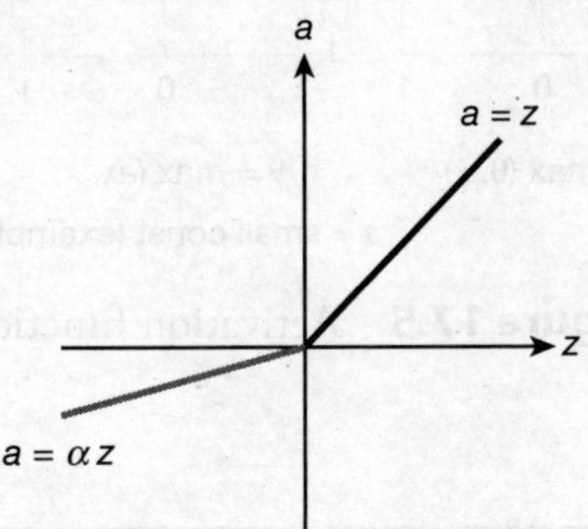

Figure 17.4 Parametric ReLU activation function

Table 17.1 Types of activation functions

Name of activation function	Description
Sigmoid	It gives output between 0 and 1. Used in binary classification.
TanH	It is a zero-centred sigmoid.
ReLU	$f(x) = \max(0, x)$, where x is the input value.
Leaky ReLU	Resolves issues of dying ReLU. It has small negative slope.
ELU	It is an exponential linear unit.
Softmax	It is used in multiclass classification. It ranges from 0 to 1.

The various activation functions are shown in Fig. 17.5.

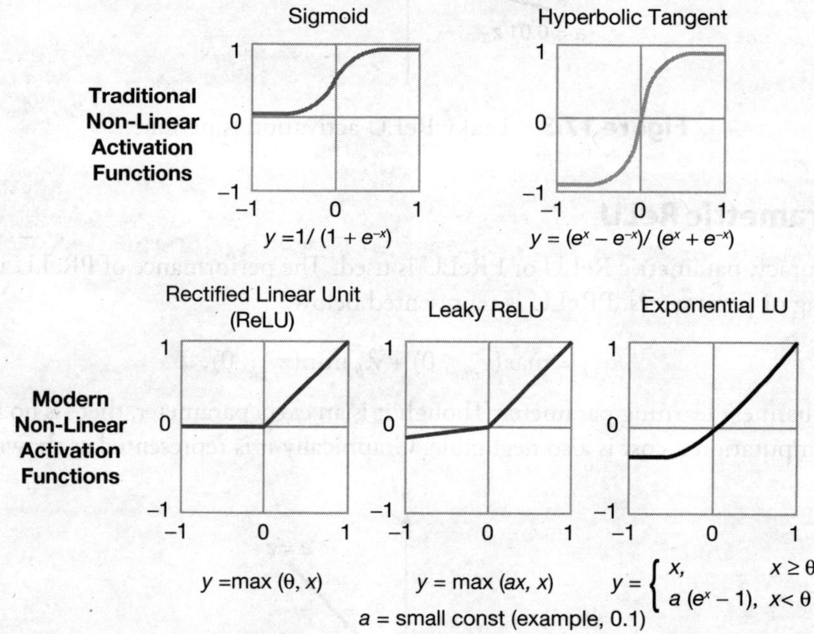

Figure 17.5 Activation functions

17.3 Loss Functions

The loss function in a neural network quantifies the difference between the expected outcome and the outcome produced by the machine learning model.

17.3.1 Softmax Loss

This is a combination of softmax and multinomial logistic loss.

Suppose a training set is given as $\{ (x^{(i)}, y^{(i)}); i \in 1,...,N, y^{(i)} \in 1,...,K\}$, where $y^{(i)}$ is the target class label for $x^{(i)}$; that is, the ith input. So, for the ith input, the prediction of the jth class using the softmax function can be given as

$$P_{(j)}^{(i)} = e^{z_j^{(i)}} / \sum_{l=1}^{K} e^{z_l^{(i)}},$$

where $z_j^{(i)}$ = activations of a densely connected layer and denoted as $z_j^{(i)} = w_j^T a^{(i)} + b_j$. The softmax loss is calculated as:

$$L_{softmax} = -\frac{1}{N}\left[\sum_{j=1}^{N}\sum_{j=1}^{N} 1\{y^{(i)} = j\} log P_j^{(i)}\right]$$

The angular boundary or θ_j is presented by large-margin softmax loss. θ_j is the angle between the jth column w_j of the weight matrix and the feature vector $a^{(i)}$.

17.3.2 Hinge Loss

Large-margin classifiers are trained using hinge loss (for example, support vector machine). This is calculated as given below:

$$L_{hinge} = \frac{1}{N}\sum_{i=1}^{N}\sum_{j=1}^{k}\left[\max\left(0, 1-\delta\left(y^{(i)}, j\right) w^T x_i\right)\right]^P,$$

where w = weight vector and $y^{(i)} \in [1,..., K]$ = class label.

$$\delta\left(y^{(i)}, j\right) = 1 \text{ if } y^{(i)} = j \text{ else } \delta\left(y^{(i)}, j\right) = -1$$

17.4 Regularization

The overfitting problem of DNN and CNN is effectively handled by regularization. The objective function is modified by adding a regularization term which can affect the model complexity. The regularization techniques used for DNN and CNN are discussed in this section.

17.4.1 Dropout

Dropout is applied to fully connected layers. It avoids the dependency of the network on specific neurons. Instead, it powers the network to be more precise even if certain information is not available. The output is described as:

$$y = r^* a\,(W^T x),$$

where W = weight matrix of size $n \times d$, $x = [x_1, x_2,..., x_n]^T$ = input of size n of fully connected layers and r = binary vector having d elements. Bernoulli distribution with parameter p is used to select elements of r; that is, r_i ~Bernoulli(p).

17.4.2 DropConnect

DropConnect is an extension of Dropout. Here, rather than randomly assigning the output of neurons to zero, it randomly assigns the weight matrix (W) elements to zero. The output of DropConnect is given by:

$$y = a\left((R * W)\, x\right),$$

where R_{ij} ~ Bernoulli(p).

17.5 Convolutional Neural Network

Some mathematical concepts of convolution neural networks (CNN) are explained in this section.

17.5.1 Preliminary Mathematical Concepts

Vector and Tensors: Different symbols are used to represent vectors and tensors. Vector representation is given as $x \in R^D$, indicating that the column vector has D elements. Capital letters are used to denote the matrix. Matrix representation given as $X \in R^{H \times W}$, indicating that the matrix consists of H rows and W columns. Higher-order matrices are called tensors. For example, the representation given as $X \in R^{H \times W \times D}$ indicates an order-three tensor and each element of the tensor is indexed by triplet (i, j, d), where $0 \leq i \leq H$, $0 \leq j \leq W$, $0 \leq d \leq D$. Tensors are very important in CNNs as all inputs, parameters and intermediate representations are in the form of tensors only.

A tensor can be converted into a vector by using notation vec, as shown below:

$$\text{vec(A)} = (3,4,5,6)^{T}$$

The recursive process is applied for vectorization of order-three matrices into order-two and then an order-one matrix or vector. The same process is applied for order-four and higher order matrices.

Chain Rule and Vector Calculus: This is very important in the learning process of CNN. For example, z is scalar, that is, $z \in R$ and the given vector is $y \in R^H$. Suppose z is a function of y, the partial derivative of z with respect to y is a vector, given as:

$$\left[\frac{dz}{dy}\right]_i = \frac{dz}{dyi}$$

This shows that the size of vector $\frac{dz}{dy}$ is the same as y and $\frac{dz}{dyi}$ is the ith element of the vector. If $x \in R^W$ is one more vector and y is a function of x, then the partial derivative of y with respect to x is given as:

$$\left[\frac{dy}{dx^T}\right]_{i,j} = \frac{dyi}{dxj}$$

The result is a matrix of size $H \times W$, and $\frac{dyi}{dxj}$ denotes the element of the ith row and j^{th} column. Hence, we can say z is a function of x and the chain rule can be applied as follows:

$$\frac{dz}{dx^T} = \frac{dz}{dy^T}\frac{dy}{dx^T}$$

17.5.2 CNN Architecture

As shown in Fig. 17.6, the CNN architecture consists of three basic building blocks: convolution layers, pooling layers and fully connected layers. Along with these building blocks, other important parameters are the dropout layer and the activation function.

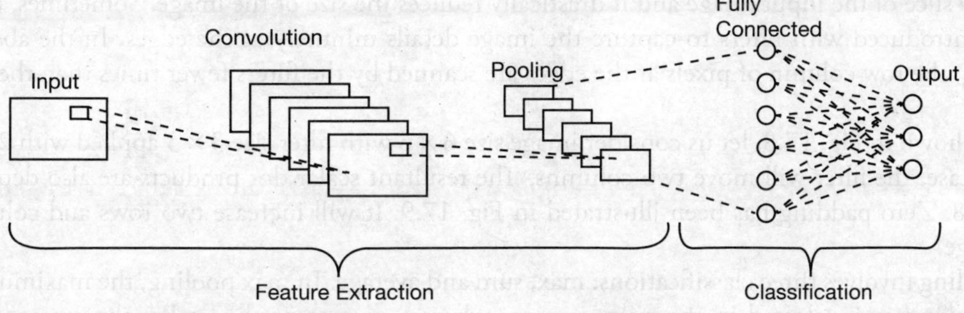

Figure 17.6 CNN architecture

Convolutional Layer

Convolution is a linear operation that involves the scalar dot product of weights with the input image weight. The multi-dimensional array used for linear operations is known as the kernel or filter. These filters are smaller than the size of the image and applied to the overall image to extract features such as edges, lines, etc. Multiple filters are applied on images which in turn produce multiple feature maps. These feature maps are combined to produce the output of the convolutional layer. Figure 17.7 shows the sliding of filters on the entire image which involves scalar dot products, thereby producing a feature map in 2D.

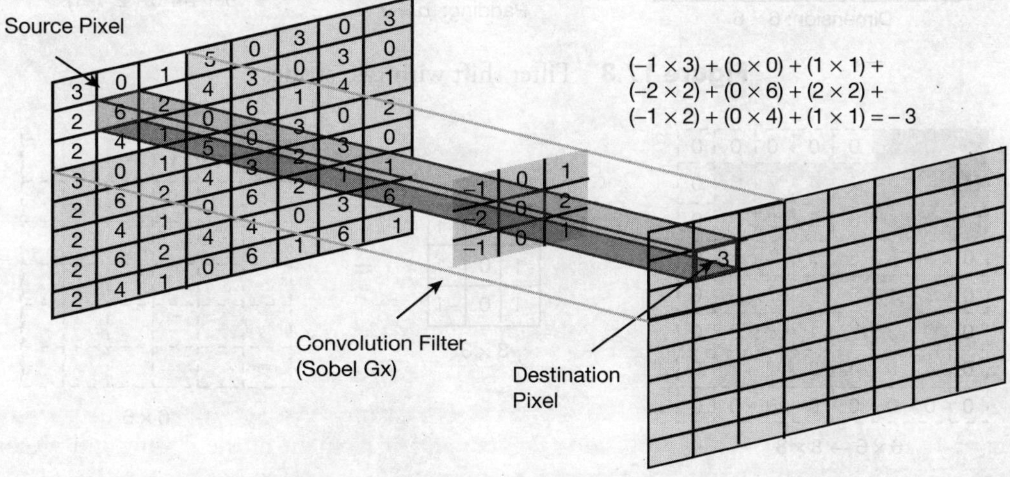

Figure 17.7 3 *x* 3 filter sliding on an image

The distance between two successive positions of a filter is called a stride. Normally, the filter moves slide by slide or pixel by pixel. In the case of two strides, the filter moves two pixels vertically and horizontally, resulting in down-sampling of the feature map.

Pooling is another way of down-sampling and is used to reduce the spatial size (number of parameters), thereby controlling overfitting issues. Generally, the pooling layer is applied independently on every slice of the input image and it drastically reduces the size of the image. Sometimes, padding is also introduced with filters to capture the image details minutely at the edges. In the absence of padding, the row column of pixels at the edges are scanned by the filters fewer times than the middle pixels.

As shown in Fig. 17.8, let us consider image size 6 × 6 with filter size 3 × 3 applied with 2 strides. In this case, the filter will move two columns. The resultant scalar dot products are also depicted in Fig. 17.8. Zero padding has been illustrated in Fig. 17.9. It will increase two rows and columns in the image.

Pooling involves three classifications: max, sum and average. In max pooling, the maximum value of each window is selected in the output vector whereas average pooling takes the average of each element of the window. The sub-region for sum pooling or mean pooling will be set the same as for max pooling, but instead of using the max function, we use sum or mean functions. Generally, data practitioners use max pooling and average pooling of the feature map, as shown in Fig. 17.10.

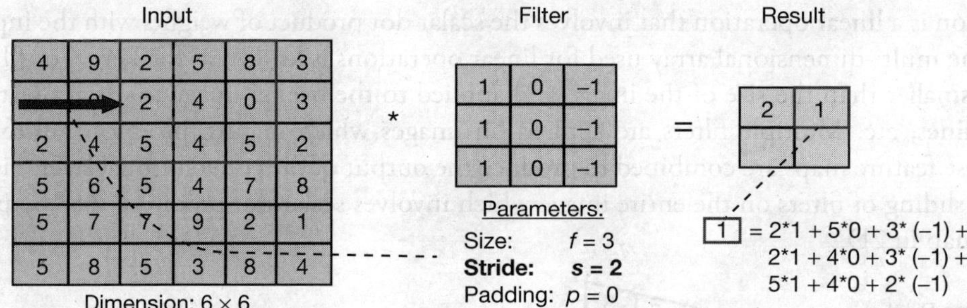

Figure 17.8 Filter shift with two strides

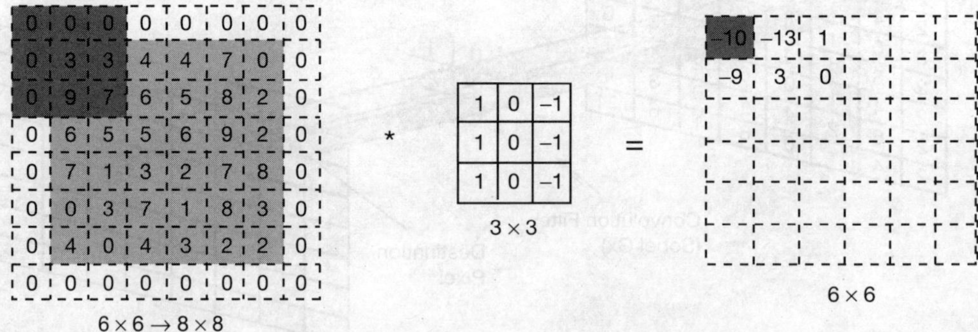

Figure 17.9 Padding illustration in feature map

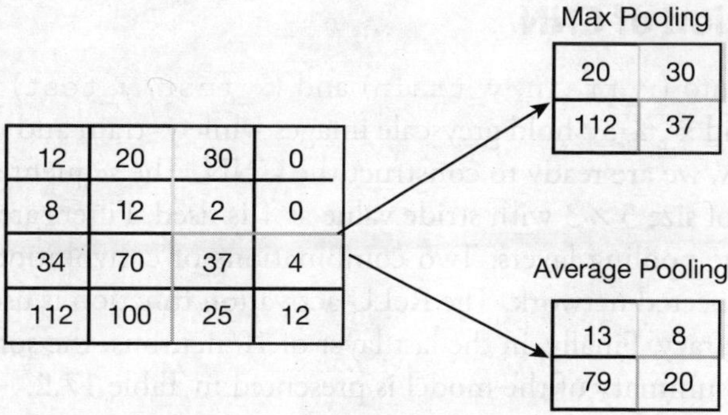

Figure 17.10 Max and average pooling

Classification

After multiple combinations of convolutions and the pooling layer with or without strides are used, the final output is obtained as a feature map. This is further flattened in a one-dimensional array for input to one or more fully connected (FC) networks. FCs are dense neural networks and classify the object in the desired classes based on probabilities. Each fully connected network uses the activation function for learning and modelling complex data used in videos, images and audio. Non-linearity in any neural network allows back-propagation as non-linear functions are derivatives. There are many non-linear activation functions, and the commonly used ones are ReLU, TanH, sigmoid and softmax. ReLU selects the maximum value from a function of input *x* and zero whereas sigmoid ranges from −1 to +1. TanH functions are hyperbolic tangent functions. Initially, TanH and sigmoid are used because they provide a mathematical representation of the behaviour of neurons. However, the most commonly used activation function is ReLU because of its simplicity in computation functions.

17.6 Implementation of CNN

17.6.1 Loading the Data Set and Importing the Required Packages

Google Colab is used here for implementation. First, packages such as NumPy, Seaborn and sklearn and their sub-packages required for pre-processing and CNN layers must be imported.

```
import cv2
import matplotlib.pyplot as plt
import numpy as np
import seaborn as sns; sns.set()
from keras.datasets import cifar10
from sklearn.metrics import confusion_matrix
from sklearn.preprocessing import OneHotEncoder
from keras.layers import Conv2D, MaxPool2D, Flatten, Dense, Dropout
from keras.models import Sequential, load_model
```

17.6.2 Construction of CNN

The data set is divided into (`x_train, y_train`) and (`x_test, y_test`) for training and testing, respectively. `x_train` and `x_test` hold greyscale images while y_train and y_test are labels as shown in the code snippet. Now, we are ready to construct the CNN. The sequential model is used.

First, a filter/kernel of size 3 × 3 with stride value as 1 is used. Filters are increased in subsequent layers before reaching the pooling layers. Two combinations of convolution-max pooling layers are used before the fully connected network. The ReLU activation function is used in all layers except the last layer, to increase accuracy. Finally, in the last layer of 10 neurons, the softmax function is applied to classify the images. A summary of the model is presented in Table 17.2.

```
X_train, y_train), (X_test, y_test) = cifar10.load_data()
X_train  = X_train/255
X_test  = X_test/255
one_hot_encoder = OneHotEncoder(sparse=False)
one_hot_encoder.fit(y_train)
X_train = X_train.reshape(X_train.shape[0], X_train.shape[1], X_train.
shape[2], 1)
X_test = X_test.reshape(X_test.shape[0], X_test.shape[1], X_test.
shape[2], 1)
model = Sequential()
model.add(Conv2D(16, (3, 3), activation='relu', strides=(1, 1),
    padding='same', input_shape=input_shape))
model.add(Conv2D(32, (3, 3), activation='relu', strides=(1, 1),
    padding='same'))
model.add(Conv2D(64, (3, 3), activation='relu', strides=(1, 1),
    padding='same'))
model.add(MaxPool2D((2, 2)))
model.add(Conv2D(16, (3, 3), activation='relu', strides=(1, 1),
    padding='same'))
model.add(Conv2D(32, (3, 3), activation='relu', strides=(1, 1),
    padding='same'))
model.add(Conv2D(64, (3, 3), activation='relu', strides=(1, 1),
    padding='same'))
model.add(MaxPool2D((2, 2)))
model.add(Flatten())
model.add(Dense(256, activation='relu'))
model.add(Dropout(0.5))
model.add(Dense(128, activation='relu'))
model.add(Dense(64, activation='relu'))
model.add(Dense(64, activation='relu'))
model.add(Dense(10, activation='softmax'))
```

Table 17.2 CNN model data set

Attributes	Values
Size of data set	60000
Number of classes in data set	10
Size of each image	32 × 32
Image type	Color
Training data set under consideration	50000
Test data set under consideration	10000
Size of each batch in training	10000
Number of batches	5
Mutually exclusive	Yes
Data downloaded	CIFAR-10 Python version

17.7 CASE STUDIES

Case Study 1: Create a CNN model of three convolution layers by considering the following parameters:

a. Input is image of size (32,32,3)
b. Pooling: Max pool
c. Activation function: ReLU
d. Output is 10 classes

Print the summary of the model.

```
importtensorflowastf
      fromtensorflow.kerasimport datasets, layers, models
      importmatplotlib.pyplotasplt
model =models.Sequential()
model.add(layers.Conv2D(32,(3,3), activation='relu',input_
shape=(32,32,3)))
model.add(layers.MaxPooling2D((2,2)))
model.add(layers.Conv2D(64,(3,3), activation='relu'))
model.add(layers.MaxPooling2D((2,2)))
model.add(layers.Conv2D(64,(3,3), activation='relu'))
model.add(layers.Flatten())
model.add(layers.Dense(64, activation='relu'))
model.add(layers.Dense(10))
model.summary()
```

Output:
Model: "sequential"

```
_________________________________________________________________
Layer (type)                 Output Shape              Param #
=================================================================
conv2d (Conv2D)              (None, 30, 30, 32)        896
max_pooling2d (MaxPooling2D  (None, 15, 15, 32)        0
)
conv2d_1 (Conv2D)            (None, 13, 13, 64)        18496
max_pooling2d_1 (MaxPooling  (None, 6, 6, 64)          0
2D)
conv2d_2 (Conv2D)            (None, 4, 4, 64)          36928
flatten (Flatten)            (None, 1024)              0
dense (Dense)                (None, 64)                65600
dense_1 (Dense)              (None, 10)                650
=================================================================
Total params: 122,570
Trainable params: 122,570
Non-trainable params: 0
```

Display the layer names of the above model.

```
layer_names = []
for layer in model.layers[:8]:
  layer_names.append(layer.name)
print(layer_names)
```

Output:
['conv2d', 'max_pooling2d', 'conv2d_1', 'max_pooling2d_1', 'conv2d_2', 'flatten', 'dense', 'dense_1']

Case Study 2: To visualize a feature map of layer 1 of the deep model to classify images. Consider that there are 64 maps.

```
model = Model(inputs=model.inputs, outputs=model.layers[1].output)
img = img_to_array(img)
img = expand_dims(img, axis=0)
feature_maps = model.predict(img)
# plot all 64 maps in an 8x8 squares
square = 8
ix = 1
```

```
for _ in range(square):
  for _ in range(square):
    # specify subplot and turn of axis
    ax = pyplot.subplot(square, square, ix)
    ax.set_xticks([])
    ax.set_yticks([])
    # plot filter channel in grayscale
    pyplot.imshow(feature_maps[0, :, :, ix-1], cmap='gray')
    ix += 1
# show the figure
pyplot.show()
```

EXERCISES

Multiple Choice Questions

1. Which of the following neural networks has memory?
   (a) 1D CNN
   (b) 2D CNN
   (c) LSTM
   (d) None of the above

2. Which of the following is true about neurons?
   (a) A neuron has a single input and a single output
   (b) A neuron has multiple inputs and multiple outputs
   (c) A neuron has a single input and multiple outputs
   (d) All of the above

3. Which of the following deep learning models uses back-propagation?
   (a) Convolutional Neural Network
   (b) Multilayer Perceptron Network
   (c) Recurrent Neural Network
   (d) All of the above

4. Neural networks can be used in:
   (a) Regression problems
   (b) Classification problems
   (c) Clustering problems
   (d) All of the above

5. In a classification problem, which of the following activation functions is most widely used in the output layer of neural networks?
   (a) Sigmoid function
   (b) Hyperbolic function
   (c) Rectifier function
   (d) All of the above

6. Which of the following is a deep learning library?
   (a) TensorFlow
   (b) Keras
   (c) PyTorch
   (d) All of the above

7. Which of the following is a loss function?
   (a) Sigmoid function
   (b) Cross entropy
   (c) ReLU
   (d) All of the above

8. Which of the following makes a neural network non-linear?
   (a) Convolution function
   (b) Batch gradient descent
   (c) Rectified linear unit
   (d) All of the above

9. Let us assume we implement an AND function to a single neuron. The tabular representation of the AND function is given below:

X_1	X_2	X_1 AND X_2
0	0	0
0	1	0
1	0	0
1	1	1

The activation function of our neuron is denoted as:

$$f(x) = \begin{cases} 0, \text{ for } x < 0 \\ 0, \text{ for } x \geq 0 \end{cases}$$

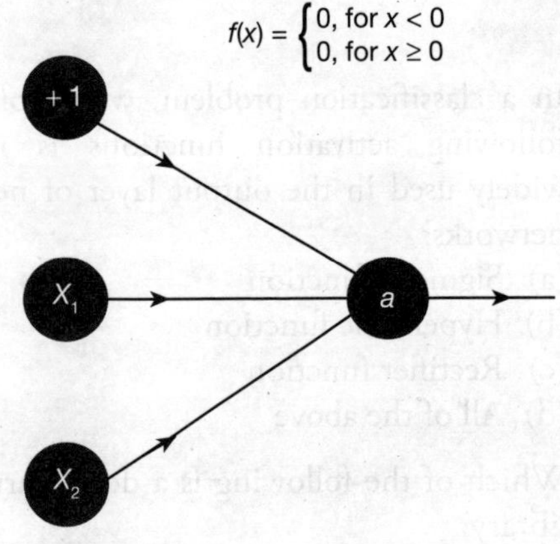

What would be the weights and bias? (Hint: For which values of w_1, w_2 and b does our neuron implement an AND function?)

(a) Bias = −1.5, $w_1 = 1$, $w_2 = 1$
(b) Bias = 1.5, $w_1 = 2$, $w_2 = 2$
(c) Bias = 1, $w_1 = 1.5$, $w_2 = 1.5$
(d) None of these

10. What is hypothesis space in deep learning?
(a) ML/DL algorithms merely searching through a predefined set of operations
(b) Searching for useful representations of some input data, within a predefined space of possibilities, using guidance from a feedback signal
(c) (a) and (b)
(d) None of the above

Answers

1. (c) **2.** (d) **3.** (c) **4.** (d) **5.** (a) **6.** () **7.** (b) **8.** (c)
9. (a) **10.** (c)

Programming/Concept-based Questions

1. What is the role of activation functions in a neural network?
Answer: At the most basic level, an activation function determines whether a neuron should be fired or not. It accepts the weighted sum of the inputs and bias as input. Step function, sigmoid, ReLU, TanH and softmax are examples of activation functions.
2. What are the steps involved in training a perceptron in deep learning?
Answer: There are five main steps that determine the learning of a perceptron:
   1. Initialize thresholds and weights
   2. Provide inputs
   3. Calculate outputs
   4. Update weights in each step
   5. Repeat steps 2 to 4

3. What are the steps to be followed to use the gradient descent algorithm?

Answer: There are five main steps to initialize and use the gradient descent algorithm:

1. Initialize biases and weights for the network.
2. Send input data through the network (the input layer).
3. Calculate the difference (the error) between expected and predicted values.
4. Change values in neurons to minimize the loss function.
5. Use multiple iterations to determine the best weights for efficient working.

4. What is the meaning of overfitting?

Answer: Overfitting is a common issue when working with deep learning. It is a scenario where the deep learning algorithm vigorously hunts through the data to obtain some valid information. The model picks up noise rather than useful data, causing high variance and low bias. This makes the model less accurate, and is an undesirable effect that can be prevented.

5. What is model capacity?

Answer: The capacity of a deep learning neural network controls the scope of the type of mapping functions that it can learn. Model capacity can approximate any given function. When there is higher model capacity, it means that a larger amount of information can be stored in the network.

6. What is a cost function?

Answer: A cost function describes how well the neural network is performing with respect to its given training sample and the expected output. It may depend on variables such as weights and biases. It provides the performance of a neural network as a whole. In deep learning, our priority is to minimize the cost function. That is why we prefer to use the concept of gradient descent.

7. Why do we prefer convolutional neural networks (CNN) to artificial neural networks (ANN) for image data as input?

Answer:

1. Feed forward neural networks can learn a single feature representation of the image but in the case of complex images, ANN will fail to give better predictions. This is because it cannot learn pixel dependencies present in the images.
2. CNN can learn multiple layers of feature representations of an image by applying filters or transformations.
3. In CNN, the number of parameters for the network to learn is significantly lower than in multilayer neural networks as the number of units in the network decreases, thereby reducing the chance of overfitting.
4. CNN considers the context information in a small neighborhood; this is important for achieving better prediction in data such as images. Since digital images are a groups of pixels with high values, CNN can be used to analyze them. CNN decreases their values, which is better for the training phase, with less computational power and less information loss.

8. What will happen if the learning rate is set too low or too high?

Answer: When the learning rate is set too low, training of the model will progress very slowly as we make minimal updates to the weights. It will take many updates to reach the minimum point.

If the learning rate is set too high, it causes undesirable divergent behaviour to the loss function due to drastic updates in weights. It may fail to converge (model can give good output) or even diverge (data is too chaotic for the network to train).

9. What is the difference between epoch, batch and iteration in deep learning?
Answer:
Epoch: This is one iteration over the entire data set (everything put into the training model).
Batch: When we cannot pass the entire data set into the neural network at once, we divide it into several batches.
Iteration: If we have 10,000 images as data and a batch size of 200, an epoch should run 50 iterations (10,000 divided by 50).

10. What are the programming elements in TensorFlow?
Answer:
Constants are parameters whose values do not change. To define a constant, we use the `tf.constant()` command. For example:

```
a = tf.constant(2.0,tf.float32)
b = tf.constant(3.0)
Print(a, b)
```

Variables allow us to add new trainable parameters to a graph. To define a variable, we use the `tf.Variable()` command and initialize them before running the graph in a session. For example:

```
W = tf.Variable([.3].dtype=tf.float32)
b = tf.Variable([-.3].dtype=tf.float32)
```

Placeholders allow us to feed data to a TensorFlow model from outside. It permits a value to be assigned later. To define a placeholder, we use the `tf.placeholder()` command. For example:

```
a = tf.placeholder (tf.float32)
b = a*2
with tf.Session() as sess:
result = sess.run(b,feed_dict={a:3.0})
print result
```

A session is run to evaluate the nodes. This is called the TensorFlow runtime. For example:

```
a = tf.constant(2.0)
b = tf.constant(4.0)
c = a+b
# Launch Session
Sess = tf.Session()
# Evaluate the tensor c
print(sess.run(c))
```

11. What will be the output of the following code?

```
layer_outputs = [layer.output for layer in model.layers]
```

Answer: The line of code returns the output objects of the layers.

12. What will be the output of the following code?

```
model.layers[0].get_weights()
```

Answer:

The `get_weights()` function returns a list consisting of NumPy arrays. The first array gives the weights of layer 0 and the second array gives the biases.

13. What will be the output of the following code? Describe.

```
from random import random

def initialize_network(n_inputs, n_hidden, n_outputs):
  network = list()
  hidden_layer = [{'weights':[random() for i in range(n_inputs + 1)]}
for i in range(n_hidden)]
  network.append(hidden_layer)
  output_layer = [{'weights':[random() for i in range(n_hidden + 1)]}
for i in range(n_outputs)]
  network.append(output_layer)
  return network

network = initialize_network(3, 2, 2)
for layer in network:
  print(layer)
```

Answer: The code creates a neural network with input layer with 3 neurons, hidden layer with 2 neurons and output layer with 2 neurons. It assigns weight and bias to each neuron using the `random()` function and finally prints each layer with each neuron's weight and bias. This may change as we apply `random()` function.

Output:

[{'weights': [0.4221165755827173, 0.029040787574867943, 0.22169166627303505, 0.43788759365057206]}, {'weights': [0.49581224138185065, 0.23308445025757263, 0.2308665415409843, 0.2187810373376886]}]

[{'weights': [0.4596034657377336, 0.28978161459048557, 0.021489705265908876]}, {'weights': [0.8375779756625729, 0.5564543226524334, 0.6422943629324456]}]

14. Apply forward propagation on the above network and check the output. The code for forward propagation is given below:

```
def activate(weights, inputs):
  activation = weights[-1]
  for i in range(len(weights)-1):
    activation += weights[i] * inputs[i]
  return activation
def transfer(activation):
  return 1.0 / (1.0 + exp(-activation))
def forward_propagate(network, row):
  inputs = row
  for layer in network:
```

```
        new_inputs = []
        for neuron in layer:
            activation = activate(neuron['weights'], inputs)
            neuron['output'] = transfer(activation)
            new_inputs.append(neuron['output'])
        inputs = new_inputs
    return inputs
```

Answer:

```
row = [1, 0, 1, None]
output = forward_propagate(network, row)
print(output)
```

Output:

After executing

[0.8695145221824447, 0.8525887873005287]

15. Write the syntax to compile a deep model.

Answer:

```
model.compile(loss='loss function used', metrics=['Name Metric used'],
optimizer='name of optimizer')
```

BIBLIOGRAPHY

1. Jojo John Moolayil. "A Layman's Guide to Deep Neural Network". Towards Data Science, published July 2019. https://towardsdatascience.com/a-laymans-guide-to-deep-neural-networks-ddcea24847fb
2. saumyasaxena2730. "Introduciton to Deep Learning". GeeksforGeeks. https://www.geeksforgeeks.org/introduction-deep-learning/
3. Anastasia Kyrykovych. "Deep Neural Networks". https://www.kdnuggets.com/2020/02/deep-neural-networks.html

CHAPTER 18

Case Studies

18.0 Digit Recognition

Digit recognition can be considered as a classification problem that deals with the identification of digits. Various algorithms including naive Bayes', random forest, decision tree, support vector machine (SVM) and convolutional neural network (CNN) can be applied to classify digits. Here, we use CNN with the Keras library of Python to classify the MNIST data set. This data set contains 60,000 greyscale images of digits from 0 to 9 in the training set and 10,000 greyscale images in the test set, each of size 28 x 28 pixels. We need to classify the given images into one of 10 classes that represent values from 0 to 9. The code given below loads the MNIST data set using the Keras library, displays the images and calculates the accuracy of the build model on the test data set.

```
# Digit Recognition
from tensorflow import keras
import numpy as np
import matplotlib.pyplot as plt
```

First load the Keras data set using `keras.datasets.mnist.load_data()`. It returns the training and test set digits along with their labels.

```
(train_digits_val, train_labels_val), (test_digits_val, test_labels_val) =
keras.datasets.mnist.load_data()
```

We now need to display 16 random images from the training set. The seed number (123) you choose will be the starting point in the generation of the sequence of random numbers. It will generate the same random numbers in multiple executions. Now, we will write the code to display 16 images in a subplot of 2 rows and 8 columns. The random images retrieved will be shown along with their labels.

```
np.random.seed(123)
rand_16digits = np.random.randint(0, train_digits_val.shape[0],16)
sample_digits = train_digits_val[rand_16digits]
sample_labels = train_labels_val[rand_16digits]
sample_labels
num_rows, num_cols = 2, 8
```

```
f, axval = plt.subplots(num_rows, num_cols, figsize=(14,6),
                    gridspec_kw={'wspace':0.04, 'hspace':0.02},
                    squeeze=True)
for r in range(num_rows):
    for c in range(num_cols):
        image_indexval = r * 8 + c
        axval[r,c].axis("off")
        axval[r,c].imshow(sample_digits[image_indexval], cmap='gray')
        axval[r,c].set_title('No. %d' % sample_labels[image_indexval])
plt.show()
plt.close()
print(train_digits_val.shape)
print(test_digits_val.shape)
```

Output:

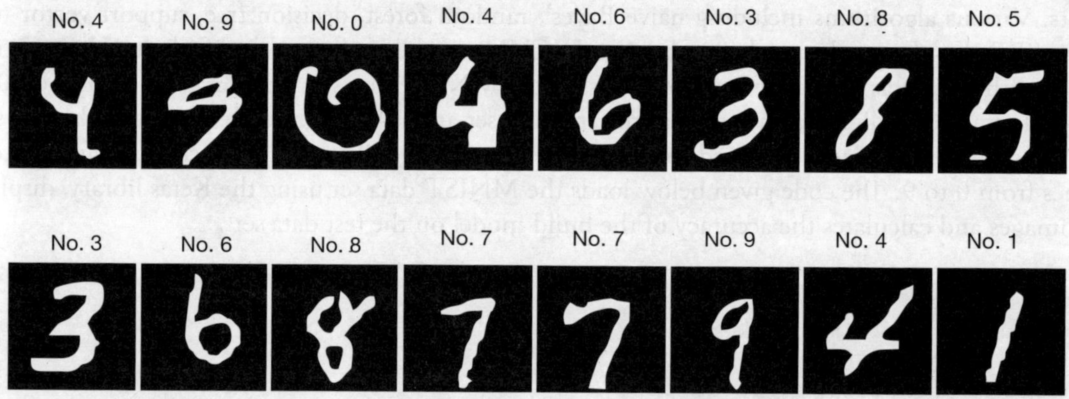

(60000, 28, 28)
(10000, 28, 28)

This is the size of the training and test data sets. So `train_digits_val` data is the feature, which is the pixel values of the 28 x 28 images of the digits 0–9. `train_labels_val` is the label (it is 0, 1, 2, 3, 4, 5, 6, 7, 8 or 9).

We then perform some pre-processing on the data. It is generally a good idea to normalize the data. This involves scaling the data to be between 0 and 1, or −1 and positive 1. In our case, each pixel is a feature, and each feature currently ranges from 0 to 255. We must rescale the data so that it is between 0 and 1 and categorize the training and test data in 10 classes, between 0 and 9. Next, we need to build the machine learning (ML) model. We can build CNN models using Keras functions. The `Conv2D()` function takes the kernel size, padding, activation function, number of kernels and input data as parameters. Kernel size is always taken in odd values, such as 1 x 1, 3 x 3, 5 x 5, and so on. Here we take 3 x 3. 1 x 1 or 3 x 3 are ideal for input size less than 128 x 128. A number of kernels are taken in the range of [32, 64,128]. In the deeper layers, it can extend to [256, 512,1024].

First we have 32 filters, then we use `MaxPooling2D()` to reduce the dimension. We will have 64 and 128 filters in the next layers. Filters are always taken as powers of 2.

```
image_heightval = train_digits_val.shape[1]
image_widthval = train_digits_val.shape[2]
num_channels = 1  # we have grayscale images
# NOTE: image_height == image_width == 28
# re-shape the images data - Preprocessing
train_dataval = np.reshape(train_digits_val, (train_digits_val.shape[0],
image_heightval, image_widthval, num_channels))
test_dataval = np.reshape(test_digits_val, (test_digits_val.shape[0],
image_heightval, image_widthval, num_channels))
# re-scale the image data to values between (0.0,1.0]
train_dataval = train_dataval.astype('float32') / 255
test_dataval = test_dataval.astype('float32') / 255
from tensorflow.keras.utils import to_categorical
num_classes = 10
#Categorise train label and test label data in 10 classes
train_labels_cat = to_categorical(train_labels_val,num_classes)
test_labels_cat = to_categorical(test_labels_val,num_classes)
train_labels_cat.shape, test_labels_cat.shape
# shuffle the training dataset (5 times!)
for _ in range(5):
    indexes = np.random.permutation(len(train_dataval))
train_dataval = train_dataval[indexes]
train_labels_cat = train_labels_cat[indexes]
# now set-aside 10% of the train_data/labels as the
# cross-validation sets
val_perc = 0.10
val_count = int(val_perc * len(train_dataval))
# first pick validation set from train_data/labels
val_data = train_dataval[:val_count,:]
val_labels_cat = train_labels_cat[:val_count,:]
# leave rest in training set
train_dataval2 = train_dataval[val_count:,:]
train_labels_cat2 = train_labels_cat[val_count:,:]
from keras.models import Sequential
from keras.layers import Conv2D, MaxPooling2D,Dense,Dropout,Flatten
def build_model():
    cnnmodel = Sequential()
    # add Convolutional layers
    cnnmodel.add(Conv2D(filters=32, kernel_size=(3,3),
activation='relu',padding='same',                input_shape=(image_
heightval, image_widthval, num_channels)))
    cnnmodel.add(MaxPooling2D(pool_size=(2,2)))
    cnnmodel.add(Conv2D(filters=64, kernel_size=(3,3),
activation='relu',padding='same'))
    cnnmodel.add(MaxPooling2D(pool_size=(2,2)))
    cnnmodel.add(Conv2D(filters=128, kernel_size=(3,3), activation='relu',
padding='same'))
    cnnmodel.add(MaxPooling2D(pool_size=(2,2)))
    cnnmodel.add(Flatten())
```

```
    # Densely connected layers
    cnnmodel.add(Dense(128, activation='relu'))
    # output layer
    cnnmodel.add(Dense(num_classes, activation='softmax'))
    # compile with adam optimizer & categorical_crossentropy loss
function ylog(p) + (1-y) log (1-p) where p is predicted observation of
class c
    cnnmodel.compile(optimizer='adam',loss='categorical_crossentropy',
                    metrics=['accuracy'])
    return cnnmodel
cnn_model = build_model()
print(cnn_model.summary())
results = cnn_model.fit(train_dataval2, train_labels_cat2,
                    epochs=20, batch_size=128,
                    validation_data=(val_data, val_labels_cat))
import matplotlib
import numpy as np
import matplotlib.pyplot as plt
plt.show(results.history)
test_loss_val, test_accuracy_val = cnn_model.evaluate(test_dataval, test_
labels_cat, batch_size=64)
print('Test loss: %.4f accuracy: %.4f' % (test_loss_val, test_accuracy_
val))
predictions_val = cnn_model.predict(test_dataval)
first_preds = np.argmax(predictions_val, axis=1)[:25]
first_true = np.argmax(test_labels_cat,axis=1)[:25]
print(first_preds)
print(first_true)
(np.argmax(predictions_val, axis=1) != np.argmax(test_labels_cat,axis=1)).
sum()
```

Output:
Displays the model summary: Model: Sequential, layer type, output shape and parameters in each layer. It also displays Total params as 241,546, Trainable params as 241,546 and Non-trainable params as 0
After that, each epoch information will be displayed:
Epoch 1/20
422/422 [==============================] - 89s 209ms/step - loss: 0.5319 - accuracy: 0.8295 - val_loss: 0.0610 - val_accuracy: 0.9805
After 20 epochs Test loss: 0.0327 accuracy: 0.9915
[7 2 1 0 4 1 4 9 5 9 0 6 9 0 1 5 9 7 3 4 9 6 6 5 4]
[7 2 1 0 4 1 4 9 5 9 0 6 9 0 1 5 9 7 3 4 9 6 6 5 4]
85

Here, the accuracy of the model after 9 epochs is 99.15% and 85 samples are misclassified. Model parameters can be further tuned and epochs can also be increased to achieve better accuracy for digit classification.

18.1 Face and Eye Detection in Images

Face detection can be performed using techniques that classify face and non-face images. Various methods exist for this, but here we use the Haar cascade classifier, which is an effective object detection method. The Haar cascade classifier is an ML method, which is trained from many positive images (with faces) and negative images (without faces). It is then used to detect objects in other images.

We use pre-trained Haar cascade models using the OpenCV (Open Source Computer Vision) library of Intel, which supports deep learning frameworks. The function `cv2.CascadeClassifierload()` is used for reading the models. Before we start coding for face and eye detection in images, we need to download the utility files (`haarcascade_frontalface_default.xml,haarcascade_eye.xml`) in Google Colab, using the commands given below. If you want to detect a smile in the given image, you can download the utility file `haarcascade_smile.xml` along with the face and eye files.

Deep neural network (DNN) models are created and used with TensorFlow and Keras; however, the Viola Jones method (Haar classifier) for face detection produces very good results. OpenCV is also widely used for image manipulation and pre- and post-processing, even in modern DNN-based systems.

```
# Download the test image and utils files
!wget --no-check-certificate \
    https://raw.githubusercontent.com/computationalcore/introduction-to-
opencv/master/assets/test.jpg \
    -O test.jpg
!wget --no-check-certificate \
    https://raw.githubusercontent.com/computationalcore/introduction-to-
opencv/master/assets/haarcascade_frontalface_default.xml \
    -O haarcascade_frontalface_default.xml
!wget --no-check-certificate \
    https://raw.githubusercontent.com/computationalcore/introduction-to-
opencv/master/assets/haarcascade_smile.xml \
    -O haarcascade_smile.xml
!wget --no-check-certificate \
    https://raw.githubusercontent.com/computationalcore/introduction-to-
opencv/master/assets/haarcascade_eye.xml \
    -O haarcascade_eye.xml
!wget --no-check-certificate \
    https://raw.githubusercontent.com/computationalcore/introduction-to-
opencv/master/utils/common.py \
    -O common.py
```

Python code

```
import numpy as np
import pandas as pd
import cv2 as cv
import matplotlib.pylab as plt
```

```
from google.colab import files
from io import BytesIO
from PIL import Image
import matplotlib.pyplot as plt
#This will upload the image file in google colab
uploaded = files.upload()
im = Image.open(BytesIO(uploaded['photo.jpeg']))
plt.imshow(im)
plt.show()
face_cascade.load('haarcascade_frontalface_default.xml')
im = np.array(im)
gray=cv.cvtColor(im,cv.COLOR_BGR2GRAY)
plt.imshow(gray)
plt.show()
```

Output:
photo.jpeg(image/jpeg) - 48611 bytes, last modified: 10/10/2020 - 100% done
Saving photo.jpeg to photo (19).jpeg

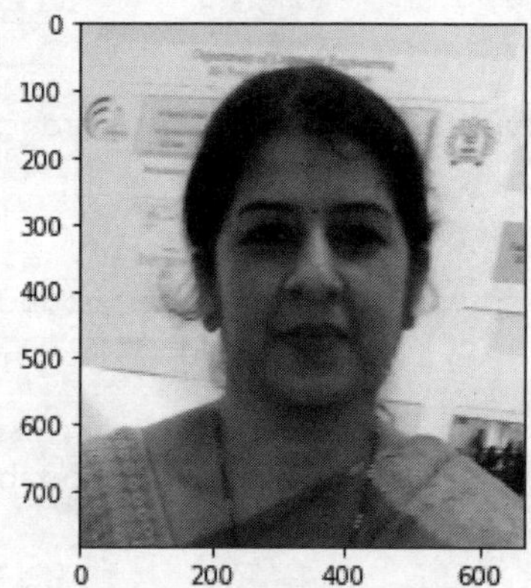

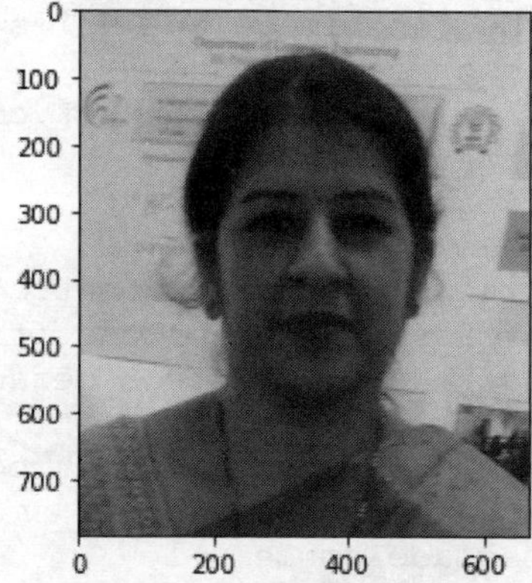

The output above shows the uploaded image and the grey-converted image.

```
#Face detection from image
face_cascade = cv.CascadeClassifier('haarcascade_frontalface_default.
xml')
faces = face_cascade.detectMultiScale(gray, 1.3, 5)
for (x,y,w,h) in faces:
     cv.rectangle(im,(x,y),(x+w,y+h),(255,0,0),2)
plt.imshow(cv.cvtColor(im, cv.COLOR_BGR2RGB))
plt.imshow(im)
plt.show()
```

Output:

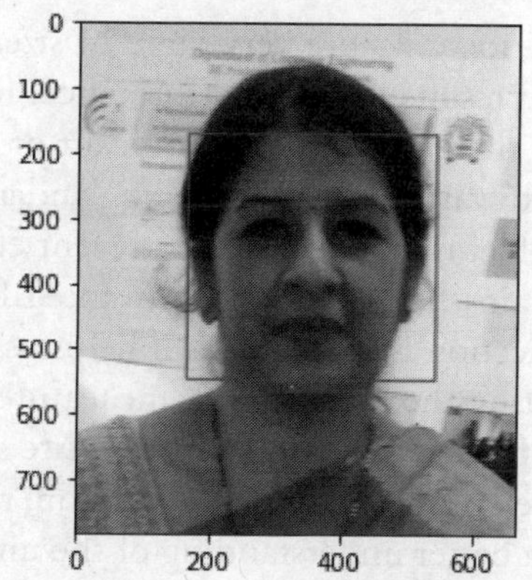


```
#Eye Detection from image
eye_cascade = cv2.CascadeClassifier('haarcascade_eye.xml')
eyes = eye_cascade.detectMultiScale(gray, 1.3, 1)
for (x,y,w,h) in faces:
  for (x_s,y_s,w_s,h_s) in eyes:
    if( (x <= x_s) and (y <= y_s) and ( x+w >= x_s+w_s) and ( y+h >= y_
s+h_s)):
      cv2.rectangle(im, (x_s,y_s),(x_s+w_s,y_s+h_s),(255,255,255),2)
plt.imshow(cv.cvtColor(im, cv2.COLOR_BGR2RGB))
plt.imshow(im)
plt.show()
cv.waitKey()
cv.destroyAllWindows()
```

Output:

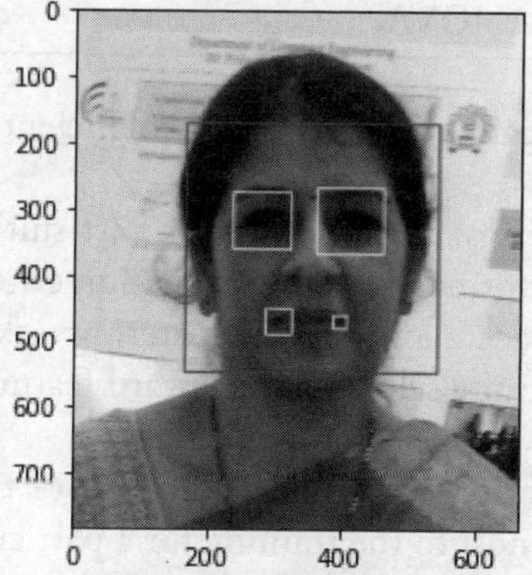

18.2 Correlation and Feature Selection

Sometimes, the data sets provided for tasks are very large in size. It becomes a bottleneck for processing and training the model and results in poor performance. It is the features that make the data sets large. Often in large data sets, there are some insignificant or unimportant features, in the sense that they do not contribute much towards system modelling and are therefore considered redundant. Moreover, these features cause problems and eventually prevent efficient modelling. Unnecessary resource allocation, more time to train the system and unwanted features that act as noise affect the system performance. So feature selection is required, as it helps us avoid all these problems.

From the given data set, selecting the most significant features to enhance the performance of a machine learning model is called **feature selection or attribute selection**. The objectives are to increase the performance of the model, provide faster computation, reduce the complexity of the model, reduce overfitting and to provide a better understanding of the underlying data.

Dimensionality reduction is sometimes mistaken for feature selection. Both methods reduce the number of features of the data set, but dimensionality reduction creates new combinations of features or attributes; in other words, they change the values of new features. This is sometimes known as **feature transformation**. In feature selection, inclusion or exclusion of features is performed without changing the feature value. Principal component analysis (PCA), singular value decomposition (SVD) and linear discriminant analysis (LDA) are examples of dimensionality reduction techniques. The three feature selection methods are filter methods, wrapper methods and embedded methods.

The **filter method** is the simplest and produces the relevant features. It uses a ranking technique for feature selection. Features are given ranks on the basis of statistical scores which determine the features' correlation with the outcome variable. Scores are defined differently for different types of data and outcome variables. Table 18.1 defines the correlation coefficients for different types of data.

Table 18.1 Correlation coefficients for different types of data

Feature\Response	Continuous	Categorical
Continuous	Pearson's correlation	LDA
Categorical	ANOVA	Chi-square

Chi-square test, information gain and correlation coefficient scores are some examples of filter methods.

The **wrapper method** searches for a feature that is best-suited for the ML algorithm. It needs one ML algorithm and uses its performance as the evaluation criteria. For classification tasks, it evaluates the features using predictive accuracy and for clustering tasks, it uses the goodness of cluster as the evaluation criteria. Forward feature selection, backward feature elimination and recursive feature elimination are some examples of wrapper methods.

Embedded methods use iteration where each iteration of the model training process extracts those features that contribute the most to the training for a particular iteration. Regularization methods are the most commonly used embedded methods.

The following code uses the Iris data set, which contains five columns: `SepalLengthCm`, `SepalWidthCm`, `PetalLengthCm`, `PetalWidthCm` and `Species`. The `Species` field is an output variable that contains only two values: Iris-setosa and Iris-versicolor. The data set contains 150 rows. We want to classify data into two classes, considering only two of the four features.

```
#Feature selection using filter method
from matplotlib import pyplot
import io
import pandas as pd
import numpy as np
import matplotlib.pyplot as plt
from google.colab import files
from sklearn.feature_selection import SelectKBest
from sklearn.feature_selection import chi2
uploaded= files.upload()
dfval=pd.read_csv(io.BytesIO(uploaded['Iris_data_sample.csv']))
#print(dfval.head())
for tcol in dfval.columns:
   print(tcol)
```

Output:
SepalLengthCm
SepalWidthCm
PetalLengthCm
PetalWidthCm
Species

```
arraydata = dfval.values
Tx = arraydata[:,1:5]
Ty = arraydata[:,5]
# Extraction of two features
testset = SelectKBest(score_func=chi2, k=2)
fitfilter = testset.fit(Tx, Ty)
# Summarize scores
np.set_printoptions(precision=3)
print(fitfilter.scores_)
```

Output: [10.43 3.591 112.935 64.832]

```
features = fitfilter.transform(Tx)
# Summarize selected features
print(features[0:2,:])
```

Output:
[[1.4 0.2]
[1.4 0.2]]

```
#Feature selection using wrapper method
from sklearn.feature_selection import RFE
from sklearn.linear_model import LogisticRegression
# Feature extraction using wrapper method
modelfit = LogisticRegression()
rfe = RFE(modelfit, 2)
fitmodel = rfe.fit(Tx, Ty)
print("No of Features: %s" % (fitmodel.n_features_))
print("Features selected are: %s" % (fitmodel.support_))
print("Feature Ranking is: %s" % (fitmodel.ranking_))
```

Output:
No of Features: 2
Features selected are: [False False True True]
Feature Ranking is: [3 2 1 1]

The results show that `PetalLengthCm` and `PetalWidthCm` have the highest scores. So they are the selected features. Both methods result in the selection of the same features.

18.3 Fake News Detection

Fake news refers to information that is untrue. Nowadays fake news spreads easily and people share information without verifying it. This is often carried out to further or impose certain ideas and is often based on political agendas.

We need to design a model for detecting fake news using Python and ML. Here, we use logistics regression, K-NN and decision tree algorithms to detect fake news.

The data set we will use for this is train1.csv, which is a news data set. This can be accessed at https://www.kaggle.com/jruvika/fake-news-detection

It has the shape 4009 x 4. It is a binary classification: news is fake or not.

This data set has four columns:

- `URLs`, gives the URL where news is available
- `Headline`, gives the headline of the news article
- `Body`, gives the body of the news message
- `Label`, labels the news as fake (0) or real (1)

```
# 1. Import Libraries
import pandas as pd
import streamlit as st
from PIL import Image
from matplotlib import pyplot as plt
import plotly.graph_objects as go
from sklearn.feature_extraction.text import TfidfVectorizer
from sklearn.linear_model import LogisticRegression
from sklearn.metrics import accuracy_score, confusion_matrix,
classification_report, precision_score, recall_score
```

```
from sklearn.model_selection import train_test_split
from sklearn.neighbors import KNeighborsClassifier
from sklearn.tree import DecisionTreeClassifier
import plotly.express as px
st.set_page_config(page_title="FAKE NEWS PREDICTION", page_
icon=":newspaper:")
def main():
st.sidebar.title("Binary Classification Web App")
st.sidebar.markdown("Is the Newspaper you are reading FAKE or REAL?□")
option = ["HOME","PREDICT", "RESULT", "ANALYSIS","INSTRUCTION"]
a = st.sidebar.selectbox("MENU", option)
# Loading the data
def load_data():
raw_news_data = pd.read_csv('train1.csv')
print(raw_news_data.head())
print("Count of null values in raw data:",raw_news_data.isnull().sum())
# Removing the Null Values
news_dataset = raw_news_data.where((pd.notnull(raw_news_data)), '')
print("Count of null values after processing: ",news_dataset.isnull().
sum())
features_dropped = ['URLs', 'Headline']
news_dataset = news_dataset.drop(features_dropped, axis=1)
print("After processing \n",news_dataset.head())
return news_dataset
def logisticregression():
model = LogisticRegression()
# train our model on training data set using.fit() method and make
predictions on test set using.predict()
model.fit(X_train_features, Y_train)
print("Logistic Regression")
# prediction on training data
X_train_prediction = model.predict(X_train_features)
training_data_accuracy = accuracy_score(X_train_prediction, Y_train)
# the set of labels predicted for a sample must exactly match the
corresponding set of labels in y_true.
print('Accuracy score of the training data: ', training_data_accuracy)
# prediction on testing data
X_test_prediction = model.predict(X_test_features)
lrtest_data_accuracy = accuracy_score(X_test_prediction, Y_test)
print('Accuracy score of the test data: ', lrtest_data_accuracy)
print('confusion matrix:',confusion_matrix(X_test_prediction, Y_test))
report = classification_report(X_test_prediction, Y_test)
print(report)
st.subheader("To check whether the news is Fake or Real")
String = st.text_input("Enter news for prediction")
input_news = [String]
input_data_features = feature_extraction.transform(input_news)
prediction = model.predict(input_data_features)
# making prediction
click = st.button("PREDICT")
```

```
# print(prediction)
if click:
if (prediction[0] == 0):
st.subheader("Prediction of the News: Looking Fake□ News□ ")
else:
st.subheader("Prediction of the News: Looking Real News□ ")
st.subheader("Logistic Regression( Result)")
st.write("Accuracy ", lrtest_data_accuracy.round(2) * 100)
st.write("Precision: ", precision_score(Y_test, X_test_prediction,
labels=class_names).round(2))
st.write("Recall: ", recall_score(Y_test, X_test_prediction, labels=class_
names).round(2))
conf = Image.open("lr confusionmatrix.png")
st.image(conf, width=400)
st.write(report)
def knn():
print("KNN")
knn = KNeighborsClassifier(n_neighbors=100, metric='euclidean')
knn.fit(X_train_features, Y_train)
X_test_prediction = knn.predict(X_test_features)
knntest_data_accuracy = accuracy_score(X_test_prediction, Y_test)
print('Accuracy score of the test data: ', knntest_data_accuracy)
print('confusion matrix:',confusion_matrix(X_test_prediction, Y_test))
print(classification_report(X_test_prediction, Y_test))
report = classification_report(X_test_prediction, Y_test)
st.subheader("To check whether the news is fake or real...")
String = st.text_input("Enter news for prediction")
input_news = [String]
input_data_features = feature_extraction.transform(input_news)
prediction = knn.predict(input_data_features)
# making prediction
click = st.button("PREDICT")
# print(prediction)
if click:
if (prediction[0] == 0):
st.subheader("Prediction of the News: Looking Fake□ News□ ")
else:
st.subheader("Prediction of the News: Looking Real News□ ")
st.subheader("K Nearest Neighbour( Result)")
st.write("Accuracy ", knntest_data_accuracy.round(2) * 100)
st.write("Precision: ", precision_score(Y_test, X_test_prediction,
labels=class_names).round(2))
st.write("Recall: ", recall_score(Y_test, X_test_prediction, labels=class_
names).round(2))
conf = Image.open("knn confusion matrix.png")
st.image(conf, width=400)
st.write(report)
def DecisionTree():
dclassifier = DecisionTreeClassifier(criterion='entropy', random_state=0)
dclassifier.fit(X_train_features, Y_train)
```

```
X_test_prediction = dclassifier.predict(X_test_features)
dttest_data_accuracy = accuracy_score(X_test_prediction, Y_test)
print('Accuracy score of the test data: ', dttest_data_accuracy)
print('confusion matrix:',confusion_matrix(X_test_prediction, Y_test))
report = classification_report(X_test_prediction, Y_test)
st.subheader("To check whether the news is fake or real...")
String = st.text_input("Enter news for prediction")
input_news = [String]
input_data_features = feature_extraction.transform(input_news)
prediction = dclassifier.predict(input_data_features)
# making prediction
click = st.button("PREDICT")
# print(prediction)
if click:
if (prediction[0] == 0):
st.subheader("Prediction of the News: Looking Fake□ News□ ")
else:
st.subheader("Prediction of the News: Looking Real News□ ")
st.subheader("Decison Tree( Result)")
st.write("Accuracy ", dttest_data_accuracy.round(2) * 100)
st.write("Precision: ", precision_score(Y_test, X_test_prediction,
labels=class_names).round(2))
st.write("Recall: ", recall_score(Y_test, X_test_prediction, labels=class_
names).round(2))
conf = Image.open("dt confusionmatrix.png")
st.image(conf, width=400)
st.write(report)
# loading the processed data into newsdata
news_data = load_data()
# separating the data and label
X = news_data['Body']
Y = news_data['Label']
class_names = ['FAKE', 'REAL']
# transform the text data to feature vectors that can be used as input to
the Logistic regression
feature_extraction = TfidfVectorizer(min_df=1, stop_words='english',
lowercase='True')
# Convert all characters to lowercase before tokenizing.
# Splitting DataSet
# split our data set in 75:25 ratio
X_train, X_test, Y_train, Y_test = train_test_split(X, Y, test_size=0.25,
stratify=Y, random_state=2)
X_train_features = feature_extraction.fit_transform(X_train)
X_test_features = feature_extraction.transform(X_test)
if a=="HOME":
st.title("FAKE NEWS PREDICTION WEB APP")
backg = Image.open("backpg.jpg")
st.image(backg)
elif a == 'PREDICT':
classifier=st.sidebar.radio("Choose Classifier",["KNN", "Logistic
```

```
Regression", "Decision Tree"])
# classifier = st.sidebar.selectbox("Classifier", ())
if classifier == 'Logistic Regression':
logisticregression()
elif classifier == 'KNN':
knn()
elif classifier == 'Decision Tree':
DecisionTree()
elif a == "ANALYSIS":
label = "Label"
news_data[label].value_counts().plot(kind='pie')
fakecount = news_data[label].value_counts()
plt.show()
category = ['Fake', 'Real']
# values = [4825,747]
fig = go.Figure(
go.Pie(
labels=category,
values=fakecount,
hoverinfo="label+percent",
textinfo="value"
))
st.header("DataSet Analysis")
st.subheader("Pie chart")
st.plotly_chart(fig)
st.subheader("Real news words")
real = Image.open("real news words.png")
st.image(real, width=600)
st.subheader("Fake news words")
fake = Image.open("fake news words.png")
st.image(fake, width=600)
elif a=="RESULT":
st.subheader("Algorithm Analysis")
image = Image.open('bargraph_ofaccuracy.png')
# displaying the image on streamlit app
st.image(image)
elif a=="INSTRUCTION":
ins = Image.open("instructions_Fake_news.jpg")
st.image(ins)
if __name__ == '__main__':
main()
```

Output:
DATA PREPROCESSING
URLs Headline Body Label
0 http://www.bbc.com/news/world-us-canada-414191... Four ways Bob Corker skewered Donald Trump Image copyright Getty Images\nOn Sunday mornin... 1
1 https://www.reuters.com/article/us-filmfestiva... Linklater's war veteran comedy speaks to moder... LONDON (Reuters) - "Last Flag Flying", a comed... 1

2 https://www.nytimes.com/2017/10/09/us/politics... Trump's Fight With Corker Jeopardizes His Legi... The feud broke into public view last week when... 1
3 https://www.reuters.com/article/us-mexico-oil-... Egypt's Cheiron wins tie-up with Pemex for Mex... MEXICO CITY (Reuters) - Egypt's Cheiron Holdin... 1
4 http://www.cnn.com/videos/cnnmoney/2017/10/08/... Jason Aldean opens 'SNL' with Vegas tribute Country singer Jason Aldean, who was performin... 1

Count of null values in raw data:
URLs 0
Headline 0
Body 21
Label 0
dtype: int64

Count of null values after processing:
URLs 0
Headline 0
Body 0
Label 0
dtype: int64

After processing
Body Label
0 Image copyright Getty Images\nOn Sunday mornin... 1
1 LONDON (Reuters) - "Last Flag Flying", a comed... 1
2 The feud broke into public view last week when... 1
3 MEXICO CITY (Reuters) - Egypt's Cheiron Holdin... 1
4 Country singer Jason Aldean, who was performing... 1
Body Label
0 Image copyright Getty Images\nOn Sunday mornin... 1
1 LONDON (Reuters) - "Last Flag Flying", a comed... 1
2 The feud broke into public view last week when... 1
3 MEXICO CITY (Reuters) - Egypt's Cheiron Holdings... 1
4 Country singer Jason Aldean, who was performing... 1
....
4004 Trends to Watch\n% of readers think this story... 0
4005 Trump Jr. Is Soon To Give A 30-Minute Speech F... 0
4006 0

KNN
Accuracy score of the test data: 0.9032901296111665
[[489 51]
[46 417]]

	precision	recall	f1-score	support
0	0.91	0.91	0.91	540
1	0.89	0.90	0.90	463

accuracy 0.90 1003
macro avg 0.90 0.90 0.90 1003
weighted avg 0.90 0.90 0.90 1003

Logistic Regression
Accuracy score of the training data: 0.9876912840984697
Accuracy score of the test data: 0.967098703888335
confusion matrix:
[[510 8]
[25 460]]

	precision	recall	f1-score	support
0	0.95	0.98	0.97	518
1	0.98	0.95	0.97	485

accuracy 0.97 1003
macro avg 0.97 0.97 0.97 1003
weighted avg 0.97 0.97 0.97 1003

Decision Tree
Accuracy score of the test data: 0.9322033898305084
confusion matrix:
[[513 46]
[22 422]]
"""

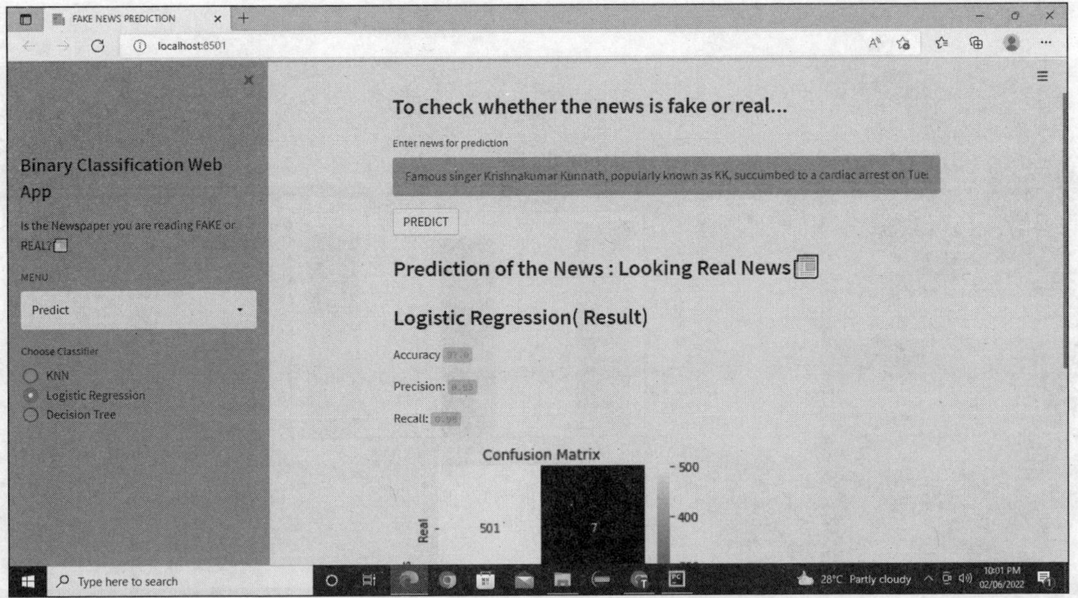
FAKE NEWS PREDICTION
localhost:8501
Binary Classification Web App
Is the Newspaper you are reading FAKE or REAL?
MENU
Predict
Choose Classifier
KNN
Logistic Regression
Decision Tree
To check whether the news is fake or real...
Enter news for prediction
Famous singer Krishnakumar Kunnath, popularly known as KK, succumbed to a cardiac arrest on Tue
PREDICT
Prediction of the News : Looking Real News
Logistic Regression(Result)
Accuracy
Precision:
Recall:
Confusion Matrix
Real
501
7
500
400
Type here to search
28°C Partly cloudy
10:01 PM
02/06/2022

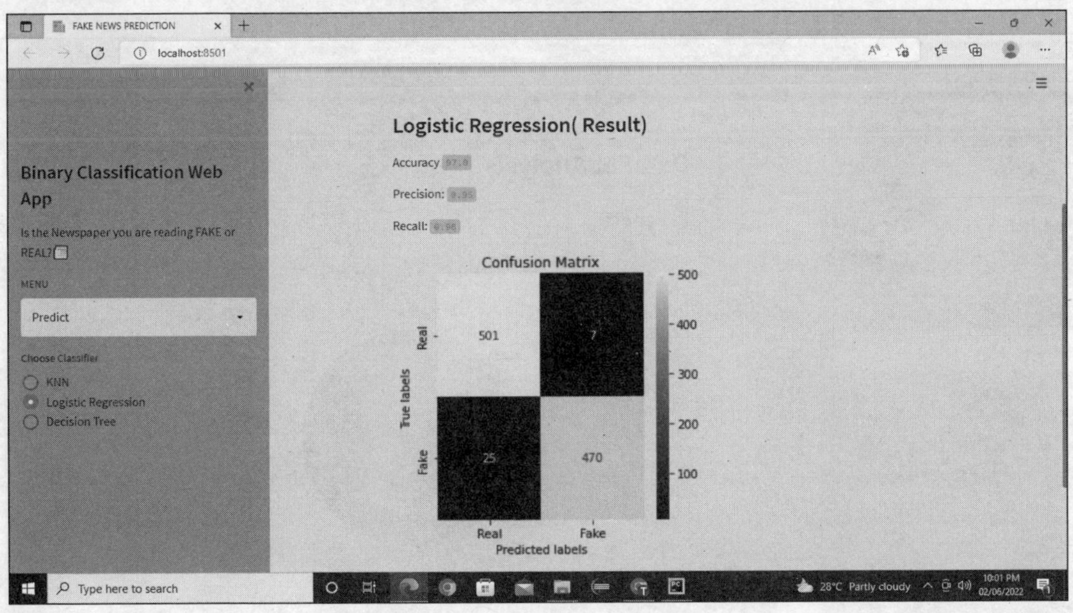
FAKE NEWS PREDICTION
localhost:8501
Binary Classification Web App
Is the Newspaper you are reading FAKE or REAL?
MENU
Predict
Choose Classifier
KNN
Logistic Regression
Decision Tree
Logistic Regression(Result)
Accuracy
Precision:
Recall:
Confusion Matrix
True labels
Real
Fake
501
7
25
470
500
400
300
200
100
Real
Fake
Predicted labels
Type here to search
28°C Partly cloudy
10:01 PM
02/06/2022

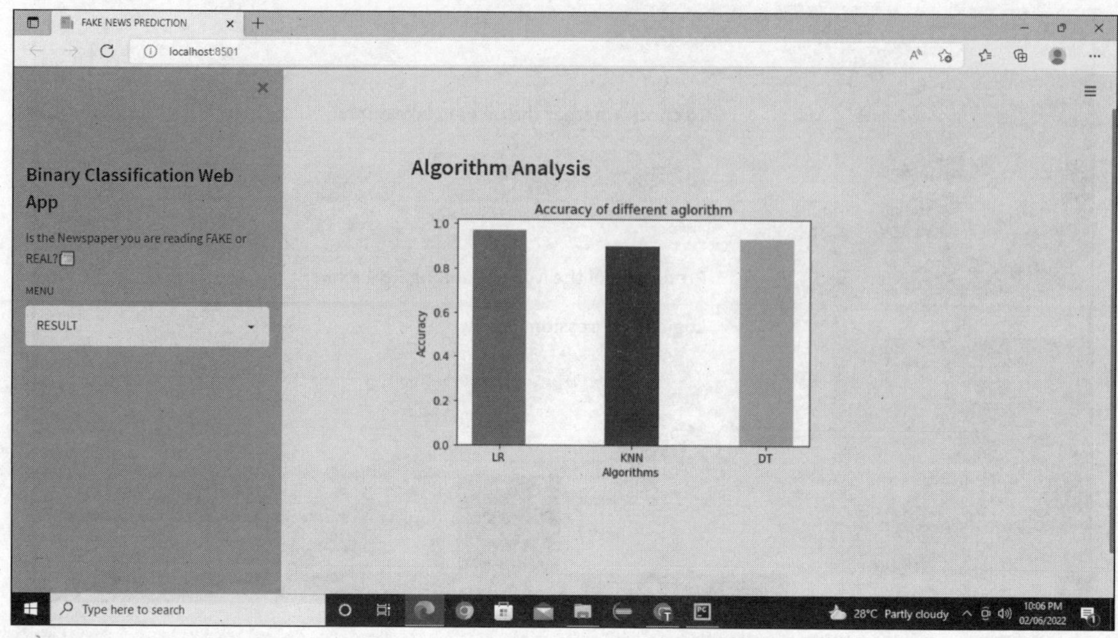
FAKE NEWS PREDICTION
localhost:8501
Binary Classification Web App
Is the Newspaper you are reading FAKE or REAL?
MENU
RESULT
Algorithm Analysis
Accuracy of different aglorithm
Accuracy
Algorithms
LR
KNN
DT
Type here to search
28°C Partly cloudy
10:06 PM
02/06/2022

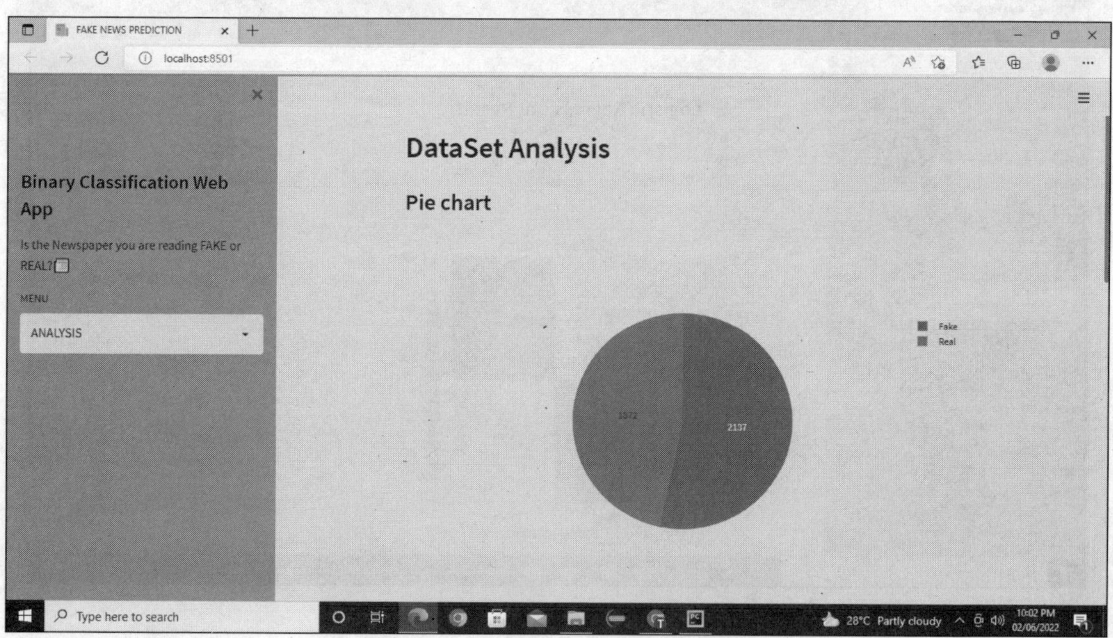
FAKE NEWS PREDICTION
localhost:8501
Binary Classification Web App
Is the Newspaper you are reading FAKE or REAL?
MENU
ANALYSIS
DataSet Analysis
Pie chart
Fake
Real
2137
Type here to search
28°C Partly cloudy
10:02 PM
02/06/2022

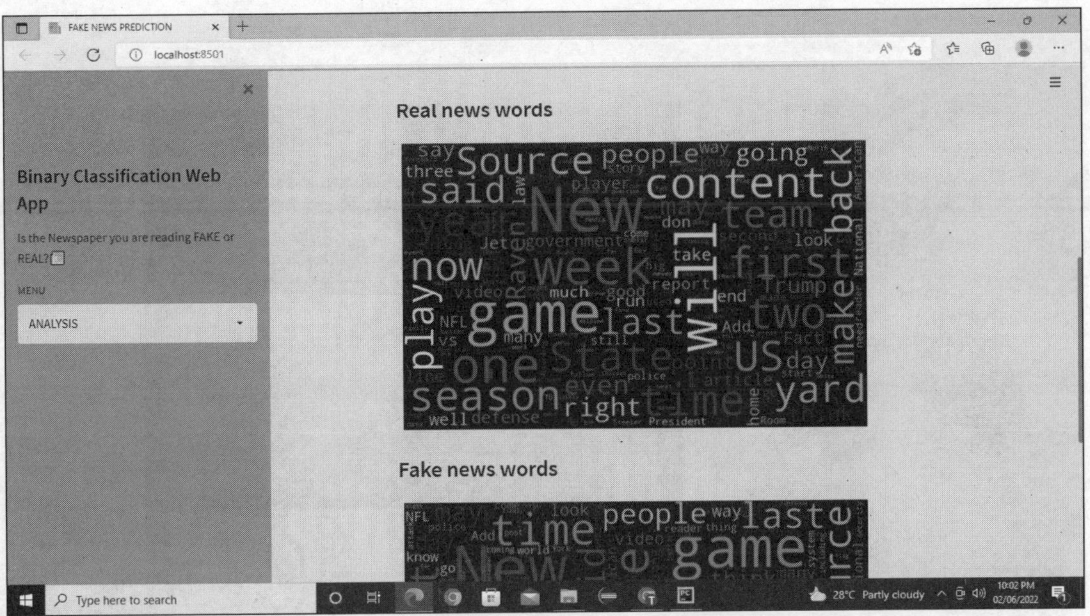
FAKE NEWS PREDICTION
localhost:8501
Binary Classification Web App
Is the Newspaper you are reading FAKE or REAL?
MENU
ANALYSIS
Real news words
Fake news words
Type here to search
28°C Partly cloudy
10:02 PM
02/06/2022

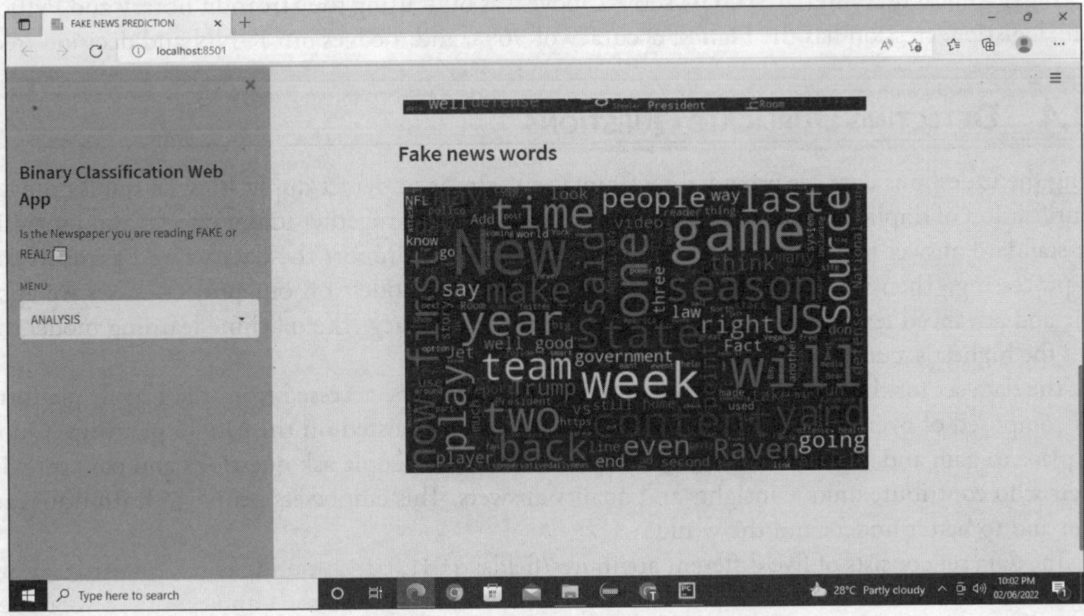
FAKE NEWS PREDICTION
localhost:8501
Binary Classification Web App
Is the Newspaper you are reading FAKE or REAL?
MENU
ANALYSIS
Fake news words
Type here to search
28°C Partly cloudy
10:02 PM
02/06/2022

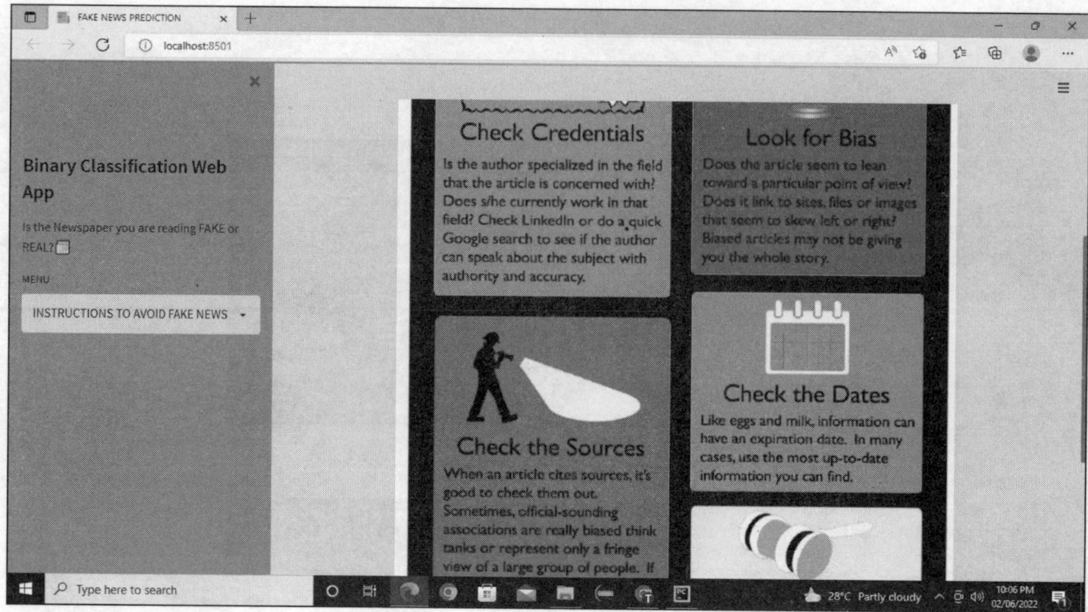

The graphical user interface (GUI) shown above was built using the Streamlit library and Python. Here, logistic regression has the highest accuracy of 96%, and it edges out K-NN and decision tree.

18.4 Detecting Duplicate Questions

Using the Questions data set provided by Quora, our aim is to detect duplication in question pairs. Identification of duplicate questions will help in clubbing them together under one set and providing one standard answer for the entire set. In our project, we first import the data set and perform data pre-processing. Then we check the accuracy of various ML models on our project. Later we apply basic and advanced feature engineering and compare the accuracy. The machine learning model that gives the highest accuracy is chosen for our final prediction.

The data set for the project is provided by Quora and can be accessed from the Kaggle platform. It is composed of over 404,290 entries of different questions posted on the Quora platform. Quora is a place to gain and share knowledge. It is a platform where people ask questions and connect with others who contribute unique insights and quality answers. This empowers people to learn from each other and to better understand the world.

The data set consists of five different attributes/fields: `qid1`, `qid2`, `question1`, `question2` and `is_duplicate`, where `qid1` and `qid2` are the unique IDs for `question1` and `question2`, respectively, and `is_duplicate` classifies whether the question is a duplicate or not.

```
#Importing necessary Libraries
import numpy as np
import pandas as pd
import matplotlib.pyplot as plt
import seaborn as sns
import re
from bs4 import BeautifulSoup
import warnings
warnings.filterwarnings('ignore')
df = pd.read_csv('C:/Users/SAMIKSHA/Documents/project/train.csv')
df.shape
df.head()
new_df = df.sample(1000,random_state=2)
new_df.isnull().sum()
new_df.head()
new_df.isnull().sum()
new_df.duplicated().sum()
# Distribution of duplicate and non-duplicate questions
print(new_df['is_duplicate'].value_counts())
print((new_df['is_duplicate'].value_counts()/new_df['is_duplicate'].
count())*100)
new_df['is_duplicate'].value_counts().plot(kind='bar')
# Repeated questions
qid = pd.Series(new_df['qid1'].tolist() + new_df['qid2'].tolist())
print('Number of unique questions',np.unique(qid).shape[0])
x = qid.value_counts()>1
print('Number of questions getting repeated',x[x].shape[0])
# Repeated questions histogram
plt.hist(qid.value_counts().values,bins=160)
plt.yscale('log')
plt.show()
# Feature Engineering
new_df['q1_len'] = new_df['question1'].str.len()
new_df['q2_len'] = new_df['question2'].str.len()
new_df.head()
new_df['q1_num_words'] = new_df['question1'].apply(lambda row: len(row.
split(" ")))
new_df['q2_num_words'] = new_df['question2'].apply(lambda row: len(row.
split(" ")))
new_df.head()
def common_words(row):
w1 = set(map(lambda word: word.lower().strip(), row['question1'].split("
")))
w2 = set(map(lambda word: word.lower().strip(), row['question2'].split("
")))
return len(w1 & w2)
new_df['word_common'] = new_df.apply(common_words, axis=1)
new_df.head()
def total_words(row):
```

```
w1 = set(map(lambda word: word.lower().strip(), row['question1'].split("
")))
w2 = set(map(lambda word: word.lower().strip(), row['question2'].split("
")))
return (len(w1) + len(w2))
new_df['word_total'] = new_df.apply(total_words, axis=1)
new_df.head()
new_df['word_share'] = round(new_df['word_common']/new_df['word_total'],2)
new_df.head()
ques_df = new_df[['question1','question2']]
ques_df.head()
final_df = new_df.drop(columns=
['id','qid1','qid2','question1','question2'])
print(final_df.shape)
final_df.head()
from sklearn.feature_extraction.text import CountVectorizer
# merge texts
questions = list(ques_df['question1']) + list(ques_df['question2'])
cv = CountVectorizer(max_features=3000)
q1_arr, q2_arr = np.vsplit(cv.fit_transform(questions).toarray(),2)
temp_df1 = pd.DataFrame(q1_arr, index= ques_df.index)
temp_df2 = pd.DataFrame(q2_arr, index= ques_df.index)
temp_df = pd.concat([temp_df1, temp_df2], axis=1)
temp_df.shape
final_df = pd.concat([final_df, temp_df], axis=1)
print(final_df.shape)
final_df.head()
import atexit
def goodbye():
print ("You are now leaving the Python sector.")
atexit.register(goodbye)
from sklearn.model_selection import train_test_split
X_train,X_test,y_train,y_test =
train_test_split(final_df.iloc[:,1:].values,final_df.iloc[:,0].
values,test_size=0.2,random_state=1
)
#from xgboost import XGBClassifier
from sklearn.metrics import accuracy_score
'''
xgb = XGBClassifier()
xgb.fit(X_train,y_train)
y_pred = xgb.predict(X_test)
accuracy_score(y_test,y_pred)'''
from sklearn.ensemble import RandomForestClassifier
from sklearn.metrics import accuracy_score
rf = RandomForestClassifier()
rf.fit(X_train, y_train)
y_pred = rf.predict(X_test)
accuracy_score(y_test,y_pred)
```

```
def preprocess(q):
q = str(q).lower().strip()
# Replace certain special characters with their string equivalents
q = q.replace('%', ' percent')
q = q.replace('$', ' dollar ')
q = q.replace('₹', ' rupee ')
q = q.replace('€', ' euro ')
q = q.replace('@', ' at ')
# The pattern '[math]' appears around 900 times in the whole dataset.
q = q.replace('[math]', '')
# Replacing some numbers with string equivalents (not perfect, can be
done better to
account for more cases)
q = q.replace(',000,000,000 ', 'b ')
q = q.replace(',000,000 ', 'm ')
q = q.replace(',000 ', 'k ')
q = re.sub(r'([0-9]+)000000000', r'\1b', q)
q = re.sub(r'([0-9]+)000000', r'\1m', q)
q = re.sub(r'([0-9]+)000', r'\1k', q)
# Decontracting words
contractions = {
"ain't": "am not",
"aren't": "are not",
"can't": "can not",
"can't've": "can not have",
"cause": "because",
"could've": "could have",
"couldn't": "could not",
"couldn't've": "could not have",
"didn't": "did not",
"doesn't": "does not",
"don't": "do not",
"hadn't": "had not",
"hadn't've": "had not have",
"hasn't": "has not",
"haven't": "have not",
"he'd": "he would",
"he'd've": "he would have",
"he'll": "he will",
"he'll've": "he will have",
"he's": "he is",
"how'd": "how did",
"how'd'y": "how do you",
"how'll": "how will",
"how's": "how is",
"i'd": "i would",
"i'd've": "i would have",
"i'll": "i will",
"i'll've": "i will have",
"i'm": "i am",
"i've": "i have",
```

```
"isn't": "is not",
"it'd": "it would",
"it'd've": "it would have",
"it'll": "it will",
"it'll've": "it will have",
"it's": "it is",
"let's": "let us",
"ma'am": "madam",
"mayn't": "may not",
"might've": "might have",
"mightn't": "might not",
"mightn't've": "might not have",
"must've": "must have",
"mustn't": "must not",
"mustn't've": "must not have",
"needn't": "need not",
"needn't've": "need not have",
"o'clock": "of the clock",
"oughtn't": "ought not",
"oughtn't've": "ought not have",
"shan't": "shall not",
"sha'n't": "shall not",
"shan't've": "shall not have",
"she'd": "she would",
"she'd've": "she would have",
"she'll": "she will",
"she'll've": "she will have",
"she's": "she is",
"should've": "should have",
"shouldn't": "should not",
"shouldn't've": "should not have",
"so've": "so have",
"so's": "so as",
"that'd": "that would",
"that'd've": "that would have",
"that's": "that is",
"there'd": "there would",
"there'd've": "there would have",
"there's": "there is",
"they'd": "they would",
"they'd've": "they would have",
"they'll": "they will",
"they'll've": "they will have",
"they're": "they are",
"they've": "they have",
"to've": "to have",
"wasn't": "was not",
"we'd": "we would",
"we'd've": "we would have",
"we'll": "we will",
"we'll've": "we will have",
```

```
"we're": "we are",
"we've": "we have",
"weren't": "were not",
"what'll": "what will",
"what'll've": "what will have",
"what're": "what are",
"what's": "what is",
"what've": "what have",
"when's": "when is",
"when've": "when have",
"where'd": "where did",
"where's": "where is",
"where've": "where have",
"who'll": "who will",
"who'll've": "who will have",
"who's": "who is",
"who've": "who have",
"why's": "why is",
"why've": "why have",
"will've": "will have",
"won't": "will not",
"won't've": "will not have",
"would've": "would have",
"wouldn't": "would not",
"wouldn't've": "would not have",
"y'all": "you all",
"y'all'd": "you all would",
"y'all'd've": "you all would have",
"y'all're": "you all are",
"y'all've": "you all have",
"you'd": "you would",
"you'd've": "you would have",
"you'll": "you will",
"you'll've": "you will have",
"you're": "you are",
"you've": "you have"
}
q_decontracted = []
for word in q.split():
if word in contractions:
word = contractions[word]
q_decontracted.append(word)
q = ' '.join(q_decontracted)
q = q.replace("'ve", " have")
q = q.replace("n't", " not")
q = q.replace("'re", " are")
q = q.replace("'ll", " will")
# Removing HTML tags
q = BeautifulSoup(q)
q = q.get_text()
```

```
# Remove punctuations
pattern = re.compile('\W')
q = re.sub(pattern, ' ', q).strip()
return q
new_df['question1'] = new_df['question1'].apply(preprocess)
new_df['question2'] = new_df['question2'].apply(preprocess)
new_df.head()
def common_words(row):
w1 = set(map(lambda word: word.lower().strip(), row['question1'].split("
")))
w2 = set(map(lambda word: word.lower().strip(), row['question2'].split("
")))
return len(w1 & w2)
new_df['word_common'] = new_df.apply(common_words, axis=1)
new_df.head()
def total_words(row):
w1 = set(map(lambda word: word.lower().strip(), row['question1'].split("
")))
w2 = set(map(lambda word: word.lower().strip(), row['question2'].split("
")))
return (len(w1) + len(w2))
new_df['word_total'] = new_df.apply(total_words, axis=1)
new_df.head()
new_df['word_share'] = round(new_df['word_common']/new_df['word_total'],2)
new_df.head()
# Advanced Features
import nltk
nltk.download('stopwords')
from nltk.corpus import stopwords
def fetch_token_features(row):
q1 = row['question1']
q2 = row['question2']
SAFE_DIV = 0.0001
STOP_WORDS = nltk.corpus.stopwords.words("english")
token_features = [0.0]*8
# Converting the Sentence into Tokens:
q1_tokens = q1.split()
q2_tokens = q2.split()
if len(q1_tokens) == 0 or len(q2_tokens) == 0:
return token_features
# Get the non-stopwords in Questions
q1_words = set([word for word in q1_tokens if word not in STOP_WORDS])
q2_words = set([word for word in q2_tokens if word not in STOP_WORDS])
#Get the stopwords in Questions
q1_stops = set([word for word in q1_tokens if word in STOP_WORDS])
q2_stops = set([word for word in q2_tokens if word in STOP_WORDS])
# Get the common non-stopwords from Question pair
common_word_count = len(q1_words.intersection(q2_words))
# Get the common stopwords from Question pair
common_stop_count = len(q1_stops.intersection(q2_stops))
```

```
# Get the common Tokens from Question pair
common_token_count = len(set(q1_tokens).intersection(set(q2_tokens)))
token_features[0] = common_word_count / (min(len(q1_words), len(q2_
words)) +
SAFE_DIV)
token_features[1] = common_word_count / (max(len(q1_words), len(q2_
words)) +
SAFE_DIV)
token_features[2] = common_stop_count / (min(len(q1_stops), len(q2_
stops)) +
SAFE_DIV)
token_features[3] = common_stop_count / (max(len(q1_stops), len(q2_
stops)) +
SAFE_DIV)
token_features[4] = common_token_count / (min(len(q1_tokens), len(q2_
tokens)) +
SAFE_DIV)
token_features[5] = common_token_count / (max(len(q1_tokens), len(q2_
tokens)) +
SAFE_DIV)
# Last word of both question is same or not
token_features[6] = int(q1_tokens[-1] == q2_tokens[-1])
# First word of both question is same or not
token_features[7] = int(q1_tokens[0] == q2_tokens[0])
return token_features
token_features = new_df.apply(fetch_token_features, axis=1)
new_df["cwc_min"] = list(map(lambda x: x[0], token_features))
new_df["cwc_max"] = list(map(lambda x: x[1], token_features))
new_df["csc_min"] = list(map(lambda x: x[2], token_features))
new_df["csc_max"] = list(map(lambda x: x[3], token_features))
new_df["ctc_min"] = list(map(lambda x: x[4], token_features))
new_df["ctc_max"] = list(map(lambda x: x[5], token_features))
new_df["last_word_eq"] = list(map(lambda x: x[6], token_features))
new_df["first_word_eq"] = list(map(lambda x: x[7], token_features))
new_df.head()
'''
from xgboost import XGBClassifier
xgb = XGBClassifier()
xgb.fit(X_train,y_train)
y_pred1 = xgb.predict(X_test)
accuracy_score(y_test,y_pred1)'''
from sklearn.linear_model import LogisticRegression
model_logistic = LogisticRegression()
model_logistic.fit(X_train,y_train)
y_pred2 = model_logistic.predict(X_test)
accuracy_score(y_test,y_pred2)
from sklearn.tree import DecisionTreeClassifier
model_decision = DecisionTreeClassifier()
model_decision.fit(X_train,y_train)
y_pred3 = model_decision.predict(X_test)
```

```
accuracy_score(y_test,y_pred3)
from sklearn.neighbors import KNeighborsClassifier
model_kneighbors = KNeighborsClassifier()
model_kneighbors.fit(X_train,y_train)
y_pred4 = model_kneighbors.predict(X_test)
accuracy_score(y_test,y_pred4)
from sklearn.svm import SVC
model_svm = SVC()
model_svm.fit(X_train,y_train)
y_pred5 = model_svm.predict(X_test)
accuracy_score(y_test,y_pred5)
from sklearn.metrics import confusion_matrix
confusion_matrix(y_test,y_pred2)
def test_common_words(q1,q2):
w1 = set(map(lambda word: word.lower().strip(), q1.split(" ")))
w2 = set(map(lambda word: word.lower().strip(), q2.split(" ")))
return len(w1 & w2)
def test_total_words(q1,q2):
w1 = set(map(lambda word: word.lower().strip(), q1.split(" ")))
w2 = set(map(lambda word: word.lower().strip(), q2.split(" ")))
return (len(w1) + len(w2))
def test_fetch_token_features(q1,q2):
SAFE_DIV = 0.0001
STOP_WORDS = stopwords.words("english")
token_features = [0.0]*8
# Converting the Sentence into Tokens:
q1_tokens = q1.split()
q2_tokens = q2.split()
if len(q1_tokens) == 0 or len(q2_tokens) == 0:
return token_features
# Get the non-stopwords in Questions
q1_words = set([word for word in q1_tokens if word not in STOP_WORDS])
q2_words = set([word for word in q2_tokens if word not in STOP_WORDS])
#Get the stopwords in Questions
q1_stops = set([word for word in q1_tokens if word in STOP_WORDS])
q2_stops = set([word for word in q2_tokens if word in STOP_WORDS])
# Get the common non-stopwords from Question pair
common_word_count = len(q1_words.intersection(q2_words))
# Get the common stopwords from Question pair
common_stop_count = len(q1_stops.intersection(q2_stops))
# Get the common Tokens from Question pair
common_token_count = len(set(q1_tokens).intersection(set(q2_tokens)))
token_features[0] = common_word_count / (min(len(q1_words), len(q2_
words)) +
SAFE_DIV)
token_features[1] = common_word_count / (max(len(q1_words), len(q2_
words)) +
SAFE_DIV)
token_features[2] = common_stop_count / (min(len(q1_stops), len(q2_
stops)) +
SAFE_DIV)
```

```
token_features[3] = common_stop_count / (max(len(q1_stops), len(q2_
stops)) +
SAFE_DIV)
token_features[4] = common_token_count / (min(len(q1_tokens), len(q2_
tokens)) +
SAFE_DIV)
token_features[5] = common_token_count / (max(len(q1_tokens), len(q2_
tokens)) +
SAFE_DIV)
# Last word of both question is same or not
token_features[6] = int(q1_tokens[-1] == q2_tokens[-1])
# First word of both question is same or not
token_features[7] = int(q1_tokens[0] == q2_tokens[0])
return token_features
def test_fetch_length_features(q1,q2):
length_features = [0.0]*3
# Converting the Sentence into Tokens:
q1_tokens = q1.split()
q2_tokens = q2.split()
if len(q1_tokens) == 0 or len(q2_tokens) == 0:
return length_features
# Absolute length features
length_features[0] = abs(len(q1 tokens) - len(q2 tokens))
#Average Token Length of both Questions
length_features[1] = (len(q1_tokens) + len(q2_tokens))/2
strs = list(distance.lcsubstrings(q1, q2))
length_features[2] = len(strs[0]) / (min(len(q1), len(q2)) + 1)
return length_features
def query_point_creator(q1,q2):
input_query = []
# preprocess
q1 = preprocess(q1)
q2 = preprocess(q2)
# fetch basic features
input_query.append(len(q1))
input_query.append(len(q2))
input_query.append(len(q1.split(" ")))
input_query.append(len(q2.split(" ")))
input_query.append(test_common_words(q1,q2))
input_query.append(test_total_words(q1,q2))
input_query.append(round(test_common_words(q1,q2)/test_total_
words(q1,q2),2))
# bow feature for q1
q1_bow = cv.transform([q1]).toarray()
# bow feature for q2
q2_bow = cv.transform([q2]).toarray()
return np.hstack((np.array(input_query).reshape(1,7),q1_bow,q2_bow))
```

```
### Graphical user Interface ###
import tkinter as tk
from tkinter import *
window=Tk()
window.title("Duplicate question detection")
window.resizable(False,False)
window.configure(bg="cyan")
button = tk.Button()
button.config(height=200, width=200)
def gui():
n=tk.StringVar()
p=tk.StringVar()
Label(window,text="Enter Question 1 here",font=("Bookman Old Style", 20,
"italic"),bg="yellow").grid(row=0,column=0)
Entry(window,width=100,borderwidth=50,textvariable=n).grid(row=0,column=1)
Label(window,text="Enter Question 2 here",font=("Bookman Old Style", 20,
"italic"),bg="yellow").grid(row=1,column=0)
Entry(window,width=100,borderwidth=50,textvariable=p).grid(row=1,column=1)
def on_click():
q1=n.get()
q4=p.get()
query_point_creator(q1,q4).shape
rf.predict(query_point_creator(q1,q4))
if (rf.predict(query_point_creator(q1,q4))):
print("The questions are duplicate.")
Label(window,text="The questions are duplicate.",font=("Bookman Old
Style", 20,
"italic"),bg="red",width=40).grid(row=4,column=1)
else:
print("The questions are not duplicate.")
Label(window,text="The questions are not duplicate. ",font=("Bookman Old
Style", 20,
"italic"),bg="green",width=40).grid(row=4,column=1)
Label(window,text="The result:-",font=("Bookman Old Style", 20,
"italic"),bg="pink",width=10).grid(row=4,column=0)
def clear():
gui()
Label(window,text=" ",width=100,height=3,bg="cyan").grid(row=4,column=1)
Label(window,text=" ",width=30,height=3,bg="cyan").grid(row=4,column=0)
Button(window,text="Reset",command=clear,font=("Bookman Old Style",15,
"italic"),bg="orange",height=3,width=7).grid(row=2,column=0)
Button(window,text="Detect",command=on_click,font=("Bookman Old Style",
15,"italic"),bg="blue",height=3,width=15).grid(row=2,column=1)
gui()
window.mainloop()
```

Output:

#Output when duplicate questions are entered.

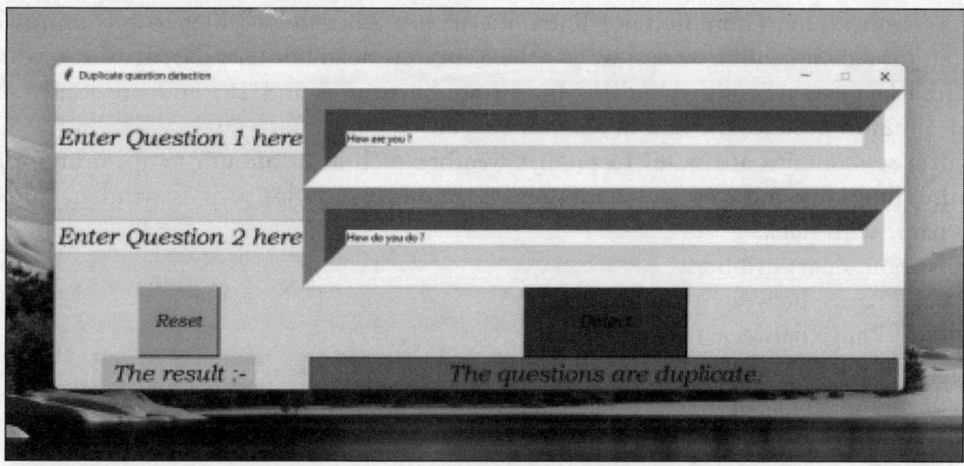

#Output after pressing the reset button.

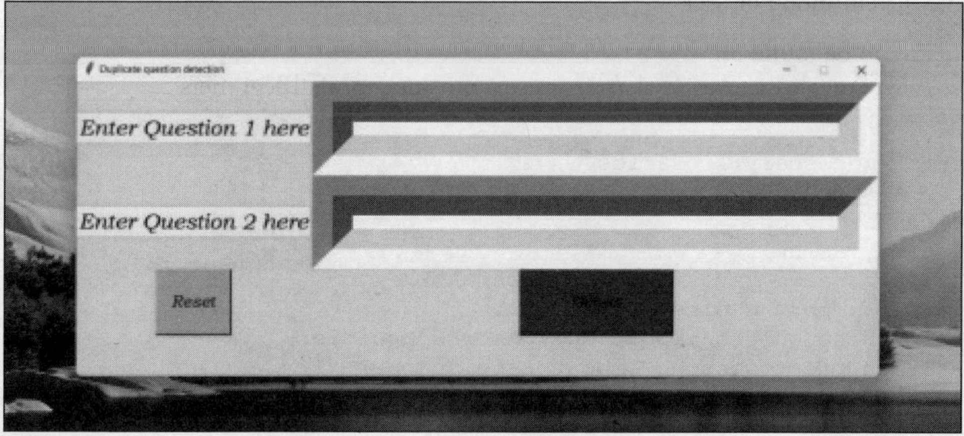

#Output when dissimilar questions are entered.

Duplicate detection can be performed using natural language processing (NLP) and ML techniques. Here, we use a random forest ML model that detects duplication in question pairs with an accuracy of 74%. This functionality can be extended towards assertive, declarative and exclamatory sentences. This can be helpful in detecting plagiarism in articles, essays and compositions. Such a model can also be incorporated in the Q/A section of online meetings/chat platforms where the participants are made aware of whether a question is redundant or not before posting it. Hence, it will be easy for the organizer to answer a limited set of questions.

18.5 Weather Prediction and Song Recommendation System

We first predict the weather using naive Bayes', giving input features such as Minimum Temperature, Maximum Temperature, Humidity and Rain. We then predict the weather to be Sunny, Rainy or Cold. Next, for recommending songs, we use the K-nearest neighbor (K-NN) algorithm which takes the preferred language (English/Hindi), Mood (rate between 0 and 10) and previously predicted weather as input to produce the best fit song as output.

The data set contains attributes to predict weather such as minimum temperature, maximum temperature, humidity and rain and attributes to recommend songs such as weather, mood rating and song name with track.

Details about data attributes:

`MinTemp`: Range between 4.1 and 20.9
`MaxTemp`: Range between 11.3 and 35.8
`Humidity`: Range between 10 and 72
`Rain today`: Yes or No
`Weather`: Sunny, Rainy or Cold
`Song`: Song names for weather
`Language`: Languages of songs
`Mood`: Current mood of user

Weather data can be found at:

https://www.kaggle.com/odisevila/min-max-temp-max-rainfallBeginners

```
#importing necessary libraries
import playsound
import pandas as pd
import numpy as np
from sklearn.naive_bayes import GaussianNB
from random import choices
from sklearn.neighbors import KNeighborsClassifier
from sklearn.preprocessing import LabelEncoder
from sklearn.model_selection import train_test_split
from sklearn.metrics import accuracy_score
import warnings
warnings.filterwarnings('ignore')
def split_data(dfv):
dfval, testing = train_test_split(dfv, test_size=0.25, random_state=0,
shuffle=False)
return dfval, testing
# weather prediction
def weather_prediction(dfval):
# stores the binarized train values of RainToday column
rt=[]
for item in dfval['RainToday']:
if(item=="Yes"):
rt.append(1)
```

```
else:
rt.append(0)
# making dataframe of features to give input to naive bayes
df={'MinTemp':dfval['MinTemp'],'MaxTemp':dfval['MaxTemp'],
'Humidity':dfval['Humidity'],'
RainToday':rt}
feature=pd.DataFrame(df)
# target variable
target=dfval['Weather']
Classifier=GaussianNB()
Classifier.fit(feature,target)
# input to test
min_temp=float(input("Enter the Min Temperature:"))
max_temp=float(input("Enter the Max Temperature:"))
humidity=input("Enter the humidity low/high/normal:")
RainToday=input("Is it raining today 1/0:")
if(humidity=="low"):
hum=choices(low,k=1)
if(humidity=="normal"):
hum=choices(normal,k=1)
if(humidity=="high"):
hum=choices(high,k=1)
test=[]
test.append(min_temp)
test.append(max_temp)
test.append(hum[0])
test.append(RainToday)
pred_weather=Classifier.predict([test])
return pred_weather,Classifier
# song recommendation
def song_recommendation(dfval, pred_weather):
lt = []
for item in dfval['Language']:
if (item == "Hindi"):
lt.append(1)
else:
lt.append(0)
Numerics = LabelEncoder()
wt = Numerics.fit_transform(dfval['Weather'])
train_f = pd.DataFrame({'Weather': wt, 'Language': lt, 'mood':
dfval['MOODS']})
train_t = dfval["Song"]
clf = KNeighborsClassifier(n_neighbors=7)
clf.fit(np.array(train_f), np.array(train_t).reshape(-1, 1))
lang = input("Enter your preferred language for song 1=Hindi,0=English:")
if (pred_weather == "Sunny"):
weather = 2
if (pred_weather == "Rainy"):
weather = 1
```

```
if (pred_weather == "Cold"):
weather = 0
mood = input("Rate your mood between 0-10:")
test_s = []
test_s.append(weather)
test_s.append(int(lang))
test_s.append(mood)
pred = clf.predict(np.array(test_s).reshape(1, -1))
print("For the weather: ", pred_weather)
print("The recommended song is:", pred)
# to play the soundtrack
tracks=dfval["Track"].tolist()
songs = dfval["Song"].tolist()
for i in range(0,len(songs)):
if(pred==songs[i]):
choice=i
track = tracks[choice]
print("Playing the song □♪♫□")
playsound.playsound(track)
# to calculate accuracy
def calcAccuracy(testing,Classifier):
#test prediction to calculate accuracy
rtest=[]
for item in testing['RainToday']:
if(item=="Yes"):
rtest.append(1)
else:
rtest.append(0)
htest=[]
for val in testing['Humidity']:
if(val=="low"):
val=choices(low,k=1)
if(val=="normal"):
val=choices(normal,k=1)
if(val=="high"):
val=choices(high,k=1)
htest.append(val)
test=pd.DataFrame({'MinTemp':testing['MinTemp'],
'MaxTemp':testing['MaxTemp'],'Humidi
ty':htest,'RainToday':rtest})
testf=np.array(test)
test_Actual=np.array(testing['Weather'])
test_pred=[]
for i in range(len(testf)):
w1=Classifier.predict(testf[i].reshape(1,-1))
test_pred.append(w1)
acc=accuracy_score(test_Actual,test_pred)
print("The Accuracy of the model is",acc)
dataset = pd.read_csv('weather.csv')
```

```
# dividing the humidity range as low,normal,high
low=list(range(10,33))
normal=list(range(34,66))
high=list(range(60,72))
dfval, testing = split_data(dataset)
pweath,Classifier=weather_prediction(dfval)
song_recommendation(dfval,pweath)
calcAccuracy(testing,Classifier)
```

Output:

Enter the Min Temperature: 16
Enter the Max Temperature: 24
Enter the humidity low/high/normal: normal
Is it raining today 1/0: 0
Enter your preferred language for song 1=Hindi,0=English: 1
Rate your mood between 0 and 10: 6.2
The accuracy of the model is 0.8333333333333334
For the weather: ['Sunny']
The recommended song is: ['Chittiyaan Kalaiyaan']
Playing the song ♬ ♪♫♬

It is concluded that ML algorithms can be used efficiently to recommend the best song based on the weather conditions provided by the user.

18.6 Spam Detection

The model detects whether the mail received is spam or not (ham) on the basis of the frequency (count) of each word that occurs in the text. This model is implemented using naive Bayes' classification.

The data set is taken from Kaggle at https://www.kaggle.com/datasets/uciml/sms-spam-collection-dataset

It consists of only two columns: category of email {'ham', 'spam'} and the text of the message. Naive Bayes' is applied to detect if the given message is spam or ham.

```
import pandas as pd
import pickle
df = pd.read_csv("spam.csv");
# print(df.head())
print(df.Category.unique()) # ['ham' 'spam']
df['spam'] = df['Category'].apply(
lambda x: 1 if x == 'spam' else 0) # new column named spam created where
spam is assigned 1 else 0
print(df.head())
from sklearn.model_selection import train_test_split
```

```
# data spliting
x_train, x_test, y_train, y_test = train_test_split(df.Message, df.spam,
test_size=0.2, random_state=42)
# print(x_train) len =4457
# print(x_test) len=1115
# count frequecy of each word
from sklearn.feature_extraction.text import CountVectorizer
v = CountVectorizer()
cv_msg = v.fit_transform(x_train.values)
cv_msg.toarray()[0:5]
from sklearn.naive_bayes import MultinomialNB
model = MultinomialNB()
model.fit(cv_msg, y_train)
# email = [
# "WINNER!! As a valued network customer you have been selected to
receivea Â£900 prize reward! To claim call "
# "09061701461. Claim code KL341. Valid 12 hours only.",
# "Ok lar... Joking wif u oni..."]
# email_count = v.transform(email)
# model.predict(email_count)
x_test_count = v.transform(x_test)
model.score(x_test_count, y_test)
# print(model.score(x_test_count, y_test))
from sklearn.pipeline import Pipeline
clf = Pipeline([('vectorizer', CountVectorizer()), ('nb',
MultinomialNB())])
clf.fit(x_train, y_train)
email = ["WINNER!! As a valued network customer you have been selected to
receive a Â£900 prize reward! To claim call "
"09061701461. Claim code KL341. Valid 12 hours only."
]
print(clf.predict(email))
print("Score:", clf.score(x_test, y_test))
pickle.dump(clf, open('spam_model.pkl', 'wb'))
model = pickle.load(open('spam_model.pkl', 'rb'))
# print(model.predict(email))
```

Output:

C:\Python310\python.exe C:/Users/Tanaya/PycharmProjects/Spam_filter/main.py
['ham' 'spam']
Category Message spam
0 ham Go until jurong point, crazy.. Available only... 0
1 ham Ok lar... Joking wif u oni... 0
2 spam Free entry in 2 a wkly comp to win FA Cup fina... 1
3 ham U dun say so early hor... U c already then say... 0
4 ham Nah I don't think he goes to usf, he lives aro... 0
[1]
Score: 0.9919282511210762
Process finished with exit code 0

BIBLIOGRAPHY

1. Khanam, Z et al. 2021. Fake News Detection using Machine Learning Approaches. *IOP Conference Series: Materials Science and Engineering* 1099: 012040. https://iopscience.iop.org/article/10.1088/1757-899X/1099/1/012040/pdf
2. Goodfellow, I, Bengio, Y and Courville, A. 2016. *Deep Learning*. MIT Press. https://www.deeplearningbook.org
3. Mehdi Saeedi. "Identify Digits with Convolutional Neural Network". https://mehdi-saeedi.github.io/MNIST-Digit-Recognizer/
   "Welcome to Colaboratory". Google Colab. https://colab.research.google.com/
4. "How to Choose a Feature Selection Method for Machine Learning". Machine Learning Mastery. https://machinelearningmastery.com/feature-selection-with-real-and-categorical-data/
5. "Python Feature Selection Tutorial: A Beginner's Guide". DataCamp. https://www.datacamp.com/community/tutorials/feature-selection-python
6. Purnendu Shukla. "Performing Email Spam Detection Using BERT in Python". Analytics Vidhya, published September 2021, https://www.analyticsvidhya.com/blog/2021/09/performing-email-spam-detection-using-bert-in-python/

Index

E

F

G

O

P

R

S